THROUGH A GLASS DARKLY

THROUGH A GLASS DARKLY

Suffering, the Sacred, and the Sublime in Literature and Theory

Edited by
Holly Faith Nelson
Lynn R. Szabo
Jens Zimmermann

Wilfrid Laurier University Press

Wilfrid Laurier University Press acknowledges the financial support of the Government of Canada through its Canada Book Fund for its publishing activities.

Library and Archives Canada Cataloguing in Publication

Through a glass darkly : suffering, the sacred, and the sublime in literature and theory / edited by Holly Faith Nelson, Lynn R. Szabo, Jens Zimmermann.

Includes bibliographical references and index.
Also available in electronic format.
ISBN 978-1-55458-184-9

1. Suffering in literature. 2. Holy, The, in literature. 3. Sublime, The, in literature. 4. Literature—Philosophy. 5. Literature, Medieval—History and criticism. 6. Literature, Modern—History and criticism. 7. English literature—History and criticism. I. Nelson, Holly Faith, 1966– II. Szabo, Lynn II. Zimmermann, Jens, 1965–

PN45.T57 2010   809'.93353   C2009-906523-1

ISBN 978-1-55458-206-8
Electronic format.

1. Suffering in literature. 2. Holy, The, in literature. 3. Sublime, The, in literature. 4. Literature—Philosophy. 5. Literature, Medieval—History and criticism. 6. Literature, Modern—History and criticism. 7. English literature—History and criticism. I. Nelson, Holly Faith, 1966– II. Szabo, Lynn II. Zimmermann, Jens, 1965–

PN45.T57 2010a   809'.93353   C2009-906524-X

Cover design by David Drummond. Cover art: *In Your Own Time*, by Alan W. Alker (2008, Digital Art). Reproduced with the permission of the artist. Text design by Daiva Villa, Chris Rowat Design.

This book is printed on FSC recycled paper and is certified Ecologo. It is made from 100% post-consumer fibre, processed chlorine free, and manufactured using biogas energy.

Printed in Canada

FSC Recycled
Supporting responsible use of forest resources
www.fsc.org Cert no. SGS-COC-003153
© 1996 Forest Stewardship Council

To the memory of

Dr. W. Stanford Reid (1913–96) and Priscilla Reid (1908–97)

Dr. Barbara Helen Pell (1945–2009), Professor of Canadian Literature

and

Simon Mortimer Poultney (1983–2004)

"In my end is my beginning."
—*Mary, Queen of Scots*

CONTENTS

ACKNOWLEDGEMENTS

A great many supporters have assisted us with this essay collection. Our greatest debt of gratitude is owed to The Priscilla and Stanford Reid Trust (http://www.reidtrust.com), which provided the funding for this project. Priscilla and Dr. W. Stanford Reid were dedicated to the pursuit of integrating faith and learning such as this volume represents. We are especially grateful to the Rev. Dr. R.J. Bernhardt, a trustee of the Reid Trust, for his thoughtful guidance and encouragement over the past two years. To them, we add the Social Sciences and Humanities Research Council of Canada (SSHRC); Jens Zimmermann, the Canada Research Chair in Interpretation, Religion, and Culture at Trinity Western University; and the Western Regional Conference on Christianity and Literature, since it was at one of its annual conferences, also sponsored by the Reid Trust, that the seeds of many of the ideas presented in this collection first took root. Alan W. Alker, artist and designer, kindly permitted us to display his striking and poignant artwork on the book's cover, for which we are most grateful. Jennifer Doede, assistant professor of English at Trinity Western University, is offered generous thanks for her insightful and creative development of the thematic focus of the collection. We are also enormously grateful to the research assistants who worked alongside us in the preparation of this volume, most notably Lise van der Eyk and Priscilla E. Tang, as well as Nicole Brandsma, Stephen Anderson, Matthew Gaster, and Paula Flink.

We would also like to acknowledge the ways in which this work has been shaped by encounters with students and colleagues, in particular Simon Poultney (1983–2004), a Trinity Western University student who was extraordinarily insightful and creative, deeply sensitive to human suffering, and highly capable of engaging the power and grandeur of the sacred and the sublime. Dr. Barbara Pell, a beloved colleague and contributor to the volume, succumbed to cancer in March 2009. Dr. Pell was an esteemed scholar of Canadian literature and a co-founder of the Christianity and Literature Study

Group (CLSG). Dr. Pell's research interests regularly drew her to the subject of the sacred and the sublime, and students will fondly remember that any "suffering" experienced in her classes led to a remarkable improvement in both mind and spirit. We celebrate her contributions to our department and the academy by this volume.

Holly Faith Nelson would like to recognize the ongoing support of Russell, Caleb, and Faith Nelson, as well as Marion Henderson, sources of inspiration and delight during the editing of this book. She would also like to thank Barbara E. Smith, author of *Women, Saints, and Servants*, whose lifelong guidance, encouragement, and spiritual generosity have fostered in her a deeper understanding of the themes of this volume. Lynn R. Szabo thanks her parents and children for their love and devoted support of her scholarly pursuits.

Finally, we are grateful to the authors, editors, and publishers that granted us permission to publish previously issued material. A version of Norm Klassen's "Suffering in the Service of Venus: The Sacred, the Sublime, and Chaucerian Joy in the Middle Part of the *Parliament of Fowls*," was published in *Tradition and Formation: Claiming an Inheritance: Essays in Honour of Peter C. Erb*, ed. Michel Desjardins and Harold Remus (Kitchener, ON: Pandora Press, 2009) 213–28, and a small portion of it appeared in *Notes and Queries* 251 (2006): 154–57. Sections of Christine Colón's "Joanna Baillie and the Christian Gothic: Reforming Society through the Sublime" were published in *Joanna Baillie and the Art of Moral Influence* (New York: Peter Lang, 2009). Versions of Richard Kearney's "Sacramental Imagination: Eucharists of the Ordinary Universe in the works of Joyce, Proust, and Woolf" and Jens Zimmermann's "Suffering Divine Things: Cruciform Reasoning or Incarnational Hermeneutics" were published in, respectively, *Analecta Hermeneutica,* vol. 1 (2009), http://journals.library.mun.ca/ojs/index.php/analecta and *Tradition and Formation: Claiming an Inheritance: Essays in Honour of Peter C. Erb*, ed. Michel Desjardins and Harold Remus (Kitchener, ON: Pandora Press, 2009) 361–79. We also appreciate the permission granted to us by Art Resource to reproduce in David Lyle Jeffrey's "Sacred Proposals and the Spiritual Sublime" photographs of Jan van Eyck's *Ghent Altarpiece* and Rogier van der Weyden's *Annunciation*, as well as the permission given by Jane Zavitz-Bond, archivist, to quote material from the Canadian Yearly Meeting Archives (CYMA), Pickering College, Newmarket, Ontario, in Robynne Rogers Healey's "Suffering in Word and in Truth: Seventeenth- and Nineteenth-Century Quaker Women's Autobiography."

ILLUSTRATIONS

TRAUMA AND TRANSCENDENCE: AN INTRODUCTION

Holly Faith Nelson

Suffering, the sacred, and the sublime, terms that frequently intersect in recent works of literature and criticism, speak to the ineffable—that which appears to transcend or operate outside of language or that which is challenging or impossible to represent. To varying degrees, these terms help us to interrogate and negotiate the gap between the spoken and the unspeakable, language and experience, the body and spirit, the immanent and the transcendent, the human and the divine. In particular historical periods and cultural traditions, the convergence of all three terms is widely accepted. This is particularly true of the Christian tradition, in which suffering, the sacred, and the sublime coalesce in the figure of the crucified and risen Christ. Nevertheless, as David Lyle Jeffrey theorizes, many postmodernists have viewed some or all of these terms as unrelated or even at odds, leading each to be examined, at times, in relative isolation.[1] However, the historical and contemporary connections between suffering, the sacred, and the sublime have repeatedly surfaced in scholarly studies and professional dialogues in the last few decades, as have the difficulties of bringing language to bear on that which appears to elude or transcend the spoken or written word. Interest in and anxieties about the ways in which suffering, the sacred, and the sublime converge are particularly evident in enquiries into trauma, religion, and aesthetics.

In trauma studies, an ongoing debate over the suitability of giving expression to suffering continues to rage. Cathy Caruth, for example, has stressed the irrepressibility of the "speaking wound," and Richard Kearney has advocated finding a "delicate balance" between employing "the narrative imagination to revisit trauma," thereby stimulating the "healing-mourning process," and acknowledging the "unspeakable evil of that trauma."[2] Scholars in Holocaust and related studies, however, warn of the dangers of attempting to give voice to, and thus to contain, make meaningful, or render sublime, incomprehensible acts of (in)human brutality.[3] While F.R. Ankersmit argues in *Sublime Historical Experience* that "trauma can be seen as the psychological counterpart to the sublime and the sublime can be seen as the philosophical counterpart of trauma," Dominick LaCapra warns of the danger of "convert[ing] trauma into the occasion for sublimity."[4] He is uneasy at "the excess of trauma" becoming "an uncanny source of elation or ecstasy"—traumatic events, including the Holocaust, becoming "occasions of negative sublimity or displaced sacralization."[5]

Trauma theorists also express intense concern about the ways in which religious discourses might potentially erase or diminish the tangible reality of extreme suffering. This apprehension is evident in Shoshana Felman's reading of the works of Paul Celan, a Jewish-Romanian poet who was confined in a labour camp during the Second World War and whose parents did not survive the concentration camps. Felman explores how Celan resists, in his poem "Todesfuge," what she sees as the Christian tendency to strip suffering of its historicity:

> The Christian figure of the wound, traditionally viewed as the mythic vehicle and as the metaphoric means for a *historical transcendence*—for the erasure of Christ's death in the advent of Resurrection is reinvested in the poem with the literal concreteness of the death camp blood and ashes, and is made thus to include, within the wound, not resurrection and historical transcendence, but the specificity of history—of the concrete historical reality of massacre and race annihilation—as unerasable and untranscendable.[6]

While Felman is not alone in viewing sacred discourse as capable of fostering harmful interpretations of human atrocities in such a context, many professionals working with victims of trauma conceive of the relation of the sacred and suffering in more complex, often affirmative, terms. For example, in *Healing from Post-Traumatic Stress*, Monique Lang reviews how religious belief can variously affect or be affected by traumatic experience; in *The Sacred Path Beyond Trauma: Reaching the Divine Through Nature's Healing Symbols*, Ellen Macfarland envisions healing in sacral, if not religious, terms; and in "Healing the Wounds Following Protracted Conflict in Angola: A Community-Based Approach to Assisting War-affected Children," Michael G. Wessells and Carlinda Monteiro consider the crucial role played by spiritual rituals in the healing of traumatized individuals and communities in particular cultural contexts.[7]

In religious studies, the inability of language to communicate fully the radical alterity of the divine Other continues to be an important issue. In many religions, the fundamental difference between positive theology (*via positiva*) and negative theology (*via negativa*) can be attributed to competing perspectives on the extent to which language can describe and illumine divine Being. The mystery of divinity and the non-linguistic nature of many encounters with God have led some religious scholars and practitioners to conceive of the sacred in the language of the sublime. In fact, despite LaCapra's belief that the sublime has simply displaced the sacred in recent years, we commonly find that the language of sacredness and sublimity are intimately related or even conflated in some theological texts.[8] The Jewish theologian Abraham Joshua Heschel, for example, writes poignantly of the theological importance of the sublime, describing it as "the silent allusion of things to a meaning greater than themselves" or as a "spiritual suggestiveness of reality."[9] In describing Heschel's meditations on the sublime, John C. Merkle explains that, for Heschel, "All things are sublime because they are divine acts of creation and because their continuous being is a way of obeying the Creator... [T]he infinite or ultimate reality which is Divine speaks through the finite or proximate which is sublime.... The experience of the sublime is not an end in itself but a means to the experience of faith."[10] Although addressing sublimity in more theoretical postmodern terms, in unfolding the thesis of his book *A Theology of the Sublime*, Clayton Crockett also merges the sacred and the sublime: "I suggest that the sublime, broadly understood, constitutes what [Paul] Tillich calls the depth aspect of existence. In a sense religion in the modern world can be defined as sublime; that is, what exceeds or resists the modern project of representation even as religion is ever the acknowledged or unacknowledged object of modern representation."[11]

Other theologians are more wary of fashioning the sacred in the language of sublimity. As Kevin Hart observes in "God and the Sublime," some Christian theologians "agree that the sublime appears in Christian theology as an element that was thought philosophically rather than theologically and that therefore has never been thought with sufficient inwardness by Christians."[12] After all, as Hart argues elsewhere, "attention to the sublime" has served in the past "to replace the practice of religion. The accent is removed from worship and placed firmly on sublime feelings and ethics." Therefore, Hart concludes that "Orthodox Christians" often claim "that God cannot adequately be discussed in terms of the sublime" since "two quite different senses of 'transcendence' are at play when talking of God and the sublime."[13]

More pressing than the relation of the sacred and the sublime in religious studies, however, is the question of why God permits such immense suffering in the world. Countless theologies of suffering—often in the form of theodicies—

continue to emerge in the face of personal and communal trauma. We might consider, for instance, David Blumenthal's *Facing the Abusing God: A Theology of Protest*, which Elie Wiesel views as a theology of suffering that looks "to reconcile memory with hope, divinity with cruelty, language and truth, absolute exile with ultimate redemption"; or we could turn to Rabbi Rebecca W. Sirbu's recent pamphlet, *Theologies of Suffering: How Judaism Can Help You Cope*, written in order "to provide Jews who are experiencing life challenges with a framework to help them cope with their suffering." While acknowledging that "[t]here are no easy answers to these questions" and that "[e]ach person must struggle to create meaning out of his or her own suffering," Rabbi Sirbu presents the theologies of suffering of, for example, Job, Rabbi Harold S. Kushner, and Rabbi Mordecai Kaplan as possibilities for managing the anguish of the traumatized.[14] However, as noted above, such theologies of suffering have been viewed by many trauma theorists not as a means of healing victims, but rather as a way (to our peril) of averting our eyes from the brutal physical realities of the human condition.

Finally, in the field of aesthetics, the notion of the sublime has historically focused on the paradoxical pleasure and pain — the delight and distress — experienced by humans when they confront the unrepresentability of experience, which involves, according to Slavoj Žižek, the straining of "the aesthetic imagination … to its utmost" as it strives in vain to represent "the transcendent, trans-phenomenal unattainable Thing-in-itself" or "suprasensible Idea." The pain that results from this recognition is mitigated by pleasure because the "sublime object" permits us to "have a presentiment of the true dimension of the Thing."[15] Though classical works on the sublime focused largely on rhetorical technique, treatises on the aesthetic of the sublime were thereafter typically written through philosophical and, later, psychoanalytic frameworks (as is evident in Žižek's writing), which resulted in a gesturing beyond the formal features of art to more abstract ideas of the unattainable and the infinite or that which is beyond human reach. "Within the domain of literary critics and aesthetics," as Judith Butler explains, this has manifested itself as "the problematic of the sublime": the reality that writing, which is unable to "reach beyond itself," "is condemned to figure that beyond again and again within its own terms."[16]

As suggested above, this fascination with the relation of art to the unrepresentable or the infinite is not necessarily a desire for the sacred or the holy. As Jean-François Lyotard relates in *The Postmodern Explained*, the "aesthetic of the sublime" for the avant-garde artists of the early twentieth century, for example, entailed a commitment "to presenting the existence of something unrepresentable," which was not envisioned as a spiritual exercise.[17] Nevertheless, the relationship of the sublime to the realm of the sacred has become more complex, since postmodern literary critics and philosophers frequently link the aesthetics of the sublime and the ethical in their writings. In this they may be partially indebted to Immanuel Kant's relation of the aesthetic and the moral in his theorization of the sublime. As Dorota Glowacka and Stephen Boos observe in *Between Ethics and Aesthetics: Crossing the Boundaries*, for Kant "the aesthetic experience of the sublime is thought ... to awaken in us a feeling of our supersensible destination (i.e. the idea of the morally good)."[18]

While the discourse of ethics or moral law, like that of infinity, is not necessarily embedded in conceptions of the sacred, at the very least traces of the language of the holy, especially biblical language, appear in many discussions of the relation of art to moral value, judgements, and obligations.[19] Such traces are evident, for example, in Julia Kristeva's reflections on ethical and unethical encounters between the self and Other in both works of art and life. In an interview with Richard Kearney, Kristeva considers the importance of the "notion of the Other"—particularly the stranger—developed by "monotheistic religions" in the West, a notion she believes should be "redevelop[ed] today." On this topic she remarks, "What does that mean? When a stranger knocks at my door, for instance, I should, as the Bible says, consider that it might be God—a sign of the sacredness and singularity of others."[20]

As is evident in Richard Lane's essay in this collection, suffering is the ethical focus of much postmodern writing on the aesthetic of the sublime; this is not wholly unexpected given the association of the sublime with the experiences of terror and pain that result from confronting that which is beyond reason or representation. Nevertheless, as argued earlier, the ability of the sublime to translate or elevate even the base, vulgar, or violently disturbing into something awe-inspiring is also a matter of much controversy, as is its emphasis on the silence that ensues from an awe-full (or awful) experience. In *Holocaust Monuments and National Memory Cultures in France and Germany Since 1989*, Peter Carrier reminds us that both Holocaust monuments and "counter-monuments" have been criticized as "architectural translation[s] of the sublime" which entail the "renunciation of sensible effects in favour of the conceptualisation of representation."[21]

As this brief overview of the exploration and interrogation of suffering, the sacred, and the sublime in trauma studies, religious studies, and aesthetics indicates, the theme of this collection is of critical significance at this historical moment, perhaps because we live in an age when debates on religious fanaticism and religious promise abound and when the ubiquitous images of war and terror are often rendered sublime aesthetic objects in a variety of media. The twenty-five essays in this volume, which were first ignited by conversations at an international symposium on the subject of trauma and transcendence, seek to participate in this scholarly conversation by attending to the ways in which literature and literary theory address these three frequently overlapping concepts. The collection brings together a series of case studies that cut across genre, geography, cultural circumstance, and historical epoch not only to reveal the shift across time and space in the conception of suffering, the sacred, and the sublime, but also to consider the remarkable number of ways in which these terms have been articulated and examined in aesthetic and theoretical contexts.

The volume opens with an expansive essay by David Lyle Jeffrey, "Sacred Proposals and the Spiritual Sublime," which traces the history and significance of the three concepts that lie at the core of the volume. In his account of the "Christian spiritual sublime," in which "sacred love and sacrificial suffering" converge (p. 19), Jeffrey examines aesthetic theories, religious texts, and works of art across time and space—from the Hebrew scriptures, Virgil's *Aeneid*, and Longinus's *Peri Hupsous* to Rogier van der Weyden's *Annunciation*, William Wordsworth's "Tintern Abbey," and Dante Gabriel Rossetti's *Ecce Ancilla Domine*. The essays that follow are arranged chronologically according to the historical period of the literary work or theory under study, beginning with the medieval English lyric and concluding with postmodern theory.

The first series of essays consider the representation of suffering, the sacred, and/or the sublime in medieval and early modern British literature. In "'Loke in: How weet a wounde is heere!': The Wounds of Christ as a Sacred Space in English Devotional Literature," Eleanor McCullough explores the image of the wounded Christ in medieval texts as a figure of both the feminized sufferer and the "feminine sublime" (p. 34). While admitting to the general abandonment of such Christological imagery (particularly its erotic aspects) after the Reformation, McCullough argues for the significance of the elements that remain in the works of Crashaw and eighteenth-century hymnists. In "Suffering in the Service of Venus: The Sacred, the Sublime, and Chaucerian Joy in the Middle Part of the *Parliament of Fowls*," Norm Klassen proposes that in the *Parliament of Fowls*, Geoffrey Chaucer interrogates the "sacred space of love and art" linked with a libidinous Venus and the suffering of her devotees (p. 39). While censuring the aesthetic vision associated with Venus, Chaucer remains dedicated to an art that combines "truth, beauty, and moral commitment" out of which emerges the joyful, almost euphoric, tone in the poem's middle portion (p. 40).

The tempered vision of suffering in Chaucer's dialogic poem stands in stark contrast to the brutality of sexual violation in Shakespeare's rape narratives in *Titus Andronicus* and *The Rape of Lucrece*. In "Listening to Lavinia: Emmanuel Levinas's Saying and Said in *Titus Andronicus*," Sean Lawrence reads Lavinia's abjection and silence through the filter of Levinasian ethics. In Lavinia's silent suffering and her family's attempts to attend to and comfort her, Lawrence perceives an absolute—if unrepresentable—demand for "ethical concern" and for a meaningful response (p. 58). Lawrence maintains that the fissure between the demand and the response in *Titus Andronicus* raises the question of the relation of ethics and language in the play, which, he concludes, shows the priority of ethics. Heather G.S. Johnson, in "Precious Stories: The Discursive Economy in Shakespeare's *Rape of Lucrece*," scrutinizes the scene of rape in Shakespearean poetry, considering the sometimes exploitive tendency to market suffering through narration. Johnson argues that in *The Rape of Lucrece*, Shakespeare takes as his theme an economy that trades in the narratives of victims, as several male characters appropriate the story of Lucrece's violation and death in order to earn cultural capital. However, this marketing of suffering, Johnson contends, is not envisioned as an entirely unethical act in Shakespeare's poem as Lucrece's gifting of her story to male members of her family is a generous ethical gesture motivated by the desire to benefit her family.

In turning to early modern metaphysical poetry, the volume narrows its focus to the spiritually beneficial effects of affliction. In "The Sacred Pain of Penitence: The Theology of John Donne's *Holy Sonnets*," David Anonby considers the nature and expression of spiritual suffering in the *Holy Sonnets*, aligning Donne's "penchant for pain" with devotional purity and "spiritual health" (p. 94). Anonby reflects on the ways in which intersecting theological traditions inform, feed, and alleviate Donne's religious angst, allowing Donne to express, if only for moments, "sublime strains" (p. 88). Daniel W. Doerksen, in "Bearing the Cross: The Christian's Response to Suffering in Herbert's *The Temple*," deals with the Christian's experience of affliction, as depicted in George Herbert's devotional poems. Doerksen asserts that, consonant with John Calvin's way of reading the Psalms and other biblical texts, Herbert portrays spiritual conflicts as "God's fatherly discipline," intended for the believer's renewal and maturing through identification with Christ and his suffering on the cross (p. 100). Herbert's picturing of such experience results not only in vivid poetry, but also in what Herbert said he intended, help for a "dejected poor Soul."

The next series of essays in the volume address trauma and transcendence in the literature of the Romantic and Victorian periods. In "Horrific Suffering, Sacred Terror, and Sublime Freedom in Helen Maria Williams's *Peru*," Natasha Duquette contends that Williams invokes and alters the Burkean trope of the "raging storm" in her political poem *Peru: A Poem in Six Cantos* (1783) to dispute Burke's suggestion in *A Philosophical Enquiry into the Origins Our Ideas of the Sublime and Beautiful* that punitive justice is sublime (p. 113). Williams, Duquette proposes, turns to poetry as a vehicle of the sublime, finding in the poetic utterance of empathy for the victims of suffering a means for preventative justice as well as freedom and rebirth. In "Joanna Baillie and the Christian Gothic: Reforming Society through the Sublime," Christine A. Colón maintains that Baillie deploys the spectacle of the Gothic in *Plays on the Passions* as a tool for ethical reform. In Baillie's introduction to *Plays on the Passions* (1798), Colón discovers a well-formulated theory on the moral purpose of the theatre that is influenced by the writings of the Scottish philosophers David Hume and Adam Smith as well as those of the Earl of Shaftesbury. Using Baillie's *The Dream* (1812) as an example of the playwright's project, Colón theorizes that Baillie includes "sublime moments" of "Gothic spectacle" that highlight human suffering to reform the audience by teaching them to restrain unwieldy passions that lead only to self-destruction (p. 129).

In "Sacramental Suffering and the Waters of Redemption and Transformation in George Eliot's Fiction," Constance Fulmer finds that in the works of Eliot, an atheist, the imagery of water, especially in a ceremonial or sacramental context, speaks not only to the novelist's understanding of the holy, but also to her overarching ethical concerns. Fulmer observes that while water is often associated with suffering in Eliot's novels, it is also linked to the process of moral development which Eliot relates to the ethical "principles of Solidarity and Continuity" (p. 147). Esther Hu, in "Christina Rossetti and the Poetics of Tractarian Suffering," challenges the common reading of Rossetti's poems as works that demand the abnegation or renunciation of the female self. Looking at poems that address pain, affliction, and sorrow in *Verses* (1893), a collection of devotional poems Rossetti produced while battling cancer, Hu uncovers a Tractarian theology which stipulates that one can experience spiritual cleansing, restoration, hope, and communion with the crucified Christ "in the crucible of pain" (p. 156). Adopting a transatlantic perspective in "Suffering in Word and in Truth: Seventeenth- and Nineteenth-Century Quaker Women's Autobiography," Robynne Rogers Healey addresses the formulaic narration of suffering in Quaker autobiographical prose of the seventeenth to nineteenth centuries, pointing to the paradox of life writing that was more public and communal than personal and individual. She considers the need for authors of such texts to provide evidence of their intense spiritual and physical affliction in order to receive approval for publication from the Meeting for Sufferings. While "a collective identity and theology" was thereby imprinted on the life writings of individual Friends, Healey is convinced that the vibrant voices of "strong, resourceful," and revolutionary Quaker women can still be heard in their memoirs (p. 172).

With the essays of Richard Kearney and George Piggford, the volume turns to the subject of transcendence in modernist literature. In "Sacramental Imagination: Eucharists of the Ordinary Universe in the Works of Joyce, Proust, and Woolf," Richard Kearney performs a close reading of epiphanic and eucharistic moments in *Ulysses*, *Time Regained*, and *To the Lighthouse*. The sacred transfiguration of embodied or fleshly experience in these moments is Kearney's focus. To uncover the "grammar of transubstantiation operating in these sacramental accounts of the sensible universe"—and to devise a method by which to reinvest the profane or secular with the sacred—Kearney draws on the incarnational phenomenology of Maurice Merleau-Ponty and Julia Kristeva as well as on the hermeneutics of Ricoeur, among others (p. 183). George Piggford, in "The *Via Negativa* in E.M. Forster's *A Passage to India*," observes a fascination with the "rhetoric of negation" in Forster's novel that allows for the possibility of transcendence and deconstruction of ontological Christian theology (p. 223). Forster's mystical approach contrasts with the embodied transcendence Kearney unearths in Woolf, Joyce, and Proust. According to Piggford, Forster's "God both is and is not," and it is the inclusion of negation that might reinvigorate what Forster's narrator calls "poor little talkative Christianity" (p. 228).

The manner in which fantasy and children's literature enable the reader to negotiate suffering and experience a measure of solace is treated in the next pair of essays. In "Consolation in Un/certainty: The Sacred Spaces of Suffering in the Children's Fantasy Literature of George MacDonald, C.S. Lewis, and Madeleine L'Engle," Monika Hilder contends that the "mythic imagination" of MacDonald, Lewis, and L'Engle works alchemically inasmuch as it "transforms suffering into a genuinely sacred space of well-being," one that encourages children to exchange an "idolatry of certainty" for the "defiant hope" of "consolation in un/certainty" (p. 240). In "The Messiah of History: The Search for Synchronicity in Miller's *A Canticle for Leibowitz*," Deanna T. Smid employs Fredric Jameson's theory of synchronicity and Walter Benjamin's conception of Messianic time to reveal strands of communal hope in the face of apocalyptic suffering—figured as "a global nuclear holocaust"—in Walter M. Miller's science fiction novel, *A Canticle for Leibowitz* (p. 243).

Turning to the subject of Canadian literature, Barbara Pell and John C. Van Rys take up the matter of trauma and transcendence in the fiction of Hugh Hood and Alice Munro respectively. In "Suffering and the Sacred: Hugh Hood's *The New Age / Le nouveau siècle*," Pell identifies in Hood's twelve-volume *New Age*—at once realistic fiction and religious allegory—a pronounced commitment to "Romantic transcendentalism" or what Hood defined as "super-realism" (p. 258). Pell believes that Hood's incarnational aesthetic ensures that earthly suffering in his novel series is sacralized. In "Fictional Violations in Alice Munro's Narratives," Van Rys enumerates many kinds of violation in Munro's short stories to demonstrate that her works situate and complicate the problem of suffering in the context of an essentially secular enigmatic existence, examining the capacity of the human spirit to confront affliction and to inspire moments of "spiritual motion" and sublime awe and longing (p. 269).

The next three essays in the volume address the interplay of suffering, the sacred, and the sublime in twentieth-century American poetry and fiction. In "Thomas Merton and the Aesthetics of the Sublime: 'A Beautiful Terror,'" Lynn R. Szabo contemplates Merton's conceptualization of the sublime, which she describes as an aesthetic of solitude and silence that engenders the acute spiritual agony and ecstasy necessary to move the seeker along an iconic pilgrimage toward contemplative prayer and mystical union. In "Belated Beloved: Time, Trauma, and the Sublime in Toni Morrison's *Beloved*," Steve Vine associates the Romantic sublime that emerged out of the Enlightenment with the "American Africanism" explored by Morrison in both her novels and literary criticism. In attending to this connection, Vine suggests, we can better comprehend Morrison's reinvention of the "*slave sublime object*" and her motion forward in time "toward an African-American freedom that is yet to come" (p. 312). The reworking of the sublime in American fiction is also the subject of Deborah Bowen's "Annie Dillard on Holy Ground: The Artist as Nun in the Postmodern Sublime." While Bowen finds useful Jean-François Lyotard's conception of the artist as one whose "business" is "not to supply reality but to invent allusions to the conceivable which cannot be presented," she feels that Lyotard's impious and pragmatic "aesthetic of the sublime" fails to account for a distinct kind of allusivity in Dillard's *Holy the Firm*, an allusivity of "*reimagined* piety" in which "suffering and the sublime are mediated by the incarnate sacred" (p. 318).[22]

Sean Somers's study, "Passion Plays by Proxy: The Paschal Face as Interculturality in the Works of Endō Shūsaku and Mishima Yukio," takes us beyond the literature of the Americas and Western Europe to the twentieth-century texts of two Japanese authors deeply concerned with the subject of Christian, or more specifically Catholic, martyrdom and sacrifice. Focusing on Endō's best-known novel, *Chinmoku* [*Silence*], and Mishima's play, *Madame de Sade*, Somers explores how both texts engage with the sepulchral meaning of sacrifice in a Japanese context.

The final three essays in the volume point to the ethical implications of ongoing research on suffering, the sacred, and the sublime in the humanities. In "Testifying to the Infinity of the Other: The Sacred and Ethical Dimensions of Secondary Witnessing in Anne Karpf's *The War After*," Bettina Stumm draws on the work of Emmanuel Levinas and Paul Ricoeur in her analysis of the ethical act of bearing witness to the traumatized other. Stumm brings such an ethics to bear on the experience of secondary witnessing of the atrocities of the Holocaust, examining the autobiographical narrative of Anne Karpf, the daughter of survivors who records her struggle to respond to the ethical call to testify to the trauma of her parents. Stumm's research on the moral dimension of secondary witnessing is applicable to the broader ethical concern in the humanities of bearing "responsibility *for-the-other*," especially for the afflicted other (p. 360).

In "Sacred Space and the Fellowship of Suffering in the Postmodern Sublime," Richard Lane argues that post-structuralist and postmodern theory must enter, as it were, a "sacred space" to reflect on its relation to religion in the humanities, an entrance encouraged by the religious turn in the later works of Derrida. Though Lane admits that such theory often fails to even acknowledge the existence of sacred space, he wonders whether it will, of necessity, be transformed in this consecrated place. In particular, Lane postulates that sublimity is inevitably bound up with the sacred, which significantly impacts how we should respond to current theory. To ground his theory in the concrete, Lane reads Rachel Whiteread's *The Nameless Library* as a sublime, sacred space of suffering that demands a transformational post-Christendom conception of post-structuralism and postmodernism.

Like Lane, Jens Zimmermann, in "Suffering Divine Things: Cruciform Reasoning or Incarnational Hermeneutics," also addresses the transformation of philosophy and literary theory in light of the shift toward religion in the late twentieth and early twenty-first centuries. Zimmermann posits that only an interpretive paradigm rooted in the Incarnation can ensure that Western culture will survive the loss of its character and educational objectives and its failure to support its ethical principles persuasively in an evolving global context. While he recognizes the limitations of a naive Enlightenment rationalism, Zimmermann proposes that we have been left "without any common ground for a universal sense of human dignity," a concern also voiced by Terry Eagleton in *After Theory* and Jean Baudrillard in *Simulacra and Simulation* (p. 378).[23] Convinced that secularist reason, or "scientific objectivism," has "run its course," Zimmermann proposes that only in an inherently ethical and intellectual incarnational hermeneutic can "an immediate transcendent unity and goal for human reason" be discovered (p. 392).

Notes

1 See David Lyle Jeffrey's essay in this collection: "Sacred Proposals and the Spiritual Sublime."

2 See, for example, Cathy Caruth's *Unclaimed Experience: Trauma, Narrative, and History* (Baltimore: Johns Hopkins University Press, 1996) 1–9; Richard Kearney, *On Stories: Thinking in Action* (London and New York: Routledge, 2002) 49.

3 In a related vein, F.R. Ankersmit, in *Sublime Historical Experience* (Stanford, CA: Stanford University Press, 2005), argues that language actually functions to distance

us from traumatic experience: "We have language in order *not* to have experience and to avoid the fears and terrors that are typically provoked by experience" (11).

4 Ankersmit, *Sublime Historical Experience*, 338; Dominick LaCapra, *Writing History, Writing Trauma* (Baltimore: Johns Hopkins University Press, 2001) 23.

5 LaCapra, *Writing History, Writing Trauma*, 23.

6 Shoshana Felman, "Education and Crisis, or the Vicissitudes of Teaching," *Trauma: Explorations in Memory*, ed. Cathy Caruth (Baltimore: Johns Hopkins University Press, 1995) 32, 36.

7 Monique Lang, "Trauma and Spirituality," *Healing from Post-Traumatic Stress: A Workbook for Recovery* (New York: McGraw-Hill, 2007) 163–76; Ellen Macfarland, *The Sacred Path Beyond Trauma: Reaching the Divine through Nature's Healing Symbols* (Berkeley, CA: North Atlantic Books, 2008); Michael G. Wessells and Carlinda Monteiro, "Healing the Wounds following Protracted Conflict in Angola: A Community-Based Approach to Assisting War-affected Children," *Handbook of Culture, Therapy, and Healing*, ed. Uwe Peter Gielen, Jefferson M. Fish, and Juris G. Draguns (New York and London: Routledge, 2004) 321–41.

8 In *Writing History, Writing Trauma*, LaCapra writes, "I have speculated that the sublime may itself be construed as a secular displacement of the sacred in the form of a radically transcendent, inaccessible, unrepresentable other" (93). LaCapra's claim is echoed by Helmut J. Schneider, who, in considering the Romantic sublime, writes, "The fascination of the sublime was largely due to the fact that in it nature assumed the quality of the 'aweful' transcendence of God; the sublime natural object provided an apt substitute for waning religious belief.... At the same time... otherworldly transcendence was conferred on the human subject" (Helmut J. Schneider, "Nature," *Romanticism*, ed. Marshall Brown [Cambridge: Cambridge University Press, 2000] 112, vol. 5 of *The Cambridge History of Literary Criticism*).

9 Abraham Joshua Heschel, *God in Search of Man*, qtd. in John C. Merkle, *Approaching God: The Way of Abraham Joshua Heschel* (Collegeville, MN: Liturgical Press, 2009) 14–15.

10 John C. Merkle, "The Sublime, the Human, and the Divine in the Depth-Theology of Abraham Joshua Heschel," *The Journal of Religion* 58.4 (1978): 376, 379.

11 Clayton Crockett, *Interstices of the Sublime: Theology and Psychoanalytic Theory* (New York: Fordham University Press, 2007) 10. See also his *A Theology of the Sublime* (London and New York: Routledge, 2001). Kevin Hart would see in Crockett's thesis evidence of his claim that some recent thinkers perceive "the sublime and indeed the category of feeling" as "the peculiarly modern way in which we are religious" (Hart, "Postmodernism," *The Oxford Handbook of English Literature and Theology*, ed. Andrew Hass, David Jasper, and Elisabeth Jay [Oxford: Oxford University Press, 2007] 184).

12 Kevin Hart, "God and the Sublime," *God Out of Place? A Symposium on L.P. Hemming's "Postmodernity's Transcending, Devaluing God,"* ed. Yves de Maeseneer (Utrecht, Neth.: Ars Disputandi, 2005) 34. Here Hart is pointing to the agreement of Karl Barth and Laurence Hemming on this issue.

13 Hart, "Postmodernism," 184.

14 Elie Wiesel's comments are published on the front cover of David Blumenthal's *Facing the Abusing God: A Theology of Protest* (Louisville, KY: Westminster/John Knox Press, 1993); Rabbi Rebecca W. Sirbu, *Theologies of Suffering: How Judaism*

Can Help You Cope, 2007, http://www.huc.edu/kalsman/articles/Rebecca.pdf. This document was produced with the support of the National Center for Jewish Healing and the Kalsman Institute on Judaism and Health.

15 Slavoj Žižek, *The Sublime Object of Ideology* (London: Verso, 1989) 203. Here Žižek discusses the Kantian sublime.

16 Judith Butler, "Desire," *Critical Terms for Literary Study,* ed. Frank Lentricchia and Thomas McLaughlin, 2nd ed. (Chicago: University of Chicago Press, 1995) 374.

17 Jean-François Lyotard, *The Postmodern Explained: Correspondence 1982–1985,* ed. Julian Pefanis and Morgan Thomas, trans. Don Barry et al. (Minneapolis: University of Minnesota Press, 1992) 11.

18 Editorial introduction, *Between Ethics and Aesthetics: Crossing the Boundaries,* ed. Dorota Glowacka and Stephen Boos (Albany: State University of New York Press, 2002) 2. It should be noted that Glowacka and Boos qualify this statement by explaining that Kant did not manage to work out in any systematic way this relation between "aesthetic experience" and moral feeling (2).

19 Editorial introduction to *Aesthetics and Ethics: Essays at the Intersection,* ed. Jerrold Levinson (Cambridge: Cambridge University Press, 1998) 1–25.

20 Julia Kristeva, "Strangers to Ourselves: The Hope of the Singular," *States of Mind: Dialogues with Contemporary Thinkers on the European Mind,* ed. Richard Kearney (New York: New York University Press, 1995) 11. See also Julia Kristeva, *Strangers to Ourselves,* trans. Leon S. Roudiez (New York: Columbia University Press, 1991).

21 Peter Carrier, *Holocaust Monuments and National Memory Cultures in France and Germany Since 1989* (New York: Berghahn, 2005) 137–38.

22 Jean-François Lyotard, "Answering the Question: What Is Postmodernism?" *The Postmodern Condition,* trans. R. Durand (1979; Manchester, UK: Manchester University Press, 1986) 78, 82; here Bowen quotes Richard Kearney's notion of the "pragmatic impiety" of Lyotard's account (Richard Kearney, *Poetics of Imagining: Modern to Post-modern* [Edinburgh: Edinburgh University Press, 1998] 209).

23 Terry Eagleton, *After Theory* (London: Allen Lane; New York: Basic Books, 2003); Jean Baudrillard, *Simulacra and Simulation,* trans. Sheila Faria Glaser (Ann Arbor: University of Michigan Press, 2004).

THE CLASSICAL AND
BIBLICAL
INHERITANCE

SACRED PROPOSALS AND THE SPIRITUAL SUBLIME

David Lyle Jeffrey

> "...look here; this is the thankfull glass,
> That mends the looker's eyes."[1]

Our terms of reference for this collection, "suffering, the sacred, and the sublime," might seem to some ears and eyes a strange conjunction, even a confusion of categories. If this be so, it is in part because much that now forms critical training in our discipline has served to make formally incongruous what in Holy Scripture is represented as uniquely God-joined. As with life, so typically with the arts: we "postmoderns" have tended to divorce with a social construct what, in liturgical language, "he has joined together." Probably most of our contemporaries have long since ceased to give such holy conjunctions as our topic implies a blessed thought.

There is nonetheless precedent for our contemporaries' sense of disjunction in these terms. For the Greeks, for example, the apogee of "sacred" aspiration was *arête*, an acquired legacy of human dignity and heroic achievement that makes of heroic man himself the transcendent: accordingly, for Protagoras of Abdera, "Man is the measure of all things, of those that are, that they are; of those that are not, that they are not."[2] Suffering for the Greeks is just one part of the price for achieving *arête*; inevitable, but best thought of as an opportunity for the operation of manly virtues, and, of course, their visible triumph. The object of human aspiration is public honour.

The Variable Sublime

Historically, the "sublime" is a more difficult concept. For Jean-François Lyotard, this difficulty is intrinsic: the "sublime" points to an aporia in human reason, expressing the "boundary" of our conceptual powers, and thus, for him, revealing the multiplicity and instability of the postmodern world.[3] In a fashion aslant from what Lyotard intends, a certain notion of aporia features in what I will attempt to characterize here as the Christian spiritual sublime. But it is appropriate first to take our bearings from more conventional notions.

For the Greeks the sublime was a rhetorical category, defining what one felt in the presence of human greatness or paragon beauty: what the pseudonymous Athenian, Cassius Longinus, called "the grand or noble elements in a work of art."[4] Although Longinus clearly associates the sublime with great ideas, enthusiasm, and lofty language, the effect of such language is dependent on an infused emotional rather than simply rational assent; the moment of sublimity ideally transports one suddenly, taking the reader "out of himself." One of his examples is the phrase "Father Zeus, kill us if thou wilt, but kill us in the light."[5] The thrill in such a rhetorical moment is to Longinus cathartic, and representative to a degree that the Greek sublime, though primarily a rhetorical conception, is akin to religious *ex-stasis*, as in the tragedies of Sophocles, with their stark antimonies of greatness and tragic destruction, captured in high moments of definitive lofty speech. (One thinks not merely of *Oedipus* but also of *Antigone*.)

The Romans located the sacred in the *civitas*, at its plenitude, in imperial power itself. The worship of godlike Caesar was a concomitant both of political aspiration and the *pietas* one owed to the glory of Rome; personal suffering was an unfortunate distraction to the pursuit of civic virtue, ideally to be borne with stoic indifference. But in Roman culture the rhetorical sublime of the Greeks persisted in writings as divergent as Virgil's *Aeneid* and the orations of Cicero, while the public worship of eroticized human beauty and a voyeuristic appetite for horror conflated destructively to undermine it.

Much later, a European revival of Longinus by figures such as Nicolas Boileau-Despréaux, the French neoclassicist, ironically turned attention away from a verbal and rhetorical sublime to a notion more often visually prompted by nature, one which came to be called the "natural sublime." The gentlemanly sense of aesthetic awe produced by a traveller's mountaintop experience, characterized in the writing of John Dennis, is of this species.[6] For Dennis, such vistas from the precipice are a pleasure to the eye, much as is music to the ear, but "mingled with Horrours, and sometimes almost with despair."[7] For Joseph Addison this effect becomes an "agreeable terror," and even Edmund Burke's definition of the sublime as a kind of edgy, narcotic unsettling produced by nightfall and darkness seems somewhat effete by comparison with the classical precedent.[8] Addison's agreeable terror, like James Thompson's "rapturous terror," is of itself neither holy nor unholy—though it may substitute for either. But in certain contexts, the "sacred" for Enlightenment neoclassicism is in effect some order of the natural sublime, as it is in Kant.[9] In Mark Aikenside's *The Pleasures of the Imagination* (1744), the sublime is simply the highest form of Beauty. Edward Young's poem "Night Thoughts" argues for the "infinite" of the nighttime starry sky as a primary source of the sublime; Edmund Burke is more expansive: "[W]hatever is in any sort terrible…or operates in a manner analogous to terror, is a source of the *sublime*; that is, it is productive of the strongest emotion which the mind is capable of feeling."[10] Among Burke's greatest sources of the sublime he lists "Vacuity, Darkness, Solitude and Silence," and one can see one way these features can come to substitute, if oddly, for traditional religious awe in Gothic novels such as Horace Walpole's *Castle of Otranto* (1765).

By the time of Wordsworth's *Guide to the Lakes* (1810), the "scary" sort of natural sublime had been tamed somewhat, drawn rather to the rustic "picturesque"; vignettes of wilderness beauty sought by the painters on their mountain hikes through the Lake District gorges, peaks, and precipices were framed by them in a mirror—a convex glass—for the sake of concentrating the sublime elements for representation on tidy little canvases for the drawing-room. In fact, the painters turned their backs on the actual landscape to find in their looking glass a new picturesque "sublimity"—already there is an aesthetic remove from the ostensible source of the sublime in nature's grandeur such as is still immediate in the painting of Caspar David Friedrich. The "Wordsworthian egotistical sublime," as the poet John Keats dubbed Wordsworth's poetic—that is, a primary focus on himself and his own inner mental processes rather than the external nature that Keats believed was merely his excuse for self-indulgence in a poem like "Tintern Abbey"—we might take to be a further turn away from objective toward subjective resources for the sublime.[11] In "Tintern Abbey," fully seven-eighths of the lines are not about the landscape but about the poet's internal musings on

> A presence that disturbs me with the joy
> Of elevated thoughts; a sense sublime
> Of something far more deeply interfused,
> Whose dwelling is the light of setting suns,
> And the round ocean and the living air,
> And the blue sky, and the mind of man. (lines 94–99)[12]

In his mystical interiority Wordsworth elides natural and supernatural, as has memorably been observed elsewhere,[13] essentially a blurring and elision of the content in all three terms: "suffering, the sacred, and the sublime."

To summarize, there have been two prominent understandings of the "sublime" in Western aesthetic theory, classical and late neoclassical, namely the rhetorical sublime of Longinus and the natural sublime of the eighteenth-century poets and landscape painters. The second of these came to be quite protean; it could apply to art in which subject matter akin to campfire ghost stories or horror movies in our own time might for some people substitute for the awe once associated specifically with primary religious encounters. Suffering in such a context tends to be suffering for dramatic effect — a kind of aesthetic component of the sublime. Real-life suffering to such a sensibility as one cultivated by the "Age of Reason" remained, of course, lamentable, but it was also liable to produce divergent reactions: to the stoic mind it might provide an occasion for exhibiting rational self-control; to others among the "rationalists," all human suffering became a proof against God, and sufficient excuse for an anti-religious tirade.

We need not detain ourselves further over this largely familiar territory. In our context, however, it is essential to note that biblical conceptions of "the sacred," of "suffering," and even, if we may stretch our sense of the term, of "the sublime" are notably at sharp variance with both classical and neoclassical formulations — this, despite some superficial similarities. In the Judaism of the Old Testament, for example, sublimity and the sacred are in some contexts (e.g., in the Psalms and Isaiah) arguably indistinguishable; yet in narrative contexts, experience of the sacred is anything but an aesthetic matter. Rather, such experience is both real and radical, compelling either abject silence or carefully prescribed worship of a deity too terrible even to name. Art may do high honour to the divine, as in the cherubim made by Bezalel, son of Uri, to hover over the ark, but representation of the divine nature itself (Exod. 20) is forbidden. Face-to-face encounter is as likely to bring about death (Gen. 32; Exod. 19:12; Isa. 6) as enlightenment simply because God's holiness is so terrible it cannot be encountered directly. Rhetorically, "a word fitly spoken" may be "like apples of gold in pictures of silver" (Prov. 25:11) — that is, lofty language is aesthetically pleasing where the ear is concerned, and one may "make a joyful noise unto the Lord" (Ps. 100:1; cf. Pss. 148–50) or praise him with the sound of harps, but no one who has not already lost his mind will approach the holy of holies for an experience of Addison's "agreeable horror."[14] The sublime encountered in the Hebrew Scriptures may find lofty rhetorical expression — one thinks of the annihilating power of God's speech from the whirlwind to Job (Job 38–42), a discourse which ends, however, not in Job's being thrilled but in his repentance. Another example might be the Vision of Isaiah (ch. 6), while the Magnificat of Mary (Luke 1:46–55) is the pre-eminent example from the Gospels. Yet, as even these most luminous examples suggest, though rhetorically grand biblical eloquence may achieve heights of the sublime, it occurs when the voice of God (or his most intimate interlocutor) is speaking, and that voice does not typically conform to the manner suggested by Longinus. There is in the Bible no equivalent whatsoever of the eighteenth century "natural sublime."

Suffering as *Problematique*

Suffering in the biblical context is metaphysically and ethically front-loaded, in its generality a consequence of sin. Extreme suffering may be taken sometimes as a sign that God has turned away from his people, as in Isaiah 51 or the Lamentations of Jeremiah (or as reflected in Ps. 102:1–10), because of his "indignation and wrath" at personal disobedience or sacrilege (102:10). Elsewhere individual suffering may be simply inexplicable in human terms, as in the book of Job, part of the great mystery of a world still held in sin's great sway, a thoroughly disagreeable *agon* through which the ultimately redemptive purposes of God may perhaps be glimpsed with the eyes of faith but certainly not comprehended in any fully satisfying rational way by a logic of cause and effect.

In the Old Testament view suffering is accordingly neither a rite of passage for heroic manhood nor an occasion for demonstrating stoic indifference. Above all, it is no proof against God — even in the extreme case of Job. In fact, in the biblical account, as evident in the Suffering Servant poems, perhaps especially Isaiah 53, there is even a divinely ordained substitutionary suffering in which one who is "wounded for our transgressions and bruised for our iniquities" (53:3, 11) "pleases the Lord" (53:10), especially when the suffering is accompanied by intercession for others (53:12).

In some biblical contexts, that is to say, suffering can become a critical component of the sublime, but hardly by way of being an aesthetic element. To wit: Isaiah 53, a Messianic poem for both Jews and Christians, has been repeatedly described as a poem exhibiting the "height of the Hebrew sublime."[15] For those of the adoption, who, to know God, must come to him through Christ, suffering of the order suggested by Isaiah's poem typically becomes the defining term, the critical presupposition for any comprehension of either the sacred or the sublime. In a Christian context the Cross is accordingly the singular axis around which all three of our collection's terms ("sacred," "suffering," and "sublime") constellate. That which to other world views is in fundamental contradiction to the sacred and the sublime, namely terminal and unmerited suffering, here becomes their common anchor and ground of being. Among myriad apostrophes to the Cross on which the Saviour died, a few lines from a seventeenth-century spiritual diary can render explicit this paradoxical yet, for Christians, essential conjunction of joy and sorrow, sublimity and appalling dishonour. For Thomas Traherne, "The Cross is the abyss of wonders, the centre of desires, the school of virtues, the house of wisdom, the throne of love, the theatre of joys, and the place of sorrows; It is the root of happiness, and the gate of Heaven."[16]

Traherne's apostrophe is a summation of what we might call the "spiritual sublime"; in fact, this passage could be an epigraph for our collection, for not only do his phrases remind us of a faith in which the Cross is "the most exalted of all objects," a paragon of sublimity, "the only supreme and sovereign spectacle in all Worlds," but Traherne also describes it as "the only *mirror* wherein all things appear in their proper colours: that is, sprinkled in the blood of our Lord and Saviour."[17] Here then, says Traherne, is the one glass through which we may hope to see less darkly than through any other—almost, as it were, to see the One whom most we would love, face to face. This notion of the sublime—a distinctively Christian conception—stands apart from all others.

Sublimity and Suffering: The Paradox
Literary critics have long seen Christian paradox as an animating theological insight in seventeenth-century poetry, particularly among the "metaphysical" poets such as George Herbert, John Donne, Richard Crashaw, and Henry Vaughan. The "paradox" is, of course, both deeper than a metaphysical conceit and of greater longstanding. Rooted in centuries of Christian theological reflection on the perpetual contradiction of God's glory by our human ignominy—between his holiness and our unholiness—is a counterintuitive understanding of reality in which that contradiction is shattered from above: the very Prince of Glory condescends to the crude inglorious human lot; his perfection and purity "become sin" for us. The way up, therefore, becomes the way down, and death may be life (John 12:24–26). In this understanding, personal suffering may, *imitatio Christi*, become a substitutionary gift of love to another, a transfiguration of misery by joy, offered up as a sacramental thanksgiving.

Take for example this brief Middle English poem from a thirteenth-century manuscript entitled *Speculum Ecclesie* ("a mirror, or glass, for the Church"):

> Nou goth sonne under wode;
> Me reweth, Marie, thi faire rode.
> Nou goth sonne under tre;
> Me reweth, Marie, thi sone and the.[18]

This compression captures our paradox even more concisely than does the passage from Traherne, if only by juxtaposing more forcibly an element of the natural sublime—a sunset over a "wood" or forest—with the thought of the beauty of Mary's countenance (her "rode" in Middle English), but here in a way which prompts a sudden flood of sorrow or pity (*rewes /rewen*, from the Old English *hreowen*) rather than simply a gasp of awe or admiration. The second two lines of the quatrain enrich the "natural" sublime by reminding us why it is that the speaker experiences both joy and sorrow simultaneously. At the literal level a superficial reader might take the third line for a repetition of the first, replacing the forest (plural) with a singular metonymic tree. But that singularity is of course the point of the entire poem; it is the Cross our anonymous poet means to be the subject of his poem, and he makes that explicit by concluding with intensification in his final line: "I pity, Mary, your son and you." The English homonym by which the "sun" which sets over the woods and the "Son" who dies on the tree coalesce gathers in resonances, of course, from many sources. But these associations are suddenly fused in the Church's liturgical memory of those three hours on Good Friday when the sky grew so dark it was almost as though the world stopped turning. Recollection of it calls up a reality we too may find deeply conflicting: the most sublime moment of salvation history occurs at just that moment when the self-offering of divine glory is almost eclipsed, as it were, by human ugliness. The Cross of Calvary is at once an "abyss of wonders" and "the centre of desires."[19] A scene of hideous suffering, justly evocative of revulsion and the deepest sorrow, has become our object most holy, the most sacred sign of the Christian Church, a point of concentration at which uniquely the sacred, the spiritual sublime, and deepest suffering meet and merge.

When we find this conjunction hard to look upon we may, as did medieval Christians, make a "rood screen," a tracery of wood reminiscent of the autumnal branches of the wood through which the red sun sets in the west, as a means of veiling our eyes. Or, in our time, we may far more dangerously seek to bypass Good Friday altogether, trying, as it were, to get straight to the Resurrection without passing through the valley of the shadow of his death. But if our reflex is of the latter sort, according to the *Speculum Ecclesie*, we will not see through the glass we have been given very well at all, darkly or otherwise. In other words, we shall misunderstand the "good" of the Good News and of Good Friday both. Moreover, we shall miss seeing into that beauty upon which the poet meditates compassionately, in his gaze upon the quiet, peaceful countenance of Mary, Virgin most beautiful, Mother most sorrowful—for these two faces cannot be separated from each other in the eyes of the Church. (One may think here of the paradox as captured by Michelangelo in his matchless *Pietà*).

Good News and Bad

It is to be expected, of course, that the altars of Christian churches should have crosses—that worship should, indeed, be under the sign of the Cross. In the Middle Ages, when the Eucharistic celebrant invariably faced the altar, he was in every overt visual as well as verbal sense made mindful of Calvary.

Altarpieces, that is to say, that particularly medieval species of reredos painting that functioned as the backdrop of the altar and its vessels, often made the
suffering of Christ on the Cross the centre of visual focus; in larger altarpieces,
such as the famous *Isenheim Altarpiece* of Matthias Grünewald, the crucifixion scene might be surrounded by other elements of the salvation narrative,
for which the grim scene at Calvary is the "centerpiece." These elements in
some cases include all the major elements of the story of human salvation. In
the *Ghent Altarpiece* of the van Eyck brothers (Figure 1.1), this means that
when we see inside an otherwise enclosed interior panel, it is precisely as we
sing in the great hymn of Prudentius, an evocation "Of the Father's love
begotten / Ere the worlds began to be," and we are specifically reminded that
Christ "is Alpha and Omega / He the source, the ending he."[20] That is, the
glory of God is here pictured as the glory of the only begotten Son of the
Father, full of grace and truth, but now seated forever in eternal majesty, surrounded by the angelic choristers and musicians, who sing "evermore and
evermore" his praises. But the outermost top frame shows us ourselves "in
Adam," under a faux relief carving of the sacrifice of Abel. That is, we see the
entire story of human redemption in the context of our desperate need for it:
Adam and Eve are ourselves, disclosed by sin, ashamed and sorrowful.

Figure 1.1 Jan van Eyck (c. 1390–1441), *Ghent Altarpiece* (open state), 1432. Cathedral of
St. Bavo, Ghent, Belgium. Photo Credit: Scala/Art Resource, New York.

The altarpiece is textually mediated with exacting theological precision: the inscriptions surrounding the supreme figure of the Deity are biblical: "*Rex regum, Dominus dominantium*" — King of Kings and Lord of Lords, a verbal harbinger of the Parousia to come (1 Tim. 6:15; Rev. 12:14). John the Baptist has his Bible open to Isaiah 40: "Comfort ye my people"; Isaiah's fortieth chapter (e.g., verses 6 and 31) was taken by medieval exegetes to anticipate John's role in announcing the Messiah. The writing over Mary has been altered, so as to refer now to her immaculate purity (rather than simply, as from Isaiah 7:14, to her virginal state). But in the lower panels the text is more straightforwardly biblical: the Adoration of the Lamb (Rev. 5) is the central painting of his polyptych thematically (Figure 1.2). On the altar is written John 1:29: "Behold the Lamb of God, which takes away the sin of the world." Above this to the left is "*Ihesus via*," to the right "*vita, V[er]ita[s]*" (John 14:6). The foreground fountain quotes from Rev. 22:1, "a pure river of water of life, clear as crystal, proceeding out of the throne of God and of the Lamb." The buildings are meant, as perhaps the palm tree indicates, to suggest the heavenly Jerusalem. The groups of personages which surround the altar, adoring the Lamb, include the just judges, the holy warriors (martyrs), the holy recluses, and holy pilgrims — metonymically, those who have given their all for Christ — in this sense, also a *speculum ecclesie*, a mirror of the faithful Church of all the ages.

The scene is intended to be one of compelling beauty, and, as an altarpiece, it occupies the place of that greatest and most holy beauty for which the

Figure 1.2 Jan van Eyck (c. 1390–1441), The Adoration of the Lamb, detail from the *Ghent Altarpiece*, 1432. Cathedral of St. Bavo, Ghent, Belgium. Photo Credit: Scala/Art Resource, New York.

Eucharist itself is the symbol. Thus, at the precise centre of this program, to remind us of that which makes a living Church possible, is that rather grotesque image of the Lamb, with its lifeblood flowing into the Eucharistic chalice: "Behold, the Lamb of God who takes away the sin of the world. Come, taste and see that the Lord is good." Here, in stark visual representation, is sacred sublimity—and acknowledgement of its steep price, immeasurable suffering.

But this is not the view that meets the eye of the casual art tourist. With the altarpiece wings closed, as would be the case through Lent and Passiontide, we see rather the Annunciation of the Incarnation, Gabriel appearing to Mary (Figure 1.3). This "outer" subject is, in fact, the most common of late medieval altarpiece subjects, conjoining the proclamation of the Good News with the preaching of the Gospel, and the treatment here is in many ways typical. Beneath the prophet Zechariah, who cries out "Rejoice greatly O daughter of Zion; shout, O daughter of Jerusalem: behold, thy King cometh unto thee" (Zech. 9:9), is a beautiful angel Gabriel, slightly bowing. He bears a lily (symbolic of the virgin's purity), but in such a way as to evoke a courtly beseeching, as St. Anselm suggests, a kind of marriage proposal. His greeting, "*Ave gratia plena, D[omi]nus tecum,*" from Luke's gospel (1:28) is only the first part of his greeting and high compliment: "Hail, highly favored one" (Gk. *kecharitomene*), but the term, both in Greek and Latin, is also such a term as may well be used in a courtly address by a suitor to a lady who is the object of his desire. It suggests that she is seen as in all ways beautiful or, as the text of Psalm 45 says, "all glorious within" (45:13). As in the commentary of St. Bonaventure on the narrative in Luke, she is thus "exceedingly comely with an incredible beauty... in the eyes of all, gracious and loveable."[21]

Over the large, discreet, empty space between Gabriel and the Virgin are two sibyls from classical mythology: on the left the Erythraean Sibyl paraphrases Virgil's *Aeneid* to suggest that Gabriel's words are not merely those we associate with a worldly courtship, but a holy proposal: "Not offering human words, you are inspired by a divinity on high."[22] The Cumaean Sibyl quotes Augustine's *City of God* to say, "Your king of future centuries is coming in the flesh."[23] Both of these phrases that "seers in old time / Chanted of with one accord," as the hymn of Prudentius has it, serve to heighten our awareness that Gabriel himself is a suitor on behalf of someone far greater and give extra resonance to the courteous manner of the angelic proposal.[24] (Such intermediation was a well-understood practice in noble courtship.) But that the proposal is of "marriage," or a mystery analogous to it, is reinforced by the messianic prophecy of Micah: "Out of thee shall come forth that one who is to rule Israel" (5:2).

Mary has been found as she almost always is in Northern annunciations of this period, kneeling before a copy of the Scriptures (sometimes it is a book of

Figure 1.3 Jan van Eyck (c. 1390–1441), *Ghent Altarpiece* (closed state), 1432. Annunciation, Prophets Zechariah and Micah, Eritrean and Cumaean Sibyls, Donors, Saints John the Baptist and John the Evangelist. Cathedral of St. Bavo, Ghent, Belgium. Photo Credit: Scala/Art Resource, New York.

hours)—a student of the Word of God (Figure 1.4). Her hands crossed over her breast indicate iconographically her assent to the sacred proposal. But here too are the words the gesture signifies: "*ecce ancilla domini*" ("Behold, the handmaiden of the Lord"). As the Spirit—iconograpically, the dove—then "overshadows" her, we note further that the words are painted upside down and written from right to left. These words are evidently neither for us nor even for the angel who has come "courting." They are positioned to show that her assent to the sacred proposal is directed upward to that Lord most holy, her coming King. If we are to read these words—which, to become part with

Figure 1.4 Jan van Eyck (c. 1390–1441), *Ghent Altarpiece*, polyptych with The Adoration of the Lamb, 1432. The Virgin Mary of the Annunciation, from the centre of the workday panels. Oakwood, 164.8 × 71.7 cm. Cathedral of St. Bavo, Ghent, Belgium. Photo Credit: Erich Lessing/Art Resource, New York.

the bride in her joy, we must — then it must be with the aid of a mirror — figuratively, the *Speculum Ecclesie*, the mirror of the Church. Only then, the painter suggests, can the meaning of the Gospel be fruitful, that is, become intelligible to us in the mirror of our own assent.

There is yet more to this altarpiece than meets the eye. But I would make two final observations, both critical to understanding this "sublime" example of sacred art, the *Ghent Altarpiece* of the brothers van Eyck. The first I borrow directly from St. Bonaventure's commentary on Luke: "Now this fruitfulness took place through *God's action*, the *angel's annunciation*, and the *virgin's consent*, so that the manner of our restoration might correspond to the manner of the fall."[25] Bonaventure quotes appropriately St. Bernard, who said, "It pleased God to reconcile humanity to himself in the same way and order in which he knew it had fallen."[26] The point of both biblical commentators is clear: the sacred proposal to Mary is a deliberate counter to the unholy proposal of the serpent to Eve; Mary's holy assent to the divine proposal is a counter to Eve's unholy seduction by an infernal proposition. This is a point which both early modern and modern painters often subvert — as, for example, in the *Annunciation* by Lorenzo Lotto, with its overt and seamy analogy to one of the rapes of Jupiter.[27] But a suggestive coupling of implied sexual violence with the holy scene is evident enough also in Dante Gabriel Rossetti's version of the "*Ecce Ancilla Domine*" theme, in which a terrified Mary huddles against the wall from the suggestive, stem-first presentation of a cut lily by the somewhat too-naturalistically portrayed angel.

Sacred Proposal, Sublime Suffering

All such subversion degrades the sacred proposal, denying Mary's agency, her gracious obedience. In quite a different fashion than Lotto's or Rossetti's depictions imagine, there will of course be dire as well as glorious consequences. In the *Ghent Altarpiece* the angel's beckoning hand points not to himself but to the Cross under whose sign he serves. In the liturgy of the medieval church and in its iconography, the sacred proposal here exemplified is an invitation not only to participate in the most sublime imaginable of human joys, but also to identify intimately with the way of the Cross. There are not only the joys of the Virgin to think of here, but also her sorrows; so too for the Church, the bride of Christ, of whom Mary in these scenes is the preeminent exemplar. The point of the juxtaposition of outer and inner panels in the Ghent polyptych — the distinction between the view from outside, as it were, and from inside the Church's story, is now clear — namely, that the Good News of human redemption will not be fully comprehended until, so to speak, before the altar we see and confess this *entire* story to be our story. Then we who still await the final consummation can, by the mediation of both word and image,

Figure 1.5 Rogier van der Weyden (c. 1399–1464), *Annunciation*, c. 1455. Left panel of a triptych (Columbia altarpiece). Oil on oak, 139.4 × 72.9 cm. Inv. WAF 1190. Alte Pinakothek, Bayerische Staatsgemäldesammlungen, Munich, Germany. Photo Credit: Bildarchiv Preussischer Kulturbesitz/Art Resource, New York.

know that "the Lamb slain before the foundation of the world" (Rev. 13:8; cf. Heb. 9:26) once came into our space by a beautiful consent but is coming again on terms none may refuse, and that of this final consummation of the entire *mysterium magnum*, we can know only part, and not the whole.

In the meantime, that to which we are beckoned by the angel's Annunciation—by his holy proposal—is the way of the Cross, a way inseparable from our desire for union with God, and conjointly an apotheosis of the sublime for Christians. When Rogier van der Weyden paints the *Annunciation* for an altarpiece (Figure 1.5) he makes the idea of a sacred proposal of marriage more explicit—there is, in this churchlike setting, a marriage bed and a descending homunculus—but the words of his greeting, *Ave Maria, plena gratia*, transverse the angel's sceptre, fusing thus the joyous proclamation with the further announcement that the Cross is inevitable. In the magnificent *Merode Altarpiece* of Robert Campin, the divine homunculus comes bearing his own cross.[28] A human analogy may be found in the more famous van Eyck brothers' *Arnolfini Marriage*, where we see a convex mirror in the background (in which we recognize the painter and another as bearing witness to the marriage) and the mirror frame itself shows a series of scenes from the Passion of Christ.

The juxtaposition of sacred proposal with the suffering of Calvary is, thus, basic not only to the late medieval altarpiece but to faithful proclamation of the gospel as our forebears understood it. I want to give, finally, some attention to a poem by John Donne which seizes upon a rare confluence of feast day and fast day in the liturgical calendar to make the paradox of grace, as we have been viewing it, verbally and theologically explicit: "Upon the Annunciation and Passion, falling upon one day. 1608 [March 25]." This poem nicely bookends, for our purposes, with our anonymous medieval poem and the hymn by Prudentius, and thus serves to complete my commentary on the *Ghent Altarpiece*:

Tamely, fraile body, 'abstaine to day; to day
My soule eates twice, Christ hither and away.
She sees him man, so like God made in this,
That of them both a circle embleme is,
Whose first and last concurre; this doubtfull day
Of feast or fast, Christ came, and went away.
Shee sees him nothing twice at once, who'is all;
Shee sees a Cedar plant it selfe, and fall,
Her Maker put to making, and the head
Of life, at once, not yet alive, yet dead.
She sees at once the virgin mother stay
Reclus'd at home, Publique at Golgotha;
Sad and rejoyc'd shee's seen at once, and seen
At almost fiftie, and at scarce fifteene.
At once a Sonne is promis'd her, and gone,

Gabriell gives Christ to her, He her to John;
Not fully a mother, Shee's in Orbitie,
At once receiver and the legacie.
All this, and all beetweene, this day hath showne,
Th'Abridgement of Christs story, which makes one
(As in plaine Maps, the furthest West is East)
Of the'Angels *Ave*,' and *Consummatum est*.
How well the Church, Gods Court of faculties
Deales, in some times, and seldome joyning these!
As by the selfe'fix'd Pole wee never doe
Direct our course, but the next starre thereto,
Which showes where the'other is, and which we say
(Because it strayes not farre) doth never stray;
So God by his Church, nearest to him, wee know
And stand firme, if wee by her motion goe;
His Spirit, as his fiery Pillar doth
Leade, and his Church, as cloud; to one end both.
This Church, by letting these daies joyne, hath shown
Death and conception in mankinde is one;
Or 'twas in him the same humility,
That he would be a man, and leave to be:
Or as creation he hath made, as God,
With the last judgement, but one period,
His imitating Spouse would joyne in one
Manhoods extremes: He shall come, he is gone:
Or as though one blood drop, which thence did fall,
Accepted, would have serv'd, he yet shed all;
So though the least of his paines, deeds, or words,
Would busie a life, she all this day affords;
This treasure then, in grosse, my Soule uplay,
And in my life retaile it every day. (lines 1–46)[29]

Liturgically, the paradox is highlighted in the superposition of the feast of the Annunciation (always March 25) and the moveable fast of Good Friday. The body of Christ in the Eucharist for the Feast of the Annunciation, real and present in the consecrated Host, is absent, of course, from the altar on Good Friday. Yet to Donne, as to Prudentius, this dialectic of presence and absence, between closed and open altarpiece, describes the course of salvation "full circle." The Virgin Mother appears twice in defining moments in her life as emblem of the whole salvation story, in the doubled moment, joy and sorrow, feast and fast of 1608, a metonym, "the Abridgement of Christ's story," making one, Donne writes, "the Angel's *Ave* and *Consummatum est*." Though at the objective level of the calendar the Church seldom experiences these two celebrations on the same day, it is nevertheless true that the conjunction forms a means of direction for the Church's journey, when the "Pole"—i.e., Calvary—

is coupled with the Annunciation (implicitly to the *stella maris*, "star of the sea," one of the names for Mary) so as to "direct our course." This method, Donne suggests, is a navigational analogy for the individual journey of a Christian toward the Church's Lord: "So God by his Church, nearest to him, we know / And stand firm, if we by her motion goe." The Church is thus indispensable. The juxtaposition also mirrors our own humanity, for "Death and conception in mankind is one; or 'twas in him the same humility." Thus his Incarnation, but also the role of his Church in receiving the gift prefigured in Mary: "His imitating Spouse would joyne in one / Manhoods extremes: He shall come, he is gone." Our calling in the Church is to model our way of life on this juxtaposition of sacred joy and suffering in the Way,

> So though the least of his paines, deeds, or words,
> Would busie a life, she all this day affords;
> This treasure then, in grosse, my Soule uplay,
> And in my life retail it every day. (lines 43–46)

Conclusion

In Donne's (quite representative) view, that which seems to the natural mind impossible to conjoin, sacred love and sacrificial suffering, becomes in the Christian life the essential nature of our marriage to Christ. Donne knew, and his poetry shows it, how hard it is to live the conjunction. The Cross, as he puts it elsewhere, is, for the Christian, hidden in every joy, present even in the most holy nuptial chamber. This is the extreme incongruity, or aporia, that makes Christianity's most sacred act of worship a horror to those outside an intimate understanding of the Gospel, which is perhaps to say, it makes them unable to assent to a holy proposal. But willing consent to the unimaginable — ultimately to the way of the Cross — is the indispensable precondition of the Christian spiritual sublime. What follows for the believer is not aporia, but kairos, the ever-present possibility of an epiphany in which, as the American poet Richard Wilbur has it, "for a flying moment one may see by what cross-purposes the world is dreamt."[30] Such a moment will be instant worship — not a detachable aesthetic experience, but a spontaneous, though deeply willed, "yes." As Bonaventure comments regarding the Annunciation to Mary, "the perfect consent of love occurs when it is said: 'Be it done to me according to your word.'" And he drives the point home by remembering again Bernard in this passage: "'Be it done' is a sign of desire, not an expression of doubt."[31] Bonaventure goes on to suggest that Mary's words of assent can also become the words of our own prayer, our own deeply willed desire, so that our own response to the Word of God in all its manifestations issues from love. On this account, whether celebrated by theologians, preachers, painters, or poets, Mary's consent to the sacred proposal anticipates that utter "yes" which the

Church, as bride of Christ, must give if we are to proceed beyond our joy in enigmatic figures to a far brighter sublime — the marriage supper where, as Prudentius sings it, our hearts are transported "evermore and evermore" in adoration of the Lamb.

Notes

1 George Herbert, "The H. Scriptures I," *George Herbert: The Complete English Works*, ed. Ann Pasternak Slater, new ed. (New York: Alfred A. Knopf, 1995) 56.

2 Qtd. in Christopher Stead, *Philosophy in Christian Antiquity* (Cambridge: Cambridge University Press, 1994) 15.

3 Jean-François Lyotard, *Lessons on the Analytic of the Sublime*, trans. Elizabeth Rottenburg (Stanford, CA: Stanford University Press, 1994).

4 *Peri Hupsous*, qtd. in *The Handbook of Classical Literature*, ed. Lillian Feder (New York: De Capo, 1998) 232.

5 Longinus, "On the Sublime," *Classical Literary Criticism*, orig. trans. T.S. Dorsch, rev. trans. Penelope Murray (1965; London: Penguin, 2000) 124.

6 John Dennis, as Phillip Donnelly has shown, misunderstood Longinus, but for his time in a representative way: see Donnelly's "Enthusiastic Poetry and Rationalized Christianity: The Poetic Theory of John Dennis," *Christianity and Literature* 54.2 (2005): 236–64.

7 John Dennis, *Miscellanies* (1693), *The Critical Works of John Dennis*, ed. E.N. Hooker, 2 vols. (Baltimore: Johns Hopkins University Press, 1939) 2.380–81.

8 Joseph Addison, "XXII. Pleasures of Imagination," *The Spectator* 411 (21 June 1712); Edmund Burke, *A Philosophical Enquiry into the Origin of Our Ideas of the Sublime and Beautiful* (London, 1757).

9 Immanuel Kant, *Observations on the Feeling of the Beautiful and Sublime* (1764).

10 Edward Young, *The Complaint, or Night Thoughts on Life, Death, and Immortality* (London, 1742); Burke, *A Philosophical Enquiry*, 36.

11 John Keats, letter to Richard Woodhouse, 27 October 1818, included in *The Poems of John Keats: A Sourcebook*, ed. John Strachan (New York: Routledge, 2003) 17.

12 William Wordsworth, "Lines written a few miles above Tintern Abbey," *William Wordsworth: The Major Works*, ed. Stephen Gill, Oxford World's Classics (1984; Oxford: Oxford University Press, 2000) 134.

13 M.H. Abrams, *Natural Supernaturalism: Tradition and Revolution in Romantic Literature* (New York: Norton, 1973).

14 All scriptural quotations are translations from the Latin Vulgate used by medieval authors, except in a few instances from Luke where the Authorized (King James) Version is employed.

15 Robert Lowth, *Lectures on the Sacred Poetry of the Hebrews*, trans. G. Gregory (1829; New York: Garland, 1971) 173.

16 Thomas Traherne, *Centuries of Meditations* (London: A.R. Mowbray, 1960; Wilton, CT: Morehouse, 1985) 28.

17 Ibid., 28 (italics mine).

18 "Nou goth sonne under wode," *English Lyrics of the XIIIth Century*, ed. Carleton Fairchild Brown (Oxford: Clarendon, 1932) 165–66.

19 Traherne, *Centuries*, 28.

20 "Of the Father's love begotten," "Ancient and Medieval Hymns," *An Annotated Anthology of Hymns*, ed. J.R. Watson (Oxford: Oxford University Press, 2002) 18.

21 Bonaventure, *Commentary on the Gospel of Luke*, ed. and trans. Robert J. Karris, 3 vols. (St. Bonaventure, NY: Franciscan Institute Publications, 2001–3) 1.1.47 (v. 28).

22 Virgil, *Aeneid*, in *Eclogues, Georgics, Aeneid 1–6*, trans. H. Rushton Fairclough, rev. and ed. G.P. Goold, Loeb Classical Library 63, rev. ed. (Cambridge, MA: Harvard University Press, 1916) 6.50.

23 See Book 18, Chapter 23 of Augustine's *Concerning the City of God against the Pagans* (London: Penguin, 1984).

24 "Of the Father's Love begotten," *Hymns Ancient and Modern, for Use in the Services of the Church, with Accompanying Tunes*, comp. and arr. under the musical editorship of William Henry Monk (Philadelphia, 1869) 39.

25 Bonaventure, *Commentary on the Gospel of Luke*, 1.1.40.

26 Ibid.

27 Massimo Firpo, "Storia religiosa e storia dell'arte. I casi di Iacopo Pantormo e Lorenzo Lotto," *Belfagor: Rassegna di Varia Umanità*, 59 (2004): 571–90.

28 For an exposition of this painting see David Lyle Jeffrey, *People of the Book: Christian Identity and Literary Culture* (Grand Rapids, MI and Cambridge: Eerdmans, 1996) 221–24.

29 John Donne, "Upon the Annunciation and Passion, falling upon one day. 1608 [March 25]," *John Donne: Selections from Divine Poems, Sermons, Devotions, and Prayers*, ed. John Booty (New York: Paulist Press, 1990) 98–99. There may be a pun in the last line, in which "retaile" is homonymous with "re-tell."

30 Richard Wilbur, "An Event," *The Poems of Richard Wilbur* (New York: Harcourt Brace, 1963) 106.

31 Bonaventure, *Commentary on the Gospel of Luke*, 1.1.69.

MEDIEVAL VISIONS
AND DREAMS

"LOKE IN: HOW WEET A WOUNDE IS HEERE!": THE WOUNDS OF CHRIST AS A SACRED SPACE IN ENGLISH DEVOTIONAL LITERATURE

Eleanor McCullough

In medieval allegories on the Song of Songs, the clefts of the rock of chapter 2, verse 14 were considered sacred spaces for contemplation on the sufferings of Christ. These places of refuge were specifically linked with the wounds in Christ's side, into which the believer could enter in a state of mystical rapture. Bernard of Clairvaux's commentary on the fourteenth verse states that "[t]he secret of [Christ's] heart is laid open through the clefts of his body; that mighty mystery is laid open ... God ... has even led us by the open clefts into the holy place."[1] Over time, such mystical expression was linked with devotion to a feminized saviour, who in his suffering and bleeding identified with women.[2] Even though explicit feminized imagery came to be suppressed in England during the Reformation, the invitation to enter into Christ's wounds as a place of safety and contemplation based on the clefts of the rock of the Song of Songs continued through the evangelical piety of the eighteenth century. Moreover, a few outcroppings of eroticized devotion to Christ's wounds appeared most notably in the poems of the seventeenth-century Catholic poet Richard Crashaw, as well as in some eighteenth-century Moravian hymns. Through an exploration of some of the developments of English devotion to the wounded Christ, this essay will argue that, despite some differences in emphasis, there is a discernible continuity of expression of contemplation on the cross between the medieval and post-Reformation writers. ·

Medieval contemplation on the wounds of Christ was based not only on allegorical commentaries on the Song of Songs, but also rather tenuously on the risen Christ's invitation to Thomas to put his hand into Christ's side.[3] The Church Fathers expanded this slight biblical evidence, and devotion to the suffering, human Saviour reached new heights of expression in the late Middle Ages, when Christ's body became increasingly connected with that of the female. According to medieval anatomical theories, the milk of a mother was formed by the mixture of blood and water.[4] Thus the pouring of blood from Christ's wounds was sometimes identified not only with menstruation, but also with the milk of a woman's breasts. In the same way that milk provided physical nourishment, Christ's blood provided spiritual nourishment for the believer during the Eucharistic meal. Moreover, the hole in Christ's side was considered a place of comfort or enclosure, like the womb, and his wounds, which were open and inviting, were the mystical means of access to his womb. This highly eroticized imagery was enhanced by a play on the Latin words *vulnus* for wound and *vulva* for womb or vagina.[5] .

The feminization of religious language, based on biblical images of God as a nurturing, caring provider, was present as early as the writings of the Church Fathers.[6] The first Christian theologian to refer extensively to God as a mother with nursing functions was the second-century Clement of Alexandria (c.150–215).[7] In the *Paedagogos* (Educator), which forms the central part of his trilogy, he devotes almost an entire chapter to the notion of a suckling, maternal God who gives the milk of Christ as spiritual nourishment to his children: "It was not the breasts of women that were blessed by the Lord ... it is he himself who has become the spiritual nourishment ... the breast that is the Word, who is the only one who can truly bestow on us the milk of love."[8] In the same passage, Clement makes a connection between the spiritual milk of Christ and the Eucharistic elements of bread and wine that were transformed, literally, into Christ's flesh: "He is Himself the nourishment that He gives. He delivers up his own flesh and pours out His own blood. There is nothing lacking His children, that they may grow."[9] The fusion of spiritual milk with Christ's blood was to become a much more multivalent image, replete with its own theology, in the Middle Ages.

The eleventh century witnessed the beginnings of affective piety, or devotion to the human Christ, with the teachings of Anselm of Canterbury (1033–1109). St. Anselm expanded the traditional nurturing images of Christ as Mother in his *Prayers and Meditations*, which were widely disseminated among the laity.[10] In his *Prayer to St. Paul*, he utters, "And you, Jesus, are not you also a mother? Are you not the mother who, like a hen, gathers her chickens under her wings? Truly, Lord, you are a mother; for both they who are in labour and they who are brought forth are accepted by you."[11]

By the twelfth century, feminized images of Christ became increasingly linked with devotion to his suffering on the cross. Aelred of Rievaulx (1109–1166), the founder of the English-based Cistercian order, compares the literal nursing of a mother with the metaphorical nursing of Christ as portrayed on the crucifix that adorned every altar in anchorholds. Moreover, Christ's body is spread out in a posture of welcome:[12]

> And as touchyngge holy ymages, haue in þyn awter þe ymage of þe crucifix hang-ynge on þe cros, which represente to þe þe passioun of Crist, which þu schalt folwe. Al-to-gydere he is ysprad abrood to bykleppe þe in his armes, in which þu schalt haue gret delectacioun; and hys tetys beþ al naked ischewd to þe to gyue þe melk of spiritual deletacioun and confortacioun.

> (And regarding holy images, have on your altar the image of the crucifix hanging on the cross, which represents to you the passion of Christ, which you shall follow. He is totally spread out to clasp you in his arms; you will experience great delight in this. And both his teats are made bare to you to give you the milk of spiritual delight and comfort.)[13]

Aelred's contemporary, William of St. Thierry (1085–1148), speaks explicitly of the open, inviting wounds of Christ, which in this case lead to sacral bliss in the partaking of the Eucharistic elements: "Open to us Thy Body's side, that those who long to see the secrets of the Son may enter in, and may receive the sacraments that flow therefrom, even the price of their redemption."[14]

One of the earliest English expressions of devotion to the wounds in Christ's side based on chapter 2, verse 14 of the Song of Songs is cited in the *Ancrene Wisse*, a guide for female anchorites written in the early thirteenth century. Drawing from St. Bernard's sermons on the Song, the anonymous author writes, "flih to his wunden. Muchel he luuede us þe lette makien swucche þurles in him forte huden us in. Creop in ham wið þi þoht—ne beoð ha al opene?"[15] ("Flee into his wounds. He loved us much who allowed such holes to be made in him for us to hide in. Creep into them with your thought—are they not entirely open?")[16] The author goes on to transliterate Song of Songs 2:14 as "'Mi culure... cum hud te I mine limen þurles i þe hole of mi side.'"[17] ("'My dove... come hide yourself in the openings in my limbs, in the hole in my side.'")[18] Although the language is not explicitly feminized, the writer deals with the theme of enclosure as it relates to the situation of female anchorites, who regarded themselves as devotees committed to living in womblike cells in imitation of Christ's choosing to dwell in his mother's womb.

As well as being linked with the safety of the clefts of the rock, enclosure imagery was further based on descriptions of the bride as an enclosed garden in Song of Songs 4:12, and it was closely connected with female virginity. Throughout the *Ancrene Wisse*, anchorites are exhorted to keep their bodies closed, not only sexually, but also through strict dietary and dress codes in accordance with the anchoritic rule. However, Christ's open body represents a subversion of the enclosure concept, while the paradoxical invitation to enter into his side-wound denotes a corresponding transgression into a forbidden area of ecstasy.

The feminization of religious terminology implied in the *Ancrene Wisse* and *De Institutione Inclusarum* is more explicitly expressed in two late fourteenth-century texts written in the English vernacular: the *Book of Showings* by the anchorite Julian of Norwich (1342–c.1416), and the anonymous religious love lyric "In a Valey of This Restles Mynde." In *Showings*, Julian speaks of how the loving, nurturing, and serving properties of earthly mothers are imaged in our "Moder Jhesu." He, in turn, lovingly sustains and nourishes us with the spiritual milk of the Eucharist:[19]

> The moder may geve hyr chylde sucke hyr mylke, but oure precyous Moder Jhesu, he may fede us with hym selfe and doth full curtesly and full tendyrly with the blessyd sacrament that is precyous fode of very lyfe.... The moder may ley hyr chylde tenderly to hyr brest, but oure tender mother Jhesu, he may homely lede us in to his blessyd brest by his swet opyn side and shewe us there in perty of the God-hed and the joyes of hevyn with gostely suernesse of endlesse blysse.[20]

> (The mother can give her child to suck of her milk, but our precious Mother Jesus can feed us with himself, and does most courteously and most tenderly, with the blessed sacrament, which is the precious food of true life.... The mother can lay her child tenderly to her breast, but our tender Mother Jesus can lead us easily into his blessed breast through his sweet open side, and show us there a part of the god-head, and of the joys of heaven, with inner certainty of endless bliss.)[21]

In her first comparison of Jesus with an earthly mother in this passage, Julian describes how his food is that of the Eucharistic sacrament, the source of life. While an earthly mother may feed her child with her own milk, Jesus feeds us with his very flesh. In her second comparison, she goes even further in speaking of Christ's wounds at his side as the opening to the mysteries of the God-head and to mystical union with him. Entrance to the feminized breasts of Christ is through his open wounds.

The religious love lyric "In a Valey of This Restles Mynde" is based on a mystical interpretation of the Song of Songs, in which Christ appears as the soul's bridegroom. The anonymous poet draws from the rich tradition of associating Christ's wounds with sexual and spiritual ecstasy in his subtle interweaving of sacred and profane literary strands. He writes in lines 54 to 58:

Alle myn humours Y have opened hir to —
There my bodi hath maad hir hertis baite,
Quia amore langueo.

In my side Y have made hir neste.
Loke in: How weet a wounde is heere![22]

(I have opened her up to all my bodily fluids —
There my body has been made bait for her heart,
Because I languish in love.

In my side I have made her nest.
Look in: How wet a wound is here!)[23]

Like Julian, the poet confidently employs erotic images with the implication that access to contemplation on the sufferings of Christ is through the wounds in his side. The "neste" or the womb as a sacred space also alludes to the clefts of the rock of the Song of Songs. Both sexual and Eucharistic meanings are implied in the reference to "humours," or the mingling of the blood and water of Christ with the milk and blood of the female.[24] When the Christ-figure invites the reader to "loke in" to his "neste" he is inviting entry, not only into mystical contemplation on his wounds but also into the place of sexual ecstasy implied by the word "weet," an allusion both to lovemaking and to the waters of baptism. The tone becomes increasingly devotional as the reader is urged to see Christ's wounds for herself: "Loke in: How weet a wounde is heere!"

In a later section of the poem, lines 105 to 112, the poet makes a more explicit reference to the concept of Christ as Mother. As with Julian of Norwich, he exploits both nurturing and sexual images of the feminized Christ in his description of the bride as a suckling baby at her mother's breast. Only in this way can she receive his nourishment:

My love is in hir chaumbir. Holde youre pees!
Make ye no noise, but lete hir slepe.
My babe Y wolde not were in disese;
I may not heere my dere child wepe;
With my pap Y schal hir kepe.
Ne merveille ye not though Y tende hir to:
This hole in my side had nevere be so depe,
But *Quia amore langueo.* (lines 105–12)

(My love is in her chamber, hold your peace!
Don't make any noise, but let her sleep.
I would not want my baby in distress;
I may not hear my dear child weep;
With my breast I shall her nurse.

Don't be surprised that I look after her in this way:
This hole in my side has never been so deep,
  Because I languish in love.)[25]

Sacred and profane imagery are further combined in the reminder that Christ's wounds are deep. There is no end to the tender love of Christ for the restless soul, or of the soul for Christ as she enters, in turn, into his suffering and into ecstatic union with him.

For the medieval mystics there were few barriers between the sacred and profane, just as there is no barrier as to who can enter into Christ's sufferings in loving contemplation. Christ transcended the barriers between the sacred and profane by becoming human, and transcended the barriers between women and men by identifying with women in his suffering. The invitation by medieval writers to enter into or to "loke" into Christ's side is an inferred refutation of the appeal for female sanctity by ensuring enclosed bodies. Christ's bloody body was open, welcoming, and warm, and so the entering into his wounds in mystical ecstasy denoted a breaking down of boundaries and margins.[26] In their focus on the graphic images of entrance and suckling, worshippers were by implication helping to restore the status of women within society. Women could be empowered not only through the identification of their bodies with that of Christ's, but also through the reintegration of the body and soul, or of the sacred and profane, in answer to the dualistic tendencies of the male hierarchy, adopted from the Church Fathers.[27]

For the Protestant Reformers, however, the association of the suffering of the Saviour with the pangs of women during menstruation and childbirth were no longer visually or theologically credible. Regardless, some vestiges of a feminized Christ remain in the poetry of Richard Crashaw (1612–49), even before his conversion from the Reformed to the Catholic faith. Although writing within the English lyric tradition, Crashaw was influenced by Continental writers and in particular by the affective piety of mystics such as Teresa of Avila and Francis of Sales. He can therefore be regarded as an important link between Catholic mysticism and evangelical piety as expressed by the eighteenth-century hymn writers.

In keeping with the sentiments of the "In a Valey" poet, Crashaw invites us to engage with the open wounds of the crucified Christ as an act of loving devotion. Indeed, he makes the appeal not only to "Loke in," but also to actively taste and intermingle with Christ's body and blood through the celebration of the Eucharist. This invitation is particularly evident in Crashaw's poem "On the wounds of Our crucified Lord" in which Christ's bloody body is depicted as being covered with mouths and/or eyes which are indistinguishable from each other.

O these wakefull wounds of thine!
Are they mouthes? Or are they eyes?
Be they Mouthes, or be they eyne,
Each bleeding part some one supplies.[28] (lines 1–4)

Mouths are connected with the sense of taste, while eyes, of course, correlate with sight. The inference may be not only that the mouths and eyes represent the communicants who actively partake of the elements, but also that Christ's bodily fluids and orifices are open and inviting, like the body of a woman.

Another instance of Crashaw's layering of sacred and profane imagery is in the very short and disconcerting epigram "Blessed be the pap" which is based on Luke 11:27–28. Crashaw paraphrases Christ's response to the woman who tells him, "Blessed is the womb that bore you and the breasts which nursed you!" In the biblical version, Jesus states, "More than that, Blessed are those who hear the Word of God and keep it." In Crashaw's epigram, a third person appears to challenge the woman, perhaps in order to elicit empathy with Jesus' mother, as well as with Christ's forthcoming suffering:

Suppose he had been Tabled at thy Teates,
Thy hunger feels not what he eates:
Hee'l have his Teat e're long (a bloody one)
The Mother then must suck the Son.[29] (lines 1–4)

The phrase "Tabled at thy Teates" in the first line carries the connotations both of the Christ-child formally sitting down to eat as he suckles at his mother's breast and of the Eucharistic table, at which the crucified Christ provides his very body as nourishment. The unusual use of the word "Tabled" as a verb marks it out for special attention. It is associated with the tablets of the Law of Moses and hence with Christ's charge to keep God's Word in the Lucan narrative. And yet, in Crashaw's poem, the implication is that the act of feeding on the body of Christ, who is the "Word become flesh," supersedes obedience to the Old Testament law.[30] In the second line, the poet suggests that the woman of the Lucan story, who cannot yet perceive what Christ "eats," or must endure, is nevertheless hungry for his spiritual milk. And by the third line, the teat of the mother has become blended with the teat, or the side-wound, of Christ as he suffers (or will suffer) on the cross. Sacred and profane imagery are more explicitly employed in the final line with the poet asserting, "The Mother then must suck the Son," perhaps at the communion table. The suggestion here that Crashaw is asking his readers to humble themselves in celebration of the Eucharist by kneeling before the altar table and feasting on the nurturing and suffering properties of Christ is linked with the word "Tabled" of the first line.[31] By the end of the epigram, the woman of the

Gospel story has merged with the Virgin Mary, and both will mystically feast on Christ's wounds.

This epigram has evoked particularly strong reactions from critics. William Empson, writing in 1930, goes so far as to state that "a wide variety of sexual perversions can be included in the notion of sucking a long bloody teat which is also a deep wound. The sacrificial idea is aligned with incest, the infantile pleasures and cannibalism."[32] However, when placed within the context of medieval devotion to Christ's wounds as a place of nurturing and mystical ecstasy, Crashaw's juxtaposing imagery of sucking and suckling, while at once sensual and provocative, cannot be deemed perverse.

In the poem "On our crucified lord, Naked, and bloody," Crashaw laments the covering of Christ's body on the cross by the purple garment that is his blood.

> Th'have left thee naked Lord, O that they had;
> This Garment too I would they had deny'd.
> Thee with thy selfe they have too richly clad,
> Opening the purple wardrobe of thy side.
> O never could bee found Garments too good
> For thee to weare, but these, of thine owne blood.[33] (lines 1–6)

In his play on the idea that the purple robe is both the physical garment that the soldiers removed before the crucifixion and a metaphor for Christ's blood, Crashaw suggests that Christ's blood is the only garment that is too good for him to wear. The exposure of his naked body in the line "Opening the purple wardrobe of thy side" invites contemplation on his wounds, as does the first line of the epigram, *I am the door*. In this emblematic poem based on Revelation 3:20, the words "And now th'art set wide ope" are reminiscent of the plea by the earlier poet to "Loke in" and see "How weet a wounde is heere!" (line 1).[34]

Crashaw may have appeared "too Catholic" for Reformed English sensibilities by placing so much emphasis on erotic and graphic illustrations of Christ's wounds.[35] He is deemed more of a Baroque poet, attuned to Spanish Catholic preferences for the ornate in liturgical devotion, than a metaphysical poet like his contemporaries John Donne or George Herbert, who largely write from within the Reformed liturgical tradition.[36] However, Crashaw's eroticized vision of the wounds, a vision indebted in many respects to Catholic devotional practices, was revived in part by the Moravian hymn writers. Originally from Bohemia, the Moravians made their way to England by the mid-eighteenth century, exerting a profound influence on English piety. Their early hymns were Christological and emphasized a personal response to the crucified Lord, such as the hymn entitled "Jesus, thy Blood and Righteousness," written by the founder of the movement, Count Nicolaus Ludwig von Zinzendorf (1700–1760), and translated by Charles Wesley (1707–88). Yet for a short period between 1743 and 1750, known as the "Sifting Time," the Moravians conveyed their devotion to Christ using excessively eroticized imagery. Note, for example, the following descriptions of Christ's "side-hole":

> I...
> Smell to and kiss each Corpse's Wound;
> Yet at the Side-Hole's Part,
> There throbs and pants my Heart.
> That dearest side-hole!
> Be prais'd O God, for this Spear's Slit!
> I thank thee, Soldier too for it
> I've licked this Rock's Salt round and round;
> Where can such Relish else be found! (lines 2, 4–11)[37]

The imagery is even more sexually suggestive than Crashaw's descriptions of the orifices on Christ's body. Such indelicate depictions of Christ's wound did not endure, however; they came to be suppressed by other Evangelicals as well as by the Moravians themselves. Nevertheless, these extreme examples serve to demonstrate that occasional outcroppings of eroticized devotion to Christ's wounds continued long after the English Reformation.

Many hymns from the Evangelical Revival express devotion to Christ's wounds, but they are more tempered than the works of Crashaw or the "Sifting Time" hymn writers. One hymn typical of the era is the moving "When I survey the wondrous cross" by Isaac Watts (1674–1748), in which the speaker contemplates the overwhelming significance of Christ's death. The listener is drawn into the scene of the crucifixion with the appeal to "See from His head, His hands, His feet, / Sorrow and Love flow mingled down!" (lines 9–10).[38] As well as expressing Christ's compassion for humanity, the phrase "sorrow and love" is a metonym for the blood and water that pour from Christ's wounded side. In a fourth stanza, not often included in current hymn books, Watts employs another metonym for Christ's blood:

> His dying crimson, like a robe,
> Spreads o'er his body on the tree;
> Then I am dead to all the globe,
> And all the globe is dead to me. (lines 13–16)

The depiction of Christ's blood as a crimson garment covering his naked body is evocative of Crashaw's image of the "purple wardrobe of thy side." And in the internal rhyming of "spreads" and "dead," Watts suggests that nothing matters so much to the speaker as that he be enveloped by Christ's all-encompassing blood.

The hymn perhaps most directly derived from Song of Songs 2:14 is Augustus Toplady's (1740–78) "Rock of ages, cleft for me."[39] The hymn writer was influenced by the Moravians, and the hymn is much more representative of Moravian piety than the earlier extreme example given. The medieval theme of entering into Christ's wounds in mystical contemplation is also revived but with a much stronger emphasis on the doctrine of atonement than in pre-Reformation expositions of the clefts of the rock. The hymn writer wishes not only to hide himself in the body of Christ, the "Rock of ages," but also to have his sins washed away in the blood that flows from Christ's side:

> Rock of ages, cleft for me,
> Let me hide myself in thee;
> Let the water and the blood,
> From thy riven side which flowed,
> Be of sin the double cure,
> Cleanse me from its guilt and power.[40]

These images of the blood and water flowing from Christ's "riven" side are striking, yet the writer stresses their salvific power — "be of sin the double cure" — rather than their erotic associations with the female body.[41]

While graphic illustrations of a feminized Christ displaying the open wounds at his side as well as his lactating nipples may seem strange, grotesque, and perhaps even shocking to contemporary readers, they are partly based on biblical illustrations of God. The appeal of the depictions of Christ's wounds, both during and after the Middle Ages, was that in his suffering and nurturing Christ identified with all of humanity, both male and female. The medieval mystics cut through exclusive language and imagery for God. In their balancing of male and female metaphors, they guide us towards a God who reveals masculine qualities in the gentle pursuit of his beloved bride of the Song of Songs and feminine qualities in the tender nurturing of his "dere child."[42] Moreover, even though the associations of Christ's wounds with the more eroticized aspects of the feminine sublime were suppressed by the eighteenth-century hymn writers, the concept of the clefts of the rock as sacred spaces for contemplation on the wounds of Christ continued to be as evocative for Evangelicals as for their medieval predecessors.

Notes

1 Bernard of Clairvaux, Sermon 61, *On the Song of Songs III: Bernard of Clairvaux*, ed. and trans. Kilian Walsh and Irene M. Edmonds (Kalamazoo, MI: Cistercian Publications, 1976) 144–45.

2 It has been established through the work of Caroline Walker Bynum and others that devotion to the wounds of Christ in the Middle Ages was at times both eroticized and feminized. See, for example, Caroline Walker Bynum, *Jesus as Mother: Studies in the Spirituality of the High Middle Ages* (Berkeley: University of Califor-

nia Press, 1982); David Aers and Lynne Staley, *The Powers of the Holy: Religion, Politics, and Gender in Late Medieval English Culture* (University Park: Pennsylvania State University Press, 1996).

3 John 20:27 (NKJV); subsequent biblical quotations are from the New King James Version.

4 See Caroline Walker Bynum, *Holy Feast and Holy Fast: The Religious Significance of Food to Medieval Women* (Berkeley: University of California Press, 1987) 270; Eleanor McLaughlin, "Christ My Mother: Feminine Naming and Metaphor in Medieval Spirituality," *Nashota Review* 15 (1975): 234.

5 Wolfgang Rhiele, *The Middle English Mystics* (London: Routledge and Kegan Paul, 1981) 46. St. Francis and St. Bonaventure spoke of Christ's wound as the *stimulus amoris* or "the pricking of love," i.e., the place of eroticized mysticism. Many pseudo-Bonaventuran texts in Middle English survive, such as *The Pricking of Love* and *The Prick of Conscience*.

6 The most deliberate feminizations of God are found in Isaiah 49:15 and 66:12b–13. Specific weaning imagery includes Isaiah 66:7–11 and Psalm 131:2. New Testament allusions to a nurturing Christ include 1 Peter 2: 2–3 and 1 Thessalonians 1:7, and in Matthew 23:37 and Luke 13:34, Christ depicts himself as a mother hen gathering her chicks under her wing.

7 Irenaeus and Justin Martyr also used maternal terminology for Christ, stemming from Jewish antecedents and directly influenced by the Hellenistic Jewish philosopher, Philo of Alexandria. Irenaeus referred to the Holy Spirit as feminine; see Jean Leclercq in his preface to *Julian of Norwich: Showings*, trans. Edmund Colledge and James Walsh (New York: Paulist Press, 1978) 19.

8 Clement of Alexandria, *Christ the Educator*, trans. Simon P. Wood, The Fathers of the Church 23 (Washington, DC: The Catholic University of America Press, 1954) 40, 41.

9 Ibid., 40.

10 Anselm's comments are based on Christ's depiction of himself as a mother hen gathering her chicks in Matthew 23:37 and Luke 13:34. Chrysostom, Clement of Alexandria, and Augustine also cite this passage as a basis for their doctrines on God as Mother.

11 St. Anselm, *The Prayers and Meditations of St. Anselm*, trans. Sister Benedicta Ward, S.L.G. (London: Penguin, 1973) 153.

12 Aelred's *De Institutione Inclusarum* was originally written in the 1160s, and there were two translations into Middle English: Oxford, Bodleian Library, MS Eng. Poet. a.1 (more commonly known as the Vernon Manuscript), in the late fourteenth century; and Oxford, Bodleian Library, MS Bodley 423, in the mid-fifteenth century. The English text cited here is taken from the Vernon Manuscript.

13 Aelred of Rievaulx, *Aelred of Rievaulx's De Institutione Inclusarum: Two English Versions*, trans. John Ayto and Alexandra Barratt, Early English Text Society, o.s. 287 (London: Oxford University Press, 1984) 35; translation mine.

14 William of St. Thierry, Meditation Six, *The Meditations of William of St. Thierry: Meditativae Orationes,* translated from the Latin by a Religious of C.S.M.V. (London: A.R. Mowbray, 1954) 52.

15 *Ancrene Wisse: A Corrected Edition of the Text in Cambridge, Corpus Christi College, MS 402 with Variants from Other Manuscripts: Drawing on the Uncompleted Edition by E.J. Dobson, with a Glossary and Additional Notes by Richard Dance,* ed.

Bella Millett, Early English Text Society, o.s. 325, vol. 1 (Oxford: Oxford University Press, 2005) 111.

16 *Anchoritic Spirituality: Ancrene Wisse and Associated Works*, trans. Anne Savage and Nicholas Watson (New York: Paulist Press, 1991) 155.

17 *Ancrene Wisse*, 111.

18 *Anchoritic Spirituality*, 155.

19 A possible source for the fusion of sacral and erotic bliss in the partaking of the Eucharistic elements is William of St. Thierry; see footnote 14, above.

20 Julian of Norwich, *The Showings of Julian of Norwich*. Norton Critical Edition, ed. Denise N. Baker (New York: Norton, 2005) 94.

21 The translation is from *Julian of Norwich: Showings*, trans. Colledge and Walsh, 298.

22 "In a Valey of This Restles Mynde," in *Moral Love Songs and Laments*, ed. Susanna Greer Fein (Kalamazoo, MI: Medieval Institute Publications, 1998) 69, lines 54–58; future citations are from this edition and will be given in the text by line number.

23 Translation mine.

24 Susanna Greer Fein translates "humours" as the bodily fluids of milk, water, and blood, all of which were associated with the wounds of Christ (*Moral Love Songs and Laments*, ed. Fein, 64).

25 Translation mine.

26 Much is made of this idea by Caroline Walker Bynum in both *Holy Feast and Holy Fast* and *Jesus as Mother*.

27 Of course, it is difficult to assess how widespread women's sense of empowerment was, and to what extent women were even conscious of this politicizing and renegotiation of their status in society because of the identification of their bodies with the suffering Christ. That this redefining of the margins of a woman's body could be empowering does not mean that it did effectively empower women on a large scale. We know of the writings of Julian of Norwich and Margery Kempe but the vast majority of extant mystical writings in the vernacular are either anonymous or authored by men. For more on this subject, see the introductions to excerpted texts in *Women's Writing in Middle English*, ed. Alexandra Barratt (London: Longman, 1992) 1–23; and *Gendering the Master Narrative: Women and Power in the Middle Ages*, ed. Mary Erler and Maryanne Kowaleski (Ithaca, NY: Cornell University Press, 2003) 1–16.

28 Richard Crashaw, *The Complete Poetry of Richard Crashaw*, ed. George Walton Williams (New York: Anchor Books, 1970) 24.

29 Ibid., 14.

30 John 1:14.

31 At the time of writing the poem, Crashaw, though not yet a Roman Catholic, was influenced by the ecclesiology of William Laud, Archbishop of Canterbury, who required that communion tables be set apart and railed off in churches and that communicants kneel at the rail to receive the sacrament.

32 William Empson, *Seven Types of Ambiguity* (London: Chatto and Windus, 1930) 122.

33 Crashaw, *The Complete Poetry*, 24.

34 Ibid., 17.

35 For example, see Lorraine M. Roberts and John R. Roberts, "Crashavian Criticism: A Brief Interpretive History," *New Perspectives on the Life and Art of Richard Crashaw*, ed. John R. Roberts (Columbia: University of Missouri Press, 1990) 19.

36 On this point, see, for example, Trevor James, *The Metaphysical Poets* (Essex: Longman, 1988) 100–107.

37 Count Zinzendorf, *Hymns Composed for the Use of the Brethren* (London, 1749) 7, qtd. in Cynthia Aalders, "'Hymns and music were poured out': Moravian Hymnody and the Evangelical Revival," unpublished paper, Regent College, Vancouver, 2007, 8.

38 Isaac Watts, *The Psalms and Hymns of the Rev. Isaac Watts, D.D.: A New Edition… corrected and revised by the Rev. G. Burder* (London: Whittingham, 1806) 424.

39 See Exodus 33:22 for another reference to the cleft of the rock as a hiding place ("So it shall be, while My glory passes by, that I will put you in the cleft of the rock, and will cover you with My hand while I pass by"). Toplady may have been alluding to either one or both biblical sources.

40 Augustus Toplady, *Psalms and Hymns for Public and Private Worship: Collected… and published by Augustus Toplady, A.B. Vicar of Broad Hembury* (London, 1776) 309–10.

41 The phrase "double cure" may also be an allusion to the doctrine of "double imputation" in which the sins of humanity are laid upon Christ and he takes them upon himself as punishment from God.

42 "In a Valey of This Restles Mynde," *Moral Love Songs and Laments*, ed. Fein, 71, line 108.

SUFFERING IN THE SERVICE OF VENUS: THE SACRED, THE SUBLIME, AND CHAUCERIAN JOY IN THE MIDDLE PART OF THE *PARLIAMENT OF FOWLS*[1]

Norm Klassen

Geoffrey Chaucer wrote the *Parliament of Fowls* in the middle of his career as a poet, sometime in the late 1370s or early 1380s, and perhaps as the first celebration of St. Valentine's Day ever written.[2] It is a dream-poem, readily recognizable to a medieval audience in that well-established genre.[3] Yet the poem has posed long-standing interpretive problems, for despite being less than 700 lines long it seems rather disconnected, dividing into three distinct parts: a reading, an exploration of the temple of Venus, and the parliament of birds proper. In the first section, a reader-narrator does a book report on Cicero's *Dream of Scipio*, a Stoic work that has two main points in the narrator's telling: know thyself, and work for common profit. Each of these is refracted in the subsequent parts of the poem: the second section, which will occupy our attention here, focuses on the solitary exploration of a sacred space of love and art by a dispassionate observer, while the third opens out into the sociality of the parliament.

The Riverside Chaucer tells us that "the dominant stream in modern criticism is that which embraces the poem's discordances, dwelling in one way or another on irony, indirectness... and inconclusiveness as part of its design."[4] In what follows, I am going to suggest that the second section of the poem does not privilege inconclusiveness but rather conveys strong authorial opinions while preserving a consistent tone. That tone is one of joy, a term the semantic range of which overlaps with such adjectives as "rhapsodic" or "sublime," where the area of overlap indicates wonder and transport beyond intellectual ken. The apparent discordances of the overall design of Chaucer's poem have perhaps led readers not to expect to find firm positions on any level. Yet Chaucer's joy is doubly paradoxical. One paradox is that joy leaves him an acute observer capable of judgment. He judges art, associating it with the temple of lascivious Venus; art in her temple depicts only the suffering and death of lovers who went into her service. The second and perhaps deeper paradox is that Chaucer's handling of the tensions in the second part of the poem manifests itself as a beautifully consistent tone, a suggestion of his own commitment to an art that reveals the beauty of complex harmonies. As we shall see, an aesthetic of participatory integrity and harmonies anticipates both an objective focusing on the requirements of the work itself and a telling of metaphysical depths. Ultimately, then, the art and the sacred associated with lascivious Venus, productive of and depicting suffering, cannot be thought to represent his final thoughts on these subjects; perhaps it would be better to say that they remain unthematizable in his work.

It can be difficult to speak negatively about either love or art in any form, as I will maintain we must if we are to appreciate Chaucer's concerns and accomplishments in this poem, without appearing to privilege a certain narrow moralism. However, I simply think that an older tradition for interpreting the poetic scene in question happens to have been right and that we have lost an appreciation for Chaucer's definite opinions and moral seriousness in the process. Recent criticism tends to leave us with only binaries for understanding the poem: dogma or the reflexive questioning of authority, moral neutrality or moral*ism*.[5] Beyond such stark oppositions we need to be able, if we are to read with Chaucer (and for our own circumstances as, collectively in the theme of these essays, we attempt to do), to imagine moral positions that do not automatically have a negative valence attached to them and to recognize that moral neutrality is not the only legitimate moral position (if it is one at all). Beyond sheer dogma and relativism Chaucer imagines a synthesis of truth, beauty, and moral commitment arguably constitutive of being human.[6] Recognition of the moral positions Chaucer conveys draws attention to the achievement of a joyful tone as one of his main accomplishments in the poem that at the same time points beyond the limits of authorial control.

Chaucer against Love and Art

The middle section of the *Parliament of Fowls* contains one of Chaucer's most strident yet artistically veiled statements against the goddess of love that we find in any of his poetry.[7] Here are the relevant lines, written after the narrator has described Venus lying on her bed, naked from the breasts up and with only a "subtyl coverchef of Valence" (line 272) covering the rest of her body:

> But thus I let hire lye,
> And ferther in the temple I gan espie
>
> That, in dispit of Dyane the chaste,
> Ful many a bowe ibroke heng on the wal
> Of maydenes swiche as gonne here tymes waste
> In hyre servyse; and peynted overall. (lines 279–84)

The clause in the *Parliament of Fowls* beginning "But thus I let hire lye" (line 279), spanning a stanza break, and culminating in the phrase "in hyre service" (line 284), is long enough to have caused confusion over the identity of the goddess in whose service certain maidens waste their time, Venus or Diana.[8] In a poem about love, and given that the girls in question are referred to as "maydenes" (line 283), one might assume that the answer is obviously Diana. Yet when one accounts for the grammatical constructions, explicates the clause line by line, and incorporates the stanza following as contextual direction, one is led inexorably to the conclusion that one wastes one's time in the service of Venus.[9] Hanging on her temple walls she has, in contempt (*dispit*) of Diana the chaste, the broken bows of maidens *who went to waste their lives in the service of love*. The maidens got their bows from Diana, and these were broken and became trophies for Venus when the girls went into the latter's service. Paintings illustrate the outcome. Described in the lines following, they show scenes from lovers' lives that the narrator summarizes when he says, "Alle these were peynted on that other syde, / And al here love, and in what plyt they dyde" (lines 293–94).

The stories of these lovers invariably end in suffering and death.[10] Chaucer expresses a logic opposite to that of male erotic desire, in which service of Diana is wasted time, a way of thinking perhaps best expressed in Marvell's famous opening gambit to his coy mistress, "Had we but world enough, and time…" The remark about wasted lives supports J.A.W. Bennett's conclusion that the Venus of the *Parliament of Fowls* is quite specifically the Venus of lasciviousness.[11] D.S. Brewer's summary of many years ago would similarly appear to stand: "The Venus passage in the Parliament is clearly a moral allegory, signifying selfish, lustful, illicit, disastrous love."[12]

The culmination of the section also sheds light on Chaucer's apprehensions of art, which for him contributes pivotally to the functioning of the temple and finds its home in her sacred precincts. The context, both the stanzas immediately following the reference to wasted lives and the larger context in which the narrator describes the temple of Venus, implicates art-as-sheer-appearance in the world and degenerate values of lascivious Venus. The temple is a scene of urbane artificiality; art is constitutive of its lasciviousness. From where we have started, in the aftermath of love, Venus *uses* art as propaganda. The bows that hang on her walls as trophies symbolize triumph, while on her walls paintings flaunt the fruitless suffering of a panoply of lovers. Art in the temple is either empty appearance or evidence of waste, and Venus's temple provides such art a home in which to thrive.

Once we see where the description of Venus and her temple precincts leads — to a blunt statement about and depiction of wasted lives — we can reread the role art has had in the section all along. Such a rereading may seem increasingly necessary in the light of recent critical reluctance to find moral judgment. However, it was always going to be part of the reading process Chaucer demands, for he achieves a remarkable tone in this section of the poem, so that the indictment of Venus and therefore of art comes as a surprise.

Art — as artifice, excess, and functionality — encompasses the numerous allegorical figures who work or dally near the temple of Venus: Aray, Curteysie, Gentilesse, Beute, Flaterye, Messagerye. Together, they contribute to a mode of being emphasizing presentation, appearance, and deportment. The manifold complementarity of the figures itself suggests the excess of art, excess being a fault later writers like Spenser will portray as going hand in hand with artifice, a point to which I shall return. Among these figures, Craft attracts particular attention: "[Tho was I war]... /... of the Craft that can and hath the myght / To don by force a wyght to don folye — / Disfigurat was she, I nyl nat lye" (lines 218, 220–22). Craft is associated with violence and disfigurement. The narrator's tag remark "I nyl nat lye" draws attention to the seriousness of the description. The narrator, at least, is shocked to discover the nature of Craft and apologizes for the indictment of her he knows he implies. That apology simultaneously indicates his desire for objective description and would distance him from the world of Craft. She works by reshaping and disfiguring; he is committed to plain speaking. She may achieve, by her various wiles, the effect of causing the beloved to look lovely to the lover; he expects us to accept the description of disfigurement as her real or natural appearance. Art happens within the world of love, but he speaks artlessly and reliably. He may not actively pass judgment on her at this point, but neither is he complicit with her in the system he is describing.

On the threshold of the temple itself the narrator finds Behest and Art, the one promise, the other appearance. Behest, a linguistic character, betokens the sweet nothings of amorous speech that we are invited to reread as the empty promises of lovers destined for a tragic and wasteful end. Such talk belongs to a world sharply contrasted to the objectivity of the narrator's recent protestation, "I nyl nat lye." Together, Behest and Art serve as the gatekeepers to Venus's temple, occupying a liminal position. They beckon one to the temple and foster desire, aurally and visually; one cannot enter into the temple of Venus without passing through them and entering into their world, yet one discovers within only a cul-de-sac of death-dealing art and lasciviousness that simply exhausts itself.

The figures clustered here belong to a world of allegoresis. For Chaucer it would appear that not only the figures but the literary form as well reinforce the values of lascivious Venus. He employs allegory very little in his oeuvre;[13] in the *Parliament of Fowls* he does so only in this section and does so indulgently. Though I above agreed with Derek Brewer's assessment of the description of the temple, I do not think I would describe it as a "moral allegory," for in the context Chaucer seems to be rejecting the form even as he employs it to single out characteristics that endorse appearances and empty promises, his allegory's contentless content.[14] Some critics tend to think of medieval allegory as itself moralizing and Chaucer as rejecting allegory because of its associations with inflexible judgment.[15] In this poem Chaucer appears to associate allegory with artifice in a process of discovery that will culminate in loss and waste and to reject it on those grounds.[16] As we saw earlier with the paintings in the recesses of the temple, Chaucer locates art, that is, art-as-artifice, as both form and content in the world of the goddess.

A later poet writing in the same tradition, Edmund Spenser, can help us interpret the indictment of both love and art that Chaucer is making throughout this section. In Canto 12 of Book 2 of *The Faerie Queene*, Spenser describes the Bower of Bliss where the good knight Guyon encounters Acrasia, "that wanton Ladie."[17] As Judith H. Anderson observes, "More than once in Spenser's description of the Bower, memories of the garden in the *Parliament* are ... explicit and verbally exact."[18] Acrasia lies upon a bed of roses, prepared for "pleasant sin" (line 686), and like Chaucer's Venus wears a scant covering: "And was arayd, or rather disarayd, / All in a vele of silke and siluer thin, / That hid no whit her alablaster skin" (lines 687–89). She has with her a young knight spending his days "in lewd loues, and wastfull luxuree.... O horrible enchantment, that him so did blend" (lines 718, 720). Acrasia dwells in a bower bedecked with the trappings of art. Nature is, by comparison, niggardly. Art dresses her daughter Flora, goddess of flowers, "too lauishly" (line 449), "like a pompous bride" (line 448), "halfe in scorne / Of niggard Nature" (lines 447–48). The bower has a porch made of vines, and they have been "beauti-fide" (line 445) by art so as to oppress the weak bows. In the Bower of Bliss, art overwhelms nature. Excess typifies art, and it works to support the ambitions of sexually wanton Acrasia. In *The Faerie Queene*, Guyon must overcome the combination of the two, which he will do, but only after a severe temptation. Similar excess describes Chaucer's sudden infusion of allegory into the middle section of the *Parliament of Fowls* and his unrelenting progression towards discovery and fulfillment that ends in a gruesome art gallery.

Though rejecting the art complicit with lascivious Venus, Chaucer does not reject art outright. If we return to the passage with which we began, we can anticipate Chaucer's subtlety on the question of art by recognizing that he appears artfully to encourage such confusion of Diana and Venus: he puts his statement about wasted time in a very long clause; he employs severe enjamb-ment, spreading the meaning of the clause over two stanzas;[19] he places Diana as the named goddess nearest to the pronoun "her" in the crucial phrase "went to waste their lives *in her service.*" Venus is not even named in the entire inde-pendent clause but reduced to a pronoun used twice. At the start of the sen-tence Chaucer invites us mentally to leave Venus behind: "But thus I let her lie… and deeper inside the temple I began to see." In other words, Chaucer uses art (his skill in poetic making) to critique art. He simultaneously makes a sharp criticism and veils it. If he is against Venus and art, on the one hand, he nonetheless affirms another approach to art, just as he obviously is commit-ted to exploring varieties of love.

Art, like love, is at issue throughout the poem. If we restrict ourselves to the middle section, art confronts us in Chaucer's invocation of planetary Venus to help him "to rhyme, and endyte" (line 119), in the black and gold lettering over the gate and, on another level, in the imitation of Dante. Once we are inside the park, art recedes in favour of nature, if only momentarily; after an initial enraptured description of the trees and the park, the narration makes its segue into an allegory of love. What appears to be a celebration of nature turns out to have points of contact with literary exemplars, both a common-place description of a "mixed forest" and Giovanni Boccaccio's own descrip-tion of a park in *Il Teseida*. To follow artists is artful, and there is no question in Chaucer's mind of doing so. Near the beginning of the poem he entwined art and nature when he compared old books to old fields and new poetry to new corn (lines 22–25). Whatever we may imagine by Chaucerian natural-ism, it cannot mean utter separation from art, which would be the equivalent of linguistic or hermeneutical naïveté.[20]

Yet Chaucer does distinguish between intertextuality, or literary embed-dedness, on the one hand, and art as artifice and excess on the other. The former art privileges careful observation of nature, though intricated with inter-textuality; the latter oppresses nature and contributes to lasciviousness. In this poem, Chaucer focuses ultimately on a parliament of birds presided over by nature and resulting in love as plenitude and joy. In the middle section of the poem, he establishes a joyful tone and, paradoxically, does so through the seemingly detached observation of nature, a stance those of us with postmod-ern sensibilities might wincingly find naive and objectivizing.[21] To this tone we must now turn our attention.

Chaucer's Tone

Chaucer's great achievement in lines 92 to 294 is to establish a joyful tone and to bring his audience to an indictment of lascivious Venus and of art without altering that tone, a feat representing an alternative to artifice, excess, and functionality and drawing attention to the nature of joy in ways that will ulti-mately go beyond the bounds of the poem itself. If the section ends in indict-ment, it begins in exuberance, and when we read the poem through, not starting with the indictment as we have here, we hardly bat an eye when the judgment comes. As modern readers, the evidence suggests we can miss it altogether.

The sequence leading to the exploration of Venus's temple begins in great optimism. The narrator, who has been led to the park by a wise guide, after some hesitation enters through the gate and soon rejoices at what he sees: "But, Lord, so I was glad and wel begoon!" (line 171). He is happy about the trees, all of them fresh and as green as an emerald: the builder oak, the boxtree piper, the sailing fir. He delights also in the birdsong he hears and the animals he sees, as well as the stringed instruments playing with "ravyshyng swetnesse" (line 198) (perhaps he hears the wind in the trees, or the music of the spheres). The air is temperate, neither hot nor cold. Boccaccio will reduce the pleasure in the particulars by the allegorical explanations in his glosses. (For instance the temperate atmosphere becomes a mere prerequisite for venereal love.) Chaucer celebrates the harmony (line 191), the sweetness (line 198), the accord (line 203) of nature. "Yit was there joye more a thousandfold / Than man can tell" (lines 208–9), he says, reiterating his perception of the scene before him and reinforcing the tone.

Throughout the ensuing description of figures just outside the temple and those inside it, discussed above, this sense of joy persists, neutralizing one's response to the ensuing information flatly delivered, even though in a hun-dred lines one will discover a gallery of suffering. The narrator now simply reports what he saw: "Tho was I war...."; "Saw I Delyt..."; "I saw Beute..."; "I saw a temple..."; "Saw I syttynge..." The neutrality of the visual language does nothing to deflect the earlier ebullient tone (though the parenthetic remark about refusing to lie produces a momentary hiccup). So we merely smile as the narrative report slips into a description of Priapus caught with his sceptre in his hand when Silenus's ass brays in the night to wake everyone while Priapus is trying to mount a nymph, even though in Ovid the story accentuates futility and humiliation. Similarly, one can remain indifferent, perhaps even wistful, about the sweet agony of love even when the stories painted on Venus's walls represent the unrelieved agony of lovers who went into her service. The audience is borne aloft by an earlier joyful tone even as the narration moves relentlessly towards considered and sober judgments.

The combination of joy and judgment suggests a tension, if not a contradiction, yet Chaucer holds the two together. As we have seen, he does so partly by artfully embedding the indictment when it comes. Chaucer uses intricate syntax, wordplay, enjambment, and a sense of ongoing report to buffer the change. Stepping back from the rhetorical detail, one perceives that the genre of the dream vision, with its ethereal fluidity, also suits Chaucer's purposes. The reader or listener overlooks apparent disjunctions, mimics the dreamlike state, and simply accepts the narrative. A medieval audience would expect a clear, authoritative conclusion in a dream vision, but Chaucer has already supplied one with the ending of the dream of Scipio. Now the narrator, and with him the reader, wanders and observes.

The narrator plays a key role in effecting and in reconciling the juxtaposition of joy and judgment. Many readers of the *Parliament of Fowls* assume that the narrator is inexperienced, naive, perhaps a bit of a dolt.[22] His joy is easily read as the uncomplicated pleasure of the simpleton or the innocent. Such a narrator could never pronounce severe, yet measured, judgment, which may account for some readers' inability to see it. Yet a different understanding of the persona allows one to bridge joy and judgment. We have already seen that his joy derives from the observation of nature, reported in some detail. His is a considered, rational joy rather than sheer effusiveness. He does not lurch from joy to judgment but maintains a level of dispassionate observation, his joy aligned with nature. Though troubled—perhaps, indeed, *because* he is troubled and in search of answers to questions virtually inarticulable, questions touching on the human condition—the narrator models an inquiring method.

Admittedly, certain features of the poem would appear to support a reading of the narrator as naive. His incompetence is hinted at in the poem's opening lines:

> The lyf so short, the craft so long to lerne,
> Th'assay so hard, so sharp the conquerynge,
> The dredful joye alwey that slit so yerne:
> Al this mene I by Love, that my felynge
> Astonyeth with his wonderful werkynge
> So sore, iwis, that whan I on hym thynke
> Nat wot I wel wher that I flete or synke. (lines 1–7)

The narrator does not feel that he has gotten very far in mastering the craft of love,[23] overwhelmed in both feeling (line 4) and thought (line 6) so that he does not know whether he is floating or sinking. His opening remarks hardly inspire confidence. A similar confusion overwhelms him when he reads the messages over the gate into the park, texts that speak first of the bliss, then of the threat, of love. These render him, again, "astoned" (line 142, cf. line 5). Africanus suggests that he has lost his taste for love, that the messages do not apply to him, and that he can observe the features of the park disinterestedly. The guide compares him to a person who still likes to watch wrestling even though he himself would not want to "stonde a pul" (line 164) or take a fall. This apparent objectivity and passivity foster the illusion that the narrator is an "innocent abroad," especially if we are inclined to privilege experience in the ways of venereal love as that which would give him credibility.

Yet Chaucer's indictment of lascivious Venus indicates that he does not value highly that particular variety of love. Chaucer's lack of experience in the ways of love, hinted at in terms of his failure to master the craft of love and Africanus's assigning to him an identity as not one of Love's servants (line 159), need not imply credulity on his part. Similarly, the joy he expresses need not issue from the innocence of one lacking urbane sophistication, but differs as much from it as from the tumultuous emotion that leads to wasted lives.

Chaucer in several ways encourages us to trust his narrator and to identify with his method. An early example of Chaucer's useful detachment comes with his description of the dreaming process. In fairly authoritative, matter-of-fact language, Chaucer tells us that dreamers tend to dream about what occupies them in their waking hours (lines 99–105). Commonplace though the wisdom of these lines may be, the passage indicates a commonsensical response to the phenomenon of dreaming, encouraging us to think of the narrator as oriented towards nature. In a further remark astonishing for its self-limitation, modelling a restrained and nascently scientific temperament, Chaucer then admits he is not sure if this explanation accounts for the dream he had after doing the reading he had done:

> Can I not seyn if that the cause were
> For I hadde red of Affrican byforn
> That made me to mete that he stod there. (lines 106–8)

Chaucer approaches his subject matter calmly, in an attitude of unblinking observation that encourages the audience similarly to avoid hasty conclusions and to trust him. Africanus himself endorses the narrator, for he has appeared to offer him a reward for being a faithful reader (lines 109–12). Whatever his limitations, this narrator has definite strengths to recommend him.

As he launches into a description of the dream sequence, Chaucer invokes a being associated with nature, Cytherea, the planetary goddess Venus, as his muse. This planetary authority compares favourably to Africanus. Chaucer diminishes the guide's authority when Africanus shoves the dreamer through the gate in an undignified and mildly violent act. Whereas readers sometimes think of the narrator as the comic character here, his freezing when he cannot interpret the conflicting messages over the gate is plausible enough. The push merely establishes the momentum needed to carry the narrator, unmotivated by an established personal agenda, through the space of love. It is Africanus who is comically reduced, and he will never recover to deliver a clear message to Chaucer, who simply outlasts him and now writes with planetary Venus as his literary guide.

This persona contributes a remarkably even tone. Evenness does not mean indifference or that caricature applied to the modern scientist, emotional frigidity. Chaucer may not serve love, but he loves trees and parks and has the capacity for saying so. Yet the steadiness of tone indicates an outlook unlikely to be swept up by the glamour of a Jazz Age Venus or the business of an art show driven by a narrow ideology.

In this tonal achievement, Chaucer differs markedly from Boccaccio. The English poet lifted almost all of the middle section of the *Parliament of Fowls* from the Italian's mid-fourteenth-century poem *Il Teseida*, yet the two present Venus Cypride's shortcomings quite differently. In the *Teseida*, a prayer has gone to find Venus to deliver a message on behalf of a lovelorn knight. Both Chaucer and Boccaccio describe the scene outside the temple, including the temperate air, the bunny rabbits, and the various allegorical figures. Both describe a similar interior temple scene as well, culminating in near identical pictures of Venus in bed. Boccaccio, however, wrote glosses, a commentary, to accompany his poem and only indicts Venus there,[24] not in the poem itself: "This Venus is twofold, since one can be understood as every chaste and licit desire, as is the desire to have a wife in order to have children, and such like. This Venus is not discussed here. The second Venus is that through which all lewdness is desired, commonly called the goddess of love. Here the author describes the temple of this goddess, and the other things that belong to it, as appears in the text."[25] The tone in the glosses differs markedly from that in the body of the poem, and he insists that virtually every detail in the poem allegorically reinforces the picture he explains in the commentary.

Chaucer reduces the indictment of Venus to a phrase paradoxically more biting and damning than any of Boccaccio's comments for its terse reference to wasted lives and to trophies of war and art depicting suffering. Most significantly, it is embedded in a syntactically complex unit *within the poem*. We are right to refer to the English poet's technique as "Chaucerian ambiguity," but wrong if we are tempted to think he withholds judgment entirely. If he is merely bland, there is no tonal achievement. The wonder of his ambiguity is that, unlike Boccaccio, he incorporates judgment directly into his poetic artifact while maintaining a consistent tone.

The tone is significant for several reasons. It reinforces a point C.S. Lewis once made about the difference between Boccaccio and Chaucer with regard to the latter's use of another poem, Boccaccio's *Il Filostrato*. Lewis argued that what Chaucer does with *Il Filostrato* in his own poem *Troilus and Criseyde* is to medievalize his exemplar.[26] Lewis claims that Chaucer's poem is more medieval than Boccaccio's because it holds together two different impulses: narrative and psychology.[27] Similarly, the English poet's rendering of *Il Teseida* compresses and holds together an exuberant, natural tone and a judgment of love and art that places his poetry well within the realm of medieval moral philosophy. As Bennett has observed generally, Chaucer has a marvellous "passion for compactness."[28]

As a second, closely related point, the tone models a method of inquiry. Chaucer reveals his commitment to observation, particularly careful attentiveness to nature. As a guide to poetic style, this method indicates understatement and technical complexity and argues for the resistance of empty artifice, excess, and, it would seem, allegory. It is not hermeneutically naive, nor is it reducible to sheer functionality. Whereas observation can conjure for us visions of scientific detachment resulting in either a refusal to make moral judgments on the grounds of a specious objectivity or the modernistic judgments belonging to those who wrongly think they have enough information and enough neutrality to make them, whether scientific or bureaucratic automatons or their fundamentalist alter egos, Chaucer has an entirely different organizing principle. Chaucer's critique of art involves his own art; the ability to combine joy and judgment suggests a deeper joy at the complex harmonies which the artist can trace.

In a participatory aesthetic, the task of the artist involves attending to the object. Beauty cannot be sought in its own right but is the product of being drawn to the inner integrity of an object and its harmony with the perceiver. The artist cannot have a moral agenda or be seeking information from the object. Rowan Williams describes this requirement: "What matters is what *this* work requires.... [Beauty] provides satisfaction, joy, for the human subject, but does not in itself *tell* you anything."[29] Chaucer's tonal achievement, I would suggest, finally works on this principle. Although he refers to joy numerous times throughout the work and engages in severe judgment, he achieves a tone that does not tell us anything, a tone that reflects the integrity of *all* of the elements of the world before him in this section of the poem, including both lascivious Venus and the objective judgment that *already* rests upon the values in this temple. Chaucer does not turn away from anything. He can take anything as his subject matter in his experience of the world as a reader and writer and look at it unblinkingly.

In such an aesthetic, beauty nonetheless does tell us something about the world. What Thomas Aquinas called *splendor formae* involves an overflow of presence beyond functionality: "The emphasis on the gratuity of the artwork, its disinterested character, suggests that the awareness of beauty is always a recognition of what is more than functional in a work, and thus is some kind of relation with an aspect of reality otherwise unknown."[30] Beauty, in the not-telling which is the work's integrity and in the tone which Chaucer achieves, on this understanding paradoxically tells us of metaphysical depth — the fact that the contrasting elements in this section of the poem can be combined in joy points beyond itself to a deeper joy not within the artist's control, not subject to his will. If art continues to be present in Chaucer's very critique of it, a dimension of the sublime is revealed the nobility of which is less grand, more subtle.

An aesthetic based on inner harmonies and correspondences between observer and object, based, that is, on the notion of participation and the ideas of Thomas Aquinas, may seem thoroughly medieval and "other" to the concerns of modern poetry. Yet one of the priorities of this aesthetic is to reveal resonances obscured by ordinary perception. For us it might be scientific quantification or historico-critical positivism that obscures; in any age it might be a preoccupation with the merely functional. To be able to catch resonances, to be able to give back to reality "a dimension that necessarily escapes our conceptuality and our control,"[31] is a source of great joy, and the desire to do so arguably shared by those involved in the arts both then and now.

Notes

1 This essay reproduces, with some expansion, alteration, and application in a direction in keeping with the themes of the present volume, material that appeared as "'Surprised by Joy': Chaucer's Tonal Achievement in *Parliament of Fowls*, 92–294," *Tradition and Formation: Claiming an Inheritance: Essays in Honour of Peter C. Erb*, ed. Michel Desjardins and Harold Remus (Kitchener, ON: Pandora Press, 2009) 213–28.

2 D.S. Brewer, ed., *The Parlement of Foulys*, 2nd ed. (Manchester, UK: Manchester University Press, 1972) 3–7; A.J. Minnis et al., *Oxford Guides to Chaucer: The Shorter Poems* (Oxford: Clarendon, 1995) 256–61.

3 A.C. Spearing, *Medieval Dream-Poetry* (Cambridge: Cambridge University Press, 1976).

4 *The Riverside Chaucer*, ed. Larry D. Benson et al., 3rd ed. (Boston: Houghton Mifflin, 1987) 994; subsequent citations are from this edition and will be given in the text by line number.

5 Of the section of the poem that will concern us and the role of Venus in it, David
   Aers insists that Chaucer causes the reader to suspend "conventional condemna-
   tions": "even here Chaucer's poem makes it quite impossible for anyone in its
   ambience to claim access to an absolute, impersonally dogmatic viewpoint from
   which to launch unequivocal moral judgements" (*The Parliament of Fowls*:
   Authority, the Knower and the Known," *Chaucer Review* 16.1 [1981]: 8–9). Helen
   Cooney, for her part, does believe that the atmosphere within the temple of Venus
   "is one of unrelieved evil" ("The *Parlement of Foules*: A Theodicy of Love," *Chaucer
   Review* 32.4 [1998]: 357) but that Chaucer balances the "moralistic perspective" of
   Jean de Meun and Dante with the morally neutral view of Guillaume de Lorris.
   These, for her, are the choices, which she also applies to the work that directly
   influences Chaucer: "Boccaccio's *Chiose* on the relevant passage in the *Teseida* are
   themselves marked by a rather disconcerting mixture of morally neutral glosses on
   the allegory, on the one hand, and rather heavy-handed, explicitly moralistic ones,
   on the other" (Ibid., 352). To slip from moral neutrality is, apparently, to become
   moralistic, with all the connotations that word has of censorious and unconsid-
   ered judgment. Aers's adjectives, "absolute," "dogmatic," "unequivocal," and, elsewhere, "transcendent," similarly represent the only apparent alternative to "a continuous self-reflexivity combined with a marked epistemological modesty" and a
   "mode utterly subversive of all dogmatizing fixities and finalities" ("The *Parliament of Fowls*," 14).

6 Literary theorist Terry Eagleton has recently explored this terrain, writing in *After
   Theory* (New York: Basic Books, 2003) that "it belongs to our dignity as moderately
   rational creatures to know the truth" (109) and that "[k]nowledge and morality ...
   are not finally separable, as the modern age has tended to assume" (132). Writing
   from a different perspective relevant to Chaucer's context, Pope Benedict XVI
   insists on the inclusion of both transcendent and material dimensions to our
   understanding of truth and love but similarly would encourage us in "the path
   leading to true humanism," which he interestingly sees consisting ultimately in
   the discovery of joy. See Joseph Ratzinger (Pope Benedict XVI), "Encyclical Letter,
   Deus Caritas Est" (2005): 9, http://www.vatican.va/holy_father/benedict_xvi/
   encyclicals/documents/hf_ben-xvi_enc_20051225_deus-caritas-est_en.html.

7 I drew attention to this Chaucerian statement in "A Note on 'Hyre' in *Parliament
   of Fowls*, 284," *Notes and Queries* 251 [2006]: 154–57 and my argument here builds
   on the conclusions reached in that piece. The substance of that brief article is
   restated in the first part of the following section with kind permission from
   Oxford University Press.

8 John H. Fisher is the only editor I know of who glosses "hyre" (line 284) (*The
   Complete Poetry and Prose of Geoffrey Chaucer* [New York: Holt, Rinehart and
   Winston, 1977] 571). He does so correctly, as Venus. Piero Boitani seems to have
   "In hyre servyse" in mind when he writes of Venus, "All around her lie the broken
   bows of the virgins of Diana who have sacrificed their chastity in her service"
   ("Old books brought to life in dreams: The *Book of the Duchess*, the *House of Fame*,
   the *Parliament of Fowls*," *The Cambridge Companion to Chaucer*, ed. Piero Boitani
   and Jill Mann, 2nd ed. [Cambridge: Cambridge University Press, 2003] 69). Elizabeth Salter, in contrast, puts considerable weight on the idea that Chaucer "presents us with the concept of the wastefulness of chastity" without wrestling with

the syntax ("Chaucer and Medieval English Tradition," in her *Fourteenth-Century English Poetry: Contexts and Readings* [Oxford: Clarendon, 1983] 137). Her misreading significantly influences Aers, "The *Parliament of Fowls*," 8. Gerald Morgan clearly thinks that "hyre servyse" refers to Diana's service, for he writes, "The dreamer in *The Parliament of Fowls* who has enthusiastically acknowledged Cupid as 'oure lord' (line 212) continues to manifest his bias when he comes to tell of the followers of 'Dyane the chaste' (line 281), for they are 'maydenes swiche as gonne here tymes waste / In hyre servyse' (lines 283–4)" ("Chaucer's Adaptation of Boccaccio's Temple of Venus in *The Parliament of Fowls*," *Review of English Studies*, n.s. 56 [2005]: 33). For Morgan, the narrator sides with Cupid against Diana and her maidens: "the dreamer, as a servant of Cupid, has no interest in the subject of chaste maidens" (34). Robert Entzminger does not appear to realize that the notion of wasting time in Venus's service nicely supports his thesis of how time functions in the poem as a whole ("The Pattern of Time in *The Parlement of Foules*," *Journal of Medieval and Renaissance Studies* 5 [1975]: 5). Kathryn L. Lynch misleadingly suggests that the bows belong to Diana when in fact they belonged to the maidens and now hang as trophies on Venus's wall. See also Minnis's comments in favour of Venus (Lynch, "Diana's 'Bowe Ybroke': Impotence, Desire, and Virginity in Chaucer's *Parliament of Fowls*," *Menacing Virgins: Representing Virginity in the Middle Ages and Renaissance*, ed. Kathleen Coyne Kelly and Marina Leslie [Newark: University of Delaware Press, 1999] 87); Minnis et al., *Oxford Guides to Chaucer*.

9 Klassen, "A Note on 'Hyre,'" 154–57.

10 Even Elizabeth Salter, one of the critics most eager to preserve narratorial neutrality in the middle section of the poem, admits that these lines allow for an interpretation consonant with the moral tone of *Divina Commedia* ("Chaucer and Medieval English Tradition," 137). See also Cooney, "The *Parlement of Foules*: A Theodicy of Love," 357–58.

11 J.A.W. Bennett, *The Parlement of Foules: An Interpretation* (Oxford: Clarendon, 1957) 95–98.

12 Brewer, *The Parlement of Foulys*, 31.

13 Helen Cooper similarly observes that Chaucer "largely avoids" this "non-naturalistic" form ("Chaucerian Representation," *New Readings of Chaucer's Poetry*, ed. Robert G. Benson and Susan J. Ridyard [Cambridge: D.S. Brewer, 2003] 24).

14 Brewer, *The Parlement of Foulys*, 31.

15 David Aers's view is typical. For him, Chaucer rejects the world of moral allegory as associated principally with a world of metaphysics, dogma, and authority in Alain de Lille's *Planctu Naturae,* cited by Chaucer in the poem ("The *Parliament of Fowls*," 9 passim). There is much that I admire in Aers's study, and I agree with him that Alain's world of Neo-Platonic metaphysics is not Chaucer's, but even though I would support his claim that Chaucer undermines "claims to dogmatic knowledge and unreflexively impersonal discourse, having shown us the human mediations involved in all human knowledge" (9), this does not leave Chaucer in the position of merely allowing a multiplicity of voices to speak or of his eschewing authoritative stances altogether. Helen Cooney argues that the middle section divides into two contrasting views, and that both Boccaccio and Chaucer follow the *Roman de la Rose* in presenting two rival versions ("The *Parlement of Foules*," esp. 352; see also n3 above). She reads Guillaume de Lorris's views on love as

morally neutral, Jean de Meun's as moralistic. While this view may apply to the *Roman* itself, with its two different authors, Boccaccio makes it clear in his glosses that Venus in his poem means only lascivious desire. For Chaucer, as for Boccaccio, the scene works towards a unified culmination. If anything, he appears resolutely to turn away here from the more purely allegorical world of Guillaume de Lorris.

16 Gerald Morgan would reinforce the point that, on the medieval understanding, poetry belongs to moral philosophy and that Chaucer is following Boccaccio, from whom he borrows the allegorical descriptions and much else in his description of the temple of Venus, in a careful and unrelenting attack on Venus in terms of Aristotelian faculty psychology ("Chaucer's Adaptation," 2–4). With Morgan, I agree that Chaucer follows Boccaccio in indicting lascivious Venus. However, beyond this basic point of contact, Chaucer shows little interest in making explicit a full-blown scholastic moral schema of the sort Boccaccio contrives in his glosses.

17 Spenser, *The Faerie Queene* (Harmondsworth: Penguin, 1987) 683; future citations are from Book 2, Canto 12 of this edition and will be given in the text by line number.

18 Judith H. Anderson, "The 'couert vele': Chaucer, Spenser, and Venus," *English Literary Renaissance* 24.3 (1994): 641.

19 "The most striking example in *PF* of *enjambment* between stanzas" (*Chaucer's Dream Poetry*, ed. Helen Phillips and Nick Havely [London: Longman, 1997] 247n).

20 Helen Cooper reminds us of Chaucer's commitment to representation not only of "what he saw around him" but also, especially, of texts. He gives us not so much a mirror of nature as a "hall of mirrors" ("Chaucerian Representation," 7, 24).

21 Chaucer's joyful tone would not appear to derive from a commitment to sheer relativism or multiplicity. David Lawton makes the most extensive argument about Chaucer's tone in such terms, arguing that Chaucer privileges "tonal unpredictability" and that "[a] multiplicity of tones and voices represents a multiplicity of attitudes" (*Chaucer's Narrators* [Cambridge: D.S. Brewer, 1985] 46).

22 Spearing, *Medieval Dream-Poetry*, 6; J.J. Anderson, "The Narrators in the *Book of the Duchess* and the *Parlement of Foules*," *Chaucer Review* 26.3 (1992): 219–20. For a view that represents an extrapolation as much as a distinction, see also Lawton, *Chaucer's Narrators*, 47 and 47n13.

23 It might have been art, given that the first line echoes the saying "*Ars longa, vita brevis est.*"

24 I am inclined to think Chaucer knew the glosses and set himself the challenge of constructing a more artful though no less condemnatory comment on Venus. For a discussion of the question, see Morgan, "Chaucer's Adaptation," 3ff, esp. n9. Even if Chaucer was not explicitly setting out to achieve a synthesis in contradistinction to Boccaccio's work, his integrative sensibility produced that effect.

25 Boccaccio, *The Book of Theseus*, trans. Bernadette Marie McCoy (New York: Medieval Text Association, 1974) 199n50.

26 C.S. Lewis, "What Chaucer Really Did to *Il Filostrato*," *Essays and Studies* 17 (1932): 56.

27 Ibid., 58.

28 Bennett, *The Parlement of Foules: An Interpretation*, 118.

29 Rowan Williams, *Grace and Necessity: Reflections on Art and Love* (London: Continuum, 2005) 12.

30 Ibid., 13–14.

31 Ibid., 37.

SHAKESPEAREAN HORROR

LISTENING TO LAVINIA: EMMANUEL LEVINAS'S SAYING AND SAID IN *TITUS ANDRONICUS*

Sean Lawrence

Of all William Shakespeare's plays, *Titus Andronicus* probably enjoys the least respect. As early as 1687, Edward Ravenscroft justified rewriting it by declaring that "[i]t seems rather a heap of rubbish than a structure."[1] The success of his new version, which displaced Shakespeare's from the English stage until 1923, bespeaks the agreement of audiences. Shakespeare's Senecan orgy of rape, murder, dismemberment, and cannibalism challenges most imaginable assumptions about artistic decorum. It is tempting to dismiss the play's violence as a young Shakespeare's concession to an audience inured to the theatre of blood and lusting for the pornography of violence. If anything, however, *Titus* exceeds in the depiction of premeditated brutality even the other revenge plays against which it competed;[2] John Dover Wilson suggests that it parodies them.[3] Eugene M. Waith concludes one of the best articles on the play by declaring that the horror of the characters' suffering leaves us cold: "[W]e momentarily forget the sufferer in the overwhelming reality of the wound."[4] In Waith's influential reading, the play fails because its horrors do not engage, but alienate us.

In what follows, I should like to emphasize the response of the characters to the onstage horrors, rather than our own, as audience or readers. Shown his raped, mutilated, and physically silenced daughter, Titus remarks, "Had I but seen thy picture in this plight, / It would have madded me; what shall I do /

Now I behold thy lively body so?"[5] As audience, of course, we encounter Lavinia only as a representation. "What shall I do?" remains Titus's concern, just as the experience remains his trauma, not ours. The play therefore engages us in an ethical problem, but intellectually, where ethics intersects with the question of language. Mary Laughlin Fawcett suggests, in 1983, that the work, if read "as a meditation on language and body," will "present a set of possibilities for language from which a theory may be derived."[6] Taking up this challenge, I argue that Shakespeare's first tragedy constitutes a sophisticated exploration of the relationship between what Emmanuel Levinas, particularly in *Otherwise Than Being*, terms *the saying* and *the said*. Whereas the said includes both the "amphibology" of the verb and the signification of the noun, the saying locates itself prior to both, in the concern that inspires language in the first place. Levinas defines it sweepingly: "Antecedent to the verbal signs it conjugates, to the linguistic systems and the semantic glimmerings, a foreword preceding languages, it is the proximity of one to the other, the commitment of one to the other, the commitment of an approach, the one for the other, the very signifyingness of signification."[7]

Perhaps we could define *saying* more briefly as a concern that elicits language. Every communication has two elements. What Levinas terms *the said* includes everything that we might consider content—the subject matter, choice of words, their arrangement, and so forth—and which might be misunderstood, intentionally or otherwise. Antecedent to this, however, is the radical fact of being addressed, the saying, which Levinas compares to sincerity and even silence: "Saying opens me to the other before saying what is said, before the said uttered in this sincerity forms a screen between me and the other. This saying without a said is thus like silence."[8] Unable to communicate reciprocally with Lavinia, Marcus and Titus remain in a position of silence, but also one of sincerity and concern. When they actually do find means of communication, their concern finds expression, but it also loses itself in the said. The play dramatizes the distinction of saying and said, since the Andronici find themselves addressed by Lavinia and called to respond to her, even though she can offer no words. By dramatizing efforts to respond to Lavinia, the play shows language to be a product of ethical concern, rather than ethical concern to be a product of language. If by language is meant the said, language's content and form, then ethics is prior to language.

Bernice Harris argues that Lavinia is herself a signifier, "a means by which power is marked as masculine and is then transferred and circulated."[9] Harris details Lavinia's role in the various exchanges in the opening scene. Rather than making an appeal, she is treated as a sign, signifying something other than herself, within what Levinas terms the said. When she first enters, Titus treats her as the gift of a grateful state, addressing her only after thanking

"Kind Rome, that hast thus lovingly reserved / The cordial of mine age to glad my heart!" (1.1.165–66). Saturninus repays Titus "for thy favours done / To us in our election this day" by offering to marry Lavinia (1.1.234–35). Titus then reciprocates, offering the new emperor "My sword, my chariot, and my prisoners" (1.1.249). Powerful men exchange Lavinia, like the prisoner Tamora, to ratify their relations.[10] Even before she enters, Bassianus calls her "Rome's rich ornament" (1.1.52), establishing her value in material terms. When Bassianus later abducts her, one of her brothers helpfully explains that "*Suum cuique* is our Roman justice; / This prince in justice seizeth but his own" (1.1.280–81). Saturninus accuses him of "rape," though Bassianus objects that he did only "seize my own, / My true betrothèd love, and now my wife" (1.1.404–6). Amazingly, Lavinia objects to neither of her claimants, not that anyone asks her opinion. She is passed from hand to hand, like the "changing piece" as which Saturninus soon denounces her (1.1.309). Moreover, if she can be used to honour the Andronici, she serves equally well as an instrument to disgrace them. Her abduction by Bassianus furnishes Saturninus with all the excuse he needs to repudiate Titus (1.1.305–7). More gruesomely, Tamora, giving Lavinia to her sons to rape and dismember, declares that she uses Lavinia to inflict revenge against her father (2.3.163–65). At least three critics have noted the difference between the definitions of rape applicable to Bassianus's abduction of Lavinia and that in Tamora's revenge. Emily Detmer-Goebel and Carolyn D. Williams both cite Nazife Bashar on the growing recognition of rape as an independent crime, separate from abduction, over the course of the sixteenth century, whereas in medieval law rape was an offence against the victim's father's property rights.[11] Harris summarizes the distinction:

> In the exchange of women, it is as if, on the one hand, when ownership presumptions are violated, rape is the resulting charge and it is the original owner who is the victim. On the other hand, if an exchange is mutually agreed upon between men, no matter how politically invested the exchange is, it is as if there were no victims.[12]

In the case of Bassianus's abduction of Lavinia, the only victim is Saturninus, whereas in Chiron and Demetrius's assault, harming Lavinia is the whole point. In both cases, however, control over Lavinia serves as a means of relating to her father. The argument that Lavinia signifies power relations seems irrefutable. She therefore serves as a sign within the said.

Her purely structural importance in the opening scene, however, makes her continued importance later in the play all the more striking. "In this world," Sara Eaton writes, "Lavinia is a 'changing piece' (1.1.309), her humanist education but an ornament, her only 'real' value the possession of her chaste femininity."[13] Raped, silenced, and mutilated, she loses this value. Marcus's famously gratuitous speech on discovering her takes the form of a blazon, a list of her charms, inventorying what has been lost. He calls her hands "sweet ornaments," "pretty fingers," and "lily hands" (2.4.18, 42, 44). Similarly, in describing "the heavenly harmony / Which that sweet tongue hath made" (2.4.48–49), Marcus only emphasizes how it, too, is gone. Raped and mutilated, Lavinia loses sexual and social value. No one tries to marry her again.

She no longer signifies in the manner of the said, such as when she signifies a value or a relation between men, but she continues to signify in the manner of the saying, eliciting an ethical response, expressed in frustrated efforts to acknowledge and understand. Marcus describes her metaphorically and proverbially, "Seeking to hide herself, as doth the deer" (3.1.89). Titus, as he often does, seizes on the expression as an occasion for a dreadful pun: "It was my dear, and he that wounded her / Hath hurt me more than had he killed me dead" (3.1.91–92). Both folio and quarto texts aid the pun by spelling both words as "Deare" (through line numbers 1229–31 in the folio). The play on words certainly displays bad taste, but also conflates two notions, of endearment and of a type of property associated with noble rank. Lavinia's fate, however, inflicts on Titus a pain greater than death, which overwhelms the metaphor. When, only ten lines later, he refers to "dear Lavinia, dearer than my soul" (3.1.102), his expression places his concern for Lavinia above concern for his personal salvation, never mind personal property. The language of possession survives, briefly, in the form of a metaphor for value, until concern for the Other overwhelms the metaphor in which it is expressed.

Precisely because Lavinia cannot be understood and thereby be reduced to a sign and a meaning, she commands enormous concern from the men in her life. On first realizing her mutilation, Marcus wishes to "rail" at the rapist "to ease my mind" but then generalizes his observation: "Sorrow conceal'd, like an oven stopped, / Doth burn the heart to cinders where it is" (2.4.36–37). If expression eases suffering, then listening already offers comfort. Unfortunately, as Detmer-Goebel emphasizes, Lavinia is not merely mutilated, but specifically silenced.[14] Marcus's first words, on encountering the mutilated and muted Lavinia, demand a response (2.4.11–12). Titus and Lucius echo him in asking her to name her assailant (3.1.66–67; 3.1.81). Of course, Lavinia can say nothing, but the male characters seek her voice all the more desperately, searching for some means of communication, and hence of comfort. Everyone listens to Lavinia, but only after mutilation reduces her to silence.

The problem of language assumes centrality after the loss of Lavinia's tongue. Unable to exchange words with her, Titus proposes mimetic expressions of sympathy:

Or shall we cut away our hands like thine?
Or shall we bite our tongues, and in dumb shows

Pass the remainder of our hateful days?
What shall we do? (3.1.130–33)

When Aaron suggests that either "Marcus, Lucius, or thyself, old Titus" (3.1.152) amputate his hand to ransom Quintus and Martius, the Andronici react with something like mania, each claiming the right to offer his own. Lucius reasons that "My youth can better spare my blood than you" (3.1.165), while Marcus argues that as a civilian, "My hand hath been but idle" (3.1.171). Finally, Titus tricks them into leaving to find an axe, in order to cut off his own hand, using another play on words to crow triumphantly to Aaron, "Lend me thy hand, and I will give thee mine" (3.1.186). Offered a means of expressing their suffering, one which Titus anticipates in his proposed responses to Lavinia, the characters embrace it eagerly. Aaron's treacherous offer not only provides the characters with a glimmer of hope but also seems to provide an answer to their achingly open question, "What shall we do?" The suffering Lavinia appears as a silent saying, demanding an ethical response.

In contrast, books frequently appear on stage, but they only demonstrate their impotence to elicit ethical concern. *Titus Andronicus* makes extraordinarily overt use of intertexts, one of which, Ovid's *Metamorphoses*, characters handle on stage as a theatrical property. Several characters independently offer comparisons between Lavinia and Philomela, raped and muted by Tereus in Ovid's *Metamorphoses*. Noticing that his niece's hands as well as tongue have been cut away, Marcus begrudgingly acknowledges that she has met with "a craftier Tereus" (2.4.41).[15] Titus's revenge, cooking the rapists' brains in a pie and serving it to their mother, shares the same literary precedent. "[W]orse than Philomel you used my daughter," he declares, "And worse than Procne I will be revenged" (5.2.194–95). All the characters appear to share a familiarity with Shakespeare's source. Aaron adopts it as his own inspiration (2.3.43), but all it teaches him is how to commit rape and get away with it. Titus even describes the scene of the rape as "[p]atterned by that the poet here describes, / By nature made for murders and for rapes" (4.1.56–57). At least in Titus's expression, nature imitates art. Marcus asks if the place was created because "the gods delight in tragedies" (4.1.59). Ovid provides a precedent for crime, perhaps even to the gods. Shakespeare's play damningly refutes the humanist claim that literary education leads to moral improvement, as Grace Starry West has shown.[16] In the play, literature teaches crime, not concern. Text, as said, proves incapable of eliciting an ethical response.

Even as a means of communication, the written text proves almost hopelessly inadequate. For one thing, multiple intertexts frustrate narrative clarity. Titus, Marcus, Lucius, and even Aaron refer to the rape of Lucrece (4.1.62–63; 4.1.90; 3.1.297; 2.1.109), but the reference misleads, suggesting Saturninus as the rapist, at least in Titus's mind. When Lavinia tries to indicate the intertext, her nephew, young Lucius, runs away from her, citing a literary precedent for his fears: "I have read that Hecuba of Troy / Ran mad for sorrow" (4.1.20–21). In this case, a text serves as an excuse to avoid communication, rather than its means. Moreover, even to those equipped with the correct intertextual key, Lavinia remains maddeningly opaque. Marcus immediately notices the Ovidian parallel, but Lavinia nevertheless has to painstakingly write the word "*Stuprum*," so it seems that he fails to recognize that she has been raped (4.1.77). When she indicates a copy of the *Metamorphoses*, Titus assumes that she seeks literary escapism: "Come and take choice of all my library, / And so beguile thy sorrow," he urges her, "till the heavens / Reveal the damned contriver of this deed" (4.1.34–36). Her father and uncle remain baffled by her signs. Raising her two stumps might indicate "that there were more than one / Confederate in the fact" or merely that "to heaven she heaves them for revenge" (4.1.38–40). Fawcett argues that the Andronici are text-bound, while West points to a general obsession throughout the play "with writing things down."[17] The instinctive reference to text, however, serves as often to frustrate as to facilitate communication. Lavinia has been robbed of speech, and writing proves a poor substitute.

Returning obsessively to the instability of text as said and the importance of the saying as ethical response, the play addresses the relationship between language and ethics. Language serves as communication, but also carries a content, sometimes inaccurately and never reliably. It can only function as a said at all, however, because first offered, generously, as a saying. Conversely, for communication to be meaningful, the saying must seek realization in the said. "The subordination of the saying to the said, to the linguistic system and to ontology," Levinas declares, "is the price that manifestation demands."[18] Lavinia's suffering body, by simultaneously eliciting and frustrating response, delays and therefore dramatizes this process.

Roman society and culture, which expressed its complex beliefs in language, law, and custom, may as a whole be placed within the said. In his funeral oration for Levinas, Jacques Derrida recalls how his late friend insisted upon "the necessary distinction between sacredness and holiness, that is, the holiness of the other, of the other person."[19] Shakespeare's play illustrates the same distinction, in that ethical response does not arise from what Tamora terms the "cruel, irreligious piety" (1.1.130) of Rome. The erasure, not the content, of this culture and language leads back to the saying and ethical response, which is revealed as the very opposite of a cultural product. The failure of the sacred reveals the holy, just as the erasure of the said reveals the saying.

Lavinia's loss of meaning as a signifier of power relations exemplifies the rapid collapse of the whole Roman political and semiotic structure. The wars with "the barbarous Goths" (1.1.28), from which Titus returns victorious, imply a binary distinction between Rome and its enemies. Marcus gives this binary aphoristic form when he scolds his brother's refusal to inter Mutius: "Thou art a Roman; be not barbarous" (1.1.378). Titus's sacrifice of Tamora's son, however, already elicits comparisons with the barbarism of Scythia and therefore casts doubt upon the distinction (1.1.131). The Goths, for their part, find themselves robbed of their identity, referring to a time past "[w]hen Goths were Goths, and Tamora was queen" (1.1.140). Rather than reclaiming their Gothic roots, they soon find themselves "incorporate in Rome" (1.1.462), as Tamora says after being chosen as empress. Marcus asks how she is "of a sudden thus advanced" (1.1.393). The Goths whom Lucius leads against Rome in act 5 seem to have disowned those brought as captives in act 1, vowing to "be advenged on cursèd Tamora" (5.1.16). Barbarity and Rome cease to be opposites when the Goths become Romans and a Roman leads the Goths. More importantly, their languages begin to come apart when such central binaries collapse.

Titus finds himself suddenly excluded from the centre of Roman political life. At the beginning of the first scene, everybody defers to Titus's greatness. Both Marcus, as tribune of the people, and a captain who serves as herald announce him in fulsome terms (1.1.23–38, 64–69). Even Tamora, pleading for her son, calls him "Thrice-noble" (1.1.120). His rage at Mutius's insubordination measures his wounded sense of his own importance: "What, villain boy, / Barr'st me my way in Rome?" (1.1.290–91). Titus's choice of terms locates the respect he feels he deserves not within the family, but within the state. He finds it particularly galling to be stopped in Rome, where he commands the status of a conquering general and popular hero. In this context, the word "villain" probably retains its meaning of "[l]ow or mean in respect of birth or position."[20] Though Titus and Mutius obviously share the same class, Titus treats his son as far beneath him. A few lines later, Titus finds to his surprise that "I am not bid to wait upon this bride" (1.1.338), and left alone, he is reduced from public declamation to private self-address: "Titus, when wert thou wont to walk alone, / Dishonoured thus and challengèd of wrongs?" (1.1.339–40). When Tamora rises to imperial power, Titus suffers a corresponding marginalization. Within a few scenes, he declares that "Rome is but a wilderness of tigers" (3.1.54), after the Tribunes refuse even to hear him plead. The symbolic silencing of Titus not only neatly counterpoints the physical silencing of Lavinia, but also shows that the value system which prized Titus and his worth, like that which prized Lavinia as "Rome's rich ornament," has been deranged.

In the opening scene, the principal figures of the Roman state exchange women, prisoners, and honours, but the relationships thus established soon collapse in mutual recrimination. Though Tamora early in the play warns Saturninus against "ingratitude, / Which Rome reputes to be a heinous sin"

(1.1.447–48), he nevertheless later returns Titus's hand, inciting the messenger to observe, "[I]ll art thou repaid" (3.1.233). This most callous gesture of ingratitude marks the collapse of the system of exchanges within which Lavinia serves as a marker of value and Titus acts as an important agent. By finally defeating the Goths, after ten years of war (1.1.31), Titus not only exhausts his own raison d'être but also destroys the central dichotomy between Roman and barbarian. Marcus describes Roman values as the opposite of barbarian and Tamora identifies gratitude as Roman. Once Rome becomes barbarian, however, "a wilderness for tigers," the exchange system ceases to apply. Not only does Lavinia lose value, but the whole system of exchanges within which she has value ceases to function.

The breakdown of Roman values and of its language as a system, a said, is also a failure of the sacred. Rituals cease to apply. Waith comments on the highly ritualistic character of the play's dramaturgy, beginning with an "almost uninterrupted series of spectacles in the first act," but this only serves to emphasize the failure of ritual.[21] A Girardian might note that the sacred violence of scapegoating fails to unify the community. Instead, as often in the myths which Girard discusses, "violence that should be present in but contained by the religious ritual is released into the community."[22] Stephen X. Mead argues that the play's world suffers from "the failure of sacrifice to protect a community from its own violence by channelling that violence into a meaningful experience."[23] On the contrary, the most spectacular ceremony, the sacrifice of Alarbus to the ghosts of Titus's dead sons, begins the whole spiral of sanguinary revenge. Tamora rejects the sacrifice of her son with an oxymoron: "O cruel, irreligious piety!" (1.1.130). The Romans, however, accept this piety as an expression of religion and concern for the dead: "Religiously," Titus says of his sons, "they ask a sacrifice" (1.1.124). Titus himself, "surnamèd Pius" (1.1.23), serves as a pillar of this value system. Although sacred traditions may be partly invented — Titus proudly claims to have "sumptuously re-edified" the family tomb (1.1.351) — they structure responses to the suffering of others, and thereby contain grief. Mutius becomes the first occupant of the monument of the Andronici to be, as Titus puts it, "basely slain in brawls" (1.1.353), but his kinsmen repeat the customary words: "No man shed tears for noble Mutius; / He lives in fame, that died in virtue's cause" (1.1.389–90). Apparently these words furnish an actual imperative, not merely an obsequious prayer: "For two-and-twenty sons," Titus tells the Tribunes, "I never wept" (3.1.10). Titus entombs his grief along with his sons in the family monument. The ethical response finds expression in a said, in words and rituals, where it is entombed like Titus's sons.

When the sacredness of Rome and its gods fails, the characters must face the suffering of others without a customary form of mourning. An image of the movement from pagan religion to human comfort appears when Titus, having chopped off one of his hands to ransom his sons, implores the gods for revenge (3.1.205–8). Mockery answers his prayers. A messenger arrives bearing the heads of Titus's sons, along with "thy hand in scorn to thee sent back" (3.1.236). Later in the play, when Titus again calls on the gods, a clown enters instead. "Shall I have justice? What says Jupiter?" (4.3.79), he demands of the uncomprehending bumpkin. The hollowness of the ceremonies of Roman piety, however, makes Lavinia's demonstration of sympathy, joining her father in prayer, all the more remarkable: "What, wouldst thou kneel with me?" (3.1.208). Even the messenger who brings the heads of Titus's sons finds an empathy beyond the demands of Roman piety: "[W]oe is me to think upon thy woes, / More than remembrance of my father's death" (3.1.238–39). Concern for the Other, the call for an ethical response that Levinas terms saying, does not evaporate with the sacred practices in which it found expression. On the contrary, revealed as a trace behind the said, it assumes renewed importance.

Hence, the difficulty of understanding Lavinia fails to discourage Titus from labouring doggedly at the task. When she frightens Young Lucius, Titus assures him that "She loves thee, boy, too well to do thee harm" (4.1.6). Titus does not base his trust of Lavinia on understanding; on the contrary, he makes an effort to understand her because he first trusts and loves her. "Fear her not, Lucius;" he explains, "somewhat doth she mean" (4.1.9). When the sight of Lavinia knocks her sole surviving brother to his knees, Titus insists that he muster courage to "arise, and look upon her" (3.1.65). A primordial ethical appeal inspires an effort to face Lavinia. Titus's response seeks semiotic form when he asks his daughter to "make some sign how I may do thee ease" (3.1.121). In the next scene, he offers to study her gestures, in order to develop a common language:

> In thy dumb action will I be as perfect
> As begging hermits in their holy prayers.
> Thou shalt not sigh, nor hold thy stumps to heaven,
> Nor wink, nor nod, nor kneel, nor make a sign,
> But I of these will wrest an alphabet,
> And by still practice learn to know thy meaning. (3.2.40–45)

Lavinia's condition frustrates, but also elicits, language, driving the men around her to construct semiotic systems, to search for means of communication. Titus anachronistically compares this search to the rigorous discipline of monastic prayer, attendance to the silent voice of the absolutely Other.

After they learn the names of Lavinia's murderers, the Andronici do not call on her again. Detmer-Goebel concludes that identifying the guilty exhausts their interest in Lavinia's voice: "As soon as Lavinia dutifully writes in the sand the names of her attackers, she is not addressed or consoled, but told to kneel down with the others present and swear revenge."[24] Nevertheless, both Marcus and Titus treat her words with extraordinary importance, and attempt to fix Lavinia's message permanently. Marcus proposes an oath, on the precedent of that taken by Junius Brutus to revenge Lucrece (4.1.88–93), while Titus quotes Seneca in Latin (4.1.80–81), before devising an elaborate allegory, practically a fable, in which the rapists, their mother, and her husband take symbolic form as animals (4.1.95–100). After resorting to literary and narrative precedents, Titus proposes to give the words physical form: "I will go get a leaf of brass, / And with a gad of steel will write these words" (4.1.101–2). Both the metal and the literary precedents fix Lavinia's words within the said, where they become separable from the person who offers them. Marcus and Titus do not address her again, because the content of what she says eclipses the fact of her address, that she faces them and commands their attention. Paradoxically, the Andronici silence Lavinia by assigning her words extraordinary importance. In the said, the saying finds both expression and betrayal.

The Andronici take revenge, at first symbolically on paper but then physically, on the bodies of their enemies. Learning the rapists' identities, Titus sends them a gift, as Aaron says, "wrapped about with lines / That wound, beyond their feeling, to the quick" (4.2.27–28). Aaron seems amused, but Chiron and Demetrius fail to even notice, and Marcus confuses Titus's revenge with forgiveness (4.1.127). Titus sends a similar message to Saturninus, but this only angers Saturninus, who orders the messenger executed (4.4.44), then plots to execute Titus himself: "For this proud mock I'll be thy slaughterman" (4.4.57). He would probably succeed if Aemilius did not immediately provide an imperative distraction with news of Lucius's Gothic army marching on Rome. Later, Titus writes "sad decrees" in blood, which seem only a desperate effort to assure himself that "what is written shall be executed" (5.2.11, 15). Titus's efforts to give his revenge textual form are futile and even self-defeating.

Only when Tamora, crazed with hubristic confidence in her own rhetorical power and cunning (4.4.94–98), brings him Chiron and Demetrius can Titus follow his Ovidian precedent to its cannibalistic climax. He does not write another word in the play, even sending Marcus to summon Lucius by word of mouth (5.2.122–30). Henceforth, literature is for Titus strictly an applied art. He dispatches Lavinia on the strength of the "pattern, precedent, and lively warrant" of "rash Virginius," who similarly killed a ravished daughter (5.3.43, 36). One might argue that Titus merely avenges his honour, but he speaks only of his pain. Moreover, Lavinia begged for death with some of her last words (2.3.173), and Chiron and Demetrius boast in their sadistic way of robbing her even of the means to hang herself (2.4.9–10). In any case, Titus finds, in actions and in literary precedent, a response to Lavinia's suffering. He answers his own question "What shall we do?" (3.1.133) in a most macabre way. We ought not to forget, however, that the question itself expresses the extraordinary ethical demand made of the Andronici by Lavinia. In finding something "to do," Titus gives this saying form in the said.

Manifestation, Levinas insists, demands betrayal. The last scene of the play shows how language as an exorbitant concern yields to a said. Marcus's speech to the Roman people constitutes a tour de force of spontaneous rhetoric, mixing claims on pity with humility before the popular judgment. Instead of introducing his nephew as *candidatus*, Marcus compares him with Aeneas, "our ancestor" and founder of Rome (5.3.79), while conflating "our Troy, our Rome" in case anyone misses the parallel (5.3.86). In a flurry of metaphors, Marcus likens the state to "a flight of fowl," "scattered corn" and finally a severed body, with "broken limbs" (5.3.67–71). Where Lavinia's body lost meaning, the body now serves as a means of expression, and even as evidence. Marcus appeals to his "frosty signs and chaps of age" as "Grave witnesses of true experience" (5.3.76–77). Lucius proclaims that "My scars can witness, dumb although they are, / That my report is just and full of truth" (5.3.113–14). Finally, the very colour of Aaron's child witnesses to Tamora's infidelity (5.3.118–20). Indeed, Marcus deploys silence as a trope, claiming to be unable to speak for weeping:

> … floods of tears will drown mine oratory
> And break my utt'rance, even in the time
> When it should move ye to attend me most,
> And force you to commiseration. (5.3.89–92)

Where Lavinia's body calls for a response, but offers no statement or meaning beyond her suffering, the bodies of Marcus and Lucius signify truths and ratify their words. Rather than mutely calling for an ethical response, the bodies of the surviving Andronici are immediately ascribed meaning within the said.

Moreover, the body's various significations serve as arguments in a political arena. Without even requesting it, Marcus obtains the empire for his nephew. It would be churlish to insist that Marcus merely feigns distress, on the grounds that he exploits the claim of silence rhetorically and for dynastic political gain. The possibility of suspecting Marcus of bad faith, however, shows that his suffering has become a said. It has been rendered into a set of potentially false signs. "In language qua said," writes Levinas, "everything is conveyed before us, albeit at the price of a betrayal."[25] As with other references to the body, Marcus's tears signify and even guarantee the truth of his claims, as does his offer, on behalf of his nephew and Young Lucius, to "hand in hand all headlong hurl ourselves, / And on the ragged stones beat forth our souls, / And make a mutual closure of our house" (5.3.131–33). The traumas which these "poor remainder of Andronici" (5.3.130) have survived render the offer creditable. As when the Andronici perform their obsequies in the play's first scene, however, rhetorical form gives feeling expression and therefore allows it to be suspected of falsehood.

One has the sense that Roman government and society undergoes a permanent change. Titus will join his sons in "our household's monument" (5.3.193), and even Saturninus receives the dignity of burial "in his father's grave" (5.3.191). Whereas Titus demanded stoicism, however, Lucius invites his son to "learn of us / To melt in showers" (5.3.159–60). Lucius ratifies his own and his son's public mourning, but forbids pity towards Aaron: "If anyone relieves or pities him, / For the offence he dies" (5.3.180–81). The coldly traditional execution of Alarbus appears merciful by comparison. Similarly, Lucius denies Tamora burial. After the semiotic crisis of the play, Lucius establishes a new order, reiterating the distinction between Roman and barbarian. New burial rites replace old obsequies. Suffering reclaims expression and social discourse assimilates its signs.

Whatever mark the events of the play leave on Shakespeare's fictive Rome, however, the play dramatizes the birth of language in ethics. Lavinia appeals silently. Despite the failure of social structures and sanctities, and the collapse of dialogue into silence, the characters struggle to find a response. Their response, however, betrays itself into a said, with all the formal conventionality of a new social organization.

Notes

1 Qtd. in Eugene Waith's introduction to *Titus Andronicus* (Oxford: Oxford University Press, 1984) 1.

2 S. Clark Hulse, "Wresting the Alphabet: Oratory and Action in *Titus Andronicus*," *Criticism* 21 (1979): 106.

3 Qtd. in Waith, introduction to *Titus Andronicus*, 9.

4 Ibid., 42.

5 William Shakespeare, *Titus Andronicus*, ed. Eugene Waith (Oxford: Oxford University Press, 1984) 3.1.103–5; future citations are from this edition and will be given in the text by act, scene, and line number.

6 Mary Laughlin Fawcett, "Arms/Words/Tears: Language and the Body in *Titus Andronicus*," *ELH* 50.2 (1983): 263.

7 Emmanuel Levinas, *Otherwise Than Being or Beyond Essence*, trans. Alphonso Lingis (The Hague: Martinus Nijhoff, 1981) 5.

8 Emmanuel Levinas, "God and Philosophy," trans. Richard A. Cohen, *The Levinas Reader*, ed. Seán Hand (Oxford: Blackwell, 1989) 183.

9 Bernice Harris, "Sexuality as a Signifier for Power Relations: Using Lavinia, of Shakespeare's *Titus Andronicus*," *Criticism* 38.3 (1996): 385.

10 Ibid., 387.

11 Emily Detmer-Goebel, "The Need for Lavinia's Voice: *Titus Andronicus* and the Telling of Rape," *Shakespeare Studies* 29 (2001): 77–78; Carolyn D. Williams, "'Silence, Like a Lucrece Knife': Shakespeare and the Meanings of Rape," *Yearbook of English Studies* 23 (1993): 99–100.

12 Harris, "Sexuality as a Signifier for Power Relations," 389.

13 Sara Eaton, "A Woman of Letters: Lavinia in *Titus Andronicus*," *Shakespearean Tragedy and Gender*, ed. Shirley Nelson Garner and Madelon Sprengnether (Bloomington: Indiana University Press, 1996) 64.

14 Detmer-Goebel, "The Need for Lavinia's Voice," 80.

15 Grace Starry West, "Going by the Book: Classical Allusions in Shakespeare's *Titus Andronicus*," *Studies in Philology* 79.1 (1982): 67.

16 West, "Going by the Book," 65.

17 Fawcett, "Arms/Words/Tears," 269; West, "Going by the Book," 68.

18 Levinas, *Otherwise Than Being*, 6.

19 Jacques Derrida, *Adieu to Emmanuel Levinas*, trans. Pascale-Anne Brault and Michael Naas (Stanford, CA: Stanford University Press, 1999) 4.

20 "Villain," Def. 4b, *The Oxford English Dictionary*, 2nd ed., 1989.

21 Waith, introduction to *Titus Andronicus*, 58.

22 William W.E. Slights, "The Sacrificial Crisis in *Titus Andronicus*," *University of Toronto Quarterly* 49.1 (1979): 20.

23 Stephen X. Mead, "The Crisis of Ritual in *Titus Andronicus*," *Exemplaria* 6.2 (1994): 463.

24 Detmer-Goebel, "The Need for Lavinia's Voice," 87.

25 Levinas, *Otherwise Than Being*, 6.

PRECIOUS STORIES: THE DISCURSIVE ECONOMY IN SHAKESPEARE'S *RAPE OF LUCRECE*

Heather G.S. Johnson

In retelling the tale of the Roman matron Lucretia's rape, Shakespeare places himself among a large and prestigious group of authors that includes Ovid and Livy as well as some of his own contemporaries who had already dealt with the same subject matter. Moreover, the poet would have been recognized as one of many rewriters of the tale by the readers of his day, who would probably have at least read Ovid's *Fasti* as part of their early education.[1] But of course, Shakespeare's adoption of the Roman story is no mere matter of outfitting old material in new language.

Though *The Rape of Lucrece* necessarily follows the story of the Roman matron's rape and subsequent death, many critics have recognized the ways in which the actual events that comprise the core of the story act as skeletal support to—and an excuse for—the discussion of pressing philosophical issues. Written as a poetic complaint—a popular genre of the time—*The Rape of Lucrece* is as much a theoretical essay as a Renaissance rendition of a classic narrative. That Shakespeare has written a philosophical treatise enclosed within a beautiful poem is indicated by his inclusion of extended speeches and sequences that are not in the original stories and which are largely irrelevant to the achievement of the plot (and even tangential to character development). As Heather Dubrow comments, "*The Rape of Lucrece* is often dismissed as 'a gorgeous gallery of gallant inventions,' a literary sampler that is crammed with tropes and schemes."[2] If we understand the poem as a philosophical essay as well as a plot-driven narrative poem, these somewhat extraneous "inventions" take on new relevance and purpose.

Though many critics agree, at least implicitly, that Shakespeare uses the Lucretia story as a scaffolding for philosophical discourse, there is far less agreement about what the central thesis of his "essay" might be. We might see this variety of critical interpretations as a positive side effect of Shakespeare's choice of genre (rather than as the failure of the poem to make its philosophical intentions clear). Because it is technically a poem rather than an essay, *The Rape of Lucrece* need not limit itself to a single central question, nor are the normal standards of argumentation enforced. In addition to the philosophical discussions of Time, Night, and Opportunity pronounced by Lucrece herself, critics have identified larger thematic arguments about historiography, the female body, narrative, and Elizabethan politics. I argue that Shakespeare's poetic "essay" also grapples with the uses and abuses of discourse itself (including his *own* discourse). The poem recognizes and discusses the poet's participation in a larger symbolic marketplace in which the ownership of stories is negotiated and cultural capital purchased with discursive coin. In this marketplace, individuals or institutions compete for the right to place a specific sequence of events in the context of a greater historical narrative. I further argue that Lucrece's story is particularly valuable precisely because she is a victim — that is, because her story carries hefty emotional weight, potentially motivating not only pity and fear, as in the classic tragedy, but also outrage, righteous indignation, and finally, *more storytelling*.

The symbolic marketplace in which successful discourse is valued is established early on, in the argument that precedes the poem proper. Bored by their lengthy siege of Ardea and looking for a fight, a group of Roman officers, including Collatine (Lucrece's husband) and Tarquin, gather together to joust with words. The competition takes the form of a boasting match in which each individual claims the superior beauty and virtuosity of his wife. Boasts, however, have little discursive value if they cannot be verified, and therefore the group sets off to prove their statements true or false (thereby proving their relative "worth" in the symbolic market). When they arrive to find all the wives but Lucrece revelling, Collatine's statement is proven to be true, while all the other combatants find their boasts to be suddenly and utterly without value. Collatine's symbolic wealth is multiplied, and he gains an important edge over his embarrassed companions.

The encounter has a second, unintended effect; it initiates Tarquin's obsession with Lucrece. Her beauty is certainly part of her appeal, but Tarquin's lust is also a response to Collatine's victory over his fellows. Tarquin is motivated in part by desire, in part by jealousy of Collatine's discursive capital:

Collatine's "boast of Lucrece's sovereignty" incites "envy of so rich a thing."[3] The "rich thing" mentioned in these lines is primarily Lucrece, who is also referred to as a "jewel," but the phrase "rich thing" may also refer to the claim itself. The narrator asks, "Why is Collatine the publisher of that rich jewel?" and we might answer that he publishes because publication multiplies the symbolic wealth contained in Lucrece's person by producing discursive capital in the form of the successful boast. Thus, Tarquin's plan to rape Lucrece — though motivated primarily by unruly lust — is also calculated to ruin Collatine, to render his boast as valueless as the others. In economic terms, the principal, Lucrece, and the interest, the boast, would be wiped out in one fell swoop.

The most blatant example of the struggle for discursive capital occurs at the end of the poem, after Lucrece's death. The men who have heard her testimony deliver their wailing laments over her body in a scene that parallels Lucrece's own behaviour in the aftermath of the rape. However, once they begin to speak, their eulogizing takes a curious form, resembling a type of contest. Father and husband fight between them about who is experiencing the greatest loss, each mounting to more and more extravagant claims to the greater anguish over her death. What becomes clear is that these two men are not merely discussing the nature of their grief, but arguing about the *ownership* of Lucrece, and most importantly *the right to tell her story*.[4] In this exchange, Lucrece's life is being transformed from a work-in-progress to a "saleable" commodity, a discourse bought with discursive capital. The father asserts his "right" to retell the story of Lucrece as the tale of a father's loss, while the husband bargains for exclusive rights to present her story as that of a husband's injury. Both parties claim to have made a substantial "investment" in Lucrece, an investment which becomes the basis for their discursive stances. In a revealing turn of phrase, Collatine begs Lucretius not to "take away / [His] sorrow's interest" (lines 1796–97), indicating not only his claim upon Lucrece as a grieving husband, but also gesturing toward the return he might expect from his cultural investment in his heroic wife. Lucretius heightens the bidding war with the classic claim of the father: "I did give that life / Which she too early and too late hath spilled" (lines 1800–1801). As the biological producer of a cultural icon, Lucretius expects to receive any profit to be made from Lucrece's victimization. Collatine counters the father's claim by reminding him that he gave away all rights to Lucrece when he gave her in marriage to Collatine: "[S]he was my wife. / I owed her, and 'tis mine that she hath killed" (lines 1802–3).[5] In the end, neither of these individuals possesses enough "discursive capital" to definitively claim Lucrece: "The one doth call her his, the other his, / Yet neither may possess the claim they lay" (lines 1793–94). The literal meaning of this line is, of course, that neither may possess Lucrece because she's dead. In another sense, neither husband nor father may possess Lucrece's story because a more aggressive—and more savvy—buyer appears on the scene.

Both father and husband are "outbid" by Brutus, who triumphantly appropriates both Lucrece's body *and* story. While Brutus has the disadvantage of not having a substantial investment in Lucrece, he gains extra cultural capital by enacting a transformation from shallow to eloquent on the spot: "[B]ut now he throws that shallow habit by / Wherein deep policy him did disguise, / And armed his long-hid wits advisedly" (lines 1814–16). Using the capital generated by the transformation, Brutus interprets Lucrece's story as a call to political change on a national level, and her story becomes one of the enabling myths of the new Roman republic. Brutus completes his economic coup by calling on the combined cultural capital of Lucrece's blood, the sun above, and the gathered crowd's rights as Romans.

Why this discursive competition for the right to claim—and tell—the dead woman's story? It is precisely Lucrece's status as a victim that makes her life story valuable. Unlike the martyr, who may have the opportunity to claim a cause or purpose (by stating religious or political motives, for example), the victim's very "silence" allows for a narrative in which meaning is malleable. This makes the victim's story particularly ripe for appropriation, and therefore particularly valuable on the "cultural market." Jean-François Lyotard makes an important distinction between the plaintiff and the victim, stating that while both figures have suffered *damage* of some sort, only the latter suffers a *wrong*. A wrong is a "damage accompanied by the loss of the means to prove that damage."[6] Thus, one who is able to bring proof to bear in an appropriate setting is merely a plaintiff, while, for the victim, "to the privation constituted by the damage there is added the impossibility of bringing it to the knowledge of others, and in particular to the knowledge of a tribunal."[7] From this viewpoint, the defining quality of the victim is *not* the affliction he or she suffers at the hands of another, but a breakdown in communication between the addressor and the addressee. Significantly, this "breakdown" may occur at a number of points in the process of communication, whether the cause be a physical or emotional inability (or unwillingness) of the victim to speak, the inadequacy of language to express, a lack of understanding in the intended audience, or any other barrier to effective communication. Essentially, the *victim* is one who is "silent"[8] on the subject of his or her own victimhood. By this definition, anyone who is able to announce his or her own victimhood and/or derive cultural capital from it is not precisely a victim, but a type of plaintiff. Martyrs, too, are akin to the type of victim discussed in this paper, but once again the key difference lies in their ability to give the damage they sustain meaning. While the "tribunal" that would understand the martyr's pronouncement may be unsympathetic or relatively powerless, the relevant communication has still been made.[9]

One of the elements that all of the Lucretia stories seem to share is that she is able, in the end, to accuse her rapist. The men who hear her utterance (whom we might call a "tribunal") seem to understand what she is saying — they proceed to punish her attacker and his family. It is an "open and shut case" as it is told in the traditional narratives: Lucretia reveals that she has been raped by Tarquin and he is punished accordingly. Under this scenario, the rape is not a "wrong" and Lucretia would more properly be described as a plaintiff than a victim. Yet this easy solution is none too satisfying — if she is vindicated, why does she kill herself? Why does her "open and shut" story continue to occasion debate in later centuries? As many have noted in response to Shakespeare's version of the story (though the point is also applicable to the other accounts), the actual rape is not Lucrece's only concern.[10] What we may see on closer inspection is that the physical violation *is not the only damage inflicted by the rape*: in fact, the physical fact of the rape may be comparatively minor in comparison to its effects. Shakespeare's portrayal of Lucrece takes little account of the bodily sensations of pain that might have accompanied the rape. The attack is figured as a mental and emotional one: though her physical reactions are graphically represented, they seem to have oddly little bearing on her sense of violation. If the "collateral" (non-physical) damage was in fact *not* communicated to a "tribunal," then Lucrece *is* a victim.

The wrong that remains unspoken (and for which there is as yet no idiom) is the destruction of Lucrece's identity as a *chaste* woman. Examining the historical record of responses to Lucretia, Sasha Roberts finds that "[d]espite [her] iconic status as an exemplary, chaste wife, her innocence as a raped woman was not universally acknowledged. The dominant view of her chastity and devotion as a wife was countered by dissenting voices, which saw her as dissembling, seductive and ultimately selfish. This tradition centered on two perceived difficulties raised by St. Augustine: her submission to rape and her act of suicide."[11] What this disagreement over Lucretia's status makes clear is that there is very little "conceptual room" between the labels "chaste" and "unchaste." In the first stanza of *The Rape of Lucrece* we are presented with an image of a lust-driven Tarquin racing from Ardea to Collatium in order to "girdle with embracing flames ... Lucrece the Chaste" (lines 6–7). "Lucrece the Chaste" is a title that she had been given earlier and which seems to identify her to the community in which she lives. It is a title which will ultimately be lost.

While her father and husband insist that she is not responsible for the rape because she did not consent, after the rape has occurred, Lucrece can no longer be titled "the chaste." Gestures are made toward an understanding of the raped woman as not accountable the crime and therefore still at least spiritually chaste even if not physically so. Yet the distinction collapses quickly and the sufferer becomes either one or the other (chaste or not chaste) in the eyes of the community at large. Her identity as a societal exemplar, the emblem of chastity, has been ripped from her.[12] While meant as reassuring, the ministrations of Lucrece's family only serve to deepen confusion about Lucrece's identity: she is simultaneously neither chaste nor unchaste. There is no *positive* way of expressing her identity (in human terms), no word that adequately describes her strangely "in-between" condition — she can be explained only by pointing out what she is *not*.[13] This collapse of boundaries between two mutually exclusive categories, and the knowledge that neither is precisely correct, places the victim in an impossibly schizophrenic position. The original identity is irrevocably lost, yet there is no viable replacement for it.[14]

That Lucrece experiences the rape as accompanied by a loss of identity is made clear by her thoughts following the event, many of which take form as attempts to orient herself to a "new" identity in accordance with her new status. Lucrece is left at loose ends, unsure of the pattern of behaviour now required of her (whereas the proper actions of a person named "Lucrece the Chaste" were clear enough). She will eventually realize, after seeking examples on which to base her conduct and on which to model the narrative of her future, that the only response proper to her neither/nor position is to end all action by giving herself death. Therefore, her eventual suicide signals her ultimate failure to find an identity with which she can live.

Lucrece's search for a pattern on which to base future behaviour is explored in the latter portion of her solitary meditations: she seeks out, through a rehearsal of history, a mirror in which to view her new self. While she finds an image of her exterior in her maid, the two figures in whom she seems to find the most accurate and satisfying reflection are mythological: Philomel and Hecuba. The most obvious link between the three women is severe trauma followed by psychological confusion and subsequent release of their roles in human society. Philomel is withdrawn from the human community when she is transformed into a bird, while Hecuba severs social connections when she commits suicide. Yet what may be more important to an understanding of Lucrece's behaviour is what happens to the voices of these women, or even more appropriately, the ways in which they may express their traumatic experiences.[15] Lucrece finds her first mirror in Philomel, a woman turned bird:

> "Come, Philomel, that sing'st of ravishment,
> Make thy sad grove in my disheveled hair.
> As the dank earth weeps at thy languishment
> So I at each sad strain will strain a tear,
> And with deep groans the diapason bear;
> For burden-wise I'll hum on Tarquin still,
> While thou on Tereus descants better skill." (lines 1128–34)

Not only is Lucrece's prime example a woman who, having been raped, became a bird who could only sing wordlessly about her own assault, but Lucrece proposes to respond in kind, with inarticulate humming and groaning. She goes on to compare herself to a stringed instrument, while the narrator describes her as a "poor frighted deer" (line 1149), both comparisons that highlight her lack of humanity and her *speechlessness*. This might seem incongruous, given her immense and oft-noted volubility in the passages which immediately follow the rape. Yet she has no contemporary human audience during her most voluble phase — she is alone, speaking only to herself and the inanimate objects around her. The failure in communication symbolized by the wordless sounds of Philomel represents not only Lucrece's abortive struggle to express her identity, but also refers to the literal lack of an audience for her innermost thoughts and most grievous emotional wounds (none of which will appear in her final statement, which does have an audience).

Another mirror is sought in a painting depicting the Trojan War. As Stephen Carter writes about this scene, "It is during her first narration of (and address to) the painting that Lucrece, in effect, crosses over into what she sees, and also into herself as representation."[16] While this may not be the very first identification with a mythological figure, it is certainly a moment when Lucrece locates a pattern into which her experience fits. She finally finds a sympathetic face in the rendering of Hecuba:

> To this well painted piece is Lucrece come,
> To find a face where all distress is stell'd.
> Many she sees where cares have carved some,
> But none where all distress and dolour dwell'd
> Till she despairing Hecuba beheld. (lines 1443–47)

Tellingly, Hecuba is yet another woman (though her lament proceeds from a different cause) who, in the traditional tale, is rendered incapable of speech: driven mad, she barks like a dog and murders her own children before killing herself. The emphasis on "distress and dolour" is significant; it gives us an indication of what Lucrece expects to be able to express now that she has assumed a new verbally inexpressible identity. The split in audience comprehension noted earlier is highlighted again here. While the readers of Shakespeare's poem experience Lucrece as highly eloquent, perhaps even too talkative, she can only understand herself as properly wordless.[17]

In addition to the inarticulate "sounds" with which Lucrece associates herself — moaning, groaning, humming, vibrating (as the strings of a violin), or barking — the new expressive space she inhabits incorporates a constellation of other types of gestures. Looking at the painting of the Trojan War, Lucrece is initially intrigued by the *expression* on Hecuba's face, the look of distress.

The non-verbal communication that she and her predecessors share replaces the verbal speech of which they are no longer capable. Thus, though Lucrece is still able to verbally accuse her attacker of the crime of rape, she is unable to express the wrong done to her good name and to her identity except by the violent gesture that ends her life. She is both plaintiff and victim.

Her victimization—her inability to express the true extent of the damage done to her—makes her story especially attractive to those who would adapt it to their own purposes. Victims are valuable because they are repositories and fountains of emotive power, like the endless song of the nightingale always re-imprinting Philomela's horror or the painted face of Hecuba's sorrow. This emotive power is "up for grabs" in the sense that it begs for explanation and retribution, and it can be used as a potent source of cultural motivation through guilt, indignation, or pity. The victim's lament mobilizes affect without directing it; it is the "buyer's" prerogative to interpret as he/she sees fit. Slavoj Žižek, writing about an entirely different set of circumstances, states that "the ideal subject" (for the individual who hopes to appropriate his or her story) is a "victim... not a political subject with a clear agenda, but a subject of helpless suffering," and remains so only "*insofar as it remains a victim.*"[18] The identification of the victim with a "pure," non-political suffering leaves her story open to political constructions from the outside, as well as signifying that she is a fit object for protection and sympathy.

Interestingly, Lucrece seems to be well aware of her value on the discursive market. One of her most immediate concerns, following the rape, is the effect that the event will have on her husband's cultural capital. She imagines that the capital she afforded him as "Lucretia the Chaste" will now be disbursed among the general population, a common coin to be exchanged frivolously by anyone who so chooses. She begs that her "good name, that senseless reputation, for Collatine's dear love be kept unspotted," lest the story be told by "[t]he nurse to still her child," "the orator to deck his oratory," and the minstrels to "tune [her] defame" in order to find feasts—that is, to earn their livings (lines 813, 815, 817). Later, she refers specifically back to the boasting contest that opens the poem, imagining a restaging of that competition, with Tarquin victoriously claiming that he has conquered Collatine's virtuous wife and is the father of her child. Lucrece's suicide is calculated to deprive Tarquin of this dubious capital: "He shall not boast who did thy stock pollute, / That thou are doting father of his fruit. / Nor shall he smile at thee in secret thought, / Nor laugh with his companions at thy state, / But thou shalt know thy int'rest was not bought / Basely with gold, but stol'n from forth thy gate" (lines 1063–68). Though she might be able to prove her "innocence," and prevent Tarquin's profit by explaining that the act was not consensual, she rejects the idea quickly, stating, "I will not poison [Collatine] with my attaint, / Nor fold my fault in cleanly coin'd excuses" (lines 1071–72). These lines imply that excuses are cheap, and being newly minted, can only add to inflation, lowering the general worth of discourse (especially, perhaps, feminine discourse).

In the stanzas that follow, Lucrece devises a plan to recover her value as an object of discourse. Following the example of Philomel and the painted Hecuba, she decides to limit her own public utterances. The emotional but non-verbal communication practised by both women inspires others, including Lucrece, to speak for them, to tell their stories for them. Contemplating the silent form of the woeful Hecuba, Lucrece exclaims, "Poor instrument, without a sound, / I'll tune thy woes with my lamenting tongue" (lines 1464–65). She seems to realize that the stories of the two victimized women are made more powerful by their silence, and she calculates her own performance accordingly. It is, according to Carter, through her identification with Hecuba "that Lucrece, in effect, crosses over into what she sees, and also into herself as representation."[19] Her announcement to the male witnesses of her suicide is intentionally short and explosively emotional, as "the life and feeling of her passion / She hoards, to spend when [Collatine] is by to hear her" (lines 1317–18). In response to her maid's request that she share her grief, Lucrece states that "if it should be told, / The repetition cannot make it less" (lines 1284–85), but the exact opposite is true of the cultural capital to be extracted from that grief. Lucrece fears that telling her tale will somehow decrease its effect and so deliberately withholds the information from her maid, reserving the story for the men whom she is trying to enrich. That her final speech is calculated for maximum cultural capital is reinforced by the fact that she is clearly capable of eloquent, extended speech. Her lengthy descant on night, time, and opportunity contrasts sharply with her halting announcement of the events of the previous night: "Three times with sighs she gives her sorrow fire, / Ere once she can discharge one word of woe" (lines 1604–5). She repeats little beyond the bare events of the case, with the exception of her final request that Tarquin be punished for his crime.[20] It is as though she is deliberately leaving her experience open to interpretation, inviting sympathetic retellings of her tale. Once she is dead — and therefore no longer capable of speaking for herself — others will take up her story, just as she took up the stories of Philomel and Hecuba. By making Collatine, Lucretius, and Brutus swear to punish Tarquin, she also implicitly gives them permission to tell, and to interpret, her story. By making them *part* of her story, she makes them partial owners of it.

Lucrece's awareness of the value of her own narrative, and her effort to transfer that value to the men who promise to avenge her, complicates her story's status in the marketplace. While it is tempting to interpret the male appropriation of Lucrece's rape as a type of stealing, Lucrece's attitude implies that her story isn't so much stolen as it is received as a gift. Lucrece wants her husband and father to profit from her famous rape in the same way that they previously profited from her famous chastity. Yet, their appropriation of her story is not entirely positive, either; Shakespeare's description of the men's petty squabbling over who gets to "claim" the dead victim adds a sour note to the whole affair. Appropriation, then, has both positive and negative features: on the one hand, some victims' stories may only find a hearing if they are appropriated by others, especially when the victim has no voice of his or her own. On the other hand, appropriated stories can be misused and misinterpreted; such appropriation can easily cross over into exploitation.

As much as the figures *within* the poem, Shakespeare is also a beneficiary of Lucrece's legacy, as are Livy, Ovid, and the others who have recounted her tale over the centuries. Each of these men retells and reinterprets her story as part of a larger narrative. Livy and Ovid, following Brutus, place the rape of Lucretia firmly in the greater scope of Roman history. Suzanne Scholz notes the ways in which, "[i]n its historical situation, the myth of Lucretia appears as a legitimizing and identity-giving narrative after a change of political organization and renders the chaste woman as an icon of unity for the early republic."[21] Shakespeare gestures toward this interpretation in the argument preceding the poem, which follows the traditional versions of the story quite closely. The poetic rendition of the rape, however, places the story in a philosophical setting. Lucrece herself does much of the work of contextualizing the rape, in an effort to give the violent, senseless crime meaning, by connecting it to the larger philosophical abstractions Time, Night, and Opportunity. Lucrece's interpretation attempts to transform the rape into a symbol, not of the Roman Republic, but of personified concepts. Though she plays with this interpretation, she eventually discards it in favour of leaving the task to the men, perhaps because, as Joyce Green MacDonald explains, "copiousness appears as a distinctively female property of language, a linguistic property often at odds with social prescriptions of female silence, retirement, and obedience."[22] Shakespeare, of course, "reinstates" Lucrece's own interpretation (which, of course, is actually *his* imagined version of her interpretation), while adding another layer of meaning by reorganizing the story to reveal the discursive marketplace, the trade in women, and political use of stories and storytelling.

That Shakespeare himself benefits from a parallel appropriation of Lucrece's story is made clear by the patronage-seeking dedication to Henry Wriothesley. Like the men within the poem, Shakespeare also "uses" Lucrece—to suit his own literary purpose, transforming her story into a vehicle for his own essay on discursive practice. The critics who write about the poem (myself included) are also among those who "profit" from the tragic tale, as well as from the more general practice of speaking for the silent victim. New, politically charged readings of texts are often formulated as an effort to restore power to oppressed groups of people by retroactively locating a voice for them, by sifting through the various representations written by men like Ovid and Livy. While there is nothing wrong with this activity per se, many practitioners fail to notice that after stripping away the exploitative interpretations of others, they must replace them with another interpretive framework, a framework which, though hopefully less exploitative than others, is necessarily always somewhat self-serving. The righteousness that accompanies any attempt to vindicate a silent victim reflects as much upon the vindicator as it does on the victim. This is not to condemn such efforts, but merely to point out that an awareness of the economy at work is necessary if one is to avoid blatantly taking advantage of the victim's story. Shakespeare neatly sidesteps any possible accusations of exploitation by arguing that appropriation is precisely what Lucrece wants (he constructs Lucrece as the guarantor of his right to write her story). The poem argues that it is the story's placement in a greater historical, philosophical, and intellectual framework which transforms it from the tale of a basely physical, violent act into a thought-provoking, nation-building narrative of sublime heroism to be retold by historians and poets.

Notes

1 In her introduction to *The Rape of Lucrece* in *The Norton Shakespeare*, Katharine Eisaman Maus notes, "Slightly different versions of the tale of Tarquin and Lucretia were available in Livy's history of Rome and Ovid's *Fasti*, both commonly read in Elizabethan grammar schools" (*The Norton Shakespeare*, ed. Stephen Greenblatt et al., 2nd ed. [New York: Norton, 2008] 663).

2 Heather Dubrow, "The Rape of Clio: Attitudes to History in Shakespeare's *Lucrece*," *English Literary Renaissance* 16.3 (1986): 425.

3 William Shakespeare, *The Rape of Lucrece*, *The Riverside Shakespeare*, gen. ed. and text. ed. G. Blakemore Evans, with J.J.M. Tobin, 2nd ed. (Boston: Houghton Mifflin, 1997) lines 36 and 39; future citations are from this edition and will be given in the text by line number.

4 While her focus is on Lucrece's body and on the theft of that body by Tarquin, Catherine Belsey also asserts that *The Rape of Lucrece* is "a story about possession" ("Tarquin Dispossessed: Expropriation and Consent in 'The Rape of Lucrece,'" *Shakespeare Quarterly* 52.3 [2001]: 315.)

5 Collatine's argument that Lucrece belongs to him works on a number of levels; she is literally his property by marriage, but he also owns her in so far as he created her — not *biologically*, like her father, but *discursively* as "Lucrece the Chaste." In "'Lucrece the chaste': The Construction of Rape in Shakespeare's *The Rape of Lucrece*" (*Modern Language Studies* 25.2 [1995]: 3–17), Sara E. Quay argues that the "verbal production" of Lucrece first by Collatine and then by Tarquin (following social constructs already in place) designs her as "rapable" (4).

6 Jean-François Lyotard, *The Differend: Phrases in Dispute*, trans. Georges Van Den Abbeele (Minneapolis: University of Minnesota Press; Manchester, UK: Manchester University Press, 1988) 5.

7 Ibid., 5. Interestingly, in *Chaste Thinking: The Rape of Lucretia and the Birth of Humanism* (Bloomington: Indiana University Press, 1989), Stephanie Jed also connects Lucretia's narrative with courtroom language, stating that "there is ample justification…both ancient and modern, for interrogating the literary tradition concerning Lucretia in a legal setting" (2).

8 Lucrece is certainly *not* technically inexpressive in Shakespeare's text, which is why I place the term "silent" in quotes. I will argue that she is silent insofar as the "courtroom"-style speech that would be necessary to remove her victimhood is concerned.

9 A figure like Anne Askew comes to mind; while she cannot save herself from being burned, she does manage to interpret her own situation in a way that would be intelligible to others in her community, as well as to future readers of the text ascribed to her. The wrong—her accusation and punishment by church officials—is described in detail to a tribunal of readers, and she becomes a martyr for the Protestant cause in England. See *The Examinations of Anne Askew*, ed. Elaine V. Beilin (Oxford: Oxford University Press, 1996).

10 While many have noted the obvious concern with chastity, other issues are also discussed in relation to her discomfort. One major strand that has occasioned comment is her concern with her own "fame."

11 Sasha Roberts, "Editing Sexuality, Narrative and Authorship: The Altered Texts of Shakespeare's *Lucrece*," *Texts and Cultural Change in Early Modern England*, ed. Cedric C. Brown and Arthur F. Marotti (New York: St. Martin's Press, 1997) 125. Laura Bromley sets out a number of very different arguments made on the topic of Lucrece's culpability in "Lucrece's Re-Creation" (*Shakespeare Quarterly* 34.2 [1983]: 200–211), noting that "it is difficult to reconcile the headstrong, willful Lucrece portrayed by some critics or the pitiful, passive, deluded Lucrece of others with…a courageous and resolute Lucrece" (205).

12 Both A.D. Cousins and Catherine Belsey come to a similar conclusion. In "Subjectivity, Exemplarity and the Establishing of Characterization in *Lucrece*" (*Studies in English Literature 1500–1900* 38 [1998]: 45–60), Cousins emphasizes the way in which Lucrece is deprived of her role: "The externality of Lucrece's selfhood, and her awareness of its being so, explains her feeling of contamination and her decision to commit suicide, for it becomes apparent that she thinks of Tarquin's assault as having stolen her main role in her world" (58). In "Tarquin Dispossessed," Belsey notes Lucrece's symbolic displacement: "[T]he symbolic Law that confers identity constructs Lucrece as a loyal wife, and Tarquin had deprived her of that 'true type'" (330).

13 This negative expression of self is also present in Livy's account of Lucretia's confession: "As for me, although I absolve myself of guilt, I do not release myself from paying the penalty. From now on, no woman can use the example of Lucretia to live unchaste." The sequence of negatives points to a fundamental difficulty of expression, but it also reveals Lucretia's anxiety concerning her future reception. The label of "unchaste" is seen as coming directly from a specific quadrant of the community: other Roman matrons like herself. See Livy, "The Rape of Lucretia,"

The History of Rome, trans. B.O. Foster, *World Civilizations: An Internet Classroom and Anthology*, ed. Richard Hooker et al., Washington State University, 1996, http://www.wsu.edu/~dee/.

14 She will, in fact, find an identity of sorts, but this identity will not be capable of sustained life.

15 Hopefully this phrasing will remind us of the "damage" which cannot be properly expressed by the victim, according to Lyotard. Though I am claiming here that the women *do* express damage, I hope to prove that the genre in which they express it is not adequate to the task of presenting it to a "tribunal," and that they therefore still qualify as victims.

16 Stephen J. Carter, "Lucrece's Gaze," *Shakespeare Studies* 23 (1995): 216.

17 Lucrece's volubility has received much critical attention. In "Speech, Silence and History in *The Rape of Lucrece*," Joyce Green MacDonald offers one explanation for the violent reaction (*Shakespeare Studies* 22 [1994]: 77–103): "copiousness appears as a distinctively female property of language, a linguistic property often at odds with social prescriptions of female silence, retirement, and obedience" (78).

18 Slavoj Žižek, *The Fragile Absolute — or, Why Is the Christian Legacy Worth Fighting For?* (London: Verso, 2000) 58, 60. Žižek is actually discussing the recent disasters in embattled Kosovo and the news coverage of the victims of both the local racial cleansing and NATO's violent intervention.

19 Carter, "Lucrece's Gaze," 216.

20 There is little doubt that Lucrece's suicide is intended as a message; it is above all a *symbolic* act, a carefully planned performance rather than a spontaneous act of desperation. Belsey notes the deliberation with which the suicide is planned and points out that "Lucrece acts before an audience — not only her family but other members of the Roman community — and by daylight explains the significance of her deed, in order to enlist their intervention. She offers her death as a model for their treatment of the rapist" ("Tarquin Dispossessed," 327). I would argue that while she does, then, suggest a punishment for Tarquin, she leaves the *political* interpretation of the events open, and that it is ultimately Brutus who decides to re-figure her story as a warning against tyranny and a celebration of righteous rebellion.

21 Suzanne Scholz, "Textualizing the Body Politic: National Identity and the Female Body in *The Rape of Lucrece*," *Shakespeare Jahrbuch* 132 (1996): 107.

22 MacDonald, "Speech, Silence and History," 78.

METAPHYSICAL
AFFLICTIONS

THE SACRED PAIN OF PENITENCE: THE THEOLOGY OF JOHN DONNE'S *HOLY SONNETS*

David Anonby

John Donne's *Holy Sonnets*, with their paradoxical wit, dramatic tension, and spiritual passion, are among the most fascinating and resonant works of Christian devotional poetry. Pulitzer Prize–winning playwright Margaret Edson aptly diagnoses Donne with "salvation anxiety," and indeed many critics have tried to uncover the theological roots of the despair in the *Holy Sonnets*.[1] Donne abandoned his Roman Catholic upbringing during the markedly anti-Catholic reign of Elizabeth I and eventually took holy orders in the Church of England at the behest of James I. Apparently, this "conversion" was not a painless process, as the *Holy Sonnets* will attest. Anthony Low traces the insecurity of Donne back to his rejection of Roman Catholicism and its objective means of grace in the Real Presence of the sacrament of Holy Communion, and its assured absolution in the sacrament of confession.[2] In the Protestant arena of the individual's private conscience, many nagging soteriological fears are likely to lurk. It may also be plausibly argued that Donne's *Holy Sonnets* exhibit tendencies of Arminianism, with its concomitant paranoia about the possibility of losing one's salvation. (Of course, it must be conceded that Donne wrote the *Holy Sonnets* before the ascendancy of his Arminian bishop, William Laud; in fact, he composed most of these poems years before he even took holy orders.) More recently, scholars such as John Stachniewski, Paul Cefalu, and Daniel Doerksen have situated Donne within the Calvinist camp of English church conformity.[3] According to Cefalu, Donne's is a "'filial' fear" of backsliding, not a "'servile' fear" of reprobation.[4] Donne's complex theological identity as apostate Catholic, Arminian doubter, and Calvinist self-critic finds expression in the *Holy Sonnets*, which cohere in the theme of repentance. I will attempt to demonstrate how each of these three traditions at once fuels and consoles Donne's anxiety about the state of his soul. As Donne discovers, major repentance can be an agonizing experience, regardless of one's theological orientation. But such functional suffering prepares the soul for a greater apprehension of the Divine Presence, as is recorded in the sublime strains of the *Holy Sonnets*.

Donne's most authoritative modern biographer, R.C. Bald, maintains that "the years 1607–10 were probably the most disturbed and anxious of Donne's life. He passed through a spiritual crisis which was in large measure concealed from those closest to him."[5] Helen Gardner convincingly argues that the majority of the *Holy Sonnets* date from this period, which authenticates these poems as products of the furnace of affliction.[6] For a religious personality such as Donne, suffering often stimulates soul-searching, and I would argue that the dominating theme of the *Holy Sonnets*—repentance—splinters into various theological shards as Donne desperately struggles to attain the assurance of salvation. In *Holy Sonnet VII*, Donne emphasizes the subjective response of repentance as the key to unlocking the salvific efficacy of the atonement—a distinctly Arminian emphasis:

> here on this lowly ground,
> Teach mee how to repent; for that's as good
> As if thou'hadst seal'd my pardon, with thy blood.[7]

Of course, there is a note of hyperbole in equating the subjective, human response of repentance with the objective, Christological initiative of self-sacrifice, but such a misplaced emphasis is perhaps characteristic of hyper-Arminianism. In *Holy Sonnet IV*, the theological tables are turned towards Calvinism, with its doctrine of total depravity, which prevents anyone from converting without the foreordination and irresistible grace of God. This poem inverts the theology of *Sonnet VII*, suggesting instead that the merits of the atonement far outweigh the benefits of penitence. If Donne may be charged with hyperbole in *Sonnet VII*, he may be guilty of understatement in *Sonnet IV*.

> Yet grace, if thou repent, thou canst not lacke;
> But who shall give thee that grace to beginne?
> Oh make thy selfe with holy mourning blacke,
> And red with blushing, as thou art with sinne;
> Or wash thee in Christs blood, which hath this might
> That being red, it dyes red soules to white. (lines 9–14)

The unmistakable influence of St. Ignatius's *Spiritual Exercises* on the *Holy Sonnets* (as noted by Louis Martz) provides a Roman Catholic theological dimension to Donne's drama of repentance.[8] An Ignatian meditation on Christ crucified forms the basis of *Sonnet XIII*. Whereas many of the sonnets focus on the pain of the penitent, this poem calls to mind the sufferings of the Saviour:

> Teares in his eyes quench the amasing light,
> Blood fills his frownes, which from his pierc'd head fell. (lines 6–7)

While the octave portrays Donne's reverent quest for the assurance of salvation through meditating on the image of the suffering Messiah, the sestet employs the most startling metaphysical conceit:

> but as in my idolatrie
> I said to all my profane mistresses,
> Beauty, of pitty, foulnesse onely is
> A signe of rigour: so I say to thee,
> To wicked spirits are horrid shapes assign'd
> This beauteous forme assures a pitious minde. (lines 9–14)

True to form, Donne's speaker draws an audacious analogy between the flattering of his mistresses to obtain sexual favours and his penitential posture in receiving grace from Christ. Whereas Donne's misogynous persona ascribes beauty to those whom he is able to seduce and ugliness to those who resist his advances, he paradoxically esteems the disfigured body of the Lord to be a "beauteous forme" because it "assures a pitious minde" (line 14). The irony is further intensified by remembering that the pleasures of sin necessitate Christ's sufferings, which are the redemptive basis for repentance. The speaker's designation of his former sexual sin as "idolatrie" (line 9) is a fascinating reversal of the archetypal Old Testament depiction of Israel's idolatry as adultery. And while the poem's status as autobiographical lyric is a thorny hermeneutical problem, the piece may support James Winny's contention that "Donne found it impossible to shake off the Catholic indoctrination that told him he was in a state of mortal sin."[9]

Incidentally, the sexual behaviour of the writer of the *Songs and Sonets* and the *Elegies* has long been a matter of speculation. Sir Richard Baker, a contemporary acquaintance, remembered Donne as one "who leaving *Oxford*, lived at the *Innes of Court*, not dissolute, but very neat; a great visiter of Ladies, a great frequenter of Playes, a great writer of conceited Verses."[10] However, Baker's account has not prevented modern critics such as David L. Edwards from painting a very different portrait of Donne: "Donne wrote about raw sex, either for the enjoyment of other lusty young bachelors or in celebration of his own promiscuity, courtship and marriage."[11] More recently, Ben Saunders reads Donne's erotic impulses as often homoerotic, though his thesis is not well substantiated in my estimation.[12]

Nonetheless, in the *Holy Sonnets* spirituality and sexuality are quite comfortable bedfellows, and often their union issues in repentance. The famous couplet of *Sonnet XIV* uses the startling metaphor of divine rape to communicate the exigency of sanctification:

> for I
> Except you'enthrall mee, never shall be free,
> Nor ever chast, except you ravish mee. (lines 12–14)

Donne thus violently revolutionizes the medieval mystics' metaphor of the marriage of God and the soul. Low argues that Donne, leaving behind the Catholic theology of his youth, seems to be suggesting "that it will take something like Calvin's irresistible grace to free him from his bondage, the kind of grace that leaves no room for cooperation or for willing consent."[13] But Donne's passionate expostulation, "Yet dearely'I love you,'and would be loved faine" (line 9), expresses a heartfelt surrender that demonstrates the very prevenient grace that Low finds absent in the poem. Upon closer theological inspection, this sonnet reflects the assumptions of Arminianism rather than Calvinism. Donne's speaker, already a lover of the Trinity, laments in Pauline fashion (see Rom. 7) that his desire to obey God is foiled because he is "betroth'd unto" the "enemie" (line 10). The idea that a Christian can easily backslide into the control of Satan is a typically Arminian emphasis. In Calvinism, the believer draws comfort from the marks of election, most notably perseverance, but Donne finds that this type of assurance eludes him. His penitential supplication is Arminian, with its assumption that the Christian can repeatedly change spiritual allegiances: "Divorce mee,'untie, or breake that knot againe" (line 11). But it appears that the Catholic, Calvinist, and Arminian strains of Donne's theology were all insufficient defences against the spiritual angst he experienced, an anxiety which produced in him a compelling need to repent. And then again, perhaps repentance helps alleviate the burden of proof in theology.

Donne continues his witty use of provocative sexual imagery in *Sonnet XVIII*, where he attempts to resolve his theological ambivalence, elucidate his philosophical polyvalence, and make peace with his ideological eclecticism by establishing the signs of the true Church, be it Roman Catholic, Reformed, or Anglican.

> Betray kind husband thy spouse to our sights,
> And let myne amorous soule court thy mild Dove,
> Who is most trew, and pleasing to thee, then
> When she'is embrac'd and open to most men. (lines 11–14)

On one level, Donne is imploring God to show him the true Church, which he expects will be marked by ecumenicity rather than sectarianism. According to this reading, "men" is used generically for humankind. By penetrating the imagery more deeply, however, one can discern that Donne is using a daring love analogy, paradoxically comparing the "most trew" Church to a promiscuous lover, who is "embrac'd and open to most men." In this interpretation, "men" refers specifically to male suitors. So in Donne's audacious metaphor, which turns on the paradox of sanctity in debauchery, the church is at once a monogamous, virtuous bride and "the mistress of the whole world."[14] The image of the Church as a wife pursued by "adventuring knights" recalls the medieval courtly love tradition, in which romance was sought in extramarital affairs, while marriage was reduced to a matter of convenience (line 9). The (dis)figuring of God's holy love as human sexual love is a favourite theme of Donne's, for as Louis Martz observes, in six of the *Holy Sonnets* "the memories and images of profane love are deliberately used in love-sonnets of sacred parody."[15] (Conversely, religious imagery pervades many of Donne's secular love poems, including "A Valediction: forbidding mourning," "The Indifferent," and "The Canonization.")

The theological tenor of Donne's ecclesiastical metaphor is remarkably revealing. Donne seems to be rejecting the limited atonement, particular redemption, and double predestination of Calvinism, and also to be indicting the exclusivity of Rome. His soteriologically inclusivist metaphor instead has an affinity with the views of Jakob Arminius, who died one year before the publication of the *Remonstrance* of 1610, which appeared during the period of Donne's composition of the majority of the *Holy Sonnets*. This Arminian document maintained that "Christ the Savior of the world died for all and every human being, so that he obtained, through his death on the cross, reconciliation and pardon for all, in such a way, however, that only the faithful actually enjoy the same."[16] Donne's ideal of the "promiscuous" Church not only anticipated (or attested to) his conversion to the *via media* of Anglicanism and his taking of holy orders in 1615 but also subtly articulated his Arminian concern for the potential salvation of every human being.

The Christological dimensions of the theology of the *Holy Sonnets* are essential to understanding Donne's theme of repentance. Catherine Gimelli Martin speaks of Donne's penitential mood as an exhibition of "Christ-like pain."[17] The author of Hebrews recounts how Christ "offered up prayers and supplications with strong crying and tears unto him that was able to save him from death, and was heard in that he feared. Though he were a Son, yet learned he obedience by the things which he suffered" (Heb. 5:7–8 AV). But the analogy between Christ's passionate prayers and the grief of the penitent may only be partially drawn. Donne's sufferings, by his own admission, were occasioned by his sin, whose consequences he cannot avoid. As he laments in *Sonnet III*, punning all the while:

> That sufferance was my sinne; now I repent;
> 'Cause I did suffer I must suffer paine. (lines 7–8)

Christ's sufferings, perfecting his sinless humanity and his atoning sacrifice as High Priest, are not only the culmination of human pain but also the antidote for it. Using the forensic language of the Protestant Reformers, Donne realizes that only the vicarious sufferings of Christ can secure his pardon, and so he prays, "Impute me righteous"(*Sonnet VI*, line 13). But for Donne the sufferings of Christ are more than simply a means to ease his conscience and to gain assurance of his salvation. His own penitential tears are a way to enter more fully into Christ's sufferings and thus to be transformed. As Martin so eloquently argues, "Donne is creating a baroquely triangulated *imitatio Christi* to fulfill his Pauline need personally and perpetually to reenact Christ's suffering and death as the most assured way to heaven."[18] Felecia Wright McDuffie also notices that "[i]n his sermons, Donne often uses the dual themes of suffering as a way of participating in Christ's atonement and suffering as a way of moving toward sanctification."[19]

Throughout the *Holy Sonnets*, Donne's desire for sanctification seeks fulfillment in suffering. In "Batter my heart," *Sonnet XIV*, he pleads:

> That I may rise, and stand, o'erthrow mee,' and bend
> Your force, to breake, blowe, burn and make me new. (lines 3–4)

One of Donne's favourite themes is the paradox of functional suffering. It reappears in *Sonnet VI*, where he identifies himself not only with Christ's sufferings, but also with the Lord's cleansing of the temple, which becomes a metaphor for the purification of Donne's body:

> And burne me O Lord, with a fiery zeale
> Of thee and thy house, which doth in eating heale. (lines 13–14)

The Roman Catholic theology of suffering which informs the *Holy Sonnets* is even more pronounced in *Goodfriday, 1613. Riding Westward*:

> O Saviour, as thou hang'st upon the tree;
> I turne my backe to thee, but to receive
> Corrections, till thy mercies bid thee leave.
> O thinke mee worth thine anger, punish mee,
> Burne off my rusts, and my deformity,
> Restore thine Image, so much, by thy grace,
> That thou may'st know mee, and I'll turn my face. (lines 36–42)

Whereas Protestant Reformers, especially Calvin, took their cue from Anselm in interpreting the Cross as the vicarious satisfaction of God's wrath, Donne follows the *Via Dolorosa* to Calvary, not just to assuage God's anger but also to intercede for it to be wisely visited upon him. Here again, repentance is an invitation and initiation into Christ's sufferings. And while mainstream Protestantism would commonly define repentance as turning from sin unto God, Donne first must turn his back to God to receive chastisement until the *Imago Dei* can be recognized in him by his divine Disciplinarian. Donne maintained this desire to be purified by suffering long after it would be extinguished in the average devotee. Even after enduring job dismissal, social disgrace and imprisonment (for his secret marriage to the minor Ann More), financial hardship, frequent illnesses, the deaths of a number of his children, and finally the death of his wife from complications of childbirth, Donne continued to emphasize the value of functional suffering in his ministry. In his famous *Devotions upon Emergent Occasions*, which were composed during his convalescence from the plague which swept London in 1623 and 1624, which Anthony Raspa believes to be either typhus or relapsing fever, Donne enthusiastically embraces all the suffering he has undergone: *"[A]ffliction* is a *treasure*, and scarce any Man hath *enough* of it. No Man hath *affliction* enough, that is not matured, and ripened by it, and made fit for *God* by that *affliction*" (Meditation 17).[20]

The physical sufferings which occasioned his *Devotions* seem manageable when compared to the anguish of soul in some of the *Holy Sonnets*. Reminiscent of the lament psalms, *Sonnet I* vividly describes Donne's feelings of spiritual desolation:

> I dare not move my dimme eyes any way,
> Despaire behind, and death before doth cast
> Such terrour, and my feeble flesh doth waste
> By sinne in it, which it t'wards hell doth weigh; (lines 5–8)

In objection to Cefalu, I would argue that the intensity of the language here denotes a traumatic fear of reprobation, not merely a "filial fear" of backsliding. Nevertheless, like the despairing psalmist, Donne finds his only consolation in God's grace:

> Onely thou art above, and when towards thee
> By thy leave I can looke, I rise againe; (lines 9–10)

Donne's confession of ongoing spiritual vacillation, however, is met by some critics with a tinge of skepticism. Robert Whalen sees in the *Holy Sonnets* "the manic-depressive turns of a lover/devotee who variously embraces and resists a radically transcendent deity."[21] And just as Donne's psychological stability has been called into question, so has his theology. Stanley Fish argues that "the God Donne imagines [is] ... a jealous and overbearing master who brooks no rivals and will go to any lengths (even to the extent of depriving Donne of his wife) in order to secure his rights."[22] Certainly Donne's handling of biblical and theological material is more passionate and urgent than typical modern or postmodern worship or scholarship, but is it really fair to regard him as neurotic or heretical?

I think that this question can only be rightly addressed by recognizing that the *Holy Sonnets* do not simply represent a problem of theology or a problem of psychology, but that both these concerns are in large measure a response to the ever-pressing problem of pain. In addition to crystallizing his theology, Donne's sufferings prompt him to repent. And if my thesis is correct, Donne's theology of repentance in the *Holy Sonnets* is eclectic, drawing from Roman Catholic, Calvinist, and Arminian wells. For a person of such spiritual depth as Donne, it is the broad expanse of Christian orthodoxy, rather than the narrow groove of denominational conformity, that furnishes a rich language for the life of the soul. But what of Donne's mental anguish? Does his poetry betray an unhealthy state of mind? Admittedly, Donne's "salvation anxiety" is not an enviable condition, but his pain apparently tends towards purity, which is synonymous with spiritual health. To the modern reader, Donne's methodology of sanctification may seem almost masochistic. In rhetoric reminiscent of the *Holy Sonnets*, Donne prays in a 1622 sermon that he may "be *vir dolorum*, a man of affliction, a vessell baked in that furnace, fitted by God's proportion, and *dosis* of his corrections, to make a right use of his corrections."[23] Perhaps Donne's penchant for pain does proceed from a melancholic frame of mind, but then again, it may betray a courageous willingness to be conformed to the image of our suffering Saviour. In a 1627 sermon Donne refers to Christ as the one "who fulfil'd in himselfe alone, all *Types*, and *Images*, and *Prophecies* of sorrowes, who was, (as the *Prophet* calls him) *Vir dolorum*, a man compos'd, and elemented of sorrowes."[24]

Notes

1 Sean McDowell, "*W;t*, Donne's Holy Sonnets, and the Problem of Pain," *John Donne Journal* 23 (2004): 161–83.

2 Anthony Low, "Absence in Donne's Holy Sonnets: Between Catholic and Calvinist," *John Donne Journal* 23 (2004): 95–115.

3 John Stachniewski, "John Donne: The Despair of the 'Holy Sonnets,'" *ELH* 48.4 (1981): 677–705; Paul Cefalu, "Godly Fear, Sanctification, and Calvinist Theology in the Sermons and 'Holy Sonnets' of John Donne," *Studies in Philology* 100.1 (2003): 71–86; Daniel Doerksen, "Polemist or Pastor? Donne and Moderate Calvin-

ist Conformity," *John Donne and the Protestant Reformation: New Perspectives*, ed. Mary Arshagouni Papazian (Detroit: Wayne State University Press, 2003) 12–34.

4 Paul Cefalu, "Godly Fear, Sanctification, and Calvinist Theology," 72.

5 R.C. Bald, *John Donne: A Life* (New York: Oxford University Press, 1970) 235.

6 John Donne, *The Divine Poems*, ed. Helen Gardner, 2nd ed. (Oxford: Clarendon, 1978) xliii.

7 John Donne, "Holy Sonnet VII," *Poetical Works*, ed. Herbert J.C. Grierson (Oxford: Oxford University Press, 1991) 296, lines 12–14; future citations of Donne's poetry are from this edition and will be referenced in the text by line number. Grierson's enumeration of the *Holy Sonnets* will also be used throughout the essay.

8 Louis Martz, *The Poetry of Meditation* (New Haven, CT: Yale University Press, 1954).

9 James Winny, *A Preface to Donne* (New York: Charles Scribner's Sons, 1970) 35.

10 Qtd. in Bald, *John Donne: A Life*, 72.

11 David L. Edwards, *John Donne: Man of Flesh and Spirit* (Grand Rapids, MI: Eerdmans, 2001) 17.

12 Ben Saunders, *Desiring Donne: Poetry, Sexuality, Interpretation* (Cambridge, MA: Harvard University Press, 2006).

13 Low, "Absence in Donne's Holy Sonnets," 112.

14 K.W. Gransden, *John Donne* (London: Longmans, Green and Co., 1954) 138.

15 Martz, *The Poetry of Meditation*, 216.

16 Qtd. in Alister E. McGrath, *Christian Theology: An Introduction*, 2nd ed. (Oxford: Blackwell, 1997) 454.

17 Catherine Gimelli Martin, "'Unmeete Contrraryes': The Reformed Subject and the Triangulation of Religious Desire in Donne's *Anniversaries* and *Holy Sonnets*," *John Donne and the Protestant Reformation*, 211.

18 Martin, "'Unmeete Contrraryes,'" 200.

19 Felecia Wright McDuffie, *To Our Bodies Turn We Then: Body as Word and Sacrament in the Works of John Donne* (New York: Continuum, 2005) 66.

20 Anthony Raspa, introduction to *Devotions upon Emergent Occasions* (Montreal and Kingston: McGill-Queen's University Press, 1975) xiv; future citations from Donne's *Devotions* are from this edition and will be referenced in the text by page number.

21 Robert Whalen, *The Poetry of Immanence: Sacrament in Donne and Herbert* (Toronto: University of Toronto Press, 2002) 69.

22 Qtd. in Edwards, *John Donne*, 10.

23 Qtd. in Roger W. Williams, "Man of Sorrows," *A Dictionary of Biblical Tradition in English Literature*, ed. David Lyle Jeffrey (Grand Rapids, MI: Eerdmans, 1992) 476.

24 Ibid.

BEARING THE CROSS: THE CHRISTIAN'S RESPONSE TO SUFFERING IN HERBERT'S *THE TEMPLE*

Daniel W. Doerksen

Faced with the question, "Why do bad things happen to good people?" Rabbi Harold S. Kushner replies that God is good, but not all-powerful.[1] Seventeenth-century poet George Herbert has a different answer: for him, God is *both* "Lord of power" and "Lord of love."[2] Herbert writes significantly of suffering in the life of a Christian believer, often in terms of "grief" or of the "afflictions" he sees as divinely sent for good purposes, even though those goals may not be understood or appreciated at the time. In my article "'Growing and Groning'" I have taken up his "Affliction" (I), a powerful picturing of human response to the seemingly baffling ways of God, which the speaker feels "crosse-bias" him. His claim in that poem, "what thou wilt do with me / None of my books will show" (lines 55–56), is only partly true, because (as Herbert recognizes elsewhere) the Scriptures and commentaries on them do shed valuable light on God's purposes in the afflictions of a believer.

Herbert's poetry demonstrably owes much to a broad Christian tradition, including medieval liturgy and iconography,[3] but I maintain that in picturing inner conflicts he reflects an approach to biblical texts, especially the Psalms,[4] fostered by writers influential in his own Church of England, particularly John Calvin.[5] The patterns he finds there help shape the poetry of suffering in his collection, *The Temple*. That afflictions come from God, that they unite the believer with Christ in a bearing of the cross, that they nevertheless involve spiritual conflicts with God himself, that they can be persistent and painful and yet must be accepted in a correct way, one that leads to spiritual renewal—all these are *pictured* for Calvin and for Herbert in the biblical writings. So important was this aspect of his own poetry for Herbert that in sending the manuscript of his poems to his friend Ferrar he singled out for attention its "picture of the many spiritual Conflicts that have past betwixt God and my Soul, before I could subject mine to the will of *Jesus my Master*: in whose service I have now found perfect freedom."[6] This focus on personal experience contributes to Herbert's distinctive frankness and vividness.

A twentieth-century reader of Herbert, L.C. Knights—not a Christian believer—admires *The Temple* not only for its literary excellence but for the substance of its depiction of conflict and resolution, praising "Affliction" (I) as "one of the most remarkable records in the language of the achievement of maturity and of the inevitable pains of the process."[7] Knights asserts that the "first condition of development was that the disturbing elements in experience should be honestly recognized."[8] Interestingly, this is rather like what Calvin (in theological language and on the basis of Scripture) suggests in the preface to his commentary on the Psalms.[9] Calvin, as much as Knights, would say one must recognize that "the universe is not constructed on our plan."[10]

Jesus notably said, "If any man will come after me, let him deny himself, and take up his cross, and follow me" (Matt. 16:24 AV).[11] In keeping with that, Calvin discusses some of the main features of the Christian life as self-denial and bearing the cross.[12] The believer participates in the death of Christ not only through self-denial—inward mortification, or the repeated dealing of death to the old nature—but also through outward mortification: the voluntary bearing of afflictions from without. Though the latter are often the same kinds of circumstantial difficulties that unbelievers also face,[13] they take on a different meaning for early modern Protestant people of faith.[14] These will tend to see them as "spiritual Conflicts that have past betwixt God and my Soul," and for them they are part of the process of renewal that constitutes the Christian life. Just as Christ had to endure "many a brunt" ("The Bag," line 21) in a life that culminated in crucifixion, his followers conform to that pattern because they are joined with him:

> Thy life on earth was grief, and thou art still
> Constant unto it, making it to be
> A point of honour, now to grieve in me,
>   And in thy members suffer ill.
>   They who lament one crosse,
> Thou dying dayly, praise thee to thy losse.
>   ("Affliction" [III], lines 13–18)

This parallels what Calvin says in the opening section on "Bearing the Cross" in the *Institutes*: "For whomever the Lord has adopted and deemed worthy of his fellowship ought to prepare [himself—corrected from "themselves"] for a hard, toilsome, and unquiet life, crammed with very many and various kinds of evil.... Christ's whole life was nothing but a sort of perpetual cross.... Why should we exempt ourselves, therefore, from the condition to which Christ our Head had to submit?" (3.8.1). This gives us none of Herbert's wit or poetry, but tells us something of how early modern Protestants interpreted the scriptural patterns of affliction (dying daily, bearing the cross).[15]

An important feature of afflictions as portrayed in *The Temple* is that they come from God. This aspect, accounting for some of Herbert's most characteristic effects in picturing spiritual conflict, is deeply rooted in his Protestant and scriptural outlook. I say "Protestant" partly because a comparison of Augustine's and Calvin's commentaries on Psalms of such conflict (both available on the Web) shows that Calvin is much readier than Augustine to acknowledge the conflicts with God and to speak of the individual believer's life in commenting on such passages as Psalms 66:11, 69:26, and 88:6.[16] The pungency of many of Herbert's finest poems, such as "Bitter-sweet" or "The Crosse," is inseparable from the Reformation belief that it is with God that we have to do in all the circumstances of life—including unpleasant ones—a belief that in turn grows out of Scriptures like the Psalms dealing with affliction.[17] Knowing that affliction comes from God is vital, but it can actually heighten the conflict for the believer. In fact Calvin admits in his note on Psalm 77:3 that often "the remembrance of God in the time of adversity aggravates the anguish and trouble of the godly, as, for example, when they entertain the thought that he is angry with them." Herbert does not shy away from the thought of an angry God, referring to divine anger in beautiful, memorable poems like "The Flower" and "Bitter-sweet."[18] In "Affliction" (II), there is a real protest in the opening stanza:

> Kill me not ev'ry day,
> Thou Lord of life; since thy one death for me
> Is more than all my deaths can be,
> Though I in broken pay
> Die over each houre of Methusalems stay. (lines 1–5)

The accusation continues, in intimate but aggrieved tones reminiscent of Jeremiah's complaints against God:

> Thou art my grief alone,
> Thou Lord conceal it not: and as thou art
> All my delight, so all my smart:

> Thy crosse took up in one,
> By way of imprest [advance payment], all my future mone.
>> (lines 11–15)

Herbert's "conceal it not" somewhat parallels but stops short of Jeremiah's direct accusation to God, "thou hast deceived me" (Jer. 20:7). In Herbert as in Jeremiah 15:16–18, the mention of God as a source of delight gives perspective but actually heightens the pain. That Christ shared and shares human suffering is a comforting thought, but the Christian's participation in the afflictions God himself has borne may have an opposite effect. In fact, in one possible reading of Herbert's "The Thanksgiving,"[19] the speaker is reminded of just how great one's suffering may become. Thus while the final stanza of "Affliction" (II) shows some balance by recognizing in God as well "all my delight," it expresses not so much release from conflict as "fellowship of suffering" in its anticipation of "future mone."[20]

In the biblical Christian view, God, the source of everything good, also sends afflictions to people but has constructive purposes in the tribulations of believers. Terry Sherwood appropriately calls attention to such purposes named in Herbert's chapter of the *Country Parson* called "The Parson Comforting."[21] Outward trials are an aid to inner mortification, or self-denial, and thus are part of the daily process of renewal without which we should "spurn / Our salvation" ("Giddinesse," lines 27–28). God's fatherly discipline is not only a matter of punishing past sin (as in "Repentance," which has a close affinity to some of the penitential psalms), but also of promoting our spiritual advance (*Institutes*, 3.8.6). Both aspects are reflected in "Easter-wings" (lines 12–13, 20) and in a section of "Affliction" (V) that recapitulates (and thus also helps interpret) "Affliction" (I):

> At first we liv'd in pleasure;
> Thine own delights thou didst to us impart:
> When we grew wanton, thou didst use displeasure
> To make us thine...(lines 7–10)

Here "we grew wanton" recalls "my wish and way" (line 20) and "my wayes" (line 54) of "Affliction" (I) and thus may indicate that the sin being treated there was wilfulness. But the "displeasure" is used to a beneficial and positive end. A more particular goal in God's afflictions of man is the maturing of character[22] through the building up of humility (in ourselves), confidence (in God), patience, and obedience (*Institutes*, 3.8.2–4) — qualities such as those Herbert celebrates in "Constancie" and "Vertue" (whose seasoned timber "never gives"). "We are the trees," he says in "Affliction" (V), "whom shaking fastens more" (line 20).[23]

Calvin says that in times of trial the believer experiences God's loving discipline but not in the full sense his punishing wrath (*Institutes*, 3.8.6). The difference between such chastening and what for the unbeliever is "a sort of entry way of hell" (*Institutes*, 3.4.32) seems to be chiefly in the beneficial effect that results; neither is dealt with (on earth) in utmost rigour. Still, the believer too may feel, as Calvin says, "not far distant from the damnation of hell" (*Institutes*, 3.4.32). Surely this is the kind of experience Herbert pictures in "A Parodie." The biblical background of this poem is the "God-forsakenness" of Psalm 22:1, which Jesus identified with on the cross — especially as interpreted by Calvin.[24] The paradox of Herbert's first stanza ("Souls joy, when thou art gone, / And I alone, / Which cannot be, / Because thou dost abide with me, / And I depend on thee") is much like the one Calvin finds in the psalm, whose two "remarkable" opening thoughts,

> although apparently contrary to each other, are yet ever entering into the minds of the godly together. When the Psalmist speaks of being forsaken and cast off by God, it seems to be the complaint of a man in despair; for can a man have a single spark of faith remaining in him, when he believes that there is no longer any succour for him in God? And yet, in calling God twice his own God, and depositing his groanings into his bosom, he makes a very distinct confession of his faith.[25]

Herbert's "when thou dost suppresse / The cheerfulnesse / Of thy abode" (lines 6–8) recalls Calvin's "[w]hen, therefore, he suffers us to lie long in sorrow, and as it were to pine away under it, we must necessarily feel ... as if he had quite forgotten us,"[26] and the poet's "No stormie night / Can so afflict or so affright, / As thy eclipsed light" (lines 13–15) is like imagery in Calvin: "With this inward conflict the godly must necessarily be exercised whenever God withdraws from them the tokens of his favour, so that, in whatever direction they turn their eyes, they see nothing but the darkness of night."[27] The absence of God is the chief feature in Calvin's idea of hell, and such is the "deadly cold" (line 26) of which Herbert speaks.[28] When he says that his state is one that "Thou and alone thou know'st" (line 25), the poet may have in mind not only God's omniscience but Christ's descent into hell as interpreted by Calvin in the *Institutes* (2.16.10–11), where the *descensus* is associated with Christ's cry of dereliction on the cross, and thus with Psalm 22:1.

It is fully within the framework of the Renaissance Protestant view of God's chastenings, and not in rejection of that framework,[29] that Herbert writes, in "Discipline":

> Throw away thy rod
> Throw away thy wrath:
> O my God,
> Take the gentle path. (lines 1–4)

Like David in Psalm 6:1, Herbert's speaker is properly asking for a mitigation not on the basis of his own righteousness but because the purpose of the chastening has already been achieved: "For my hearts desire / Unto thine is bent" (lines 5–6); "Though I fail, I weep" (line 13). To quote Calvin on Psalm 6:1, "[David] does not altogether refuse punishment, [since] to be without it… would be more hurtful than beneficial to him, but what he is afraid of is the wrath of God, which threatens sinners with ruin and perdition. To anger and indignation David tacitly [and Herbert more explicitly: 'Take the gentle path'] opposes fatherly and gentle chastisement, and this last he was willing to bear." Relying on "thy book alone" (line 12), Herbert is appealing like David (or like Jeremiah at 10:24) to the grace (line 16) and love (lines 18–28) of God, who "not only mingles with [the punishment of believers, who are also "sinners"] some of the sweetness of his grace to mitigate their sorrow, but also shows himself favourable to them, in moderating their punishment, and in mercifully drawing back his hand."[30] In saying "Throw away thy rod," Herbert is not so much rejecting the instrument of affliction itself, though that would be a human enough impulse, as desiring God to make a "scepter" of the rod, "To guide and govern it to my relief" ("Affliction" [III], lines 4, 3). What he aspires to is a "full consent" (line 8), a participation in Christ, and the love he seeks from God is not an unprincipled indulgence but a potent two-way sharing, which involves both God and man in bearing the cross:

> That which wrought on thee,
> Brought thee low,
> Needs must work on me. (lines 26–28)

"Affliction then is ours," declares Herbert, in his fifth and final poem entitled "Affliction," signalling acceptance. That insight, however, does not end the conflicts over adversity. It is one thing to look at past struggles and see value in them in retrospect — "shaking fastens more." It is another to face fresh onslaughts, which may be persistent and unrelieved (as in "Longing") despite repentance and prayer. That "sinne is dead" (line 67) implies that a chief purpose of affliction, the bringing about of repentance (see lines 65–66) has already been fulfilled, and the opening stanza certainly recalls passages in the penitential psalms, such as Psalms 32:3–4 and 51:8. (Also, the fifth stanza, though it alludes overtly to afflictions, echoes a literary pattern [what…, what…!] found in 2 Corinthians 7:11, which speaks clearly of repentance.) The whole poem is a prayer, and Herbert appeals to God on the basis of a penitent response to affliction: "I fall, / Yet call" (lines 11–12). Yet the affliction continues, and the poem, like Psalm 39 which it significantly resembles at points, ends on an almost despairing reference to death. The poem concludes this way, I suggest, because Scriptures (like this psalm) read in Herbert's Protestant manner caused him to pay attention to actual experiential patterns in the life of the believer. His is an "unvarnished tale." (However, the poem which next follows in *The Temple*, "The Bag," begins, "Away despair: my gracious Lord doth heare," and thus reflects the same movement out of despair that one may find in the shift from Psalm 39 to Psalm 40:1: "I waited patiently for the Lord; and he inclined unto me and heard my cry.")[31] Sometimes afflictions may be subtly and painfully penetrating, as described in the second stanza of "Confession":

> No scrue, no piercer can
> Into a piece of timber work and winde,
>   As Gods afflictions into man,
>   When he a torture hath design'd.
> They are too subtill for the subt'llest hearts;
> And fall, like rheumes [rheumatic pains], upon the tendrest parts. (lines 7–12)

Such language of violence is remarkable for its honesty and boldness, but has scriptural warrant from passages in Job 6:4 and Psalm 38:2 that speak of God's arrows piercing the believer.[32]

While the Christian must patiently prepare himself to face adversity, Calvin emphasizes (on the basis of experiential examples in Scripture) that he cannot like the Stoics seek indifference to it, but must "feel it as a man."[33] Groaning and weeping are not inappropriate in those who are sharing the cross of one who, as Calvin says, "groaned and wept both over his own and others' misfortunes."[34] It is surely because of such an outlook that Herbert so often mentions sighs, groans, and tears (regarded, as in Calvin, as part of a constructive process) and, more significantly for his poetry, pays enough attention to inner feelings so that he can give an "anatomy of all parts of the soul." Herbert's greatest depictions of human spiritual agony, such as "The Crosse" or "A Parodie," could never have been written but for this willingness to respond with feeling to God's afflictions.[35]

A believer must not deaden himself against adversities, but respond, and the actual nature of his response is extremely important:

> ev'n the greatest griefes
>   May be reliefs,
> Could he but take them right, and in their wayes.
>   ("Mans medley," lines 31–33)

When Herbert says, in "The Water-course," "If troubles overtake thee, do not wail," he is not objecting to tears per se, as the second stanza (and the rest of his poetry) reveals. Rather he is warning himself and others against the "loud complaints," the "improper and sinful excess of passion" in grieving to which Calvin finds the Psalmist succumbing at times (see his commentary on Ps.

39:3, 4). Herbert, like Calvin, objects to "loud complaints" (in "The Familie," line 3), and contrasts with them what Calvin commends in other parts of Psalm 39, "griefs without a noise" (line 18).[36] The second stanza of "The Water-course" shows another aspect of coping with the "waters of affliction"— one should repent, and be renewed by God:[37]

> But rather turn the pipe and waters course
> To serve thy sinnes, and furnish thee with store
> Of sov'raigne tears, springing from true remorse:
> That so in purenesse thou mayst him adore,
>
> Who gives to man, as he sees fit $\begin{cases} \text{Salvation.} \\ \text{Damnation.} \end{cases}$ (lines 6–10)

Like Calvin, or for that matter like Paul (Phil. 2:12–13), Herbert is at pains to insist on human responsibility and at the same time God's complete sovereignty.[38]

Taking griefs "right, and in their wayes" includes seeing them in perspective. The "temper" manifested in Herbert's lyrics[39] is much like the dynamic balance described in Calvin's account of David's "many spiritual conflicts." In both cases there is a basic assurance that is sustained in the face of real and repeated struggles. Such an outlook cannot adequately be expressed without the use of paradox, which has the capacity to capture within itself the tension of opposites while at the same time bringing them into unity.[40] Herbert's poems are characterized by a living poise of "Content and care" ("The Size," line 34). Herbert himself presents the vital equilibrium beautifully in the second stanza of "Bitter-sweet," a poem which describes not so much God and man as their relationship:

> Ah my deare angrie Lord,
> Since thou dost love, yet strike;
> Cast down, yet help afford;[41]
> Sure I will do the like.
>
> I will complain, yet praise;
> I will bewail, approve:
> And all my sowre-sweet dayes
> I will lament, and love. (lines 1–8)

Herbert's title might well derive from a Calvin passage such as the following, which offers a perfect epitome of the poem: "the godly heart feels in itself a division because it is partly imbued with *sweetness* from its recognition of the divine goodness, partly grieves in *bitterness* from an awareness of its calamity" (*Institutes*, 3.2.18; italics mine). The as-yet-imperfect believer's appropriate response to the "tempering" vicissitudes which reveal to him God's "power and love" — goodness in the midst of afflictions, and even through them — is a balanced "temper" or faith that manifests itself in praise and trust but also in the groans and laments (found too in the Psalms) which in their own way are "musick for a King" ("Sion," line 24). Herbert's poetry in this respect should not be seen as pessimistic, nor as too determined to be "optimistic," but relished as realistic.[42]

In sending the manuscript of his poems to Nicholas Ferrar, Herbert told his friend that "if he can think it may turn to the advantage of any dejected poor Soul, let it be made publick."[43] One purpose of the suffering the poet experiences is thus what Paul writes about in addressing the Corinthians: suffering in order to be able to console others (2 Cor. 1:5, 6). And the expression of that suffering (David's, Paul's, Herbert's) can have beneficial effects.

I suggest that Herbert's lyrics have in fact functioned in much the way he intended. Following patterns in the Psalms and other Scriptures as read by Reformation Protestants, he depicts experiences of the Christian life, including those of conflict with God in suffering afflictions. He does not versify theology, but creates beautiful, moving poems — like the Psalms, in their own way. In the seventeenth century *The Temple* became a bestseller, appealing (like the Psalms) to a wide range of readers, including both King Charles I awaiting his execution and the Puritans, some of whom rearranged the poems into *Select Hymns* for singing. In a later century Coleridge admitted finding "substantial [personal] comfort" in *The Temple*, in particular naming "The Flower," a poem par excellence of spiritual conflict and resolution, as "especially affecting."[44] A similar poem is likely in Coleridge's mind when he writes a few years later to the effect that two stanzas of Herbert have helped him to face a "tendency to self-contempt, a sense of the utter disproportionateness of all I can call *me*, to the promises of the Gospel."[45] And Gerard Manley Hopkins, somewhat like Herbert and the biblical writers before him, wrestled with "(my God!), my God" ("[Carrion Comfort]," line 14).[46] As the writings of Herbert make evident, poetry, whether in the Psalms or in later writers, has the capacity to *picture* afflictions and responses to them in a way that helps deal with those afflictions.

Notes

1 Harold S. Kushner, *When Bad Things Happen to Good People* (New York: Schocken, 1981).

2 "The Flower," lines 15, 43, in George Herbert, *The Works of George Herbert*, ed. F. E. Hutchinson, corr. ed. (Oxford: Oxford University Press, 1945); future citations from Herbert are from this edition and will be given in the text by line number.

3 See, for example, Rosemond Tuve, *A Reading of George Herbert* (Chicago: University of Chicago Press, 1952), and Louis L. Martz, *The Poetry of Meditation*, rev. ed. (New Haven: Yale University Press, 1962).

4 Regarding the Psalms and Herbert, see Martz, *Poetry of Meditation*, 273–82; Heather Asals, "The Voice of George Herbert's 'The Church,'" *ELH* 36.3 (1969): 511–28; Barbara K. Lewalski, *Protestant Poetics and the Seventeenth-Century Religious Lyric* (Princeton, NJ: Princeton University Press, 1979) 300–304 and passim; Chana Bloch, *Spelling the Word: George Herbert and the Bible* (Berkeley: University of California Press, 1985) 231–305; and Elizabeth Clarke, *Theory and Theology in George Herbert's Poetry: 'Divinitie, and Poesie, Met'* (Oxford: Clarendon, 1997) 127–78. Martz on this topic makes a connection to the verse translation of the Psalms by Sir Philip Sidney and his sister; the latter has been described as a "Calvinist theologian" (Wikipedia).

5 See Daniel W. Doerksen, *Conforming to the Word: Herbert, Donne, and the English Church before Laud* (Lewisburg, PA: Bucknell University Press, 1997) esp. 16–17, and sources cited there. The works of Calvin dominated English publications for many decades, and were widely read and respected in the universities. Donne, Herbert's friend, cited Calvin frequently in his sermons and considered him "worthy to be compared to the *Ancients*, for the exposition of the Scriptures" (Donne, *Sermons*, ed. G.R. Potter and E.M. Simpson [Berkeley: University of California Press, 1953–62] 3.177). Calvin has often been seen by literary critics as having chiefly harmful influences in England, and as mainly linked to puritanism, and for this reason some Herbert critics, such as Stanley Stewart (*George Herbert* [Boston: Twayne, 1986]), have worked hard to distance him from Calvin. By contrast, A.D. Nuttall acknowledges Calvin's influence in the English church and specifically on Herbert, but views both authors unfavourably, as in spite of their intentions portraying a God who is *not* good. Nuttall, an unbeliever, justifiably admits to being "an ill-conditioned and rebellious reader" (*Overheard by God: Fiction and Prayer in Herbert, Milton, Dante and St. John* [London: Methuen, 1980] 58). In *Love Known: Theology and Experience in George Herbert's Poetry* (Chicago: University of Chicago Press, 1983), Richard Strier frequently cites Calvin as relevant, but makes more of Luther as background for Herbert. In *Theory and Theology*, Clarke acknowledges Herbert's Calvinism (10), but concentrates on Savonarola and Valdes as likely influences.

6 Izaak Walton, *The Lives of John Donne, Sir Henry Wotton, Richard Hooker, George Herbert, and Robert Sanderson* (1927; London: Oxford University Press, 1962) 314.

7 See L.C. Knights, "George Herbert," *Scrutiny* 12 (1944): 171–86; also Daniel W. Doerksen, "'Growing and Groning': Herbert's 'Affliction' (I)," *English Studies in Canada* 8 (1982): 1–8. Clarke (*Theory and Theology*, 215–16) and Barbara Leah Harman ("George Herbert's *Affliction (I)*: The Limits of Representation," *ELH* 44.2 [1977], 267–85) view the frustration in the poem less favourably.

8 Knights, "George Herbert," 180.

9 John Calvin, *Commentary on the Book of Psalms*, trans. James Anderson, Calvin Translation Society, 1843–55, 5 vols. rpt. (Grand Rapids: Eerdmans, 1963) 1.xxxvi–xxxvii.

10 Knights, "George Herbert," 182.

11 Unless otherwise noted, subsequent biblical quotations are from the Authorized (King James) Version.

12 See John Calvin, *Institutes of the Christian Religion*, ed. John T. McNeill, trans. F.L. Battles, 2 vols. (Philadelphia: Westminster, 1960) 3.7 and 3.8; future citations from the *Institutes* are from this edition and will be given in the text by book, chapter, and section number. Also see use of these categories in Gene Edward Veith Jr., *Reformation Spirituality: The Religion of George Herbert* (Lewisburg, PA: Bucknell University Press, 1985) 145–67. Calvin, in keeping with his reading of the Old Testament, regards bearing the cross as a chief pattern in the Psalms (*Commentary on the Book of Psalms*, 1.xxxvi–xxxvii). For Calvin's distinction between the old and the outward man in relation to these two major features of the Christian life, see R.S. Wallace, *Calvin's Doctrine of the Christian Life* (Edinburgh: Oliver and Boyd, 1959) 51–53.

13 Herein lies one important reason for the valuing of Herbert's poetry by those who do not share his religious beliefs: he depicts "realistically" the facing of adverse circumstances with which, in varying degrees and ways, we all have to cope. See Knights, "George Herbert," 178–86. But Calvin and John Donne recognize that while "every man hath afflictions … every man hath not crosses," because the latter involve "conformity with Christ" (Donne, *Sermons*, 2.300); see also Calvin, *Institutes*, 3.8.1.

14 See Keith Thomas, *Religion and the Decline of Magic* (New York: Charles Scribner's Sons, 1971) 78–85. But at note 5 on page 85, Thomas incorrectly attributes to Calvin himself the foolish view of the "Profane men with their absurdities" cited by Calvin.

15 Since these are biblical patterns they are of course not *limited to* Renaissance Protestants. I say more about Herbert's scriptural patterning in a book-length work under consideration by a press. A few relevant biblical references are: Ps. 44:22; Luke 9:23; Rom. 8:35–36; 1 Cor. 15:31; 2 Cor. 4:8–11, 16–17; Col. 1:24; and 1 Pet. 4:13.

16 Augustine is more like Calvin in comments on Psalm 80:4. In recommending commentaries on the Psalms as helpful for reading Herbert's poems, Asals cites Calvin once, but concentrates on Augustine's *Enarratio in Psalmum*, which she quotes entirely in Latin.

17 See Clarke, *Theory and Theology*, 110, who places Herbert's wrestling with God in the context of a Protestant "acknowledgement of God's interest and presence in all circumstances of life." Clarke shows clear distinctions between Protestant and Counter-Reformation poetry, as at 136–39. As McNeill has pointed out, Calvin teaches that "every man in all circumstances has dealings with God (*negotium cum Deo*)" (*Institutes*, 1.212.n2). This is deeply related to Calvin's insistence that man and God cannot be understood, humanly speaking, apart from each other. See Calvin on Psalm 6, among many passages; and Wallace, *Calvin's Doctrine*, 259–61. Because of its origin in the Scriptures, this insight is of course not limited to Renaissance Protestants, but they give it distinctive emphasis.

18 On "Bitter-sweet" and divine anger see Strier, *Love Known*, 165–67.

19 Dealt with in my book manuscript under consideration by a press.

20 Anne C. Fowler ("'With Care and Courage': Herbert's '*Affliction*' Poems," "*Too Rich to Clothe the Sunne*": *Essays on George Herbert*, ed. Claude J. Summers and Ted-Larry Pebworth [Pittsburgh, PA: University of Pittsburgh Press, 1980] 129–45), gives a very different reading of Herbert's "Affliction" (I) and (II). Thus

she reads the third stanza of "Affliction" (II) in metaphysical and Petrarchan terms rather than in the light of biblical theology. For her, "the speaker's personal grief... never becomes a felt presence in the poem." Also she unnecessarily finds censoriousness in the final lines of "Affliction" (III), where the speaker's point is how to give sufficient praise to God (131–32), and in the final stanza of "Affliction" (V), where "destroy the wanton bowres" likely refers to the speaker's own cleansing by the wind.

21 Terry Sherwood, *Herbert's Prayerful Art* (Toronto: University of Toronto Press, 1989) 113.

22 See also Rom. 5:3–4, which Calvin cites, and James 1:3–4.

23 Clarke, *Theory and Theology*, 272, in contrast to Knights's reading cited above, maintains that there is no spiritual progress and that (citing the Calvin scholar W. Niesel) because of the need of continual mortification, "progress is properly the recognition of our lack of progress."

24 A related point is made in Strier, *Love Known*, 242–43.

25 Calvin, *Commentary on the Book of Psalms*, 1.357. This passage is also effectively cited in Strier, *Love Known*, 177–78.

26 Calvin, *Commentary on the Book of Psalms*, 1.358

27 Ibid., 1.357–58.

28 On experiencing the absence of God, see also Veith, *Reformation Spirituality*, 158–67, where reference is made to Luther, too. The works of St. John of the Cross were first published in 1618. Doubtless his insights into the "dark night of the soul" are related to the same source in the Psalms.

29 In *The Poetry of George Herbert* (Cambridge, MA: Harvard University Press, 1975), Helen Vendler gives an interesting reading of this poem, but ascribes one kind of twentieth-century outlook to Herbert (242–46). For a clear seventeenth-century parallel (in John Donne) to what is happening in "Discipline," see Doerksen, *Conforming*, 104. Veith's treatment of "Discipline" (153–56) shows a good comprehension of how the poem relates to the Reformation understanding of Scripture.

30 Calvin, comment on Ps. 6:1 (*Commentary on the Book of Psalms*, 1.66–67). In dealing with Ps. 39:10–11, a passage that parallels this verse, Calvin makes a similar remark, in which he explicitly refers to God's "love."

31 In *Spelling the Word*, Bloch notes this shift in Herbert's poems but does not relate it to those Psalms (270–71).

32 An interesting analogue and perhaps even a source for the image of God's penetration in this stanza is Psalm 39:11, where God's afflictions are compared to the inroads of a moth; see also Calvin's comment on this verse, where he discusses the propriety of the comparison and speaks of the moth's "secret gnawing" of "a piece of cloth or *wood*" (italics mine); the comment of the editor James Anderson in Calvin, *Commentary on Psalms*, 2.86.n1; and the more explicit scriptural parallel to this verse in Hosea 5:12.

33 I am here borrowing Macduff's words (*Macbeth* 4.3.221). See Strier, *Love Known*, 177 regarding anti-stoicism in Calvin and other Reformers.

34 Calvin, *Institutes*, 3.8.9, referring of course to Gethsemane and to Jesus' tears over Jerusalem; see also ibid., sec. 8 and Wallace, *Calvin's Doctrine*, 191–92, where this teaching of Calvin is put into the context of his emphasis on Christian moderation. Herbert's religious background would encourage both the emotional sensi-

tivity and the control that we find in his verse. On Calvin, Herbert, and emotional experience, see Strier, *Love Known*, 144–45, 174, and passim.

35 In dealing with "affliction" Psalms like 38 and 39, Calvin counsels moderation and yet repeatedly makes allowance for human factors and feelings. For example, he says, with regard to Psalm 38:21, that "it is not at all wonderful that the saints, when they unburden themselves of their cares and sorrows into the bosom of God, should make their requests in language according to the feeling of the flesh. They are not ashamed to confess their infirmity, nor is it proper to conceal the doubts which arise in their minds." It is on such grounds, I suggest, that Herbert can imply, in the first line of "The Crosse," that the ways of God as he is experiencing them are "strange and uncouth." ("Uncouth" in Herbert's time could mean not only "unknown" but also "Of an unfamiliar or strange appearance or form; *spec.*, having an odd, uncomely, awkward, or clumsy shape or bearing" *OED* 6.)

36 See especially on vv. 1, 2, 9–10; on the last of these verses Calvin says that "our desires and prayers, if they are framed according to the rule of God's word, are not inconsiderate and noisy..., but proceed from the calm stillness which faith and patience produce in our hearts." For a fuller treatment of Herbert's poem, see my *Conforming* 118–21, where I note important parallels to Richard Sibbes. For a different reading of "The Familie," see Claude J. Summers and Ted-Larry Pebworth, "The Politics of *The Temple*: 'The British Church' and 'The Familie,'" *George Herbert Journal* 8.1 (1984): 1–15. For "noise" and the limits of emotional experience, see Strier, *Love Known*, 188–89, 218ff.

37 Compare Calvin's comment on Psalm 25:7, where, having noted David's outwardly unmerited persecution, he goes on to say that the psalmist "teaches us by his example, that when any outward affliction presses upon us, we must entreat God not only to deliver us from it, but also to blot out our sins, by which we have provoked his displeasure, and subjected ourselves to his chastening rod." A precedent for Herbert's combination of water images might perhaps be found in Psalm 69:1–3, which deliberately or otherwise collocates the overwhelming flood waters of affliction with the flowing of tears, possibly those of repentance (see v. 5). Elsewhere in Herbert, water imagery is used to link baptism, the redemption, and repentance ("H. Baptisme," 4–9).

38 On Phil. 2:12–13, Calvin remarks: "It is God who calls us and offers us salvation; it is our part to embrace by faith what He gives, and by obedience to respond to His calling. But we have neither from ourselves." In treating of God's purpose and man's response in afflictions, Calvin, somewhat like Herbert in the poem under discussion, also paradoxically employs a reference to double predestination in close conjunction with an appeal to man to respond as God wants him to, even saying "Now you must choose" (*Institutes*, 3.8.6). Water-pipe imagery with regard to divine predestination and man's response may be found not only in Herbert's poem but also in the *Institutes* (4.24.3), where Calvin uses it to distinguish human faith and assurance, based on the revealed word, from the eternal decrees of God himself. See Jeanne Hunter, "Herbert's 'Water-Course': Notorious and Neglected," *Notes and Queries* 34 (1987): 310–12. Viewing life dynamically (a water-course, water *flowing*, rather than *objects* pre-sorted into two bags), predestinarians like Calvin or Herbert seem willing to trace *events* as much as *created beings* to the "spring, whence all things flow" ("Miserie," 60).

39 See the excellent treatment of this topic in Fredson Bowers, "Herbert's Sequential Imagery: 'The Temper,'" *Modern Philology* 59 (1962): 202–13.

40 Although Herbert (like Calvin and the Scriptures) makes frequent use of polarities, one should note that this does not bespeak an ultimate dualism but an attempt in the face of human and linguistic limitations to describe experiential realities which are dynamic. In *The Poetry of Grace: Reformation Themes and Structures in English Seventeenth-Century Poetry* (New Haven, CT: Yale University Press, 1970), William H. Halewood argues that the opposites in English Reformation poetics "are related to a theological conception of reality" and are not absolute but directed toward ultimate reconciliation (23–24).

41 The first part of this poem seems strongly reminiscent of Calvin's reading of life, as in the following passage: "Gods shewing of himselfe angrie with us, is bicause [*sic*] he loveth us, and ... if he should alwayes shew us a loving countenance, it would overthrowe us and destroy us. Therefore it behoveth us to feele his anger effectually. Neverthelesse, the same is a record of his goodnesse, and a meane whereby he calleth us to him.... And ... as he striketh us with his one hande, so he setteth us up agayne with the other: and if he send us to the grave, it is to lift us up afterward above the heavens" (*Sermons vpon the Booke of Iob*, trans. Arthur Golding [London, 1584] 664). The latter part of this quotation also seems related in thought and expression to lines in "The Flower" ("Killing and quickning, bringing down to hell / And up to heaven in an houre," lines 16–17) ; and shortly afterward follows a passage that is akin to lines 13–16 of "Praise (III)" ("when thou dost on businesse blow, / It hangs, it clogs: / Not all the teams of Albion in a row / Can hale or draw it out of doore"): "Let us learne that all our abilitie is lesse than nothing, specially when wee have to deale with our God, for he will do no more but *blowe* upon it. Wee may well gather togither all the strength in the worlde, not only which might be in any one man, yea though he were the strongest that ever was: but also all the strength that is in all creatures above and beneath: and yet shall it be nothing woorth at all if wee have the hand of God agaynst us" (emphasis added to the word that Herbert also uses). So many parallels to Herbert's verse all on one page of Calvin make it appear likely that the poet was familiar with this part of the Reformer's writings. Calvin's sermons on Job appeared in four English editions.

42 Clarke, *Theory and Theology,* 272; Fowler, "'With Care and Courage,'" 130.

43 Walton, *Lives,* 314.

44 Samuel Taylor Coleridge, *Coleridge on the Seventeenth Century,* ed. Roberta F. Brinkley (Durham, NC: Duke University Press, 1955) 533.

45 Ibid., 540. The stanzas, not identified in that portion of the letter which has been preserved, are described with the same phrase that Coleridge has used in the earlier letter, "especially affecting," and may even be from the same poem, "The Flower."

46 *Poems and Prose of Gerard Manley Hopkins,* ed. W.H. Gardner (Harmondsworth, UK: Penguin, 1963) 61.

THE ETHICAL
ROMANTIC SUBLIME

HORRIFIC SUFFERING, SACRED TERROR, AND SUBLIME FREEDOM IN HELEN MARIA WILLIAMS'S *PERU*

Natasha Duquette

By presenting preventative, as opposed to punitive, justice as sublime, eighteenth-century poet Helen Maria Williams modifies the categories of Edmund Burke's *Philosophical Enquiry into the Origin of Our Ideas of the Sublime and Beautiful*. In her *Peru: A Poem in Six Cantos*,[1] specifically, she chronicles Peru's colonial history by repeatedly using the image of a relentless "raging storm" (6.211) to symbolize unjust political oppression,[2] thus questioning Burke's fascination with the "raging storms" of punitive justice.[3] Williams then presents poetry as key to societal movement beyond cycles of vengeance and violence, drawing heavily on Burkean imagery of horror but refusing to label such imagery "sublime." Instead, she presents poetic expressions of compassion for suffering as ushering in forms of liberation and social regeneration that, for her, are truly sublime. For Williams, poetry helps communities move past destructive rage to envision greater sublimity in a peaceful radiance that powerfully binds and limits hostile passions, thus preventing future harm. Ultimately, in advocating for preventative rather than punitive justice, Williams acknowledges horrific suffering, with sacred terror, moving towards sublime freedom.

In *Peru*, Williams challenges Edmund Burke's severe dichotomy between a raging, masculine passion for punitive justice and an indulgent, feminine desire for mercy. Burke insists on a "wide difference" (*Enquiry*, 113) between the respected masculine virtues that he defines as sublime and the lovable feminine virtues that he defines as beautiful. This gendered dualism has been problematic for feminists from Mary Wollstonecraft onwards.[4] Burke's dichotomizing sets the masculine "virtues" of "fortitude, justice, [and] wisdom," realized by severe "punishments," against the feminine virtues of "compassion, kindness and liberality," which he claims are "more lovely, though inferior in dignity," and therefore not sublime (*Enquiry*, 110–11). He thus excludes the feminine from the sublime.

Williams questions Burke's dichotomy by presenting sublimity not in severe judgment *or* in soft mercy but in a third category, characterized by a peaceful radiance that actively enables social justice. Her belief in the transcendence of Burkean dichotomies, through prayerful calls for justice and poetic visions of freedom, reflects her participation in London's dissenting religious and intellectual circles. She was raised in the Presbyterian Church. A Scottish, Presbyterian minister, Dr. Andrew Kippis, first urged her to publish.[5] The diverse list of subscribers to Williams's 1786 *Poems* includes Kippis, as well as the Presbyterian poet and playwright Joanna Baillie and her brother Dr. Matthew Baillie.[6] Modern critics have not fully considered the connections between Williams's poetic modifications of Burkean aesthetic theory, her dissenting focus on human incarnations of merciful justice, and her portrayal of social virtue and political freedom as sublime.

Williams's poems build on the definition of sublimity within the sermons of Andrew Kippis, for example.[7] In his "Sermon VII" Kippis asserts that prayer can "draw off our affections from the vanities, follies, and vices of the world, and lead them to worthy, noble and sublime objects," thus promoting "our benevolence."[8] Kippis, unlike Burke, does not oppose feminine compassion to masculine justice, but asserts that sincere prayer makes us "more just, *and* more compassionate."[9] Joanna Baillie echoes this phrase when she writes that the exercise of "sympathetic curiosity" makes us "more just, more merciful, more compassionate."[10] In his "Sermon X," Kippis emphasizes the "inward peace" and "sublime serenity" of prayerful Christians.[11] The practice of prayer, according to Kippis, can "fill our hearts with sublime consolation," which we then extend to others through loving action.[12]

Critics have viewed Williams's political commentary apart from her Christian vision of a dauntless and peaceful sublimity that prompts social action through visionary poetics.[13] In *Peru*, Williams deploys visionary figures to denounce the "hideous horror" (6.83) of oppression and to prophesy enactments of social justice. Williams thus couches political commentary within the rhetoric of prophecy, a move of which Edmund Burke would disapprove.[14] Jon Mee highlights Burke's resistance to dissenting visionaries who "were little better than playthings of enthusiasm to Burke, men [and women] who were sacrificing a proper sense of self and the stability of the commercial and social order to their improbable visions of futurity."[15] Williams's *Peru* does indeed stake high value on idealized social visions of a utopian future. By boldly invoking poetic visionaries, Williams affirms links between prophetic enthusiasm, dissenting spiritual community, and social justice.[16]

Williams could draw on the history of women's prophetic utterance in doing so. Bishop Robert Lowth's *Lectures on the Sacred Poetry of the Hebrews* (published in Latin in 1753 and English in 1787) may have encouraged her in her deployment of prophetic figures.[17] Lowth not only presents biblical prophecy as sublime but also praises the only female prophet who was also a judge and a poet: Deborah.[18] When Lowth admires Deborah's biblical "ode" for its "great force," he implies that it expresses the strength of sublime poetry.[19] Anne Mellor astutely places Williams among female poets who likewise "claimed divine authority...for their prophetic verse."[20] In her article on the "maternal sublime," feminist critic Patricia Yaeger protests the divide between the domestic world of the "labouring female and the Old Testament world of the prophetic male";[21] and Williams's verse challenges the assumptions of such a dichotomy early on.

Near the beginning of Williams's *Peru*, a female personification, "Peruvia's genius," prophesies the violence of Spanish colonization. Williams first uses the word "sublime," however, not to refer to such colonial violence but to the social virtues of Peruvia:

> Nor less, Peruvia, for thy favour'd clime
> The virtues rose, unsullied and sublime:
> There melting charity, with ardour warm,
> Spread her wide mantle o'er th'unshelter'd form;
> Cheer'd with the festal song, her lib'ral toils,
> While in the lap of age she pour'd the spoils.
> Simplicity in every vale was found,
> The meek nymph smil'd, with reeds, and rushes crown'd; (1.41–48)

In this idealistic vision of pre-colonial Peru, Williams includes the recognizably Christian virtues of agape, encouragement, charity, and meekness.[22] In doing so, she does contribute to the eighteenth-century stereotype of the "noble savage,"[23] but her poem's ability to imagine ethical conduct in Peru before the arrival of the Spanish nevertheless offers a refreshing corrective to the projection of absolute depravity onto pre-colonial cultures by other eighteenth-century poets.

In Williams's poem, it is the conquistadors, not the indigenous Peruvians, who are the source of horrific, depraved transgression. Peruvia's genius foresees that "the unrelenting storm" (1.131) of colonialism will "rend [Peruvia's] soft robe, and crush her tender form" (1.132). The metaphor of physiological violation is underlined when treasures are taken "from lost Peruvia's bleeding land" (1.184). The Spanish gouge Peruvia in their quest for gold and silver, leaving her with gaping "wounds" (6.280). Feminist critics have, not surprisingly, tended to view Williams's Peruvia as a passive victim. Janet Todd, for example, observes that for Williams, "Peru becomes an appealing feminine victim."[24] However, every tragic event in *Peru* has an impact on the entire Peruvian community, men and women, whose "sublime public virtues"[25] are paradoxically strengthened by Spanish persecution.

Williams's "Peruvia" is not just an individual victim but also a personification of the multitude of Peruvian people both wounded by and actively resisting Spanish attacks. Williams describes one such attack by "stern Pizarro" (2.2)[26] in the lines "sudden, while frantic zeal each breast inspires, / And shudd'ring demons fan the impious fires, / The bloody signal waves" (2.25–27). This imagery of sudden violence meets Burke's criteria for sublimity.[27] Williams continues to deploy very Burkean diction by referring to the attack's "thund'ring cannon" (2.30), "sanguine rage" (2.31), and "rush" (2.32) of passion. Burke claims that "sublime" passion "anticipates our reasonings and hurries us on by an irresistible force" (*Enquiry*, 57). The "sanguine" passion of the "Sons of Spain" as they rush at Peruvia with phallic-sounding "naked sabers" (2.28) at first appears Burkean due to its hurried force, but Williams does not label this attack "sublime."

Williams continues to use the rush of "raging storms" (*Enquiry*, 82) to represent unjust oppression in her portrayal of the corrupt priest "stern Valverda" (3.28), who is driven by a "fanatic fury" (3.15) to murder indigenous Peruvians. Valverda's raging fanaticism does not meet Williams's ideal of a Christian faith "founded on the principles of rational enquiry, and on the sublime morality and the eternal truths of the Gospel."[28] The "impious" (3.23) profanations of Valverda's "rising storm" (3.27) are not labelled sublime but "hideous" (3.28). Williams presents the force of fanaticism as ugly and repulsive. She notes of Valverda, "His bosom never felt another's woes / No shriek of anguish breaks its dark repose" (3.29–30). His raging cruelty towards the Peruvians excludes him from Williams's construction of a sublime typified by just compassion and constructive social action.

In Williams's poem, Valverda meets his opposite in Bishop Bartolomé de Las Casas, whose "God, is Love" and who rescues an indigenous Peruvian man from Valverda's grip. The historical atrocities that occurred in South America were recorded by Las Casas in his *Brevisma Relación de la Destruyción de las Indias* (1542) and later illustrated by Theodore de Bry in woodcuts created for a 1599 English translation of Las Casas's work, *A Short Account of the Destruction of the Indies*. This English translation would have been the text available to Williams. In her poem, Williams intentionally parallels the entrapment and torture of a Peruvian man by Valverda with the imprisonment, taunting, and crucifixion of Christ. She is very loyal to Las Casas in doing so, as Las Casas once explained to a friend that he saw "in the Indies, Jesus Christ, our God, scourged and afflicted and buffeted and crucified, not once but millions of times."[29] There is heavy irony in Williams's description of Spanish church leaders judging and torturing a "meek spirit" who "humbly sought its God" (3.34). It becomes even more clear that Williams is asking her audience to see the Peruvian as a Christ figure when he maintains his peaceful composure, and does not strike back, as the Spanish tie him, tear his hair, and rend his robe. The speaker comments, "Ah, see his uncomplaining soul sustain / The sting of insult, and the dart of pain" (3.85–86). At this point the kind Las Casas appears, sheds tears for the Peruvian man, burns with righteous indignation at his treatment, and prays to Christ, before he rebukes Valverda "in grace severe" (3.122).

Las Casas's prayer draws parallels between the Spanish leaders who tortured and murdered Peruvians and the individuals directly involved in Christ's death; but instead of seeking vengeance for these acts, Las Casas meets them with forgiveness:

> Oh suff'ring Lord! he cried, whose streaming blood
> Was pour'd for man — Earth drank the sacred flood —
> Whose mercy in the mortal pang forgave
> The murd'rous band, thy love alone could save;
> Forgive — thy goodness bursts each narrow bound,
> Which feeble thought, and human hope surround;
> Forgive the guilty wretch, whose impious hand
> From thy pure altar flings the flaming brand,
> In human blood that hallow'd altar steeps,
> Libation dire! while groaning nature weeps— (3.103–12)

The word "forgive" is repeated twice, at lines 107 and 109, alluding to Christ's statement from the cross, "Father, forgive them; for they know not what they do" (Luke 23:34 AV).[30] Williams ends Las Casas's prayer by connecting the suffering of incarnate divinity to the wounds of Peruvia's landscape, through the phrase "groaning nature weeps," which itself alludes to Romans 8:22: "the whole creation groaneth and travaileth in pain." By drawing parallels between the tortured Peruvians, the wounded landscape, and Christ's crucified body, Williams gestures towards the possibility of material restoration in the light of resurrection.

Williams further counters the oppressive rage of the "Sons of Spain" through the visionary perceptions and creative forms of fictional Peruvian poet Zamor. Zamor loves both beauty and terror in the landscape but is also sensitive to a third category typified by glowing light, which he labels sublime.[31] This light is first literal, perceived by Zamor as he views the Andes at sunset (5.19–20), and then symbolic, used by Williams to represent her hope for the

rapid spread of "freedom" (6.332) across the Peruvian landscape. Zamor functions as the active social bard of the Peruvian people, thus illustrating how a
social consciousness supported by sublime poetics can supersede political
horror. Zamor unites the Peruvians while they are still in Peru and consoles
them once they have taken refuge in Chile. Williams records in the prefatory
"Argument" for Canto Five that she will sketch the "character of Zamor, a
bard," and conclude with "a reflection on the influence of poetry on the
human mind" (line 123). Williams believes that sublime poetry arises out of
the transparency and virtue of communities where artifice does not veil "the
soul" (5.6) and convention does not "warp" (5.6) the heart. It is Zamor's reverence for such social virtue paired with his love for natural sublimity that
results in his passionate and benevolent capability as a bard.

Williams first describes Zamor's experience of sublimity in the Peruvian
landscape in terms of recognizably Burkean elements and then suggests that
what most appeals to him is the inclusion of glowing light and intimate affection in a sublimely rugged scene:

> Nature, in terror rob'd, or beauty drest,
> Could thrill with dear enchantment Zamor's breast:
> He lov'd the languid sigh the zephyr pours,
> He lov'd the murm'ring rill that fed the flow'rs;
> But more the hollow sound the wild winds form,
> When black upon the billow hangs the storm;
> The torrent rolling from the mountain steep,
> Its white foam trembling on the darken'd deep —
> And oft on Andes' height with eager gaze,
> He view'd the sinking sun's reflected rays,
> Glow like unnumber'd stars, that seem to rest
> Sublime, upon his ice-encircled breast. (5.9–20)

Williams does not exclude love from Zamor's response to aspects of the landscape that fit the Burkean sublime. Zamor loves "wild winds" (5.13), stormy
"billows" (5.14), rolling torrents (5.15), "steep" (5.16) mountains, and "dark-
'ned" depths (5.16). However, Williams chooses to reserve the term "sublime"
(5.18) for reference to a unique vision of radiant, multi-faceted, and tranquil
light. Through her depiction of Zamor's reverence for the innumerable "rays"
(5.18) of light resting on Andean "heights" (5.17), which draw his "eager gaze"
(5.17), Williams suggests that higher sublimities of light can generate a sustaining repose more beneficial than hurried passion. The image of sunrays
resting (5.19) like "unnumber'd stars" (5.19) upon the mountain's "ice-encir-
cled breast" (5.20) suggests a person resting on the breast of a loved one.

Zamor's "wild warblings" (5.21) of song "whose theme was love" (5.24) are
inspired not only by the sublimity of the landscape but also by the virtues of

his love Aciloe. The speaker notes of Zamor, "Aciloe's beauties his fond eye confest, / Yet more Aciloe's virtues warm'd his breast" (5.25–26). Zamor's love for the sublime, in the natural landscape and in Aciloe's virtues, is mixed with reverence. Modern linguist Julia Kristeva envisions a similar form of love when she suggests that erotic desire can be transformed into "a *sublime love*, indebted to God."[32] Williams presents Zamor's affection and respect for Aciloe in terms of such sublime love. Later in the poem, Zamor, Aciloe, and Las Casas together form a small community of resistance to colonial oppression. Bishop Bartolomé de Las Casas's ability to engage in bold social action, rescuing the indigenous Peruvian from Valverda's grasp and taking him to "safer plains" (3.128), links him to Zamor's role as social bard of the Peruvian people. When the Spaniard Alphonso attempts to force Aciloe to marry him, Las Casas takes Aciloe and Zamor to Alphonso and pleads, "by every horror bleeding passion knows / By the wild glance that speaks her frantic woes" (5.287–88), for Alphonso to "let mercy's pleading voice [his] bosom move" (5.291).

Just as Williams imagines the bishop Las Casas actively intervening and mediating on behalf of the indigenous Peruvians, she envisions the bard Zamor bringing a degree of healing to the Peruvian people through his poetry. After he and Aciloe are released by Alphonso, Zamor "leads Aciloe, and her sire, to Chili's [*sic*] meads" (5.318) where Peruvian refugees, "condemn'd to roam, / By hard oppression, found a shelt'ring home" (5.319–20). Here, amongst this community of exiles, "Zamor to pity, tun'd the vocal shell / Bright'ning the tear of anguish as it fell" (5.321–22). Zamor's poetry brightens "the tear of anguish" (5.322) in active social restoration. This idea of sublime poetry's power to brighten the darkness of suffering leads Williams's speaker to a more general meditation on the healing capacity of the "heav'nly muse" (5.324). A female embodiment of sublime verse, this muse is able to "still" (5.325) destructive rage, lessen political "affliction" (5.326), subdue the "stormy passions" (5.327), and "lift the soul" (5.328).

Zamor's appearance in *Peru* ushers in active Peruvian resistance to colonial oppression.[33] In Canto Six, the Peruvian rebel Cora runs through the landscape in search of her love, indigenous leader Manco-Capac. In her construction of Cora as a subject "of true pathos," Williams imaginatively mixes characters from Spanish history, Peruvian legend, and French fiction.[34] In Williams's half-historical and half-imaginative account of events in sixteenth-century Peru, Cora searches for Manco-Capac until she falls down exhausted. When this happens the landscape shudders in sublime compassion:

O'er the fair valley sudden darkness throws
A hideous horror; thro' the wounded air
Howl'd the shrill voice of nature in despair;

> The birds dart screaming thro' the fluid sky,
> And, dashed upon the cliff's hard surface die;
> High o'er their rocky bounds the billows swell,
> Then to their deep abyss affrighted fell;
> Earth groaning heaves with dire convulsive throws,
> While yawning gulfs her central caves disclose. (6.82–90)

With its sudden darkness, heaving earth, and yawning gulfs, this passage continues to affirm Las Casas's comparison of the suffering of indigenous Peruvians to the suffering of Christ by alluding to imagery in the Gospels of Matthew and Luke. Luke notes that as Christ died "the sun was darkened" (23:45), and Matthew records, "the earth did quake, and the rocks rent; and the graves were opened" (27:51–52). Williams combines this biblical imagery with the Burkean sublime of darkness, danger, abrupt angles, boundless heights, sudden depths, and terrifying, giddy plunges. She might also be drawing on Marmontel's *Les Incas*, within which the narrator describes the heroine Cora's entrapment amidst a volcanic eruption in the Andes,[35] a decidedly Burkean image.

Such physical upheaval in nature ultimately serves a constructive, redemptive purpose in Williams's poem. It causes the other Peruvians who have fled Cuzco to run in Cora's direction and to "pitying paus[e]" (6.97) at her side, creating a tableau of community bonded through grief. Cora sees Manco-Capac standing among the members of this community and their "melting souls unite" (6.99) in a moment of affective bonding that brings them a sublime "wild delight" (6.100). The pause motivated by pity that facilitates such mixture of Burkean delight with love helps define Williams's idea of sublimity. After Cora dies, Manco-Capac is left with deep grief mixed with traces of the sublime delight brought about by loving reunion. The speaker remarks, "[s]carce could his soul in one short moment bear / The wild extreme of transport, and despair" (6.111–12). The wild and sublime transport brought through the joy of Cora and Manco-Capac's reunion is intensified by its sharp juxtaposition with Cora's sudden death.

Though Capac has acted as a great, even terrible, military leader of the Peruvian rebels, Williams also chooses to portray his soulful emotional vulnerability. This prepares the reader for the casting of Capac in a maternal role when he takes "his lov'd babe" (6.123) from Cora's arms and bathes the infant in "showers of softer sorrow" (6.124) before carrying Cora's corpse along with their child to Chile. Again, Williams draws on yet modifies Burke's definition of sublimity, blending death and love in her creation of a familial sublime. Capac's wild and sublime love for Cora motivates his journey "o'er many a pathless wood and mountain hoar" (6.135) to the political "freedom" (6.134) of Chile.

The pathos of loss is again met with a politicized compassion and sublime love in *Peru* when Las Casas dies and a personification of Sensibility descends to consecrate his grave:

> But ah! Whence pours that stream of lambent light,
> That soft-descending on the raptur'd sight,
> Gilds the dark horrors of the raging storm —
> *It lights on earth — mild vision! gentle form —*
> *'Tis Sensibility! She stands confest,*
> With trembling step she moves, and panting breast;
> Wav'd by the gentle breath of passing sighs
> Loose in the air her robe expanded flies;
> Wet with the dew of tears her soft veil streams,
> And in her eye the ray of pity beams. (6.213–22; italics mine)

The feminine figure of Sensibility brings about a calm spiritual repose through the pouring out of light around her body, metonymically represented through her "trembling" (6.214) feet, "panting breast" (6.214), and pitying "eye" (6.222). The mantle of light that surrounds Sensibility, though it inspires, does not threaten to overpower or ravish the viewer. Williams's feminine sublime is transformative but also gentle and full of trembling compassion. In *Peru* Williams responds to the fearful, angry, trembling, and prophetic figure of Peruvia's Genius with the consolations of Sensibility, who trembles back in sorrow and compassion. She thus defines prophecy as a painful witness to impending political injustice, and to its future reparations, which is enabled through, met with, and contained by the sublime grace and light of merciful feminine friendship. Like Las Casas's patient work towards social justice, Sensibility's power resides not in any ability to dominate but in her very mildness, a form of power excluded from Burke's system.

After chronicling the Peruvians' suffering, struggles, and setbacks, Williams sketches the potential birth of freedom out of the country's strife. In the final canto, the speaker envisions a glowing personification of freedom sweeping over Peruvia's landscape and lighting up the mountaintops.

> A brighter glory gilds the passing hour,
> While freedom breaks the rod of lawless power:
> Lo on the Andes' icy steep she glows,
> And prints with rapid step th'eternal snows;
> Or moves majestic o'er the desert plain,
> And eloquently pours her potent strain. (6.331–36)

Recalling Zamor's earlier reverence for sublime light, freedom gilds the Andean mountaintops with her bright glory. Williams depicts freedom as sweeping from the utmost heights of the Andes to the edges of the coastal desert in a journey of feminine expansion. Freedom spreads her influence through a rhetorically sublime eloquence (6.336), thus linking political action to the rhetorically persuasive voices of women. After sweeping over Peruvia's landscape, freedom treads the "dark laurel" (6.342) of oppression beneath her "graceful feet" (6.341). Williams's poem prophesies the merciful healing and strengthening of Peruvia's injured body through the constructive enactment of social justice.

Williams depicts the endurance of sublime, active virtues within Peruvia, a female personification of the Peruvian people and landscape that is ultimately covered over with a sympathetic light in resistance to the "dark repose" of colonialist indifference. The narrative of *Peru* reveals how the human capacity for dauntless action in aid of others can endure amidst international conflict and political oppression. Furthermore, Williams presents visionary spiritual figures — like the historical Bishop Las Casas and fictional bard Zamor — as encouraging and facilitating such social action. Once such facilitation occurs in her poems, mild yet powerful female personifications of Peace, Sensibility, and Freedom can bind and limit the hostile passions, thus allowing for social regeneration.

Notes

1 Printed in Helen Maria Williams, *Poems, in Two Volumes* (1786), a collection of poetry which has been reprinted in its entirety and introduced by Jonathan Wordsworth in a modern facsimile edition (Oxford: Woodstock, 1994). *Peru* appears in volume 2, pages 41–178 of this facsimile edition, but the poem was originally published singly by Thomas Cadell in 1784. Future citations from *Peru* are from Wordsworth's 1994 facsimile edition of Williams's 1786 *Poems in Two Volumes* and will be given in the text by canto and line number. Citations from Williams's prose introductions to each canto and from her footnotes are also from the Wordsworth facsimile edition and will be given by volume and page number. Irregularities in spelling, such as "Chili" for "Chile," have been left unaltered.

2 In her 1823 "Introductory Remarks" to *Poems on Various Subjects* (London: Whittaker, 1823), Williams notes that what she refers to as her "Peruvian Tales in Verse" were "chiefly composed of facts taken from Robertson's History of Spanish America" (x). Here, Williams refers to the dissenting Scottish minister William Robertson, whose *History of America* — which included social histories of both Mexico and Peru — was first published in 1777. Williams also refers to Robertson's *History of America* in a 1786 footnote to *Peru* (*Poems in Two Volumes*, 2.77).

3 Edmund Burke, *A Philosophical Enquiry into the Origin of Our Ideas of the Sublime and Beautiful* (1757; London and New York: Routledge; New York: Columbia University Press, 1958) 82. Future citations from *A Philosophical Enquiry* are from this edition and will be referenced in the text by short title (*Enquiry*) and page number.

4 Mary Wollstonecraft protests Burke's inability to blend respect with love. In a critical allusion to Burke's exclusive and hierarchical dichotomy, she argues that it restricts women to passive amiability and robs them of "fortitude, justice, wisdom" (*The Works of Mary Wollstonecraft*, ed. Janet Todd and Marilyn Butler, 7 vols. [London: William Pickering, 1989] 5.45).

5 In the preface to her two-volume 1786 *Poems*, Williams writes, "My first production, the Legendary Tale of Edwin and Eltruda, was composed to amuse some solitary hours, without any view to publication. Being shewn to Dr. Kippis, he declared that it deserved to be committed to press, and offered to take upon himself the task of introducing it to the world" (iii–iv). For more background on Williams's early connection to dissenting culture see Roger Lonsdale, ed., *Eighteenth-Century Women Poets: An Oxford Anthology* (Oxford: Oxford University Press, 1990) 413; and Deborah Kennedy, *Helen Maria Williams and the Age of Revolution* (Lewisburg, PA: Bucknell University Press; Cranbury, NJ: Associated University Presses, 2002) 23–24.

6 Later, in 1791 Williams held a gathering in Hampstead that included Joanna Baillie and her brother Dr. Matthew Baillie, as well as *Man of Feeling* author Henry Mackenzie. In his diary entry titled "April 21, 1791.—At Miss Williams's" (qtd. in Peter Clayden, *The Early Life of Samuel Rogers* [London: Smith, Elder and Co., 1887] 165–74), Samuel Rogers records meeting "Miss Baillie, a very pretty woman with a very broad Scotch accent" (166), "Dr. Baillie" (168), and publisher "Cadell" (168), as well as "Dr. Kippis" (171). Both Clayden (165) and Kennedy (77) have identified "Miss Williams" as Helen Maria Williams.

7 Though Kippis's sermons were not published until 1791, Williams heard him preach in the Princes Street Presbyterian Church of Westminster from her youth onwards (Kennedy, *Helen Maria Williams*, 23–24).

8 Andrew Kippis, *Sermons on Practical Subjects* (London: T. Cadell, 1791) 170.

9 Ibid., 171.

10 Joanna Baillie, "Introductory Discourse" (1798), *Joanna Baillie: A Selection of Plays and Poems*, ed. Amanda Gilroy and Keith Hanley (London: Pickering and Chatto, 2002) 14.

11 Kippis, *Sermons on Practical Subjects*, 242, 248.

12 Ibid., 179. In Ann Radcliffe's gothic novel *Romance of the Forest*, published the same year as Kippis's sermons, the word "sublime" is used in a parallel manner when Adeline addresses "a prayer to that Being who had hitherto protected her in every danger. While she was thus employed, her mind gradually became elevated and re-assured; a sublime complacency filled her heart" (*The Romance of the Forest*, ed. Chloe Chard [Oxford: Oxford University Press, 1986] 140). This sublime peace allows her to take action that brings about justice in the case of her father's murder.

13 For commentary on Williams's abolitionist poem see Moira Ferguson, *Subject to Others: British Women Writers and Colonial Slavery, 1670–1834* (London and New York: Routledge, 1992) 158 and Robert Edward Mitchell "'The soul that dreams it shares the power it feels so well': The Politics of Sympathy in the Abolitionist Verse of Williams and Yearsley," *Romanticism on the Net* 29/30 (2003): 7–12, http://id .erudit.org/iderudit/007719ar. For commentary on her recording of events in France see Matthew Bray, "Helen Maria Williams and Edmund Burke: Radical

Critique and Complicity," *Eighteenth-Century Life* 16 (1992): 2–18; Vivien Jones, "Women Writing Revolution: Narratives of History and Sexuality in Wollstonecraft and Williams," *Beyond Romanticism: New Approaches to Texts and Contexts, 1780–1832,* ed. Stephen Copley and John Whale (London and New York: Routledge, 1992) 190–97; Chris Jones, *Radical Sensibility: Literature and Ideas in the 1790s* (London and New York: Routledge, 1993) 136–59; Steven Blakemore, *Crisis in Representation: Thomas Paine, Mary Wollstonecraft, Helen Maria Williams* (Madison, NJ: Fairleigh Dickinson University Press, 1997) 18–19 and 154–61; and most recently Kennedy, *Helen Maria Williams,* 317–30. Bray claims that Williams's letters present "a sustained critique of the ideas of Edmund Burke" (2) but does not mention her poetry. Vivien Jones compares the sublime in Williams's letters to that of Wollstonecraft's *Historical and Moral View* and does not mention Burke. Chris Jones compares her account of the revolution to that found in Wordsworth's *Prelude* but ultimately concludes that her sublime is closer to Shelley's celebration of an inner creative "spark" than to Wordsworth's "sublime self-forgetfulness" (159). Blakemore notes that Williams "angrily read Burke's *Reflections*" (154) upon her return to France in 1791, but he does not mention the sublime. Kennedy focuses on Williams's use of "the discourse of sensibility" (323) in her letters, but, again, does not mention the sublime.

14 Burke generally dismisses the mixing of aesthetics with moral philosophy as "whimsical theory," despite his own division between sublime masculine justice and beautiful feminine compassion. When Burke proceeds to claim that such theory rests on "foundations altogether visionary and unsubstantial," he reveals an even deeper resistance to couching theory in the rhetoric of dissenting visionaries (*Enquiry*, 112).

15 Jon Mee, *Romanticism, Enthusiasm, and Regulation* (Oxford: Oxford University Press, 2003) 47.

16 Shaun Irlam notes the political implications of prophecy in *Elations: The Poetics of Enthusiasm in Eighteenth-Century Britain* (Stanford, CA: Stanford University Press, 1999), claiming that after the Civil War, enthusiasm "became a labile political term liberally applied to almost all perceived enemies of Church and State, every variety of theological and political discontent (Puritan, Papist, Quaker, Antinomian, Leveller)" (23). Williams's use of prophecy to denounce tyranny and to propose merciful modes of bringing about future social justice illustrates that there were concrete reasons to associate visionary rhetoric with dissenting politics.

17 Through her connection to Andrew Kippis, Williams would most likely have been aware of Lowth's work. Kippis prompted G. Gregory to translate Lowth's lectures from Latin to English in the 1780s. In his "Translator's Preface," Gregory writes, "By the advice and encouragement of Dr. Kippis, I was in a great measure induced to undertake this translation; by a continuance of the same friendly disposition I was enabled to cheerfully proceed in it" ("Translator's Preface," *Lectures on the Sacred Poetry of the Hebrews,* by Robert Lowth, trans. G. Gregory [New York: Garland, 1971] xvii). Kippis supported this translation while introducing Williams into London's dissenting circles and encouraging her own poetic vocation.

18 Carol Myers argues, "Deborah occupies a unique role in Israelite history. Not only is she a judge in the sense of a military leader, but also she is the only judge in the law-court sense of that title (Judg. 4:5) in the book of Judges. Of all the military

leaders of the book, only Deborah is called a 'prophet.' She is also the only judge to 'sing' of the victory, illustrating the creative role played by women" (Myers, "Deborah," *The Oxford Companion to the Bible*, ed. Bruce Metzger and Michael Cogan [Oxford, Oxford University Press, 1993] 161).

19 Lowth, *Lectures on the Sacred Poetry of the Hebrews*, 291, 293.

20 Anne Mellor, "The Female Poet and the Poetess," *Women's Poetry in the Enlightenment*, ed. Isobel Armstrong and Virginia Blain (London: Macmillan, 1999) 82.

21 Patricia Yaeger, "The 'Language of Blood': Toward a Maternal Sublime," *Genre* 25 (1992): 9.

22 Here, Williams may be drawing on Immanuel Kant's *Observations on the Feeling of the Beautiful and Sublime* (1763). This early work by Kant creates a degree of gender flexibility by positing three types of sublimity — the terrible sublime, the noble sublime, and the splendid sublime — and then making room for women within the noble sublime. For Kant, the qualities of feminine sublimity include "a sort of noble simplicity and innocence in great excellences. Out of [which] shines a quiet benevolence and respect towards others, linked at the same time with a certain *noble trust* in oneself, and a reasonable self-esteem that is always to be found in a sublime disposition" (*Observations on the Feeling of the Beautiful and Sublime*, trans. John Goldthwait [Berkeley: University of California Press, 1965] 85–86). In the references to trust in oneself and self-esteem, we can see the germs of the Kantian autonomy that will become more troublesome in *Critique of Judgment*; but in this early work these qualities are prefaced by the more humble values of simplicity, innocence, "quiet benevolence," and respect towards others.

23 In historical fact, there was not an absolute moral dichotomy between the "good" pre-contact Incan culture of Peru and the "evil" Spanish colonists. Pre-colonial Peru was hardly a non-violent utopia. The Incan culture condoned the sacrifice of children, for example (Carmen Bernand, *The Incas: People of the Sun* [London: Harry N. Abrams, 1994] 32).

24 Janet Todd, *Sensibility: An Introduction* (London: Methuen, 1986) 60. Postcolonial critic Alan Richardson suggests, "Williams hints at the feminine character of the Peruvian culture at the outset" ("Epic Ambivalence: Imperial Politics and Romantic Deflection in Williams's *Peru* and Landor's *Gebir*," *Romanticism, Race, and Imperial Culture, 1780–1834*, ed. Alan Richardson and Sonia Hofkosh [Bloomington: Indiana University Press, 1996] 268). Richardson continues, "[T]he very fact that the Spanish travel without women, in contrast to the salient presence of women in Peruvian society (at least as Williams represents it), sets up a gendered dichotomy" (269). Gary Kelly argues that the entire poem "*Peru* is again 'feminine' in treatment because it portrays the evils of war and imperialism through their effects on individual sensibilities" (*Women, Writing, and Revolution 1790–1827* [Oxford: Clarendon, 1993] 32). Jonathan Wordsworth agrees, noting that *Peru* "condenses the epic scope into the frame of the more acceptably feminine epyllion, and surveys the impact of war through the lens of individual tragedy" (52).

25 Williams, "Introductory Remarks," xix.

26 Francisco Pizarro was a conquistador who first began to explore South America, in quest of El Dorado, in 1524 (Bernand, *The Incas*, 14). Bernand notes further, "[B]y 1532 Pizarro had returned to Peru, this time for good" (31).

27 In his section entitled "Suddenness," which immediately follows his reference to the sounds of "raging storms, thunder, or artillery," Burke writes, "In everything sudden and unexpected, we are apt to start; that is, we have a perception of danger" (*Enquiry*, 82–83).

28 Williams, "Introductory Remarks," xxxviii. Williams's ideal of rational faith and moral conviction founded on the sublime revelation of the gospel influenced her nephew, Athanase Coquerel, who went on to serve as a pastor within Reformed church communities in Paris and later Amsterdam. Coquerel explains how, "après de bien sérieuse et longues méditations, j'ai trouvé le christianisme dans l'Évangile"; he then asserts, "Notre foi aura une base solide, si toutes les vérités de notre religion reposent sur une vérité simple, clair, facile, à la portée de tous" (*Cours de Religion Chretienne* [Paris: Ab. Cherbuliez, 1833] 1).

29 Qtd. in Gustavo Gutiérrez, *Las Casas: In Search of the Poor of Jesus Christ*, trans. Robert Barr (New York: Orbis, 1993) 62.

30 Subsequent biblical quotations are from the Authorized (King James) Version.

31 Here Williams directly diverges from Burke's emphasis on the sublimity of darkness as opposed to the beauty of light. Burke emphasizes, "how greatly night adds to our dread" (*Enquiry*, 59). For him, "dark, confused, uncertain images" are sublime (*Enquiry*, 62). He claims, "Darkness is more productive of sublime ideas than light," and writes, "An association that takes in all mankind may make darkness terrible; for in utter darkness, it is impossible to know in what degree of safety we stand" (*Enquiry*, 80, 143). See also "Why darkness is terrible" (*Enquiry*, 145–47). The connection between darkness and sublimity was central to *Philosophical Enquiry*.

32 Julia Kristeva, *Tales of Love*, trans. Leon Roudiez (New York: Columbia University Press, 1987) 162. Similarly, Mary Wollstonecraft envisions the possibility of such sublime affection between the sexes, when she writes, "Supposing…for a moment, that women were, in some future revolution of time, what I sincerely wish them to be, even love would acquire more serious dignity, and be purified in its own fires" (*Works* 5.188–89).

33 Zamor's role as a people's poet who enables active resistance to tyranny appealed to early nineteenth-century French readers as it resonated with the ideals of the French Revolution. The description of Zamor was the only part of *Peru* included in an 1808 French translation of poetry by Williams, for example. The translator M. Stanislas de Boufflers entitled this section "Zamor, Fragment Tiré du Cinquième Chant d'un Poème Intitulé *Pérou*" (*Recueil de Poésies Extraites des Ouvrages d'Helena Maria Williams, Traduites de l'Anglais par M. Stanislas de Boufflers et M. Esménard* [Paris: Fr. Cocheris Fils, 1808] 113–17).

34 In the "Argument" (*Poems* 2.54) that prefaces the canto she recounts the defeat of "Manco-Capac" at the Peruvian city of Cuzco, after which his love "Cora" runs from the Spaniards in search of him (54). Manco-Capac is not the name of a sixteenth-century indigenous leader but the name given to the first man in Incan creation narratives. According to these narratives, Manco-Capac's bride was not Cora but "Queen Mama Huaco, his sister" (Bernand, *The Incas*, 26). Williams may have become aware of Manco-Capac through Françoise de Graffigny's *Lettres d'une Peruvienne* (1747). In the 1748 translation, *Letters Written by a Peruvian Princess*, Aza refers to "the history of Manco-capac [*sic*]" (133). In *Les Incas ou la destruction*

de l'empire du Pérou (1777), Jean-François Marmontel gives the name "Cora" to a Peruvian sun priestess (Bernand, *The Incas*, 37). These French texts could be sources for Williams's knowledge of Peruvian suffering, in addition to the two works she points to explicitly: Bartolomé de Las Casas's *A Short Account of the Destruction of the Indies* (1542 and 1599) and William Robertson's *The History of America* (1777).

35 Bernand, *The Incas*, 37.

JOANNA BAILLIE AND THE CHRISTIAN GOTHIC: REFORMING SOCIETY THROUGH THE SUBLIME

Christine A. Colón

Theatre audiences in early nineteenth-century Britain were well acquainted with the world of violence that existed just beyond their borders. They had witnessed the terrors of the French Revolution and were now embroiled in a new set of horrors as their troops went off to fight Napoleon. For some playwrights, the Gothic plays that filled the London stages may have been created simply as an escape for these audiences: an entertaining ghost story to take their minds off the very real dangers in the world around them. For others, the Gothic horrors were a means of exploring the chaotic political and social situations of their own society at a safe distance: one that could escape the careful eye of the censor. For Joanna Baillie, the premiere British playwright of the Romantic era, the Gothic became a means for her to enact her unique theories of moral reform. While we may not immediately associate mysterious forests, dreary castles, threatening ghosts, and hideous corpses with the process of learning to live a good, moral life, Baillie does. This seemingly odd connection between Gothic spectacle and moral reform is seen most clearly in her play *The Dream*, where Baillie uses the Gothic to emphasize the dangers of a world in which Christianity has become so infused with worldly values that, for most of the characters, it is no longer an influence for good. For Baillie, the mysterious dreams and long-buried skeleton of *The Dream* are not simply a capitulation to the popular tastes of her audience but rather a surprising means by which Baillie enacts her theories of moral reform by using the audience members' fascination with terror to focus their attention on the need to control their passions and live moral lives.

When Joanna Baillie published her first volume of *Plays on the Passions* in 1798, she crafted an Introductory Discourse that delineated her theories of drama and explored the potentially powerful moral effect that well-crafted plays could have on an audience. Her plan was to create a series of plays based on various passions. She would compose a tragedy and comedy on each of these passions so that she could focus the audience's attention on the development of that passion and reveal the dangers of allowing it to grow out of control. The foundation for Baillie's theories is an idea that she calls "sympathetick curiosity." She believed that all individuals are intensely interested in the people around them, proposing that "[t]here is, perhaps, no employment which the human mind will with so much avidity pursue, as the discovery of concealed passion, as the tracing the varieties and progress of a perturbed soul."[1] Rather than seeing this curiosity as a sinful invasion of privacy, Baillie contends it has been given to individuals by God so that they may learn from the examples of others, for "[i]n examining others we know ourselves."[2] Real life, however, limits the opportunities for individuals to use sympathetic curiosity effectively, for they are not given access to the hidden emotions and motivations that are generally revealed only in private.

With her plays, Baillie attempts to remedy this problem, for she allows the audience to "[follow] the great man into his secret closet … [stand] by the side of his nightly couch, and [hear] those exclamations of the soul which heaven alone may hear."[3] By granting her audience deeper access into the minds of her characters than is granted to them in real life, Baillie hopes not only to create a close connection between her audience members and the character so that they may identify with his or her struggle but also to help them discern where the character might have made other choices so that he or she would not have been destroyed by the seemingly all-consuming passion. Baillie contends, "We cannot, it is true, amidst [passion's] wild uproar, listen to the voice of reason, and save ourselves from destruction; but we can foresee its coming, we can mark its rising signs, we can know the situations that will most expose us to its rage, and we can shelter our heads from the coming blast."[4] Her plays, then, are designed to help her audiences become attuned to this process of controlling the passions so that in their own lives they may avoid the mistakes that destroy so many of her characters.

As her theories demonstrate, Baillie was not interested in simply entertaining her audience; instead, she wished to use her plays to transform individuals and, through them, all of society. While Francis Jeffrey, one of her harshest critics, objected to her project, claiming that "[p]lays have, for the most part, no moral effect at all," Baillie was actually following in a long tradition of other writers who saw drama as a powerful means of influencing society.[5] From the time that the English theatres were reopened in 1660, the debate over the proper use of drama raged. Whether they were arguing that theatre was corrupting English audiences with its representations of evil or proposing that theatre could reform English audiences by showing how evil is combatted effectively, writers such as Jeremy Collier and John Dennis repeatedly asserted that theatre was very influential. The English government certainly agreed with this assessment, for in 1737, it passed the Licensing Act, which strictly controlled all spoken drama, carefully censoring any political, religious, or sexual content that might be considered offensive or potentially dangerous for the masses. This act, which remained in effect until it was reworked in 1843, had particular resonance during the revolutionary decades of the late eighteenth and early nineteenth centuries, when fear of revolution made controlling the masses a high priority. As Julie Carlson argues in her study of Romantic drama, theatre became "a model for revolutionary politics" and had to be treated very seriously.[6] Interestingly, thinkers with such varied political opinions as Edmund Burke and Samuel Taylor Coleridge agreed on the power of theatre, with Burke proclaiming that "theatre is a better school of moral sentiments than churches" and Coleridge arguing that theatre is "a delightful, yet most effectual remedy for this dead palsy of the public mind."[7] While writers might disagree on the purpose to which theatre should be used, they concurred that it had the potential to be a powerful influence on audiences, and the English government wanted to ensure that it could not be used to foment revolution.

In her Introductory Discourse, Baillie addresses this issue directly, criticizing eighteenth-century dramas and comedies for inflaming the passions of audiences rather than helping the audience members control them. She then sets her own theories in opposition to those of the playwrights she has discussed, arguing that her own philosophy of drama will promote a positive moral effect rather than a negative one. Baillie declares, "[W]e cannot well exercise [sympathetick curiosity] without becoming more just, more merciful, more compassionate."[8] But how can Baillie be sure that her unique plan for drama will have this positive effect? Rather than relying simply upon her own ideas, Baillie places them within the context of two already well-established discourses of moral reform: Christianity and eighteenth-century moral philosophy. Using this foundation enables Baillie to assure her audiences that, unlike many other plays, her dramas will have a positive moral influence.

Baillie's Christianity proves to be very important to her overall project, for it gives her a strong argument for the use of the imagination in moral reform.[9] In contrast to many Christians of her time period who were suspicious of the theatre because they felt it was, in Baillie's words, "unfriendly to the principles and spirit of Christianity,"[10] Baillie felt that Christians needed to embrace the theatre and recognize the powerful moral effect it could have. In the preface to her second volume of miscellaneous dramas, Baillie confronts her Christian critics, declaring, "We cannot...allege that dramatic representations are contrary either to the precepts or spirit of the Christian religion."[11] As support for her assertion, Baillie turns first to human nature and then to Scripture. She argues that "[i]t is in the nature of man to delight in representations of passion and character. Children, savages, learned and unlearned of every nation, have with more avidity received instruction in this form than in any other."[12] For Baillie, the imagination that draws individuals to these representations is a powerful component in the process of learning. As she expresses earlier in her Introductory Discourse, she believes that God crafted human beings with this tendency to be fascinated by other people's emotions and experiences so that they may learn to live moral lives from the examples they observe. By acting as the force that draws individuals to these stories, the imagination, then, is perfectly consistent with the values of Christianity.

As further support for this theory, Baillie turns to the example of Christ, arguing that he, "who knew what was in man, did not contradict nor thwart this propensity of our nature, but, with that sweetness and graciousness which peculiarly belonged to His divine character, made use of it for the instruction of the multitude, as His incomparable parables so beautifully testify."[13] For Baillie, Christ's cultivation of the imagination with his parables becomes a model for her own project of reform through drama, for as she captures her audience members' imaginations through her plays, she makes them more receptive to the moral lessons revealed implicitly through the story. Baillie believes so strongly in her project that she ultimately asserts that "if [representations of strong passions] are exhibited as warnings, and as that which produces, when indulged, great human misery and debasement, they teach us a lesson more powerful than many that proceed from the academical chair or the pulpit."[14] With this preface, then, Baillie reveals the strong Christian foundation that supports her project and helps to ensure that, unlike many other plays, hers will have a positive moral influence upon her audience.

Baillie also turns to eighteenth-century moral philosophy as support for her theories, demonstrating how, even from a more secular perspective, drama may have a powerful, positive effect upon the audience if it is crafted carefully. Throughout the eighteenth century, the concept of sympathy became an important measure of the morality of society, for sympathy allowed individuals to transcend selfish motivation as they were guided instead by their interest in and concern for others. Writers such as the Earl of Shaftesbury and David Hume explored how this process of sympathy might work, and novelists such as Samuel Richardson popularized their ideas, crafting fictional works designed to cultivate this sympathy within the hearts and minds of the readers as they reacted to the plights of characters such as Pamela and Clarissa. By the end of the eighteenth century, these ideas had so permeated British society that many writers began to react against them, seeing this cultivation of sympathy as potentially hypocritical, for it could compel individuals to enact emotions that they did not actually feel. Baillie herself criticizes sentimental comedies in her Introductory Discourse for exactly this reason.

Despite this criticism, Baillie does accept some of the basic principles of this philosophy and uses them to provide a strong foundation for her own project. She relies particularly on Adam Smith's work *The Theory of Moral Sentiments*. In his discussion, Smith presents sympathy as the first step in the process of moral reform, as individuals experience "analogous emotion[s]" when they observe anyone struggling with passion.[15] He then expects them to examine these emotions within themselves, think about how they might appear to an "impartial spectator," and moderate the passions accordingly.[16] The overall process that Smith describes is very similar to the one that Baillie proposes in her Introductory Discourse. While she does modify Smith's ideas in certain respects by focusing more on the individual's internal struggle rather than his or her acceptance in society, she locates her project firmly within this tradition, drawing upon its established authority.[17]

By placing this process on stage, however, Baillie believes that she is able to enhance it, crafting stronger emotions than we generally see in the people around us, providing glimpses of the private struggle that is usually hidden from observers, and demonstrating the entire process as an example of how to subdue passions in the early stages before they become too powerful. In addition, she argues that drama is a more effective venue for this type of moral reform than the history, philosophy, poetry, or novels that have conveyed it in the past because "[t]he impressions made by [drama] are communicated, at the same instant of time, to a greater number of individuals than those made by any other species of writing; and they are strengthened in every spectator, by observing their effects upon those who surround him."[18] The philosophical tradition of moral sympathy may have started to fall out of favour because of its potential to create social hypocrites who display the sympathy that they do not truly feel, but Baillie proposes that it may be rejuvenated for a stronger moral purpose through her plays.

By building upon her Christian heritage and the tradition of moral sympathy, Baillie assures her readers that she is able to create a type of drama that will have a positive moral influence on her audiences and combat the many negative examples they have received from other plays. In order for her plays to have the effect that she desires, however, she must work to ensure that the emotions she portrays on stage will make the strongest impression possible.

That is when she often turns to the Gothic. Many of Baillie's plays rely on typical Gothic devices such as ghosts, witches, and mysterious secrets, and in her
Introductory Discourse, she reveals why she thinks this tactic will be successful. Baillie's project relies upon the fascination that individuals have with
observing others who are undergoing severe trials: the more severe the trial is,
the stronger the interest an observer will have. As she describes this process,
Baillie begins with examples such as hangings and torture — severe tests of
will and emotion that cannot help but captivate viewers. She then turns to the
supernatural and argues that "[a]mongst the many trials to which the human
mind is subjected, that of holding intercourse, real or imaginary, with the
world of spirits: of finding itself alone with a being terrific and awful, whose
nature and power are unknown, has been justly considered as one of the most
severe."[19] For Baillie, the supernatural provides one of the strongest means of
testing an individual and seeing how he or she will withstand the emotions
uncovered by this world of spirits; therefore, she believes it will also firmly
capture the imagination of the audience. As Baillie remarks, "No man wishes
to see the Ghost himself... but every man wishes to see one who believes that
he sees it, in all the agitation and wildness of that species of terror."[20]

In his work *A Philosophical Enquiry into the Origin of Our Ideas of the Sublime and Beautiful* (1757) Edmund Burke suggests one reason why the supernatural might have such a strong effect on an audience. He asserts, "Whatever
is fitted in any sort to excite the ideas of pain, and danger, that is to say, whatever is in any sort terrible, or is conversant about terrible objects, or operates
in a manner analogous to terror, is a source of the *sublime*; that is, it is productive of the strongest emotion which the mind is capable of feeling."[21] Burke
does acknowledge that "[w]hen danger or pain press too nearly, they are incapable of giving any delight, and are simply terrible," but he ultimately concludes that "at certain distances, and with certain modifications, they may be,
and they are delightful."[22] For Burke, the sublime, which links this terror with
the delight of experiencing it at a distance, can awaken individuals to the
intensity of life and is far more effective at reaching an audience than the
beautiful, which simply lulls the audience into complacency. And as J.T. Boulton remarks in his introduction to this work, Burke's ideas provide a good
explanation for "[t]he growing taste for ruins and melancholy terror, for
graveyard poetry, for wild and desolate scenery."[23] In a sense, Burke "system-
atiz[es] a change in aesthetic values" that transformed much of the literature
of the late eighteenth and early nineteenth centuries.[24] With her Gothic plays,
Baillie participates in this shift in aesthetic values, using a character's interaction with the supernatural (or a force that he or she thinks is supernatural) to
provide a sublime moment for the audience members that will not only grab
their attention but also allow them to reflect on the passions that they see dis-

played. At the time that Baillie was writing, the Gothic was at its height and many playwrights used supernatural spectacles to captivate their audiences; however, as Baillie's plays reveal, the Gothic may be used for more than just spectacle. By capturing the attention of the audience in such a powerful way, Baillie feels that she can more easily convey the moral truths that lurk behind the Gothic trappings.

The Dream, published in 1812, provides us with an excellent example of the way that Baillie uses the Gothic to enhance moral sympathy and ultimately reaffirm the Christian values she believes to be important to her society. In this play, Baillie uses the Gothic not only to reveal the dangers of excessive passion, as she does in all of her *Plays on the Passions*, but also to explore the deeper dangers of an immoral society that is so permeated by the values of self-preservation and revenge that love and mercy have almost entirely disappeared. *The Dream* is set in a Gothic world of evil and danger. At the beginning of the play, we are introduced to a gloomy monastery in the midst of a plague-ridden land, to monks who repeatedly dream of a mysterious stranger demanding that someone undergo penance for an unknown crime, to the skeleton of an unknown man discovered in the bowels of the monastery, and to a soldier named Osterloo who is chosen by lot to expiate the sin that threatens the existence of the monastery. We soon discover, however, that the true evil in this society lies not in these Gothic conventions but rather in the hearts of two characters: Osterloo, an imperial general who some years before murdered a romantic rival, and the prior of the monastery, who desires to take revenge for this murder.

At first, Baillie uses the Gothic to draw the audience's attention to the character of Osterloo and the extreme trial he is about to face. His character provides the audience members with the sublime moments necessary to focus their attention and generate the sympathy that initiates moral reform. The mysterious dreams of the monks and the fact that Osterloo is chosen by lot to provide penance for the unknown crime set him apart as a character that fate has chosen to undergo a severe test. Audience members, then, are curious to see why he has been chosen and how he will withstand it. At first, he is as brave as one would expect a respected general to be. This bravery disappears, however, when he discovers that the supposedly unknown sin is actually a murder he committed years before when he was enraged by a rival's success with the woman they both loved. This revelation, which occurs in a typical Gothic scene meant to heighten the audience's emotions, initiates Osterloo's process of deterioration from which the audience must learn.

With this scene, Baillie follows the scenario that she describes in her Introductory Discourse, expecting that Osterloo's plight will create the terror mixed with delight that will captivate her audience. The scene begins with stage directions that describe "[a] burying vault, almost totally dark; the monuments and grave-stones being seen very dimly by the light of a single torch, stuck by the side of a deep open grave."[25] It is the perfect Gothic setting for Osterloo's trial, and his terrified response focuses the audience members' attention on his plight even before they fully grasp the depths of his struggle. As Osterloo encounters the skeleton of the man he murdered, the powerful warrior cowers in fear with "his whole frame ... moved by some sudden convulsion" (172). He may not actually see the ghost of his rival, but he is so thoroughly haunted by his guilt that it is almost as if he saw the ghost rise up before him. In fact, he is so afraid, one of the monks must lead him out of the vault because every few steps Osterloo imagines that the open grave lies before him ready to receive his guilty soul. Baillie uses this Gothic moment to emphasize Osterloo's distress, compelling him to reveal not only his guilt but also the dangerous passion of fear he must learn to control before it destroys him. The Gothic, then, not only captures the audience's attention with this dark and frightening scene, it also reveals the intensity of Osterloo's struggle with which the audience must sympathize so that they may avoid the mistakes that lead to Osterloo's death.

As the play continues, Osterloo's plight becomes only more difficult, for he remains confined within a Gothic world where ghosts of the afterlife haunt his thoughts and provoke even deeper fears of the retribution he will have to suffer after death. When the prior, who turns out to be the brother of the murdered man, condemns Osterloo to death without a trial and without much time for Osterloo to grapple with his remorse, Osterloo's panic increases, for the prior tells him that "heaven, sooner or later, will visit the man of blood with its terrors. Sooner or later, he shall feel that he stands upon an awful brink; and short is the step which engulphs him in that world, where the murdered and the murderer meet again, in the tremendous presence of him, who is the Lord and giver of life" (176). From this moment on, Osterloo is fixated on "this smothered horror" of "the invisible dead" (178). He is so overcome by his fear that when help finally arrives, it is too late. Osterloo dies of fear on the scaffold before the executioner drops the axe. Baillie uses these Gothic imaginings to demonstrate the extremes of Osterloo's passion that her audience members must escape if they are to control the passions in their own lives. Osterloo is not simply struck by a momentary fear when he must face the crime he has hidden for so many years, but he becomes obsessed with ideas of eternal punishment that not only consume every waking hour but also lead to his death.

As she does throughout her *Plays on the Passions*, Baillie uses her protagonist to explore the dangers of allowing a passion such as fear to grow out of control. Fear is natural for a man in Osterloo's predicament; but, as Baillie emphasizes, Osterloo knows that the tenets of Christianity provide forgiveness for those who repent. After Osterloo's tortured confession, Jerome reminds him that "the mercy of Heaven is infinite" (187), but Osterloo holds on to his fear so tightly that he cannot fully grasp this truth. Instead, he imagines a horrific afterlife, crying, "The dead are there; and what welcome shall the murderer receive from that assembled host? Oh the terrible form that stalks forth to meet me! the stretching out of that hand! the greeting of that horrible smile!" (187). Even God is seen only as "Incomprehensible and dreadful" (187). Osterloo's destruction comes because he cannot accept the truth of God's grace and forgiveness and, thereby, overcome his terror of the afterlife. With Osterloo's death, then, Baillie emphasizes that the danger of the passions lies not only in the power that they have to control an individual but also in the power that they have to distance the individual from God, and she asks her audience members to acknowledge that they cannot allow their passions to overshadow God's truth.

In order for this lesson to resonate with her audience members, they must be able not simply to feel sorry for Osterloo but also to identify with him even though he is eventually revealed to be both a murderer and a coward. In her Introductory Discourse, Baillie points out the potential similarities between her audience members and her characters, remarking, "But many a miserable being, whom firm principle, timidity of character, or the fear of shame keeps back from the actual commission of crimes, is tormented in obscurity, under the dominion of those passions which place the seducer in ambush, rouse the bold spoiler to wrong, and strengthen the arm of the murderer."[26] With her plays, then, Baillie asks her audience members to recognize that even though they may not act on their passions, the potential for evil still exists within them, and Baillie's use of the Gothic helps them in this process. Like Osterloo, her audience members are brought out of their regular lives into the dreary atmosphere of the monastery, and as they descend with him deep into the burial vault to view the opening of the coffin and the revelation of the skeleton of the man he murdered, they are asked to experience his horror if not his guilt. Osterloo provides the audience members with access into this Gothic world, and as they experience its terrors, they get a taste of the fear that consumes him. When her earlier play *De Monfort* was produced on the London stage, Baillie was criticized for asking her audience to sympathize with a murderer. Here, she does the same but, perhaps, more successfully. By situating the murder in the distant past, emphasizing Osterloo's remorse, and cultivating a similar response of fear in her audience through the Gothic, Baillie does create sympathy for his plight. Through the Gothic, then, Baillie compels her audience members not only to experience the thrill of fear generated by the terrifying story but also to sympathize with Osterloo's struggle and understand that they, too, may be easily overcome by passion if they are not attuned to the process of controlling it.

The connection that Baillie creates between Osterloo and the audience also proves to be important for another element of Baillie's social critique, for even though she concentrates primarily upon Osterloo's process of deterioration, she also widens the focus of her play from Osterloo's struggle to include a strong critique of the society in which Osterloo is placed: a society in which his violent act of murder is only one manifestation of the jealousy, rivalry, and revenge that permeate it. While Osterloo's crime is treated as a serious sin, he is presented far more positively than the prior who is so consumed by revenge that he ignores not only the laws of the land but also his responsibilities as a man of God in order to orchestrate Osterloo's death. And it is through the character of the prior that Baillie reveals the flawed morality that endangers not only Osterloo but also the entire community, for it has permeated even the monastery that should be the stronghold of God.

At the beginning of the play, the audience members assume that the dreams of a mysterious stranger arriving at the monastery and demanding penance for a terrible crime are truly supernatural occurrences. As the play progresses, however, they begin to realize that these dreams may have natural causes. When the monk Benedict confronts Jerome, who had the first dream, the audience members discover that Jerome was the deathbed confessor of the hermit who buried the mysterious corpse in the vaults of the monastery. They also discover that Jerome described his supposed dream in great detail to Paul, the other monk who later had the same dream. This dream, then, may have been provoked by the hermit's words on his deathbed, or it may even have been orchestrated by Jerome. Benedict seems to suspect Jerome of sinister intentions when he suggests that Jerome knew that Osterloo's army would be marching through the nearby mountain pass and would, therefore, have been able to construct the plan to single out Osterloo through the supposedly random casting of lots. Did Jerome know that the murdered man was the prior's brother? Did he share the hermit's confession with the prior? Did they work together to orchestrate Osterloo's punishment? Baillie leaves these questions unanswered, but the prior's actions after the arrival of Osterloo certainly suggest that he had some knowledge of the events before they occurred and that he would go to great lengths to take revenge on the man who killed his brother.

Baillie uses these Gothic conventions, then, not only to forge a connection with Osterloo but also to highlight the evil that exists within the human heart. The true danger to Osterloo lies not in any ghosts that may exist within the dark, mysterious vaults of the monastery but rather in the embittered heart of the prior: an evil that has corrupted almost the entire monastery. In her play, Baillie suggests that this monastery was once the nurturing moral centre of the community. It has become corrupt now because, rather than holding to its original values of love and compassion, it has turned to the values of self-preservation and revenge that the prior embraces. At the beginning of the play, Baillie reveals that the nurturing role that once made the monastery so important to the community is being ignored by most of the monks as they put their own physical welfare above the spiritual welfare of the wider community. In the first scene, the peasants, who long for the consolation from the monks that they used to receive, are prevented from entering the monastery by Jerome, who fears that they will spread "death and contagion" (157). This fear is echoed later in the play when one after another the monks refuse to leave the monastery to minister to a woman on her deathbed who desperately desires a confessor. While Benedict readily agrees to go and comfort the woman, the other monks are so concerned with their own well-being that they neglect their Christian duty, leaving the peasants to die without last rights. These are not the actions of true men of God, and the fact that the prior allows these events to occur within his monastery demonstrates his flaws as a Christian and as a leader that foreshadow the even deeper sins that are revealed through his actions toward Osterloo.

With the character of the prior, Baillie reveals the dangers of a society in which Christian values have been replaced by worldly ones. While the prior should be infused with the love of God that he should then demonstrate to those around him, he is instead controlled by the same feelings of anger and revenge that caused Osterloo's downfall. In fact, he is worse than Osterloo because he never expresses any remorse for what he has done. When Osterloo confesses, the prior can see him only as a murderer. Benedict repeatedly reminds the prior that Osterloo is also their penitent, but the prior "can think of nothing but revenge" (177) and seems to enjoy "leav[ing] [Osterloo] to the bitterness of his thoughts" (176). The prior is the one who paints for Osterloo such a horrific vision of the afterlife, and he is quite willing to let Osterloo wallow in this fear without providing any consolation. Benedict recognizes the danger that the prior poses to Osterloo, exclaiming, "Then Heaven have mercy on [Osterloo], if he must find none here!" (177). Rather than fulfilling his role as a man of God and helping Osterloo turn to God in repentance, the prior can think only of his immediate execution—an act of supposed justice, which, as Benedict points out, is not the role of the monastery. Benedict declares, "Though guilty, by his own confession, of murder, committed, many years since, under the frenzy of passion; it belongs not to us to inflict the punishment of death upon a guilty soul, taken so suddenly and unprepared for its doom" (184). Benedict does not deny the seriousness of Osterloo's act, but he recognizes that, as a house of God, the monastery is not the appropriate place for this violent act of supposed justice. By having the prior deny that truth,

Baillie emphasizes how far he has fallen from his true role and demonstrates the dangers that this poses for the rest of the community which can no longer rely on this man of God to act in a godly fashion.

As the lone voice of love and compassion among the many monks, Benedict is the only one to recognize how far the monastery has strayed from its original purpose. While Benedict's insights do not change Osterloo's plight (even though Benedict does participate in a failed attempt to free Osterloo), Baillie does allow his character to provide a glimmer of hope for the future. In his final speech, the Ambassador, who had come to save Osterloo, reveals that the governance of the monastery will be taken out of the prior's hands and given to Benedict. Condemning the prior for making "the general weal of the community subservient to [his] private revenge" (198), the Ambassador turns to Benedict, desiring to give him the power that the prior "so greatly abused" (198). With this conclusion, Baillie emphasizes not only the inappropriate actions of the prior and many of his monks but also the qualities that will be necessary for the monastery and the surviving community to recover. Throughout the play, Benedict has been the voice of reason as well as of compassion and mercy. He is the one who senses a devious plot behind all of the supposedly supernatural occurrences. He is also the one to plead for the peasants and to endanger his life by going to comfort a dying woman. And, finally, he is the one who is more concerned about Osterloo's soul than with revenge. Baillie places this hope, however, within a world that is still consumed by anger and revenge, for even as the Ambassador speaks of entrusting the monastery to Benedict, he declares that the monks shall not "cheat our imperial master of his revenge for the loss of his gallant general" (198). The cycle of revenge, which began the play, continues in this final speech. By using the Gothic to emphasize the evil that exists within the prior's heart and contrasting him with Benedict, Baillie demonstrates where the true moral centre of this world lies, and implicitly she asks her audience to embrace its values of love and compassion rather than the values of self-preservation and revenge that have destroyed both Osterloo and the prior. But she also reveals what a difficult task this may be in a world consumed by revenge and hostility.

Considering the chaos and violence of early-nineteenth-century Europe, a lesson on the value of love and compassion seems particularly appropriate for Baillie's audience. What is interesting, though, is that Baillie never criticizes Osterloo for being a general and leading his soldiers into battle. She seems to accept war as a necessary evil, for she never links Osterloo's role as a soldier to his downfall. While she does acknowledge that "[t]he active and adventurous life of a soldier is most adverse to reflection" and has allowed Osterloo to repress his feelings about the murder he committed (176), she also portrays Osterloo as a noble man whose soldiers "would go through flood and flame for his sake" (161). It is not the violence of warfare, then, that concerns her but rather the violence that exists within the human heart. With her use of the Gothic, Baillie provides a harsh critique of a world in which the dangerous values of rivalry and revenge have come to permeate not only the heart of an otherwise noble character but also the walls of the monastery where the monks should be devoted to Christian love. For Baillie, however, the terrors of the Gothic also lead to a deeper truth: the fact that these same inclinations may lie in the hearts of her audience. By using the Gothic to ally her audience members with Osterloo's plight and to provide the sublime moments necessary to provoke strong emotion, Baillie asks them to search their own hearts for these destructive passions so that they may learn to control them, thereby enacting the moral sympathy she believes God has given humanity as a powerful means of reform. While the horrors of the Gothic may provide Baillie's audience members with the thrill of terror, Baillie hopes that they will also lead them out of a world of anger and revenge and into a world of love and forgiveness that is necessary to withstand these evils and repair the community.

Notes

1 Joanna Baillie, Introductory Discourse, *The Dramatic and Poetical Works* (1851; New York: Georg Olms, 1976) 4.

2 Ibid., 4.

3 Ibid., 8.

4 Ibid., 11.

5 Francis Jeffrey, rev. of *A Series of Plays (Vol. II)*, by Joanna Baillie, *Edinburgh Review* 2 (1803): 275.

6 Julie Carlson, "Command Performances: Burke, Coleridge, and Schiller's Dramatic Reflections on the Revolution in France," *Wordsworth Circle* 23.2 (1992): 117.

7 Edmund Burke, *Reflections on the Revolution in France*, ed. Frank M. Turner (1790; New Haven, CT: Yale University Press, 2003) 69; Samuel Taylor Coleridge, *Notes and Lectures upon Shakespeare and Some of the Old Poets and Dramatists with Other Literary Remains of S.T. Coleridge*, ed. H.N. Coleridge, vol. 1 (London: William Pickering, 1849) 49.

8 Baillie, Introductory Discourse, 4.

9 Baillie had a very complex relationship to orthodox, Protestant Christianity. She was raised in the Scottish Presbyterian Church but began attending an Anglican congregation when she and her family moved to England when Baillie was in her early twenties. She remained within the Church of England for the rest of her life but also had close connections with a Unitarian congregation. In fact, her tract *A View of the General Tenour of the New Testament Regarding the Nature and Dignity of Jesus Christ* (London, 1831) reveals her disbelief in the doctrine of the trinity. Baillie, however, refused to define herself as Unitarian, preferring to remain within

the Church of England even as she dissented from several of its core doctrines. As her religious tract reveals, Baillie believed strongly that each Christian has the responsibility to read the Bible for herself and come to her own conclusions. For Baillie, the result was a Christian faith that transcends traditional denominational boundaries.

10 Joanna Baillie, Preface to the Second Volume of Dramas, *The Dramatic and Poetical Works*, 528.

11 Ibid., 528–29.

12 Ibid., 528.

13 Ibid.

14 Ibid., 529.

15 Adam Smith, *The Theory of Moral Sentiments*, 2 vols. (1759; New York: Duyckinck, 1822) 1.2.

16 Ibid., 1.92.

17 For detailed discussions of how Baillie uses the ideas of eighteenth-century moral philosophy as she crafts her theories of drama, see Sean Carney's "The Passion of Joanna Baillie: Playwright as Martyr," *Theatre Journal* 52 (2000): 227–52; Aileen Forbes's "'Sympathetic Curiosity' in Joanna Baillie's Theater of the Passions," *European Romantic Review* 14.1 (2003): 31–48; Barbara Judson's "'Sympathetic Curiosity': The Theater of Joanna Baillie," *Tulsa Studies in Women's Literature* 25.1 (2006): 49–70; Julie Murray's "Governing Economic Man: Joanna Baillie's Theatre of Utility," *ELH* 70 (2003): 1043–65; and Victoria Myers's "Joanna Baillie's Theatre of Cruelty," *Joanna Baillie, Romantic Dramatist: Critical Essays*, ed. Thomas C. Crochunis (New York: Routledge, 2004) 87–107.

18 Baillie, Introductory Discourse, 14.

19 Ibid., 3.

20 Ibid.

21 Edmund Burke, *A Philosophical Enquiry into the Origin of Our Ideas of the Sublime and Beautiful* (1757; New York: Columbia University Press, 1958) 39.

22 Ibid., 40.

23 J.T. Boulton, introduction to *A Philosophical Enquiry into the Origin of Our Ideas of the Sublime and Beautiful*, by Edmund Burke (New York: Columbia University Press, 1958) lvii.

24 Ibid.

25 Joanna Baillie, *The Dream*, Six Gothic Dramas (Chicago: Valancourt, 2007) 170; subsequent citations from *The Dream* are from this edition and will be referenced in the text by page number.

26 Baillie, Introductory Discourse, 14.

SUFFERING AND SACRAMENT IN THE NINETEENTH CENTURY

SACRAMENTAL SUFFERING AND THE WATERS OF REDEMPTION AND TRANSFORMATION IN GEORGE ELIOT'S FICTION

Constance M. Fulmer

In spite of the fact that George Eliot is acclaimed as an atheist, many of her scenes borrow freely from religious imagery and use religious rituals and the sacramental language of religious ceremonies in both traditional and non-traditional ways. Eliot's characters suffer and cause others to suffer as a result of their self-centred egotism and a narrow vision of life which does not include a concern for the needs of others. However, many of these selfish sufferers as well as their suffering victims do experience moral growth, and in a remarkable number of instances, this moral growth occurs in scenes involving water which frequently include the idea of drowning. This water may provide a ceremonial washing of regeneration or may serve as a means of transportation from one spiritual state to another. In every case, contact with water involves a holy encounter in which the character who is suffering is resolving significant moral turmoil, is being rewarded for moral growth, or is enduring moral punishment. In all of these holy encounters moral growth comes about through a more mature consciousness of self and a deeper understanding of the importance of sympathetic understanding, which Eliot calls Solidarity, and/or a more profound comprehension of what she calls Continuity and defines as the impact of past generations on the present. Near the end of her career Eliot composed several notes related to her ideas on aesthetics and morality.[1] In the same note in which she defines Solidarity as "the interdependence of co-existing men" and Continuity as "the dependence of one generation on the preceding," she says, "Neither can be broken while the race lasts," not even by a "cataclysm of waters." Her use of water in a sacramental sense always involves the intervention into the lives of her characters of her highest moral authority.

The positive moral lessons Eliot teaches in her novels are based on her own unique system of morality which replaced the orthodox religion she renounced. Her personal conception of morality is completely devoid of supernatural sanction; there are no ties or allegiances higher than family relationships. There is no divine being higher than the individual who facilitates the moral growth of another person. In her last work, *Impressions of Theophrastus Such*, Eliot defines true morality as "the conduct which, in every human relation, would follow the fullest knowledge and the fullest human sympathy."[2] On November 26, 1862, she wrote to her friend Barbara Bodichon, "I have lost all interest in mere antagonism to religious doctrines. I care only to know, if possible, the lasting meaning that lies in all religious doctrines from the beginning till now."[3] That continuous meaning which is derived from generations past is her highest spiritual authority. Good and evil are measured in terms of an individual's response to his or her inheritance from the past and concern for generations to come. And in her novels the impact of the past on the present operates as a deterministic force which is similar to the orthodox conception of Providence and is specifically associated with water, floods, and drowning.

These principles which define Eliot's moral authority also provide the foundation for her artistic practice. She made it clear that she intended every aspect of her writing to be "the highest art ... consciously devoted to the deepest moral problems."[4] She accomplishes this by portraying her characters at various stages of moral maturity and illustrates their moral growth or moral depravity through the choices they make and in their interactions with others. More often than not, the expiation of suffering is associated with the transportation by water from one level of moral understanding to another, and the intervention of the past into the inner consciousnesses of her characters frequently involves water.

For Eliot and for her characters, moral authority is an extremely personal matter. She is always very careful to insist that no one moral choice or set of moral principles fits everyone but that what is morally right depends upon the individual and the circumstances. However, the moral turmoil that accompanies the intense physical, mental, and/or emotional suffering which inspires moral growth is frequently depicted in the language of baptismal cleansing, new birth, and the washing of regeneration. Her characters who experience moral growth gradually come to understand and apply the principles of Solidarity and Continuity, and a character who is morally mature in his or her understanding of the principle of Continuity is motivated to leave a legacy which will benefit posterity.

Viewing Eliot's own moral choices and the moral choices of her characters in this conceptual framework helps to explain some of the seeming moral contradictions and inconsistencies of which she has been accused. Eliot's use of water in a sacramental sense not only depicts the intervention of the divine in human form into the daily lives and inner consciousnesses of her characters but also emphasizes the fact that moral punishments and moral rewards are inevitably ambiguous. In *The Mill on the Floss*, Eliot's novel in which water is used most dramatically as a divine force, the omniscient narrator reminds us that "moral judgments must remain false and hollow unless they are checked and enlightened by a perpetual reference to the special circumstances that mark the individual lot" (628).[5]

Like Ludwig Feuerbach, whose *Essence of Christianity* she translated, Eliot uses water in an emblematic but non-religious way.[6] Her secular use of water illustrates what is sacred to her even as she illustrates the principles which for her characterize the insufficiency of traditional religion. She felt that, like her Spanish Gypsy and the Virgin Mary, she was called to fulfill a lot different from that of ordinary women.[7] In answering her higher calling she believed that she performed a godlike task by making incarnate the purely human moral concepts. She wrote to Mrs. Henry Frederick Ponsonby, "[T]he idea of God, so far as it has been a high spiritual influence, is the ideal of a goodness entirely human."[8] Within her personal belief system, Eliot felt that she served a divine function by creating these scenes in which water plays a profound role in teaching truths which contributed to the spiritual wealth of mankind.

Eliot uses the phrase "the spiritual wealth of mankind" in another of her notes entitled "Judgments of Authors," where she comments, "[I]n endeavouring to estimate a remarkable writer who aimed at more than temporary influence, we have first to consider what his individual contribution was to the spiritual wealth of mankind."[9] When she pays a compliment to any author, this lasting spiritual contribution is what she has in mind. For example, in her comments on Goethe she actually connects his spiritual contribution with water; she says, "He quietly follows the stream of act and of life; and waits patiently for the moral processes of nature."[10]

Significantly, she also uses references to water when she quotes the sermons delivered by her characters. For example, in *Adam Bede*, Eliot's first novel, Dinah Morris describes the streams of God's love which reach the whole creation and goes on to say, "[I]f the earth was to be burnt up, or the waters come and drown us — nothing could part us from God who loves us"

(33). And in *Romola* Savonarola's preaching at the Dominican convent in Florence is described as bringing "a flood of waters upon the earth" (207). And he specifically identifies what is good as "a river that flows from the foot of the Invisible Throne" (360). When Romola runs away from her marriage, Savonarola tells her, "You are seeking your own will, my daughter. You are seeking some good other than the law you are bound to obey. But how will you find good? It is not a thing of choice: it is a river that flows from the foot of the Invisible Throne, and flows by the path of obedience" (360).

One of the more familiar examples of a ceremonial washing with sacramental implications occurs in *Silas Marner* when Eliot's omniscient narrator refers to Silas's introduction to "a great ceremony with soap and water" from which Eppie "came out in new beauty" (121). When Epple arrived, Silas had little or no sense of solidarity or continuity: "He hated the thought of the past; there was nothing that called out his love and fellowship toward the strangers he had come among; and the future was all dark, for there was no Unseen Love that cared for him" (17). But as he bathes and cares for the child, she brings this divine unseen love into his life, and he undergoes a complete spiritual transformation.

Sacramental ceremonial washing also plays a critical role in *Daniel Deronda*. During Deronda's visit to the Cohen home, which takes place long before he realizes his own Jewish heritage, Mrs. Cohen "placed a china bowl near her husband that he might wash his hands in it" (396). Mr. Cohen not only "washed his hands, pronouncing Hebrew words," but "afterwards, he took off the napkin covering the dish and disclosed" the bread of which he broke "small pieces and gave one to each [member] of the family"—including Deronda—while uttering blessings (397). This simple scene is the sacramental beginning of Deronda's initiation into Jewish ceremony, of his acceptance of his own sacred mission, and of his relationship with Mordecai—who is the incarnation of all of the Hebrew prophets.

A cleansing scene with a different sort of spiritual significance occurs in *The Mill on the Floss* when Lucy—"wet and discoloured with mud" (161)—has to be washed up after Maggie deliberately pushes her into the "cow-trodden" mire (164). The scene obviously points toward Maggie's drowning because Maggie's mother expresses her habitual fear: "They're such children for the water, mine are"—"They'll be brought in dead and drowned some day" (166). In addition to foreshadowing the negative impact of Maggie's betrayal of Lucy, this scene also implies that Maggie's drowning will eventually have a redeeming and cleansing effect in Lucy's life.

There are a number of times when Eliot uses drowning as moral judgment of the person who drowns and as both reward and punishment to those left alive. In *Adam Bede* Adam and Seth Bede find their father's body beside the stream where he has drowned. With his death both brothers are freed from the burden and disgrace of his irresponsibility and drinking. Adam immediately feels guilty for being so hard and unloving and unforgiving toward his father. When Adam tells his mother, "Father's tumbled into the water," his "mind rushed back over the past in a flood of relenting and pity" (54–55). However, Thias Bede's death is also a blessing since it provides an opportunity for Dinah to come into the Bede home and eventually to bring Adam and Dinah together.

In *Silas Marner* Dunstan's skeleton is discovered at the bottom of the Stone Pit where he drowned after stealing Silas's gold. His death freed his family from his irresponsibility and Godfrey from the threat of having his secrets revealed. Ironically, when the water is drained from the Stone Pit and his secrets come to light, Godfrey learns that Nancy is more understanding and forgiving than he ever dreamed possible. She even helps him to deal with his past and to accept the fact that he is being punished by having no heirs because for so many years he failed to claim Eppie as his own child.

In *Daniel Deronda*, Grandcourt also conveniently drowns, thereby freeing Gwendolen from her miserable marriage. Like Godfrey, Grandcourt has violated the principle of continuity by failing to acknowledge his own children by Lydia Glasher. All of the circumstances involving Grandcourt's drowning have spiritual overtones and provide opportunities for Deronda "to be in the stead of God" to Gwendolen (763). For example, when—by Fate, chance, or a sort of Providence—Deronda sees Gwendolen and Grandcourt boarding the boat in Genoa, they were "moving like creatures who were fulfilling a supernatural destiny" (681). And after the drowning, as Gwendolen pours out her fears to Deronda, he comforts her by saying, "I believe that you may become worthier than you have ever yet been—worthy to lead a life that may be a blessing" (700). Significantly the encounter also enables him to see more clearly the life that he is destined to lead.

In *The Mill on the Floss* the river not only appears in the title of the novel but, through the motif of drowning, becomes a fit symbol for the river of tradition and the moral growth which is associated with the principle of continuity. Legends about the river and Saint Ogg, the boatman who is "the patron saint" of the "ancient town," have become sacred by being handed down from generation to generation (182). With respect to these beliefs, the narrator comments, "One sees little trace of religion, still less of a distinctively Christian creed. Their...moral notions, though held with strong tenacity, seem to have no standard beyond hereditary custom" (362). The ending of *The Mill on the Floss* illustrates the fact that hereditary custom is for Eliot the highest moral sanction.

The river Floss has been tied to the Tulliver family for generations past, and Maggie understands this. From the perspective of Eliot's sense of continuity, Maggie's ties to the river and to her family—particularly her brother Tom—

are stronger than any obligation she might have to Stephen Guest or to Philip Waken. In fact, she tells Philip with grave sadness, "I desire no future that will break the ties of the past. But the tie to my brother is one of the strongest. I can do nothing willingly that will divide me always from him" (463–64). In spite of the fact that Tom's harshness and his severity in passing judgment on Maggie contributed to and was largely responsible for Maggie's suffering, the narrator approves of the fact that Maggie forgives him and says to her readers, "Tom, like every one of us, was imprisoned within the limits of his own nature.... If you are inclined to be severe on his severity, remember that the responsibility of tolerance lies with those who have the wider vision" (630).

After Maggie returns from her extended excursion with Stephen Guest and her brother Tom renounces her forever for what he considers to be her lack of moral judgment (612), in the agonizing days to follow, all of "St. Ogg's passes judgment" (619) and Maggie is strongly advised to leave home. However, she says that she can't leave: "I should feel like a lonely wanderer, — cut off from the past" (626). Maggie has been unable to find any avenue of service which allows her to fulfill her obligations to the past or to leave a meaningful legacy for coming generations. Drowning solves this problem; she will not betray her father and brother's wishes by marrying Philip. Her drowning also frees Stephen from any obligation to her and makes it possible for his love to help to heal Lucy's sorrow which resulted from Maggie's betrayal of her. In many ways, her drowning is a blessing upon Maggie rather than a punishment. On the night of the flood, as she sits in solitude in her room by the river, waiting for her spiritual rebirth, "the long past came back to her" (648).

Every aspect of Maggie's drowning is related to her spiritual dilemmas. In a touching scene, as Maggie's inevitable drowning draws near, Lucy comes and forgives Maggie, and Maggie asks Lucy to forgive Stephen also: "He struggled too.... Forgive him — he will be happy then." Of this comment the narrator observes, "These words were wrung forth from Maggie's deepest soul with an effort like the convulsed clutch of a drowning man" (642). Then it was as Maggie agonized over her response to Stephen's letter that "[t]he long past came back to her and with it the fountains of self-renouncing pity and affection, of faithfulness, and resolve" (648). By this time, Maggie has matured spiritually to the extent that she is ready to face death. She has the wider vision, the moral maturity, which enables her to forgive all those in St. Ogg's who have condemned her and who now refuse to accept her. When she drowns, her life is subsumed into the river of tradition. She is delivered from her suffering which resulted from the moral ambiguity of her situation.

The narrator explains Maggie's drowning in language which sounds incredibly Christian: "Maggie fell on her knees against the table and buried her sorrow-stricken face. Her soul went out to the Unseen Pity that would be with her to the end.... At that moment Maggie felt a startling sensation of sudden cold about her knees ... water flowing under her.... [T]he stream was flowing under the door ... she knew it was the flood!... and she was alone in the darkness with God" (649, 651). Maggie immediately forgets her brother Tom's harshness toward her and hastens to rescue him; when she arrives in her borrowed boat, she says, "God has taken care of me, to bring me to you. Get in quickly" (654). Brother and sister drown together "in an embrace never to be parted" (655). Maggie's drowning is both sacred and sublime.

For Eliot, even near drownings—which are a common occurrence in her novels—are fraught with spiritual significance. In Eliot's first published volume, *Scenes of Clerical Life*, Caterina, in "Mr. Gilfil's Love-Story," runs away in moral turmoil and total despair. She was already suffering because the cruel and selfish Anthony Wybrow betrayed her, and now she fears that she will be accused of murdering him. Mr. Gilfil immediately has "the fatal conviction that Caterina's body would be found in the water" (174). To him the pool "looked black and cruel under the sombre sky, as if its cold depths held relentlessly all the murdered hope and joy of Maynard Gilfil's life" (174). Fortunately, Caterina survives.

In *Adam Bede*, Hetty is suffering because she has been cruelly betrayed by the selfish Arthur Donnithorne. In her lonely despair just before her baby is born, Hetty considers drowning herself but loses her courage when she actually contemplates the dark pool (386). The narrator emphasizes the spiritual significance of the scene by commenting, "You would misunderstand her thoughts during these wretched days, if you imagined that they were influenced either by religious fears or religious hopes.... Religious doctrines had taken no hold on Hetty's mind" (385–86). And so Hetty escapes death by drowning because of her innocence which results from her ignorance of traditional religious belief.

In stark contrast to Caterina in "Mr. Gilfil's Love-Story" and Hetty in *Adam Bede* is Mirah in *Daniel Deronda*, who is preparing to drown herself when Deronda providentially drifts by in his boat and rescues her. Her life has been strongly influenced by religious hopes. Even though her selfish father has literally taken her to a far country, separated her from her loved ones, and denied her the opportunity to worship as she has been taught, she is proud of her Jewish heritage, mature enough to forgive her father, loyal to her own family, and able to identify herself imaginatively with the past history of her people.

Mirah herself is destined to have a special divine role in Deronda's life. At this point Deronda is still unaware of his own Jewish heritage, but when he rescues Mirah, she compels him to assert himself to save her and teaches him that he has his own place in the continuous stream of history. His helping Mirah is his first step toward recognizing his own kinship with the Jewish people and toward his decision to devote his life to preserving the Jewish heritage.

Mirah's entirely positive spiritual role is in distinct contrast to the entirely negative influence of Tito in *Romola*; Tito is at odds with his own heritage and makes every attempt to separate Romola from hers. It is fitting that Tito—who is never what he claims to be—only pretends to drown himself. Tito is "The Shipwrecked Stranger" who comes from an unknown past. He has deliberately cut himself off from his own heritage by abandoning and betraying his foster father (545). In a decisive moment, Tito jumps from the bridge; he plans to pretend to drown and then to swim away in order to escape the angry mob which is pursuing him. Instead, destiny, chance, or Providence delivers Tito out of the water and into the arms of his wronged father, who is conveniently waiting beside the river to kill him.

Tito violates every aspect of the principles of Eliot's morality. Through deception, Tito wins the heart and confidence of Romola and of her father. Romola marries Tito full of high hopes, believing "their young lives should flow in one current and their true marriage would begin" (244). However, unknown to her, Tito is totally selfish and unprincipled; he betrays her trust and literally destroys her tangible ties to the past when, as soon as Romola's father is dead, Tito sells all of the manuscripts and art objects which were so dear to him and which symbolize not only Romola's close ties to her father but her reverence of the past (331).

Savonarola helps Romola to turn her disappointment and grief into an active life of service to others. After a famine comes to Florence, Romola spends her life tending the sick and relieving the hungry; in fact, "[s]he becomes the visible Madonna" (371). Then after Savonarola's martyrdom and Tito's death, Romola is literally transported on water into a whole new level of spiritual existence. She purchases a boat and pushes off into the clear waters of the Mediterranean. A divine force takes hold of her and guides her (504). In the boat, she falls into a long, deep sleep but awakes to discover that "[i]nstead of bringing her to death, it had been the gently lulling cradle of a new life" (551). She lands at a spot where the villagers are suffering from the pestilence. She tells them, "I came over the sea. I am come to take care of you" (554). After some months have passed, during which Romola works to alleviate their suffering, the narrator comments, "The experience was like a new baptism to Romola. And then the past arose with a fresh appeal to her" (561).

One March morning the "little flock" of people she has lovingly served gather together to see "the Blessed Lady," their Madonna, mount her mule and make her triumphal exit (562). She returns to Florence to establish a new family and lasting loving ties with Tito's mistress, Tessa, and his two children by Tessa. Ironically, Tito has quite unintentionally provided Romola with a meaningful way to leave a lasting legacy to generations to come.

In Eliot's long verse drama *The Spanish Gypsy*, Fedalma — whose name means "spiritual fidelity" — knows nothing of her past.[11] Born a Zincali but stolen as an infant by Spanish marauders, she has been brought up as a member of the Spanish royal family and is to marry Don Silva, a Catholic knight, who is heir to the throne. Her unknown past and her future calling are revealed to her when Zarca, her father, appears like the angel Gabriel to announce that she is destined to assume the leadership of the Zincalis and become the saviour of her gypsy tribe. She willingly chooses to assume her inherited messianic role in spite of the fact that she must be forever separated from everyone and everything she has known — including her intended husband. Even after the death of her father, Fedalma's resolve remains firm. At the end of the poem, in a series of profoundly solemn scenes, Fedalma is waiting on the coast to be transported over the sea to accompany the Zincali tribe to the shore of Africa. There she will fulfill the hereditary claim of the past and provide a lasting legacy for generations to come.

Eliot's last novel, *Daniel Deronda*, ends in a similar way, with Deronda and Mirah leaving Mordecai's body and all of their family and friends behind and setting off across the sea to carry out Mordecai's sacred mission. Deronda will fulfill his promises to Mordecai, and together he and Mirah will leave a meaningful legacy to coming generations.

Eliot's characters who allow themselves to be carried away by currents of water to become more fully a part of the stream of tradition seem to receive her highest moral commendation. Deronda's discovery of his past and realization of his mission begin with his floating aimlessly along the Thames. This same sense of letting the water take control is also felt by Romola as she drifts toward her new life. And Maggie also allows herself to flow with the current as she drifts along with Stephen. This willingness to be subsumed in the river of tradition may be enough to ensure that Maggie is indeed blessed by Eliot's providence. Always the consummate artist, Eliot repeatedly uses water in scenes which depict the intervention of her highest moral authority into the lives of her characters.

George Eliot died on December 22, 1880, and was buried in the unconsecrated section of Highgate Cemetery.[12] Her coffin bore an inscription from Dante's *Inferno* (lines 79–80), which may be translated as "That fountain / Which spreads abroad so wide a river of speech."[13] It had been her conscious aim during her lifetime to write books that contained the moral truths which would become a part of the continuous stream of tradition that flows from generation to generation.

Notes

1 Thomas Pinney, "More Leaves from George Eliot's Notebook," *Huntington Library Quarterly* 29.4 (1966): 353–76.

2 "Moral Swindlers," *Impressions of Theophrastus Such*, ed. Nancy Henry (Iowa City: University of Iowa Press, 1994) 173.

3 *The George Eliot Letters*, ed. Gordon S. Haight, 7 vols. (New Haven, CT: Yale University Press, 1955) 4.65.

4 *Letters*, 4.220–21, in correspondence with Frederic Harrison about the composition of *The Spanish Gypsy*. Eliot says of Frederic Harrison's comments on *The Spanish Gypsy*, "Genuine words from one capable of understanding one's conceptions are precious and strengthening" (*Letters*, 4.221). He had said on January 18, 1866, that it was "the highest art for the first time consciously devoted to the deepest moral problems" (*Letters*, 4.220).

5 Quotations from all of George Eliot's novels are from the following Penguin editions and are referenced by page number: *The Mill on the Floss*, ed. A.S. Byatt (London: Penguin, 1979); *Adam Bede*, ed. Stephen Gill (London: Penguin, 1980); *Romola*, ed. Andrew Sanders (London: Penguin, 1980); *Silas Marner*, ed. David Carroll (London: Penguin, 1996); *Daniel Deronda*, ed. Terence Cave (London: Penguin, 1995); *Scenes of Clerical Life*, ed. Jennifer Gribble (London: Penguin, 1998).

6 Ludwig Feuerbach, *The Essence of Christianity*, trans. Marian Evans (London: Trübner, 1854).

7 Included by J.W. Cross as an introduction to *The Spanish Gypsy*, entitled "Notes on the Spanish Gypsy and Tragedy in General," *The Works of George Eliot*, 21 vols. (Boston: Little, Brown, 1908) 1.15–16.

8 "To Mrs. Henry Frederick Ponsonby on December 10, 1874," *Letters*, 6.98.

9 "Judgments of Authors," Leaves from a Notebook, *Works of George Eliot*, 2.355–56.

10 "The Morality of Wilhelm Meister," *Leader* 6 (21 July 1855): 247–51, reprinted in *Essays of George Eliot*, ed. Thomas Pinney (New York: Columbia University Press, 1963) 47.

11 *George Eliot: Collected Poems*, ed. Lucien Jenkins (London: Skoob, 1989).

12 George Willis Cooke, *George Eliot: A Critical Study of Her Life, Writings and Philosophy* (Boston: J.R. Osgood, 1883) 101–2.

13 Ibid., 103.

CHRISTINA ROSSETTI AND THE POETICS OF TRACTARIAN SUFFERING

Esther T. Hu

Beginning with Gilbert and Gubar, feminist critics have read Rossetti's poetry as a poetry in which the poet must "learn to suffer and renounce the self-gratifications of art and sensuality."[1] Gilbert and Gubar argue that Rossetti, as "a representative female poet-speaker," must "learn to sing selflessly, despite pain"; they see an "extraordinary, masochistic vision" illuminating the moral aesthetic of poems like "Goblin Market" and "From House to Home." In "From House to Home," for example, "the Christ-like poet of Rossetti's vision drinks the bitterness of self-abnegation, and *then* sings." The woman artist can be "strengthened 'to live' only through doses of paradoxically bittersweet pain"; Rossetti, banqueting on bitterness, must "bury herself alive in a coffin of renunciation."

Gilbert and Gubar's highly influential reading continues to inform the general understanding of Rossetti and her art. Yet placing her work in its Victorian religious context adjusts, and sometimes corrects, this traditional feminist view of her poems as enactments of self-repression, masochism, or self-renunciation. But how *did* the poet approach pain and suffering? In this essay, I will examine several Rossetti poems that especially address suffering, grief, and pain from *Verses* (1893), her collection of 331 poems published a year before her death and culled from her *Called to be Saints: The Minor Festivals Devotionally Studied* (1883), *Time Flies: A Reading Diary* (1885), and *The Face of the Deep: A Devotional Commentary on the Apocalypse* (1892). Significantly, Rossetti herself was suffering from breast cancer while she arranged and revised the poems in *Verses*; the creation of the volume thus occurs at "a point

in Rossetti's life where her poetry, her religion, and her terminal illness intersect."[2] Since Rossetti's understanding of human suffering was informed by
Tractarian theology,[3] reading her work in relation to sermons by Oxford
Movement leaders John Keble, E.B. Pusey, and John Henry Newman helps
clarify her religious emphases and investments. Within a Tractarian context,
we see that suffering is part of a position that was central to Tractarian theology, rather than simply an expression of individual temperament or pathology. Pain and tribulation might offer opportunities to correct faults and
cleanse the soul. Suffering affords a way of identifying with and coming close
to the suffering Christ in his Passion and provides a conduit to experiencing
the Divine. Submitting to pain and sorrow also might constitute a voluntary
sacrifice that can appropriately be given to the Creator. For Rossetti, suffering,
beginning with a wrestling with the angel of God, offers a way for the Christian to seek Christ's blessing; her poems reflect, and often enact, the grasping
of faith as it is being tested and refined in the crucible of pain. The ultimate
challenge is for the poet-speaker to trust in divine goodness, or to *will* to trust,
even amidst bleak and barren external circumstances or while drinking the
bitter cup of pain and sorrow.

By 1843, Rossetti was worshipping at Christ Church, Albany Street, whose
incumbent minister, William Dodsworth, followed the teachings of Edward
Pusey. In "The Value and Sacredness of Suffering," Pusey preaches that suffering is Christ's "healing medicine, to burn out our wounds and purify us for
His Presence";[4] all sufferings, from "the most passing pain of the body to the
most deep-seated anguish of the soul" are messengers from Christ, the Physician of our souls. The "great Physician [looks] graciously upon our spots and
sores, checking our diseases ere they take deep root ... cutting deeply and
healthfully into our very souls, if He have compassion upon us, when we have
deeply offended Him."[5]

The Tractarian view of suffering grounds itself in a startling conviction:
God's character and purposes remain good even when his children endure
pain. Thus Christ's incisions in the Christian soul show his compassion; suffering purges and purifies the soul as the Maker's hand fashions the soul's
"imperfect or decayed substance." Despite the pain, suffering paradoxically
exemplifies God's "Fatherly care": He "temper[s] our cup with pain and sorrow, as He sees most needful for us." Pusey exhorts that all suffering—"pain,
sickness, weariness, distress, languor, agony of mind or body, whether in ourselves or others"—should be treated with a spirit of reverence: in itself, "it
were the earnest of Hell," but through Christ's mercy, "it is a purifying for
Heaven." Earthly suffering prepares souls for eternity.[6]

In a passage congruent with Tractarian theology, Rossetti observes that suffering is a means of refining the Christian soul.[7] Sorrow is a kind of teaching,

a way of purification and cleansing, and tribulation, rather than ease, "constructs the safe road and the firm stepping-stone."[8] Possibly recalling "whom the Lord loveth he correcteth" (Prov. 3:12 AV),[9] she continues, "Better to be taught with thorns of the wilderness and briars, than in no wise to be taught. Better great tribulation now than unexampled tribulation hereafter."[10] The poem following this reflection, also sandwiched between the poems for "Ash Wednesday" and "Lent" in *Verses*, reads:

> Good Lord, today
> I scarce find breath to say:
>   Scourge, but receive me.
> For stripes are hard to bear, but worse
> Thy intolerable curse;
>   So do not leave me.
>
> Good Lord, lean down
> In pity, tho' Thou frown;
>   Smite, but retrieve me:
> For so Thou hold me up to stand
> And kiss Thy smiting hand,
>   It less will grieve me.[11]

Smiting, akin to Pusey's violent imagery, becomes a necessary corrective to faults. "If Thou smite us," Rossetti reflects, "let it be with the sores of holy Job unto amendment and perfection.... By pain bring back our pleasure.... Be our pangs schoolmasters to bring us to Christ."[12] Asking Christ to "scourge" and to "smite" is part of the "sifting" that comes with tribulation: in suffering and pain, Christ separates the wheat of the soul from the chaff and adjusts the soul's condition. Elsewhere Rossetti says that "sifting reclaims and releases good from bad, while aught of good remains." The process is painful, but it yields a harvest of eternal rewards: "Now no chastening for the present seemeth to be joyous, but grievous: nevertheless afterward it yieldeth the peaceable fruit of righteousness unto them which are exercised thereby."[13] In Rossetti's own life, physical illness and pain may be instruments for "sifting"; in a January 1893 letter to Mrs. Henry Sutton, Rossetti describes her experience recovering from her mastectomy in spiritual terms: "1892 was a year of severe illness, and I little knew how much I had to learn till thus tried and *sifted*. Now I too am very much stronger and better, yet I do not expect ever to be quite what I was before this *salutary* experience."[14] Apparently she viewed the removal of cancer as also an occasion for spiritual surgery: while physically she will never be the same, spiritually she has become "stronger."

The story of Job provides the most famous example of spiritual sifting in suffering. Traditionally, Christian exegesis of the narrative works to reconcile the essential goodness and trustworthiness of God with the apparent evil of suffering. "Though He slay me, yet will I trust in Him" (Job 13:15), Job's utterance—still hopeful despite having lost both the fruit of his loins and the fruit of his labours in one fell swoop (Job 1:1–2, 2:7)—appears as a recurring theme in Tractarian writings and in Rossetti's devotional work. And just as Job asserts his trust in God's sovereignty and purpose amidst unfathomable loss, grief, and physical pain, the Tractarians insist that such suffering ultimately proves useful and may even be salutary:

> For, mostly, those severe blows whereby God brings the soul to itself, are a rending from it part of itself, since they are a rending from it, what it loved, as, perhaps, more than, itself—Yet torn, bleeding, scarce alive, except for suffering, as the soul may thus be; bewildered, dead to all interest, or care, or pleasure in things around it; as if it were dead, yet are these the lightest trials of the returning soul.[15]

In Pusey's sermon, the violent language of Divine Chastisement sounds alien to a twenty-first-century reader. But the suffering strips the soul bare and makes it dead to "all interest, or care, or pleasure in things around it," facilitating a homecoming for the soul ("returning soul").[16] An opportunity for the suffering soul to experience God's presence becomes superior to enjoying his blessings:

> For to feel a nearness of God, even in chastisement, is a deeper, stiller, aweful indeed, yet more thrilling joy, than the intensest, or the most even tide of joy, on which the soul rested, even as the gift of God. Even in the most penetrating of this life's chastisements, God replaces His gifts with the hope of Himself. Chastisement is blessed to the trusting soul, because, though an aweful Form of His Presence, it *is* His Presence. "The Lord," saith the Psalmist, "hath chastened and corrected me: but He hath not given me over unto death."... To know that one is chastened, is to know that one is not abandoned.[17]

Furthermore, the soul re-enacts the choice of Christ on the Cross, and the promise of the Resurrection: "'Though He slay me, I will trust in Him'.... The great holy words will mean yet more, 'Lo! If He slay me, I will trust in Him,' not 'although' only, but '*because*' He slayeth me. It is life to be touched by the hand of God; to be slain is, through the Cross of Christ, the pledge of the Resurrection."[18] Like Christ, through death one will rise again; suffering marks one for eternity.

Rossetti's speaker places a similar confidence in her Maker during the soul's purging process. "Though He slay me, yet will I trust in Him" appears as a recurring theme in her devotional poetic, but here Rossetti's poems enact Pusey's sermons. The first stanza of an eight-line poem in *Verses* reads:

> Shall not the Judge of all the earth do right?
> Yea, Lord, altho' Thou say me nay:

Shall not His Will be to me life and light?
Yea, Lord, altho' Thou slay.
("Shall not the Judge of all the earth do right?" lines 1–4)

What first appears as a dialogue between a soul and her Maker is in actuality a monologue: the speaker who asks is the speaker who responds. Though slaying and sifting, smiting and scourging are natural steps preparing a heaven-bound soul, in the refinement process the speaker still anxiously requests her Maker to "turn" and "see," not so much to watch but to *watch over* her. Like Job, who amidst suffering and confusion entreats God to "remember" him (Job 14:13), here the poet-speaker pleads for the Lord to "remember"—He should "remember [her]" (line 7)—five times in four lines. After reminding the Lord of her heart's desires and her very self, she simply lets go and trusts him to "do" (line 8):

Yet, Lord, remembering turn and sift and see,
Remember tho' Thou sift me thro',
Remember my desire, remember me,
Remember, Lord, and do. (lines 5–8)

In other poems Christ not only turns and sees, but also responds to the speaker, assuring her that he is near and urges her to trust in him. In "Palm Sunday," Christ says,

"Judge not before that day:
Trust Me with all thy heart, even tho' I slay:
Trust Me in love, trust on, love on, and pray." (lines 28–30)

And in "I, Lord, thy foolish sinner low and small," Christ comforts a bewildered soul:

I see
The measure and the number of thy day:
Keep patience, tho' I slay;
Keep patience till thou see My Face.
Follow thou Me. (lines 29–33)

Complementing the patience that Christ asks the soul to keep is a conviction not to see a hopeless situation of suffering or sorrow as final but to remember that life can spring from lifeless sorrow. Rossetti writes, "Let us encourage ourselves though He slay us yet to trust in Him, by help of some of those parables of nature familiar to us all which speak of life reborn from lifelessness, or from death or decay. A leafless tree, a chrysalis, a buried seed, an egg."[19]

Just as life may sprout from lifelessness in the natural world ("buried seed"),[20] life may yet burst forth from spiritual desolation; as she says in "Judge not according to the appearance," we should purge our eyes to see "Within the seed a tree, / Within the glowing egg a bird, / Within the shroud a butterfly" (lines 2–4)—until we see God himself. Trusting in God stems from an inner, visceral conviction that may be divorced from outward appearances or circumstances, even as it may be challenging to *will* such trust. Rossetti discusses the difficulty but also the sufficiency of achieving such trust when she reminds readers of Job's resolution during the dark night of his soul. She exhorts:

> "Though He slay me, yet will I trust in Him."—This is one sort of dead man who shall live, together with Christ's once-dead Body shall he arise. Perhaps for us the main point of the text roots itself in the word *will*. None predicates of him *he can* nor yet *he ought*: he alone says, and says only, *I will*. He says not, I do; for far from him be lying lips and a deceitful tongue. He says, I will: and the man who has the will to say, I will, has latent within him the power to bring to pass by God's assisting grace the purpose of that good will. His dew is as the dew of herbs, his earth shall cast out her dead.[21]

A corollary to trusting in the ultimate goodness of divine will is approaching suffering with a grateful attitude. For the Tractarians, suffering constitutes a sacrifice of *thanksgiving*. In a sermon entitled "Our Sacrifice of Pain and Sorrow," John Keble preaches that one may bring one's troubles to Christ "to be pitied and assuaged and healed," or at least to obtain grace to bear them "patiently and thankfully."[22] Christ permits the Christian to offer up her "fears and sorrows"; "afflictions and miseries" can be made "an acceptable sacrifice of thanksgiving to Him Who sends all for our good."[23] This offering of pain requires the relinquishing of the self, the soul, and the body to Christ, "to be helped no otherwise than by His merciful Right Hand…when He will and as He will."[24] Taking the leper from the Gospel (Matt. 8) as an example, Keble observes that although the leper had nothing to offer but a body corrupted with disease and a soul wounded and weakened by sin, his offering to God was "true sacrifice, because he gave himself up so entirely," saying, "Lord, if Thou wilt, Thou canst make me clean."[25] For Keble, this kind of self-surrender constitutes an appropriate offering to God; it remains valuable even if the self offered does not seem to be.

Keble offers a counterintuitive response to the bitterness that usually accompanies suffering; he exhorts Christians to approach suffering with a grateful spirit and to offer up pain and sorrow as a personal sacrifice so that Christ may help and heal. It is in this Tractarian theological context that we are to understand the poet-speaker's offering. She gives the Lord her burdened heart, the Keblean equivalent of giving up soul and body, even as she doubts its acceptability:

A burdened heart that bleeds and bears
    And hopes and waits in pain,
And faints beneath its fears and cares,
    Yet hopes again:

Wilt Thou accept the heart I bring,
    O gracious Lord and kind,
To ease it of a torturing sting,
    And staunch and bind?

Alas, if Thou wilt none of this,
    None else have I to give:
Look Thou upon it as it is,
    Accept, relieve.

Or if Thou wilt not yet relieve,
    Be not extreme to sift:
Accept a faltering will to give,
    Itself Thy gift.
        ("When I was in trouble I called upon the Lord," lines 1–16)

The poem itself enacts her offering Christ a suffering heart, with pauses between stanzas as caesuras waiting for Christ's response. First she asks him to take and cure her heart ("ease it of a torturing sting"), "staunch" and "bind" implying that Christ's healing touch can restore her heart to health. But as if receiving no reply to her request that he cure her heart, she asks him to take it "as it is" (line 11) — to "accept" and "relieve" it in its present broken condition (line 12). But again there is no reply, so she pleads that at least he may accept her *will* to give her heart to him; this is itself a worthy gesture, a poetic reification of Keble's exhortation to offer up to Christ one's pain and sorrow. If he won't accept her heart, he will accept her will to give it, even though it is a faltering will. The gesture of offering up a broken heart to Christ stems from humility: the speaker asks Christ to "[b]e not extreme to sift" in case the offering proves unacceptable, in case there is a disproportionate amount of chaff with the grain, or (heart) debris among treasure (line 14). Look not to the bleeding heart, but to the will — albeit faint and weak — the speaker says, when deciding whether or not to accept this heart gift. Whether God replies to this last request, the poem does not say.

    We observe the progression of feeling in the poem: with each absence of positive response, the speaker goes down to something more fundamental, so that in the end she asks Christ to accept not her heart, but her heart's desire to give him a gift, hoping that the desire in itself will prove acceptable in Christ's sight. "Accept" appears in three of the four stanzas, reinforcing both the speaker's desire to present and offer the seat of her volition ("heart") to Christ and her determined plea for unconditional acceptance of her will, her very being. The hope she yearns for in stanza one points to restoration, renewal, relief, and, above all, Christ's acceptance of her in her present condition. Like the woman who (literally) suffered from twelve years of bleeding and believed that touching Christ's cloak would heal her (Matt. 9:20–22; Mark 5:25–34), Rossetti's speaker hopes that Christ would staunch and bind her bleeding heart. But restoration does not stop at the level either of flesh or of metaphor: just as Christ publicly acknowledges the woman's physical healing, commends her faith and restores her back to her community, Rossetti's speaker yearns for a restoration not only of a bleeding heart, but also of her faltering will and her very self. In paring down her gift from heart to will, the speaker peels off layers to arrive at the essence of her being.

Yet occasionally it is not possible to offer to Christ one's broken heart without his help; offering one's brokenness as a sacrifice of pain and sorrow, stated so simply in Keble's sermons, entails struggle. The speaker in "Sursum Corda" entreats Christ to bend down and take up her heart since she remains powerless to lift it up. The poem's emotional trajectory curves towards the speaker giving her heart and self and Christ receiving the speaker's heart and self, even as in the first line she quotes people saying what she cannot:

> "Lift up your hearts." "We lift them up." Ah me!
> I cannot, Lord, lift up my heart to Thee:
> Stoop, lift it up, that where Thou art I too may be.
>
> "Give Me thy heart." I would not say Thee nay,
> But have no power to keep or give away
> My heart: stoop, Lord, and take it to Thyself today.
>
> Stoop, Lord, as once before, now once anew
> Stoop, Lord, and hearken, hearken, Lord, and do,
> And take my will, and take my heart, and take me too. (lines 1–9)

The poem begins with varied voices. A priest asks congregation members to "Lift up [their] hearts," and they are able to, apparently easily. But the speaker cannot, and so she responds with an imperative of her own. She repeatedly asks Christ to stoop and lift her heart for her, to take the heart that she struggles to give. All she can give is the *will* to give, and the will to have Christ bend down in tender mercy as he once did before (line 7). Such hope presupposes a God who remembers her "low estate" (Ps. 136:23).

"Have I not striven, my God, and watched and prayed?" is unique in its Rossettian response to pain and suffering. The speaker neither welcomes adversity as a possibility for improvement nor thinks of pain as a worthy offering to the Creator. Instead, she asks four hectoring questions that illuminate her current painful condition:

> Have I not striven, my God, and watched and prayed?
>   I not wrestled in mine agony?
>   Wherefore still turn Thy Face of Grace from me?
> Is Thine Arm shortened that Thou canst not aid? (lines 1–4)

The litany of verbs in the present perfect — have striven, have watched, have prayed — attests to the intense effort and energy that the speaker has devoted to her religious endeavours, pious exercises completed in her wrestling with suffering, but without the anticipated effect of divine solace. The speaker matches the intensity of her disappointment with the parallelisms of intensification in the questions "Have I not striven" and "Have I not wrestled," the accretion of each verb building towards the stark description of her emotional state: she is "in … agony" (line 2). Confiding and personal, she vents her frustrations to God; her tone prepares the reader for the complaints bordering on lament. Lines three and four introduce doubts about God's character: there is something cruel about the Face of Grace *still* being turned from her, instead of towards her, and she wonders if God's arm is too short to assist her. This ludicrous suggestion borders on sarcasm, since surely God's reach is not limited by a physical arm. The speaker's complaints sound hauntingly similar to the ones voiced by Gerard Manley Hopkins's speaker in a sonnet of religious desolation:

>   and why must
> Disappointment all I endeavour end?
>   Wert thou my enemy, O thou my friend,
> How wouldst thou worse, I wonder, than thou dost
> Defeat, thwart me?"[26]

Like Hopkins's speaker, who calls God "[his] friend" (line 6), Rossetti's speaker presupposes that God is on her side. But in facing disappointment and unremitting suffering, both speakers become indignant and question God's purposes. Unlike Hopkins's speaker, though, Rossetti's speaker continues to hope for a response:

> Thy silence breaks my heart: speak tho' to upbraid,
>   For Thy rebuke yet bids us follow Thee.
>   I grope and grasp not; gaze, but cannot see.
> When out of sight and reach my bed is made,
>
> And piteous men and women cease to blame
>   Whispering and wistful of my gain or loss;
>   Thou Who for my sake once didst feel the Cross,

> Lord, wilt Thou turn and look upon me then,
> And in Thy Glory bring to nought my shame,
> Confessing me to angels and to men? (lines 5–14)

Even though her prayers have met a reticent heaven, she requests that Christ break the silence even if only to reprimand her, for at least she would have his voice to guide her when she blindly searches for direction and cannot see the end of her pain. Her tone changes in the second half of this octet, and she cannot keep up with her verbal wrestling because she is just too sad. "I grope and grasp not; gaze, but cannot see" (line 7) — the alliterative gs perhaps an auditory insistence in reaching for God, even if her attempts appear futile. Christ can neither be touched nor seen, no matter how far she reaches or how intensely she looks. The end rhymes "Thee" and "see" in lines 6 and 7 emphasize the speaker's longing for her Creator even in her protracted agony and with the possibility of chastisement. But whereas she can neither grasp nor gaze on Christ in line 7, in line 8 it is the speaker herself who is "out of sight and reach" — far from everyone else's grasp and gaze. And it is at the volta, when we turn to the sestet, that we realize that "piteous men and women" cease to blame her and whisper about her because she no longer remains in their midst.

The world's gossip and the speaker's shame both belong to the world of erotic poetry, but here Rossetti uses worldly shame for spiritual purposes, the gossip and whispering propelling her speaker to ask God to turn and look on her. It is in the afterlife that she asks God to be both her adjudicator and her witness, "confessing [her] to angels and to men" (line 14); she believes that the Cross of Christ can blot out both her shame and her loss, as reinforced by the "Cross" and "loss" end rhymes. She couches her hope, however, in the form of a question: "Lord, *wilt Thou* turn and look upon me then, / And in Thy Glory bring to nought my shame, / Confessing me to angels and to men?" (lines 12–14, italics mine). Given that Christ already for her sake "once [did] feel the Cross," the answer to the question would be an emphatic "Yes," since by Rossetti's logic, if Christ already gave his life for her, surely he would be willing to "turn and look" upon her and speak on her behalf. Though the sonnet ends with a question mark, her question is rhetorical: Rossetti's speaker poses a situation that has already been scripted, since Christ, who is seated at the right hand of God, already intercedes on her behalf (Rom. 8:34). The sonnet ends in a recovery from its initial desolation with a hope that Christ will turn his "Face of Grace" (line 3) towards, not away from, the speaker (line 12). "Have I not striven" thus points to the comfort of knowing that ultimately Christ would acknowledge her agony and "bring to nought" her shame. And it is only in finishing the sonnet that we realize that Rossetti's speaker suffers not from some physical ailment or debilitating illness. Her mental pain and emotional suffering because of other people's words and looks have forced her to seek refuge in the Divine, though on this side of paradise he has not yet acted on her behalf: absent is the self-assurance found in Sonnet 11 of *Monna Innominata* ("Even let them prate; who know not what we knew" [line 5]).

In his sermon "Affliction, a School of Comfort," John Henry Newman says that suffering draws God's saints closer to Christ:

> He brings them into pain, that they may be like what Christ was, and may be led to think of Him, not of themselves. He brings them into trouble, that they may be near Him. When they mourn, they are more intimately in His presence than they are at any other time. Bodily pain, anxiety, bereavement, distress, are to them His forerunners. It is a solemn thing, while it is a privilege, to look upon those whom He thus visits.... He who has been long under the rod of God, becomes God's possession. He bears in his body marks, and is sprinkled with drops, which nature could not provide for him.[27]

Newman's words echo Keble's and Pusey's exhortations; pain and sorrow draw the Christian soul closer to God and help her identify with Christ's Passion. Yet Christ does not leave the suffering soul by herself. The theological premise that Christ has borne the Christian's sorrows, and continues to bear the Christian upon her hill of sorrows, provides the theme for "Good Friday Morning":

Up Thy Hill of Sorrows
    Thou all alone,
Jesus, man's Redeemer,
    Climbing to a Throne:
Thro' the world triumphant,
    Thro' the Church in pain,
Which think to look upon Thee
    No more again.

Upon my hill of sorrows
    I, Lord, with Thee,
Cheered, upheld, yea, carried,
    If a need should be:
Cheered, upheld, yea, carried,
    Never left alone,
Carried in Thy heart of hearts
    To a throne. (lines 1–16)

There is no main verb in either stanza; no grammatical completeness. The rhythms are mimetic, with Christ carrying the speaker step by step as marked by the commas ("Cheered, upheld, yea, carried," lines 11, 13). That Christ carries the speaker in her sorrows "if a need should be" should provide solace for the grieving Christian: Christ endured his sorrows alone, but the Christian need not suffer alone. Since Christ is a "Man of Sorrows, and acquainted with grief" (Isa. 53:3), he can carry the suffering Christian in her sorrow with empathy. As Rossetti writes elsewhere, "In sickness, let Thy cross sustain us; in bereavement, Thy desertion by Thy friends; in depression, the hiding of Thy Father's Face: and in death, hold Thou us fast in Thine everlasting Arms."[28] "Good Friday Morning" was the only previously unpublished poem added to *Verses* (1893). In her own suffering with breast cancer, the poet-speaker still hopes and trusts: we see no grave but a throne, and the speaker's "resting place is now the heart of Jesus."[29]

In her devotional prose, Rossetti acknowledges that at the Apocalypse she will witness the abolition of all tears, death, sorrow, crying, and pain.[30] Revelation 21:4 says, "And God shall wipe away all tears from their eyes, and there shall be no more death, neither sorrow, nor crying, neither shall there be any more pain: for the former things are passed away." On this side of paradise, however, suffering draws a soul closer to her Maker, offering opportunities to experience Christ's presence as he helps carry her and her sorrows uphill. Sorrow and pain are instruments Christ uses to purify and heal a heaven-bound soul. As a sacrifice of thanksgiving and hope, suffering might restore and reorient the soul. Rossetti's, then, is hardly a masochistic vision of suffering where the poet-speaker "drinks the bitterness of self-abnegation, and *then* sings";[31] it is a vision that lends suffering dignity and hope for renewed intimacy with Christ. As spiritual preparation for eternity, suffering strengthens the Christian soul. Through trusting Christ, the Christian soul learns to sing.

Notes

1 Sandra Gilbert and Susan Gubar, *The Madwoman in the Attic: The Woman Writer and the Nineteenth-Century Literary Imagination* (New Haven, CT: Yale University Press, 1979) 571; future citations from this work are taken from pages 571–75.
2 Diane D'Amico, "Christina Rossetti's Breast Cancer: 'Another Matter, Painful to Dwell Upon,'" *Journal of Pre-Raphaelite Studies* 15 (Fall 2006): 39.
3 Recent scholarship has examined Rossetti's indebtedness to Tractarian tradition. Diane D'Amico and David Kent's review, "Rossetti and the Tractarians" (*Victorian Poetry* 44.1 [2006]: 93–103), traces contributions by Raymond Chapman, G.B. Tennyson, Linda Marshall, Anthony Harrison, Mary Arseneau, Lorraine Kooistra, Lynda Palazzo, and others who have explored the connections between Rossetti and the Oxford Movement. See also Diane D'Amico's *Christina Rossetti: Faith, Gender and Time* (Baton Rouge: Louisiana State University Press, 1999); Mary Arseneau's *Recovering Christina Rossetti: Female Community and Incarnational Poetics* (New York: Palgrave, 2004); Dinah Roe's *Christina Rossetti's Faithful Imagination: The Devotional Poetry and Prose* (New York: Palgrave, 2007); Esther T. Hu's "Christina Rossetti, John Keble, and the Divine Gaze" (*Victorian Poetry* 46.2 [2008]: 175–89).

4 E.B. Pusey, *Parochial Sermons*, 3 vols. (Oxford: James Parker, 1873) 3.129.

5 Ibid., 130.

6 Ibid., 130–31.

7 Christina Rossetti, *The Face of the Deep: A Devotional Commentary on the Apocalypse* (London: Society for Promoting Christian Knowledge, 1892) 235.

8 Ibid., 235.

9 Subsequent biblical quotations are from the Authorized (King James) Version.

10 Rossetti, *The Face of the Deep*, 235.

11 *Christina Rossetti: The Complete Poems*, text by R.W. Crump and notes and introduction by Betty S. Flowers (London: Penguin, 2001) 430, lines 1–12; subsequent citations from Rossetti's poetry are from this edition and will be referenced in the text by line number.

12 Rossetti, *The Face of the Deep*, 381, 382.

13 Ibid., 236.

14 Christina Rossetti, letter to Mrs. Henry Septimus Sutton, 2 Jan. 1893, *The Letters of Christina Rossetti: Vol. 4*, ed. Antony H. Harrison (Charlottesville: University of Virginia Press, 2004) 308; italics mine.

15 Pusey, *Parochial Sermons*, 3.162.

16 Ibid.

17 Ibid.

18 Ibid., 166.

19 Rossetti, *The Face of the Deep*, 42.

20 Ibid.

21 Ibid., 87.

22 John Keble, Sermon XXXV, "Our Sacrifice of Pain and Sorrow," *Sermons for Christmas and Epiphany* (Oxford: James Parker, 1875) 349.

23 Ibid.

24 Ibid., 352, 350.

25 Ibid., 350.

26 "Thou art indeed just, Lord," *Poems and Prose of Gerard Manley Hopkins*, ed. W.H. Gardner (1953; New York: Penguin, 1985) 67, lines 3–7.

27 John Henry Newman, *Parochial and Plain Sermons*, vol. 5 (London: Longmans, Green, 1907) 307.

28 Christina Rossetti, *Annus Domini: A Prayer for Each Day of the Year, Founded on a Text of Holy Scripture* (Oxford: James Parker, 1874) 139.

29 D'Amico, "Christina Rossetti's Breast Cancer," 41.

30 Rossetti, *The Face of the Deep*, 486.

31 Gilbert and Gubar, *The Madwoman in the Attic*, 572.

SUFFERING IN WORD AND IN TRUTH: SEVENTEENTH- AND NINETEENTH-CENTURY QUAKER WOMEN'S AUTOBIOGRAPHY

Robynne Rogers Healey

"Who hath writ more than a Quaker?" asked the late-seventeenth-century polemicist (and former Quaker) Francis Bugg.[1] Who indeed? The Society of Friends is well known for its commitment to the written word. Since the sect began in the mid-seventeenth century, Friends have meticulously recorded their meetings, crafted works of faith and practice, and exhorted one another with epistolary correspondence, producing a body of corporate literature that rivals that of other sects in its extent. Within this body of collective literature, autobiography emerges as a singularly central genre of individual Quaker writing. It is so prevalent that one early-twentieth-century Quaker apologist was led to observe that "no sect has ever been so autobiographical as we."[2] Posthumously published memoirs, diaries, narratives, meditations, religious exercises, and journals all provide examples of Quakers who exhibited sterling qualities in their spiritual lives. According to the Society's Book of Discipline, "commemorate[ing] the lives of the righteous" provided an "incentive to the living to emulate their virtues."[3] Quakers' written expression of their devotion to the Word and to Truth is rooted in part in the theology of Christopresentism (the belief that God is in everyone) and the conviction among the earliest Friends that the Inner or Inward Light—the Word—was manifest both corporeally and linguistically. The term "Quaker," after all, was a derisive one

coined by Friends' detractors in reference to the emotional shaking and trembling experienced at early meetings for worship. For Quakers, the deep connection between the body and the divinely inspired Word created an alternative language.[4] As Nigel Smith explains, "the body [became] scripture in the
Quaker imagination."[5] Michele Lise Tarter argues that Friends' awareness that
the power of prophetic language could be transmitted in writing resulted in
the creation of "their own literary theory for the writing, printing, and reading of texts" wherein "literature…was a most forceful medium for reaching
and convincing readers throughout the world, and…reading was potentially
the most powerful agent for apocalyptic change."[6]

Certainly, the vision of Quaker literature as an important spiritual and
political force created an ongoing commitment to the production of transformational writing. Women's voices figured prominently in this work; this is
reflected in the large body of current scholarship focusing on seventeenth-
century Quaker women's self-writings.[7] The enthusiastic faith expressed in
the literature of the first generation of Friends gave way to something strik-
ingly different in subsequent generations. A marked increase in persecutions,
incarcerations, and even deaths among Friends, in part related to the bizarre
behaviour of some of the Society's members, led to a perceived need for
change. Based on its stated desire "that Truth should not suffer," and the
necessity for an outward expression of corporate spiritual unity, some of the
Society's leaders implemented a system of discipline and governance that
allowed it to rein in any "fringe" elements. The case of James Nayler was particularly important in this regard. Nayler took over leadership of Friends in
1656 when George Fox was arrested and jailed on a charge of sedition. During
Fox's incarceration, Nayler engaged in public behaviours that suggested he
was claiming to be Christ. At one point, reminiscent of Christ's triumphant
entry into Jerusalem, Nayler rode into Bristol preceded by his followers who
cried, "holy, holy, holy" and strewed their garments in his path. The response
of Parliament was swift and punitive. The response of the Society's leadership
was transformational for Friends.

In 1657 steps were taken to organize a national assembly, and in 1660 the
first representative meeting of Quakers in England was held. Fox and his ministerial supporters organized a system of business meetings that culminated in
the London Yearly Meeting. They also created a series of "advices" to counsel
Quakers on their behaviour and way of life. These included a set of queries,
established in 1700, that pertained to the observance of Quaker testimonies.
This provided a mechanism by which the yearly meeting could monitor the
behaviour of members in subordinate meetings. Shortly after the queries were
introduced, a collection of rules for behaviour, the Book of Discipline, was
adopted. From that point, the Discipline governed a Quaker's life from birth

to death, codifying appropriate behaviour. The structure the leadership imposed on the Society effectively brought what threatened to become an unruly flock into a framework where control was centralized and monitored.

Part of the extensive structure of meetings that emerged among British Friends was the Second Day Morning Meeting (initiated in 1672), a censoring committee that approved every publication of the Society, "leav[ing] out what they see not of Service to the Truth."[8] A similar task was carried out in the British North American colonies by each of the yearly meetings' respective Meeting for Sufferings, the first of which was established in 1756. The effect of regulation was, as scholars have frequently noted, an increasingly formulaic literature both in language and content, Luella Wright even suggesting that what transpired after the first generation of Quaker writing was "barrenness."[9]

Did Quaker literature become barren in the wake of its fecund origins in prophetic, enthusiastic, and transformative language that was located both in the body and on the page? I suggest that the scant interest paid to nineteenth-century Quaker literature especially by non-Quaker scholars is no doubt the result of the perception that later Quaker autobiography is indeed "barren." This is especially the case for women's writing, which under the hand of male censors, appears to have lost much of its female voice.[10]

Without a doubt, by the nineteenth century, Quaker autobiography had become invariably formulaic. It documented a deep spiritual suffering through which the writer had to pass, demonstrating the importance of denying the temporal world and taking up the cross of the spiritual life. The eventual step of denial was often foreshadowed with divine visitations in childhood followed by a series of crises, most of which occurred when the individuals in question were in adolescence or early adulthood. These spiritual crises, which always included severe mental or physical trials, provided the fodder for instruction in the moral and virtuous life. Pressed as they were through the censor's mould, these works appear to reflect few of the transformative qualities of the earliest journals. Yet, if we place nineteenth-century Quaker women's self-writings into the context of the tumultuous period of evangelical fervour and the doctrinal schisms that tore apart many of the North American yearly meetings and seriously damaged the London Yearly Meeting (the mother of all other Quaker meetings), an interesting link to the literature of the prophetic period emerges. In both eras, the corporeality of suffering in Word and Truth was central as a proof text to the narrative of rebirth. Stories of violent physical suffering, either as brutal persecution in the seventeenth century or intense illness and trials in the nineteenth century, embodied the regeneration of the Inner Light. Moreover, within the context of the rigidly gender-codified world of the nineteenth century, women's bodies once again spoke as their own texts from within written works heavily edited by men.

What appear on the one hand to be standard nineteenth-century stories of the frail female body—the weaker vessel—are also accounts of strong, resourceful activists. Read within the context of Quaker informal education—and this is certainly how they must be considered[11]—the memorials and autobiographies of the Society's women ministers across time reveal a vibrant female leadership dedicated to reform and renewal both within and without the Society.

Seventeenth-Century Bodies in Quaker Literature

During the Restoration, Friends throughout the British world endured immense persecution or "sufferings" that included public ridicule, the seizure of property, incarceration in cruel conditions, flogging, disfiguration—tongue borings were particularly popular—and public execution.[12] In response to persecution, the Society developed a number of strategies to minimize the effects of these attacks. The Meeting for Sufferings was created by the London Yearly Meeting in 1675 and performed a number of tasks. It enlisted public support for Quakerism by giving maximum publicity to sufferings and to portraying Friends in a positive light. It also lobbied for changes to the law that would declare certain types of persecution unlawful. Friends also encouraged one another with promises of the dire fate awaiting their persecutors.[13] Central to these strategies was the development of a theology of suffering. Rosemary Moore describes this as "a unity with the experience of Christ through which suffering came to be seen as a necessary part of salvation and entry into God's kingdom."[14] This theology was critical to shifting the way in which suffering was understood. Instead of viewing suffering as punishment from God, a common perception in the seventeenth century, suffering came to be seen as part of God's plan for the Society of Friends. Quakers believed themselves to be united with Christ. There were a number of biblical texts, such as Revelation and Mark 13, that connected the persecution of the righteous to the coming Kingdom of God; Christ himself had endured persecution. Persecution, then, was not punishment, it was a privilege; more so, it was evidence of one's unity with Christ.[15] This was not a veneration of martyrdom, nor were Quakers expected to seek out suffering. Rather, it was well known that membership among Friends would likely lead to a dispute with the law. The consequences of those disputes had to be accepted, not avoided.

The violence portrayed in the seventeenth-century texts speaks to the extent to which the theology of suffering was embraced. Women's accounts of the persecuted body were vivid and frequently gruesome. Consider Rebecca Travers's account of James Nayler's punishment: "[T]here was not a space bigger than the breadth of a man's nail free from stripes and blood from his shoulder to his waste [*sic*]."[16] Autobiographical accounts were equally grisly in conveying the violation of the body at the hands of others. Dorothy Waugh's 1655 description of her confinement to a scold's bridle relates an attempt of the English authorities to silence her physically:

> The Mayor … called to one of his followers to bring the bridle, as he called it, to put upon me, and was to be on three houres, and that which they called so was like a steel cap … they tare my Clothes to put on their bridle as they called it, which was a stone weight of Iron by the relation of their own Generation, & three barrs of Iron to come over my face, and a peece of it was put in my mouth, which was so unreasonable big a thing for that place as cannot well be related.[17]

The authorities may have succeeded in keeping Waugh's mouth shut for three hours; they could not silence her. Her account spoke volumes.

We see similar reports from early North American Friends, which all focus on the physicality of suffering. The treatment New England authorities meted out to Quakers Anne Austin and Mary Fisher was labelled "inhumane" and subsequently described in detail:

> [They] stript them stark naked, not missing head nor feet, searching betwixt their toes, and amongst their hair, tearing and abusing their bodies more than modesty can mention, in so much that Anne, who was a married woman and had born 5 children said, That she had not suffered so much in the birth of them all, as she had done under their barbarous and cruel hands.[18]

Elizabeth Hooton's "Account of her experiences during her visits to New England, 1661 and 1663–65/6" also points to the body as the locus of suffering. Hooton recounts that when she questioned a priest, "[t]he people violently flew upon me young and old, and flung me down on the ground." When she challenged their laws and "den[ied] [them as] being contrary to the law of God and the King" she was imprisoned for "two days and two nights," after which she was sentenced "to be whipped from the prison door to the town's end at the cart's tail and so all along out of their jurisdiction, which was between 20 and 30 miles, but they whipped me to the town's end and the next time I came I was to be hanged, such a law had they now made."[19] Finally, the execution of Mary Dyer in 1660 in Boston Common — the only woman ever executed as a Quaker — serves as the ultimate example of physical suffering and persecution in the name of Truth. As Anne G. Myles concludes, "[h]anged, Dyer's corpse is translated into the textual space of the Protestant martyr's body."[20] Desirous of martyrdom or not, Dyer's persecuted body spoke deeply into the canon of Quaker literature and the faith community from which it was born.

Nineteenth-Century Bodies in Quaker Literature

By the nineteenth century, the Society of Friends in North America had undergone a tightening of the Discipline.[21] In an attempt to purify the Society, a vigilant implementation of the Discipline had led to growing legalism and an increase in disownments. The transatlantic Society was also fraught by a number of doctrinal disputes;[22] the most severe of these was the long-simmering Hicksite-Orthodox schism that boiled over in 1827 to 1828 and rent the North American meetings asunder. That separation was based on doctrinal differences that developed as a result of religious revivalism in the late eighteenth and early nineteenth centuries set against a backdrop of social upheaval. Jacksonian democracy, the shift from an agrarian to a commercial economy, and the expansion of urbanization and industrialization all contributed to the development of a new society in the United States. In Upper Canada, the political fallout from the War of 1812, the Alien Question, and the arrival of large groups of ethnically and religiously diverse immigrants from the British Isles fuelled discontent. Disputes emerged among Friends over the true definition of Quakerism as espoused by George Fox. Unlike earlier schisms, which were localized, the Hicksite-Orthodox rupture divided all but two of the North American yearly meetings.[23] Spurred on by these events, the Quaker leadership on both sides of this dispute called Friends to repentance and a reawakening of the Inner Light.

As in the prophetic period, the body once again became the text of regeneration. Women's bodies, especially, recited the transformative power of the Inner Light. Suffering in Word and in Truth was written onto the frailty of the female body, but instead of the message being one of weakness in the face of suffering, what emerged was a narrative of transcendence. As Ann Byrd reported in 1827, "Affliction is not to these an evil; for in the midst of their trials and privations, the souls of his servants can rejoice in God their Saviour — even though the oppressor may hold their bodies bound in chains, yet the mind is free."[24] Imminent death appears as a constant companion in these women's stories. Sarah Fish Tucker wrote that shortly after her marriage to James Tucker, who already had a number of children, she

> was soon overtaken with unexpected trials and deep baptisms, being plunged into the very depths of distress both as to my outward and inward conditions. I was for six or seven years successively, visited with sickness by which I was often confined to my room and bed for weeks and months, and almost may I not say for years; not being able to go out sometimes more than twice or thrice in the course of a year, reduced at times as it were to the very brink of the grave.[25]

One wonders if the demands of her new family affected her health. Nevertheless, she overcame her grave illness to become heavily involved in ministry, frequently leaving her husband to travel in ministry. At one point she returned from a ministerial trip finding her husband quite unwell "with a cancer in the nose." While he was in obvious physical pain, Tucker makes certain to note, "[W]e both had to rejoice in that I had been enabled to perform this service, which I had long felt as a burthen upon me."[26]

This commitment to the perceived direction of the Inner Light, at all costs, recaptures the significance of the authority of the Inner Light that drove seventeenth-century Quaker prophetesses to suffer persecution and even death. The body made manifest the Word; its burden was so great that physical suffering once again became the proof text of the narrative of rebirth. Consider the manner in which Sarah Lynes Grubb expressed this to one of her children in 1834. Fearful of the damage being wrought by doctrinal disagreements between Friends, she declared:

> Until this day, my mouth has been sealed in silence in our Women's Meeting; but at length "the word was like a fire in my bones, and I could not stay;" and this I was engaged to tell them. I had a brave time of unburdening, which I am sure you will be glad to hear. Notwithstanding I feel that I have not lost more than a *part* of my load with respect to this Yearly Meeting, and whether any further way may open or not, must be left. On First Day our meetings here were very large. In the morning I had to lift up my voice like a trumpet for perhaps nearly an hour, which brought considerable relief to my exercised and oppressed spirit.[27]

The memorial of Lucy B. Cadwallader also attests to a similar experience "that when her trials seemed deepest she was most lively in the exercise of her gift, bringing forth things both new and old to their edification."[28]

Huldah Hoag's memoir presents us with an interesting example of autobiographical texts interspersed with commentary, if not provided then approved by the Meeting for Sufferings. Just as divine direction empowered seventeenth-century women to speak and behave outside social norms, nineteenth-century women recorded a similar experience. As with other travelling ministers, Hoag frequently speaks of being unburdened through the act of preaching. She also associated severe illness with failing to heed the Inner Light. Writing to her husband, who was away on his own ministerial travels, she assessed the reasons for "an alarming inflammation" of her lungs which had left her bedridden and coughing up large quantities of blood: "[T]he hand of the wise Disposer was laid upon me in judgment, as a prospect of visiting Philadelphia was with me continually."[29] Once she "gave up to resign all and go," she was pleased to note, "my health has improved to my own admiration. My cough, which was more severe than I ever experienced before is improving much."[30]

Probably no tract demonstrates more the nineteenth-century Friends' fixation on the physicality of suffering than *A Short Account of the Last Sickness and Death of Maria Mott,* who died at the age of eighteen. Because she was not a recognized minister, accounts of her life and death would not be considered for publication by the Meeting for Sufferings. The introduction to the account is interesting: "The following memoir, written by the parents of the deceased, was not originally designed for publication; but having been perused with much interest by some of their friends, it is deemed by those persons (who also prefix this note) to be worthy of general circulation."[31] The account is twenty-eight pages long and goes into great detail about Mott's illness as well as the patience and fortitude with which she bore it. For instance, her parents tell us that her "puking… [was] attended with violent spasms, and her sufferings were so exquisite as deeply to affect those about her; but she bore them with a patience almost unexampled, nor did a murmur escape her."[32] Nearing the end of her illness, "the violence of the pain abating about this time, as did also the extreme restlessness which had been occasioned by the state of the nervous system, she became quite calm and composed, being evidently in the full enjoyment of her mental powers." This allowed her to speak clearly some of her last words, "The fear of the Lord is round about to preserve us, yes, to preserve all."[33]

Clearly the Meeting for Sufferings wanted to convey a particular message. At a time of profound social and political change, superior meetings heightened their efforts to imprint a standard collective identity and theology on Quaker literature. The fractious splits that divided the body of Friends were reflected in the stories of individual Quaker's sufferings. But this is not simply a chronicle of weakness and dismembering within the Society. If we compare published journals and memorials to the unpublished journals of travelling women ministers, we see Quaker women in both instances speaking through temporal suffering, calling Friends to the triumph of the sacred. Consider Deborah Clark's memorial. During the last fifteen years of her life, Clark "was much afflicted with a complication of diseases which caused her much suffering"; by the end of her life her "sufferings were extreme."[34] Nonetheless, she remained an example of how suffering should be borne. According to her husband, "it was a pleasure to be with her, so sweet was the serenity that was felt. We could behold in her countenance the evidence of the work of the Lamb of God which takes away the sin of the world."[35] This was the same woman who, over the course of nine years, regularly walked seven miles to "faithfully attend" meetings.[36] Sarah Hunt had experienced similar trials. Both in her "early womanhood" and "later in life," perhaps periods associated with the onset of menstruation and menopause, "she suffered from physical debility and extreme nervous prostration." Regardless of her bodily trials, she commented, "I had to pass through these sufferings that I might… testify to the sufficiency of His grace."[37]

What at first glance appears to be conformation to nineteenth-century dictates of female frailty emerges as a vital expression of the transcendence of the

44

Inner Light. Travelling women ministers in nineteenth-century North America endured enormous physical trials, journeying thousands of miles through bush and swamp over virtually impassable "roads," fending off hazards of all kinds, not the least of which was the ubiquitous mosquito. These women could be absent from their families for many weeks or months and in rare cases they could be away for years. Certainly the record for endurance in this effort must go to Elizabeth Robson, who left her family in England for almost four years to visit the North American meetings in the mid-1820s. During that time she travelled over 18,000 miles, attending 1,134 meetings and recording 3,592 family visits.[38] Even though she herself commented that she was "sensible of being a poor weak creature," her diary does not reveal a "weak" woman.[39] On the contrary, it proclaims a woman utterly devoted to her faith and prepared to suffer the physical trials that accompany such devotion. As she recorded on her last day in North America: "I have been mercifully sustained [*sic*] in many deep and painful conflicts and my head kept about the waters—preservation has been witnessed in perils amongst false brethren—I have been privileged with many dear brethren and sisters in the truth which I account no small favour ... and I believe my Great and Blessed master has been pleased to grant me a release from the field of labour."[40] The Society's testimony of her life and death is instructive: "[H]er purified spirit [was] freed from the shackles of mortality.... Her remains were interred in Friends burying ground ... on which occasion ... many testimonies were born to the power and efficacy of that Grace by which she had become what she was."[41] In Robson's life, as in the lives of the other nineteenth-century Quaker "saints," the Word was expressed corporeally as well as linguistically. In suffering they declared the sublime.

Notes

1 Qtd. in Luella M. Wright, *The Literary Life of Early Friends, 1650–1725* (New York: Columbia University Press, 1932) 79.

2 Anna Cox Brinton, *The Function of Quaker Literature: An Address delivered at the Friends' Meeting House in Dublin, April 27th, the first day of the Yearly meeting of 1932* (Leominster, UK: The Orphans' Printing Press, n.d.) 16 (Canadian Yearly Meeting Archives, hereafter CYMA).

3 *Discipline of the New York Yearly Meeting, 1810,* 106 (CYMA).

4 Michele Lise Tarter, "Reading *A Quaker's Book:* Elizabeth Ashbridge's Testimony of Quaker Literary Theory," *Quaker Studies* 9.2 (2005): 180.

5 Nigel Smith, "Hidden Things Brought to Light: Enthusiasm and Quaker Discourse," *The Emergence of Quaker Writing: Dissenting Literature in Seventeenth-Century England*, ed. Thomas N. Corns and David Loewenstein (London: Frank Cass and Co., 1995) 68.

6   Tarter, "Reading *A Quaker's Book*," 180.

7   A small sampling of the extensive body of scholarship on early Quaker women's writing includes David Booy, *Autobiographical Writings by Early Quaker Women* (Aldershot, UK: Ashgate, 2004); Mabel Richmond Brailsford, *Quaker Women 1650–1690* (London: Duckworth, 1915); Rosemary Foxton, *"Hear the Word of the Lord": A Critical and Biographical Study of Quaker Women's Writing, 1650–1700* (Melbourne: Bibliographical Society of Australia and New Zealand, 1994); Catie Gill, *Women in the Seventeenth-Century Quaker Community* (Aldershot, UK: Ashgate, 2005); Hilary Hinds, *God's Englishwomen: Seventeenth-Century Radical Sectarian Writing and Feminist Criticism* (Manchester, UK: Manchester University Press, 1996); Bonnelyn Young Kunze, *Margaret Fell and the Rise of Quakerism* (London: Macmillan, 1994); Phyllis Mack, *Visionary Women: Ecstatic Prophecy in Seventeenth Century England* (Berkeley: University of California Press, 1992); Rosemary Moore, *The Light in Their Consciences: Early Quakers in Britain, 1646–1666* (University Park: Pennsylvania State University Press, 2000); Sheila Ottway, *Desiring Disencumbrance: The Representation of the Self in Autobiographical Writings by Seventeenth-Century Englishwomen* (Groningen, Neth.: University of Groningen Press, 1998); Nigel Smith, *Perfection Proclaimed: Language and Literature in English Radical Religion, 1640–1660* (Oxford: Clarendon, 1989); Christine Trevett, *Women and Quakerism in the 17th Century* (York, UK: Sessions Book Trust, Ebor Press, 1991); Christine Trevett, *Quaker Women Prophets in England and Wales, 1650–1700* (Lewiston, NY: Edwin Mellen, 2000); Catherine M. Wilcox, *Theology and Women's Ministry in Seventeenth-Century English Quakerism* (Lewiston, NY: Edwin Mellen, 1995); Luella Wright, *The Literary Life of Early Friends, 1650–1725*.

8   Qtd. in Gill, *Women in the Seventeenth-Century Quaker Community*, 184.

9   Wright, *The Literary Life of Early Friends*, 97; see also Brinton, *The Function of Quaker Literature*; Robynne Rogers Healey, *From Quaker to Upper Canadian: Faith and Community among Yonge Street Friends, 1801–1850* (Montreal and Kingston: McGill-Queen's University Press, 2006); and Mack, *Visionary Women*.

10 The exception here is scholarship devoted to Elizabeth Ashbridge, the eighteenth-century Quaker who recorded the story of her life in a narrative she titled "Remarkable Experiences." Ashbridge's life and story are so unique that they have been the subject of a sizeable body of research. See, for example, D. Britton Gildersleeve, "'I Had a Religious Mother': Maternal Ancestry, Female Spaces, and Spiritual Synthesis in Elizabeth Ashbridge's *Account*," *Early American Literature* 36.3 (2001): 371–94; Cristine Levenduski, "'Remarkable Experiences in the Life of Elizabeth Ashbridge': Portraying the Public Woman in Spiritual Autobiography," *Women's Studies* 19 (1991): 271–81; Cristine Levenduski, *Peculiar Power: A Quaker Woman Preacher in Eighteenth-Century America* (Washington: Smithsonian Institution Press, 1996); Etta M. Madden, "Quaker Elizabeth Ashbridge as 'The Spectacle & Discourse of the Company': Metaphor, Synecdoche, and Synthesis," *Early American Literature* 34 (1999): 171–89; Daniel Shea, Jr., "Elizabeth Ashbridge and the Voice Within," *Journeys in New Worlds: Early American Women's Narratives*, ed. William L. Andrews (Madison: University of Wisconsin Press, 1990) 119–46; Julie Sievers, "Awakening the Inner Light: Elizabeth Ashbridge and the Transformation of Quaker Community," *Early American Literature* 36.2 (2001): 235–62; and Tarter, "Reading *A Quaker's Book*."

11 For a discussion on the socialization of Quaker children and the role of Quaker literature in that process see Healey, "Building, Sustaining, and Reforming Quaker Community in Upper Canada: Informal Education and the Yonge Street Women Friends," *Quaker History* 94.1(Spring 2005): 1–23; and *From Quaker to Upper Canadian*, chapters 4 and 5.

12 Joseph Besse, *A Collection of the Sufferings of the People Called Quakers*, 2 vols. (London, 1753).

13 Rosemary Moore, *The Light in their Consciences*, 155–63.

14 Ibid., 157.

15 Ibid., 160–61.

16 Qtd. in William M. Bittle, *James Nayler (1618–1660): The Quaker Indicted by Parliament* (York, UK: Friends United Press, 1986) 35.

17 Qtd. in Gill, *Women in Seventeenth-Century Quaker Community*, 71–72.

18 Ibid., 62.

19 Booy, *Autobiographical Writings by Early Quaker Women*, 70.

20 Anna G. Myles, "From Monster to Martyr: Re-Presenting Mary Dyer," *Early American Literature* 36.1 (2001): 13.

21 Jack D. Marietta, *The Reformation of American Quakerism, 1748–1783* (Philadelphia, PA: University of Philadelphia Press, 1984).

22 These included those led by Hannah Barnard's "New Lights"; Jemima Wilkinson, the Public Universal Friend; and David Willson and the Children of Peace.

23 See Robert W. Doherty, *The Hicksite Separation: A Sociological Analysis of Religious Schism in Early Nineteenth Century America* (New Brunswick, NJ: Rutgers University Press, 1967); Thomas Hamm, *The Transformation of American Quakerism: Orthodox Friends, 1800–1907* (Bloomington: Indiana University Press, 1988); Thomas Hamm, *The Quakers in America* (New York: Columbia University Press, 2003); Nancy Hewitt, "The Fragmentation of Friends: The Consequences for Women in Antebellum America," *Witnesses for Change*, ed. Elizabeth Brown and Susan Stuard (New Brunswick, NJ: Rutgers University Press, 1989) 93–108; David E.W. Holden, *Friends Divided: Conflict and Division in the Society of Friends* (Richmond, IN: Friends United Press, 1988); Larry H. Ingle, *Quakers in Conflict: The Hicksite Reformation* (Knoxville: University of Tennessee Press, 1986).

24 *Narratives, Pious Meditations, and Religious Exercises of Ann Byrd, Late of the City of New York, deceased* (Philadelphia: J. Richards, Printer, 1843) 97 (CYMA).

25 *Memoirs of the Life and Religious Experience of Sarah Tucker, a Minister of the Society of Friends, Written by Herself* (Providence, RI, 1848) 25 (CYMA).

26 Ibid., 47.

27 *A Selection from the Letters of the Late Sarah Grubb (formerly Sarah Lynes)* (Sudbury, UK: J. Wright, 1848) 303 (CYMA).

28 *A Testimony of Falls Monthly Meeting of Friends, Concerning Lucy B. Cadwallader, a Minister, deceased* (Philadelphia: William H. Pile's Sons, 1900) 7 (CYMA).

29 *Memoir of Huldah Hoag*, 17 (CYMA).

30 Ibid., 17–18.

31 *A Short Account of the Last Sickness and Death of Maria Mott, Daughter of Richard and Abigail Mott, of Mamaroneck, in the State of New York* (New York: Samuel Wood and Sons, 1817) 2 (CYMA).

32 Ibid., 25.

33 Ibid., 27.
34 *A Memorial Concerning Deborah Clark, Deceased, by Her Husband, Freeman Clark; Reprinted by Direction of Genesee Yearly Meeting* (Rochester, NY: William S. Falls, 1874) 4, 7 (CYMA).
35 Ibid., 7.
36 Ibid., 3.
37 *Journal of the Life and Religious Labors of Sarah Hunt: (Late of West Grove, Chester County, Pennsylvania)* (Philadelphia: Friends' Book Association, 1892) 258 (CYMA).
38 "Elizabeth Robson, American Diary, 1824–1828," in "Quaker Women's Diaries: The Diaries of Elizabeth Robson, 1813–43," *Quaker Women's Diaries of the 18th and 19th Centuries, from Friends House Library*, reel 6.
39 "American Diary," 27th of 7th month 1828.
40 Ibid.
41 "A Testimony, 1843," in "Quaker Women's Diaries: The Diaries of Elizabeth Robson, 1813–43," *Quaker Women's Diaries of the 18th and 19th Centuries, from Friends House Library*, reel 7.

SACRED
MODERNISM(S)

SACRAMENTAL IMAGINATION: EUCHARISTS OF THE ORDINARY UNIVERSE IN THE WORKS OF JOYCE, PROUST, AND WOOLF

Richard Kearney

Introduction

Three of our great modern novelists — Proust, Joyce, and Woolf — epitomize a sacramental imagination which celebrates the bread and wine of the everyday. In Joyce this takes many forms but culminates in the passing of the seedcake from the mouth of Molly to Bloom on Howth Head in the last scene of *Ulysses*. In Proust it assumes the guise of a sonata of epiphanies, most famously those which occur at a Parisian supper party *chez les Guermantes* in *Time Regained*. In Woolf, the eucharistic vision expresses itself in a magical feast of *boeuf en daube* presided over by Mrs. Ramsay in *To the Lighthouse*, recalled in a painting by Lily Briscoe composed after Mrs. Ramsay's death.

In all three narratives we witness the consecration of ordinary moments of flesh and blood *thisness* as something strange and enduring. These acts of transfiguration transpire in an embodied space and time far from the otherworldliness of Platonic or metaphysical formalism. My suggestion in what follows is that a specific phenomenology of incarnation — adumbrated by Maurice Merleau-Ponty and Julia Kristeva, in the wake of Husserl and Heidegger — may help us discern a grammar of transubstantiation operating in these sacramental accounts of the sensible universe. I begin with a sketch of such a phenomenology before moving on to consider in more detail certain eucharistic events in these three modernist novels. In conclusion I will examine our findings in light of a new hermeneutics of the religious imaginary, advanced by Paul Ricoeur and other contemporary thinkers, and I will propose, finally, the paradigm of *ana-theism* as a manner of returning the sacred to the secular and profane.

Merleau-Ponty: A Phenomenology of Flesh

Husserl blazed a path towards a phenomenology of the flesh when he broached the crucial theme of embodiment in *Ideas 2*, a theme largely ignored by Western metaphysics since Plato. This may seem strange given that almost 1500 years of the history of metaphysics comprised what Étienne Gilson called the "Christian synthesis" of Greek and Biblical thought.[1] But metaphysics (with some exceptions) managed to take the flesh and blood out of Christian incarnation, leaving us with abstract conceptual and categorical equivalents. It would take Husserl and the modern phenomenological revolution to bring Western philosophy back to the flesh of pre-reflective lived experience.

Husserl himself, however, for all his talk of returning us to the "things themselves," remained caught in the nets of transcendental idealism and never quite escaped the limits of theoretical cognition. Heidegger took a step closer to the flesh with his existential analytic of "moods" and "facticity," but the fact remains that Heideggerian *Dasein* has no real body at all: it does not eat or sleep or have sex. It too remains, despite all its talk of "being-in-the-world," a captive of the transcendental snare. While Scheler made sorties into a phenomenology of feeling and Sartre offered fine insights into shame and desire, it was really only with Merleau-Ponty that we witnessed a credible return to the flesh; and not just as cipher, project, or icon, but as *flesh itself*, in all its ontological depth.

Here at last the ghost of Cartesian and Kantian idealism is laid to rest, as we finally return to the body in all its unfathomable *thisness*. It is telling that Merleau-Ponty chose to describe his phenomenology of the sensible body in sacramental language, amounting to what we might call—without the slightest irreverence—a Eucharist of profane perception. In the *Phenomenology of Perception* (1944), we read:

> Just as the sacrament not only symbolizes, in sensible species, an operation of Grace, but *is* also the real presence of God, which it causes to occupy a fragment of space and communicates to those who eat of the consecrated bread, provided that they are inwardly prepared, in the same way the sensible has not only a motor and vital significance, but is nothing other than a certain way of being in the world suggested to us from some point in space, and seized and acted upon by our body, provided that it is capable of doing so, so that sensation is literally a form of communion.[2]

This is a bold analogy for an existentialist writing in France in the 1940s, a time when close colleagues like Sartre, de Beauvoir, and Camus considered militant atheism de rigueur. Merleau-Ponty goes on to sound this eucharistic power of the sensible as follows: "I am brought into relation with an external being, whether it be in order to open myself to it or to shut myself off from it. If the qualities radiate around them a certain mode of existence, if they have the power to cast a spell and what we called just now a sacramental value, this is because the sentient subject does not posit them as objects, but enters into a sympathetic relation with them, makes them his own and finds in them his momentary law."[3]

We shall have occasion to refer to numerous idioms of eucharistic empathy in the work of our three novelists below. Suffice it for now to note the curious paradox that it is precisely when Merleau-Ponty traces the phenomenological return all the way down to the lowest rung of experience (in the old metaphysical ladder, the *sensible*) that he discovers the most sacramental act of communion, or what he also likes to call "chiasmus." What exactly is meant by this notion of "chiasmus"? The crossing-over of ostensible contraries: the most in the least, the highest in the lowest, the first in the last, the invisible in the visible. Here we have a reversal of Platonism and Idealism: a return to flesh as our most intimate "element," namely, that which enfolds and envelops us in the systole and diastole of being, the seeing and being seen of vision. Phenomenology thus marks the surpassing of traditional dualisms (body/mind, real/ideal, inner/outer, subject/object) in the name of a deeper, more primordial chiasmus where opposites traverse each other.

This is how Merleau-Ponty describes the enigma of flesh as mutual crossing-over in his posthumously published work, *The Visible and the Invisible* (1964): "[T]he seer is caught up in what he sees.... [T]he vision he exercises, he also undergoes from the things, such that, as many painters have said, I feel myself looked at by the things." So much so that "the seer and the visible reciprocate one another and we no longer know which sees and which is seen. It is this Visibility... this anonymity innate to Myself that we have... called flesh, and one knows there is no name in traditional philosophy to designate it."[4] It is here, I suggest, that Merleau-Ponty gets to the heart of this nameless matter and descends—in a final return, a last reduction that suspends all previous reductions—to the incarnate region of the "element": "The flesh is not matter, in the sense of corpuscles of being which would add up or continue on one another to form beings. Nor is the visible (the things as well as my own body) some 'psychic' material that would be—God knows how—brought into being by the things factually existing and acting on my factual body. In general, it is not a fact or a sum of facts 'material' or 'spiritual.'" No, insists Merleau-Ponty, "the flesh is not matter, is not mind, is not substance. To designate it, we should need the old term 'element,' in the sense it was used to speak of water, air, earth, and fire, that is, in the sense of a *general thing* midway between the spatio-temporal individual and the idea, a sort of incarnate principle that brings a style of being wherever there is a fragment of being. The flesh is in this sense an 'element' of Being."[5]

Returning to examples of painting—Cézanne and Klee—in *Eye and Mind* (1964), Merleau-Ponty expounds on this chiasmic model of the flesh as a mutual transubstantiation of the seer and the seen in a "miracle" of flesh: "There really is inspiration and expiration of Being, action and passion so slightly discernible that it becomes impossible to distinguish between what sees and what is seen, what paints and what is painted.... There is no break at all in this circuit; it is impossible to say that nature ends here and that man or expression starts here. It is... mute Being which itself comes to show forth its own meaning."[6]

In *Signs* (1960), a collection of essays devoted to questions of language and art, Merleau-Ponty repeats his claim that the flesh of art is invariably indebted to the bread of life. There is nothing so insignificant in the life of the artist, he claims, that is not eligible for "consecration" in the painting or poem. But the "style" which the artist creates converts his corporeal situation into a sacramental witness at a higher level of "repetition" and "recreation." The artwork still refers to the life-world from which it springs, but opens up a second-order reference of creative possibility and freedom. Speaking specifically of Leonardo da Vinci, he writes, "If we take the painter's point of view in order to be present at that decisive moment when what has been given to him to live as corporeal destiny, personal adventures or historical events, crystallizes into 'the motive' [i.e. the style], we will recognize that his work, which is never an effect, is always a response to these data and that the body, the life, the landscapes, the schools, the mistresses, the creditors, the police and the revolutions which might suffocate painting are also *the bread his work consecrates*. To live in painting is still to breathe the air of this world."[7] In short, the bread of the world is the very stuff consecrated in the body of the work.

We will return to this aesthetic of transubstantiation in the discussion of our three authors below. But before leaving Merleau-Ponty, I wish to mention one other intriguing passage in *Signs* where the author—no theologian and certainly no Christian apologist—has an interesting interpretation of Christian embodiment as a restoration of the Divine within the flesh, a kenotic emptying out of transcendence into the heart of the world's body, becoming a God beneath us rather than a God beyond:

[T]he Christian God wants nothing to do with a vertical relation of subordination. He is not simply a principle of which we are the consequence, a will whose instruments we are, or even a model of which human values are the only reflection. There is a sort of impotence of God without us, and Christ attests that God would not be fully God without becoming fully man. Claudel goes so far as to say that God is not above but beneath us—meaning that we do not find Him as a suprasensible idea, but as another ourself which dwells in and authenticates our darkness. Transcendence no longer hangs over man: he becomes, strangely, its privileged bearer.[8]

This insight of "immanent transcendence" is not of course original to Merleau-Ponty. Many Christian mystics—from John of the Cross to Hildegard of Bingen and Meister Eckhart—said similar things, as did Jewish sages like Rabbis Luria and Rosenzweig or Sufi masters like Rumi and Ibn 'Arabi. Indeed I am also reminded here of the bold claim by Teilhard de Chardin that God does not direct the universe from above but underlies it and "prolongs himself" into it. But what Merleau-Ponty provides is a specific philosophical method—namely, a phenomenology of radical embodiment—to articulate this "nameless" phenomenon of sacramental flesh. And it is arguable that a number of recent phenomenologists have followed Merleau-Ponty's lead (or parallel path) when seeking to inventory the sacred dimensions of the flesh—I am thinking especially of Jean-Luc Marion's writings on the "flesh" as a saturated phenomenon in *On Excess* or Jean-Louis Chrétien's phenomenological commentary on the Song of Songs.[9] But Merleau-Ponty has the advantage, in my view, not only of being the first phenomenologist to explicitly identify the sacramental valence of the sensible but also of maintaining a certain methodological agnosticism with regard to the theistic or atheistic implications of this phenomenon. Indeed his philosophy of "ambiguity," as he liked to call it, is particularly well suited when it comes to interpreting the sacramental idioms of eucharistic epiphany in Joyce, Proust, and Woolf.

Merleau-Ponty is no crypto-evangelist, as several of those belonging to the "theological turn" in phenomenology have been accused. On the contrary, he keenly observes the methodic suspension of confessional truth claims recommended by Husserl. And this chimes well, it seems to me, with the poetic licence enjoyed by artists and writers when it comes to the marvel of transubstantiation in word, sound, or image; for poetic licence entails a corollary confessional licence from which no reader is excluded. In this respect, we could say that the phenomenological method—which brackets beliefs—is analogous to the literary suspending of belief and dis-belief for the sake of all-inclusive entry to the "kingdom of as-if." And this suspension, I will argue, allows for a specific "negative capability" regarding questions of doubt, proof, dogma, or doctrine, so as to better appreciate the "thing itself," the holy *this-ness* and *thereness* of our flesh and blood existence.

The attitude of pure vigilance and attention that follows from such exposure to a "free variation of imagination" (the term is Husserl's) is not far removed, I believe, from what certain mystics have recognized to be a crucial preparatory moment for sacramental vision, calling it by such different names as "the cloud of unknowing," the "*docta ignorantia*," or, in Eastern mysticism, the "*neti / neti*" — neither this nor that — which paves the way for the highest wisdom of reality. True belief comes from non-belief; or, as Dostoyevsky put it, real "faith comes forth from the crucible of doubt." In the free variation of imagination, indispensable to the phenomenological method, as in all great works of fiction and art, everything is permissible. Nothing is excluded except exclusion. All is possible. By allowing us to attend to the sacramental marvel of the everyday without the constraints of any particular confession, Merleau-Ponty offers fresh insights into a eucharistic character of the sensible.

For reasons of economy, and limited competence, I will confine my remarks exclusively to three modernist writers of fiction. That similar arguments could be made — and perhaps more cogently — with regard to the sacramental vision of musicians, painters, and poets is undeniable, especially when one considers how such artists work more closely with the sensible and carnal than novelists do. But that is a task for others more expert than I in those disciplines.[10]

Julia Kristeva: The Sacramental Imagination

Before moving on to a close reading of our novelists, however, I wish to mention one other contemporary philosopher — Julia Kristeva — who also has had much to say on the sacramental imagination, especially as it relates to what she explicitly calls an aesthetic of "transubstantiation" in Proust and Joyce. As a linguist and psychoanalyst by formation, Kristeva adds new perspectives to the phenomenological vision of Merleau-Ponty which she also espouses. In particular she ventures rich insights into the workings of unconscious tropes and associations in modernist writing about sense and sensibility.

In *Time and Sense*, Kristeva offers this example, among many others:

> A sensation from the past remains within us, and involuntary memory recaptures it when a related perception in the present is stimulated by the same desire as the prior sensation. A spatio-temporal association of sensations is thus established, relying on a link, a structure, and a reminiscence. Sensation takes refuge in this interwoven network and turns into an *impression*, which means that sensation loses its solitary specificity. A similarity emerges out of all these differences, eventually attaining the status of a general law in the manner of an idea or thought. The "general law," however, is no abstraction, for it is established because the sensation is *immanent in it*. ... This process keeps the structure from losing its sensorial foundation. Music becomes word, and writing becomes a *transubstantiation* in those for whom it "creates new powers."[11]

Kristeva links this aesthetic of transubstantiation—that she finds in Joyce and Proust—back to the writings of the later Merleau-Ponty, which she calls "mystically significant" (247).[12] Indeed, her notion of a "general law" of ideational sensation is surely not unrelated to Merleau-Ponty's reference to a "momentary law" cited above. Most specifically, Kristeva relates the eucharistic aesthetic to the chiasmic relation between the visible and invisible, the inner feeling and outer expression, that Merleau-Ponty describes as a reversible interpenetration of *flesh*. Refusing the dualistic division of spirit and body into two separate substances, both Kristeva and Merleau-Ponty counsel us to rethink flesh more phenomenologically as an "*element*, as the concrete emblem of a general manner of being" (246; italics mine). And in this respect, Kristeva keenly endorses Merleau-Ponty's claim that "[n]o one has gone further than Proust in fixing the relations between the visible and the invisible," though she (like us) would want to add Joyce to the list (246). Indeed identifying Merleau-Ponty's model of reversibility with the notion of "transubstantiation" in Proust and Joyce, Kristeva sees this miracle of the flesh as a model both for therapeutic healing and for reading literary texts.

In both cases, the reversible transubstantiation of word and flesh expresses itself as a certain catharsis (247).[13] Kristeva goes on, rather boldly, to suggest that it is their aesthetic of transubstantiation which saves writers like Proust and Joyce (and we would venture to include Virginia Woolf) from the prison of linguistic idealism, to which certain structuralist readings have consigned them. This, mind you, is a linguistic semiotician speaking: "Although Proust never stops 'deciphering,' his world does not consist of 'signs.' At any rate, his world is not made of sign-words or idea-signs and certainly not of signifiers and signifieds" (251). Proust, Kristeva observes, was "disappointed or amused" by "empty linguistic signs" and preferred instead the fluidity of "'atmospheric changes,'" a "'rush of blood,'" a sudden silence, an "'adverb' springing from an involuntary connection made between two unformulated ideas" (251–52). Kristeva finds support for this aesthetic of "real presence" in the young Proust's aversion to "'signs'" and "'strict significations'" and points to the fact that Jean Santeuil (Marcel *avant la lettre*) conceives of art as a "'work of feeling'" which focuses on a "'sort of obscure instinct of permanent brilliance'" or "'lava about to flow over,'" as well as on "'what is not yet ready to come forth'" (252). The paradigmatic Proustian text, she avers, rises up "against the abyss between language and lived experience" and operates as a work which expresses "the vast array of impressions that the hero's sentence strives to communicate (despite his reservations about language) by associating weather, villages, roads, dust, grass and raindrops through a mass accumulation of metaphors and metonymies" (252).

This, Kristeva surmises, "paves the way" in Proust "for the *impression*, which…
makes up for the weakness of linguistic signs" (252). And so words are only useful for Proust when they exert an "'evocative power' over our 'sensibility'" and
"display a kinship with a sort of 'latent music'" (the terms are Proust's) (252).
Resisting the temptations of semiology and Platonism, Proust's eucharistic
writing aims for a "lively, physical expressiveness that resists the passivity of
the civilized sign" (252). It strives instead towards a language of the lived body:
what Proust called "the vigorous and expressive language of our muscles and
our desires, of suffering, of the corruption or the flowering of the flesh."[14]

What pertains to Proust, I will suggest, also pertains to Joyce and Woolf, and
it is to a closer reading of their novels that I now turn. Whether we are concerned
in these works with an aesthetic religion or a religious aesthetic — or both — is
something I wish to bear in mind throughout. In any case, I believe that a
deep phenomenology of flesh, elaborated respectively by Merleau-Ponty's
ontology and Kristeva's semiotics, may helpfully guide and illuminate our
investigation into the sacramental imaginary of our three modernist authors.

Three Modernist Magi: Joyce, Proust, and Woolf

James Joyce

Joyce invokes idioms of transubstantiation to describe the writing process.
Already in the *Portrait* Stephen Dedalus describes himself as a "priest of the
eternal imagination," transmuting the "bread of daily experience" in the
"womb" of art.[15] This is more than irony. Taking his cue from the sacramental operation of transubstantiation in its liturgical formulation, Joyce treats
the transformative act of writing as the "advent of new signs and a new
body."[16] In a discussion with his brother Stanislaus, he has this to say: "Don't
you think, said he reflectively, choosing his words without haste, there is a certain resemblance between the mystery of the Mass and what I am trying to do?
I mean that I am trying in my poems to give people some kind of intellectual
pleasure or spiritual enjoyment by converting the bread of everyday life into
something that has a permanent artistic life of its own."[17] The act of life-text
transfiguration is echoed at several key junctures within Joyce's texts. I have
written elsewhere of the pivotal role of "epiphanies" of repetition in *Ulysses*
where Joyce treats a remembered event as both past (separated by time) and
really present (regained miraculously in the epiphany of the moment).[18] And
yet there is a deeply deconstructive lining to many of Joyce's sacramental allusions. Indeed, *Ulysses* itself may be read as a series of anti-Eucharists or
pseudo-Eucharists leading, I will suggest, to a final eucharistic epiphany at the
close of Molly's soliloquy.

Let's start at the beginning. *Ulysses* opens, significantly, with Buck Mulligan's mimicry of Mass on the turret of the Martello tower. He is carrying a shaving bowl for a chalice and mockingly intoning the liturgical "*Introibo ad altare Dei*."[19] Holding the sacrificial bowl he addresses Stephen as a "Jesuit" before adopting a priestly tone: "For this, O dearly beloved, is the genuine Christine: body and soul and blood and ouns. Slow music, please. Shut your eyes, gents. One moment. A little trouble with those white corpuscles. Silence all" (1). Mulligan's Black Mass is followed, in the next episode, by Bloom's morning feast of fried kidneys, during the course of which, as Molly later recalls, he delivers himself of "jawbreakers about the incarnation" before burning the bottom of the pan (893). Later again in the novel we witness Stephen's parodic Mass in Nighttown and Bloom and Stephen's failed Mass over a cup of cocoa in the penultimate *Ithaca* chapter. Not to mention the mock allusions to transubstantiation in the Oxen of the Sun and Scylla and Charybdis episodes.

This series of pseudo-Eucharists may be read as a long *via negativa* which eventually opens up the space for the "kiss" of the seedcake on Howth Head in the final chapter. This "long kiss" between Molly and Bloom when they first went out, as recalled by Molly in her soliloquy, is redolent with sacramental associations. It could be said, for example, to reprise not only the "kisses of the mouth" celebrated by the Shulammite woman in the Song of Songs but also the Eucharistic Passover of Judeo-Christian promise. Molly's remembrance of the "long kiss" where she gave Bloom the "seedcake out of … [her] mouth" might be thought of as a retrieval of a genuine eucharistic gift of love after the various deconstructions of failed or parodied Eucharists — and loves — recurring throughout the narrative (931). And it is this kiss which triggers off — in true kairological fashion — the earlier memory of Molly's first kiss as a young woman in Gibraltar: a first kiss which becomes the final kiss of the novel itself, climaxing in the famous lines, "… how he kissed me under the Moorish wall…. and then I asked him with my eyes to ask again yes and then he asked me would I yes to say yes my mountain flower and first I put my arms around him yes and drew him down to me so he could feel my breasts all perfume yes and his heart was going like mad and yes I said yes I will Yes" (933).[20] This kiss may, of course, also be read as an epiphanic repetition of the particular moment on June 16, 1904, when Joyce finally went out and found pleasure with Nora Barnacle, the day subsequently known as Bloomsday, on which *Ulysses* is set. Nor should we forget that the closing chapter in which Molly remembers times past (and future) is, according to Joyce's notes, dedicated to the "flesh" and that it crowns a narrative which Joyce described as his "epic of the body."

In repeating a past moment, epiphany gives a future to the past. It some-how transubstantiates the empirical *thisness* of a particular lived event into something sacred and timeless.[21] So when Molly recalls her first kiss as a young woman she does so — tellingly — in the future tense! "Yes I *will* yes." And we might be tempted to suggest that Molly's promissory "yes" here epit-omizes Walter Benjamin's intriguing notion of "messianic time" as an open-ness to "each moment of the future as a portal through which the Messiah may enter."[22] This is, in short, epiphany understood as a transfiguring of an ordi-nary moment of secular, profane time (*chronos*) into sacred or eschatological time (*kairos*).

It is also worth noting that epiphany, in its original scriptural sense, involved witnesses who come as strangers from afar. This could be read, in terms of a sacramental hermeneutics, as an event of textual openness to new, strange, and unprecedented meanings through the textual encounter between *author, narrator*, and, above all, *reader*. Such a sacramental reading epitomizes the "desire to open writing to unforeseeable effects, in other words, to the Other. It is a function of a responsibility for the Other — for managing in writ-ing a place for the Other, saying *yes* to the call or demand of the Other, invit-ing a response."[23] And here we might recall Derrida's invocation of Elijah (also a favourite figure for Leopold Bloom) as a messianic model of the reader: the unpredictable Other par excellence who calls the text forth and is called forth in turn by the text. This notion of *Ulysses* as an open textual invitation to "re-figuration" in the reader finds confirmation in Joyce's repeated appeal to the "ideal reader," a gesture somewhat akin to Proust's appeal to his future reader who would discover in his book the book of his/her own life. One of Joyce's most telling refrains in the letters is — "is there one who understands me?" In other words, both Joyce and Proust (as we shall see) invoke the sacramental idiom of transubstantiation to convey the miracle of textual composition and reception. In both cases, we are confronted with a miracle of *repetition* that recalls the past forward and explodes the chronology of time.[24]

But how are we to read these novelistic "repetitions," in Kierkegaard's sense of *repeating forward* rather than merely recollecting backward?[25] What is the particular genre, idiom, or style which performs such gestures? To borrow a term from Joyce himself, we might call it "jokoserious." For it is a way of cele-brating the eternal in the moment by bringing us back to earth. Molly, for example, is a mock-heroic parody of the elevated and aristocratic Penelope. She repeats her Homeric prototype forward by opening up new modes of re-inscription. One only needs to compare Molly's all-too-mundane musings with the following description of Penelope in the last scene of Homer's *Odyssey*: "So upright in disposition was Penelope the daughter of Icarius that she never forgot Odysseus the husband of her youth: and therefore shall the fame of her goodness be conserved in the splendid poem wherewith the Immortals shall celebrate the constancy of Penelope for all the dwellers upon earth."[26] This is a far cry from Molly's final cry. Certainly Penelope could never say of her beloved what Molly says of hers — "as well him as another" (933)! And yet it is typical of Joyce's irony that in turning Homer's epic heroism on its head, his characters curiously maintain the truth of the situation in a kind of creative repetition. Bloom is strangely blessed with his wife (however unfaithful) and does manage to defy his rivals (Boylan, the Citizen, however indirectly and passively); Molly does not forget Bloom, and her ultimate affirmation is "celebrated" by many "dwellers upon earth." In short, by transliterating Penelope and Odysseus into Molly and Bloom, Joyce performs a daring act of eucharistic comedy. And, so doing, he proves his conviction that the "structure of heroism is a damned lie and that there cannot be any substitute for individual passion."[27]

Molly's rewriting of Penelope conforms to the basic features of comedy outlined by Aristotle and Bergson: namely, the combining of more with less, of the metaphysical with the physical, of the heroic with the demotic, of Word with flesh. And we might add, bearing in mind a central motif of comedy, the combining of death with love. (Recall that the novel begins with a series of death and burial themes, lived or remembered — Stephen's mother, the Blooms' son, Paddy Dignam — and that it ends with a call to love: eros defying the sting of thanatos.) Molly's ultimate passing from thanatos to eros is prefigured several times during her soliloquy, from fantasies of being buried (e.g., "well when Im stretched out dead in my grave then I suppose I'll have some peace I want to get up a minute if Im let O Jesus.... O Jamesy let me up out of this pooh sweets of sin") to the climatic cry of eschatological bliss, "Yes I will yes." And it is surely significant that Molly herself is "full with seed" as she records her fantasy of death and rebirth, just as Bloom himself is described as a "manchild in the womb" (913–14, 933, 870).

In her final memory of the kiss, Molly echoes the Shulammite woman's celebration of wild flora in the Song of Songs as she affirms that "we are flowers all a womans body" (932). Indeed the culminating Moorish and Mediterranean idioms of sensory ecstasy and excess are deeply redolent of the Shulammite's Canticle — itself styled after the Jewish-Babylonian nuptial poem or epithalamium. And this impression is amplified, I think, by the multiple allusions to seeds, trees, waters, and mountains, and irresistible passions between men and women. "[W]hat else were we given all those desires for"? Molly asks (925). If there is something irreducibly humorous in this replay of the Song of Songs, there is something deeply serious too. As always in Joyce, the scatological and the eschatological rub shoulders — as do Greek and Jew, Molly and Bloom, life and death. And they do so without ever succumbing to some totalizing synthesis. Joyce's comic transubstantiations do not amount to Hegelian sublations (*Aufhebungen*), in spite of Derrida's one-time suspicions.[28] Joyce keeps the dialectic open to the end, refusing the temptation of metaphysical closure. The eucharistic transformation of death and rebirth is carried out on earth. Word is always made flesh of our flesh.

Epiphanies — as Joyce knew from his studies with the Jesuits in Clongowes (especially Father Darlington) — imply Magi.[29] The three Magi who bear witness to the textual epiphany of meaning are Stephen, Bloom, and Molly, and each reincarnates a seminal moment in the author's own life. But, as suggested above, the Magi may also be interpreted more textually as *author, actor,* and *reader.* Thus we might say that while (a) the lived action of Joyce's world "prefigures" the text, and (b) the voice, style, and plot of the actors (Stephen-Bloom-Molly) "configure" the meaning in the text, it is (c) the reader who completes the narrative arc by serving as a third witness who "re-figures" the world of the text in his or her return to lived experience. Our own world as readers may thus be said to be enlarged by the new meanings proposed by the text.

This triangular model of epiphany — celebrated in the sacrament of Word-made-flesh — always implies a rebirth. It constitutes something of a miracle of meaning, the *impossible* being transfigured into the *newly possible.* And here we might invoke those famous biblical epiphanies when, for example, the three angels appear to Abraham (Gen. 18) to announce the conception of an "impossible" child (Isaac) by Sarah; or, in Christian literature, when the three Magi bear witness to the "impossible" child Jesus in Bethlehem; or, again, when the three persons of the Christian Trinity herald the birth of an "impossible" kingdom, as in Andrei Rublev's icon of the Blessed Trinity. Indeed this last Rublev example — featuring the three persons of the Trinity seated around a Eucharistic chalice — could be said to foreground the pivotal role of the free space (*chora*) at the centre of the triadic epiphany. The movement of the three persons/angels/Magi around the still womb — which the Patristic authors named *peri-choresis* or the dance around the open space — may be read, hermeneutically, as the creative encounter of *author/narrator/reader* in and around the locus of the word. This suggests, moreover, that the triadic model of epiphany always implies a fourth dimension — namely, *chora* understood as the space of advent for the new (Isaac, Jesus, Pleroma). Eucharistic epiphany might thus be said to signal a miracle of reversible semantic innovation: of flesh into word and of word into flesh.

That the witnessing of the three personas is usually met with a celebratory "yes" (Sarah's "laugh" in Genesis 18, Mary's "Amen" in the Gospels, Molly Bloom's final "yes I will yes"), is itself a significant illustration of how kairological time cuts across conventional time and opens up a surplus of possible meaning hitherto unsuspected and unknown. The epiphanic event may be seen, accordingly, as one which testifies simultaneously to the *event* of mean-ing (it is *already* here) as an *advent* always still to come (it is *not-yet* here). And in this wise it re-enacts the Palestinian formula of the Passover/Eucharist which remembers a moment of saving while at the same time anticipating a future ("until he comes").[30]

So I repeat: Molly's final cry blends and balances past and future tenses in a typically kairological way — "I *said* yes I *will* yes." Her scatological memories of all-too-human eros are repeated forward to the rhythm of eschatological time. Word becomes flesh as flesh becomes word. The secular and sacramen-tal traverse each other.

Marcel Proust

Sacramental idioms are also central to the work of Marcel Proust. Tropes of "transubstantiation," "resurrection," and "revelation" occur in several key pas-sages of *In Search of Lost Time*. They generally signal a grammar for recover-ing the timeless in time, as in the famous madeleine episode, but also a gram-mar of artistic transformation, as in Marcel's final disquisition on the writing process in *Time Regained* (the final volume of the novel). If food and taste are the sensible idioms which produce the quintessential epiphany of the madeleine, I would suggest it is another epiphany at the end of the labyrinthine narrative which brings us even closer to Proust's sacramental vision. I refer to the penultimate scene *chez les Guermantes*, when Marcel is left waiting in the library antechamber as a preprandial music recital is being performed. Hav-ing arrived late, Marcel experiences a clusters of epiphanies as he waits before entering the Guermantes's salon. Here in this antechamber of remaindered time certain achronic moments return to him.

Marcel's first involuntary memory is of entering the San Marco Cathedral in Venice, a site of Eucharistic celebration par excellence. This flash of memory is triggered by his stumbling on some uneven cobblestones as he traverses the Guermantes's courtyard. Though he had been unable to take in the sacramental epiphany at the time (when he first visited Venice with his mother), he relives it now many years later here in Paris. We shall return to this momentarily.

This "miracle of the courtyard" is followed by another involuntary mem-ory brought on by the sound of a spoon striking a plate as a waiter in the din-ing room prepares the banquet table (for the feast to come). Then we have a third quasi-Eucharistic epiphany as Marcel wipes his lips with a starched table napkin, the sensation suddenly recalling a luminous moment in his childhood when he sat in the dining room of the Grand Hotel at Balbec. And, finally, Marcel experiences a very formative (if forgotten) moment in his childhood: fetching a volume of George Sand's novel *François le Champi* from the Guer-mantes's library shelves, he suddenly relives an evening when Maman read

this same book to him at bedtime in Combray. And it was this nocturnal reading which coincided, as we know from the opening scene of the book, with the
inaugural moment when his mother left the dinner table with Marcel's father
and Swann to come kiss her son, Marcel, goodnight. Reading and feasting are
thus intimately associated with the maternal kiss which set Marcel on his
search for lost time, eventually culminating in the composition of the novel of
that name.[31]

Samuel Beckett has described this cluster of epiphanies as a "single annunciation," and I think this allusion to the miracle of Incarnation is telling. For
in this scene Marcel comes back to the flesh. He is reminded, at this same
Guermantes's party, that most of his loved ones are dead (Robert de Saint-
Loup, Grandmaman, Maman, Swann, Odette, Françoise), that Charlus is
dying, and that he himself (Marcel) has just escaped a brush with death in a
sanatorium. Marcel is brought back to earth, so to speak, and sees behind the
masks of Parisian show and snobbery to the underlying reality of mortal flesh,
transience, and passing away. And it is only then, the author seems to imply,
that Marcel is ready, at last, after many thousands of pages questing for the
perfect work of art, to renounce his elite romantic pretensions and acknowledge that real art is an *art of flesh* — a literary transubstantiation of those contingent, fragile, carnal, and seemingly inconsequential moments that our conscious will is wont to consign to oblivion. (One recalls Merleau-Ponty on Da
Vinci above.) Marcel can finally assume his vision of "Combray and its sur-
roundings... taking shape and solidity" out of a "cup of tea."[32]

In her reading of Proust in *Time and Sense*, Julia Kristeva lays special
emphasis on the San Marco epiphany, recalling as it does an earlier chapter in
the novel, and an earlier moment in Marcel's life, when he visits Venice with
Maman. Kristeva interprets this pivotal episode as central to the understanding of Proust's eucharistic aesthetic. Examining various drafts of Proust's novels and a number of notebook entries on John Ruskin, whose "religious aesthetic" greatly influenced Proust (*Time and Sense*, 101), Kristeva traces
Proust's growing fascination with liturgical terms of "transubstantiation,"
"real presence," and the incarnational mystery of "time embodied" and time
resurrected.[33] She herself uses these same terms, deployed in the Catholic
Eucharistic rite, to describe the way in which Proust's characters relate to
themselves, each other, and the textual style of the novel through a mystical
model of criss-crossing times: "As combinations of past and present impressions, the characters contaminate one another and fuse their contours; a *secret
depth* attracts them. Like the madeleine soaked in tea, they allow themselves to
be absorbed into Proust's style. These Proustian heroes and visions will eventually leave us with a singular and bizarre taste that is pungent and invigorat-
ing. It is the taste of the sense of time, of *writing as transubstantiation*" (23).

Kristeva goes on to cite many scenes which elaborate on this sacramental idiom of transubstantiation in terms of "translation," "incarnation," "metaphor," and "superimposition" (102, 106, 108, 133). For Proust it is the task of the writer to "search for 'an object' in which 'each hour of our life hides,'" for he believes that each time we achieve such a task we resuscitate those hidden moments in the form of epiphanies.[34] In his writings on the aesthetics of Ruskin and Male, for example, Proust identifies two particular such moments: a bit of toast that will become a "madeleine" and a Venetian paving stone — namely, two of the key epiphanies of *In Search of Times Past.* Commenting on the example of the paving stone in San Marco Cathedral, Kristeva writes:

> Tripping on the stone and then stumbling . . . would thus be a way of having faith in the sacred. Indeed, the sacred is made of stone: a "living stone, rejected by men but in God's sight chosen and precious . . . (1 Peter 2: 4–5) . . . The cornerstone, along with its manifestations in Proust's writings, is thus presented as a sign of the cult of Jesus, as the real presence of essence. The cornerstone appears to have been Proust's under-lying motif, for between the cathedrals and the Mass . . . Proust wished to fathom the mystery of "transubstantiation." He managed to do so by . . . clearing his own path through everyday sensations, and by acknowledging an eroticism that influenced and increasingly overwhelmed the future narrator's involuntary memory. (106)

Or again, "In contact with the 'living stone,' he [Marcel] himself becomes a 'living stone,' a 'stream of light,' a participant in the sacred, in 'transubstantiation'" (108).[35]

Proust himself, of course, describes the coming together of different times and scenes as both "metaphor" and "resurrection." And for Proust these terms are curiously allied if not identical. Both involve the translation of one thing in terms of another. True art, Marcel comes to realize, is not a matter of progressively depicting a series of objects or events ("describing one after another the innumerable objects which at a given moment were present at a particular place"); it occurs only when the writer "takes two different objects" and "states the connexion between them."[36] And here we return to Merleau-Ponty's logic of sacramental perception. For it is identification of "unique connexion[s]" and hidden liaisons between one thing and another that enables the writer to translate the book of life (that "exists already in each one of us") into the book of art (6.290–91). This is how Marcel puts it: "[T]ruth — and life too — can be attained by us only when, by comparing a quality common to two sensations, we succeed in extracting their common essence and in reuniting them to each other, liberated from the contingencies of time, with a metaphor" (6.290). That Marcel privileges figures of resurrection and transubstantiation in this work of metaphor is once again a confirmation of what I am calling — in Proust no less than in Joyce — a sacramental aesthetic.

But let us say a little more about the famous "Trip to Venice" episode which occurs immediately after the death of Albertine. The scene "opens with a golden angel on San Marco campanile" "announcing" a certain "joy" (*Time and Sense*, 112). Kristeva notes, "Several themes... are tightly woven into this... short chapter" to "reaffirm Proust's notion of art as transubstantiation": Combray and Venice, childhood and adulthood, France and Italy, and the two distinct temporal sensations of past and present "condensed into a metaphor" (112). The scene plays out a dream of death and rebirth: "Death plays a role in this condensation. A reference to the grandmother's death echoes Albertine's more recent disappearance, which is now ready to be internalized and transformed into the innermost depths of writing" (112). Recalling the mother's presence under the window, the narrator confesses an impression of "getting closer and closer to *the essence of something secret*" (112). Kristeva reads this visit to San Marco as pivotal to the entire development of the novel. It is, she claims, a crucial station in the initiatory journey between "The Death of the Cathedrals" chapter and the concluding volume, *Time Regained*, comprising what she calls a "voyage toward a *living* meaning" (113). This is how Kristeva interprets the scene:

> The mystery of this incarnate Venice resides... in the mother's presence... the incorporation of mother and city.... A strange fusion is established between the mother's body and Venice's body. Sitting and reading underneath the pointed arches of an ogival window, the mother inscribes herself in the beautiful stones of Saint Mark's. The window is identified with "a love which stopped only where there was no longer any corporeal matter to sustain it, on the surface of her impassioned gaze.... It says to me the thing that touches me more than anything else in the world: "I remember your mother so well." Through the magic of this infiltration, the Venetian window becomes the matter sustaining maternal love—the window *is* love for the mother. The same process applies to the baptistery, where we find devoted women who appear to have been taken right out of a Carpaccio painting: "She [the mother] has her place reserved there as immutably as a mosaic." (113)

The word "fusion" here is telling, I suspect, given the French association with brewing beverages, that is, the *infusion* of Linden tea in the madeleine episode. So that we might say that mystical fusion and liquid fusion brush shoulders across memory and time. Nor is it insignificant that Marcel's anamnetic retrieval of the Venice baptistery in the epiphany of the Guermantes's paving stone is contiguous with the related recall of Maman reading the story of François le Champi and his foster mother, *Madeleine* Blanchet: a mystical-maternal association which Kristeva makes much of (3–22,116).[37] Kristeva concludes her psychoanalytic reading by suggesting that the Venice scene is best understood as an "incarnation founded on the love between a son and his mother" (114). She is well aware of the Marian and Catholic connotations of this Madonna and Child imaginary (analogous perhaps to the Mrs. Ramsay and James relationship in Woolf's *To the Lighthouse*) and deems it highly significant that Proust redrafted the chapter several times and was revising it right up to his death, as witnessed in certain deathbed notes to Celeste Albaret — e.g., "cross out everything that occurs before my arrival with my mother in Venice." Hurried by his final illness, Proust concentrated on communicating his own "aesthetic credo" in this pivotal episode, which, for Kristeva, expresses itself in "the integration of the spiritual theme with the sensual theme, which includes the love for the mother in the celebration of Venice" (115).

Proust chose ultimately "to emphasize the interpenetration between Venice and his mother, between the angel's light and the body"; and this choice "endure[s] until the final typescript," inviting us to consider "the trip to Venice…as an apotheosis of the madeleine and paving-stone episodes" (*Time and Sense*, 115). For Kristeva, accordingly, Venice powerfully assumes the mystical role of a "sensual and symbolic Orient," a city that becomes "maternal and thus stresses its own incarnation" (116). (We shall return to such "Oriental" allusions in our discussion of Woolf below.) This, concludes Kristeva, is the "cornerstone" of Proust's entire eucharistic aesthetic, treating Venice as a "world within a world" (Proust's words), the very character of "time embodied." In this manner the visit to Saint Mark's Baptistery may be read as the crucial link between the "erotic bildungsroman" — running from Maman and Ghilberte to Albertine — and the annunciation of epiphanies in the "final pensive pages" of the novel (117).

But Venice is not the last station on Marcel's journey, and Maman is not the last object of his affections. On the contrary, by the end of the novel it seems that Maman has been accepted as the "lost object" par excellence, prompting him to move from an aesthetic of melancholy to one of mourning and resurrection. As the novel progresses I believe that Marcel moves increasingly beyond the various transfers of amorous want and returns to the Madonna of the ordinary universe: Françoise. The menial maid of the opening chapters now returns as "the Michelangelo of our kitchen," a quotidian creature capable of transforming a farmyard chicken into a delicious family feast of *poulet roti*.[38] I would even suggest that by the final volume of the novel, *Time Regained*, Françoise — as everyday cook and seamstress — has become Marcel's model for writing the novel. The narrator now confesses, after all, that "(he) should work beside her…almost as she worked herself" (6.509). This conjecture is confirmed, I believe, if we recall how Françoise is compared to Giotto's *Caritas* in her being as well as her appearance (*pace* Swann) in the opening volume.[39] Replacing the endless litany of elusive metonymic muses — from Maman and Ghilberte to Mlle de Guermantes and Albertine — Françoise re-emerges in the end as a post-muse of the everyday microcosm. The ethereal and unreal Albertine transmigrates back, as it were, into the Françoise of flesh and blood. The death of Marcel's exotic fantasy lover is the occasion for the rebirth of the forgotten scullery maid. Curiously, it is Françoise's very qualities of patient craft and endurance, grounded in a sharp sense of mortality and earthiness, that Walter Benjamin celebrates in his famous concluding image of Proust — "for the second time there rose a scaffold … on which the artist, his head thrown back, painted the Creation on the ceiling of the Sistine Chapel: the sickbed on which Marcel Proust consecrates the countless pages which he covered with his handwriting … to the creation of his microcosm."[40] Kitchens and cathedrals. Dying and creating. Earthly frailty as the portal to art. Moreover, it is also Benjamin who would observe — whether thinking of the culinary seamstress Françoise or not — that "[t]he eternal is in any case far more the ruffle on a dress than some idea."[41]

So where does this leave Maman? I suspect that by the time Marcel recalls Maman in the final Paris epiphanies — which trigger the involuntary memories of both the Venice visit and the bedtime reading of *François le Champi* — it is less a question of "fusion" than of trans-fusion. Or of "transversal," as Proust himself uses the term in Marcel's final contemplative musings on time embodied and regained. In other words, rather than embracing a form of immediate or magical union, Proust introduces the preposition *trans* to capture the sense of both identity and difference over time. Transfusion, transversal, translation, transubstantiation.

But a final word on Françoise. If Françoise is indeed Marcel's ultimate guide, it is perhaps no accident that the novel becomes fragmented in a number of different directions in *Time Regained* just when it appears about to reach closure and become whole (in the manner of some Hegelian teleology). Resisting the Hegelian temptation, the book remains undecided as to whether Marcel's projected novel is Proust's *In Search of Lost Time* or not. That is for the reader to decide. Indeed, it is curious how each original reading of Proust — think of those by Ricoeur, Deleuze, Levinas, Benjamin, Ginette, Beckett, De Man, Blanchot, Kristeva, Nussbaum, Murdoch, Girard — manages in almost every case to *translate* the novel into their own reading! It is the ultimate definition, perhaps, of an "open text." Or what we might also call — taking our cue from Merleau-Ponty's passage on eucharistic reciprocity and reversibility — a sacramental text.

So we might conclude that just as the marginalized Molly eventually returns as Stephen's promissory mentor, the previously mocked Françoise is now retrospectively restored as Marcel's most reliable guide. It was this housemaid, we recall, who was always the one pointing Marcel away from literature-for-literature and in the direction of literature-for-life. She was the mundane servant who, "like all unpretentious people," had a no-nonsense approach to literary vainglory and saw through all Marcel's literary rivals as mere "copiators" (6.510). It was Françoise, Marcel now realizes, who had "a sort of instinctive comprehension of literary work" capable of "divin[ing]" Marcel's "happiness and respect[ing]" his "toil" (6.509). And so Marcel ultimately resolves to labour as she did, stitching and threading from bits and pieces of cloth — "construct[ing] my book, I dare not say ambitiously like a cathedral, but quite simply like a dress" (6.509). The muse is displaced by the maid. The fantasy persona of Albertine, the main source of Marcel's tormented jealousies and deceptions, is finally replaced by the seamstress of the real.

In this respect, Françoise — no less than Molly — is a reincarnation of Penelope. Proust operates a return from heroic wanderings to the weavings of the everyday. The marvels of literature are no longer to be sought in monumental basilicas of grandiose design (or in great battle scenes — the novel is set in 1916) but in the intricate weft and warp of ordinary existence. And in this embrace of writing as weaving we find the literary trope of "metaphor" being allied to that of "metonymy." The transformative and synthetic power of metaphor, which turns contingency into essence, is here supplemented by a second moment which returns essence to contingency — that is, to metonymy as a process of displacement and replacement, of humble stitching and restitching, of one thing ceding itself to another in the quotidian play of existence. This double process is what we have been calling transubstantiation: the reversible translation of word into flesh and flesh into word.

This new understanding of writing as a stitching of webs, tapestries, textures, and texts leads Marcel to the insight that he is the "bearer" of a work that has been "entrusted" to him and which he will, in time, "deliver" into other hands (that of the reader). The connotations of pregnancy and birth are pronounced. This intuition of the basic intertextuality of writing comes to Marcel as a sort of deliverance from his own long fear of death. Affirming that genuine literature is a form of messianic "repetition" or remembering forward — from natality to mortality and back to natality again — Marcel finds himself "indifferent to the idea of death" (6.515). Learning to die is learning to be reborn. "[B]y dint of repetition," as he says, "this fear had gradually been transformed into a calm confidence. So that if in those early days, as we have seen, the idea of death had cast a shadow over my loves ... the remembrance of love had helped me not to fear death. For I realized that dying was not something new, but that on the contrary since my childhood I had already died many times" (6.515).[42] Invoking the scriptural passage about the seed dying in order to flourish, Marcel's authorial self now faces the possibility of being posthumously reborn again as another, as one of those many harbingers of new life, epitomized by Mlle de Saint-Loup or, more generally, by his future readers. Natality re-emerges from mortality, so that the final passage of the novel—recalling the dead Albertine and the dying count Charlus—invokes an enveloping movement of time which swings back and forth, up and down, carrying us towards vertiginous and terrifying summits, higher than the steeples of cathedrals, before eventually returning us to earth again, "descending to a greater depth within." In short, if time is all too wont to raise mortals "to an eminence from which suddenly they fall," might we not say that the Proustian acknowledgement of the inevitability of this fall back into the ordinary universe enables fear to become love and literary delusion true writing? (6.530–31).[43]

Virginia Woolf

My third example of sacramental aesthetics is Virginia Woolf's *To the Lighthouse*. Mrs. Ramsay is also a mistress of the feast. Like Françoise before her, though in somewhat more urbane attire, Mrs. Ramsay is introduced in the first part of the novel as both cook and seamstress. She has a singular gift for "summoning together": for bringing couples into liaison; for holding her brood of eight children in maternal connection, and her husband in marriage.[44] On the day we meet her, she has two main tasks: to give her son, James, some hope that he may sail to the lighthouse; and to prepare a magnificent supper of *boeuf en daube* for her family and guests that evening.

But this is no ordinary boat trip and this is no ordinary meal. Mrs. Ramsay is frequently depicted by Woolf in mystical terms. Woolf's use of indirect discourse—*le style indirect libre*—to convey what is going on in her various characters' minds gives the reader the impression, from the outset, that Mrs. Ramsay's soul is somehow porously interconnected with the scattered souls of those around her. And this sense of mysterious inter-being is confirmed in the last part of the novel when we find her devoted friend and painter, Lily Briscoe, recalling the same thoughts and qualities of Mrs. Ramsay herself (the term "unfathomably deep," for example, recurs in the minds of both, as do curiously sacred sentiments of "emptiness" as "fullness," or the three "strokes" of the lighthouse beam which Mrs. Ramsay contemplates repeated in the three "strokes" of Lily's brush on the white canvas). Virginia Woolf writes in her diary how she used this narrative voice as a "tunnelling process" deep into the minds of all her characters, which would reach a point where they could all connect, have similar thoughts, and move to the same deep "rhythm,"[45] a rhythm which she describes as "resonant and porous, transmitting emotion without impediment … creative, incandescent and undivided."[46] Through this free indirect voice Woolf experiments with a "multi-personal representation of consciousness … with synthesis as its aim."[47]

When dinnertime eventually arrives, the tone is sacramental. We read how the gong announces solemnly, authoritatively, that all those scattered about (the house and garden) must "assemble in the dining room for dinner" (82). And the meal unfolds accordingly as a eucharistic ritual. Mrs. Ramsay takes her place at the head of the table and assigns each person their proper seat. As she ministers the meal she presides over the assembly with a quasi-mystical sense of "being past everything, through everything, out of everything" (83). The convened guests and family members unite around the candlelit dinner table:

> Now all the candles were lit up, and the faces on both sides of the table were brought nearer by the candle light, and composed, as they had not been in the twilight, into a party round a table, for the night was now shut off by panes of glass, which, far from giving any accurate view of the outside world, rippled it so strangely that here, inside the room, seemed to be order and dry land; there, outside, a reflection in which things wavered and vanished, waterily. Some change at once went through them all, as if this had really happened, and they were all conscious of making a party together in a hollow, on an island; had their common cause against that fluidity out there. (97)

There are many antagonisms and rivalries between different people at the table, but Mrs. Ramsay contrives to deftly negotiate and mollify these differences, letting each person find their voice and making various marriage plans for various guests (Paul and Minta, Lily and Mr. Bankes). By the end of the meal, everyone seems united in eucharistic communion. The messianic Mrs. Ramsay has worked her gracious magic on the gathering. The eschatological feast is at hand:

> Everything seemed possible. Everything seemed right. Just now... she had reached security; she hovered like a hawk suspended; like a flag floated in an element of joy which filled every nerve of her body fully and sweetly, not noisily, solemnly rather, for it arose, she thought, looking at them all eating there, from husband, children and friends; all of which rising in this profound stillness (she was helping William Bankes to one very small piece more, and peered into the depths of the earthenware pot) seemed now for no special reason to stay there like a smoke, like a fume rising upwards, holding them safe together. Nothing need be said; nothing could be said. There it was, all round them. It partook, she felt, carefully helping Mr Bankes to a specially tender piece, of eternity.... [T]here is a coherence in things, a stability; something, she meant, is immune from change, and shines out... in the face of the flowing, the fleeting, the spectral, like a ruby; so that again tonight she had the feeling... of peace, of rest. Of such moments, she thought, the thing is made that endures.... (The Boeuf en Daube was a perfect triumph.) (104–5)

Mrs. Ramsay's credo, as Lily will remember it in the final section of the novel, was "of the nature of a revelation. In the midst of chaos there was shape.... Life stand still here, Mrs. Ramsay said" (161). But this epiphany of union is shrouded with irony. Life does not stand still. A sense of elegiac doom hovers

over the proceedings. In the midst of her musing, Mrs. Ramsay is caught by
the awareness that "this cannot be." She finds herself "dissociating herself
from the moment" (104). And for us, readers, it is equally short-lived. Within
pages Mrs. Ramsay is dead and the novel descends—in the middle section,
"Time Passes"—into an unconsoling exposé of transience and war. We also
learn that Mrs. Ramsay's ideal matchmaking has come to naught and that two
of her most beautiful children have perished during the war. In retrospect, the
"smoke" rising from the dinner table takes on connotations of a sacrificial
offering. The paschal feast seems less a Passover than a passing away. But this
is not the end of the story. And we are still left asking, in the third part of the
novel, what Mrs. Ramsay meant when she spoke of "the thing is made that
endures." Was she thinking of the "perfect" meal itself remembered by those
who live after her and finally make their way to the lighthouse? Or of the work
of art wherein Lily will resurrect Mrs. Ramsay and enable her to endure in the
"finished" portrait? Or of the novel itself which invites us, the readers, to
revive Mrs. Ramsay's eucharistic feat in the very act of reading and rereading?

The connection between things *lived* and things *made* brings us to the
heart of the rapport between Mrs. Ramsay and Lily. Here we encounter a complex mysticism at work. Lily's final brush "stroke" is, as mentioned above, a
repetition of the "stroke" of the lighthouse with which Mrs. Ramsay intimately identifies. This identification occurs in the first part of the novel when
Mrs. Ramsay sits down late one night when her children are in bed and, taking out her knitting, feels a strange peace as she unites with the world outside
her window. A "wedge-shaped core of darkness" deep inside her, we are told,
merges with the beam of light emitted by the lighthouse far out at sea. With
the third stroke of the light on water, her own "unfathomable deep" blends
with the depths of the ocean. We read that "[o]ften she found herself sitting
and looking, sitting and looking, with her work in her hands until she became
the thing she looked at—that light" (62–63).[48] Losing herself in the things she
beheld, leaving behind the "fret, the hurry, the stir" of her anxious self, there
rises to her lips "some exclamation of triumph over life when things came
together in this peace, this rest, this eternity." And it is in this moment of mystical communion with the surrounding universe, as deep calls upon deep, that
Mrs. Ramsay adds: "We are in the hands of the Lord" (63).

No sooner has she uttered this prayer, however, than she revokes it: "But
instantly she was annoyed with herself for saying that. Who had said that?"
Who indeed. And why feel so ashamed to have fallen back into the fold of
common prayer? Because, apparently, it is somehow unearned. Too easy, too
quick. "[S]he had been trapped into saying something she did not mean" (63).
A "lie," Mrs. Ramsay calls it, referring no doubt to the lure of an otherworldly
deity, some Supreme Omnipotent Cause aloof and detached from the world

of flesh, adjudicating our destinies. Resisting the temptation to escape into the hands of such a convenient God, Mrs. Ramsay embraces another kind of mysticism, where one is "alone with the alone" (as the Upanishads say) and where the natural universe of ordinary things is loved rather than abandoned: "It was odd, she thought, how if one was alone, one leant to inanimate things; trees, streams, flowers; felt they expressed one; felt they became one; felt they knew one, in a sense were one; felt an irrational tenderness thus (she looked at that long steady light) as for oneself. There rose, and she looked and looked with her needles suspended, there curled up off the floor of the mind, rose from the lake of one's being, a mist, a bride to meet her lover" (63–64).[49]

But what is this post-theistic mysticism that Mrs. Ramsay incarnates? In a classic admission shortly before her death, Virginia Woolf spoke of the sudden shocks and surprises of life as tokens of "some real thing behind appearances." She intimated that "behind the cotton wool is hidden a pattern" and that all human beings are somehow "connected with this." In short, she espoused the view that the "whole world is a work of art." But no sooner had she made this confession than she added, "But there is no Shakespeare, there is no Beethoven; certainly and emphatically there is no God."[50] What does she mean by this triple denial? It would seem that Woolf is implying that the "pattern," the "real thing," is not *made* but *given*. It is not the product of creators—human or divine—but an intimation of some anonymous unfathomable love which connects all beings behind and beneath the appearances of agency and artifice. And this is, of course, where the problematic role of "art" informs the novel, represented as it is by Lily Briscoe's attempt to capture Mrs. Ramsay in a painting. For how can art—be it Lily's painting, Mr. Carmichael's poem, or Woolf's own novel—ever hope to represent this miracle of ordinary life? Confronting her canvas, Lily too, we are told, is aware of something not herself, some "other thing" which is "truth" or "reality," something both there in the lampshade and also timelessly abstracted from it, a thing emerging "at the back of appearances" (158). There is, Lily realizes, something suspect in art's attempt to reduce the contingency and transience of life to "[b]eautiful pictures" and "[b]eautiful phrases." What Lily needs to get hold of is the "jar on the nerves, the thing itself before it had been *made* anything." She seeks to achieve that "razor edge of balance between two opposite forces," namely art and life (193).[51] The problem therefore arises: how can art imagine the mystery of flesh without betraying it?

Let us take a closer look. Here we return to Lily's final gesture. In the closing sequence of the book, Lily is seeking a particular stroke of her paintbrush which will, in a "leap" into the gap between art and life, somehow bring the two together, make the impossible possible; just as Mrs. Ramsay found that special "stroke of light," beamed from the lighthouse at night, with which she could connect. Lily eventually has her "vision," as she sacrifices the goal of some pure, transcendental aesthetic for an aesthetic of ordinary things. And it is just as her anamnetic portrait of Mrs. Ramsay is being completed that she expresses this sentiment of disclosing the marvel of the everyday: "One wanted, she thought, dipping her brush deliberately, to be on a level with ordinary experience, to feel simply that's a chair, that's a table, and yet at the same time, It's a miracle, it's an ecstasy. The problem might be solved after all" (202).

Everything, it seems, revolves on this reversibility of upper and lower case "It/it." The miracle consists in the transubstantiation of the higher into the lower, the extraordinary into the ordinary, transcendence into immanence. And vice versa. It is a moment both kenotic (the emptying of Word into flesh) and eucharistic (the celebration of the infinite in the finite bread and wine of quotidian experience).

It is the same "It" that Virginia Woolf writes of in February 1926, while she was composing this section of the novel, as she crossed Russell Square in London: "I see the mountains in the sky: the great clouds; and the moon which has risen over Persia; I have a great and astonishing sense of something there, which is 'it.'" This "it" is something "out there," some "other thing" beyond one's will and personality. It is at once "frightening and exciting," for it refuses to be humanized by our subjective projections and names—including the anthropomorphic name of "God."[52] But for Lily Briscoe to achieve this aesthetic "vision," for her to effect the final brush stroke, draw "a line there, in the centre" of her canvas, so that she can finally say "It was done; it was finished," for Lily to do this she first has to acknowledge the reality of Mrs. Ramsay's death and absence (209). She has to let go her ideal imago, accept the cut of mortality, and take the leap into the gap left behind.[53]

In terms of the novel's characters, this means allowing Mr. Ramsay's atheism to cut through Mrs. Ramsay's mysticism. Lily has to admit what is "other" to her fused and nostalgic memory of Mrs. Ramsay whom she has been invoking for solace and reunion: "Oh, Mrs Ramsay, Mrs Ramsay!" Mr. Ramsay is the "opposite force" which resists her retrieval of Mrs. Ramsay and compels Lily to take a leap from the "narrow plank, perfectly alone, over the sea ... into the waters of annihilation" (172, 181). Before she can finish her painting, Lily has to accept that Mrs. Ramsay is *gone*, passed away, past; for only then can she recall her again, posthumously, through the gap of atheism, the caesura of separation, the final stroke that cuts, like a sword-blade, even as it reconnects. Reconnects what? Lily to memory, a future to the past. To put it in other terms, Mrs. Ramsay is the "lost object," the deceased saviour-friend whom Lily must relinquish if she is to move from obsessive melancholy to a mourning which accepts the real. And for Lily it is Mr. Ramsay—atheist and empiricist, irritant and exigent—who represents this cutting edge of the reality principle. As

Martin Corner observes, "Mr. Ramsay is an unwavering witness to the non-humanity of the world; he therefore represents to Lily that otherness which must somehow be got into the picture if it is not to be false."[54] Mr. Ramsay testifies to the "thing itself before it has been made anything" (by knitting, cooking, painting, dreaming, fictionalizing) (193). And this thing, it transpires, is a no-thing. It is that emptiness, that void, that "unfathomable deep" which haunts the imaginations of both Mrs. Ramsay and Lily, the "wedge of darkness" which has to be faced and acknowledged before it can well up into fullness and Lily can say, "Empty it was not but full to the brim" (192). But first the letting go ... The renunciation of the illusion of a grandiose revelation, be it of art, metaphysics, or religion, which trumps the world of flesh and blood, denies the universe of little things: "The great revelation perhaps never did come. Instead there were little daily miracles, illuminations, matches struck unexpectedly in the dark" (161).

Here, I submit, we encounter a mysticism less of fusion than of equipoise, less of triumph than of that "razor edge" balance between opposites, celebrated by the Vedic sages of the Upanishads (and certain Jewish and Christian mystics). In this regard, what we have been calling Lily's — and Woolf's — atheistic mysticism takes on a more positive valence, recalling as it does the Asiatic features of Lily's countenance (those "Chinese eyes" the narrator frequently refers to). The letting go of Mrs. Ramsay and the harmonious memory of the opening meal is also a letting go of our image of the all-powerful "Lord" who "saves us," namely, the anthropomorphic deity of Western myth and metaphysics. It is only in the letting go — in the kenosis of "truth" emptying itself of Godhead — that Lily can complete her painting at the very moment that Mr. Ramsay fulfills Mrs. Ramsay's dream of bringing their son James (and daughter Cam) to the lighthouse. The passage is significant: "He rose and stood in the bow of the boat, very straight and tall, for all the world, James thought, as if he were saying, 'There is no God,' and Cam thought, as if he were leaping into space, and they both rose to follow him as he sprang, lightly like a young man, holding his parcel, on to the rock" (207). It is precisely at this moment of *grounding* that Lily, watching from the shore, draws her final stroke and says, like a certain deity on the Cross yielding up to death, "It is finished." *Consumatum est.* A moment of death and rebirth, of letting go and gaining back. A time when, at last, "empty flourishes ... form into shape" (180).

The mystical allusions of this closing paragraph of the novel are resonant and deep. And I believe they confirm Woolf's numerous mentions in her autobiographical writings of a reality which goes beyond God to achieve its epiphany of the ordinary, a sentiment not unlike the move made by Advaita and Buddhist mysticism, which refuses to think transcendence apart from immanence. Nor is it unlike the famous prayer of Meister Eckhart that "God might rid him of God." This mysticism *after God*, is, I suggest, an affirmation of a Eucharist of the everyday, of a sacrament of common "reality," of an epiphany of "It/it" residing at the core of Woolf's own vision. In short, Lily has now found her miracle "on a level with ordinary experience" (202), a world at once itself and yet simultaneously transfigured into what Woolf calls "a reality of a different order"[55] —a world poised on a razor's edge, where opposites balance without collapsing into sameness.

Conclusion

So what is the significance of the fact that our three witnesses of sacramental imagination — Joyce, Proust, and Woolf — are all agnostics, and that the three characters who best embody their aesthetic vision are women (Molly, Françoise, and Lily)? Is this not a different kind of Eucharistic language than the one which informs our traditional male-dominated liturgies (where usually no women need apply)? This is surely a sacramental vision of a new sort, or at least of the old revisited otherwise. It deploys the poetic licence of fiction to suspend confessional creeds and doctrines in order to offer "free variations" of transubstantiation, namely, the reversible "miracle" of word-made-flesh and flesh-made-word.

Recalling the canonical definition of transubstantiation as "the transforming of one substance into another," we may say that we have identified three main kinds in our readings above: (1) *intra-textual*, (2) *intertextual*, and (3) *trans-textual*. As instances of the first kind we may cite the numerous examples of one character being transfused into another (Mrs. Ramsay into Lily, Maman into Françoise, Penelope into Molly) or one spatio-temporal moment translated into another (the madeleine epiphany or the involuntary memory of Maman reading in Combray and Venice recalled years later in the Guermantes's library). As examples of the second (*intertextual*) kind, we might cite the transmuting of one narrative into another (Homer's *Odyssey* into Joyce's *Ulysses*, the Biblical stories of Elijah and St. Stephen into the tales of Bloom and Dedalus, George Sand's novel into Proust's; or the numerous instances of the Scriptural Eucharist transliterated into the sacramental re-enactments of Mrs. Ramsay and Molly or of Marcel in his final epiphanies). Finally, we can identify key examples of the *trans-textual* transubstantiation of author into narrator, character, and reader. This third model — involving the very process of writing and reading, of configuring and re-figuring — is the one highlighted in the phenomenological analyses of Merleau-Ponty, Kristeva, and Ricoeur. And it is with this final model, I suggest, that we encounter an opening of the world of the text beyond itself — both forward to the post-textual world of the reader, and backward (by way of implied regress from character to narrator to author) to the pre-textual world of the writer. This acknowledgement, however tentative and mediated, of some *extra-textual* element — intimating a life of action before and after the text — is in keeping with the sacramental paradigm of transubstantiation: a paradigm which, I have been suggesting, testifies to the unbreakable liaison between the body of the text and the bread of life. Or, to revisit the language of epiphany, between Word and Flesh.

Our three novelists may well be, by turns, agnostics, apostates, or atheists, but this does not in the least prevent them from being haunted by a singularly mystical vision of things. It may, in a paradoxical sense, even contribute to such insight by predisposing them to something beyond the reach of many orthodox religious conventions. (The history of religions, let us not forget, attests to a deep complicity between mysticism and so-called atheism.) Each writer, as I hope to have shown, bears witness to a special sacredness at the heart of the profane. But in each unique instance the mutual transfiguring of material bread and mystical body is anything but "sacrificial" — in the dogmatic sense of an expiatory victim sacrificed to redeem sins and appease an omnipotent Father. The sacramental aesthetic of our three authors is, I suggest, far removed from an economy of penalty, reward, and judgment. On the contrary, it bears witness to literary epiphanies of radical kenosis and emptying, where the sacred unhitches itself from absolute Being ("equality with the Father," as Paul put it) in order to descend into the heart of finite flesh so that the birth of the Son as an incarnate historical being attests to the demise of the Father as immutable Master of the universe. Unless the divine seed dies, there can be no Eucharistic rebirth. Or, to put it in the words of the young Jewish mystic Etty Hillesum, "by excluding death from one's life we deny ourselves the possibility of a full life."[56]

I suggested at the outset that a certain phenomenology of flesh, outlined by Merleau-Ponty and Kristeva, might offer guidance in sketching a sacramental aesthetics that goes beyond sacrificial theology and dualist metaphysics. Several other contemporary philosophers, also hailing from the phenomenological movement, have, I believe, usefully discussed this possibility of a post-sacrificial sanctity, and I would like, in these concluding pages, to engage with this debate about possibilities of a religion beyond religion. Jacques Derrida and John Caputo, for example, have both explored the idea of "religion without religion," or a messianicity without metaphysics. Caputo's own notion of the "weakness of God" stems from a reading of Christian kenosis in light of a deconstructionist complicity between mysticism and atheism as identified by Derrida in *Sauf le nom*. Here Derrida, who claims that he "rightly passes for an atheist," has this to say: "The desire of God, God as the other name of desire, deals in the desert with radical atheism.... [The] most consequent forms of declared atheism will have always testified... to the most intense desire for God.... Like... mysticism, apophatic discourse has always been suspected of

atheism.... [I]f atheism, like apophatic theology, testifies to the desire of God...
in the presence of *whom* does it do this?"[57] In an intriguing dialogue with
apophatic theology, contemporary thinkers like Stanislas Breton and Gianni
Vattimo have shown how a kenotic moment of "nothingness" and "emptiness" resides at the core of a post-metaphysical faith. Faith, says Breton, "must...
inhabit the world and give" back to God "the being he has not"; speaking more
specifically of kenosis, he talks of a process that follows "the descent of the
divine into a human form, obedience unto death, the ignominy of the Cross.
But at the very moment that the paroxysm of abasement touches the depth of
nothingness, the shock of the negative, in its paradoxical power, commands
the exultant ascent toward the point of origin."[58] In the case of Vattimo, kenosis entails a reading of 1 Corinthians 13 (on love) which treats the Incarnation
as God's relinquishing of all power and authority so as to turn everything over
to the secular order. Vattimo considers "God's self-emptying and man's
attempt to think of love as the only law" as two sides of the same coin. And the
conclusion of his "fragile" hermeneutic, while startling, is entirely consistent:
namely, that "secularization... is the constitutive trait of 'authentic religious
experience.'"[59] Copernicus, Freud, and Nietzsche need no longer, on this
account, be seen as enemies of the sacred but, on the contrary, as "carrying out
works of love."[60] And I think that Gilles Deleuze is making a somewhat similar point when he declares that we must abandon the sacrificial instinct for
scapegoating and instead identify with the lamb: "The God who, like a lion,
was given blood sacrifice must be shoved into the background, and the sacrificed god must occupy the foreground.... God became the animal that was
slain, instead of the animal that does the slaying."[61]

But it is, in my view, Paul Ricoeur who most poignantly struggles with this
post-sacrificial notion of death and resurrection in his final testament, written as he was dying, *Vivant jusqu'à la mort* (2007). Speaking of a certain kind
of "grace" accompanying the experience of death, Ricoeur notes that "it is not
important for this moment of grace that the dying person identifies with a
particular religion or confession. Indeed maybe it is only when faced with
death that the religious becomes one with the Essential and that the barrier
dividing religions (and non-religions like Buddhism) are transcended.
Because dying is trans-cultural it is also trans-confessional and trans-reli-
gious."[62] Admitting his basic suspicion of "immediacy and fusion," Ricoeur
makes one exception for "the grace of a certain dying" (45). Ricoeur talks
about this grace as a "paradox of immanent transcendence," of an especially
"intimate transcendence of the Essential which rips through the veils of confessional religious codes" (47). To encounter such authentic grace one must,
Ricoeur suggests, forgo the will for one's own personal salvation by transfer-
ring this hope onto others. He also speaks, in this respect, of renouncing the

metaphysical fiction of an otherworldly Being dispensing punishment and reward in some kind of celestial tribunal. Theodicy must be resisted. Invoking instead the great Rhine mystics, Ricoeur remarks how they "renounced themselves" for the sake of opening to the Essential, to the point of being, in their contemplative detachment, incredibly active in the creation of new orders, in teaching, in travelling, and tending to the forgotten of this world. By being available like this to the Essential, they were motivated to "transfer the love of life onto others" (76). God thus becomes a God *after* God, a god of the living rather than of the dead, of service rather than mastery, the dichotomy between "before" and "after" death suddenly dissolving.

And so here again we confront the basic scriptural paradox, so oft invoked by Proust, that he who clings to his life loses it and he who lets it go gains it.[63] Or to put it in Joyce's terms, "without sundering there is no reconciliation." In this context Ricoeur offers a startlingly refreshing reading of the Eucharist as a celebration of blood-as-wine, transubstantiation being taken as a sign of life and sharing rather than a token of sacrificial bloodletting (90). The Eucharistic commemoration of the giving of one's life — "Do this in memory of me" — thus becomes an affirmation of the gift of life to and for the other rather than an anxiety about personal physical survival after death. In other words, when Christ said "it is finished," he meant it. He was offering up his own personal life, in a second gesture of kenotic emptying (the first being the descent of divinity into flesh), so as to give life to others, in service (Luke 22:27) and in sacrament: the breaking of bread at Emmaus, the cooking of fish for his disciples when he returned — incognito — in the form of the risen servant, and ever after, down through human history, in the guise of feeding the "least of these" (*elachistos*). Ricoeur concludes his terminal testament with this remarkable note:

> The Son of Man came not to be served but to serve. Hence the link between *death-rebirth in the other* and *service as gift of life*. And the link between service and feast. The Last Supper conjoins the moment of dying unto oneself and the service of the other in the sharing of food and wine which joins the man of death to the multitude of survivors reunited in community. And this is why it is remarkable that Jesus never theorized about this and never said *who* he was. Maybe he didn't *know*, for he *lived* the Eucharistic gesture, bridged the gap between the imminence of death and the community beyond. He marked a passage to glory (through suffering and death) without any sacrificial perspective. (91)

Ricoeur is rejecting here, it seems to me, the notion of Christ's death as a scapegoating ritual of bloodletting to propitiate and recompense a blood-lusting deity, not Christ's act of "sacrificing" his life out of love for others.

The fact that Ricoeur calls himself a "Christian who writes philosophically" rather than a "Christian philosopher" seems to me significant here, for he is acknowledging the importance of a certain gap, a certain non-confessional space occupied by philosophy and art, which allows us to freely and imaginatively revisit, and at times anamnetically retrieve, the often forgotten, concealed, or taken-for-granted resources of traditional religion. God must die so that God may be reborn. Or, as Ricoeur puts it, "we must smash false idols so that genuine symbols can speak."[64]

I am struck by the relevance of these philosophical accounts for comprehending the sacramental vision of our three novelists. In each case, I have suggested, we find the letting go of a certain fetish or fixation serving as a *via negativa*, which permits the return of a *second naïveté* (Ricoeur): a repetition after the experience of death and nothingness which signals a new kind of "miracle," "resurrection," "grace," this time in ordinary events ignored first time around. For Joyce and Proust these moments of sacramental remembrance occur when their literary heroes—Stephen and Marcel—come to renounce their initial great expectations and ultimately acknowledge the muse of the everyday (Molly and Françoise, respectively). For Woolf it occurs when Lily finally recalls the failed painting of the "purple triangle," depicting Mrs. Ramsay and James in the first part of the novel, with the final stroke which enables her, as a reincarnation or rememoration of Mrs. Ramsay, to have her "vision" and declare the painting "finished" (52, 209). The bread and wine of quotidian existence are thus celebrated as eucharistic epiphanies—the kiss of the seedcake between Molly and Bloom, the touch of a table napkin for Marcel, Mrs. Ramsay's empty glove (like empty burial clothes?)—such that hitherto ignored moments are "resurrected" out of passing time, retrieved for a new life which assumes and subsumes death, for a new generation of survivors (James and Cam, Mlle de Saint-Loup, Stephen), and for a new community of readers. Unless the seed dies, the wheat cannot grow and the bread cannot be shared.

I am not suggesting that our three "sacramental" novelists are in any sense religious apologists. Or secret advocates of Christian liturgy. There are certain confessional writers who might be said to fit such a category—G.M. Hopkins, Claudel, Bernanos, even the later Eliot, not to mention Dante and many traditional religious writers throughout the centuries. My purpose here has not been to engage in doctrinal apologetics or to expose our three novelists as crypto-Catholics *après la lettre*. No, it has been to explore the possibility of a certain post-credal mysticism embracing a eucharistic aesthetic where the secular and sacred unite. Thus while not wishing to exclude confessional writers from adherence to such an aesthetic, I wish to suggest that it is particularly valuable for us in this secular era to consider how certain non-confessional authors deploy an art of transubstantiation to explore a mysticism of *God-after-God*, or, as some might prefer to say, of spirituality-after-religion. I have suggested, at the outset, that this after-faith may be helped by critical application of the sacramental phenomenology of flesh advanced by thinkers like Merleau-Ponty and Kristeva. The "after" here should not be read as privative but as an affirmative function of "ana"—that is, of retrieval and resurrection *après coup*[65]—as in ana-mnesis or, as I formulated it elsewhere, in *ana-theism*.[66]

I use the term *anatheism* to refer to the return of the divine in the secular world after the death of God (taken in the metaphysical sense of a causal Being of otherwordly omnipotence and theodicy). Anatheism thus signals, as I understand it, a *via affirmativa* following the *via negativa* of modern doubt and disenchantment: the yes to a God after God (*ana-theos*), the return to God after the setting aside (*ana-thema)* of God. And here anathema takes on the double sense of not only heretical condemnation but also of a primary consecration or setting apart as holy. Anathema originally carried the sense of a thing devoted to the divine. In this light, the agnosticism of Joyce (self-styled "heresiarch"), Woolf, and Proust might, I submit, be read as a "negative capability" which carves open a space of sacramental mysticism, beyond the traditional dichotomy between theism and atheism. In other words, anatheism signals the possibility of a God apart from metaphysics and dogmatism, the possibility of a God of inter-religious hospitality. Meaning what? An opening towards a God who neither is nor is not but may be—depending on our response to the sacred seed of each profane moment. This calls for a special attentiveness to infinity embodying itself in daily acts of eucharistic love and sharing. An endless crossing over and back between the infinite and infinitesimal. The highest deity becoming—kenotically, sacramentally—the very "least of these" (Matt. 25:40). The Word made everyday flesh. Ongoing and interminable gift. Transubstantiation.

Notes

I am very grateful to all my colleagues in the Meaning and Transcendence Seminar at the Jesuit Institute at Boston College for several of the insights in this essay, in particular those with whom I had an extensive creative correspondence on Joyce, Proust, and Woolf, namely, Mary-Joe Hughes, Dennis Taylor, Anne Davenport, Marty Cohen, Vanessa Rumble, and Kevin Newmark.

1 Étienne Gilson, *The Unity of Philosophical Experience* (1937; San Francisco: Ignatius Press, 1999) 221.

2 Maurice Merleau-Ponty, *Phenomenology of Perception*, trans. Colin Smith (London and New York: Routledge, 2002) 246; italics mine. I am grateful to John Panteleimon Manoussakis for this reference. See his extended discussion of this theme in *God after Metaphysics: A Theological Aesthetics* (Bloomington: Indiana University Press, 2007).

3 Merleau-Ponty, *Phenomenology of Perception*, 248.

4 Maurice Merleau-Ponty, *The Visible and the Invisible*, ed. Claude Lefort, trans. Alphonso Lingis (Evanston, IL: Northwestern University Press, 1968) 139.
5 Ibid.
6 Maurice Merleau-Ponty, *Eye and Mind* in *Continental Aesthetics: Romanticism to Postmodernism: An Anthology*, ed. Richard Kearney and David Rasmussen (Oxford: Blackwell, 2001) 292, 303.
7 Maurice Merleau-Ponty, *Signs*, trans. Richard C. McCleary (Evanston, IL: Northwestern University Press, 1964) 64.
8 Ibid., 71.
9 See also the work of Catherine Keller, *Face of the Deep: A Theology of Becoming* (London and New York: Routledge, 2003) and John Panteleimon Manoussakis, *God after Metaphysics*. Nor should we omit reference here to Gabriel Marcel's intriguing philosophical reflections on incarnation and embodiment, which exerted a considerable influence on the "religious" phenomenological writings of Ricoeur and Levinas.
10 See for example the work of my colleagues Frank Kennedy on music and Steven Schloesser on painting (especially Rouault) and what Schloesser calls "mystic modernism" in *Jazz Age Catholicism: Mystic Modernism in Postwar Paris: 1919–1923* (Toronto: University of Toronto Press, 2005).
11 Julia Kristeva, *Time and Sense: Proust and the Experience of Literature*, trans. Ross Guberman (New York: Columbia University Press, 1996) 251; italics mine in the second and third instance. Future quotations from *Time and Sense* are from this edition and will be referenced in the text by page number.
12 Transubstantiation is defined as (a) "The changing of one substance into another" and (b) "The conversion in the Eucharist of the whole substance of the bread and of the wine into the blood of Christ, only the appearances (and other 'accidents') of bread and wine remaining: according to the doctrine of the Roman Catholic Church 1533" (*The Shorter Oxford English Dictionary*, 5th ed. [Oxford: Oxford University Press, 2002] 2349). What fascinates both Joyce and Proust about this process, according to Kristeva, is that such an act, mixing the secular and the sacred, combines both an "imaginary" and "real" character.
13 "*A state of flesh*," writes Kristeva, "appears to underlie the therapeutic act, but it can become a true *therapeutic act* only if language is led to the reversible and chiasmic sensation that supports it" (what Proust calls the "impression" or "transubstantiation") (247). For Kristeva this reversibility of flesh can take the form of (a) a literary act of writing and reading as a "two-sided sensoriality" (247) or (b) a psychoanalytic act of transference and counter-transference. Interestingly, neither Proust nor Joyce was insensitive to the powers of psychotherapy, any more than they were to the powers of religion, without practising either. Kristeva cites and comments on a number of key passages from Merleau-Ponty's *The Visible and the Invisible* (*Time and Sense*, 269ff).
14 Marcel Proust, *Against Sainte-Beuve*, qtd. in Kristeva, *Time and Sense*, 252. I think Kristeva is close here to the hermeneutic model of extra-linguistic ontological refiguration of which Paul Ricoeur speaks in *Time and Narrative*, trans. Kathleen McLaughlin and David Pellauer, vol. 1 (Chicago: University of Chicago Press, 1984). See Ricoeur's claim, for example, that "What a reader receives is not just the sense of the work, but, through its sense, its reference, that is, the experience it

brings to language and, in the last analysis, the world and the temporality it unfolds in the face of this experience" (78–79). Or again in "Life in Quest of Narrative" (*On Paul Ricoeur: Narrative and Interpretation,* ed. Derek Wood [London and New York: Routledge, 1991] 26): "My thesis is here that the process of composition, of configuration, is not completed in the text but in the reader and, under this condition, makes possible the reconfiguration of life by narrative. I should say, more precisely: the sense or the significance of a narrative stems from *the intersection of the world of the text and the world of the reader*" (which is already "prefigured" by the world of the author). Ricoeur goes so far as to construe this surrendering of author to implied author (of the text), and the subsequent surrender of implied author to the reader, as acts of kenotic gift and service to the other, which ultimately amounts to a sacramental transubstantiation of author into reader: "[W]hereas the real author effaces himself in the implied author, the implied reader takes on substance in the real reader" (Paul Ricoeur, *Time and Narrative,* trans. Kathleen McLaughlin and David Pellauer, vol. 3 [Chicago University Press, Chicago, 1988] 170). In short, the author agrees to die so that the reader may be born.

15 James Joyce, *A Portrait of the Artist as a Young Man* (London: Penguin, 1992) 240.

16 See Julia Kristeva, "Joyce 'The Gracehoper' or Orpheus' Return," *New Maladies of the Soul,* trans. Ross Guberman (New York: Columbia University Press, 1997) 172–88. Other informative treatments of Joyce's sacramental aesthetic include William T. Noon, *Joyce and Aquinas* (New Haven, CT: Yale University Press, 1957); Robert Boyle, *James Joyce's Pauline Vision: A Catholic Exposition* (Carbondale: Southern Illinois University Press, 1978); Jean-Louis Houbedine, "Joyce, Littérature et religion," *Excès de langage: Holderlin, Joyce, Duns Scot, Hopkins, Cantor, Sollers* (New York: Denoël, 1984). Although Stephen Dedalus rejects the Eucharist of Jesus for the art of Icarus early in *A Portrait,* later in the novel he revisits an aesthetic of the sacred in his reading of Thomistic radiance (*claritas*) (Joyce, *Portrait,* 231). It is typical of Joyce's incarnational aesthetic to link Aquinas's transcendental category of beauty here with the more physiological category of heart and flesh. Tellingly, we are told in the concluding lines of *A Portrait* of the wish that Stephen "may learn in [his] own life and away from home and friends what the heart is and what it feels … So be it. Welcome, O life!" (275).

17 Conversation with Joyce recorded in Stanislaus Joyce, *My Brother's Keeper: James Joyce's Early Years,* ed. Richard Ellmann (Cambridge, MA: Da Capo, 2003) 103ff. I am grateful to Fran O'Rourke for bringing this passage to my attention.

18 See my "Joyce: Epiphanies and Triangles," *Navigations: Collected Irish Essays 1976–2006* (Dublin: Lilliput, 2006) 131ff; and "Traversals and Epiphanies in Joyce and Proust," *Traversing the Imaginary: Richard Kearney and the Postmodern Challenge,* ed. Peter Gratton and John Panteleimon Manoussakis (Evanston, IL: Northwestern University Press, 2007). On epiphany in Joyce see also George Steiner, *Real Presences* (London: Faber and Faber, 1989) 112ff. On parodied, failed, or deconstructed Eucharists in Joyce's stories "Sisters," "Clay," and "The Dead," see the work of the theologian Joseph O'Leary, for example, "Enclosed Spaces in 'The Dead,'" *English Literature and Language,* vol. 34 (Tokyo: University of Sophia, 1997) 33–52.

19 James Joyce, *Ulysses,* introd. Declan Kiberd, Modern Penguin Classics (1960; London: Penguin, 2000) 1; future citations from *Ulysses* are from this edition and will be referenced in the text by page number.

20 On the subject of the eschatological kiss see also my comparison between Molly and the bride of the Song of Songs in "The Shulammite's Song: Divine Eros, Ascending and Descending," *Toward a Theology of Eros: Transfiguring Passion at the Limits of Discipline*, ed. Virginia Burrus and Catherine Keller (New York: Fordham University Press, 2006).

21 See my discussion of Joyce's proximity to Duns Scotus's notions of *haecceitas* (thisness) and *ensarkosis* (the ongoing enfleshment of the Divine in the world) in "Joyce: Epiphanies and Triangles," *Navigations*, 131ff.

22 Walter Benjamin, "On the Concept of History," *Walter Benjamin: Selected Writings, Volume 4, 1938–1940*, ed. Howard Eiland and Michael W. Jennings (Cambridge, MA: Belknap-Harvard University Press, 2006) 397.

23 Rodolphe Gasché, *Inventions of Difference: On Jacques Derrida* (Cambridge, MA: Harvard University Press, 1994) 230. Gasché is here elaborating on Derrida's reading of Joyce in "Ulysses Gramophone: Hear Say Yes in Joyce," *Acts of Literature*, ed. Derek Attridge (London and New York: Routledge, 1992).

24 On this later point see Kristeva, *Time and Sense*, 3–22. For a eucharistic hermeneutics of reading see also Valentine Cunningham, *Reading after Theory* (Oxford: Blackwell, 2002) 148ff: "Here's a body of text and the text as body, the body of the other, the text as other, to be consumed, ingested, in a memorial act...an act of testimony, of worldly witness.... In...holy communion the believer is blessed and graced, signed as Christ's own, marked as sanctified. In reading on this (Eucharistic model), the reader is, in some way or another, also graced, blessed, marked as the text's own" (148).

25 Søren Kierkegaard, *Repetition*, trans. Walter Lowrie (Princeton, NJ: Princeton University Press, 1941).

26 *The Odyssey of Homer*, ed. T.E. Lawrence (New York: Oxford University Press, 1991) 318–19.

27 James Joyce, letter to his brother Stanislaus, 1905, quoted by Declan Kiberd in his introduction to *Ulysses* (x). The letter begins, "Do you not think the search for heroics damn vulgar?"

28 Derrida offers a useful gloss on the language of Molly/Penelope in an intriguing footnote to his commentary on the relationship between Greek and Jew in Emmanuel Levinas; see "Violence and Metaphysics: An Essay on the Thought of Emmanuel Levinas," *Writing and Difference*, trans. Alan Bass (Chicago: University of Chicago Press, 1978) 320–21. Commenting on a phrase in *Ulysses*—"Jewgreek is greekjew. Extremes meet"—Derrida attributes this not only to "woman's reason," as in Joyce's text, but he also identifies Joyce here as "perhaps the most Hegelian of modern novelists" (153). The implication here seems to be that the discourse of "feminine logic," associated with Molly/Penelope, is one which, for Levinas at least, suggests an "ontological category" of return and closure: namely, Ulysses returning to Penelope in Ithaca, Stephen and Bloom returning to Molly in Eccles Street where they may find themselves "atoned" as father-son, jew-greek, greek-jew, etc. It is not quite clear where Derrida himself stands towards Joyce in this early 1964 text, though it is evident that he thinks Levinas would repudiate the Joycean formula as overly Hegelian and Greek (that is, not sufficiently respectful of the strictly Jewish/Messianic/eschatological need for a radically asymmetrical relation of self and other). In his later essay, "Ulysses Gramophone," first delivered

as a lecture to the International Joyce Symposium in Frankfurt, 1984, he makes it clear that the "yes" of Molly/Penelope marks an opening of the text beyond total-ity and closure to an infinite and infinitely recurring "other" (*Ulysse Gramophone: Deux mots pour Joyce* [Paris: Galilee, 1987]). Even if it is a response to oneself, in interior dialogue, "yes" always involves a relay through an Other. Or as Derrida cleverly puts it, *oui-dire*, saying yes, always involves some form of *oui-dire* or hearsay. "A yes never comes along, and we never say this word alone" (300). With this relay of self through the other, this willing of yes to say yes again, "this differ-ing and deferring, this necessary failure of total self-identity, comes spacing (space *and* time), gramophoning (writing *and* speech), memory" (254). And this "other" clearly implies a reaching beyond the text of *Ulysses* itself to the listener, the reader, an open call for our response.

In this sense we would say that *Ulysses* is a deeply anti-Hegelian book. Molly's finale does not represent some great teleological reconciliation of contradictions in some absolute synthesis of Spirit but an ongoing affirmation of paradoxes, struggles, contraries, and contingencies, spoken in a spirit of humour and desire. "What else were we given all those desires for?" asks the polymorphously perverse Molly, a far cry from the Hegelian triumph of Identity. We may conclude, there-fore, that the story of struggle and trouble does not end when Stephen follows Bloom out of the library, it only begins. And by the same token, Molly, when she finally arrives, does not put paid to Trinities as such; she simply reintroduces us — along with Stephen and Bloom — to another kind of trinity, one without a capital T and more inclusive of time, movement, natality, and desire (all those things banned from the Sabellian Trinity of self-enclosed Identity parodied by Stephen in the National Library scene). And, one might add, more inclusive of the reader. For like any epiphany, Molly's too calls out to an open future of readers.

29 My understanding of eucharistic epiphany in literature is deeply indebted to Proust's understanding of sacred "repetition" over time and space, as articulated by Ricoeur in the following passage on the way in which all of Combray appeared in a teacup: "What is more, it is when the direct short-circuit between two similar sensations, obtained in happy moments, is supplanted by the long meditation on the work of art, that repetition takes on its full signification, which appeared to me to be summed up in the admirable expression of distance traversed. In happy moments, two similar instants were miraculously brought together. Through the mediation of art, this fleeting miracle is stabilized in an enduring work. Time lost is equated with time regained" (Ricoeur, *Time and Narrative*, vol. 3, 135). Such eucharistic epiphanies in literature are a connection across distance in time and space, just as the Christian sacrament is a remembrance of the Last Supper of the past (which itself repeats the Passover) which it repeats forwards "*until he (the Messiah) comes*" in the future.

30 See my discussion of the eschatological temporality of the Palestinian formula in both Judaic and Christian messianism in "Enabling God," *After God: Richard Kear-ney and the Religious Turn in Continental Philosophy*, ed. John Panteleimon Manoussakis (New York: Fordham University Press, 2006) 39–54; see also my "Hermeneutics of the Possible God," *Givenness and God: Questions of Jean-Luc Marion*, ed. Ian Leask and Eoin Cassidy (New York: Fordham University Press, 2005) 220–42. My sketch of micro-eschatological possibility, temporality, and

carnality is powerfully articulated in Denise Levertov's poem "The Annunciation"; see *Denise Levertov: Selected Poems* (New York: New Directions, 2002)
162–63.

31 Contrast this inaugural — and ultimately lost — kiss of maternal "fusion" with the
disastrous kiss of "diffusion" which Marcel experiences with Albertine later in the
novel. The closest Marcel may be said to come to achieving a eucharistic kiss,
beyond these two extremes, might be the brushing of his lips on the table napkin
chez les Guermantes which recalls the meal at the Grand Hotel in Balbec, or perhaps more emblematically, the image of the "star-shaped" crossroads where the
two diverging paths of his youth — *le chemin de Méséglise* and *le chemin de Swann* —
converge almost mystically, chiasmically, "transversally," in the figure of
Ghilberte's daughter, Mlle de Saint-Loup, at the final party. But this final kiss is a
kiss deferred for others, in the future, just as the final meal *chez les Guermantes* is
a feast postponed: his lips touch the napkin but he does not eat.

It is significant, I think, that Proust's novel does not end with the epiphanies
in the library. Marcel does not stay in the Guermantes's library any more than
Stephen stays in the National Library after his great insight into Hamlet. And
though Marcel takes this occasion to announce an extremely elaborate theory of
literature and life (as does Stephen), the text does not culminate with theory. Marcel leaves the library and re-enters the everyday universe. And it is here, in the
midst of the chaos and commotion of a fragmenting Parisian community, that
Marcel has what we might consider his ultimate epiphany: his meeting with Mlle
de Saint-Loup (Ghilberte's daughter). Mlle de Saint-Loup is to Marcel what Molly
(via Leopold) is to Stephen. Both appear at the end of the story and lead the
author-artist beyond the vain play of mimetic triangles and abstract trinities back
to the ordinary universe of generation and gratuity.

32 Marcel Proust, *Swann's Way, In Search of Lost Time*, trans. C.K. Scott Moncrieff and
Terence Kilmartin, rev. D.J. Enright, vol. 1 (New York: Modern Library, 1998) 64.

33 "Transubstantiation" and "time embodied" are Proust's terms, qtd. in *Time and
Sense*, 101. Kristeva comments interestingly on Proust's fascination with the
Catholic Eucharist and links it with his aesthetic interest in John Ruskin; she goes
on to argue that Ruskin's seduction was "aesthetic *as well as* religious" (101).

34 Proust qtd. in Kristeva, *Time and Sense*, 106.

35 Kristeva cites this telling passage from Proust's *Contre Sainte-Beuve*: "Crossing a
courtyard I came to a standstill among the glittering uneven paving-stones.... In
the depth of my being I felt the *flutter* of a past that I did not recognize; it was just
as I set foot on a certain paving-stone that this feeling of *perplexity* came over me.
I felt an invading *happiness*, I knew that I was going to be enriched by that *purely
personal thing, a past impression, a fragment of life in unsullied preservation* (Suddenly, *I was flooded by a stream of light*). It was the sensation underfoot that I had
felt on the smooth, slightly uneven pavement of the baptistery of Saint Mark's"
(*Time and Sense*, 107). It is interesting that the other two novels under consideration here also end with touchstones of a telling kind: the rock of the lighthouse
which Mr. Ramsay touches in *To the Lighthouse* and the rock of Gibraltar where
Molly's final anamnetic fantasy concludes.

36 Marcel Proust, *Time Regained, In Search of Lost Time*, trans. Andreas Mayor and
Terence Kilmartin, rev. D.J. Enright, vol. 6 (New York: Modern Library, 1999)

289–90; future citations from *Time Regained* are from this edition and will be referenced in the text by volume and page number.

37 Kristeva also identifies revealing nominal associations here with Marie Madeleine in the Scriptures.

38 Marcel Proust, *Within a Budding Grove, In Search of Lost Time,* trans. C.K. Scott Moncrieff and Terence Kilmartin, rev. D.J. Enright, vol. 2 (New York: Modern Library, 1998) 39.

39 Marcel Proust, *Swann's Way,* 110–11.

40 Walter Benjamin, "The Image of Proust," *Illuminations: Essays and Reflections,* ed. Hannah Arendt, trans. Harry Zohn (New York: Schocken, 1985) 210.

41 Walter Benjamin, *The Arcades Project,* trans. Howard Eiland and Kevin McLaughlin (Cambridge, MA: Belknap-Harvard University Press, 1999) 69. One might also mention here John Caputo's notion of holy "quotidianism" in *The Weakness of God: A Theology of the Event* (Bloomington: Indiana University Press, 2006) 155ff.

42 The point is not that epiphanies never happened before the library scene; it is that Marcel was not yet ready to see and hear them for what they really were. He had not yet, to cite Gilles Deleuze, been fully trained in his "apprenticeship to signs" (Deleuze, *Proust and Signs,* trans. Richard Howard [London: Athlone, 2000]). It is not until such apprenticeship is accomplished, through his recapitulative awareness of "being-towards-death" in the library, that Marcel can finally acknowledge the preciousness of even the most banal and discarded events through the lens of time recaptured (*le temps retrouvé*). Art is less a matter of romantic creation than of epiphanic recreation. For, as Marcel asks, "was not the re-creation by the memory of impressions which had then to be deepened, illumined, transformed into equivalents of understanding, was not this process one of the conditions, almost the very essence of the work of art as I had just now in the library conceived it?" (*Time Regained,* 525). Such epiphanic understanding marks the moment of *anagnoresis.* Otherwise put, time has to be lost before it can be recovered. Unless the seed dies, accidents cannot be retrieved as essences, contingencies as correspondences, obsessions as epiphanies. Only through the veil of mortality, can the sacred radiate across the profane world which the arrogant repudiate as ineligible for art. It is only after he renounces his promethean Will-to-Write that Marcel's previously in-experienced experience is re-experienced in all its neglected richness. (And the greater the neglect, the greater the richness). For it is precisely the rejected and remaindered events of Marcel's existence which return now, in and through literature, as "resurrections." The three personas of Marcel — as character, as narrator, and as author — seem to criss-cross here for the first time, like three Proustian Magi recognizing that the deepest acts of communion are to be found in the most fortuitous acts of ordinary perception.

43 So what do these Proustian conclusions tell us about epiphany? They indicate, I suggest, that epiphany is a process which is "achieved" in a series of double moves. First, that of mortality and natality. Second, that of metaphor (the translation of one thing into another) and metonymy (the disclosure of new meaning through the accidental contiguity of contingent things). Third, that of constructing and deconstructing. Moreover, it is in this last double-gesture that the text surpasses itself and finally reaches out towards its future readers. If we begin with the notion that literature "constructs" an epiphany based on the recreation of impressions

recalled in involuntary memory, the literary text in turn "deconstructs" itself in order to allow for the recreation of the reader. That is how Penelope's tapestry and Françoise's sewing works—stitching and unstitching, weaving and unweaving, endlessly. In a form of hermeneutic arc, the text configures an epiphany already prefigured by a life which is ultimately re-figured by the reader (see Paul Ricoeur, *Time and Narrative*, vol. 2, especially the section entitled "The Traversed Remembrance of Things Past" in chapter 4). And this reader is one who not only co-creates the text with the author but recreates it again as he or she returns from "text to action." If epiphany invites a first move from life to literature, it re-invites us to come back again from literature to life. In both Proust and Joyce, it is indeed Penelope who has the last word.

44 Virginia Woolf, *To the Lighthouse* (New York: Harcourt Brace Jovanovich, 1927; rpt. Orlando, FL: Harcourt, 1981) 63; future citations from *To the Lighthouse* are from this edition and are referenced in the text by page number.

45 Qtd. in J. Hillis Miller, "The Rhythm of Creativity: *To the Lighthouse*," *Tropes, Parables, Performatives: Essays on Twentieth-Century Literature* (Durham, NC: Duke University Press, 1991) 159.

46 Virginia Woolf, *A Room of One's Own*, qtd. in Hillis Miller, "The Rhythm of Creativity," 169.

47 Erich Auerbach, "The Brownstocking," *Mimesis: The Representation of Reality in Western Literature* (Princeton, NJ: Princeton University Press, 1968) 536; see also pages 540 and 552.

48 The references to Lily leaping into a "gap" and finding the third, final stroke which draws the "line, there in the centre" is interesting when we consider the image of the wedge, so intimately and recurrently associated with Mrs. Ramsay. This trope carries connotations of a deep inner emptiness or nothingness—as in references to "the wedge of darkness" or "the wedge-shaped core of darkness"—which holds out the possibility of some mystical fullness or completion. When we recall that Lily has been trying to compose a portrait of Mrs. Ramsay and James in the form of a "purple triangle," one might be tempted to construe Lily's finishing brush stroke as the line which completes the two-sided wedge (the missing third side, so to speak), after which she can say, "it was done.... I have had my vision" (209). This vision coincides with the exact moment that the missing father, Mr. Ramsay, lands on the rock of the lighthouse and finds acknowledgement in the hearts of his children, James and Cam. He is, as it were, finally accepted back into the picture of mother and child. This is the moment that Lily, back on shore before her painting, suddenly finds her "razor edge" balance between "art and Mr. Ramsay." The final "cut" is made. The third stroke applied to the wedge. The triangle completed. The work done. The novel concluded. This charged figurative imagery of wedge and triangle may be read, I suggest, in aesthetic, psychoanalytic, or Trinitarian terms— or all three combined.

49 This approximates to the Buddhist and Hindu view that the sacred is in every sentient being. See the teaching, for example, of Dilgo Khyentse Rinpoche in this regard: "Pure perception is to recognize the buddha-nature in all sentient beings and to see primordial purity and perfection in all phenomena" (qtd. in John Makransky, *Awakening through Love: Unveiling Your Deepest Goodness* [Boston: Wisdom Publications, 2007] 92.) The sacramental reference for all natural things is

also evidenced in certain biblical texts, such as the Song of Songs (which Mrs. Ramsay's vision echoes in the final lines just cited), but also in the mystical nature visions of certain Christian mystics like St. Francis and Hildegard of Bingen (see in particular her notion of *veriditas*, or the divine "greening" of all things), not to mention Gerard Manley Hopkins or Teilhard de Chardin. Woolf's English Protestant culture may not, however, have made her familiar with such writings. Either way, Woolf's mysticism, however "Asiatic" its allusions at times, remains nondenominational and non-confessional. One might even say non-theistic or post-theistic (or ana-theistic, as I suggest in my conclusion below).

50 Virginia Woolf, *Moments of Being*, qtd. in Martin Corner, "Mysticism and Atheism in *To the Lighthouse*," *Virginia Woolf's* To the Lighthouse, ed. Harold Bloom (New York: Chelsea House, 1988) 43. In a diary entry of 9 May 1926, Woolf notes how she had quarrelled with her husband, Leonard, who "disliked the irrational Xtian in me" (*The Diary of Virginia Woolf*, ed. Anne Olivier Bell, with Andrew McNeillie, 5 vols. [New York: Harcourt Brace Jovanovich; London: Hogarth, 1977–84] 3.801).

51 The metaphor of the "razor's edge" is a famous verse from *Katha Upanishad*, Valli 3, verses 14–17. Here is the full passage concerning the discovery of the true mystical sense (Atman-Brahman): "Arise! Awake! Pay attention, / when you've attained your wishes! A razor's sharp edge is hard to cross— / that, poets say, is the difficulty of the path." And the passage goes on, "[W]hen a man perceives it, / fixed and beyond the immense, / He is freed from the jaws of death"; or, again, if a person "proclaims this great secret / ... during a meal for the dead, / it will lead him to eternal life!" (Eliot Deutsch and Rohit Dalvi, eds. *The Essential Vedanta: A New Source Book of Advaita Vedanta* [Bloomington, IN: World Wisdom, 2004] 33). Eucharistic echoes abound. One might also cite here the mystical notions of immanent transcendence to be found in Hindu sages like Ramana and Ramakrishna or Christian-Hindu swamis like Abhishiktananda and Bede Griffiths.

52 Virginia Woolf, *A Writer's Diary*, qtd. in Corner, "Mysticism and Atheism," 48.

53 See Hillis Miller, "The Rhythm of Creativity," 152–53. Hillis Miller extends his reading of Woolf's spiritual-aesthetic vision to her novel *Mrs. Dalloway* in chapter 7 of *Fiction and Repetition* (Cambridge, MA: Harvard University Press, 1982), subtitled "Repetition as the Raising of the Dead."

54 Corner, "Mysticism and Atheism," 50.

55 Qtd. in Corner, "Mysticism and Atheism," 51. For a more ecological account of Woolf's vision of cosmic interconnection, explicitly related to the ontology of flesh and entwining in Merleau-Ponty, see Louise Westling, "Virginia Woolf and the Flesh of the World," *New Literary History* 30.4 (1999): 855–75. Westling cites Woolf's 1908 vision of "symmetry by means of infinite discords, showing all the traces of the minds [sic] passage through the world, (achieving) in the end, some kind of whole made of shivering fragments." She also makes much of Woolf's famous claim in 1925 that "life is a luminous halo, a semi-transparent envelope surrounding us from the beginning of consciousness to the end." She endorses the view that for Woolf, as for Merleau-Ponty, the world is no longer to be conceived in terms of a Platonic/Cartesian dualism but rather a "sacramental engagement within the body of the world," as a "pulsating field of mind and matter in which everything is interconnected."

56 Etty Hillesum, *An Interrupted Life* (London: Jonathan Cape, 1983).

57 Jacques Derrida, *On the Name*, ed. Thomas Dutoit, trans. David Wood, John P. Leavey, and Ian McLeod (Stanford, CA: Stanford University Press, 1995) 80, 36–37; italics mine.

58 Stanislas Breton, *The Word and the Cross*, trans. Jacquelyn Porter (New York: Fordham University Press, 2002) 114, 84.

59 Gianni Vattimo and Richard Rorty, *The Future of Religion*, ed. Santiago Zabala (New York: Columbia University Press, 2005) 38, 35. One might also note here Dietrich Bonhoeffer's affirmation of the sacred in the secular, albeit in a more explicitly Christological vein (see Bonhoeffer, *Ethik,* ed. Eberhard Bethge, vol. 6, *Dietrich Bonhoeffer Werke* [Munich: Chr. Kaiser Verlag, 1992] 44ff). I am grateful to Jens Zimmermann for bringing this passage to my attention.

60 Vattimo and Rorty, *The Future of Religion*, 38. See also in this regard, Jean-Luc Nancy, *La Déclosion; Déconstruction du Christianisme, 1* (Paris: Galilée, 2005).

61 Gilles Deleuze and Felix Guattari, *A Thousand Plateaus: Capitalism and Schizophrenia*, trans. Brian Massumi (Minneapolis: University of Minnesota, 1987) 135 (citing D.H. Lawrence, *Apocalypse* [New York: Viking, 1932] 33–34).

62 Paul Ricoeur, *Vivant jusqu'à la mort* (Paris: Editions du Seuil, 2007) 45; future citations from *Vivant jusqu'à la mort* are from this edition and will be referenced in the text by page number; translations are mine.

63 See John 12:25.

64 Paul Ricoeur, "The Critique of Religion," *The Philosophy of Paul Ricoeur: An Anthology of His Work*, ed. Charles E. Regan and David Stuart (Boston: Beacon, 1978) 213ff. Ricoeur talks about the related notion of returning to a second naïveté of authentic faith after the dogmatisms and prejudices of one's first naïveté have been deconstructed and purged; to which critical act of purgation and return one might add his more recent notions of "linguistic hospitality" and "Eucharistic hospitality." See Paul Ricoeur, *On Translation*, trans. Eileen Brennan (London and New York: Routledge, 2006) 23–24. See also in this connection Louis-Marie Chauvet, *Symbol and Sacrament: A Sacramental Reinterpretation of Christian Experience*, trans. Patrick Madigan and Madeleine Beaumont (Collegeville, MN: Liturgical Press, 1995).

65 See Jean-François Lyotard on the notions of "post" and "ana" (which he links specifically with a postmodern attitude to time and history) in *The Postmodern Condition*, trans. Geoffrey Bennington and Brian Massumi (Manchester, UK: Manchester University Press, 1984). Lyotard does not, however, consider these terms in the same religious light as we are doing here. We might also note the importance here of not only the Platonic model of *ana-mnesis* but also the Aristotelian idea of *ana-gnoresis*, a special kind of re-cognition through poetic awareness whereby we recall something previously forgotten and realize how different things are connected, how "this" relates to "that," etc. See the *Poetics* 4.4.1448ff and *Rhetoric*, 1.2.23.1371ff.

66 For a development of this ana-theistic aesthetic, see my related texts, "Epiphanies of the Everyday: Toward a Micro-Eschatology" and "Enabling God," *After God*, 3–20, 39–54; "Traversals and Epiphanies in Joyce and Proust," *Traversing the Imaginary*, 183–208; and "Hermeneutics of the Possible God," *Givenness and God*, 220–42.

THE *VIA NEGATIVA* IN FORSTER'S *A PASSAGE TO INDIA*

George Piggford

The year after the publication of *A Passage to India*, E.M. Forster wrote an essay about language and meaning titled "Anonymity: An Inquiry" (1925), in which he imagines language as a continuum between the vehicular and the mythic, between signs and symbols. In Forster's parlance, at one end is language that conveys "information" and at the other is language that creates an "atmosphere" or mood.[1] The first kind of language includes not only conventional and public communications such as "Stop" or "Mind the Gap" but also the author's name attached to many texts, and most notably literary ones: "S.T. Coleridge, William Shakespeare, or Mrs. Humphrey Ward."[2] And in a move that would no doubt warm the hearts of Michel Foucault and Roland Barthes, Forster claims that the authorial appellation distracts us from what is more important in literature. Naming calls our attention to the "conscious and alert" "upper personality" that we traditionally associate with imaginative literature at the expense of what Forster calls the "lower personality," which moves us from the individual to something beyond: "[W]ithout it there is no literature, because unless a man dips a bucket down into it occasionally he cannot produce first-class work."[3]

Forster notes the association of this personality with not just the imaginative capacity but also the spiritual. It "has something in common with all other deeper personalities, and the mystic will assert that the common quality is God, and that here, in the obscure recesses of our being, we near the gates of the Divine. It is in any case the force that makes for anonymity. As it came from the depths, so it soars to the heights."[4] What I propose is to read Forster's last novel in relation to this very notion of the mystical sublime, that is, what surfaces *sub* or "up to" the *limis* or *limen*: the threshold of our consciousness in literary texts. This experience is connected by Forster with our being, significantly, "near" not Divinity but its doorsill or "gates." To arrive at this space of the near presence or possibility of a God beyond the ontological, we must move through atheism, the nihilism of the Marabar Caves, along what is termed in Western traditions the *via negativa* or the path of spiritual negation. This journey in *A Passage to India* allows by the end of the novel for a surprising return to the language and narratives of the Judeo-Christian tradition.

Many critics have noticed the spiritual strain in Forster's writing, but very few have known what to make of Forster the mystic. The author himself expressed anxiety about the "muddle" of mysticism, notably in a 1910 letter to Syed Ross Masood, Forster's intimate friend and the dedicatee of *A Passage to India*. In the letter he implicitly contrasts unhealthy mysticism with healthy, which was brought about for him in conventional Romantic fashion via a walk in the English countryside: "It isn't bad being alone in the country—the nearest approach we Anglo Saxons can make to your saints. There's such a thing as *healthy* mysticism, and our race is capable of developing it, I think. But perhaps you don't understand, and if you did, it isn't likely you'd agree."[5] This "healthy" mysticism has been associated in secondary literature with Forster's emphasis on the fantastic in his short stories as well as on pagan myth, which provides motifs for the novels, most notably *The Longest Journey*. Max Saunders, for example, claims that "[t]here had always been a mystical tendency in [Forster's] fiction: a pagan alternative to the Christianity he eschewed, which connects the world of Pan and the dryads with the world of tea-parties and tourism; a spirit of place with money and society; the unconscious and the conscious."[6] The scene of "panic"—associated etymologically with the terror-inducing god "Pan"—is one to which Forster's texts compulsively return, in scenes that combine both violence and sexuality. We might think here of Lucy Honeychurch in the plaza outside Santa Croce in *A Room with a View*, the "panic and emptiness" associated with Beethoven's Fifth Symphony in *Howards End*, and the collapse of conventional faith and the sexual assault associated with the Marabar Caves of *A Passage to India*.

The last novel, however, invites us beyond the pagan mythical structure of the earlier texts into a much more syncretistic vision that takes into account the Abrahamic religions of Islam and Christianity as well as non-Semitic traditions, including the Buddhist and most prominently Hindu. We are invited into Islamic culture with the introduction of the novel's first characters in chapter 2: Dr. Aziz, Hamidullah, and Mahmoud Ali. The first section of three, "Mosque," features a meditation on the relationship between Christianity and

Islam, embodied by Mrs. Moore and Aziz, but these two faiths are juxtaposed eventually with the Hinduism of the Brahman Godbole. Framing our relationship with all such characters, however, is Forster's peculiar third-person narrator, who introduces us to the world of *A Passage to India* through the celebrated rhetoric of negation in the novel's first chapter. As Gillian Beer has pointed out, in its first three pages we find terms such as "not," "never," "nor," and "neither," with "nothing" and "no" recurring in mantra-like rhythms.[7] The first word in the text, "except," introduces the caves at a distance from Chandrapore as the only "extraordinary" sight on the horizon.[8] The tone of this voice is, one might say, bored and touristic, rooted in prose familiar to Forster from the Baedeker series of travel guides. Forster himself utilized such a voice for his 1922 *Alexandria: A History and a Guide*, which is based upon his experiences in that Egyptian city during World War I. The narrative voice in *A Passage to India* is also a Western, likely British one, which finds the civil station of the Raj's sahibs to be "sensibly planned" and the Indian town below it to be decidedly not so (3).

This voice is, however, not only that of the seasoned tourist but also that of the mystic, allowing for the possibility of what Michael Roeschlein has termed a "modernist spirituality."[9] It is not only "periphrastic," as Brenda Silver has pointed out, but also apophatic.[10] Above both the Indian and Anglo communities, according to this voice, is the sky, "a dome of blending tints, and the main tint blue" (3). This core of blue—associated with the Hindu god Krishna—persists at all times of day and even at night, "when stars hang from the immense vault." The distance between vault and stars "is as nothing to the distance behind them, and that farther distance, though beyond colour, last freed itself from blue" (3). The ultimate frame here is void—no colour, nothing. It is this very lack that is circumscribed and echoed in the caves, which are described by both the narrator and Professor Godbole in terms of what they are not. It is these utterly negative spaces that will challenge the spiritual beliefs and religious convictions of the novel's Abrahamic protagonists, most prominently Mrs. Moore.

Although Islam and Christianity are presented in Forster's novel as in many ways distinct, both emerged elsewhere than in the space of India and were imported by invasive forces, whether the Persian kings whom Aziz romanticizes or the Christian missionaries accompanying British and other European colonizers. And both religions, significantly, conceptualize space for Forster in relation to the binary of the sacred and the profane. This is most obvious when Aziz and Mrs. Moore first meet in the ruined mosque near the British club from which the elderly lady has wandered. When he encounters Mrs. Moore, originally mistaken for a ghost, the first thing that Aziz insists upon is that she is an unwelcome interloper into Muslim sacred space.

"Madam," he says, "this is a mosque, you have no right here at all; you should have taken off your shoes; this is a holy place for Moslems." When Mrs. Moore points out that she left her shoes "at the entrance" of the mosque, Aziz asks her "pardon," noting "so few ladies take the trouble, especially if thinking no one is there to see." The lady's reply is that "it makes no difference. God is here" (14–15). Notable in this exchange is the Englishwoman's and Indian Muslim's shared belief in a God who is "here," a God not of absence but of presence, as well as their common emphasis on the sacredness not of all space but of certain spaces where one might encounter this presence, here the holy ground of Aziz' mosque.

In contrast to these monotheists who tend to binarize space are the novel's Hindus, who are figured in Forster's text as radical inclusivists. When Christian missionaries teach that "In our Father's house there are many mansions," and that "no one shall be turned away...be he black or white," their Hindu interlocutors inquire into the limits of this God's hospitality: "May there not be a mansion for the monkeys also?" The older of the two missionaries balks at this, but the younger, Mr. Sorley, is "more advanced" and expresses an openness to this possibility. "And the jackals?" ask the Hindus. "Jackals were indeed less to Mr. Sorley's mind," Forster's narrator tells us, "but he admitted that the mercy of God, being infinite, may well embrace mammals." But it soon becomes clear that this "infinite" mercy is in actuality finite in relation to the order of being. When asked about a place in heaven for wasps—a leitmotif associated in the novel with Mrs. Moore herself—the younger Christian missionary becomes "uneasy...and...apt to change the conversation. And oranges, cactuses, crystals, and mud? And the bacteria inside Mr. Sorley? No, no, this is going too far. We must exclude someone from our gathering," Forster's narrator explains, "or we will be left with nothing" (32). This logic of exclusion is precisely what characterizes the ontological Christianity of Forster's novel: a faith that reifies the presence of the sacred in order to keep the void, nothing, absence—the possibility of God's non-existence—at bay.

Antony Copley in his book *A Spiritual Bloomsbury* has noted that homosexual writers such as E.M. Forster, J.R. Ackerley, and Christopher Isherwood found, or believed they found, in Hinduism a religion of inclusion, not of condemnation and exclusion, "a valuable tradition, one of a more fluid, less formulaic male sexuality."[11] And it is Forster's version of Hindu spirituality in *A Passage to India* that provides the corrective for the limitations of "poor little talkative Christianity" and its theology of presence (141). Godbole, who personifies the Hindu world view, is unruffled by a God who is absent and unavailable. He makes this clear through a religious song that he performs in the presence of Aziz, Mrs. Moore, Adela, and Cyril Fielding. In it, he claims, "I placed myself in the position of a milkmaiden. I say to Shri Krishna, 'Come!

Come to me only.' The god refuses to come. I grow humble and say: 'Do not come to me only. Multiply yourself into a hundred Krishnas, and let one go to each of my hundred companions, but one, O Lord of the Universe, come to me.' He refuses to come." Mrs. Moore, fixated on her God of presence, asks, "But He comes in some other song, I hope?" Godbole replies, "Oh no, he refuses to come.... I say to Him, Come, come, come, come, come, come. He neglects to come" (72). Godbole the mystic is comfortable with this God who is not yet and not here, who never quite arrives. Such an exchange might bring to mind the notion of the Messianic that we find in writers such as Emmanuel Levinas and the late Derrida: a God who is on his way and never arriving. In Levinas, for example, this is the very definition of Messiah, the God "who reveals himself as absence rather than presence."[12]

It is likely Godbole's comfort with a God of absence that allows him to remain unthreatened by the space of the Marabar Caves, which he characterizes for his English companions via negation: they are "not large," "not at all" like the caves at Elephanta, not "ornamented," nor even "holy" (68). When Aziz, frustrated, asks Godbole to describe the caves in positive terms, the Brahman replies, "It will be a great pleasure," but immediately, as the narrator informs us, "he forwent the pleasure" (68). The implication here is that the best description of the Marabar is silence itself. When, at the beginning of the novel's second section, our touristic/mythic/mystic narrator provides the description that Godbole forgoes, the voice returns to the rhetoric of negation with which the novel begins: "no water" has ever covered them (116). They "bear no relation to anything dreamt or seen. To call them 'uncanny' suggests ghosts, and they are older than all spirit" (117). Here we move beyond even the Hinduism that Forster privileges elsewhere in the novel. Even that ancient tradition has managed only to "scratch" and "plaster" "a few rocks. The Buddha himself "shunned" at the Marabar "a renunciation more complete than his own, and has left no legend of struggle or victory" there (117). "Nothing, nothing attaches to them, and their reputation ... does not depend upon human speech," we are told (117). All that they produce is the famous "utterly dull" echo: "bou-oum" or "ou-boum," which some critics have associated with the Hindu Om (138–39).[13]

The effect of the caves' echo is to flatten out all meaning, or to transform all meaning to meaninglessness, especially any potential ethical significations: "Hope, politeness, the blowing of a nose, the squeak of a boot, all produce 'boum'" (139). The lesson that Mrs. Moore learns in her experience in a cave is that "[p]athos, piety, courage — they exist, but are identical, and so is filth. Everything exists, nothing has value." "Vileness" and "lofty poetry" all come out the same in the echo of Marabar: "ou-boum" (140). Here is a space, in Nietzschean fashion, *Beyond Good and Evil.* It is therefore only a spirituality that values nothingness, which encompasses its own negation, that can stand up to the challenge of the caves.

Mrs. Moore's Christianity, which she at one point reduces to "the desire to behave pleasantly," is no match for this total annihilation (45). Her conventional ethics, her manners, and her well-meaning attempts at connection are all nullified by the Marabar. After exiting one of the caves Mrs. Moore attempts to compose a letter to her children: "She tried to go on with her letter, reminding herself that she was only an elderly woman who had got up too early in the morning and journeyed too far, that the despair creeping over her was merely her despair, her personal weakness, and that even if she got a sunstroke and went mad the rest of the world would go on" (141). She is, however, overcome with lethargy and inertia, realizing "that she didn't want to communicate with anyone, not even with God. She sat motionless with horror" (141). We might say that what surfaces with her experience in the caves is the doubt that underlies her faith, just as Adela's own sexual repression and revulsion arguably enter into her own consciousness in the caves, leading to the disastrous rape charge against Aziz. Forster's text is intentionally coy on the latter point. Although early drafts included a rape narrative, the final published version of *A Passage to India* wants the mystery of Adela's encounter in the caves to remain just that: mysterious, unspeakable, unknown.[14] The narrator himself seems excluded from the space of the caves, at least when others are within: we are made aware of Mrs. Moore's experience only after the fact and of Adela's really not at all (138, 144–45).

Despite its overwhelming nature, the spiritual experience of total negation is not the last word in Forster's text. It gives way to the very different spiritual experiences narrated in the third section, "Temple," just as the dry, hot season gives way to that of the rejuvenating monsoons. After the death of faith is a narrative of resurrection. Further, it is not necessarily Christianity that dies in the caves, but Mrs. Moore's limited, "poor little talkative Christianity": a cataphatic theology of presence untempered by the apophatic. What is reborn in Forster's text is the possibility of a new kind of Christianity, or at least Christian imagination, what we might call an inclusive and agnostic Christianity, perhaps even what Richard Kearney has recently termed "anatheism."[15]

In the "Temple" section of *A Passage to India* we encounter again a celebration of Hindu inclusiveness through the description of the Gokul Ashtami festival—the re-enactment of the birth of Krishna, which Forster himself witnessed while private secretary to the Maharajah of Dewas State Senior.[16] As with the other two sections, "Temple" begins with the voice of a geographically expansive, mythic, and mystical narrator: "Some hundreds of miles westward of the Marabar Hills, and two years later in time, Professor Narayan Godbole stands in the presence of God. God is not born yet—that will occur at midnight—but He has also been born centuries ago, nor can He ever be born, because He is Lord of the Universe, who transcends human processes. He is, was not, is not, was" (274). Perhaps it is obvious to claim that this all-inclusive God is beyond ontology, overarching the binarism of existence and non-existence. This is also the God of negative theology, who is, as Pseudo-Dionysius puts it in the *Mystical Theology*, beyond "everything perceived and understood, everything perceptible and understandable, all that is not and all that is," the one who is "beyond all being and knowledge."[17] It is important to note that what we find in Forster's description of Gokul Ashtami is a God who encompasses both absence and presence. The latter provides a decided rejoinder to the utter negation of the Divine, the holy, and meaning itself in the space of the Marabar Caves. There is in the experience of the mystic Godbole a God both of negation and of incarnation: "Infinite Love took upon itself the form of Shri Krishna, and saved the world" (278).

It does not seem that there is much Christian in such a description, and indeed Forster's narrator explicitly states that Hinduism includes crucial characteristics of God that Christianity traditionally excludes: not just God's non-being, but God's comedy and "merriment" (279). At the same time the feast that provides the centerpiece of the novel's last section allows for a coming together of Hinduism and a reinvigorated Christianity: Godbole "was a Brahman" and Mrs. Moore "a Christian," the narrator tells us, "but it made no difference.... It was [Godbole's] duty to place himself in the position of the God and to love her, and to place himself in her position and to say to the God, 'Come, come, come, come'" (281). Here the novel's religious circle completes in a vision of syncretistic love that crosses the boundary even of life and death. This Christianity informed by the inclusiveness of Hinduism allows for a freeing of the anonymous narrator's imagination not just generally but in a uniquely Christian way.

This interplay of the Christian and the Hindu provides one explanation for the narrator's account of the festival in the precise language of Judeo-Christian beliefs and traditions.[18] Gokul, we are informed, is "Bethlehem," and King Kasa is "Herod, directing the murder of some Innocents, and in a corner, similarly proportioned, stood the father and mother of the Lord, warned to depart in a dream" (278). These references point directly to Matthew 2:1–16 and its story of King Herod's attempts to find and kill Jesus and of Jesus' oneirically guided escape. The scene of Krishna and his parents is clearly a version of the Christian nativity. Similarly, the palanquin or platform upon which Krishna sits in Godbole's festival is compared to the "Ark of the Lord" from Hebrew scripture, here "covered with cloth of gold and flanked by peacock fans and by stiff circular banners of crimson" (296). The gold cloth suggests the material with which Moses' ark was overlaid, the crimson banners with the veil of Solomon's temple where the ark was eventually kept, and the peacock feathers, resurrection.[19] The narrator interprets elements of this Hindu spectacle through the language and symbolic patterns of Hebrew and Christian scripture and tradition.

The very phrase "God si love," which becomes a refrain of the "Temple" section, conveys both John the Evangelist's equation God is love (1 John 4:8) and its reversal or deconstruction. This is not to claim that God is "hate" or some other binary oppositional term to love, but that God both "is" and is not "is," or is "si." This seeming error maps an inversion of the category of being: the meontological riposte to the God of ontotheology. The phrase "God si love" suggests a God "against nature" "who turns our nature inside-out, who calls our ontological will-to-be into question."[20] Emmanuel Levinas associates such a figure with an "ethical call to conscience" that "occurs, no doubt, in other religious systems besides the Judeo-Christian but... remains an essentially religious vocation."[21] The narrator calls our attention to the phrase "God si love" as a prominent inscription at Gokul Ashtami, and these words recur as the festival comes to a close (276, 306). It is, perhaps, "the final message of India," a space in which Christian verity encounters its reverse (276). Forster's play with the Johannine maxim suggests a double critique: first of human religiousness, and specifically Christian doctrinal belief, and second a "simultaneous critique of the bluff dismissal of human religiousness," allowing for "sweeping reversals of perspective."[22] God both is and is not. "God is other than Being," and it is this that Hinduism can teach Christianity, according to Forster.[23]

The ethical implication of Forster's is/si wordplay is that ontological Christianity is in dire need of a religion of inclusiveness, here represented by Hinduism, if it is truly to reinvigorate its mystical heritage. Christian language might very well be used to point to a God beyond being, but this can only be done by demolishing the impoverished and wordy version that accompanied and in many ways underwrote the whole project of European colonization. The implication is that Western Christianity must undertake the way of negation if it is to return or resurrect from its own imminent collapse. Forster's novel indicates that if the God of love is to come into the world, then theologies of exclusion and the binarized logic of ontotheology must die or at least undergo a deconstruction via reversal and exoticization. To prepare for ethics beyond ethics and religion beyond religion one must be, like Godbole, unthreatened by the no-space of the caves and that negative region in the sky finally "freed... from blue" (3). In the terms of a narrative language that is both specifically Judeo-Christian and inclusive of the apophatic, Mrs. Moore then makes her return to the mystic Godbole. He, having "once more developed the life of his spirit," sees this Christian woman with "increasing vividness" at Gokul Ashtami (284). Christianity in a sense reincarnates in Forster's novel, just as Mrs. Moore comes back in the form that made the young missionary Mr. Sorley so uneasy: a wasp (326). By dying, "poor... talkative" Christianity might return as something beyond the binarisms of life and death and being and non-being and thus make room for the contemplation of nothing, and its language.

Notes

1   E.M. Forster, *Two Cheers for Democracy*, ed. Oliver Stallybrass, Abinger Edition, vol. 11 (London: Edward Arnold, 1972) 82.

2   Ibid.

3   Ibid., 82–83.

4   Ibid., 83.

5   *Selected Letters of E.M. Forster: Vol. 1 1879–1920*, ed. Mary Lago and P.N. Furbank (London: Arena, 1983) 113.

6   Max Saunders, "Forster's Life and Life-Writing," *The Cambridge Companion to E.M. Forster*, ed. David Bradshaw (Cambridge: Cambridge University Press, 2007) 16.

7   Gillian Beer, "Negation in *A Passage to India*," *A Passage to India: Essays in Interpretation*, ed. John Beer (Towtowa, NJ: Barnes and Noble, 1986) 46.

8   E.M. Forster, *A Passage to India*, ed. Oliver Stallybrass, Abinger Edition, vol. 6 (1924; London: Edward Arnold, 1979), 2–4; future quotations from *A Passage to India* are from this edition and will be referenced in the text by page number.

9   Michael Roeschlein, "E.M. Forster and 'The Part of the Mind that Seldom Speaks': Mysticism, Mythopoeia and Irony in *A Passage to India*," *Religion and Literature* 36.1 (2004): 70.

10   Brenda Silver, "Periphrasis, Power, and Rape in *A Passage to India*," *Novel* 22.1 (1988): 86–88.

11   Antony Copley, *A Spiritual Bloomsbury* (Lanham, MD: Lexington Books, 2006) 167.

12   Emmanuel Levinas, "Ethics of the Infinite," *States of Mind: Dialogues with Contemporary Thinkers on the European Mind*, ed. Richard Kearney (New York: New York University Press, 1995) 197.

13   See Peter Childs, "*A Passage to India*," *Cambridge Companion*, ed. Bradshaw, 192.

14   See E.M. Forster, *The Manuscripts of* A Passage to India, ed. Oliver Stallybrass, Abinger Edition, vol. 6a (London: Edward Arnold, 1978) 242–43.

15   See Richard Kearney, *Anatheism: Returning to God after God* (New York: Columbia University Press, 2009) 6–7.

16   See E.M. Forster, *The Hill of Devi and Other Indian Writings*, ed. Elizabeth Heine, Abinger Edition, vol. 14 (London: Edward Arnold, 1983) 60–73.

17   Pseudo-Dionysius, *Complete Works*, ed. and trans. Colm Luibheid (New York: Paulist Press, 1987) 135.

18   This technique is also culturally imperialistic, in that it interprets unfamiliar practices and images from the normative perspective of Judeo-Christian tradition.

19 See, respectively, Exodus 25:11, 2 Chronicles 3:14, and R. Kevin Seasoltz, *A Sense of the Sacred: Theological Foundations of Christian Architecture and Art* (New York: Continuum, 2005) 112.

20 Levinas, "Ethics of the Infinite," 190.

21 Ibid.

22 Roeschlein, "E.M. Forster," 68.

23 Levinas, "Ethics of the Infinite," 190.

THE FELLOWSHIP OF SUFFERING AND HOPE IN FANTASY LITERATURE

CONSOLATION IN UN/CERTAINTY: THE SACRED SPACES OF SUFFERING IN THE CHILDREN'S FANTASY LITERATURE OF GEORGE MACDONALD, C.S. LEWIS, AND MADELEINE L'ENGLE

Monika B. Hilder

It is not uncommon to think of children's literature as a sacred space that is or ought to be separate from the darker aspects of human experience. Many educators and readers associate children's literature with a sort of sweet sentimentality that must somehow be good for the very young but that older, more sophisticated readers have long left behind. There are excellent reasons, of course, to wish to protect children from the very graphic portrayals of evil. But the wish to shelter children from the visceral details of horrific violence in narrative is not quite the same thing as creating an imaginary world where very few, if any, bad things could happen.

In answer to the question of addressing evil in their literature for children, some writers declare that their intention is to arm the young for the realities of the world that they inhabit. On this subject, C.S. Lewis agrees that writers of children's literature should guard against creating narrative that would likely give children phobias. But, he maintains, it would be very wrong to wish to protect children from the knowledge that they live in a dangerous world. In his words, "Since it is so likely that [children] will meet cruel enemies, let them at least have heard of brave knights and heroic courage. Otherwise you are making their destiny not brighter but darker."[1] Similarly, Madeleine L'Engle observes, "Our responsibility to [children growing up] is not to pretend that if we don't look, evil will go away, but to give them weapons against it."[2] Children's narrative that addresses significant evil then may be regarded as a profound means of imaginative moral education that prepares children to face the disturbing perplexities and dangers of their world. Moreover, alongside providing children with the weapons to fight evil, the particular achievement of some writers is to give their readers the experience of consolation in the midst of suffering. In response to the terrible and important existential questions surrounding suffering — such as "What hope is there in the midst of deep pain?" "Is there purpose?" and "If there is purpose, can it truly speak to my sorrow?" — these writers craft a deep-going consolation in the midst of un/certainty. The very spaces of suffering then become *sacred* because they both honour the human story and also point to how the human story is interwoven with the active presence of the divine.

In this essay, I will explore the work of three related authors, George MacDonald, C.S. Lewis and Madeleine L'Engle, the two latter of whom claim MacDonald's direct influence. Their narratives may indeed be regarded as "golden" because their mythic imagination creates an alchemy that transforms suffering into a genuinely sacred space of well-being. Informed by their Christian faith, which asserts the soul-stretching, gut-wrenching paradox of the kingdom of heaven that is both within and yet to come, and of the heavy cross that is at once a mild and easy yoke, these writers pursue the idea of suffering as a sacred space which calls for the old virtues of patience and courage to flourish in what L'Engle calls "the *faithfulness* of doubt."[3] It is no coincidence that MacDonald, Lewis, and L'Engle achieve this experience of consolation with the tenuousness of an un/certain hope, a belief in ultimate wholeness in the face of adversity and brokenness and plain lack of understanding. Theoretical discourse often articulates what many creative writers have explored, and MacDonald, for instance, has been thought to have a "prescient postmodernist spirit."[4] Indeed, these writers have a truly fluid stance toward un/certainty, a hope that allows for long bouts with doubt. Unlike the uncertainty of postmodernists, who seem unlikely to consider the possibility of an essential or external substance to the human choice of faith, which is surely a dogmatic rigidity of another kind, these authors allow for both/and — doubt and the possibility of certainty, real fear and the determination to counter this with defiant hope. In this perplexity of doubt/faith, these writers address a wide range of children's experiences of suffering, such as bullying (*The Magician's*

Nephew, The Silver Chair, A Wind in the Door), the unexplained absence of a parent (*A Wrinkle in Time*), domestic violence (*A Swiftly Tilting Planet*), poverty (*At the Back of the North Wind*), sexual harassment (*The Horse and His Boy, A Swiftly Tilting Planet*), racism (*A Swiftly Tilting Planet*), terminal illness (*The Magician's Nephew, A Wind in the Door*), death through natural disaster (*At the Back of the North Wind*), and planetary destruction (*The Last Battle, A Wrinkle in Time, A Swiftly Tilting Planet*).[5] Their narratives plunge readers into un/certainty. As Meg realizes in *A Wind in the Door*, "suddenly the whole world was unsafe and uncertain ... their safe little village was revealing itself to be unpredictable and irrational and precarious.... Now a cold awareness of the uncertainty of all life, no matter how careful the planning, hollowed emptily in the pit of her stomach" (*Wind*, 33–34).

I will turn my attention now to three episodes from these stories. Each of these episodes features distinct characteristics of the bold mythic vision of consolation within the landscape of doubt.

First, in C.S. Lewis's *The Magician's Nephew*, readers explore the timeless quest for eternal youth. This is particularly heightened in the context of impending death for Digory Kirke's mother, Mabel. The central pain of the novel is, in fact, Digory's sorrow over his mother's imminent death, an echo of C.S. Lewis's own lived experience—his mother died of cancer when he was nine years old. The central temptation of the novel is that posed to Digory by the witch: grab the apple on the special Narnian tree, and so imbibe the elixir of youth. Moreover, seize the magical fruit to save his dying mother, if indeed he loves her so very much. So the boy negotiates this "most terrible choice" (*MN*, 150)—whether to grasp apparent certainty out of love for his mother or heed the whisper of conscience warning him that the offer of certainty will elude him and result in spiritual death. Though the witch taunts him with the universal fear of weakness, "Think of me, Boy, when you lie old and weak and dying, and remember how you threw away the chance of endless youth!" (*MN*, 152), he hesitates. As Digory wrestles with the temptation, he grasps the sense of "getting your heart's desire and getting despair along with it" when stealing forbidden fruit as he witnesses the unexpectedly dark, horrid stain around the witch's mouth: "For the Witch looked stronger and prouder than ever, and even, in a way, triumphant: but her face was deadly white, white as salt" (*MN*, 149). As Aslan later explains to him, there are far worse things than mortal weakness, pain, suffering, and death. In the lion's explanation, "length of days with an evil heart is only length of misery and already [the witch] begins to know it. All get what they want: they do not always like it" (*MN*, 162). Aslan assures Digory that he and his mother would have rued the day she had obtained immortality in this life: "The day would have come when both you and she would have looked back and said it would have been better to die in that illness" (MN, 163). Digory contemplates "that there might be things more terrible even than losing someone you love by death" (MN, 163).

Still, Digory is very sad and not at all sure "that he had done the right thing" (MN, 152), and it is in this dejected place of uncertainty that he finds consolation. Earlier he had been impressed by the sensation that Aslan perhaps cared for his mother even more than he himself did (MN, 131–32). Now "whenever he remembered the shining tears in Aslan's eyes he became sure" (MN, 152). When he looks to Aslan he forgets his troubles and is "absolutely content" (MN, 154). It is Digory's orientation to the mythic character of Aslan which inspires resilient hope. The boy freely obeys the instruction to toss away the apple that will, Aslan says, seed the tree that is to protect Narnia. With this sort of abandonment, no longer insisting on certainty, Digory demonstrates the un/certain faith that is life-giving. He is ready to embrace the everlasting joy that, in this case, will also grant several more years to his mother's mortal life. When Digory brings his ailing mother "the Apple of Youth," he senses the mystical brightness which suggests that "there was a window in the room that opened on Heaven" (MN, 167). The fact that his mother will now live is extremely important. However, what is ultimately more important is the fact that the memory of the "sweetness and power [that] rolled about [him] and over [him] and entered into [him in his encounter with Aslan] stayed with [him] always, so that ... if ever [he was] sad or afraid or angry, the thought of all that golden goodness, and the feeling that it was still there, quite close, just round some corner or just behind some door, would come back and make [him] sure, deep down inside, that all was well" (MN, 165). In a word, in The Magician's Nephew, the temptation of the promise of certainty, which must be a cheat, pales beside the offer of timeless joy and love. Digory Kirke resolves to be willing to live with un/certainty in order to contemplate such hope.

Second, Madeleine L'Engle's A Swiftly Tilting Planet raises the difficult question of the value of human life for those who are physically and/or mentally and emotionally maimed. What, all of us may ask at some time, is the purpose of a life so wounded that the person is unable to participate in most of the usual activities of family, work, and social engagement? Or of one who simply resents life? In this space-and-time travel story, the protagonist, Charles Wallace, is sent within the mind-and-body of several characters in the past, one at a time, not in order to "possess" them, as it were, but rather to join with them in order to avert tragedy. In this he experiences great pain, such as in the case of entering Chuck Maddox, whose skull was fractured by his stepfather so that "[n]othing went in straight lines for him any more, not time, not distance. His mind was like the unstable earth, full of faults, so that layers shifted and slid" (STP, 200). Charles Wallace is tempted by the dark side to leave the body of the brain-damaged boy and take control of events with his own extraordinary IQ (*STP*, 199); instead, he remains within "Chuck's shifting universe" (*STP*, 203) and learns about the history that could develop into planetary disaster as well as about what will indeed prevent it.

Similarly, Chuck's sister, Beezie, who became Meg Murry's mother-in-law, appears to be a ruined human being. She became a woman who "learned not to feel, not to love, not even her children, not even Calvin. Not to be hurt" (*STP*, 253). As the narrator describes, "Yes. That was a victory for the enemy, indeed. That Beezie, the golden child, should have become the old hag with missing teeth and resentful eyes was unbearable" (*STP*, 197). And yet, in all her sullenness and apparent confusion she holds to the one thing that swings the balance in the spiritual battle against rising darkness—love informed by faith. Remembering and embodying the power of prayer that she learned from her grandmother, Beezie O'Keefe gives this important weapon to Charles Wallace, and then successfully places herself between her loved ones and evil with this ancient rune, declaring, together with Meg,

> "*I place all Heaven with its power*
> *And the sun with its brightness,*
> *And the snow with its whiteness,*
> *And the fire with all the strength it hath,*
> *And the lightning with its rapid wrath,*
> *And the winds with their swiftness along their path,*
> *And the sea with its deepness,*
> *And the rocks with their steepness,*
> *And the earth with its starkness,*
> *All these I place*
> *By God's almighty help and grace*
> *Between myself and the powers of darkness!*" (*STP*, 247–48)

With this embodied prayer-rune, light and healing returns. Planetary disaster and Charles Wallace's own death are averted.

In brief, in *A Swiftly Tilting Planet* readers experience the paradox of the beatitudes where deep solace is extended to those who mourn (Matt. 5:4). It is in fact the maimed, the ones who have the least worldly recognition and who suffer most, who may become the best vehicles for life-giving spiritual power in a dark world, helping turn the tide. Through their pain, without the props of health and wealth, they are able to tap into "[t]hat joy in existence without which the universe will fall apart and collapse" (*STP*, 40). Their very existence, with its tenuous but firm grasp on hope, undoes the idolatry of certainty with the iconography of faith.[6]

Third, in *At the Back of the North Wind* George MacDonald explores the most troubling aspect of the problem of pain—that a loving God would permit, even welcome pain, in the design for greater good. In the midst of a wild storm

that the North Wind causes in apparent obedience to orders, the boy Diamond contemplates the existential dilemma in which the North Wind cares
for him with one arm while she sinks a passenger ship with the other. How can
it be that there is only one North Wind, all good, without evil? Or, is God
indeed both omnipotent and all-loving, both at once?

North Wind speaks to this crisis of consciousness,[7] claiming that what
allows her to bear the cries of the drowning people is her growing sense of "the
sound of a far-off song" (*ABNW*, 65), a song which she believes will "swallow
up all [the] fear and pain [of the drowning people] and set them singing it
themselves" (*ABNW*, 66). The story illustrates some of the greater good that
is a result of the sunken passenger ship: financial ruin allows a wealthy man to
grow honest (Mr. Coleman, *ABNW*, 103), and a "foolish…wicked" one to
pursue his true love (Mr. Evans and Miss Coleman, *ABNW*, 196). Diamond
resists such consolation at first, focusing only on the anguish of the dying. But
gradually, as he experiences his own death as well-being in the arms of the
North Wind, he embraces consolation in uncertainty. Pointedly, he asks her,
"You ain't a dream, are you, dear North Wind? Do say *No*, else I shall cry, and
come awake, and you'll be gone for ever. I daren't dream about you once again
if you ain't anybody" (*ABNW*, 278). With a faith like postmodern tenuousness, North Wind answers, "I'm either not a dream, or there's something better that's not a dream" (*ABNW*, 278). In short, in *At the Back of the North
Wind* readers experience existential angst in the context of ultimate hope.

In conclusion, these narratives offer the consolation that J.R.R. Tolkien
claims is one of the chief purposes of fairy stories.[8] They help repair, arguably,
the angst we experience with suffering through their glimpses of ultimate well-
being. Reading them invites us to contemplate living in fellowship with our fel-
low-sufferers, fellow-joy-givers, in humble, sometimes feisty hope. As Rabbi
Harold S. Kushner muses in *Overcoming Life's Disappointments*, "It may be that
instead of giving us a friendly world that would never challenge us and therefore never make us strong, God gave us a world that would inevitably break our
hearts, and compensated for that by planting in our souls the gift of resilience."[9]
He concludes, "Instead of exhausting ourselves trying to reshape the world to
fit our dreams, we are better off using our strength to comfort one another in
a world that is almost certain to mock our dreams and break our hearts."[10] It is
my claim then that children's narratives like these help us fulfill Rabbi Kushner's hope for us. They invite us to consider participating in the communion of
sufferers, and certainly St. Paul's idea of embracing "the fellowship of [Christ's]
sufferings" (Phil. 3:10)[11] has everything to do with ultimate wellness. These
stories replace the idolatry of certainty with the hope of consolation in un/cer-
tainty. Somehow, for these writers and their many readers, the presence of fellowship in the midst of suffering, both human and divine, is enough.

Notes

1 C.S. Lewis, "On Three Ways of Writing for Children" (1952), *The Riverside Anthology of Children's Literature*, ed. Judith Saltman, 6th ed. (Boston: Houghton Mifflin, 1985) 1079.

2 Madeleine L'Engle, *A Circle of Quiet* (New York: HarperSanFrancisco, 1972) 99.

3 Madeleine L'Engle, *Walking on Water: Reflections on Faith and Art* (Wheaton, IL: Harold Shaw, 1980) 118.

4 Roderick McGillis, ed., Introduction, *For the Childlike: George Macdonald's Fantasies for Children* (Metuchen, NJ: Scarecrow, 1992) 5.

5 C.S. Lewis, *The Magician's Nephew* (1955; Harmondsworth, UK: Puffin, 1975), cited in the text as *MN*; C.S. Lewis, *The Silver Chair* (1953; Harmondsworth, UK: Puffin, 1975), cited in the text as *Silver Chair*; Madeleine L'Engle, *A Wind in the Door* (New York: Dell, 1973), cited in the text as *Wind*; Madeleine L'Engle, *A Wrinkle in Time* (New York: Dell, 1962), cited in the text as *Wrinkle*; C.S. Lewis, *The Horse and His Boy* (1954; Harmondsworth, UK: Puffin, 1975), cited in the text as *HHB*; Madeleine L'Engle, *A Swiftly Tilting Planet* (New York: Dell, 1978), cited in the text as *STP*; George MacDonald, *At the Back of the North Wind* (1871; London: Octopus, 1979), cited in the text as *ABNW*; C.S. Lewis, *The Last Battle* (1956; Harmondsworth, UK: Puffin, 1975), cited in the text as *LB*. All quotations from these novels are taken from these editions and will be referenced in the text by page number.

6 In "Beowulf: The Monsters and the Critics," *The Monsters and the Critics, and Other Essays*, ed. Christopher Tolkien (Boston: Houghton Mifflin, 1984), J.R.R. Tolkien links the quest for certainty and literalism with idolatry. In his words, "[I]n history ... and in Scripture, people could depart from the one God to other service in time of trial—precisely because that God has never guaranteed to His servants immunity from temporal calamity, before or after prayer. It is to idols that men turned (and turn) for quick and literal answers" (44).

7 Diamond's "crisis of consciousness" in which he is faced with the possibility that suffering, even death, may lead to ultimate good, may also be thought of as a "crisis of conscience." As C.S. Lewis has observed in *Studies in Words* (1960; Cambridge: Cambridge University Press, 1990), the word "consciousness" was developed after the word "conscience," not "to express a new meaning," but "at first [as] a useless synonym" (210). In this passage the boy Diamond contemplates for the first time what would have seemed to him a logical impossibility, and now suggests itself as paradoxical truth. His new awareness has ethical and theological implications.

8 In "On Fairy-Stories," J.R.R. Tolkien discusses the functions of "Recovery, Escape, Consolation" in terms of flight from the ugliness of modernity to "the Consolation of the Happy Ending" (*The Tolkien Reader* [New York: Ballantine, 1977] 55, 63, 68).

9 Harold S. Kushner, *Overcoming Life's Disappointments* (New York: Alfred A. Knopf, 2006) 55.

10 Ibid., 63.

11 The biblical quotation is from the Authorized (King James) Version.

THE MESSIAH OF HISTORY: THE SEARCH FOR SYNCHRONICITY IN MILLER'S *A CANTICLE FOR LEIBOWITZ*

Deanna T. Smid

Walter Miller's science fiction novel, *A Canticle for Leibowitz*, first published in 1959, addresses the connections between history, time, and suffering. The novel opens in the aftermath of a global nuclear holocaust, then traces the efforts of a group of Catholic monks of the Order of Leibowitz to preserve the written history of the world before the Flame Deluge, and ends hundreds of years later than the time of the first chapter, describing the second nuclear destruction of the world. The novel is divided into three books — "Fiat Homo" ("Let there be man"), "Fiat Lux" ("Let there be light"), "Fiat Voluntas Tua" ("Let your will be done") — all of which end in death or war. Miller's novel is not only about time, it is of its time, one of a number of apocalyptic texts produced during the Cold War. Brian Baker posits that the significantly large number of dystopian texts written in the 1950s were the result of "the collapse of ideas of 'progress,' perhaps brought about by images of death camps and the destruction at Hiroshima, and the 'exhaustion' of Communist political influence in the intellectual life of the United States."[1] While Miller's depiction of death camps and nuclear destruction in the third book of *A Canticle* certainly suggests that the future does not hold the promise of progress, critics of the novel disagree about Miller's conclusions about time and history and their relation to hope. Because the novel both begins and ends in the near-total destruction of Earth, Susan Spencer identifies Miller's idea of history as a "negative, cyclical view"[2] because whatever "progress" humans make in the course of the novel only leads to a second holocaust. Dominic Manganiello, however, views the novel optimistically, focusing on one monk, Brother Joshua, who manages to escape Earth before the second nuclear holocaust. Manganiello emphasizes the Catholicity and Christian faith of *A Canticle* when he writes, "Miller's eschatological optimism, even if it seems oblique, is ... grounded in the biblical experience of divine renewal, which permits the individual and the race to make a fresh start by going back to the past in the hope of resurrecting a new self and a new world from the ashes of the old."[3] David Seed writes about time in the novel: "Dates give us linear time; recurrences and resemblances suggest cycles; and the constant presence of the old Jew adds another premessianic time scale again ... [and] early scenes recede into the past of the text itself, undergoing a constant process of revision and modification."[4] Building on Seed's recognition of the complexity and ambiguity of time in the novel, I suggest that time in *A Canticle for Leibowitz* can be best understood in terms of what Fredric Jameson calls, in *Archaeologies of the Future: The Desire Called Utopia and Other Science Fictions,* "synchronic or systematic modeling."[5]

Jameson distinguishes between "diachronic thinking" and systematic modelling, asserting that diachronic, or linear, history hypothesizes a string of connected events in which one event causes another, which in turn causes another, creating linear causality, whereas systematic modelling is a web, "an immense synchronic interrelationship" (87, 88). Jameson describes his systematic view of time: "[It is a] general sense of the present as an immense and interrelated web from which not even a dead butterfly can fall at the peril of the whole. The theory of history has certainly moved in this direction: and it is as though the ever greater accumulation of facts about a given period (very much including our own) determines a gravitational shift from diachronic thinking (so-called linear history) to synchronic or systematic modeling" (87). He warns, however, that synchronic time cannot "be grasped in terms of lived or existential time" because synchronic time does not consider temporality in a linear progression of past, present, and future, but as multiple, time-spanning "factors or facts" (89).

In Miller's novel, those "factors or facts" are foundational to the Order of Leibowitz, for the monks are mandated to collect and preserve as many remnants of human history as possible. Much of the monks' collecting is already completed by the novel's opening, and Miller focuses attention instead on whether or not the monks are able to comprehensively safeguard the facts they have gathered, and whether or not their efforts are even worthwhile. Miller already emphasizes some of the practical difficulties of the monks' attempt to create a synchronic model of history when he describes the disconnect between the monks' different experiences of the passage of time. Rita Felski's term, "synchronous nonsynchronicity," or "disjunctive temporalities" — which signifies that individuals and communities perceive time in different ways and at different tempos — describes the way the monks of the Order of Leibowitz experience time when they adopt new technologies while simultaneously following the same practices, organizing themselves on the same monastic structure, and using the same language from the beginning of the novel to the end.[6] Felski's "synchronous nonsynchronicity" both amplifies and complicates the place of Jameson's synchronic modelling in *A Canticle*, emphasizing the difficulty of reducing time to a single model, no matter how complex. The monks, as they seek to make sense of and define time, are themselves experiencing temporality in various layers. The novel, therefore, while it evinces synchronous time, complicates even that theory and calls attention to the complex experiences of those who try to make a model of the past while their own perception of time is various. The disjunction and connection between Jameson's synchronicity and Felski's synchronous nonsynchronicity highlights the essential tension in the novel, the tension of the monks who want to but ultimately cannot create a synchronous model of time. While the monks desire a single, synchronic understanding of the past, even their lives deny such a model.

Synchronic modelling operates through the accumulation of facts, which also motivates Isaac Leibowitz, the man who establishes the novel's network of bookleggers and memorizers who seek to protect books from the survivors of the first nuclear holocaust who are determined to destroy every vestige of the history and technology that made the Deluge possible. Leibowitz's program, Miller writes, is "aimed at saving a small remnant of human culture from the remnant of humanity who wanted it destroyed."[7] The monks carefully preserve the historical artifacts in their collection called the "Memorabilia," but their collection does not allow them to piece together a linear, causal timeline of the past. For example, at the beginning of the novel, already hundreds of years after Leibowitz's death, Brother Francis finds a number of pre-Flame Deluge documents, of which Seed writes, "The contents of Francis' box can be constructed as an enigmatic and perhaps random collection of metonymies, parts of a whole narrative and culture that have disappeared."[8] The objects in the box, however, are not merely, as Baker names them, random "remaining artefacts of the devastated civilisation"[9] but are a carefully chosen collection of objects that demand a synchronic understanding of the artifacts and of the text. The racing form, grocery list, address book, and blueprint Francis finds do not help him or the monks construct a fuller linear, chronological understanding of the past, but instead allow them, if they could decipher any of the artifacts, more insight into the life of the owner of the objects, Isaac Leibowitz, and through him, the monks hope, the civilization of which he was a part. Moreover, Miller uses the discovery of Leibowitz's possessions to underscore the role of the historiographer in the synchronic modelling of the past. Leibowitz, who worked diligently to preserve a record of history, is himself the subject of historical debate, and he is therefore located firmly in the synchronic model that he had hoped to facilitate. Historians then, in A Canticle, are inseparable from the histories they generate, and history is not necessarily an ordered progression through time; rather, it is a web of factors that seem unrelated and unimportant but are interconnected and maintained in the Memorabilia, evidence of the synchronicity of time.

Although the monks understand the concept of synchronic modelling and gather the plethora of facts a synchronic model of history demands, they cannot decipher history. They have the factors, but not the ability to map them together to come to an understanding of the past. In the novel, Miller questions the utility of synchronic modelling without a person who can draw connections—are facts interrelated if no one can see the interrelations? Leibowitz, who possibly could have mapped the artifacts in the Memorabilia, is dead, so the monks, who do not comprehend the content of the data in their collection, simply preserve the Memorabilia. Miller writes,

> The monks waited. It mattered not at all to them that the knowledge they saved was useless, that much of it was not really knowledge now, was as inscrutable to the monks in some instances as it would be to an illiterate wild-boy from the hills; this knowledge was empty of content, its subject matter long since gone. Still, such knowledge had a symbolic structure that was peculiar to itself, and at least the symbol-interplay could be observed. To observe the way a knowledge-system is knit together is to learn at least a minimum knowledge-of-knowledge, until someday— someday or some century—an Integrator would come, and things would be fitted together again. So time mattered not at all. (66)

Without a synchronic map, time for the monks is empty—a concept reminiscent of Walter Benjamin's discussion of time and history. In his "Theses on the Philosophy of History," Benjamin invokes the image of empty time, filled with progress, but his idea of messianic time is especially pertinent to A Canticle. Benjamin writes that, for the Jews, "every second of time was the strait gate through which the Messiah might enter."[10] For Benjamin, time has a purpose because it is "shot through with chips of Messianic time"[11] as people wait for God to return to Earth. Critics of A Canticle have rightly identified the messianic quality of the novel, Ralph Wood writing, for example, "[the monks] live in the eschatological confidence that the God who in Jesus Christ has indwelt time has all of time to work His purposes out."[12] The Messiah the

monks await is never named as Christ, however, but as the Integrator, someone who can map the synchronicity of history, for the messianic Integrator
will give meaning to the future only by explaining the past.

Although the monks await the Messiah of history, he or she does not
appear in the text. In the first book of the novel, "Fiat Homo," the monks copy
rather than comprehend the Memorabilia; in the second book, "Fiat lux," a
man named Thon Thaddeo comes to examine only a limited part of the Memorabilia; and in the third book, "Fiat Voluntas Tua," neither the monks nor any
scholars have any contact with the Memorabilia except to transport it away
from Earth. In the second book, when Thon Thaddeo, the secular scholar, visits the Abbey in order to inspect the pre-Deluge documents, Miller discusses
the monks' expectations for the visit, for they hope that Thaddeo is the Integrator. Benjamin, the enigmatic old Jew who appears in all three of the books,
and who has been waiting for centuries for the Messiah, after he meets Thaddeo and stares "hopefully into the scholar's eyes," announces sadly, "It's still
not *Him*" (216). Thon Thaddeo tries to integrate the different facts in the
Memorabilia, explaining to the abbot, "[T]he pieces have to be fitted together,
and they don't all belong to the same puzzle" (199), but he ignores or misin-
terprets any text that does not deal with science or technology. He investigates
and tries to understand all of the scientific texts, but he is not, for example,
"acquainted with the suggestions of Saint Augustine" (213), and he mistakes
a satirical drama for a scientific assertion that "man was not created until
shortly before the fall of the last civilization" (231). Thaddeo is therefore not
the Messiah of history, but someone who wants only to examine one specific
aspect of history rather than making a synchronic map of the interconnec-
tions of the facts, including documents like shopping lists and racing forms as
well as blueprints for electrical generators. Moreover, Thaddeo's investigations
in the Memorabilia ultimately lead to the technology that allows the second
holocaust to occur. Lewis Fried explains, "The irony of the Abbey's nourish-
ing what is our best sense of ourselves is the ever repeating destruction that
shall come from the Abbey's collection: another cycle of war made possible by
deciphering past technological achievements."[13] Thon Thaddeo's investigations lead to war precisely because he does not attempt a synchronic modelling of the past — he cannot understand the interrelations of the factors of history and he accordingly does not acknowledge his own connections to the rest
of humanity and the implications his research may have. When the abbot asks
Thaddeo, "Why do you wish to discredit the past, even to dehumanizing the
last civilization? So that you need not learn from their mistakes?" the scholar
replies angrily, "These records should be placed in the hands of competent
people," clearly believing that he is one of those people (235). Thaddeo is not
competent, at least not as the Integrator, for he cannot even place himself in a

synchronic model of time, choosing instead to study only certain artifacts and to dissociate himself from the people who created them.

If Thon Thaddeo is not the Messiah, the "Integrator" who can give meaning to the empty time the monks experience as they wait, does Miller provide another? Does he end the novel in hope or in despair? Critics point to the departure of Brother Joshua with the Memorabilia and a ship full of children as Miller's hope for the future. Manganiello writes, "As the new inheritors of God's promises, these voyagers are prefigured by the faithful Remnant of Israel, who survived various cataclysms. Their space exodus acts as a providential sign that the human race, if not the planet, will go on."[14] Manganiello does not, therefore, view the repetition of the novel as pessimistic, but states instead that "repetition is foremost a 'recollection forward' to the final coming of the Integrator or Lord of history, who, as Alpha and Omega, is able to join the beginning and the end, fold up the narrative of the human story like a book, and fit things together again."[15] Although Joshua escapes with the Memorabilia, can he avoid the wilful madness of humanity, or can he do anything more than the Order of Leibowitz had done for centuries: wait for a Messiah to understand and make useful the synchronicity of history? Miller gives no indication that Joshua or the children accompanying him away from Earth are distinct from any other humans — the "race of madmen" — so they carry the violence and ignorance of Earth with them (278). The Memorabilia they carry is meaningless without an Integrator, so although Joshua and his spaceship represent hope, it is a deferred hope that is not realized by the end of the novel, and the advent of the Messiah of history does not seem to be any nearer than it was at the beginning of A Canticle. Although the ability to keep waiting is optimistic, does Miller provide any more concrete and active assurance to his reader?

The only person in, or rather outside of, the text who can integrate and connect the Memorabilia and the events of the story as Miller describes them is the reader, and the novel itself becomes another factor in the synchronicity of the text. Baker writes about the place of the reader, "The text must assume some status as a surviving found object, which places the readers as ourselves survivors of the apocalyptic moment."[16] Just as the monks and abbots in the text read and memorize texts, Miller encourages the reader of A Canticle to trace the symbols he employs from the beginning of his text to the end. The reader, for example, is the only person who can realize that the skull that the last abbot of the Order of Leibowitz sees before he dies is the same one Brother Francis discovers in the opening of the text. However, although the reader can see connections between the beginning and the end of the text, that does not mean that Miller is proposing a linear view of history, one which the reader has to string together. Seed proposes instead that "Miller sets up countless obstacles to reading history as linear progress by inverting his images, shifting contexts, and introducing reversals."[17] The skull, for example, has a different significance during the second nuclear holocaust than it does when Francis discovers it in the fallout shelter. While Miller encourages the reader to connect historical factors, he does not allow for an uncomplicated linear reading of the past but forces the reader to attempt the role of the Integrator, the Messiah who can make sense of time synchronically. Nevertheless, although the reader can, and is encouraged to, try to make a synchronic model of the facts presented in the text, the reader cannot make a comprehensive synchronic map. Too many elements in the text, such as the character of Benjamin, who appears to live for thousands of years, defy mapping. As well, the reader does not have full access to the Memorabilia, which is itself a very limited collection of history. Any Integrator of history must, therefore, be able to transcend text, which is itself only one "factor" in a synchronic map.

From one perspective, then, text and narrative cannot be synchronic models, and reading is not the means to mapping synchronicity. Miller emphasizes the limitations of reading in the text, for, as Seed notes, "his main characters all become readers but all suffer from a lack of competence in varying degrees."[18] Accordingly, Miller does not end the text with a description of the Memorabilia leaving Earth, but focuses instead on a shark who, after the nuclear fallout had killed the shrimp and the whiting, "swam out to his deepest waters and brooded in the old clean currents. He was very hungry that season" (338). Commenting on the same quotation, Scholes and Rabkin write, "At first one might take this as a sign of the end of the world, but it is not. The shark will be hungry, but to be hungry it must survive."[19] Moreover, it is hungry for only a season, emphasizing the cyclical character of nature — human cycles bring destruction upon humanity, but cycles in nature are renewing and bring new life, although the shark's life depends on the destruction of another's: the shrimp and whiting he eats. The human cycle of destruction affects nature, for the shrimp and whiting die, and since the first nuclear holocaust genetic mutations in humans are common, but even death and mutation are positive at the end of the novel. After the chapel is destroyed in the novel's final nuclear blast, Mrs. Grales's previously inanimate second head, named Rachel, awakens when Mrs. Grales sleeps. Rachel, a mutation resulting from the first nuclear war, is a new innocent life, associated with the Immaculate Conception, and, because she is not born, is exempt from original sin. A consequence of the first holocaust, Rachel awakens in the second and survives, completing a cycle of hope. Hanzo opines that Rachel, "the new child born without sin who inherits the history of the Earth belongs to a new order of being,"[20] one that is formed from the events of the past but is neither conscious of nor concerned about history.

At the end of the novel, Miller gives the reader three different possibilities of hope — the escaping Joshua, the living shark, and the reborn Rachel. Nevertheless, none of them can be the Integrator and understand or redeem history, for Joshua comes from the race of madmen who continue to destroy Earth and themselves; the shark is oblivious to anything but hunger and can only live by feeding off other creatures; and Rachel, although the dying abbot can see "primal innocence in [her] eyes, and a promise of resurrection" (336), is innocent and hopeful only because she has disconnected herself from history rather than understood it. Joshua, Rachel, and the shark cannot help each other or anyone else, but they — especially Rachel and Joshua — do have something in common, something that includes them in a synchronic model of the text and of time. In the midst of the second nuclear deluge, an event of horrifying and incomprehensible destruction, both Joshua and Rachel sing, suggesting that Miller presents music as a link between experience and innocence, as an inarticulate expression of hope and life, and as a possible method for understanding synchronic models.

Miller begins and ends the novel with singing, for in the dedication of the novel, Miller calls the text "my clumsy song," and at the end of the novel, the monks sing as they help the children into the spaceship. Although Miller writes, "[W]hen the horizon erupted, the singing stopped," the song never does stop (337). The novel is Miller's "song," and it, as Baker writes, survives the fictional nuclear holocaust as an artifact for the reader. Music even survives the second nuclear holocaust in the text, for after Rachel awakens, she skips away from the dying abbot, singing wordlessly, "la la la, la-la-la ..." (336). Joshua's songs are historically based, "old space chanteys," while Rachel's are wordless, empty even of the history contained in language (337). While their singing is very different and signifies different emotions, their reaction to the nuclear holocaust is the same. It is always difficult to define the effects of music, especially in relation to literature, but I find Martin Boykan's text *Silence and Slow Time* especially useful in the context of *A Canticle*. Boykan writes, "Music belongs to another order of experience where time ... has a different flow."[21] Boykan objects to the synchronic model of time being applied to music for, he writes, "Musical structure is not a map, even one that gradually unfolds. Or to put it another way, the synchronic model, in which everything somehow is seen together, fundamentally distorts the way music is perceived."[22] Miller, however, employs a very specific genre of music in his text: a canticle, which is a song or chant of praise commonly employed in church services.[23] A canticle is a song praising God, sung and heard by a group, a community. Even if music itself should not or cannot be understood by synchronic modelling, canticles encourage people to think of themselves as a part of a group dedicated to God and connected in a web of interrelations.

The shark, although it does not sing, represents the presence of God in history, for Miller argues that synchronic models are not complete if just the factors are interconnected; God and humans must be included in the model as well. Throughout the novel, the narrator has told the story from a third-person, omniscient point of view, but the story has always followed the lives of people. Then, after the narrator concludes that while the last abbot of the monastery waits for death and "Nothing else ever came—nothing that he saw, or felt, or heard" (336), the story continues even after most of humanity in the area has been wiped out and Joshua and the other monks have left in their spaceship. The abbot's senses, and the senses of most of the people around him, are gone, but the text does not die along with the people. Indeed, the last two paragraphs of the novel, describing the hungry shark and the ruined ocean in which it lives, are utterly void of the human presence that pervades the rest of the novel. The shark is comforting only in its ability to survive, and the sea is full of "sportive brutality" (338), so nature—the created earth—is not messianic or redeeming in itself. Rather, when the humans are gone from the book, the narration continues and the omniscient—or perhaps Omniscient—narrator remains. *A Canticle*, then, ends with a reassurance that the monks, and indeed all people, are not alone, but their story is controlled by a power beyond even death. The canticle, the song of praise, which unites people in community and communication, also unites God and those who sing to him.

When he encourages his readers to transcend the text, Miller not only emphasizes the importance of community by means of music, but he also urges the importance of communion, a connection between humans and between humans and God. After Rachel awakens, the abbot tries to baptize her, but she shies away. Instead, she offers the Eucharist to the dying abbot, who receives communion from her hand. He thinks, "She who could not yet use words nor understand them, had done what she had as if by *direct instruction*" (335), as if her actions are prompted and authorized by God. Even before she can communicate verbally, she can experience, and even give, communion. Communion is a practical and physical demonstration of the interconnectedness of synchronic modelling, therefore, which connects people beyond the level of verbal or written communication. Rachel communicates, through gestures, what the abbot interprets as, "I do not need your *first* Sacrament, Man, but I am worthy to convey to you *this* Sacrament of Life" (335), demonstrating that life and hope come from communion and community. Moreover, Rachel is worthy to give communion even though she is not an ordained priest and is separate from the Church hierarchy the abbot had been so careful to maintain even among the group of clergy who escaped Earth in the spaceship. Just as a canticle is sung by the whole congregation, so communion unites all those who partake of it, and the sacrament is one of "Life," even in the presence of so much death and imminent death.

Why, then, is Miller's canticle for Leibowitz? Underlying the entire text is the act of waiting—waiting for the advent of the Messiah of history, who can transcend the limits of text and of human understanding and make sense of history and thereby give meaning to the future: someone who can control time. The "canticle" gives direction for how to live while waiting. Neither the monks nor any other character in the text can construct a comprehensive synchronic model that will make sense of all of the suffering in the history of the world, but the monks can sing canticles. They can live in synchronicity with each other and with historical characters such as Leibowitz, for they are interrelated by their faith in God, their desire to learn from the past, and their shared hope for the future. Attempting to understand the past by means of synchronic models, therefore, encourages a sense of interrelated community in the present and looks forward to the coming of the Integrator, the Christ.

Notes

1 Brian Baker, "The Map of Apocalypse: Nuclear War and the Space of Dystopia in American Science Fiction," *Histories of the Future: Studies in Fact, Fantasy, and Science Fiction*, ed. Alan Sandison and Robert Dingley (London: Palgrave, 2000) 125.

2 Susan Spencer, "The Post-Apocalyptic Library: Oral and Literate Culture in *Fahrenheit 451* and *A Canticle for Leibowitz*," *Extrapolation* 32.4 (1991): 341.

3 Dominic Manganiello, "History as Judgment and Promise in *A Canticle for Leibowitz*," *Science-Fiction Studies* 13, pt. 2 (1986): 166–67.

4 David Seed, "Recycling the Texts of the Culture: Walter M. Miller's *A Canticle for Leibowitz*," *Extrapolation* 37.3 (1996): 268.

5 Although Fredric Jameson's is not the only definition of synchronicity, I invoke his discussion of the term because his definition is quite comprehensive and he also considers synchronicity in the context of utopian fiction. See Fredric Jameson, *Archaeologies of the Future: The Desire Called Utopia and Other Science Fictions* (New York: Verso, 2005) 87; future citations from Jameson's work are from this edition and will be referenced in the text by page number.

6 Rita Felski, *Doing Time: Feminist Theory and Postmodern Culture* (New York: New York University Press, 2000) 23, 25.

7 Walter Miller, *A Canticle for Leibowitz* (1959; New York: Bantam, 1997) 65; future citations from Miller's work are from this edition and will be referenced in the text by page number.

8 Seed, "Recycling the Texts of the Culture," 258.

9 Baker, "The Map of Apocalypse," 129.

10 Walter Benjamin, "Theses on the Philosophy of History," *Illuminations: Essays and Reflections,* ed. Hannah Arendt, trans. Harry Zohn (New York: Schocken, 1985) 264.

11 Ibid., 263.

12 Ralph C. Wood, "Lest the World's Amnesia Be Complete: A Reading of Walter Miller's *A Canticle for Leibowitz*," *Religion and Literature* 33.1 (2001): 31.

13 Lewis Fried, "*A Canticle for Leibowitz*: A Song for Benjamin," *Extrapolation* 42.4 (2001): 367.

14 Manganiello, "History as Judgment and Promise," 166.

15 Ibid., 167.

16 Baker, "The Map of Apocalypse," 133.

17 Seed, "Recycling the Texts of the Culture," 262.

18 Ibid., 265.

19 Robert Scholes and Eric Rabkin, *Science Fiction: History, Science, Vision* (New York: Oxford University Press, 1977) 225.

20 Thomas Hanzo, "The Past of Science Fiction," *Bridges to Science Fiction*, ed. George W. Slusser, George R. Guffey, and Mark Rose (Carbondale: Southern Illinois University Press, 1980) 142.

21 Martin Boykan, *Silence and Slow Time: Studies in Musical Narrative* (Oxford: Scarecrow, 2004) 23.

22 Ibid., 27.

23 Miller is, by far, not the first to discuss the relationship between music and text. Although Miller concludes that song can transcend text, even labelling his novel a canticle, the Roman Catholic Church has long debated the interactions between words and music. For example, the Council of Trent, which met between 1554 and 1563, argued over the role of music in the Church liturgy, for "[t]he complaint was that the music had become overly complex and 'luxurious,' making the religious text that it was supposed to express impossible for the congregation to hear or (therefore) understand. Music, the churchmen insisted, was supposed to be servant to the text, not its master" (Peter Kivy, *Introduction to a Philosophy of Music* [Oxford: Clarendon, 2002] 161).

VIOLATION AND REDEMPTION IN CANADIAN FICTION

SUFFERING AND THE SACRED: HUGH HOOD'S *THE NEW AGE / LE NOUVEAU SIÈCLE*

Barbara Pell

Like François Mauriac in France, Graham Greene in England, and Flannery O'Connor in the United States, Hugh Hood was the finest Catholic novelist in his country of Canada. However, perhaps because the comparative group — Canadian Catholic novelists — is so small, or because the Canadian critical establishment was generally hostile or indifferent to this conservative Catholic writer, most readers of this volume will not even have heard of Hood's works.[1] Nevertheless, I would suggest that Hood, in his fictional treatment of the suffering and the sacred, merits inclusion in the ranks of Northrop Frye's "major writers" whose mark is that "their readers can grow up inside their work without ever being aware of a circumference."[2]

In addition to twenty other books, Hood published a brilliant, beautifully written twelve-volume *roman-fleuve*, *The New Age / Le nouveau siècle*, between 1975 and 2000. The first few novels won approval for the most ambitious literary project ever undertaken in Canada, but the later volumes received little critical attention and fewer readers. It is true that Hood's novels are not like most Canadian fiction: no paranoid victims, postmodern plots, or politically correct obliteration of all Western culture, to be replaced by the current literary fad. Rather they are intellectually demanding, undeniably religious, and unfashionably optimistic. In fact, they are unique in Canadian literature: Hood wrote Christian allegory in a postmodern age.

Consequently, his treatment of suffering and the sacred is also unique in Canadian fiction. Throughout his religious epic, these themes represent the struggle between original sin and God's grace. The theological resolution of suffering comes through Christ's sacrifice, enables our sanctification, and finally transcends mortality in the eternal sacred.

Hood's neo-Thomist Catholic theology centred on "the Christian mystery of the incarnation" as "the central event in universal history."[3] Because of this, "the entire world, that is, the physical universe and everything that exists in it, in time, is redeemed and made absolutely valuable by the intrusion of God.... Everything is full of God" (*Governor's Bridge*, 144). This incarnational theology resulted in his literary aesthetic of Romantic transcendentalism or "super-realism" (*Governor's Bridge*, 130). Like Wordsworth, Hood believed "the human moral imagination," by concentrating, can perceive the "illuminations in things" originally "put there by the divine act of creation" (*Governor's Bridge*, 132–33). Hood's professed desire to make fiction "a secular analogy to Scripture"[4] and his commitment to "virtuous action" as "the most important thing in literature"[5] led to his increasing rejection of "the psychological novel of character and incident." Rather, he revealed character in "the same way that Dante and Spenser did ... by the description of the movement of icons."[6] Thus, the realistic novels of *The New Age* must also be read as a "Christian allegory"[7] of sin, suffering, and the sacred.

The first four novels introduce the allegorical essentials of the whole series, creating a "documentary fantasy" or "social mythology"[8] that demonstrates within the events of this real world, and especially Canada, the sacred values that redeem all human suffering in a divine grace. The theme of the first book, *The Swing in the Garden*, is the fall from grace to nature—sin and suffering. It tells the story of Matthew Goderich, the central narrator of the entire series, during his childhood in Toronto. His movement from innocence to experience, from the garden to the world, serves as a metaphor for Canadian society during the traumatic decade before World War II. The title, referring to Matthew's two-seater swing, allegorically symbolizes humanity's fall from grace in the pendulum swing of time and its redemption through the Cross of Christ in the red-and-white crosspieces of its construction.[9] In this "garden" Matthew also discovers original sin in the game of "Executioner" when he inflicts suffering on an archetypal sinner/saviour, his friend Adam Sinclair, whose name, signifying *sin* and *clear*, represents both sin and sacrifice—the first and second Adam.

Matt's sense of life as both "progress" and "regress" is strengthened when the birth of his brother Tony gives him a "sense of exile from a very good place," and he inflicts suffering on himself in jealousy: "the mark of Cain" (*Swing*, 47). Consequently, his "successive expulsions outward toward larger, larger, less enclosed spaces" are associated with the judgment of God, with that first expulsion from Eden (*Swing*, 9). Matt's archetypal desire for freedom from restraint moves him from the "garden" to the "fall" (the last word in the novel) through increasingly larger space and less time as a metaphor for human mortality, while the five chapters become increasingly eventful and stressful leading up to the beginning of World War II (*Swing*, 210).

The second novel, *A New Athens*, depicts the adult Matthew from 1952 to 1966 in his courtship and marriage to Edie Codrington near Athens, Ontario. Here the boy who was exiled from "the garden" in Book I discovers a "doorway" back into "the green garden, the magical lost world of childhood" associated with his first vision of Edie, who represents Eden.[10] In a series of Wordsworthian "spots of time," Matt unites the present and the past as "History traces the footpaths of the Divine Being" (*New Athens*, 11). Matt and Edie's marriage in the "One True Church" is a sacramental union symbolizing Christ and his church and, supposedly, issuing in a lifelong divine "comedy" (*New Athens*, 120, 140). It is bought with the sacrificial death of Edie's father and celebrated in her mother's twelve Pentecostal paintings (religious allegories, like Hood's novels, that portray "the heavenly and eternal rising from the things of this earth"), including a triptych depicting "The Population of Stoverville, Ontario, entering into the New Jerusalem" (*New Athens*, 210–11). The theme of the novel is the interpenetration of the earthly and heavenly cities, the secular and the sacred: "A New Athens and a New Jerusalem. They cover everything" (*New Athens*, 222).

Volume 3, *Reservoir Ravine*, tells the story of Matt's prehistory, his parents' courtship and marriage in Toronto during the 1920s, that epic decade between "the War" and "the Crash." The theme of the novel is the unity, continuity, and redemption of all time and space in the eternal will of God. Andrew Goderich (a Catholic socialist philosopher) and Isabelle Archambault have "one of the great human love affairs" as a mythological Adam and Eve, "a kind of sexual and spiritual Eden" from which Matt is later excluded.[11] However, the Goderiches (from *Godes rice*—God's kingdom) still live in a post-lapsarian world. As a Christian ethicist, Andrew learns through love to connect the sacred and the suffering. But he cannot save his Jewish colleague, Samuel Aaronsohn—who views the era between the world wars as a time between the "recapitulation of the original fall of man" and a new Armageddon[12]— from returning to Germany and the Holocaust. Nevertheless, Matt's birth at the end of this novel symbolizes God's salvation of history: "In the beginning was the Word and the Word was with God and the Word was God. We are all, every one of us at any time, the precursor and the evangelist too, both John, in for the beginning, in for the end."[13]

The fourth book, *Black and White Keys*, was Hood's response to criticism of the earlier books as "Pollyanish" or "Pelagian" in their failure to depict the sufferings caused by human evil.[14] Set during World War II, this novel portrays the Nazi death camp from which Matt's father rescues Georg Mandel, a renowned Jewish philosopher; it is a salvation allegory that bears witness to, as the title of Andrew's Nobel Prize-winning book on genocide puts it, "Sin Quantified." In the brotherhood of Christian and Jew that symbolizes sacred love, Andrew and Aaronsohn at Eastertide descend "into the inferno, followed by a miraculous ascent."[15] In this harrowing of hell, they rescue Mandel from a heap of corpses, and Andrew physically resurrects him in a life-saving embrace. Therefore, at the end of this novel that portrays the depths of human suffering, and the deaths of Mandel and Aaronsohn, the ultimate theme is sacred hope: the triumph of God's grace over the most horrific human sin — Easter after Good Friday.

Hood's self-described "Marriage Group" comprises the central four volumes of *The New Age*. These books narrate the history of Matt's marriage to Edie (1953–73), his brother Tony's love affair with Linnet Olcott in England (1962–69), the breakup of Matt's marriage when Edie leaves him for Tony (summer 1973), and Matt's love affair with Linnet and her sudden tragic death (spring 1980). However, behind the events of this epic romance/soap opera we still find the central pattern of sin and suffering redeemed by the sacred.

Book 5, *The Scenic Art*, parallels Matt and Edie's early marriage with the growing confidence of Canada between 1953 (the founding of the Stratford Festival) and 1967 (Canada's centennial). Quintessentially "Canadian," Matt, in his "transparent" honesty and holy matrimony, is contrasted with Adam Sinclair, whose acting talent, "the artist's mode of Divine Grace," enables him "to play roles" but also, tragically, to disguise his homosexuality in a "PR marriage" of convenience.[16] Ironically, Matt, the naive narrator here, does not recognize Hood's depiction of human duplicity, not homosexuality, as the original sin — the "deeply fissured" sense of self — that leads to all human suffering.

These central volumes in *The New Age* focus on the central tenets of the Ten Commandments, and their violation introduces new suffering to the narrator's life. Matt's overzealous observation of the fifth commandment — honour thy father and thy mother — is clearly undermining his marriage. And in volume 6, *The Motor Boys in Ottawa*, he is devastated when Ottawa officials break the sixth commandment by engineering the political exile that "kill[s]" his father.[17] At the midpoint of *The New Age* series, the end of book 6, Andrew's death represents the death of God in Matt's universe: "The Father is in the Son and in the Holy Spirit.... My father is in me ... in an analogous way."[18]

Tony's Book (1988), the seventh novel, invokes the seventh commandment, "Thou shalt not commit adultery," in portraying the breakup of Matt and Edie's marriage by his brother Tony. Therefore, the "Fall of the house of Goderich"[19] is the destruction of *Godes rice* — God's kingdom. The novel ends with Matt in the abandoned "swing at the bottom of the garden" that symbolizes his loss of Eden again, suffering the "apocalypse" of Edie's farewell note (*Tony's Book*, 209, 215). However, the hope of salvation has already been introduced at the beginning of this novel with the portrayal of Linnet Olcott, Tony's rejected English lover, and the idealized woman of English Romanticism. Named after Wordsworth's poem "To the Green Linnet," she represents a sacred intimation of immortality within a world of sin, suffering, and death, and symbolizes the theological hope of the liturgical colour green (*Tony's Book*, 13).

In book 8, *Property and Value*, Matt has a brief love affair with Linnet Olcott in Venice, where she is starring in a film version of Marcel Proust's *À la recherche du temps perdu*. Hood's novel is divided into ten sections (like the Ten Commandments), with elaborate intertextual parallels with Proust's themes of love, loss, and the "value" that time gives to "property." The difference between Proust and Hood, however, is that for Hood the ultimate value of time lies within the scope of eternity: the sacred redemption of human sin and suffering. This theological context is indicated by his pre-Lent-to-Easter time frame.

Their affair begins the week before Lent with very positive theological allusions to their love as analogous to sanctification: "Well, we're all saved aren't we — that is, if we go about things in the right way? It's ourselves we've got to look to for salvation now that we've got the Redemption and Atonement behind us."[20] Nevertheless, as they first make love at the end of chapter 7, we remember the seventh commandment that condemns adultery and the sacrifice of Lent that requires "penitence and contrition" (*Property*, 112). When Linnet discovers she is pregnant, she faces a moral impasse: "[Matt] was a Roman Catholic. He could neither divorce nor allow himself to be divorced, on about the same grounds as would make it impossible for her to contemplate the possibility of an abortion. They were caught up in beliefs so fundamental for them, so rooted in their being, that any deviation from them was just not on" (*Property*, 215).

As she accidentally drowns in a Venetian canal, Hood allegorically constructs Linnet to take the sins of Matt on herself. She dies a sacrificial death on Easter Monday, her final hours marked by images associated with the Last Judgment, the Assumption of the Virgin Mary, and the Crucifixion of Christ. Consequently, Matt recognizes his responsibility for her death in a tortured stream of consciousness that connects Linnet with Christ's sufferings: "If nothing happens by chance, she either chose [death] or was driven to it. And since she didn't choose it freely ... she was driven to it. And if she was driven to it, friend, who was sitting in the driver's seat? ... Which of you can drink of the cup that I drink? ... They drove nails in. The wrists" (*Property*, 247).

Since *The Swing in the Garden*, Hood has used actors, like the symbolically named Adam Sinclair and Linnet Olcott, to represent archetypal sinner/saviours because they can take on roles and assume other identities in a way not possible for the naive, transparent Matt. Allegorically, they are not strictly Christ-figures, since their sins and consequent sufferings represent fallen human nature (like the first Adam). Nevertheless, in their tragedies, they take the sins of the world on themselves (like the second Adam—Christ). Hood treats them, like all of his characters, with unfashionable moral judgment and immense theological compassion. For, in Hood's allegorical universe, the sacred has triumphed over sin, but we still live in a world full of human suffering. Linnet dies after Easter: the Atonement and the Resurrection have guaranteed our salvation, but our sanctification is still up to us (*Property*, 130).

The final four books of *The New Age* complete Matthew Goderich's story on a vast canvas that spans the history of Canada from the early twentieth to the early twenty-first century and moves from Western to Eastern Canada, and even to the far reaches of outer space. Theologically connecting history to personal allegory, Hood unites the stories of five generations—from Matt's grandparents to his grandchildren—in the eternity of God's providence. These four books constitute the Bible of Matt's salvation: Genesis, Incarnation, Redemption, and final Revelation. In them we move allegorically from human sin and suffering to sacred grace.

The book of Genesis, *Be Sure to Close Your Eyes*, tells the story of Matt's future mother-in-law and spiritual mentor, May-Beth Sleaford, whose father, an agriculturist "visionary," aims to "ease and mollify the consequences of the Fall" and re-establish "the kingdom of God on earth."[21] In 1920s Saskatchewan, May-Beth falls in love with a brilliant Pentecostal cornetist: "In [his] God-given tones the blues became a music that anticipated a happier state, a better world, a closer walk with Thee" (*Close Your Eyes*, 74). However, his tragic death again heralds an exile from paradise, and May-Beth must go "eastwards from the garden" alone to "make something out of [her] life," nursing the sick and suffering in Toronto's Hospital for Sick Children (*Close Your Eyes*, 131, 158). She eventually marries a pragmatic, less-talented "trumpeter," who helps her discover her sacred vocation in the prophetic paintings that become her attempt to compensate for the Fall by transmuting the world back into the garden (*Close Your Eyes*, 176).

Dead Men's Watches is the gospel according to Hood. In this novel, Matt finally comes to understand Christ's Incarnation as unconditional sacred love that overcomes sin, suffering, and death. In Part I, after the death of his Uncle Philip (whom he had always "suspected ... of the sin" of coveting his sister-in-law Isabelle), Matt investigates Philip's secret love life with a "guardian angel" Cree woman from Moose Factory.[22] He leaves his privileged, Eurocentric apartment in Toronto to make a pilgrimage to the sacralized "margin" of Canada's North, in a post-colonial version of the post-lapsarian quest for a new Eden: "The post-modernist, despairing of the past, looks to the empty North and to space exploration [see Hood's next novel, *Great Realizations*] and sees his or her chance to escape from the past and the errors of humankind into a boundless and so far meaningless future, wholly uninscribed, without privilege" (*Watches*, 87, 53). Here he discovers "liberating love" overcoming sin and "divine knowledge" triumphing over death (*Watches*, 83–85).

More intimately, in the second part of the novel, Matt himself must demonstrate postmodern inclusiveness as sacred love when, for several years, he accepts and cares for his gay friend Adam Sinclair, who is dying of AIDS. In the 1980s context of a world coming to terms with the AIDS epidemic, "meanly and callously called the gay plague" and wrongly characterized as "an instrument of divine justice," Matt must finally repudiate his own homophobia (*Watches*, 226). As Adam again allegorically represents both the "sin" of the world and the one "sent into the world" "to suffer" for it, Matt abandons human judgment and justice for divine compassion, realizing, "He had always loved me and I had always turned him away, rejected him and his love, the wrong kind of love. You can't turn away love; you need any love that's going" (*Watches*, 137, 143, 223). The epiphanies of love—agape and eros—that Matt experiences in this novel are symbolized by the two "dead men's watches" that he inherits. Uncle Philip's is an elegant, gold, 1920s "stem-wound Gruen wristwatch" representing his family history; Adam's is a "surreptitiously pornographic" "Mickey Mouse wristwatch" that displays "Mickey [giving] Minnie a slow feel about once an hour" (*Watches*, 113–14, 160). At the end, Matt wears one on each wrist, symbolizing the triumph of sacred love over temporal sin and suffering.

In Hood's redeemed world, Dickens's *Great Expectations* have become *Great Realizations*, the title of his penultimate novel. Set in "the new age" of the twenty-first century, but in six sections symbolizing the six days of Creation, it tells two parallel stories: Matt's redemption of the past by reuniting with Edie to save a lost allegorical painting, and their son John's revelation of the future in his space journey to Mars and the birth of his son, a new Andrew Goderich.[23]

In part 1, Matt recognizes that he is nearing the last things of his spiritual quest: "an end to things, perhaps the first day of the new age, like the Day of the Resurrection, the first Easter or the approaching days of wrath, when all things shall be made otherwise than they are."[24] He reconciles with Edie in order to sell the family company and buy a lost masterpiece for the National Gallery of Canada. This allegorical painting, entitled *King Priam before the Tent of Achilles, Begging the Body of Hector from the Hero, for Burial*, symbolizes the futility of all human wars as sin that results only in suffering and death: "the nihilism of every kind of human contest. All struggle, war, passionate love and hate, domination of one person by another, all contention is idle.

What it leaves behind is desolation, the death of the hero and lover."[25] However, in the final image of the novel, suffering is redeemed in the sacred, as the allegorical painting "turns on its base winter and summer, in and out of light and darkness, like a magnificent vane or wing" or angel,[26] reminding us of T.S. Eliot's definition of Christ as the "still point of the turning world."[27]

In Hood's final novel, *Near Water*, on Midsummer Day 2012, Matthew Goderich dies of a stroke (coincidentally, the cause of Hood's own death just one month before the publication of the novel). This Book of Revelation consists solely of Matt's twenty-eight hour stream-of-consciousness before death; it announces itself as an epic like the *Odyssey*, an allegory like *Pilgrim's Progress*, and a theology like The Acts of the Apostles, and like all of these, a *periplum*: "a literary work having the overt and public form of...an account of an epic journey, as well as a private and concealed purpose."[28] Matt has reached the allegorical conclusion of his theological epic; *Near Water* is his apocalyptic eschatology: "Novel turning into allegory from Homer to Dante, the greatest of endings, the essential arrival, SAFE AT HOME! Nine choirs of angels.... It is better to reach home than to continue the search. The deepest narrative of all with the supreme usefulness of high allegory. Safe at home in Eden... the history of our salvation, *periplum!*" (*Near Water*, 9)

At the beginning of the novel, Matt returns to the Goderich family cottage (symbolizing "God's kingdom") to await a final reunion with his wife Edie (allegorically, the lost Eden). As he approaches the lake, he meditates on the suffering and salvation implied in the book's title:

I thirst.
Which of you can drink of this cup?
Save me, O Lord, or I will drown! (*Near Water*, 55)

Almost immediately after arrival, he has a stroke while resting by the lakeshore; the rest of the book consists of his martyred suffering as he crawls across the ground ("My back, from shoulders to waist, is being whipped and bloodied by the lashing branches") and up the nine stairs (symbolizing the ranks of angels) to the porch, where he dies in an "old swing that only swings in one direction" (*Near Water*, 193, 236). As he waits "for the circle to complete itself" that started in *The Swing in the Garden*, he meditates, "Don't push the swing backwards! Let it find its own centre-point, and then be still and try to put a name to the experience of love" (*Near Water*, 237).

Matt has spent his life as a near celebrity: son of a Nobel Prize-winner; husband of a popular painter; father of an astronaut; friend of a famous actor. His final reflections and memories embrace all the major characters of *The New Age* in a benediction of hope and love. But the book is primarily an allegory of faith, structured (with a couple of revisions) according to the fifth-century textbook of mysticism, *The Celestial Hierarchy* by Pseudo-Diony-sius.[29] The nine chapters parallel the nine ascending orders of the angels that mediate God to humanity: angels, archangels, powers, virtues, principalities, dominions, thrones, cherubim, and seraphim. Matt's passage from mortal suffering to sacred transcendence is marked by his progression through the "triad of triads" toward knowing God: philosophy, theology, and narrative; discipline, reason, and suffering; and finally, divine action, thought, and love as he enters into the "Divine Presence" (*Near Water*, 54, 251). At the end of *The New Age*, no longer "waiting for Edie" to re-establish his temporal Eden without sin and suffering, Matt rests at the "still" "centre-point" of the turning world, to welcome "three heavenly forms … [c]oming across the water for [him] now" (*Near Water*, 159, 237, 251). His sacred pilgrimage is finished.

In my introduction I compared Hood to Mauriac, Greene, and O'Connor as Catholic novelists. I have spent over thirty years dealing with the paradox of the suffering and the sacred, the problem of faith and fiction, in the modern novel.[30] Georg Lukacs said, "The novel is the epic of a world that has been abandoned by God."[31] In "Novelist and Believer," Flannery O'Connor expressed the frustration of the religious writer when she said, "I don't believe we shall have great religious fiction until we have again that happy combination of believing artist and believing society."[32] François Mauriac articulated the conflict between sin and the sacred: "How can I reconcile such a distorted view of the human animal with the faith I claim to have in his vocation to sanctity?"[33] Graham Greene attempted to avoid the struggle by calling himself "a Catholic who was a novelist, not a Catholic novelist."[34] And, in the end, they both stopped writing Catholic novels. Hugh Hood's solution to the paradox of Catholic faith in modern fiction was to write realistic novels that also function as religious allegories. He deliberately allied himself with the kind of literature Frye espoused: "Frye talks of a kind of fiction which begins with a genesis and ends with an apocalypse, and it's like the Christian scripture. That's what I'm doing."[35] Hood's Christian allegories may not be popular postmodern novels, but the serious Christian reader can, as I again quote Frye, "grow up inside [his] work."[36] In this postmodern but eternally redeemed world, Hood's theology transforms sin into grace, and his novels transform suffering into the sacred.

Notes

1 Hugh Hood (1928–2000), born in Toronto of a Nova Scotian father and French Canadian mother and educated in Roman Catholic schools, received his Ph.D. from the University of Toronto, and taught at Université de Montréal for most of his career. In all, he wrote five non-fiction books, seven short story collections (he

is regularly anthologized as one of the best Canadian short story writers), and four novels plus *The New Age* series, "the most ambitious literary undertaking to date in English-speaking Canada" (W.J. Keith, *Canadian Odyssey: A Reading of Hugh Hood's* The New Age / Le nouveau siècle [Montreal and Kingston: McGill-Queen's University Press, 2002] 3). The first two novels in this series were well received, and a special edition of *Essays on Canadian Writing* was devoted to Hood's work to 1978. In it he alienated many critics with the very un-Canadian statement that "I really want to endow the country with a great imperishable work of art. If I do, it will be the first one that we have" (J.R. [Tim] Struthers, "An Interview with Hugh Hood," *Hugh Hood's Work in Progress, Essays on Canadian Writing* 13/14 [Winter/Spring 1978–79]: 85). The next ten volumes of *The New Age* were increasingly ignored. In the past twenty years there have been only five scholarly articles (by Dave Little and me), one introductory book after his death (W.J. Keith's *Canadian Odyssey*), and a few book reviews. He was always published by major Canadian publishers (Oberon, Anansi, and Stoddart), but his final five volumes were never issued in paperback because of poor sales. He was a Companion of the Order of Canada and received a number of writing awards, but never the most prestigious ones for fiction (the Governor General's Award and the Giller Prize). In his defence of Hood's work, Keith argues that contemporary readers were reluctant "to persevere with a series that demands application, sustained attention, and the outlay of a considerable amount of time and intellectual effort" (*Canadian Odyssey*, 194). Lawrence Mathews, more cynically, says of the poor reception of Hood's "brilliant, original work," "No one ever went broke underestimating the taste of the Canadian literary establishment" (review of *Near Water, Essays on Canadian Writing* 72 [Winter 2000]: 109). I have argued that these brilliant Christian allegories are antithetical to secular, postmodern, post-colonial narrative fashions and expectations (Pell, "Divine Tragicomedy: A Theological/Tropological Reading of Hugh Hood's 'Marriage Group,'" *English Studies in Canada* 28 [2002]: 685–713).

2 In one of the most famous documents of Canadian literary history, ten years before Hood began his epic allegory, Northrop Frye said, "There is no Canadian writer of whom we can say what we can say of the world's major writers, that their readers can grow up inside their work without ever being aware of a circumference" (Northrop Frye, "Conclusion," *Literary History of Canada: Canadian Literature in English*, ed. C.F. Klinck [Toronto: University of Toronto Press, 1965] 821).

3 Hugh Hood, *The Governor's Bridge Is Closed* (Ottawa: Oberon, 1973) 141; future citations from this work are from this edition and will be referenced in the text by short title and page number.

4 Struthers, "An Interview with Hugh Hood," 32.

5 Victoria Hale, "An Interview with Hugh Hood," *World Literature Written in English* 11.1 (1972): 36.

6 Hugh Hood, "Letter," *Essays on Canadian Writing* 9 (1977–78): 140–41.

7 Hugh Hood and John Mills, "Hugh Hood and John Mills in Epistolary Conversation," *Fiddlehead* 116 (Winter 1978): 145.

8 Robert Fulford, "An Interview with Hugh Hood," *Tamarack Review* 66 (1975): 65.

9 Hugh Hood, *The Swing in the Garden* (Ottawa: Oberon, 1975) 5; future citations from this work are from this edition and will be referenced in the text by short title and page number.

10 Hugh Hood, *A New Athens* (Ottawa: Oberon, 1977) 8; future citations from this work are from this edition and will be referenced in the text by short title and page number.

11 Patrick J. Mahony, "Hugh Hood's Edenic Garden: Psychoanalysis among the Flowerbeds; with a reply by Hugh Hood," *Canadian Literature* 96 (Spring 1983): 46.

12 Hugh Hood, *Reservoir Ravine* (Ottawa: Oberon, 1979) 233–34.

13 Ibid., 192.

14 Hood and Mills, "Epistolary Conversation," 133–46.

15 Hugh Hood, *Black and White Keys* (Toronto: ECW, 1982) 129.

16 Hugh Hood, *The Scenic Art* (Toronto: Stoddart, 1984) 62, 49, 99, 158.

17 Hugh Hood, *The Motor Boys in Ottawa* (Toronto: Stoddart, 1986) 291.

18 Ibid., 203.

19 Hugh Hood, *Tony's Book* (Toronto: Stoddart, 1988) 241; future citations from this work are from this edition and will be referenced in the text by title and page number.

20 Hugh Hood, *Property and Value* (Toronto: Anansi, 1990) 130; future citations from this work are from this edition and will be referenced in the text by short title and page number.

21 Hugh Hood, *Be Sure to Close Your Eyes* (Toronto: Anansi, 1993) 12, 111; future citations from this work are from this edition and will be referenced in the text by short title and page number.

22 Hugh Hood, *Dead Men's Watches* (Toronto: Anansi, 1995) 105; future citations from this work are from this edition and will be referenced in the text by short title and page number.

23 Struthers, ed., *Work in Progress*, 12.

24 Hugh Hood, *Great Realizations* (Toronto: Anansi, 1997) 15.

25 Ibid., 239.

26 Ibid.

27 T.S. Eliot, "Burnt Norton," *Four Quartets* (London: Faber and Faber, 1944) 9.

28 Hugh Hood, *Near Water* (Toronto: Anansi, 2000) 3; future citations from this work are from this edition and will be referenced in the text by title and page number.

29 Keith, *Canadian Odyssey*, 201.

30 Barbara Pell, *Faith and Fiction: A Theological Critique of the Narrative Strategies of Hugh MacLennan and Morley Callaghan* (Waterloo, ON: Wilfrid Laurier University Press, 1998) 1–13.

31 Qtd. in T.R. Wright, *Theology and Literature* (Oxford: Blackwell, 1988) 110–11.

32 Flannery O'Connor, *Mystery and Manners: Occasional Prose*, ed. Sally Fitzgerald and Robert Fitzgerald (New York: Farrar, Straus, and Giroux, 1969) 74.

33 Qtd. in Philip Stratford, *Faith and Fiction: Creative Process in Greene and Mauriac* (Notre Dame, IN: University of Notre Dame Press, 1964) 304–5.

34 Ibid., 289.

35 Linda Sandler, "Between Proust and Yonge," *Books in Canada* 4 (December 1975): 5.

36 Frye, "Conclusion," 821.

FICTIONAL VIOLATIONS IN ALICE MUNRO'S NARRATIVES

John C. Van Rys

In his review of Alice Munro's 1996 *Selected Stories*, John Updike offers the following assessment of the composite heroine at the heart of Munro's work: "She is neither virtuous nor a victim; what she is is vital."[1] Munro's readers will undoubtedly recognize that vitality in characters as far apart as Helen from "The Peace of Utrecht," Almeda from "Meneseteung," and Carla from "Runaway." Such characters exist in vital narratives crafted by Munro to express the complex mysteries of how people live in time—the psychologically tricky and emotionally bewildering experiences of their own wills and of the forces beyond their control. The paradox of Munro's fiction is that such vitality is closely linked with violence. Munro's exploration of what is alive, of what is vital and spiritual, is embedded in various forms of violence and violation: her characters experience physical, emotional, and psychological violence, experiences that Munro's readers share through the narrative violations at the heart of her technique. Through such violence, both characters and readers experience a fruitful suffering, a suffering—desacralized to an extent— that nevertheless initiates "lines of spiritual motion," to borrow a memorable phrase from Flannery O'Connor, a writer whose work is critical to understanding Munro's own work.[2] In fact, understanding this spiritual motion, these stirrings generated by suffering linked to violence and violations, is a complex, painfully productive challenge for Munro's readers. To that end, this study aims to clarify the place of violence and suffering in Munro's work; develop a reading of these vital operations in Munro's female künstlerroman, *Lives of Girls and Women*; and examine the "progress" of suffering in Munro's later work.

The Place of Violence and Suffering in Munro's Work

As Updike's review suggests, Munro has frequently been characterized as a writer's writer, an author's author. That authority is rooted in authenticity, in an appreciated realism involving both an attentiveness to material surfaces and an insight into what lies below those surfaces. Such realism in Munro's fiction is, of course, a complex matter. In a recent appreciation of Munro's work, novelists Russell Banks and Michael Cunningham both locate Munro's authority in the characters she creates and the fictional techniques she marshals to those creations. Banks describes how Munro's stories initially invite the reader in, but "once you are in this fictional world, it becomes more threatening.... You realize that issues of life and death are going on, and Munro's fiction takes hard swerves abruptly."[3] Violent shifts in the narrative are related to forces that can potentially harm or violate. Similarly, Cunningham praises as unparalleled by any other writer Munro's ability "to chart the intricacies of human beings, the incredible complexity and ambiguity of emotions." He continues, "Munro has a firm grasp on the complicated interplay between our will, our desires, and the outside forces over which we have almost no control.... Munro isn't afraid of a mess; she knows that the mess enhances us.... [S]he understands that a fiction writer's job is to further complicate the world."[4] That complex interplay of internal and external forces, some of which are explicitly violent and violating, produces a complex mess, a mess including human suffering, a mess that nevertheless develops us as creatures. "Munro," concludes Cunningham in an allusion to Flannery O'Connor, "is a master of the mystery that resides in the human heart."[5] More than a half century ago, O'Connor characterized modern fiction as reflecting "the man of our time, the unbeliever, who is nevertheless grappling in a desperate and usually honest way with intense problems of the spirit."[6] In this sense, Munro's characters are people of our times, people experiencing various bewilderments of the spirit, and Munro's fictions seek to expose and elaborate these mysteries.

Munro has frequently acknowledged her debt to Flannery O'Connor, who was herself clearly an authority on violence and suffering in relation to the human spirit, specifically in a Catholic Christian context and within her own Lupus-plagued body. In a 1994 interview, Munro described her own living in books up until she was about thirty years old, reading primarily Southern women because "[t]here was a feeling that women could write about the freakish, the marginal."[7] Munro's fictions are written out of a fascination for the basic, the bare, the marginal, the weird, and the grotesque, all associated with a violent vitality. In the introduction to her *Selected Stories*, Munro shares a key moment that inspired her writing life. She recalls a winter evening with snow falling straight down, when she was preparing to leave the town library and saw a farmer, his horses, and a wagon on the town scales. That scene, she relates, did not function as a painting, "framed and removed"; rather, she says, "I saw it alive and potent, and it gave me something like a blow to the chest. What does this mean, what can be discovered about it, what is the rest of the story? The man and the horses are not symbolic or picturesque, they are moving through a story which is hidden, and now, for a moment, carelessly revealed."[8] Not the artistry of the scene but its vitality and its potency, its revelation and its secrecy — these offer the apprentice author a physical jolt, a metaphoric blow to the chest that presses her in search of meaning. That blow to the chest is what Munro has sought to communicate in story after story, through her portrayal of characters such as this farmer and by engaging us in revelation.

Not that these revelations are easy, orthodox, or even sympathetic to Christianity. In a 1982 interview, Munro discussed with Geoff Hancock her debt to O'Connor while also expressing her own distinct sense of life. Speaking of the Southwestern Ontario world that she grew up in and that dominates her fiction, Munro describes that culture as one "that has become fairly stagnant. With a big sense of righteousness. But with big bustings-out and grotesque crime.... There's always this sort of boiling life going on."[9] Later in the interview, she tells Hancock, "When I was a kid, like all kids, I felt that about objects and their becoming animated by sort of hostile or benevolent spirits according to what is happening in one's life. Of course, I didn't know it was because of what was happening in my life. I just felt the whole world was seething around me."[10] Munro, in other words, fills her fictions with that boiling life, that seething world populated by spirits — whether external or internal — and characterized by violations of righteousness. When Hancock asks her whether she sees her characters moving towards discovery, she responds that such discovery is highly problematic; traditional resolutions especially for female characters, whether marriage or flight from marriage, seem too restrictive:

> What I have is people going on. Just as if every day had its own pitfalls and discoveries and it doesn't make much difference whether the heroine ends up married or living in a room by herself. Or how she ends up at all. Because we finally end up dead.
> There are just flashes of things we know and find out. I don't see life very much in terms of progress. I don't feel at all pessimistic. I rather like the idea that we go on and we don't know what's happening and we don't know what we'll find. We think we've got things figured out and then they turn around on us.[11]

While claiming that she is not pessimistic, Munro nevertheless resists notions of progress (whether in life or in fiction), offering instead a notion of unpredictable discovery tempered by death's potency.

In a more recent interview with Eleanor Wachtel, Munro describes this view of life and fiction in more positive language, perhaps. Explaining the surprising changes that happen in her stories, the unexpected occurrence after some form of thwarting, Munro says, "I like the change *not* to be the change that you thought you were finding — and for something to come that is completely unexpected, as if life had a mind of its own and would take hold of you and present you with something that you hadn't anticipated."[12] What Munro seems to be suggesting of her fiction — for herself as author, for her characters, and for her readers — is that life can one moment deal us a blow and the next release us through a surprise, through a violation of our wills and our desires and our reason. This is the idea that Munro has been developing, testing, elaborating, and stretching in her fictions for decades.

It is no surprise, then, that Munro scholars have long been attentive to the presence of violence in Munro's stories. Already in his 1977 thematic study, *Sex and Violence in the Canadian Novel*, John Moss linked sexuality and violence in Munro's work as part of a distinctively Canadian fictional issue. When he focuses on *Lives of Girls and Women*, it is on the dualities and double vision that run through her work.[13] Almost thirty years later, Caitlin J. Charman, in her reading of Munro's "Fits," continues this focus on violation by teasing out "the disturbing and comic connection between sex and violence" in this story of murder-suicide, while Carrie Dawson explores the connection between taxidermy and pedophilia in Munro's "Vandals," a narrative that is preoccupied with various forms of "assault on bodily integrity."[14] What these three studies share, with their divergent critical approaches, is a focus on the intersection of violation and sexuality in Munro. Indeed, as Coral Ann Howells points out in her review of Munro scholarship, much of this criticism focuses on "the way [Munro's] language 'violates the familiar' by 'speaking about things not to be mentioned.'"[15] Some critics, such as Lorraine McMullan, have read these violations in terms of narrative paradox, or "the art of disarrangement."[16] Many others have read such violations through the lens of gender. For example, Georgeann Murphy, while pointing to death in Munro's work as "a violent, transforming upheaval," focuses her attention on the risks faced by the female body: "As if rape and childbirth were not enough sexual danger, the female body itself is forever threatening Munro's characters with humiliation and exposure."[17]

As this brief review indicates, while these studies have stressed the thematic, gendered, and formal qualities of violence in Munro, few have traced the spiritual implications of her fictional violations, whether in characters' lives, in the reader's experience, or in the story's form itself.[18] It is quite striking, then, that Margaret Atwood has recently linked Munro's narrative art with the explicitly Christian violations of the Incarnation: the human-divine mystery of Christ. In her introduction to *Alice Munro's Best: Selected Stories*, Atwood argues that the cultural Christianity that lies behind Munro's stories gives rise to "one of the most distinctive patterns in her image-making and storytelling."[19] Key to understanding Munro, claims Atwood, is the "central Christian tenet... that two disparate and mutually exclusive elements — divinity and humanity — got jammed together in Christ, neither annihilating the other."[20] Concluding that "Christianity thus depends on a denial of either/or classifying logic and an acceptance of both-at-once mystery," Atwood then explains that "[m]any of Munro's stories resolve themselves — or fail to resolve themselves — in precisely this way."[21] That is to say, within the story, "a thing can be true, but not true, but true nonetheless.... The world is profane *and* sacred. It must be swallowed whole."[22] In this sense, suggests Atwood, the mysterious spiritual violations of Christianity, its both-at-once nature, inform Munro's fiction. Tracing the implications of these violations, starting with their presence in *Lives of Girls and Women*, should deepen our sense of religious, spiritual motion in Munro's body of work.

Violations in *Lives of Girls and Women*

Munro's *Lives of Girls and Women* (1971), characterized as a set of linked stories or an episodic novel, offers a helpful starting point for thinking about the relationships between violence, suffering, vitality, and story in her work. In this story of Del Jordan's growth and development as a young woman and a young writer, Munro shows Del in a complex struggle with various forms of violence and violation, forces that are both external to and within Del herself. In a sense, as we move from one story of Del's growing up to the next, we participate in one "unavoidable collision"[23] after the other: between Uncle Benny's violent world and her parents' ordinary world, between family deaths and communal hope, between her mother's and her uncle's versions of the past, between life and religion, between Miss Farris's theatrical energy and her suicide by drowning, between fantasies of total depravity and the reality of Art Chamberlain's vacuity, between her sexual awakening with Garnet French and her spiritual deceitfulness, between the "black fable" she has constructed in her writer's mind and the reality of Bobby Sherriff serving her cake and lemonade. In other words, in *Lives of Girls and Women*, violence, vitality, and the fictions that contain these are sweeping concerns.

For example, in the narrative, violence is both a microcosmic phenomenon and a macrocosmic framework for experience. "The Flats Road," the first story in *Lives*, opens with an image of the Wawanash River, where, with her brother, Owen, Del is catching frogs as bait for Uncle Benny's fishing. Del describes chasing and stalking frogs "along the muddy riverbank under the willow trees and in marshy hollows full of rattails and sword grass that left the most delicate, at first invisible, cuts on our bare legs" (3). Such tiny cuts, small violations of Del's body, function as emblems of her physical vitality and vulnerability. Conversely, on the macrocosmic scale, Munro frames Del's life within the context of global violence, violation, and suffering. Without stressing this context, Munro periodically reminds readers that her characters have experienced the Great Depression and are living through and within World War II and the Cold War. This global context is evoked by Del's brief reference to Canada's effort "to help save England from Hitler" (27) and by her description of Bobby Sherriff's house, with its "souvenirs that had been sold when the King and Queen visited Canada in 1939" (233). We also learn of this framework of political, economic, and cultural violence through the more extensive discussions and debates between Del and Jerry Storey as they make post-high-school plans. In the period just after World War II, Del and Jerry go to the movies together, with many of the movies being war movies, and Jerry bombards Del with information about the war, with "unbeatable atrocities, annihilating statistics" (184); he talks of scientific discoveries that would create "prodigious catastrophe" (185). Thus, whether in tiny cuts inflicted by grass blades or reminders of destruction unleashed through split atoms, Munro establishes violence and suffering as an underlying motif in the narrative.

Violence and its correlative suffering are, in fact, portrayed as part of the natural order of things, as part of humanity's experience of and participation in nature. Uncle Benny, that living emblem of the swamp and its vitality, fishes the river and captures and tames animals. Del comments, "Much as he enjoyed taming and feeding animals, he enjoyed also their unpleasant destinies" (5). Perhaps in a more complex way, Munro shows how our perceptions of nature are transformed by human violations. When Del travels through the countryside with Mr. Chamberlain towards what she believes will be a sexual encounter, the landscape becomes vacant of the "secret, strong exaltation," of the emotion that she "used to hope for, and have inklings of, in connection with God" (157). Now, confesses Del, "with Mr. Chamberlain I saw that the whole of nature became debased, maddeningly erotic" (157). And after his theatrical masturbatory performance, Del explains that "[t]he landscape was post-coital, distant and meaningless" (160). For Del, at least, the violations that she participates in and witnesses radically alter her perception of and connection with the natural world; as a creature, she becomes alienated from creation.

While the relationship between humans and nature thus involves violence and violation, *Lives* also portrays human nature itself in this light. Munro's narrative locates much suffering in people's capacity for violence directed towards others and the self. The threat of violence exists in characters as far apart in the narrative as Mrs. Sherriff, the Anglican tartar, and Garnet French, guilty of beating a man outside a bar in Porterfield before he, Garnet, became a Baptist. An early example in the narrative that sets this threatening tone is Madeline Howey, also a tartar and Uncle Benny's wife. Described as "mentally deranged" or "borderline" by Del's mother, Madeline at one point threatens

Del with the stove-lifter. Del is fascinated by this threat. "Her violence," explains Del, "seemed calculated, theatrical; you wanted to stay to watch it, as if it were a show, and yet there was no doubt, either, when she raised the stove-lifter over her head, that she would crack it down on my skull if she felt like it — that is, if she felt the scene demanded it" (18). The threat of such personal violence, both theatrical and real, remains, then, an undercurrent throughout the narrative, and such violence does indeed erupt, violence that is real, both brutal and fascinating.

Perhaps not surprisingly, Munro locates much of the violence, violation, and suffering within the family. Such violence is the dark subtext of Ada Jordan's childhood as Addie Morrison, living on a remote, rocky farm in an old frame house "enclosing evil, like a house where a murder has been committed" (71). Feeling robbed by her fanatically religious mother, Addie hates her brother Bill, who tormented her when they were children. In fact, his tortures included sexual violations. Yet this is the same brother who then visits Del's family and functions as "Uncle Bill," an overly generous but dying-from-cancer man with a very different version of the family history. When Ada shares that Bill will be leaving her some money, she turns it into a bitter joke, rooted in their own mother's actions: Ada says that perhaps she will use the money to buy and give away Bibles. At that moment, Del receives a revelation of the pain that can exist within families: "[T]here was something in the room like the downflash of a wing or knife, a sense of hurt so strong, but quick and isolated, vanishing" (86). The family, then, is frequently the location of complex forms of suffering rooted in powerful struggles played out over generations.

As the examples above indicate, male-female relationships (both within and outside the family) are highly potent sites for both vitality and suffering, particularly because of the presence of the sexual. Clearly, Del's relationships with Mr. Chamberlain and Garnet French are foregrounded in this regard, with each offering a variation on the theme of attraction and violation. With the fraudulent Art Chamberlain, Del's fantasy makes her "feel endangered and desired" (143). Del's fantasy becomes violently real, however, when she performs her seal impression for Mr. Chamberlain. As he brings his whiskey to her lips as a reward, Del relates, he does the following: "Then with the other hand he did something nobody could see. He rubbed against the damp underarm of my blouse and then inside the loose armhole of the jumper I was wearing. He rubbed quick, hard against the cotton over my breast. So hard he pushed the yielding flesh up, flattened it. And at once withdrew. It was like a slap, to leave me stung" (150). Mr. Chamberlain's sexual communication with Del involves short and brutal contact, made as an "open secret," linked with performance and animal play. When Del reflects on Mr. Chamberlain's act, she characterizes it as "[i]mpertinent violation, so perfectly sure of itself, so authoritative, clean of sentiment" (152). As the violations continue, with Del conspiring to make them happen, Del confesses, "And this was what I expected sexual communication to be—a flash of insanity, a dreamlike, ruthless, contemptuous breakthrough in a world of decent appearances.... In the secret violence of sex would be recognition, going away beyond kindness, beyond good will of persons" (152). In her encounters with Mr. Chamberlain, violations that culminate in his masturbatory performance and end in his skipping town, Del experiences the debased, the erotic. In the end, she cannot turn him into "a funny, though horrifying, story"; he will not get back into his role as "the single-minded, simple-minded, vigorous, obliging lecher of [her] daydreams. [Her] faith in simple depravity had weakened" (162).

In her relationship with Garnet French, the violations are multiple in both directions. Del confesses that they rearrange each other, do violence to parts of the other, in order to be together. In fact, the violence that they do to each other's characters contributes to the dissolution of their relationship, particularly on Del's side. After making love by the Wawanash River and talking about babies and marriage, Del refuses to be baptized. This refusal turns from play to serious struggle. At the heart is Garnet's awareness that Del had simply been playing with him. "[T]his was what he knew," explains Del, "that I had somehow met his good offerings with my deceitful offerings, whether I knew it or not, matched my complexity and play-acting to his true intent" (222). As the struggle in the river escalates, Del describes her emergence from delusion and her attempts to save herself: "I thought of him kicking and kicking that man in front of the Porterfield beer parlour. I had thought I wanted to know about him but I hadn't really, I had never really wanted his secrets or his violence or himself taken out of the context of that peculiar and magical and, it seemed now, possibly fatal game" (222–23). After Garnet attempts to dip Del backwards and she kicks him in the lower belly, they separate and see that the fight cannot be continued. They break apart violently and permanently, believing in the "finality of some fights, unforgivability of some blows" (223). In her suffering over this breakup, however, Del herself re-emerges and repossesses the world; she experiences pain yet also the revival of her self back into "real life" (225–26).

This battle over baptism reminds us again of that "unavoidable collision ... of religion and life" that Del experienced as an adolescent. Indeed, *Lives of Girls and Women* is deeply concerned with issues of faith and suffering. Of course, it is in the story "Age of Faith" that Munro explores most fully the problematic relationship between faith and reality. A key episode centred on violence occurs at the end of the story. When the family dog, Major, takes to sheep killing in his old age, the decision is made that he must be killed. When Del imagines her father shooting Major, Del relates,

I did see again the outline of that reasonable, blasphemous face. It was the deliber-
ateness I dwelt on, deliberate choice to send the bullet into the brain to stop the systems working—in this choice and act, no matter how necessary and reasonable,
was the assent to anything. Death was made possible. And not because it could not
be prevented but because it was what was wanted—*wanted*, by all those adults,
and managers, and executioners, with their kind implacable faces. (108)

Reasonableness as blasphemy, death as wanted, the kindness of execution: in
her nightmare and her imagining, Del is confronted with grim certainties about
the spiritual implications of the human will. When her brother, Owen, on whom
she has been testing her faith, tries to stop the execution by praying, Del is dis-
mayed. As Owen swipes at her with clenched fists and closed eyes, his prayer
becomes a series of "desperate, private grimaces," for Del "hard to look at as
skinned flesh." She relates, "Seeing someone have faith, close up, is no easier
than seeing somebody chop off a finger" (109). In terms of her own faith, Del
can only question: "*Could there be God not contained in the churches' net at all,
not made manageable by any spells and crosses, God real, and really in the world,
and alien and unacceptable as death? Could there be God amazing, indifferent,
beyond faith?*" (109). In this questioning, one senses Del imagining that God
himself violates our religious institutions and our deepest spiritual sensibilities.

What all these various forms of violation and violence, the blending of
vitality and suffering, seem to point to is Del's experience of reality and fiction
themselves as unstable and vulnerable. Lives, stories, narrative, history, writing, fiction: all of these are made problematic in *Lives of Girls and Women*
because of the forces that operate on and within them. In particular, Del's stories will not hold together; her own imaginings get violated. When her relationship with Garnet ends, Del begins to study the want ads, saying, "Now at
last without fantasies or self-deception, cut off from the mistakes and confusion of the past, grave and simple, carrying a small suitcase, getting on a bus,
like girls in movies leaving home, convents, lovers, I supposed I would get
started on my real life" (226). While Del claims now to be past fantasy and self-
deceit, to be embarked on her real life, she pictures that real life in terms of
inhabiting a borrowed and already constructed narrative.

Perhaps more potently, in the epilogue, Munro questions Del's authority
and authorship with respect to the novel in her mind. Early in the epilogue, we
learn that Del has turned the Sherriff family into the Halloways, placing them
at the centre of a rather gothic, violent narrative. This story, carefully stored in
her mind, seems more truthful than the reality she knows. But Del finds it
impossible to actually commit the narrative to writing without ruining it, and
when she meets the real, living Bobby Sherriff, Del is confronted with the mystery of the ordinary, with what is stubbornly there. Del's novel is damaged,
violated by reality. It is as if the imagined narrative cannot withstand the

assault of what is concrete — words recorded on paper, a flesh-and-blood encounter and conversation. Del confesses,

> The truth was that some damage had been done to it that I knew could not be put right. Damage had been done; Caroline and the other Halloways and their town had lost authority; I had lost faith. But I did not want to think about that, and did not.
> But now I remembered with surprise how I had made it, the whole mysterious and as it turned out unreliable structure rising from this house, the Sherriffs, a few poor facts, and everything that was not told. (234)

As the author of the Halloways, Del has lost authority. Reality has dealt a violent blow to her fiction, a blow that has destroyed her faith in that particular narrative, a house built on a poor foundation. At the end of the narrative, then, Del is left with a faith-full fiction. She is left with the challenge of more authentically engaging reality through imagination. She confesses that while young she ignored Jubilee imaginatively; however, later she became greedy for it, making heart-breaking lists that failed to capture "every last thing, every layer of speech and thought, stroke of light on bark or walls, every smell, pothole, pain, crack, delusion, held still and held together — radiant, everlasting" (236). Del's imaginative and authorial longing comes to be located in getting a hold on reality and enclosing it in an everlasting light. By the end of *Lives of Girls and Women*, Del and the readers of her life have thus experienced a series of interrelated violations, from grass cuts to undercut metanarratives, that leave them bewildered but longing.

The Progress of Suffering in Munro's Work

Since the publication of *Lives of Girls and Women* in 1971, Munro has obviously continued to develop as a writer of short fiction. With respect to vitality and violence, what directions has this development taken? As an episodic novel or set of linked stories, *Lives* clearly gave Munro the opportunity to explore these matters in a thoroughgoing way. Essentially, her later stories elaborate and complicate the concerns and strategies that she implements in *Lives*. These developments can be seen through a brief survey of her work and a close reading of the story "Carried Away."

In many respects, Munro's stories after *Lives*, from those in *Something I've Been Meaning to Tell You* (1974) to those in *The View from Castle Rock* (2007), continue to disrupt characters' and readers' lives with unavoidable collisions. However, we can discern a few patterns. First, while *Lives of Girls and Women* effectively used the first-person narrative point of view, many more of Munro's stories since then have used the third person (though not exclusively). Such a shift has allowed Munro greater flexibility in narrative perspective and tale-telling — giving her more opportunity for multiple perspectives (with some violating each other), surprising swerves or turns in the narrative, and formal experiments (e.g., introducing epistolary voices, obituaries, news stories, and so on) that can develop jarring contrasts. What this shift in narrative voice also indicates as a second trend in Munro's later stories is a shift from more personal writing material to less personal material, though *The View from Castle Rock* returns to the personal with its powerful attention to ancestral history in a form of family chronicle. While all Munro's writing gets its start in reality, *Lives* functions much more as a fictionalized autobiography with its starting points in Munro's personal experience. In a sense, *Lives* exhausted that material and Munro began to turn more and more to real, if less personal, material. The result is that her subsequent stories show violence, suffering, and vitality at work in more diverse ways in the lives of more diverse characters at different stages of their lives.

With this turn to less personal material, another trend that readers can discern in Munro's later fiction is her dealing with violations in a greater geographical, temporal, and formal range. While much of her fiction remains rooted in Huron County, she frequently has taken excursions, notably to British Columbia and to the Ottawa Valley, but even to Montana and to Albania. Violence, her fiction shows, is not peculiar to Huron County, Canada, though there its nature may be distinctive. Perhaps more notably, her stories address this issue both thematically and structurally through a more sweeping and more overtly non-linear, non-progressive approach to time. Munro will present her characters' lives through many decades, but more through a back-and-forth, filling in, jump-ahead method that violates our sense of linear life time but effectively captures the swerves and surprises of a person's will experienced within the forces operating on that will. As this description also suggests, Munro's treatment of violence in terms of character, theme, and narrative technique has also been deepened and complicated by her tendency to write longer stories, many of which approach novella length. As Munro herself relates in the introduction to her *Selected Stories*, "In later years my short stories haven't been so short. They've grown longer, and in many ways more disjointed and demanding and peculiar."[24] These stories have grown longer, I would argue, at least in part because of Munro's exploring in greater complexity and depth the mysteries of violence, vitality, and the human spirit. These disjointed, demanding, and peculiar stories develop complex narrative puzzles that deliver a blow to the chest through rich images, statements, and surprises. In other words, these later stories resist the epiphanies (dark or otherwise) that characterize the stories of Del Jordan's growth and development as a young woman and writer.

Munro's "Carried Away," from her 1994 collection *Open Secrets*, offers a particularly rich instance of the spiritually significant violations at work in her later fiction. With the suggestive motif in its title; with multiple examples of physical, personal, and textual violence and violation; and with its tentative exploration of grace's presence in the neighbourhood of trickery, "Carried Away" opens up an intricate intersection for various lines of spiritual motion. Ostensibly, the story focuses on the intersecting lives of four characters: Louisa, the librarian of Carstairs; the man who becomes her husband, Arthur Doud, the owner of the primary industry in town; and Jack Agnew and Jim Frarey, her earlier love interests. In a sense, the story narrates the violations that bring these characters together or drive them apart. However, the larger context of the story creates a rich historical framework inextricably tied to the characters' personal histories. The action ranges over decades, from World War I to the Spanish flu epidemic of 1918–19 to World War II to the 1950s. Within this time frame, Munro alludes to tuberculosis and sanatoriums, Bolshevism, the Depression, the Tolpuddle Martyrs, trade unions, and Mennonites. The story, in other words, embeds the action within the twentieth-century history of struggle, warfare, deadly illness, economic and political strife, and religious persecution. Through these motifs, Munro involves both characters and readers in a history of suffering.

From the story's beginning, the narrative is shot through with meaningful, life-altering physical suffering, the body subjected to violence and violation. For example, Louisa has recovered from tuberculosis, and in the course of the story she becomes feverish with flu, painfully loses her virginity with Jim Frarey, and develops heart problems as she ages. However, the central moment of physical violence in the story is the decapitation of Jack Agnew in an industrial accident. Jack's head is physically carried away, first by the saw and then by Arthur Doud, who must return it to Jack's body. Jack's brutal, bloody death is rife with meaning and irony: the soldier who survives the war dies at home, the man who has injured Louisa's heart loses his head, and his death leads to the marriage of Louisa and Arthur. Moreover, Jack's decapitation involves Arthur in a highly public ritual. When Arthur is summoned to the accident site, his workers witness him "[p]ressing the face out of sight, as if comforting it, against his chest. Blood seeped through his shirt and stuck the material to his skin. Warm. He felt like a wounded man. He was aware of them watching him and he was aware of himself as an actor must be, or a priest."[25] Coming in contact with Jack's head, Arthur takes on Jack's blood and receives his own wound, feeling himself connected with theatrical and religious ritual that makes sense of catastrophic violence. In this way, Jack's death prompts profound questions about man and machine, about an attitude to life and the consequences. Arthur muses about the possible connection between such fatal carelessness and Jack's odd habit of sneaking books out of the library: "Was there any connection? Between thinking you could do things a little differently that way and thinking you could get away with a careless move that might catch your sleeve and bring the saw down on your neck?" (36). In this instance and in others, physical suffering prompts ontological questions about being, character, and fate.

As the relationships alluded to suggest, the violence and violations at the heart of "Carried Away" are deeply cultural, social, and personal. Having survived tuberculosis in a sanatorium, Louisa arrives in Carstairs and takes up the librarian position after learning that Miss Tamblyn, the dragon-like and disorganized librarian, has died (4). Bringing order to the library, Louisa nevertheless experiences disorder in her life. While her epistolary relationship with Jack deepens, she grows connected to the war and to others, feeling "a constant fear and misgiving and at the same time this addictive excitement" (11). With his proximity to death having made him feverishly careless to record his love for Louisa (11), Jack violates her trust by returning to Carstairs without a word to her and then marrying Grace Horne. Jack's death a few years later leaves Louisa "fierce in her solitude" (25). However, it is Jack's death and the discovery of his book-borrowing violations that bring Louisa in contact with Arthur. Strangely, their somewhat painful and awkward discussions of Jack's death, which verge on verbal violations, lead to attraction. In the wake of a powerful summer storm, Arthur is "visited by a clear compulsion" beyond his imagining but not his preparedness, and he asks Louisa to marry him (40–41). Louisa, we learn later in the story, was initially provoked by Arthur's being in the library and wanted to hit him in the back of the neck with something, but then she realized that she really wanted the opposite: "[I]t turned out to be something else I wanted entirely. I wanted to marry him and get into a normal life" (48). In this way, Munro intimately links and contrasts death and life, suffering and release, entrapment and risky escape.

These complex threads of living and dying, both literal and metaphoric, are thoroughly tied up in "Carried Away" with textual violations of a broad range. Clearly, Munro's method involves narrative violations that force readers to rethink conclusions constantly, to navigate swerves and tricks, confusions and surprises. Moreover, textual violations deepen the overall pattern of violations that the characters live and that readers experience. The story opens with a section entitled "Letters," comprising the exchanges between Jack Agnew and Louisa. The letters establish and deepen a relationship that is then violated by silence and supplanted by contrary texts: the newspaper announcement of Jack's marriage to Grace Horne, his brief note of explanation slipped under Louisa's desk blotter, the newspaper account of his death. Towards the story's end, one of the speakers at the rally honouring the Tolpuddle Martyrs, those men punished for illegal oaths, is bizarrely named John (Jack) Agnew. While the narrative maintains a degree of ambiguity, it appears that Jim Frarey has taken Jack Agnew's name, a textual turn that amounts to identity theft.

Even more strange is the working out of this final episode in "Carried Away." Having visited the heart specialist in London and fled the celebration of the Martyrs in Victoria Park because she begins to feel "a faintly sickening, familiar agitation" (43), Louisa is sitting in the temporary bus depot waiting to return to Carstairs, when she finds herself visited by Jack Agnew. Through much of this encounter, it is unclear what is happening: Was Jack's death not real? Is Louisa hallucinating, her mind drifting into senility? Sitting with Jack, Louisa experiences a "giddiness," "a widespread forgiveness of folly" related to an "amorous flare-up of the cells, of old intentions" (48–49). However, when some Mennonite families arrive at the depot, Jack identifies them as the Tolpuddle Martyrs, long dead, and saying that he must go talk with them, leaves Louisa. It is as she watches Jack walk away that Louisa realizes that she has been tricked, that this Jack Agnew is actually the Jim Frarey of her past, violating Jack's identity and Louisa's confidence, just as he had violated her (with her consent) in their sexual encounter decades before, again making her "dizzy and humiliated" (50). Her suffering is captured powerfully in this extended metaphor:

> No wonder she was feeling clammy. She had gone under a wave, which nobody else had noticed. You could say anything you liked about what had happened—but what it amounted to was going under a wave. She had gone under and through it and was left with a cold sheen on her skin, a beating in her ears, a cavity in her chest, and revolt in her stomach. It was anarchy she was up against—a devouring muddle. Sudden holes and impromptu tricks and radiant vanishing consolations. (50)

For Louisa and for the readers of her life, this moment of literal and psychological trickery delivers one of those blows to the chest, felt physically but also ontologically in an attack on her being and metaphysically in relation to the forces that govern life.

The power of this moment, however, is infinitely deepened by the presence of the Mennonite families. At the beginning of the narrative, Louisa had shared with Jack Agnew, "*I am not very religious*" (7). Similarly, decades later and six years after the death of her husband Arthur, she explains to Jim Frarey disguised as Jack that she remains close to Arthur: "I am very close to him still but it is hardly in a mystical way. You would think as you get older your mind would fill up with what they call the spiritual side of things, but mine just seems to get more and more practical, trying to get something settled" (47–48). As a character, Louisa does not experience her life in terms of orthodox religion and spirituality, and Munro resists infusing Louisa's life with clear turnings toward grace; instead, Louisa experiences a profound unsettlement in her life, a dis-ease. However, Louisa's encounter with the Mennonites in the bus depot offers her an at least temporary settlement, in the form of a rescue from the violating trickery of Jim Frarey, from the wave that has washed over and threatened to drown her. Initially confused about the identity of the Mennonites, experiencing them as a mass of black clothes that "melt into a puddle," she comes to see them as multicoloured, as cheerful rather than shy and dejected (49–50). In the wake of the wave, the narrator shares, "[T]hese Mennonite settlings are a blessing. The plop of behinds on chairs, the crackling of the candy bag, the meditative sucking and soft conversations" (50). When a child shares a candy with Louisa, "[s]he sucks on it as they do on theirs, not in a hurry, and allows that taste to promise her some reasonable continuance" (50). In the temporary bus depot, these fellow travellers experience a moment of communion, for Louisa in particular a blessed settlement into existence. Nevertheless, the encounter ends with Louisa's question, "What place is this?" reintroducing ontological uncertainty and disorientation (50).

Leaving Louisa with this question hanging, Munro ends "Carried Away" by taking readers back to the beginning, to the Louisa who has just taken the bold step of replacing the dead dragon Miss Tamblyn as Carstairs's town librarian. "She would be glad of a fresh start," we read, "her spirits were hushed and grateful. She had made fresh starts before and things had not turned out as she had hoped, but she believed in the swift decision, the unforeseen intervention, the uniqueness of her fate" (51). In the end, readers are left with profoundly spiritual questions: Does the story bear out Louisa's belief in intervention and fate? Has her lived life, with its illnesses, its heartbreaks, its near drownings, and its rescues, expressed the marvel of being alive? The story closes with the resonant image of horse-drawn sleighs moving into the dark winter landscape, the sound of their bells lost to each other, with multiple hidden stories fanning out from Louisa's. With the story's emphasis on physical, social, and psychological violations, with its terrible accidents and hidden pains, with its unstable realities but also its blessings, its interventions, its grace, "Carried Away" powerfully portrays life as an ambiguous school of suffering.

In Munro's fiction, whether in the early *Lives of Girls and Women* where Del Jordan experiences problematic epiphanies through unavoidable collisions or in the later "Carried Away" where Munro narrates the "open secrets" of Louisa Doud's violated but Mennonite-blessed life, readers can experience lines of spiritual motion. Munro's stories deepen our sense of human suffering in the larger view of life's mysteries, probing various realities and insights, exploring various deceptions and self-deceptions, testing the limits of the human will in the light of those forces that impinge on that will, involving us in surprise and wonder and yearning. Margaret Atwood claims that Munro has the gift of showing the gap between expectations and actual outcomes. "In Alice Munro stories," she writes, "people go into a house and find that someone has been murdered. Every expectation is met; and then, there is an event, a surprise — and that's the story."[26] In typically understated fashion, Atwood praises the violations of Munro's art. While readers may find these surprises desacralized in Munro's fiction, such swerves are not demystified. In this way, readers may learn something of what Munro sees at the heart of all stories: "the ways people discover for getting through life."[27]

Notes

1 John Updike, "Magnetic North," rev. of *Selected Stories*, by Alice Munro, *New York Times*, 27 Oct. 1996: 11.

2 Flannery O'Connor, *Mystery and Manners: Occasional Prose*, ed. Sally Fitzgerald and Robert Fitzgerald (New York: Farrar, Straus and Giroux, 1969) 113.

3 Russell Banks, contribution to "Appreciations of Alice Munro," comp. Lisa Dickler Awano, *Virginia Quarterly Review* 82.3 (2006): 94.

4 Michael Cunningham, contribution to "Appreciations of Alice Munro," 92.

5 Ibid.

6 O'Connor, *Mystery and Manners*, 158.

7 Alice Munro, "Art of Fiction," interview with Jeanne McCulloch and Mona Simpson, *Paris Review* 137 (1994): 255.

8 Alice Munro, introduction, *Selected Stories* (New York: Vintage Books, 1996) xvi.

9 Alice Munro, "An Interview with Alice Munro," interview with Geoff Hancock, *Canadian Fiction Magazine* 43 (1982): 92–93.

10 Ibid., 100.

11 Ibid., 102.

12 Alice Munro, "Alice Munro: A Life in Writing," interview with Eleanor Wachtel, *Queen's Quarterly* 112.2 (2005): 270.

13 John Moss, *Sex and Violence in the Canadian Novel: The Ancestral Present* (Toronto: McClelland and Stewart, 1977) 57.

14 Caitlin J. Charman, "There's Got to Be Some Wrenching and Slashing: Horror and Retrospection in Alice Munro's 'Fits,'" *Canadian Literature* 191 (Winter 2006): 24; Carrie Dawson, "Skinned: Taxidermy and Pedophilia in Alice Munro's 'Vandals,'" *Canadian Literature* 184 (Spring 2005): 77.

15 Coral Ann Howells, *Alice Munro* (Manchester, UK: Manchester University Press, 1998) 138.

16 Lorraine McMullan, "'Shameless, Marvellous, Shattering Absurdity': The Humour of Paradox in Alice Munro," *Probable Fictions: Alice Munro's Narrative Acts*, ed. Louis MacKendrick (Downsview, ON: ECW Press, 1983) 193.

17 Georgeann Murphy, "The Art of Alice Munro: Memory, Identity, and the Aesthetics of Connection," *Canadian Women Writing Fiction*, ed. Mickey Pearlman (Jackson: University Press of Mississippi, 1993) 18, 19.

18 In fact, few focused studies of religion in Munro have been undertaken. In *Locations of the Sacred: Essays on Religion, Literature, and Canadian Culture* (Waterloo, ON: Wilfrid Laurier University Press, 1998), William Closson James briefly dis-

cusses Munro's *Lives of Girls and Women* in terms of how "the religion of Protestant Christianity represents an entire system excluding their central characters or inhibiting their growth and freedom" (35). He then posits that this decentring relocates the sacred, prompting a religious quest (37). In "Temples and Tabernacles: Alternative Religions in the Fictional Microcosms of Robertson Davies, Margaret Laurence, and Alice Munro" (*International Fiction Review* 31.1–2 [2004]: 67–71), Nora Foster Stovel focuses specifically on Munro's presentation of Christian denominations, on the institutional church as a presence, particularly in the story "Age of Faith." Stovel claims that in the end "Munro discovers mystery in the very heart of established Protestant religion" (77). These competing conclusions, I argue, can be reconciled by shifting the focus to spiritual motion in her stories.

19 Margaret Atwood, introduction, *Alice Munro's Best: Selected Stories* (Toronto: McClelland and Stewart, 2006) xvii.
20 Ibid.
21 Ibid.
22 Ibid.
23 Alice Munro, *Lives of Girls and Women* (1971; Toronto: Penguin Canada, 2005) 108; future citations from *Lives of Girls and Women* are from this edition and will be referenced in the text by page number.
24 Munro, introduction to *Selected Stories*, xiv.
25 Munro, "Carried Away," *Open Secrets* (New York: Alfred A. Knopf, 1994) 34; future citations from "Carried Away" are from this edition and will be referenced in the text by page number.
26 Atwood, contribution to "Appreciations of Alice Munro," 94.
27 Munro, interview with Geoff Hancock, 108.

THE AMERICAN SUBLIME

THOMAS MERTON AND THE AESTHETICS OF THE SUBLIME: "A BEAUTIFUL TERROR"[1]

Lynn R. Szabo

> "If you want to find a satisfactory formula you better
> deal with things that can be fitted into a formula.
> The vocation to seek God is not one of them.
> Nor is existence. Nor is the [human spirit]."[2]

Throughout the course of his twenty-six years of monastic life at the Cistercian Abbey of Our Lady of Gethsemani near Louisville, Kentucky, Thomas Merton continually sought to find and create the conditions that nourished his spirituality as a religious and his creativity as a poet. Such conditions both enchanted and eluded him, as does God's spirit in the dance that silence and language, presence and absence, music and ritual, darkness and light perform in the deepest, most intimate yearnings and discoveries of our search for unity with him. Merton records his quest's narrative and leaves for us, in his voluminous literary corpus of poetry, journals, and essays, a record of his iconoclastic and illuminating pilgrimage from Prades, France, the home of his birth, to Bangkok, Thailand, the site of his death.

In addressing the essential conditions and disciplines that ground Merton's ontotheology of the sublime or what one might also describe as his aesthetics of the sublime, one is led to his mysticism—what he called that "beautiful terror"—whose powers forever mark those who encounter it. Merton's oxymoron captures the confounding beauty of the mystic's apprehension of the sublime, transcendent God, whose presence leaves in its wake the "burnt men" of the Hebraic prophetic tradition, including Moses, Elijah, Isaiah, the Apostle John, and all whom God calls to this holy vocation, seemingly even Merton himself. In the haunting epilogue to his autobiography, *The Seven Storey Mountain,* now a spiritual classic, Merton evokes these searing experiences in the poetic language of a prayer in which God responds to the yearnings of his servants whose vocation is the mystery of solitude and the burden of its prophetic call:

> I will give you what you desire. I will lead you into solitude. I will lead you by the way that you cannot possibly understand.... Therefore all the things around you will be armed against you, to deny you, to hurt you, to give you pain, and therefore to reduce you to solitude.... Everything that touches you shall burn you, and you will draw your hand away in pain, until you have withdrawn yourself from all things.... Everything that can be desired will sear you, and brand you with a cautery, and you will fly from it in pain, to be alone.... But you shall taste the true solitude of my anguish and my poverty and I shall lead you into the high places of my joy and you shall die in Me and find all things in My mercy which has created you for this end.... That you may become the brother of God and learn to know the Christ of the burnt men.[3]

This first and ultimate condition/discipline essential to Merton's aesthetic of the sublime is solitude. It is, in all of Merton's aspirations, his quest, the ground of his epistemology throughout the course of his monastic vocation and his engagement with language, literature, art, and contemplation. The more he sought solitude, the more elusive it became, resulting in the claim by those who knew him and who study his journals that he talked about it much more than he lived it. In one of his many self-flagellating journal entries, written, ironically, after he had been granted his long-sought hermitage away from the abbey walls, he says, "I see more and more that solitude is not something to play with. It is deadly serious. Much as I have wanted it, I have not been serious enough. It is not enough to like solitude or love it even.... Solitude is a stern mother who brooks no nonsense. The question arises: am I so full of nonsense that she will cast me out? I pray not and I think it is going to take much prayer."[4] Merton's longing for solitude and his contingent need for community result in tumult and vexation as he enters into and withdraws from solitude in sometimes frenetic, sometimes highly orchestrated patterns of retreat and engagement throughout his monastic life.

The desert fathers remind him of the price of the wisdom he so desires, found only in intimacy with God in Christ. In the introduction to a helpful and concise collection of these desert teachings, *The Wisdom of the Desert*, he describes the desert fathers as

the first Christian hermits, who abandoned cities of the pagan world to live in solitude.... What the Fathers sought most of all was their own true self, in Christ. And
in order to do this, they had to reject completely the false, formal self, fabricated
under social compulsion in 'the world.' They sought a way to God that was uncharted
and freely chosen, not inherited from others who had mapped it out beforehand.[5]

Merton clearly links solitude with the wisdom of God that is revealed in the
abandonment of oneself fully to him. It is a solitude filled with work, prayer,
study, penance, and contemplation, learned as spiritual disciplines, with the
commitment to the unity of the love of God and one's community. This was
the radical nature of Merton's ontology in his pursuit of life in Christ and God.

Merton, deeply indentured in his monastic life of silence and later, his life
as America's first Cistercian hermit monk, embraced this ontology from his
comprehensive study and his highly prized solitary life. His hard-won discoveries and their unexpected revelations had made it undeniably clear that solitude is not a condition one seeks in order to retreat from the world; rather, it
is the nexus into which one must enter and where one inevitably finds intense
spiritual anguish as well as profound spiritual joy. In solitude, one discards
one's self and its pursuits and painfully divests oneself of all self-absorption,
seeking the emptying of self sought and taught by the Apostle Paul: "I am crucified with Christ, nevertheless I live; yet not I, but Christ liveth in me" (Gal.
2:20 AV).[6] Solitude is not something outside one; it is not an absence of people or sound. It is an abyss opening at the center of the soul.[7] In true solitude,
one defers to the hiddenness, complexity, and significance, in Christian terms,
of an encounter and engagement with the mysteries of the Holy Spirit.[8] Merton articulates his understanding of solitude in his well-known book of meditations entitled *Thoughts in Solitude*, in which he writes:

> To love solitude and to seek it does not mean constantly travelling from one geo-
> graphical possibility to another. [One] becomes a solitary at the moment when, no
> matter what may be [one's] external surroundings [one] is suddenly aware of
> [one's] own inalienable solitude.... But this has to be properly understood: for we
> lose the actuality of the solitude we already have if we try, with too great anxiety, to
> realize the material possibility for greater exterior solitude that always seems just
> out of reach.[9]

The second condition/discipline of the "beautiful terror" of sublimity is
silence itself. John Cage, in his seminal study, *Silence*, determined that, ultimately, there is no such thing as pure silence even in a completely soundproof
chamber. Silence is, if nothing more, the sound of the body's rhythms of pulse
and breath, the music of the spheres. Cage concluded that silence is, ultimately, an absence of all being — impossible and inconceivable.[10] But the

silence to which Merton refers, the attending, listening silence into which God speaks his presence, is not limited to the metaphysics of silence. It is an emptying silence; for the Christian, the Christlikeness of kenosis.[11] Through kenosis, Christ does not, in his emptying of his divinity, exchange his strength for weakness, but rather, it is precisely out of his strength that he chooses to be weak.[12] St. Paul elaborates this exchange in explaining the life of Christ's spirit in the Christian believer: "My grace is sufficient for thee: for my strength is made perfect in weakness" (2 Cor. 12:9). This silent exchange occurs, as described by the Psalmist, in the stillness in which the knowledge of God is predicated.[13]

In his illuminating essays on basic principles of monastic spirituality, Merton states that "God is heard when we realize we don't know the sound of His voice. The words he utters are full of silence: they are bait to draw us into silence."[14] This silence is the point at which words run out, not only because we have exhausted them, but because we reach the point at which we wish to celebrate things just as they are; to give up the need to interpret; to stop looking and begin seeing; to stop talking and begin listening.

In this primordial silence reside light and music, reality and transcendence.[15] As with these faculties, words and language are but a limited mimesis by which to decode and encode the transcendent mysteries of the abyss of silence. Merton said it finely in his beautifully poetic deference to solitude and silence: "[N]o writing on solitude can say anything that hasn't already been said by the wind in the pine trees."[16] I would wish to add here that it is in such metaphor that Merton's best poetry creates its own mimesis of the silence he is here describing; Merton, as poet, silences himself in order to listen and to gain the category of knowledge that "cannot be gained by any other means, for the poet is concerned with the aspects of experience that can never be well-described, but only reproduced or imitated."[17]

For Merton, silence was the condition in which the contradictions in us are reconciled so that even though they remain in us, they "cease to be a problem."[18] He posited that we "put words between ourselves and things"; that "words stand between … the silence of the world and the silence of God"; that we cannot "trust entirely in language to contain reality."[19] But for him, God's silence is the presence of the sublime in the attendant aporia. It is this sublimity that gives rise to Merton's ontotheological aesthetics and the rubric of meaning in unknowing and despair.

In the discipline of the attendant and listening silence, Merton's ontology of God's presence in the world reveals itself: "Truth rises from the silence of being to the quiet … presence of the Word of God [being Christ]. Then, sinking again into silence, the truth of words bears us down into the silence of God. Or rather, God rises up out of the sea like a treasure in the waves, and when language recedes His brightness remains on the shores of our own being."[20] Merton as poet-prophet evokes words from the silence of the contemplative experience; such evocations then prompt the return to silence. Herein resides Merton's reproduction of the mystical experience which directed him towards silence, and the poetic vision which compelled him to speak. In such poetry, he allows us into the sacred places where speech and silence dance as partners who know the iconography of their journey well, leading us into the nexus of holy mysteries. In the language of his anti-poetry, he tells us that "words are in [the] feet as [we] walk without them" on "speechless pavements... printed with secrets";[21] that true communication is beyond words at the same time as it is reflected by them.[22]

This silence, for the person who seeks God and the true self, reveals itself in contemplative prayer, from which Merton's aesthetics of the sublime produces its rewards. First published as *The Climate of Monastic Prayer*, Merton's essay "Contemplative Prayer" explains that "monastic [contemplative] prayer is a special way of following Christ.... [I]ts dimensions... are those of [our] ordinary anguish, [our] self-searching, [our] moments of nausea at [our] own vanity, falsity and capacity for betrayal."[23] The prayers of contemplation come into play over and over again, every time that we face the existential dread of our own spiritual decay and the pathology of its failed experiments in aesthetic aspiration. Such prayer flourishes in the absence of comfort and in pure faith. For Merton, this prayer was embedded in psalmody, liturgy, and *lectio divina*. Additionally, he posited that the inseparability of the spoken and silent Word/word was the daily sustenance of the Cistercian monk, elected to silence and solitude:

> To separate meditation from prayer, reading and contemplation is to falsify our picture of the monastic way of prayer... rather, prayer, meditation and contemplation fill the apparent "void" of solitude and silence with the reality of God's presence... in it, we come to experience the emptiness and futility of these forms of distraction and useless communication which contribute nothing to the seriousness and simplicity of a life of prayer.[24]

Contemplative prayer, whatever our tradition, opens into the ground of being, the abyss in which is the unknown, silent God. It is the language of a life lived in commitment to hope and desire (which Gabriel Marcel so movingly engages) in one's utter abandonment to the Divine will in the matter of desires deferred to one's existential commitment to hope.[25] Influenced by such Christian existentialists, Merton's study of inter-religious dialogue additionally led him to the literary and religious traditions of Zen consciousness, which gave him an understanding of the transparency of perception and realization without the necessity for abstraction, conceptualization, rationalization, and other

Western ways of knowing. He came to believe that the ground of being and one's comprehension of it is not so much an activity as a receptivity—for the Christian, a receptivity to the Holy Spirit of Christ and its attendant hopes and desires. As a Christian writer, Merton sought the experience of Christ's presence as the ground of his creative impulses and aesthetic aspirations.

In this ethos, the natural world often becomes the medium of Merton's engagement of solitude in the same way that it has for the psalmist and the lyric poet, through which contemplation and prayer offer their liturgical and affective intimations of reality—apprehensions of the immanent/transcendent—of God himself, in the highest sacrament of the poet's vocation. Arguably the most beautiful of Merton's poems metaphorizing this particular and unique experience of the poet/mystic is "Night-Flowering Cactus," which functions as an icon from which the numinous and transcendent radiate.[26] The night-flowering cactus indigenous to the desert (both a geographical and spiritual archetype in the poem) "shows [its] true self only in the dark and to no man" but "belongs neither to night nor day."

The narrative paints the beauty of the "deep white bell" that opens to the "timeless moment of void"—a picture of the "extreme purity of virginal thirst." In this case, the thirst is for the Eucharistic wine which comes "sudden[ly], out of the earth's unfathomable joy." The image of innocent virginity is further enriched when it is described as a "white cavern without explanation." And the drama is completed as the flower divulges its secrets: "when I open once for all my impeccable bell / No one questions my silence." The power of the icon in this striking poem resonates not only as the virginity is completed by the echo of the "all-knowing night bird which flies out" of the cavern, but also in the "wrought passion" which bursts from the flower's blossoming with a union of mysteries reserved for sexual and spiritual encounters of orgasmic resonance. Merton concludes the poem with this profound question which is related to the reader's experience of both the natural and spiritual realms:

> Have you seen it? Then though my mirth has
> quickly ended
> You live forever in its echo:
> You will never be the same again.[27]

Iconoclasm radiates from our experience of this poem. In its moment of (de)flowering, the cactus has bloomed for us as we have visited its dark obedience and entered into its "excellent deep pleasure" beyond which is "the silent life of God." Such a poem may be the finest literary representation of Merton's aesthetics of the sublime.

In a short but helpful article, "What Merton Came to Know through Icons," Jim Forest (an intimate colleague of Merton's in peace activism) explains that the icon is concerned with the invisible and silent.[28] It leads its beholder to the awareness of the transcendent, what Merton calls the Divine: "Icon is a sacramental medium of illumination ... [a] sort of theology of light."[29] In the silence of the icon, one sees an "interior presence of light not reached by scientific study but through direct faith."[30] The icon serves as the sacred means by which one enters the sacred/mystical moment. Infinity transcends time, consciousness transcends being, and reality transcends the empirical. We enter the quantum.[31]

In his insightful discussion of the quantum mind and the meaning of life, physicist Evan Harris Walker engages what he entitles *The Physics of Consciousness*. Walker posits the physical universe as we know it as a sort of icon which is accessed by human consciousness. He explains that "quantum fluctuations" (i.e., those apprehended by Einstein, Planck, et al.) "are the stuff of consciousness and will"; "that quantum states and mind are one and the same thing"; and that the "Quantum Mind" (which some might call God) is "a first cause, itself time-independent and nonlocal, that created space-time and matter-energy."[32] I believe that it is this reality which the mystic encounters, beyond language, beyond ritual and religion, beyond light, beyond music, beyond science, beyond imagination and human will, beyond everything but God.

In *What Is Contemplation?* Merton teaches us that we must "be content to remain in loneliness and isolation and dryness and anguish waiting upon God in darkness; 'that our inarticulate longing for Him in the night of suffering' will be [our] most eloquent prayer and will be more valuable to [us] ... and will give more glory to God than the highest natural flights of the intelligence or the imagination."[33] This must surely be the condition/discipline of intuitions of mystery — in other words, mysticism. For Merton, this was the realization of a Hidden Wholeness. One is immediately reminded here of the haunting words of Merton's "Hagia Sophia," his long verse poem in celebration of the female figure of Scripture (Prov. 8) and Wisdom traditions in Christian thought:

> There is in all visible things an invisible fecundity, a dimmed light, a meek namelessness, a hidden wholeness. This mysterious Unity and Integrity is Wisdom, the Mother of all, *Natura naturans*. There is in all things an inexhaustible sweetness and purity, a silence that is a fount of action and joy. It rises up in wordless gentleness and flows out to me from the unseen roots of all created being, welcoming me tenderly, saluting me with indescribable humility. This is at once my own being, my own nature, and the Gift of my Creator's Thought and Art within me, speaking as Hagia Sophia, speaking as my sister, Wisdom.[34]

In this pivotal expression of the feminine in the character of the Godhead, as in all of Merton's best poems, metaphor finds its way into and out of the wisdom of God's universe. As "liberation from the ontology of substance," metaphor sets words free of an agenda to reduce everything to the known and knowable.[35] It represents an infinite desire to acknowledge invisible and unknown realities; it finds its own radiant complexities (and one could here argue that it is in his poetry that Merton intimates the essence of his literary power which he connected deeply with his spiritual vocation as poet/mystic).

Ultimately, one discovers in Merton's iconic journey into the desert wherein resides the "beautiful terror," the conditions of solitude, silence, and contemplative prayer, wherein the immanent/transcendent abyss brings forth from its hidden fecundity the intuitions of mystery — the experience of the realization of the Divine, of the Voice of the Universe, of God.

Notes

1 I am indebted to the Trustees of the Merton Legacy Trust, Paul M. Pearson, Archivist of the Thomas Merton Studies Center at Bellarmine University, and to the Social Sciences and Humanities Research Council of Canada for funding support for the research that this essay elaborates.
2 Thomas Merton, journal entry, 15 Nov. 1957, *The Intimate Merton: His Life from His Journals*, ed. Patrick Hart and Jonathan Montaldo (San Francisco: HarperSanFrancisco, 1999) 119.
3 Thomas Merton, *The Seven Storey Mountain* (1948; New York: Farrar, Straus and Giroux, 1998) 462–63.
4 Merton, journal entry, 26 Feb. 1965, *The Intimate Merton*, 238–39.
5 Thomas Merton, *The Wisdom of the Desert* (New York: New Directions, 1960) 3–6.
6 Subsequent biblical quotations are from the Authorized (King James) Version.
7 Thomas Merton, *New Seeds of Contemplation* (New York: New Directions, 1961) 59.
8 Merton's most detailed study of solitude is found in his essay "Notes for a Philosophy of Solitude" in *Disputed Questions* (New York: Farrar, Straus and Giroux, 1960) 177–207.
9 Thomas Merton, *Thoughts in Solitude* (New York: Farrar, Straus and Giroux, 1958) 77.
10 John Cage, *Silence* (Middletown, CT: Wesleyan University Press, 1961) 208.
11 See George Kilcourse, *Ace of Freedoms: Thomas Merton's Christ* (Notre Dame, IN: University of Notre Dame Press, 1993) 29.
12 Thomas Merton, *The New Man* (New York: Farrar, Straus and Cudahy, 1961) 5.
13 "Be still and know that I am God" (Ps. 46:10).
14 Thomas Merton, *Seasons of Celebration: Meditations on the Cycle of Liturgical Feasts* (New York: Farrar, Straus and Giroux, 1977) 210.
15 George Steiner, *Language and Silence: Essays on Language, Literature, and the Inhuman* (New York: Atheneum, 1967) 39.
16 Thomas Merton, *"Honorable Reader": Reflections on My Work*, ed. Robert E. Daggy (New York: Crossroad, 1991) 91.

17 Thomas Merton, "John Crowe Ransom — Standards for Critics," rev. of *The World's Body*, by John Crowe Ransom, *New York Herald Tribune* 8 May 1938. This review was later included in *The Literary Essays of Thomas Merton*, ed. Patrick Hart (New York: New Directions, 1981) 462–63.

18 Max Picard, *The World of Silence* (Chicago: Henry Regnery, 1952) 66–67.

19 Merton, *Thoughts in Solitude*, 82–83. In this, Merton thinks along with the post-structuralists and deconstructionists who interrogate the relationships between language, reality, and meaning (i.e., Derrida, Lyotard, Foucault, and Lacan).

20 Merton, *Thoughts in Solitude*, 83.

21 Thomas Merton, "The Geography of Lograire," *The Collected Poems of Thomas Merton* (New York: New Directions, 1977) 497–98.

22 Lynn Szabo, "The Sound of Sheer Silence: A Study in the Poetics of Thomas Merton," *The Merton Annual* 13 (2000): 208–21.

23 Thomas Merton, *The Climate of Monastic Prayer* (Spencer, MA: Cistercian Publications, 1969) 35–36. I recommend Merton's *Dialogues with Silence: Prayers & Drawings*, ed. Jonathan Montaldo (San Francisco: HarperSanFrancisco, 2001) as the quintessential combining of Merton's prayers with his Zen calligraphy and line drawings that evoke a sublime presence in their silent dialogues.

24 Thomas Merton, *Contemplative Prayer* (New York: Doubleday, 1996) 29.

25 Gabriel Marcel, "Desire and Hope," *Readings in Existential Phenomenology*, ed. Nathaniel Lawrence and Daniel O'Connor (Englewood Cliffs, NJ: Prentice-Hall, 1967) 277–85.

26 Thomas Merton, "Night-Flowering Cactus," *In The Dark Before Dawn: New Selected Poems of Thomas Merton*, ed. Lynn R. Szabo (New York: New Directions, 2005) 98.

27 Ibid.

28 James Forest, "What Merton Came to Know through Icons," *U.S. Catholic* 20 (1993): 26.

29 Merton, qtd. in Forest, "What Merton Came to Know," 21–29.

30 Merton, "Letter to June Yungblut," *The Hidden Ground of Love: The Letters of Thomas Merton on Religious Experience and Social Concerns*, ed. William H. Shannon (New York: Farrar, Straus and Giroux, 1985) 637.

31 Quantum denotes the smallest quantifiable atomic space in which the indefinable and unknowable difference in energy states in electrons occurs because their energy is not discharged continuously but seemingly in random exchanges in modality between wave and particle; it is used to describe the unknowns associated with this unpredictable phenomenon and their profound implications for the origins and state of the universe.

32 The parenthetical phrases are mine, but they align with Walker's argument; Evan Harris Walker, *The Physics of Consciousness: The Quantum Mind and the Meaning of Life* (Cambridge, MA: Perseus, 2000) 326.

33 Thomas Merton, *What Is Contemplation?* (Springfield, IL: Templegate, 1950) 74–77.

34 Merton, "Hagia Sophia," *In The Dark Before Dawn*, 65–71.

35 Susan H. Handelman, *The Slayers of Moses: The Emergence of Rabbinic Interpretation in Modern Literary Theory* (Albany: State University of New York Press, 1982) 82–83.

BELATED BELOVED: TIME, TRAUMA, AND THE SUBLIME IN TONI MORRISON'S *BELOVED*

Steve Vine

> The politics of transfiguration strives in pursuit of the sublime,
> struggling... to present the unpresentable.[1]

"Without Defense"

In her searching critique of the tradition and ideology of "whiteness" in American literature, Toni Morrison argues that "American [cultural] coherence" is produced through "a distancing Africanism."[2] "American Africanism," she writes, constructs blackness as the generative other of American identity, projecting it as "the not-me... a fabricated brew of darkness, otherness, alarm, and desire that is uniquely American." "Africanism," she says, "is the vehicle by which the American self knows itself as not enslaved, but free; not repulsive, but desirable; not helpless, but licensed and powerful" (*Playing in the Dark*, 52). In a different historical context, she might have been talking about the eighteenth-century or Romantic sublime.[3]

In Enlightenment Europe, the sublime is a "vehicle" for underwriting the bourgeois, cultural, and aesthetic self, not the American national self—but the eighteenth-century Romantic sublime is a principle of self-confirmation that mirrors what Morrison identifies in "American Africanism." Formalized in Burke's *Enquiry into the Origin of Our Ideas of the Sublime and Beautiful* (1757) and Kant's *Critique of Judgement* (1790), the sublime is an affective labour, for Burke, of "self-preservation" in the face of threat, while for Kant it is a discipline of rational self-elevation in the presence of magnitude.[4] In both cases, the self is defended against external danger. The feeling and thinking subject is maintained in the face of the thunderous sublime object, whether that object is conceived as nature, terror, power, size, infinity, death, otherness, revolution, or war. Thus, in Burke, the sublime emerges in the spatio-temporal "distances"[5] between the self and the sublime object, to the extent that the object denotes a deferred threat to the self's life. In Kant, the size or power of the sublime object is also overcome by the self's being distanced from it, but even more by the self's generating "ideas"[6] about the object, rather than being overwhelmed by it. Morrison's American "Africanism" defends against "blackness" in the same way that Burke and Kant defer the danger of the sublime, for Africanism arises from "collective needs to allay internal fears"; in it, American identity is confirmed against alterity, and white subjectivity consolidated against Africanist otherness (*Playing in the Dark*, 38).[7]

In her 1987 novel *Beloved*, however, Morrison presents a vision of the sublime that — while acknowledging it as a force of endangerment — shifts the sublime from being a drama of ideological or national self-confirmation into a poetics of temporal and historical transformation, an adventure in cultural renovation and reimagining. For it is not white, American national self-invention that is the subject of *Beloved*'s sublime, but black, slave, African-American historical survival, witnessing, and reinvention. In *Playing in the Dark*, Morrison describes the Africanist population in American literature as an "ego-reinforcing presence": a marginalized, subordinated, and othered presence, a dark sublime object, against which white American identity defines and defends itself (*Playing in the Dark*, 45). But *Beloved* reinvents this sublime object — this *slave sublime object* — as desiring and "beloved," as well as terrifying, ravaged, othered, and devastated. In *Beloved*, the fearful, dark, "black" sublime object of American-Africanist othering comes back — just as Beloved herself does in Morrison's narrative — to lay claim to a different story, a different history, a different symbolic inscription: and to call for a transformed historical future.[8]

"124 was spiteful. Full of a baby's venom," begins *Beloved*.[9] Morrison describes the opening of her novel as an infraction — a sublime rupture — that "confront[s] the reader with what must be immediately incomprehensible." It is "excessively demanding," she says, "abrupt": for the "reader is snatched, yanked, thrown into an environment completely foreign."[10] Imposing disturbance from the start, *Beloved* propels the reader into a realm of instability. If we recognize the terrain of the sublime here, Morrison insists that it is a landscape that does not provide the reader with any security. Instead, "[t]he reader is… [s]natched just as the slaves were from one place to another, from any place to another, without preparation and without defense." Morrison promotes a sublime in which, for both "the reader and the novel's population," for black and white, "something is beyond control" — and she invents what Barbara Claire Freeman calls an "aesthetics of the incalculable."[11] Morrison instates sublimity, then, as an encounter with the historically unmasterable and exorbitant, but she also offers the sublime as a "way of confronting" historical horror, and of "making it possible to remember."[12]

Morrison's remarkable link between the reader's textual disorientation and the slaves' literal depredation means that, at the level of aesthetic inscription, her novel seeks to answer to the reality of slave historical trauma. Indeed, Morrison "refuse[s] to believe that that period, or that thing [slavery] is beyond art," and insists that "the consequences of practically everything we do, art alone can stand up to" — as if only "art" had the resources necessary to broach the historically excessive and unspeakable (*Conversations*, 244). In this way, *Beloved* is an enterprise in what Paul Gilroy, referring to Morrison's text, calls the "slave sublime": a sublime that resides, for him, in the "vital" symbolic "work of enquiring into terrors that exhaust the resources of language."[13] As an example of the slave sublime, *Beloved* contests and bears witness to the "chok[ing]" of the African-American slave presence in American tradition, for the novel's searing narrative grimly haunts and harries white America's national self-image with its traumatic, ineffable, slave repressed (*Playing in the Dark*, 17). This symbolic encounter with the slave sublime, however, is something that opens up terror as well as historical reclamation, for, as Morrison says to Bonnie Angelo in 1989, with reference to the pain of revisiting the slave past in *Beloved*, "the book is about something that the characters don't want to remember, I don't want to remember, black people don't want to remember, white people won't want to remember. I mean, it's national amnesia" (*Conversations*, 257).

This "national amnesia" of the horrors of slavery is not just a cultural repression, but a historical obliteration, too; for a key dimension of the sublime in Morrison's text is the *silence* or *absence* that characterizes the very object that it takes as its focus of representation. Morrison comments, for example, that in the slave narratives of early American literature there is a "veil drawn over proceedings too terrible to relate," since these narratives hold back from representing the horrors of slavery and maintain an anxious Burkean distance in relation to the slave authors' sufferings.[14] The need to "resist devastation" in the name of survival, however, means for Morrison that there is "no mention of [the] interior life" in these slave narratives, no phrasing of internal suffering and longing—yet it is the "unwritten interior life of these people," their historically silenced life, that is most of interest to her ("Site of Memory," 192).[15]

The "absence of the interior life" in the slave narratives — "the deliberate excising of it from the records that the slaves themselves told" — enjoins, says Morrison, a strange historical responsibility on the writer who, like her, wishes to bear witness to it: a responsibility less to a presence than an absence ("Site of Memory," 192). Consequently, Morrison speaks of the need for a "fidelity to the milieu out of which ... my ancestors actually lived," a milieu not defined by a documented presence but an absence, not by speech but silence, not by articulation but obliteration, not by the presentable but the unpresentable ("Site of Memory," 192).

And it is Morrison's "fidelity" to this historical unpresentable that defines the sublime aesthetic of *Beloved*, for while her text strives to "rip th[e] veil" that is drawn over the "unspeakable thoughts, unspoken" (*Beloved*, 199) of the slave narratives, it also scrupulously embodies this unspeakable in the spectral, ghostly, unreadable figure of Beloved herself ("Site of Memory," 191). For — as well as being the ghost of the murdered child of the main character, Sethe, killed by her in order to save her from recapture under the Fugitive Slave Law of 1850 — Beloved is the enigmatic, unmanageable, and unassimilable symbol of the shared terror, desire, and suffering of the nameless victims of the 300-year history of African-American enslavement.

"Flesh That Needs to Be Loved"

Beloved's presence in the narrative brings the return of innumerable slave "voices" that, late in the novel, howl around and inside the very house of trauma, 124 Bluestone Road: the voices of the slave repressed of African-American life. As he approaches 124, Stamp Paid hears these voices as "recognizable but undecipherable" (*Beloved*, 199), insistent yet unmanageable, and the narrative comments, "So, in spite of his exhausted marrow, he kept on through the voices and tried once more to knock at the door of 124. This time, although he couldn't cipher but one word, he believed he knew who spoke them. The people of the broken necks, of fire-cooked blood and black girls who had lost their ribbons. What a roaring" (*Beloved*, 181).

Beloved's embodiment of this unmanageable historical excess appears most forcibly in the novel's epigraph to the "*Sixty Million and more*": to those who, says Morrison, "died either as captives in Africa or on slave ships" — the victims of the historical lesion of the Middle Passage, the passage across the Atlantic from Africa to the West Indies or Americas.[16] Morrison speaks about her novel's injunction to "assum[e] responsibility for people no one's ever assumed responsibility for. They are those that died en route. Nobody knows their names, and nobody thinks about them. In addition to that, they never survived in the lore; there are no songs or dances or tales of these people. The people who arrived—there is lore about them. But nothing survives about... that" (*Conversations*, 247).

Beloved herself is the "sublime" materialization of these Middle Passage slave-ship dead, the erased of the transatlantic trade. Morrison says that Beloved

> is a spirit on one hand, literally she is what Sethe thinks she is, her child returned to her from the dead.... She is also another kind of dead which is not spiritual but flesh...a survivor from the true, factual slave ship. She speaks the language, a trau-matized language, of her own experience.... So that when they say "What was it like over there?" they may mean—they do mean—"What was it like being dead?"... because the language of both experiences—death and the Middle Passage—is the same. Her yearning would be the same, the love and yearning for that face that was going to smile at her. (*Conversations*, 247)

As a plural figure for the "*Sixty Million and more*" of the captive and slave-ship dead, for the "people who arrived," *and* for the main character's murdered daughter, Beloved is a sublime, overdetermined sign of slave historical unpre-sentability. Her "traumatized language" remembers fragments, shards, traces, splinters, and echoes of an unavailable, inaccessible, and untellable history. Her scarred throat, her permanent smile, her sweet tooth, her dropping head, her insatiable hunger, her desire for stories, her demand for sexual usage, her crouching and rocking, all "rememory" (*Beloved*, 36), in the novel's idiom, the elements of an overwhelming slave trauma: Sethe's murderous assault, the slave bit, the sugar plantations, the physical deprivation, the effacement from story, the necks broken from lynching, the rapes, the suffocating slave-ship holds. Beloved is the sublime sign of an unappeasable story of slave suffering and longing.

The fact that Morrison says that one of the levels on which Beloved func-tions is not "spiritual but flesh"—that she can be read as a "survivor from the true, factual slave ship," a material rather than mental figure—is crucial for *Beloved*'s reconfiguration of the sublime. For while in the Enlightenment-Romantic sublime threat is overcome by internalizing transcendence—through elevated feeling in Burke and elevated thought in Kant—Morrison transgresses this subject-based, self-consolidating, idealizing idiom. The sub-lime of *Beloved* does not affirm transcendent individual selfhood or self-con-firmation, but material, fleshly, temporal, and historical existence. In *Beloved*, the sublime object—"the beloved"—is not the narcissistic, self-affirming sub-ject, but the transfiguring, transformative, historical, communal, and loved other. Speaking of *Beloved* as she was writing it in 1985, Morrison comments that she is concerned in the novel to "project the self not into the way we say 'yourself,' but to put a space between those words, as though the self were really a *twin* or a thirst or a friend or something that sits right next to you and watches you, which is what I was talking about when I said 'the dead girl'" (*Conversations*, 208). In this idiom, the self is projected into the other, the desired or beloved: "displace[d]" (*Conversations*, 208) from itself, it is reinvented not in self-confirmation but transformation. This othering of the self — its finding of itself in the other — is materialized in the fugue-like chapters late in the novel when "the thoughts of the women of 124, unspeakable thoughts, unspoken" (*Beloved*, 199) are given, and Sethe, Denver, and Beloved speak individually, then indistinguishably, in a threnody to mutual loss and reclamation, their voices joining finally without separation:

> Beloved
> You are my sister
> You are my daughter
> You are my face; you are me
> I have found you again; you have come back to me
> You are my Beloved. (*Beloved*, 216)

Morrison's reinvention of the sublime as a relation to the beloved rather than the self means that her novel flouts the subjectivist transcendences of Kant's sublime. In Kant, the sublime points to the transcendent sphere of reason and law that is embedded in the faculties of the self and enthrones supersensible ideas above the body; but *Beloved* affirms what Baby Suggs calls the "Flesh that needs to be loved" (*Beloved*, 88). Morrison's text transgresses the dualism of spirit and matter because Beloved returns from the dead *in the flesh*; she figures not a sublime of the idea but the body, or rather, she collapses the very distinction between the spirit and body, ghost and matter. Against the Kantian principle of supersensible transcendence or ideality, Morrison finds the sublime in the beloved itself: in the body, not the spirit, of the sublime object, in its fleshly, material, historical being, in the flesh that "needs to be loved."

The scandal of Sethe's murder of Beloved is that while her act shatters all canons, creeds, and codes of morality — and no appeal to any system or law justifies it — it is an act that is performed out of love.[17] Sethe kills because she loves; she does not kill in the name of a cause, principle, or law to which she defers or yields. She does not instate transcendence through her act, for she does not sacrifice Beloved to an *idea*. Rather, Beloved is in the place of this idea. In Slavoj Žižek's formula for love, Beloved is "put ... into the place of the Thing, the unconditional Object."[18] For Žižek, Sethe's act is an "exemplary case of the properly *modern* ethical act." For, rather than "sacrific[ing] everything ... for the Cause-Thing that matters ... more than life itself" — sacrificing it to a principle of transcendence, or idea, as in the traditional ethical (and sublime) situation — Sethe sacrifices the very thing that matters to her more than life itself: Beloved. In Žižek's terms, this means that the transcendence or "Exception" of the "Thing" from sacrifice is "suspended," and the Thing itself—Beloved, the Thing in the place of transcendence—is foregone (*Fragile Absolute*, 154). He argues:

> In the modern ethical constellation...one *suspends [the] exception of the Thing*: one bears witness to one's fidelity to the Thing by *sacrificing (also) the Thing itself* (in the same way, Kierkegaard enjoins a true Christian believer to hate the beloved himself out of love). And is this not the very unbearable crux of Sethe's act—that she killed her children *out of her very fidelity to them*, not as a "primitive" act of brutal sacrificing to some obscure superego gods? (*Fragile Absolute*, 154)

For Žižek, the strange, monstrous, traumatic, sublime logic of this act that involves the "Exception" of the transcendent Thing from sacrifice—that involves "striking" (150) or "shooting" (153) at "what is most precious to [one]self" (150)—is a logic of "uncoupling" (123–30) or "unplugging" (125): an unplugging of the subject and beloved from their inscription in the socio-symbolic network that harnesses them to its meanings, laws, and demands, that contains, constrains, and positions them in its system. Žižek says that this "unplugging from the social body" and "hierarchic social order" performs the strange Christian logic in which, in Kierkegaard's reading of Christ's injunction, the believer is enjoined to "*hate the beloved* out of love and in love": to hate the beloved because of love for the beloved (*Fragile Absolute*, 125, 126).[19] He writes, "The proper way to understand this is to ask a precise question: *what dimension* in the beloved other am I enjoined to hate?"—and he answers with the example of the son's hostility to the father in the Oedipal scenario, a "hate" or hostility that "disappears the moment the son perceives his father no longer as the embodiment of his socio-symbolic function but as a vulnerable subject 'unplugged' from it" (*Fragile Absolute*, 126). It is in this sense, Žižek argues, "that, in true love, I 'hate the beloved out of love': I 'hate' the dimension of his inscription into the socio-symbolic structure on behalf of my very love for him as a unique person" (*Fragile Absolute*, 126).

Although Žižek does not develop his account of *Beloved* in relation to this, his argument about "hating the beloved out of love" can be read in terms of Sethe's traumatic plight. For Sethe kills Beloved out of love: she takes a handsaw to Beloved's throat as Schoolteacher and the Sweet Home slave-hunters arrive to recapture her and her family after a month of freedom, following their escape from bondage, and she does it to save Beloved from a life of slavery. In the antiphonal articulation of Sethe's thoughts late in the text, Morrison has Sethe muse, "I'll explain to her.... How if I hadn't killed her she would have died and that is something I could not bear to happen to her" (*Beloved*, 200). Later, Sethe insists to Beloved that "what she had done was right because it came from true love" (*Beloved*, 251). Sethe's fearful logic replays that of Margaret Garner, the slave mother who tried to kill her children in 1856 to prevent their recapture by slave-hunters, and whom Morrison used as a model for her text: when Garner was asked why she did it, she said that she was "unwilling to have her children suffer as she had done," or be "murdered by piece-meal" in slavery.[20] The terrible reasoning used by Sethe is also that she is putting her children outside, or apart, from slavery: "She ... carried, pushed, dragged them through the veil, out, away, over there where no one could hurt them," Morrison writes. "Over there. Outside this place, where they would be safe" (*Beloved*, 163). Sethe's deed is a violent act of "unplugging" Beloved from slavery, from the brutal regime of African-American bondage — from what Morrison calls "slavocracy" (*Playing in the Dark*, 25).

By "unplugging" Beloved in this way from the slave system, Sethe flouts slavocracy's literal and symbolic economy: the regime that declares the slave child to be the property of the slaveholder, not the child of its mother.[21] For Sethe's fearful act puts Beloved "outside" the economy of slavery, outside its use-value and exchange-value; indeed, a murdered slave is worth nothing, and is not a slave. The fearful emancipation Sethe secures for Beloved is a fatal one, for she asserts her claim on and responsibility for her child infanticidally. But Žižek argues that this act of striking at oneself, of shooting at what is most precious to oneself, is "far from ... a case of impotent aggressivity turned against oneself"; rather, it "changes the co-ordinates of the situation in which the subject finds himself: by cutting himself loose from the precious object *through whose possession the enemy kept him in check*, the subject gains the space of free action. Is not such a radical gesture of 'striking at oneself' constitutive of subjectivity as such?" (*Fragile Absolute*, 150, italics mine). According to this argument, Sethe's traumatic action becomes an assertion of maternity and subjectivity insofar as it projects itself outside the slaveholders' material and symbolic regime or domain. By "claiming" (*Beloved*, 164) Beloved and subjectivity, Sethe transgresses slavocracy's vicious protocols, and points sublimely beyond them — albeit self-laceratingly. Hers is an act of "liberat[ion] ... from the grip of existing social reality" and bears witness to what Žižek calls "the unbearably painful birth of African-American subjectivity" (*Fragile Absolute*, 149, 152).

The monstrous character of Sethe's act contains, then, an element of the future. For Sethe cannot be a mother in the "present" of slavery; her children are not her own, even though she "claims" them. Sethe can only be a mother in the future, outside slavery — and that is what Morrison gives her with Beloved's untimely return in the narrative.

"Idioms Which Do Not Yet Exist"

Beloved's presence in the novel bears witness to an itinerary of silences: the absent interiority and suffering inscribed in the slave narratives, the experience of death and survival in the Middle Passage, the force of filial love between the slave mother and slave child.

In each of these cases, Morrison's text confronts the force of an erasure and an abeyance of presence. Morrison's "fidelity" to this historical privation means that—as a textual figure or sign of slave suffering—Beloved remains at some level unreadable, indecipherable, and unassimilable. She is the spectral signifier of an immeasurable and irrecoverable loss; but, as a figure, she seeks at the same time—impossibly and necessarily—to speak the unspeakable, articulate the inexpressible, and present the unpresentable.

In Jean-François Lyotard's terms, Beloved is a rhetorical figure that attempts to "phrase" something that cannot, or has not, been spoken—here, slave interiority, slave fatality, and slave maternity. She is an effort, or assay, to invent or frame an "idiom" for the historically unpresentable.[22] She is an articulation of the silenced. In this light, Beloved is a sublime sign of what Lyotard calls the "differend." For Lyotard, the differend is an "unstable state and instant of language wherein something that must be able to be put into phrases cannot yet be.... In the differend, something 'asks' to be put into phrases, and suffers from the wrong of not being able to be put into phrases right away."[23]

As we saw, the brutal erasure that Sethe resists in her infanticide is slavery's obliteration of slave maternity. In *Playing in the Dark*, Morrison shows how slavocracy effaces slave maternity not only through law but also through the silence it imposes on historical discourse. She shows that in Willa Cather's *Sapphira and the Slave Girl* (1940) there is a "void" inhabiting the novel, one that comes from "the silence of four hundred years"—the "void of historical discourse on slave parent-child relationships and pain" (*Playing in the Dark*, 22). This "silence" that the novel displays inflicts an "unbearable violence" on communication: a violence coming from the fact that "there is no available language to clarify or even name the source of unbelievability" surrounding the absence of slave mother–child connection in the novel (*Playing in the Dark*, 22–23). This situation arises because of the fact that "slave women are not mothers; they are 'natally dead,' with no obligations to their offspring or their own parents" (*Playing in the Dark*, 21). It is this natal death, or effacement of filial relationship, that Sethe refuses in her terrible deed. In her act, Sethe "claims" the maternal obligation that slavery denies her. As Morrison says in an interview, "Under those theatrical circumstances of slavery, if you made that claim, an unheard-of claim, which is that you are the mother of these children—that's an outrageous claim for a slave woman" (*Conversations*,

252). The "unheard-of claim" that Sethe makes is a claim that cannot be heard—that is unpresentable—in the discourse of slavery: it is a claim that exceeds slavery's regime and points beyond it. It is a transgressive, projective, and sublime claim. It is a claim, or phrase, whose time is yet to come.

In *The Inhuman*, Lyotard says that the sublime in Burke poses the threat of silence, a threat that "language will cease." This means that the sublime invokes a "challenge posed by this failure of the word"—a challenge to "accept... the advent of an 'unheard of' phrase," a challenge to speak the unheard-of, to present the unpresentable, to bear witness to an absence in the face of silence.[24] And it is as a *refusal of the silencing* that she is "mother of these children" that Sethe kills Beloved in *Beloved*. In this light, the "advent of [the] 'unheard of' phrase" in *Beloved* is, in Lyotard's terms, the advent of the "phrase" of slave maternity itself: a phrase that Sethe cannot articulate as a mother in slavery. Grotesquely and monstrously, the only way Sethe *can* "claim" or "phrase" maternal love and responsibility for her children in slavery—and in the framework of the novel's story of slave recapture—is to kill them, to put them outside slavery, so they cannot be reclaimed by the slave-hunters and slaveholders.

Lyotard defines a "wrong" as the inflicting of a "damage accompanied by the loss of the means to prove the damage." A wrong occurs if the "victim is deprived of life... of all his or her liberties... of the freedom to make his or her ideas or opinions public... of the right to testify to the damage, or... if the testifying phrase is itself deprived of authority."[25] Sethe is a victim of all but one of these privations. Her "testifying phrase" of maternal love—indeed, her bid to take her children to freedom—is "deprived of authority" by the slave-hunters, and her only recourse to "testify" to that love is by removing her children altogether from slavery in her desperate deed. Sethe's monstrous act of infanticide—she murders Beloved, and is prevented from killing her three other children—is a traumatic-sublime "phrasing" of slave maternity, a fearful "idiom" for maternal love in slavocracy's impossible regime. Her attempt is the sublime sign of an unpresentable love.

Lyotard's idea that something in the differend "asks" to be put into phrases, but "cannot yet be"—that something suffers the "wrong of not being able to be put into phrases *right away*"—introduces the idea of temporal lag into the notion of phrasing, or finding an idiom, for the unpresentable. The fact that in the differend, and in Lyotard's notion of the sublime, something asks to be put into phrases that cannot yet be means that Lyotard's sublime projects itself into futurity—as does Morrison's narrative. Lyotard says that confronting the differend means "human beings... recognize that what *remains to be phrased* exceeds what they can presently phrase, and that they must be allowed to institute idioms which do not yet exist."[26] He might have been talking about Morrison's sublime in *Beloved*, for her text points to the fact that slave history occurs in excess of its phrasing: in relation to its historical unpresentability, slavery is an event that calls for idioms that do not yet exist. "Beloved" is in this sense a trope of symbolic quest: she phrases a story of slave loss and longing, of privation and desire, of devastation and demand — and imposes a differend that calls for articulation. "What is at stake in a literature," writes Lyotard, "is to bear witness to differends by finding idioms for them."[27]

Morrison's narrative "bears witness" to the slave differend, or unpresentable, in the figure of Beloved by telling the story of Sethe's rediscovery of her dead daughter in the ghost of the girl who returns eighteen years after her killing. But, as a ghost or spectre, Beloved does not belong to the *time* or history that she rejoins belatedly in 1873: the time of African-American, post-Abolition slave freedom, eight years after the ending of slavery with the close of the American Civil War. Instead, Beloved belongs to, or is tied to, another time, the time of African-American enslavement and silencing. This time haunts the present of the novel with both loss and desire: it is a time that cannot be reclaimed but that demands to be spoken or made present because it has been lost. It is a time that, like Beloved, is looking for "a place to be" (*Beloved*, 213) in historical discourse.

"No-Time"

After Beloved has been recognized by Sethe as her returned daughter, the women of 124 Bluestone Road — Sethe, Beloved, and Denver (Beloved's sister) — enter a period of mutual acknowledgement and reclamation that the novel calls "no-time" (*Beloved*, 191): for this time unfolds as a story of desire, wish-fulfillment, and symbolic reinvention that rewrites, rather than represents, privative slave historical experience.

The fact that Beloved inhabits a "timeless place" or "timeless present" in the novel means that she is positioned out of the frame or jointure of historical time (*Beloved*, 182, 184). As a figure in excess of her own narrative inscription, Beloved is temporally anachronistic. She belongs to "no-time" in the sense that she incarnates the African-American slave past, the African time before capture and enslavement,[28] and the promise of an African-American future: after her exorcism from 124 Bluestone Road by the women of the town, she flees, naked and pregnant with Paul D's child, into a history that is literally waiting to be born, an African-American futurity that is incalculable and unknowable.[29] Ella is "not so sure," indeed, that Beloved "is truly gone" after her exorcism, for she ruminates, "Maybe [gone] ... maybe not. Could be hiding in the trees waiting for another chance" (*Beloved*, 263).

Arguably, at the end of the novel, Beloved is necessarily "waiting for another chance" to "be loved," or acknowledged, in time — for her desire for acceptance is unassuaged owing to the fact that her story has not been (and perhaps cannot be, because of its effacement) told in American history (*Beloved*, 274). The final, lyrical chapter of the novel captures this sense in which Beloved's story is still waiting to be told when Morrison insists, "Disremembered and unaccounted for, she cannot be lost because no one is looking for her, and even if they were, how can they call her if they don't know her name? Although she has claim, she is not claimed" (*Beloved*, 274). With a searching ambivalence, Morrison writes, "This is not a story to pass on" (*Beloved*, 275): and "pass on," here, means both — as Barbara Claire Freeman says — "to transmit and forget," gesturing to the fact that Beloved's story is both traumatically irrecoverable (it cannot or must not be "passed on") and ineffaceable (it cannot be denied or "passed" on).[30] At once untellable and ineradicable, Beloved's story spectrally haunts the novel's present and our own, persisting and obtruding itself with an irresistible — or sublime — "claim" to be heard. Beloved remains the "girl who waited to be loved" (*Beloved*, 274).

Jacques Derrida writes of the spectre that it has "several times" and that it "is a proper characteristic of the specter…that no one can be sure if by returning it testifies to a living past or to a living future, for the *revenant* may already mark the promised return of the specter of living being." A ghost, he says, imposes an "untimeliness and disadjustment of the contemporary," for it belongs neither to the present nor to the past but haunts the present with what it can neither articulate nor obliterate. In this way, the spectre or ghost belongs to the *future*, for it is part of what has not yet been made present in the contemporary but is waiting to be made present — or come back — in the future. Derrida writes, "a ghost never dies, it remains always to come and to comeback."[31] And Beloved, of course, does not die but remains or "waits" to come back — waits to be loved, to be made present in history. To this extent, Beloved belongs to a sublime of temporal *belatedness*: a sublime that calls for a rewriting of the past, of slave history, so that Beloved can live, so that she can love, so that she can *be* "loved." Beloved configures a sublime that demands a rewriting of historical silence and obliteration — a rewriting of the past in the name of the future.

In *The Inhuman*, Lyotard links the "postmodern" sublime to the question of "rewriting"[32] — to a project of recollection or anamnesis. He sees the postmodern not as the temporal successor to modernity, but as a critical or revisionary *relationship* to modernity. He considers the postmodern as the "anamnesis of the Thing" of the modern — an anamnesis of the unpresentable, unspoken, or unknown of modernity — and thus a broaching of the "sublime," or ineffable, of modernity. This "Thing," he says, "haunts the 'language,' the tradition and the material with, against and in which one writes. In this way rewriting comes under a problematic of the sublime."[33] To "rewrite" modernity, he suggests, is to re-inscribe the repressed or unspoken "Thing" of modernity *within* modernity—to recollect, as it were, what modernity forgets in order to constitute itself. In the context of *Beloved* this, among other things, is the anamnesis of the repressed Thing of *slave* modernity—for American modernity, while a project of liberty and progress, founds itself contradicto-rily on the history of slavocracy. In *Playing in the Dark*, Morrison writes that America's self-invention as the "New" world is "distinctive … first of all, [in] its claim to freedom·and, second, [in] the presence of the unfree within the heart of the democratic experiment"—the presence of the black population as free-dom's "echo, shadow, and silent force" (*Playing in the Dark*, 48). The repressed Thing of American, Enlightenment, democratic modernity is the slave or black repressed.

In a remarkable interview with Paul Gilroy, Morrison states that "modern life begins with slavery.… From a woman's point of view … black women had to deal with 'post-modern' problems in the nineteenth century and earlier … certain kinds of dissolution, the loss of and the need to reconstruct certain kinds of stability."[34] Morrison suggests that the body of nineteenth-century, democratic, "free" America is haunted by a non-modern alterity—by the black man and black woman—and that, in this way, American modernity is always already, and constitutively, fissured by a troubled and troubling "post-modernity": by modernity's black, unfree other.[35] The repressed other of slav-ery ruptures America's emancipated modernity.

This inhabitation of emancipatory modernity by its repressed other leads Homi K. Bhabha to read Morrison's *Beloved* as diagnosing modernity's dis-ruption by what he calls a "postcolonial contra-modernity."[36] Moreover, it is the lagged or belated character of this disruption that interests him. For Bhabha, while Enlightenment modernity identifies itself in the "now"[37] of performative political self-awareness—for example, in America's declaration of itself as "free" in the Declaration of Independence of 1776—the racial other is excluded from this self-recognizing modernity. The racial other does not belong to Western modernity's liberated self-present "now" or time, says Bhabha, whether that now is conceived as revolutionary, republican, or dem-ocratic; instead, the racial other is thrown backwards, into the past, into the archaic, into a "time" before Western modernity declared itself or recognized itself. The racial other is not identified with the Western, "modern" social col-lective of political freedom and enlightenment. Bhabha traces this temporal belatedness, the temporal caesura of "race" within modernity, in the work of Franz Fanon, calling it Fanon's "sense of the *belatedness of the Black man*"—Fanon's sense that the "Black man" comes too late in Western history—and he reads Morrison's narrative as an enactment of this lagged structure.[38] For, as a narrative-historical figure, Beloved is shot through with temporal lag:[39] returning as a ghost to post-Abolition America in the 1870s, Beloved comes too late in American history to belong to emancipation or to the dawn of free African-American subjectivity.

What this means, for Bhabha, is that the history to which Beloved belongs is one of the "projective past," a past that is "projective" because it has not yet been spoken or written in history: it does not belong to the story that American modernity tells about itself, but instead to "forms of social antagonism and contradiction that are not yet properly represented." Bhabha says that this "*projective past*" consequently takes the form of "cultural reinscription," or rewriting, that *re-inscribes* what is historically repressed and "moves *back to the future*": back to the future in the sense that, as unarticulated, the "projective" past must come back *belatedly*—like Beloved—to interrupt the time of white modernity.[40] Beloved belongs to the "projective past" because hers is a past that has not yet been made present in historical discourse—specifically, the discourse of colonial, Enlightenment, American modernity. Beloved's is a past that is still *waiting* to be spoken, just as she herself waits to be loved. Beloved is not part of the story of emancipation—the "time" of white modernity—but haunts it with its African-American, slave repressed. She is "time-lagged."[41] Projected into the future, and freighted with historical excess, her story is yet to be made present: in Bhabha's formulation, her disjunctive time lag "*keeps alive the making of the past*"—keeps the past alive as a question still to be answered by and in American modernity.[42]

Though Bhabha relates the temporality of belatedness to Morrison's *Beloved*, he does not connect this temporality to the sublime. Lyotard's notion of "rewriting" the unpresentable of modernity, however, allows Bhabha's "projective past" to be understood as a sublime demand, or call, for the belated historical presentation of what has not been presented. While Beloved's ghostly existence in the narrative is *out of time*—anachronistic—in relation to the post-Abolition America of the 1870s, her spectral reappearance calls sublimely to the future that was denied to her: it calls for her story to be articulated, and for the healing of the survivors of "slavocracy." In her *Nobel Lecture*, Morrison writes that "Word-work is sublime...because it is generative."[43] Although Sethe's act of murdering Beloved is not "generative" like Morrison's text, it points projectively (if monstrously) to the sublime, unrealized future of African-American autonomy—as does Morrison's "Word-work." Sethe's infanticide, even as it obliterates Beloved, steps outside the present and projects itself into the future. Her act gestures toward an African-American freedom that is yet to come, and her deed, like the novel, reaches forward. Sethe's murderous act cannot, in the time of the narrative, master slavery or pin it down. But, Morrison suggests, neither can language itself. Rather, she says, "language can never live up to life once and for all. Nor should it. Language can never 'pin down' slavery, genocide, war. Nor should it yearn for the arrogance to be able to do so. Its force, its felicity, is in its reach toward the ineffable."[44]

Notes

1 Paul Gilroy, *The Black Atlantic: Modernity and Double Consciousness* (London: Verso, 1993) 38.

2 Toni Morrison, *Playing in the Dark: Whiteness and the Literary Imagination* (Cambridge, MA: Harvard University Press, 1992) 8; future citations from *Playing in the Dark* are from this edition and will be referenced in the text by short title and page number.

3 In a reading to which mine is indebted, Barbara Claire Freeman, in *The Feminine Sublime: Gender and Excess in Women's Fiction* (Berkeley: University of California Press, 1995), says that Morrison's Africanism "mirrors [the function] of the Kantian sublime: to contain the fear of boundlessness and primal terror; to give the unnameable a name and thereby defend against it; to aggrandize (or create) identity; and to keep the fear of unrepresentability at bay." Freeman's elegant reading finds "another sublime" in Morrison than the one found in Kant, a sublime that "does not eradicate alterity but ... seeks to articulate and bear witness to it"; this is what she calls the "feminine sublime" (108). Without questioning her reading, my concern here is to relate *Beloved* to a historical, postmodern, and temporal — rather than specifically feminine — sublime.

4 Edmund Burke, *A Philosophical Enquiry into the Origin of Our Ideas of the Sublime and Beautiful*, ed. David Womersley (London: Penguin, 2004) 86.

5 Ibid.

6 Immanuel Kant, *Critique of the Power of Judgment*, ed. Paul Guyer, trans. Paul Guyer and Eric Matthews (Cambridge: Cambridge University Press, 2000) 129.

7 Morrison insists, "In this country ... American means white" (*Playing in the Dark*, 47).

8 In "From the Sublime to the Beautiful: The Aesthetic Progression of Toni Morrison" (in *The Aesthetics of Toni Morrison: Speaking the Unspeakable*, ed. Marc C. Conner [Jackson: University of Mississippi Press, 2000]), Marc C. Conner argues that while the "sublime is the aesthetic realm that dominates Morrison's fiction," her work negotiates a shift from the sublime to the beautiful — from the "individual" sphere of the sublime to the social realm of the beautiful (50). He contends that Beloved is a "figure of the sublime, offering in her very body intimations of the unrepresentable" and that she "represents the crossing of boundaries, excess and overflow" (66), but he concludes that the novel's ending is "quintessentially 'anti-sublime'" (71) because it affirms community over the severance of the individual from community. My reading differs from this by seeing Morrison's sublime as temporally defined; although Morrison celebrates community, *Beloved*'s African-American community belongs to a sublime futurity.

9 Toni Morrison, *Beloved* (London: Picador, 1987) 3; future citations from *Beloved* are taken from this edition and will be referenced in the text by title and page number.

10 Toni Morrison, "Unspeakable Things Unspoken: The Afro-American Presence in American Literature," *Michigan Quarterly Review* 28.1 (1989): 32.

11 Ibid., 32; Freeman, *The Feminine Sublime*, 123.

12 Toni Morrison, *Conversations with Toni Morrison*, ed. Danille Taylor-Guthrie (Jackson: University Press of Mississippi, 1994) 248; future citations from *Conversations* are taken from this edition and will be referenced in the text by short title and page number.

13 Gilroy, *The Black Atlantic*, 187–223, 218.

14 Toni Morrison, "The Site of Memory," *Inventing the Truth: The Art and Craft of Memoir*, ed. William Zinsser (New York: Mariner Books, 1998) 191; future citations from "The Site of Memory" will be taken from this edition and will be referenced in the text by short title and page number.

15 Toni Morrison, "Rediscovering Black History," *New York Times Magazine*, 11 Aug. 1974: 18.

16 Walter Clemons, "A Gravestone of Memories," *Newsweek*, 28 Sept. 1987: 75.

17 In relation to the impossible ethical question that Sethe's deed poses, Morrison comments, "It was the right thing to do, but [Sethe] had no right to do it" (Morrison, *Conversations,* 272). She also says: "I got to a point where in asking myself who could judge Sethe adequately, since I couldn't, and nobody else that knew her could, really, I felt the only person who could judge her would be the daughter she killed. And from there Beloved inserted herself into the text" (Ibid., 248).

18 Slavoj Žižek, *The Fragile Absolute — or, Why Is the Christian Legacy Worth Fighting For?* (London: Verso, 2000) 128; future citations from *The Fragile Absolute* are from this edition and will be referenced in the text by short title and page number.

19 "If any man come to me, and hate not his father, and mother, and wife, and children, and brethren, and sisters, yea, and his own life also, he cannot be my disciple" (Luke 14:26 Authorized [King James] Version).

20 These words come from a report of Garner's recapture and imprisonment in *American Baptist* of 12 February 1856, given by Christian abolitionist the Reverend P.S. Bassett, who visited her (see Morrison, *Conversations*, 40).

21 In *The Location of Culture* (London and New York: Routledge, 1994), Homi K. Bhabha comments, "In her fine account of slave resistance in *Within the Plantation Household*, Elizabeth Fox-Genovese considers murder, self-mutilation and infanticide to be the core psychological dynamic of all resistance…. [I]nfanticide was recognised as an act against the system and at least acknowledged the slave-woman's legal standing in the public sphere. Infanticide was seen to be an act against the master's property — against his surplus profits — and perhaps that, Fox-Genovese concludes, 'led some of the more desperate to feel that, by killing an infant they loved, they would be in some way reclaiming it as their own'" (17).

22 Jean-François Lyotard, *The Differend: Phrases in Dispute*, trans. Georges Van Den Abbeele (Minneapolis: University of Minnesota Press; Manchester, UK: Manchester University Press, 1988) 171.

23 Ibid., 13.

24 Jean-François Lyotard, *The Inhuman: Reflections on Time*, trans. Geoff Bennington and Rachel Bowlby (Cambridge: Polity, 1991) 84.

25 Lyotard, *The Differend*, 5.

26 Ibid., 13.

27 Ibid.

28 Some of the fleeting, fragmentary images in the narrative and Beloved's consciousness place her in an Africa before slavery. The last chapter, for instance, situates her in "the place where the long grass opens," and she herself seems to "rememory" the scene of her capture by slave traders: "I wanted to help [Sethe] when she was picking the flowers, but the clouds of gunsmoke blinded me and I lost her" (*Beloved*, 274, 36, 214). For a fascinating account of Beloved's plural identities and locations

in her recollection of the African and slave past, see Jennifer L. Holden-Kirwan's "Looking into the Self That Is No Self: An Examination of Subjectivity in *Beloved*," *African American Review* 32.3 (1998): 415–26.

29   Morrison regarded *Beloved* as part of a thematic trilogy with *Jazz* (1992) and *Paradise* (1998). She makes it clear, for instance, that she is still writing Beloved's story when, in 1985, with reference to the story of *Jazz*, she says: "I call her Beloved [in *Beloved*] so that I can filter [the] confrontations and questions that she has in that situation, which is 1851, and then … extend her life, you know, her search, her quest, all the way through as long as I care to go, into the twenties where it switches to this other girl [Dorcas in *Jazz*]. Therefore, I have a New York uptown-Harlem milieu in which to put this love story, but Beloved will be there also" (*Conversations*, 208). Though Dorcas in one sense plays Beloved's role in *Jazz*, in another sense Beloved inhabits the strange, marginal figure of "Wild" in the narrative: Dorcas is Joe Trace's lover, and Wild the woman he believes to be his lost mother. Like Beloved in *Beloved*, then, Dorcas and Wild in *Jazz* function as images of black longing and loss.

30   Freeman, *The Feminine Sublime*, 145.

31   Jacques Derrida, *Specters of Marx: The State of the Debt, the Work of Mourning, and the New International*, trans. Peggy Kamuf (London and New York: Routledge, 1994) 99.

32   See Lyotard, "Rewriting Modernity," *The Inhuman*, 24–35.

33   Ibid., 33.

34   Gilroy, *The Black Atlantic*, 221.

35   Morrison speaks of the African-American presence as the "ghost in the machine" of nineteenth-century American literature ("Unspeakable," 11).

36   Bhabha, *The Location of Culture*, 244–55. Bhabha uses this term rather than the more familiar "postmodernity" because he sees the latter as the identifying moniker of late capitalist Western societies and regards his own project as an attempt to "rename the postmodern from the position of the postcolonial" (175).

37   Ibid., 37.

38   Ibid., 236.

39   In "The Belated Postmodern: History, Phantoms and Toni Morrison," *Psychoanalytic Criticism: A Reader*, ed. Sue Vice (Cambridge: Polity, 1996), Peter Nicholls reads Morrison's novel as enacting the temporality of Freudian *nachträglichkeit*, or "deferred action": a temporality that also characterizes Lyotard's idea of the postmodern (50–74). My argument echoes that of Nicholls in some respects, but Nicholls does not discuss the link between postmodern temporality and the sublime.

40   Bhabha, *The Location of Culture*, 252.

41   Ibid., 254.

42   Ibid.

43   Toni Morrison, *The Nobel Lecture* (New York: Norton, 1993) 22.

44   Ibid., 21.

ANNIE DILLARD ON HOLY GROUND: THE ARTIST AS NUN IN THE POSTMODERN SUBLIME

Deborah C. Bowen

Annie Dillard's non-fiction novella of 1977, *Holy the Firm*, is one of those favourite books that are included in my course on contemporary fiction, even though it is more spiritual autobiography than fiction—even though it is so dense as to have some students gasping for breath after a page and a half. And even though, after teaching this book at least a half-dozen times, I still have not grasped it in the way I might say I have grasped *A Tale of Two Cities* or *Animal Farm* or even *In the Skin of a Lion*. Something is present here that is more elusive than the Victorian historical novel, or the realist political fable, or even the postmodern web of identity-as-responsibility. What is it that pulls me back to this little book over and over again? Not that it is one of Roland Barthes's "scriptible" texts that provide spaces of free play for the reader—no, more that it is a text that plays with *the nearness of the unnameable that overwhelms our space*. Here is a kind of literature that is in constant tryst with the sublime—a text about holy ground.

When Jean-François Lyotard talks about "the aesthetic of the sublime" he associates it with a falling-short of imagination in face of "ideas of which no presentation is possible"—the totality of things, the undecomposably simple, the infinitely great.[1] Immanuel Kant suggested that though imagination cannot represent the infinite, reason can comprehend it, and Lyotard is Kant's disciple in this: "The real sublime sentiment," he says, "is in an intrinsic combination of pleasure and pain: the pleasure that reason should exceed all presentation, the pain that imagination or sensibility should not be equal to the concept." However, he postulates a third mode of approach to the sublime: not "the powerlessness of the faculty of presentation," that is, imagination; nor "the power of the faculty to conceive," that is, reason; rather a new hybrid, the "increase of being and the jubilation which result from the invention of new rules of the game" through allusion. The business of the postmodern artist and writer, according to Lyotard, is "not to supply reality," by which he means some kind of totalized systematic presentation of the world, "but to invent allusions to the conceivable which cannot be presented."[2]

It seems that the focus of the postmodern sublime is less likely to be an awe-inspiring experience of mountains than an encounter with incomprehensible cultural extremes, and perhaps in particular the threat of alienation created by the complexities of our techno-scientific culture. Some of those who write about these particularly contemporary manifestations of the sublime return to the Kantian valorization of reason as a way of overcoming any threat: as Bert Olivier puts it, for instance, "Reason... circumscribes that which overwhelms the senses."[3] Others foreground rhetoric rather than metaphysic: Timothy H. Engström writes that "Sublimity, in general, seems to refer more to one's rhetorical skill in managing the normal than to a revolutionary, metaphysical fracture in the narratizable altogether."[4] But "skill in managing the normal" of course raises a number of questions about normalcy and what "managing" it might mean; does Lyotard's notion of art's "allusion to the unpresentable by means of visible presentations" count as "managing"? In fact, Lyotard suggests that the postmodern artist is more akin to the philosopher than the rhetorician, as he (or she) does not work with pre-established rules but in the event of the artwork itself is formulating new ones which will explain "what *will have been done.*" Lyotard's concern is to avoid any return to those totalizing unities which he sees as having produced the worst terrors of the nineteenth and twentieth centuries; instead, he advocates what he calls an "anti-theological," because plural and non-totalizing, approach to narrative— "let us be witnesses to the unpresentable."[5]

I want to suggest that in *Holy the Firm* Annie Dillard is working with art's "allusion to the unpresentable by means of visible presentations" but that she rescues such allusiveness from what Richard Kearney calls Lyotard's "pragmatic impiety" and from the calculated but helpless limitlessness of the postmodern sublime by being thrown into a contemporary narrative where suffering and the sublime are mediated by the incarnate sacred.[6] Dillard's narrator exercises a "dissenting imagination" against the hubristic monolith of a theological system, but she does so not through *im*piety so much as through a *reimagined* piety, which is her response to first thinking about and then experiencing a vision of the transcendentally sublime Other.[7] The narrator is forcibly confronted with the disfigurement by a freak accident of the face of a young girl and struggles with the seeming impossibility of responding adequately to this injustice as a person of Christian faith. In such a case of unmerited suffering, the sublime in the sense of the imaginatively unpresentable is also the uninterpretable before which reason is disarmed. In this book its only adequate expression is by allusion to the immanence-in-transcendence of Christ, baptized into what Edward Said would call "worldliness" and thus into the world's pain; and the narrator's only adequate response is by allusion to the self-immolation of the artist-as-nun. The figure of the nun has in Christian tradition been understood as one deeply connected to the social reality of the world by her conscious participation in it and her intervention on its behalf through prayer; the artist-as-nun will then similarly participate in the sacramental nature of reality by fulfilling her artistic responsibility to set light to firm and holy ground before the face of the human other who will then be "held fast by love in the world."[8]

Julie Norwich is the little seven-year-old girl whose face is burnt by a gob of ignited fuel as a small plane crashes. Her father was flying the plane; no one else is hurt at all; there is no one to blame except God. Julie is in the hospital; as Dillard writes, "No drugs ease the pain of third-degree burns, because burns destroy skin: the drugs simply leak into the sheets" (*HF*, 60). This event causes a crisis of both faith and hope for the narrator, whom Dillard has admitted that she sees as herself.[9] She identifies with Julie Norwich because Julie looks like the narrator, leggy and fair; also Julie played all of one fall day with the narrator's cat Small, dressing it in doll's clothes that made it look like a nun. The "evidence of things seen" in what has now happened to Julie seems initially to Dillard to assert the "truth" that "this one God is a brute and a traitor, abandoning us to time, to necessity and the engines of matter unhinged," as she thinks of "one Julie, one sorrow, one sensation bewildering the heart, and enraging the mind, and causing me to look at the world stuff appalled" (*HF*, 46). If God is good, which the narrator "know[s]...as given," then "[t]he question is...whether God touches anything. Is anything firm, or is time on the loose?" (*HF*, 47).

Julie Norwich: Julian of Norwich—the intentional link is clear. Julian of Norwich was a fourteenth-century mystic, an anchoress who lived in a cell attached to St. Julian's Church in Norwich, England, the door sealed, only a window giving contact with the outside world. We know little about her— not even her real name; she is chiefly famous for her writings, collected in a single book, *Showings, or Revelations of Divine Love,* a commentary on visionary experiences that occurred during a serious illness in 1373. The focal point of Julian's visions is the crucifix that had been placed before her as part of medieval rites for the dying. This image of the dying Christ, which seemed to sum up all the pain and violence in the world, also gave profound comfort to Julian, because she saw it as an image of divine love "so all-encompassing that even sin cannot mar its perfection."[10] The image is in fact Julian's primary "evidence" of the form and nature of God's beneficent power exercised so that, in her oft-repeated words, "All shall be well, and all shall be well, and all manner of thing shall be well." *Holy the Firm* will become, then, Dillard's "revelation" of narrative imagination: how to read the story of Julie Norwich through the story of Julian of Norwich.

This is obviously more than a matter of rhetoric; there is a kind of correspondence here — it is an issue of truth to experience. As Julie has experienced utter trauma, so Julian experienced both extreme illness and those visionary "revelations," evidence less of what Engström terms "deference for the obscure" than of something extraordinary breaking in beyond the normal.[11] Engström and other rationalists argue that an experience beyond what is culturally normative can be brought within the paradigm by being re-described — that rhetoric has effectively a domesticating power. But Julian's experiences, her "shewings," have remained extraordinary, subliminal, for 700 years; she spent the second half of her life figuring out how to figure them forth — they are unnarratizable in the sense that narrative cannot control or exhaust or domesticate their deeply mysterious nature. This is neither Kant's sublime of the natural world nor Lyotard's sublime of modern or postmodern art; it is the mystical sublime of an experience beyond the powers of reason to comprehend. Not, then, "the conceivable which cannot be presented," but the imaginable which cannot be conceived.

In his work on imagination, Richard Kearney allows for just this kind of incomprehensibility. He asserts that Kant himself theorized imagination to be the primary faculty, the "transcendental imagination" without which we can't even form images of reality in the first place, and though Kant recanted, apparently in deference to the culturally dominant belief in the supremacy of reason over imagination, Kearney rejoices.[12] He talks about the need for imagination to be not only active but also receptive, listening to the senses, "suffering [in the sense of receiving] rather than acting."[13] When imagination falls short, he says, it can only "wait on" the other;[14] we might say imagination must become an anchoress of sorts. "What Julian proposes," writes Frederick Bauerschmidt, is in direct contradistinction to the human desire for mastery and control — "that we embrace the mystery of suffering, and it is only from within that embrace that action can grow that truly accords with God's love."[15] And for Dillard, this "waiting" is key. She draws a direct parallel between the life of the nun, the one who prays and waits and suffers, and the work of the artist, the writer, who experiences a listening and waiting and suffering of her own.

One of the criticisms levelled at this kind of imagining, this kind of mysterious embrace, this kind of allusion to the sublime, is its apparent uselessness. What difference will such imagining make to Julie's suffering? As Pamela A. Smith puts it, Dillard seems to "exhibit ... that familiar twentieth-century phenomenon: an inability to move from observation to ethic ... a tendency to let things alone."[16] Bruce Bawer is even more damning: Dillard's book, he declares, is more interested in making sure we all know "how sensitive its author is to the glorious mysteries around her" than in saying anything useful. In Bawer's opinion, the intent of books like *Holy the Firm* seems to be to "steer clear of ideas — to eschew cognition, as fully as possible, the more purely to experience and express physical and spiritual sensation";[17] in fact, Dillard's view of artistic creation "amounts to a nearly wholesale abdication of the intellect, a New Age-style surrender to forces beyond oneself."[18] The Christian believer can hardly avoid a certain kind of sadness in response to Smith and Bawer, at their lack of "another way of seeing," at their functionalist and rationalist approach to meaning. This is a head-on clash of world views about notions of reality, for of course if you discount, a priori, the possibility of a mystical Other, then you will be led to speak disparagingly of someone like Dillard who, Bawer concedes, "really has quite a good mind," but ironically fails to use it.[19]

If, on the other hand, you accede to the reality of a mystical Other who will always and necessarily exceed both reason and imagination, you will likely agree with Samuel O'Neill that "the merely human faculties of rationality and intellect are insufficient for knowing the ways of the Spirit."[20] "These things are not issues; they are mysteries," Dillard has written in another context.[21] But even if you accept the possibility of mysteries that are "not so much to be interrogated as experienced," you must still confront Smith and Bawer's ethical challenge: is experience-qua-experience enough?[22] When is the ascription of sublimity an excuse for quietism, that "deference for the obscure" that, as Engström puts it, abdicates responsibility "for what it is discourses do, whether sublime or not"?[23] In fact, in the reaction against the oppression of totalities and absolutes, the most serious critique of the unrepresentable "aesthetic of the sublime" judges it as well-nigh synonymous with narrative irresponsibility: in particular, if we cannot represent or retrieve the totality of the past, then we may come to abandon the claim to recount it. Kearney argues that any such "eclipse of historical narrative" is as dangerous for the exemplary as for the monstrous, since we need reimaginings of both to understand and to guide human behaviour.[24] Certainly any celebration of the "sublime" unrepresentability of experiences of terror will compel the response that "if the silence imposed on imagination in such circumstances can be described as aesthetically *sublime* it is morally *suspect*."[25]

I would like now to consider Dillard's own response to these questions, her reimaginings of the monstrous and the exemplary, in *Holy the Firm*. The tripartite structure of the book moves through three days from creation to fall to redemption, or, in terms more consonant with the vocabulary of the mystics, from illumination to purgation to union, from *via positiva* to *via negativa* to *via creativa*. I want to look specifically at the third section, Dillard's own *via creativa*, to explore her conclusion. Julie Norwich lies burned in the hospital; how can the person of faith respond? Does God touch the world? Is there any relationship between time and eternity? Between observation and ethic? Can doing nothing ever be doing something? Dillard's journey to wisdom has three stages.

First, faced by the incomprehensibility of suffering, the narrator is reminded in her angry reading that love is greater than knowledge. the angels of the highest order are so aflame with love for God that they perpetually dissolve back into flames. Moreover, she is confronted by her lack of knowledge even of the sensate world. Incomprehensibility invades space as well as time: a new land appears on the edge of the sea's blue horizon, and she names it Julialand, Time's Bad News, God's Tooth. And so even in her exasperated and wretched questioning where, to use Kearney's phrase, her "subjective security empties itself out,"[26] she recognizes she needs reminding that "we are created, *created,* sojourners in a land we did not make, a land with no meaning of itself and no meaning we can make for it alone. Who are we to demand explanations of God?" (*HF*, 61–62). Thus in the experience of God's silence "it's time to toss things, like our reason, and our will." The narrator, says O'Neill, "has reached the point of surrender," where "the only plausible response to the mystery of existence is worship."[27] And so, on the third day, her response is to say, "I know only enough of God to want to worship him" (*HF*, 55).

Second, it is in this place of surrender that the narrator has two epiphanic experiences. She is returning home to her writer's retreat on Puget Sound, having gone to her local grocery store to buy communion wine for her little church. She marvels that she is carrying in her knapsack "a backload of God … Christ with a cork … very God of very God" (*HF*, 64). She experiences the wine as light through her clothing; it "fills the buttressed vaults of my ribs with light pooled and buoyant" so that she herself becomes light and each thing in the world is translucent, a reality she had lost sight of within the incommensurable grief of the previous day. As she comes out to the top of the hill overlooking the bay, where yesterday she experienced the world as brittle and unreal and time and space as cruel illusions, now "everything, everything is whole" and aflame with light (*HF*, 66). "I remember this reality. Where has it been?" (*HF*, 65).

And then, in this place of floating and translucence, she has a vision of Christ being baptized in the ocean by John, Christ being held under the water, "coiled and white":

Water beads on his shoulders. I see the water in balls as heavy as planets, a billion beads of water as weighty as worlds, and he lifts them up on his back as he rises. He stands wet in the water. Each one bead is transparent, and each has a world, or the same world, light and alive and apparent inside the drop: it is all there ever could be, moving at once, past and future, and all the people. I can look into any sphere and see people stream past me, and cool my eyes with colors and the sight of the world in spectacle perishing ever, and ever renewed. I do; I deepen into a drop and see all that time contains, all the faces and deeps of the worlds and all the earth's contents, every landscape and room, everything living or made or fashioned, all past and future stars, and especially faces, faces like the cells of everything, faces pouring past me talking, and going, and gone. And I am gone.

For outside it is bright. The surface of things outside the drops has fused. Christ himself and the others, and the brown warm wind, and hair, sky, the beach, the shattered water — all this has fused. It is the one glare of holiness; it is bare and unspeakable. There is no speech or language; there is nothing, no one thing, nor motion, nor time. There is only this everything. There is only this, and its bright and multiple noise.

I seem to be on a road, standing still. It is the top of the hill. The hedges are here, subsiding. My hands are in my pockets. There is a bottle of wine on my back, a California red. I see my feet. I move down the hill toward home. (*HF*, 67–8)

The narrator sees Christ not crucified but triumphant, as his baptism readies him to begin his earthly ministry. He is under the water, but then he is also lifting worlds on his back. He holds "all there ever could be" in both the past and the future, the riches of the earth and its people and history and culture and the universe beyond, and everything outside fused into the "one glare of holiness" which is the sublimely "unspeakable." Holiness infuses the water, the stones, the hedges, the bay, the narrator's jacket, the wine, the road home: "There is only this everything." This oneness must be seen as a challenge to the kind of totalized and systematized unity against which Lyotard and others inveigle. It is clearly nothing of "theory": what the narrator is describing is a vision to which the familiar philosophical categories don't apply. New rules must be invented to explain "what *will have been done*," what will have been experienced. In this passage narrative strives to present the experience of sublime vision. It can never encompass the vision, but it can allude to it. And the work of language, always allusive, never identical with the referent, is to bridge the gulf from visionary to reader in such a way that she or he may catch the vision too.

And now in the third stage of her journey to wisdom, the narrator herself becomes the reader. She reads with the vision engulfing her, informing also everything she can't see. In this timeless place of light, more new islands aplenty on the horizon to remind her of how much she does not know, she reads of the esoteric substance Holy the Firm, which is "in touch with the Absolute, at base" (*HF*, 69). This substance links the immanence and the emanance of God: "[m]atter and spirit are of a piece but distinguishable; God has a stake guaranteed in all the world," because all things have emanated from God, but are linked back to God through the presence of this sublime Christ in and through them all.[28] "Holy the Firm is in short the philosopher's stone" (*HF*, 71). It is in light of this revelation, this substantial ground newly uncovered, that the narrator can move forward to meditate on her own role, her own position, at this point in the narrative of the world and Julie Norwich within it.

For what of the artist? The artist is the wick for the candle, the burnt sacrifice "lighting the kingdom of God for the people to see" (*HF*, 72). Linda L. Smith suggests that the artist with his work *is* Holy the Firm: the artist as a Christ-figure who links heaven and earth, spiritual and material: "He is holy and he is firm, spanning all the long gap with the length of his love, in flawed imitation of Christ on the cross stretched both ways unbroken and thorned" (*HF*, 72).[29] It is not that he (or she) is particularly special; it is just that, like Isaiah, he — or she — is there when God calls. And so the narrator turns again to Julie Norwich, who, she imagines, has lost all chance of happiness in this world, and "might as well be a nun" learning to "wreck [her] heart in prayer," and around the pattern of the day's monastic services learning too the power of beauty in the world which is "the smash of the holy" (*HF*, 75). The nun, like the artist, is one who is "[h]eld, held fast by love in the world like the moth in wax, your life a wick, your head on fire with prayer, held utterly, outside and in, you sleep alone, if you call that alone, you cry God" (*HF*, 76). The narrator's final wisdom is to realize that Julie's life will move on, she will likely be healed and married and a mother, for it is the narrator's own life that has now been transformed: "So live. I'll be the nun for you. I am now" (*HF*, 76). In embracing the emotional pain, the isolation and the all-or-nothing commitment of the writer, this final acceptance of writing-as-sacrifice unites the nun, the artist, and the flame-faced child. Like the moth aflame in the wax of a candle in Part I of the book, the artist and the nun must burn to illumine the world.[30] Thus Dillard's journey to wisdom provides an answer to the question of how observation becomes ethic, how doing what appears to be nothing can in fact be doing something profound, how the *via creativa* unites time and eternity in an experience of the sublime that is not quietism or abdication of responsibility but a willing complicity in a discourse of suffering on behalf of another.

Dillard is not in an obvious sense a postmodernist. Her narratives are carefully balanced and structured; the role she gives to the artist is at least modern if not late-Romantic; her ultimate appeal is to a mystery that exceeds language. But insofar as she espouses a very different model of the imagination from either the solipsistic Romantic or the apocalyptic postmodern, she speaks to Kearney's concern for a "postmodern hermeneutic of imagination," aware that meaning "does not originate within the narrow chambers of its own subjectivity but emerges as a response to the *other*, as radical interdependence."[31]

In *Holy the Firm*, the invading transcendental reality is at once sublime and personal, the ethic is one of kenosis, and Dillard as artist-nun finds her meaning in relation to her service of Julie through her art. St. Paul taught that whoever is "baptized into Jesus Christ" is "baptized into his death" (Rom. 6:3 AV). As for Paul, so for the artist-nun: though the suffering is acute, so is the vision. This book enacts an ethical poetics of the sublime. And so the "indescribably more" that takes place in its interaction with the reader will enable her or him "not just [to] see the divine in an ethics of suffering but also in a poetics of the beautiful… the celebration of… the beautiful in the everyday moment."[32] For, as the narrator's vision of Christ's baptism revealed, "[t]here is only this everything. There is only this, and its bright and multiple noise" (*HF*, 68).

Notes

1 Jean-François Lyotard, "Answering the Question: What Is Postmodernism?" *The Postmodern Condition*, trans. R. Durand (1979; Manchester, UK: Manchester University Press, 1986) 78.

2 Ibid., 82, 80, 82.

3 Bert Olivier, "The Sublime, Unpresentability and Postmodern Cultural Complexity," *South African Journal of Philosophy* 16.1 (1997): 7–13.

4 Timothy H. Engström, "The Postmodern Sublime? Philosophical Rehabilitations and Pragmatic Evasions," *Boundary 2* 20.2 (1993):194.

5 Lyotard, "Answering the Question," 82.

6 Richard Kearney, *Poetics of Imagining: Modern to Post-modern* (Edinburgh: Edinburgh University Press, 1998) 209.

7 Ibid., 207.

8 Annie Dillard, *Holy the Firm* (New York: Harper and Row, 1977) 76; future citations from *Holy the Firm* are from this edition and will be referenced in the text by the abbreviation *HF* and page number.

9 Karla M. Hammond, "Drawing the Curtains: An Interview with Annie Dillard," *Bennington Review* 10 (1981): 33.

10 Frederick Christian Bauerschmidt, "Loosening Our Grip: Julian of Norwich," *Mysticism* (Waco, TX: Baylor University Center for Christian Ethics, 2005) 30.

11 Engström, "The Postmodern Sublime?" 204.

12 Richard Kearney, "The God Who May Be," conversation with David Cayley, *Ideas*, CBC Radio, 20 Feb., 27 Feb., and 6 Mar. 2006 (*Ideas* Transcripts ID 2964).

13 Ibid., 33.

14 Ibid., 32.

15 Bauerschmidt, "Loosening Our Grip," 35.

16 Pamela A. Smith, "The Ecotheology of Annie Dillard: A Study in Ambivalence," *Cross Currents* 45.3 (1995): 355.

17 Bruce Bawer, "Quiet—Author Suffering," rev. of *The Writing Life*, by Annie Dillard, *American Scholar* 59.3 (1990): 447.

18 Ibid., 449.

19 Ibid., 447.
20 Samuel O'Neill, "The Mystic Way in Two Works by Annie Dillard" (master's thesis, Georgetown University, 1993), 11.
21 Annie Dillard, *Teaching a Stone to Talk: Expeditions and Encounters* (New York: Harper, 1982) 64.
22 O'Neill, "The Mystic Way," 28.
23 Engström, "The Postmodern Sublime?" 204.
24 Kearney, *Poetics of Imagining*, 255.
25 Ibid., 231–32.
26 Richard Kearney, *The Wake of Imagination* (London: Hutchinson; Minneapolis: University of Minnesota Press, 1988) 397.
27 O'Neill, "The Mystic Way," 45.
28 Sandra Humble Johnson, *The Space Between: Literary Epiphany in the Work of Annie Dillard* (Kent, OH: Kent State University Press, 1992) 88.
29 Linda L. Smith, *Annie Dillard* (New York: Twayne, 1991) 75.
30 Smith, *Annie Dillard*, 79.
31 Kearney, *The Wake of Imagination*, 392, 387.
32 Kearney, "The God Who May Be," 22.

JAPANESE (RE)VISIONING OF THE SUFFERING CHRIST

PASSION PLAYS BY PROXY: THE PASCHAL FACE AS INTERCULTURALITY IN THE WORKS OF ENDŌ SHŪSAKU AND MISHIMA YUKIO

Sean Somers

Akihabara is renowned as an electropolis: a neon-encrusted district, pulsing with digital blips and pixels. Unparalleled as a shopping place for technology, this borough of Tokyo offers up-to-the-minute technologies for entertainment, as well as all the latest updates in communications gadgetry. Wandering there in awe, amidst such microchips and circuitry, I was surprised to come across, in a side street, a rather anachronistic religious goods shop. A display window showcased a variety of chipped plaster saints, sterling silver rosaries, and holy-water basins. With such pious appearances, this venue seemed not altogether different from the sacramental boutiques of Dublin, Sienna, or Lourdes. Inside, my eyes took in an even larger assortment of the art and imagery that inspire the Christian faith. Most noticeably, the farthest wall displayed countless crosses — woods, textures, and gildings — in all types and sizes. A young man was thoughtfully perusing this vast collection, looking carefully but remaining uncommitted. A clerk approached him and asked, "Anything in particular you're looking for?" He had an air of uncertainty. "Utsukushii desu kedo…" "They're beautiful," he said, "but, well, have you got one with the little man on it?"

This introductory anecdote is not meant to censure Tokyoites in particular. Our world is marked by multiple geographies of belief, and when transferred, religious ideas and icons take on new faces or appearances. The *world religions* scenario, one of dialogue, translation, and miscegenation, has thereby revealed instabilities within dogma considered universal. When religious doctrines and aesthetic forms enter new cultural spaces, they are inevitably modified and detached from the foundational ideologies out of which they emerge. We need only also look at the West, with its Zen breakfast cereals or lawn ornament Buddhas, to find other examples of religious tradition being turned into commodified tropes or decontextualized tokens. As Raymond Cohen notes, "cross-cultural encounters" in various manifestations can engender an intense sense of "misunderstanding" or "dissonance."[1] Precisely how this intercultural dissonance manifests in art, particularly in relation to the meaning of suffering and salvation through Christ, is a crucial issue for Christian writing in Japan.

In this essay, I will investigate this theme through two case studies of post–Pacific War writing: one from a Christian believer, Endō Shūsaku, and one from a non-believer, Mishima Yukio. Both writers compose Passion plays that fail to maintain the official narrative of the paschal sacrifice, although they are filled with Catholic imagery. Endō's novel *Chinmoku* [*Silence*] (1966) is conceptually histiographic in approach but deeply personal in its attempt to visualize faith and atonement in Japan. Mishima stages aesthetic theology, which is subject to much revision, in an unstable setting of pre-revolution France. The manner in which characters in these works attempt to adopt the model of Christ, with themselves as his proxy united to his suffering, exposes world-view dissonance as a clash between aesthetics and theology. In these works, Endō and Mishima forcefully reveal fundamental problems of cultural pluralism and a universal Christology. By confronting these problems, the writings of Endō and Mishima illustrate and illuminate the aesthetic controversy between two contemporary theologians of religious aesthetics, Hans Urs von Balthasar and Roger Haight, and address the extent to which Christian truth can and should be adapted to new linguistic and aesthetic contexts.

Against the iconoclasts, Orthodox and Catholic theologians have argued that religious adoration finds necessary expression through aesthetic sites for uplifted meditation. Christological piety is invited, and enhanced, through these visual windows to heaven. Catholicism further makes allowance for three-dimensional forms of theological expressivity, ones generally not permitted in Eastern Orthodox churches. The latter prefers relief-style imagery, while in Catholicism statuary can also be objects of reverence. But the purpose of such aesthetics, as not being mere idolatry contrary to divine ordinance, requires theological explication. Hans Urs von Balthasar, on this question, emphasized the correlation of the visual component, the sacramental item, to an interiority of faith that has *imaginative empathy* (*Mitfühlen*) with the human face of Christ as one "who renounces the form of God" and chooses the way of "the cross."[2] Accepting the doctrine of hypostatic union — "the substantial union of divine and human nature in the one person of Jesus Christ" — is necessary for viewing the true form of Jesus as a manifestation of the reality of God.[3] Any *theological aesthetics* must have "the essential content of faith" to properly possess "vision (*theoria*)."[4] Without the proper relationship of vision and faith, art and universal dogma, Christians will be guilty of revering the idol, as Eric Fromm puts it; they will simply be worshipping themselves.

In his formulation of Christological artistry, however, Balthasar does not adopt a permissive, liberal attitude in assessing how much allowance should be made for socio-historical transposition, as seen in the influence of cultural forces that alter the reception and re-presentation of Christ's humanity. I do not wish to press Balthasar's thinking into a narrow formula for approaching Christ. Indeed, Balthasar can accept cultural mediation, to a guided extent, as a way of spreading Christian truth. In such works as *Dare We Hope "That All Men Be Saved"?* Balthasar may be seen to approach a form of optimistic universalism. And, in agreement with Karl Barth, Balthasar asserts in this short work that the Word is never a formula, because the formula is always that which has already become form, merely attesting to the Word that remains unsayable (or, as Endō will describe, *silent*).[5] However, in his multi-volume work on theological aesthetics, Balthasar often takes a conservative position, limiting the versatility of creative art for enacting, and thereby interpreting, theology. For Balthasar, aesthetics are necessarily important, but must be cautiously *subsumed* within theology: "It is that, in everything the Church, as steward of the sacraments, does to give visible form, the manner and measure of this form-giving is determined by the event which is to be made present in that form and which is itself the archetypal form of all revelation. Nothing in the Church — not even the Church herself — can lay claim to an autonomous form that would compete with the Christ-form or even replace it."[6] Aesthetics opens up the drama of transcendent sacramental theology, which itself is unchanging and beyond visuality. In terms of human societies, then, intercultural encounters between ethoi must not (and ultimately cannot) undermine the proper relation of theology and icon.

Roger Haight has recently presented some challenges to Balthasar's theological aesthetic. Haight finds that the pluralistic conditions of the postmodern, as represented by interculturality, interrogate a single objective truth necessarily exhibited in a single luminous form (*splendor formae*).[7] And, complicating the situation, scholars such as Masuzawa Tomoko have argued that the very procedures of religious pluralism, such as interfaith dialogue, are covert methods of missionarianism.[8] Theological aesthetics in such a formulation encode and perpetuate the strategies of European universalism. Looking at a little man on the cross, no matter what his face looked like, might mean absorbing an ethos of Western expansionism. However, a culture's reception of a foreign theology, and its accompanying aesthetics, divulges distinct cultural differences, as is evident in the Japanese modification of visual Christologies. By investigating this process of acculturation in imaginative literature, Endō Shūsaku and Mishima Yukio expose the universalist presumptions of theological aesthetics and reveal that the relationship between aesthetics and theology is characterized by complex and unstable intersections of culture, image, and belief. In Japan, with its historical legacy of suffering and martyrdom, the paschal narrative, as salvific message, becomes a flashpoint for contested depictions of the crucified Christ and, more generally, for competing views on the presence of Christian ideas and images in Japan.

Christianity—unlike the other Abrahamic faiths of Islam and Judaism—has an incarnate God as its message of atonement. The human-ness of God, as mortal form, thus becomes the central theme of salvation. A theological aesthetics, as explicated by Balthasar, must match the expressivity of its semiotic forms with the preordained module of Christ as universal truth. The imaginations of diverse global communities, which come into cohesion through a Christian visual scheme, absolutely derive their reference from a transcendental Word. Acting on the Word's behalf, a universal authority [*magisterium*] must regulate cultural or historical expressions to prevent heterodoxy. Revelational art embodies theological intent, and these visual intermediaries must be safeguarded from pluralistic adaptations. Dogma maintains the proper connection between *affect* and *piety* that prevents Christological imagery from being turned into corrupt simulacra of bad faith. Typological formulas of devotion—such as the Stations of the Cross, the rosary, or other orthodox forms of affective piety—are meant to reinforce and regulate an aesthetic experience as faithful to a Catholic/universal catechism.

This is Balthasar's *theoretical* cornerstone for religious art, but what have intercultural encounters revealed in *actual* transcultural histories? In reviewing Christianity in Japan, Yasuoka Shōtarō identifies a serious predicament when it comes to national identity and a relationship with the Roman church.[9] Japanese Christianity, he argues, will always seem divided, because ethnicity presupposes a split in allegiances. In considering the tension that results from such a fracturing of identity, Roger Haight, from the perspective of postmodern Christology, argues that cultural pluralism—specifically, the ways in which different cultures understand Christ—is the most pressing topic for meaningful theological dialogue.

Endō Shūsaku, a practising Catholic, was continually troubled both theologically and socially by a seemingly insurmountable gap between Caucasians [*shiroi hito*] and Orientals [*ki'iroi hito*] and their respective societies. Christ is proclaimed as universal—Endō believes and accepts this. But Endō proposes that rather than shunning or ignoring the obvious variety in aesthetic treatments of Christ's humanity, theology should learn from multiple expressivities. He wonders: How do differing ethnic perspectives influence meditation on the features of Christ's face? How does one tell a mask from a true messiah? And what becomes of the salvific message if the aesthetic theology that approaches Calvary is misconfigured? The question that both Endō and Mishima explore is one of great theological importance: to what extent, if at all, can universal Christian truth be expressed in different cultural media? To explore this question, Mishima and Endō both present unorthodox images of the incarnated Christ, as one who experienced both suffering and the sublime, through the medium of Japanese literature.

Mishima Yukio's *Sado kōshaku fujin* [*Madame de Sade*] makes for a compelling contrast with Endō's *Chinmoku* [*Silence*].[10] Both texts question, in divergent ways, how the suffering humanity of Christ is culturally mediated. Mishima's potential contribution to the Balthasar/Haight debate—absolute transcendence or cultural plurality in the visual form of Christ—is to show how the excesses of aesthetics overwrite canonical presumptions. As a Japanese writer manipulating the paschal narrative, Mishima offers, in an anticlimactic fashion, a version of a visual Christ who is made present only because of a sensual fascination with miracles and martyrdom. In this reversed way, the incarnation of Christ is actually *preceded* by the Passion. Only through the performance of suffering and death does Christ become meaningfully corporeal. Mishima makes the object of worship attainable only by first indulging in sin, which stands in contrast to Karl Barth's more standard view of salvation as *prior* to sin. A visualization of the *crucifixion* owes its form to self-indulgent fantasies. Aesthetics is ennobled by its romantic resemblance to theology. In *Madame de Sade*, Sade derives satisfaction through a personalized *crucifixion* as a melodrama of suffering. In this regard, Mishima exemplifies what Ellis Hanson called "the dialectic of shame and grace": the sublime is subordinated to a sensual dynamic of the subject.[11] Thus, a fundamental agnosticism, figured as the limits of human perception and ego, pervades Mishima's play. Christ, in terms of Balthasar's sense of him as transcendental signifier, cannot be sustained in the variability of physical form. In fact, by keeping Christ in the drama only through reference and not appearance, Mishima denies the messianic face any visibility, except as a visage created out of the psychosexual sublime. Religious icons are a form of interactive role play.

Endō Shūsaku, most notably, emerged in this era as a prominent spokesman for a postwar Christianity that offered a gospel of pacifism and redemption. That does not mean he offered facile pronouncements that conversion is easy or that the Latinate world view is inerrant. Indeed, problematically, such essays as *Kamigami to kami to* [*Gods and God*] (1947) analyze the linguistic and cultural difficulties of a Japanese Catholicism. It is useful to think of Endō's envisioning of Christ within these layered contexts: the historical recollection of the first Japanese Catholic converts as a legacy of suffering for the sublime; a recent era of militant Shintō; and the postwar growth of *shin-shin shūfkyō* [new-new religions] such as *Sōka gakkai*. Key theological terms, such as transcendence and Trinitarianism, are not so readily turned into equivalent cognates in the Japanese language. But Endō sought to expound Christian beliefs in a non-catechetical way as well as to negotiate interfaith difficulties. In an interview with William Johnston, a Jesuit scholar of Zen Buddhism (and Endō's translator), Endō observes that "[t]heology has been based on Western thought patterns for too long. We Japanese were taught that it was dangerous to depart from them."[12] He goes on to explain that he desires a pluralistic view of Japanese Catholicism that is orthodox in belief but innovative in method.

At the same time, Endō is concerned with socio-historical conditions in Japan that inhibit ready identification with a humble, crucified Christ. As he wrote, tellingly, in the preface to the American edition of his *A Life of Jesus* [*Iesu no shōgai*], "The religious mentality of the Japanese is — just as it was at the time when the people accepted Buddhism — responsive to one who 'suffers with us' and who 'allows for our weakness,' but their mentality has little tolerance for any kind of transcendent being who judges humans harshly, then punishes them."[13] According to Endō, the difficulty arises from fundamentally dissimilar attitudes in Buddhism and Christianity in regard to the human condition. Buddhism takes a radically different approach to suffering and the problem of evil than does Christianity. Endō understood that while interculturality is a necessary dimension of dialogue that world Christianities recognize they must partake in, "there are differences in the two religions and these differences must be made clear; otherwise something fundamental might be lost."[14] Endō speculates, for example, that Western Christians, eager to adopt Buddhist methods — Zen meditation, for example — may find themselves overlooking the essential personage of Christ.

Endō's own faith journey thus stressed the compatibility of Abrahamic religion and a Japanese believer, initiated by the contemplation of Jesus. Johnston is fascinated by Endō's commitment to Christ, as saviour God with a human face. Endō's biography exhibits his prayerful commitment to the human condition of Christ, explored through the *via crucis*, which Endō emulated through affective meditation and pilgrimage. Endō visited important holy sites in Israel and took walking tours that allowed him to follow in the footsteps of St. Paul. He found that the spiritual discipline of the Stations of the Cross was enhanced by such apostolic tourism. Much of Endō's writing, including *Shikai no hotori* [*Near the Dead Sea*], benefited from the visual contact with the landscape of the gospel. And Endō's experiences of the Holy Land were thereby journeys of affective piety, as experiential practices that connected a historical Christology to his work as a Japanese novelist. So, despite the various conflicts he experienced, Endō also says Catholicism "had become a part of me after all."[15]

Endō reflects on the obligations of Christian testimony in his novel *Silence*, which imagines the missionary efforts of Sebastian Rodrigues, a Portuguese priest. This Jesuit, as bearer of *logos*, must traverse geographies and societies so that the Word is made communicable to all peoples, that Christ as global sacrifice becomes united through the multicultural Mass. In Matthew's Gospel, Christ on several occasions instructs his disciples to *teach all the nations* (Matt. 12:18; Matt. 28:19). This is the challenge of Rodrigues's missionary project, to translate Christ as both image and word for the Japanese people. The Eucharist, as *memory* of Christ, must operate as both a transcendent event and a translatable idiom. Yet Rodrigues struggles in a new cultural context with the notion of a redeemer who is at once human and divine, a redeemer whose human suffering can be demonstrated through the visual imagination, but the mystery of whose resurrection has no physical manifestation.

Endō's novel wants to reunite a crucified Christ (human) with the resurrected God (divine). The imagery of the paschal sacrifice, as the penultimate feature of the Gospels, might provide the translatable discourse for the performance of salvation. If Christ were a common criminal, then his death would have no significance. If he is redeemer, then the depiction of his suffering must connect to an ineffable truth. The man on the cross is both incarnate God and final Adam. The sacraments also represent the communicability of Christ's Real Presence, linking human experience with divine transcendence.[16] Such images and sacraments permit Rodrigues to dedicate himself to the belief that *logos* is universal utterance. Word-become-flesh can be understood both as physical reality and universal transcendent. Following the principle of Romans 10:13–14 (how can one hear the name unless it is uttered, and how can it be uttered unless it is preached), the missionary, as extension, delivers the name of Christ.

The competing cultural forces in this novel, however, produce differing modes of *silence* that relate in complicated ways to Rodrigues's sharing of the Word. The gospel's message, as presenting the personage of Christ, can be muted, but quietness does not mean silence. Indeed, Endō shows that *silence* can be, in fact, polyphonic. Silence speaks volumes in different ways: to signal an abdication of faith, or a keeping of it; a lack of disclosure from God (104), or an inner working of the Holy Spirit (190). For example, *Kirishitan*, the Japanese Christians, were told that to end the agony of torture they had only to signify their abdication of faith through a motion of the hand. Later,

Rodrigues imitates Peter's rejection of Christ when he is captured by the Japanese authorities. But *silence* for Rodrigues also meant *not* becoming an apostate. To withhold an expression of apostasy meant to remain committed to Christianity (133). To believe or not believe are forms of dialogue, actually, with both officialdom and the suffering of Christ: "I was not silent. I suffered beside you" (190). This comment, spoken internally, seems to answer Rodrigues's own question about the purpose of suffering and silence. He has not been able to fathom why, despite the enormous suffering of the Japanese Christians, God does not intervene with speech or miracle. Despite Rodrigues's pleading for the little man on the cross — on his religious symbols — to speak out, no response comes. The *logos* does not directly speak into the ear of the believers.

To compensate for silence(s), Rodrigues attempts to formulate his own utterances according to seminary texts on Christ's Passion; he develops his priestly role as *alter Christus* to speak on behalf of heaven. Salvific truth can be communicated through imitation of Christ as testimony; the ontology of sacrifice and redemption can come into being through the faith-acts of Christ's proxies. Such is particularly incumbent on the priest, who consecrates the bread and wine at Mass, where transubstantiation takes place and the Real Presence of Christ is made known: "The Eucharist effects our participation in the Paschal Mystery and thus constitutes the Church, the body of Christ."[17] In becoming a Christic "image-form, which bears the impress of the dying" and martyred Christ, Rodrigues fashions himself as a kind of Eucharist.[18] This is evident in passages in which the images used to describe Christ are related to his own haggard appearance (67).

In his evangelical mission, therefore, Rodrigues finds that both a theological and an aesthetic sensibility are needed to overcome silence. In order to convey the notion of resurrection, Rodrigues must sketch a human face for Christ — first in his own mind, and then make it manifest through preaching. The novel spends a great deal of time examining this effort towards a personal Christology. Rodrigues's inner monologue — shown in both first- and third-person perspectives — fluctuates between apophatic and kataphatic methods for envisioning the Godhead. Initially, as a seminarian, he ponders why the Gospels are silent in regard to Christ's face (44). Jesus weeps, but we do not see (nor are we told of) the tears sliding down his cheeks. Christ becomes angry, but his lips do not twist in rage. The Gospel narratives do not describe the physical contours of his face. Therefore, what visage is most truly identifiable as Christ's? God becoming man, in the hypostatic union of Christ, is either a mystery so complex that the soul is emptied before it (*apophasis*), or a reality so compelling that the body seeks to unite its sacrifices to it (*kataphasis*).

Rodrigues compensates for a lack of biblical imagery by expanding the visual scope of his own narrative to recreate models of affective piety, as Golgotha prototypes derived from the paschal sacrifice, furthered by exemplary figures such as Francis Xavier. These intentional overlayings of paschal imagery on Japanese landscape strive to unify, through a biblical template, the disparate experiences encountered through cultural diversity. In making himself a sacrificial Christic figure, Rodrigues inserts himself on the cross, regardless of the cartographic location of his own martyrdom. Envisioning himself in the sacrificial role, he adopts the Passion play theology, with him as Christ's proxy. The spiritual meaning of suffering is thus derivative, connected with, and framed by, Christ as the first martyr. If the aesthetic image of Christ is absent, Rodrigues can present an aesthetic theology of the face through his own example. His activities in Nagasaki will demonstrably merge, at least in Rodrigues's spiritual imagination, with the crucifixion near Jerusalem. But the triumphant arrival on Palm Sunday becomes aligned, instead, with a humble inverse, a secretive beach landing near Nagasaki. When Rodrigues watches the *Kirishitan* being forcibly drowned, he notes the disparity between hagiography and reality: "I had long read about martyrdom in the lives of the saints.... But the martyrdom of the Japanese Christians I now describe to you was no such glorious thing" (60).

Diverse socio-historical circumstances, after all, do not make for tidy analogues. This missionary has been preparing himself for a surrogate Calvary scene, one in Japan rather than Jerusalem. Mentally, Rodrigues has been fashioning vignettes of Gospel-esque scenarios, with himself replicating the role of Christ: "And as I speak there often arises in my mind the face of one who preached the Sermon on the Mount .... As for me, perhaps I am so fascinated by his face because the Scriptures make no mention of it" (43–44). As with the stations of the cross, his paschal narrative must be shown to be performable both in the orthodoxy of the church and in a living encounter with the Japanese landscape. To emphasize this relationship between official pattern and dynamic performance, *Silence*'s point of view vacillates between omniscient and first-person perspectives. The Godlike voice of the remoter narration gives way to the personal pathos of the first person. What is thereby apparent, however, is how the modelled formality of the stations, as the universal *via dolorosa*, does not easily mesh with the social circumstances of Japan. This gap, which Endō exposes through Rodrigues's unstable paschal performance, exemplifies the points of contention between Balthasar and Haight about aesthetic Christologies. As Haight maintains, "Historical relativity forces the Christian to define more exactly the content of what is mediated by Jesus."[19] Assertions of pure catholicity and pre-configured visual models of Jesus do not accomplish this end.

Rodrigues maintains his own role of Christ as the most apparent expression of the message of salvation. Thus, his proxy-Passion narrative has been building up to crucifixion: "every day he had dramatically pictured the scene as being like the meeting of Pilate and Christ ... Christ standing silent" (107). As he strives to unite his life with that of Jesus, other elements of the gospel emerge in the narrative. Kichijirō, Rodrigues's disciple, turns out to be the Judas who hands him to the authorities. The Palm Sunday procession is mirrored by a prisoner's march, in which Rodrigues rides "through the streets of Nagasaki on a donkey" (157). And then, in this unfolding typology, the apostate priest Christavão Ferreira plays the role of Caiaphas, or religious authority. His Kurtzian betrayal of the Portuguese Jesuits is legendary. And, leading up to the moment of martyrdom, Rodrigues's examination by the Shogunate authorities is supposed to have the silent heroism of Christ before the Sanhedrin. At the critical moment of sacrifice, however, the paschal sequences become reversed, and thereby so does the theology guiding the aesthetics.

Ferreira, under his Buddhist name Sawano Chuan, finds a weakness in Rodrigues's dependence on the visuality of the passion narrative. He uses a multipronged form of inquisition to cut into the doctrinal stability of Rodrigues's *imitatio Christi*. Ferreira's arguments (144–50) are complex. However, distilled into a central thesis, the various points mesh into one clear assertion. Divergent cultural ethoi in Japan and Portugal prevent a meaningful communication of the gospel in image or word. Catholic claims of universality, through the theology of Christ as a hypostatic Man-God, appear suspect when transposed in Japanese discourses, especially when errors can be easily introduced as ideas and images are transmitted from one culture to the next. Key terms can be mistranslated or iconic traditions (for example, *Kannon-sama* and Mary) can be inappropriately conflated. Such forces disfigure the theological and aesthetic identity of the Christ. Ferreira gives an example: "From the beginning those same Japanese who confused 'Deus' and 'Dainichi' twisted and changed our God and began to create something different. Even when the confusion of vocabulary disappeared the twisting and changing secretly continued" (148). This results, according to Ferreira, in a *corpus Christi* completely altered in appearance and thus no longer indicating a theological source. Affect has overruled piety because cultural pluralism has perverted both the name and image, and therefore the substance, of God. What if the sacramental figures that the Japanese have sculpted are, after all, surrogate Buddhas? Is that statue one of St. Joseph cradling Christ in a nativity scene, or an O-Jizō-san with child? Contrary to Balthasar, Ferreira states that cultural subjectivities *invariably* reconfigure and alter both the appearance and essence of the *imago Dei* into an *imago clipeata*, a kind of reframed portrait that is a disconnected simulacrum of the original Person. The meaning of these altered Christian images, and the doctrine that informs them, are no longer authoritative or worthy of esteem.

Balthasar, of course, believes that it is possible to enjoy a "clear vision of the things of Christ" regardless of circumstance as long as vision (*theoria*), in the aesthetic sense, is rooted in the power of an eternal and unchangeable theology.[20] In Japan, as elsewhere, however, the precise nature of *clear vision* cannot necessarily be taken for granted. Haight asserts that "any given Christology in any given community should enter into dialogue with other communities."[21] In a similar vein, and in line with Endō's vision in *Silence*, the noted theological commentator Inoue Yōji proposes that acculturation can, in fact, augment a European understanding of Christ. His seminal work *Japan and the Face of Jesus* [*Nihon to Iesu no kao*] considers the critical issue of how perceptions of Christ's divinity and humanity become re-faced through the "the sensibilities of Japanese everyday life."[22] Inoue is faithful to the classical Christology of the Incarnation, of a God becoming man and dwelling among us (John 1:14). However, taking a comparativist approach, Inoue explores a biblical theology that develops within a Japanese aesthetic. For example, he suggests that Christian teaching becomes more fluently Christological by engaging with and attending to the socio-cultural realities of Buddhism, for example. Haight, in his own way, makes the same point as Inoue: "Christians of the West must have the freedom to enter into this dialogue in the terms that the culture [African, Asian, etc.] dictates."[23] However, the question remains: when does permissible augmentation end and heretical obfuscation begin?

For Rodrigues, the development of Christology, as a process of missionary activity, is a crisis of systematic theology clashing with cultural adaptation, and outright xenophobic hostility. Haight's vision of cross-cultural theological dialogue depends on a presumption of goodwill that Rodrigues does not enjoy. This, ultimately, is the meaning of silence in Endō's portrait: a form of Christ that no longer conforms to, or speaks from, orthodox theological expectations. Thus, a crucial Christophanic moment in *Silence* does not occur. Instead, Rodrigues comes face to face with the *fumie*, a distorted mask intended in every way to be a farcical imitation of the Blessed Sacrament. The *fumie* is a crude circumvention of Renaissance ideals. Christ is portrayed as a grotesque human, sickly and without salvation: "A simple copper medal is fixed on to a grey plank of dirty wood on which the grains run like little waves. Before him is the ugly face of Christ" (170). Unlike Jesus, Rodrigues is not tortured: those final, redemptive stations of the *via dolorosa* are denied him. Instead, this missionary hears the wailing agony of his flock, all of whom have already renounced their new faith. Their suffering—they are slowly tortured through *anazuri* rather than martyred outright—will only end if Rodrigues forsakes his own religion and thus his Christ-priest role. By blaspheming the image of Christ, he in turn is rejecting the God in whose name he speaks.

Apostasy is formally accomplished by stomping on this *fumie*, which means *defacing* the aesthetic personhood of Christ as God.

Having so long yearned for the materialization of the body of Christ, Rodrigues encounters instead an aesthetic of something anti-Eucharistic. Thus, the novel's key scene rebukes piety by effacing the beauty of its affect. To stop the suffering of these *Kirishitan*, Rodrigues must only add his stomp to the pile of apostate footprints. Rodrigues, having acted throughout as the proxy Christ, now commits to a counter-Christophany, erasing the form of a perverted *imitatio Christi*. The salvific irony of the novel thus becomes the first words of Christly speech; this false image of Christ is the one that becomes animate and alive, addressing Rodrigues: "Trample! Trample! I more than anyone know of the pain in your foot. Trample! It was to be trampled on by men that I was born into this world. It was to share men's pain that I carried my cross" (171). *Speech* trumps visual imagery; the significance of the icon is irrelevant compared to the mystery of Christ's mercy, which adapts to horrible circumstances. As Rodrigues defaces this pseudo-Christ, the form which actually speaks his truth, he commits himself to a martyrdom of the heart rather than the body. His foot goes down, stuffing the *fumie*'s mouth. The cock crows in the distance, calling to mind Peter's denial of Christ (171). But, according to the *fumie*, a silent message of salvation has been given, one that overrules the theological image that the senses claim to understand and behold.

Although in ways highly contrary to Endō, the subjectivity of martyrdom also fascinates Mishima, as is evident in his fiction as well as in his public exhibitionism. His novel *Haru no yuki* [*Spring Snow*] (1968) includes a sacrificial death of the protagonist. This suffering youth, Masugae Kiyoaki, and his failed love are modelled on the quasi-historical legend of Komachi, whose suitor perished in a snowstorm while trying to complete one hundred consecutive nights of visitation.[24] In terms of Catholic holy card imagery, Mishima produced a series of self-portraits in which he posed as St. Sebastian: a loincloth hangs loosely on his body, his arms bound to a tree, his belly shot full of arrows. It does not require a complex psychoanalytic framework to grasp that Mishima saw in Catholic versions of martyrdom a kind of spiritual-erotic chic. The seemingly sado-masochistic dimensions of Catholic martyrdom appealed to the ego's need to heroicize itself. Freud, of course, had posited decades before that affective piety was a psychical mechanism for negotiating sexual taboos.[25] But, at the same time, *Madame de Sade* seeks a theological legitimacy by approaching the subject of Christ and considering what motivates individuals to die in his name. In this respect, Mishima's novel is more nuanced than a pornographic carnival of self-flagellation. It recognizes that suffering, as a personal commitment to an ideal, depends on an enigma of the sublime. Mishima makes this point clearly in his epilogue: "I was sure that something highly incomprehensible, yet highly truthful, about human nature lay behind this riddle."[26] Therefore, this enigmatic mechanism of Madame de Sade's suffering rises above mere farce, and Mishima generates dramatic tension in the novel that is distinctly different from, for example, Genet's absurdist spectacle of saints farting on ceilings.

Madame de Sade, like *Silence*, manipulates the conventions of the passion play in the performance of martyrdom. In this case, Renée, Sade's wife, speaks from the vantage point of her own suffering, as one waiting perpetually for her imprisoned, unscrupulous husband. She acts as an apostle, speaking of the larger-than-life Marquis through Christological references, as one who is "without sin" (53). Certainly, this account of her husband is knowingly absurd. Sade was imprisoned for publicly turning blasphemy into his own gospel, making a reputation out of public pasquinades that mocked the sanctity of Christ.

The Marquis takes upon himself the role of *alter Christus*, but his martyrdom is a soteriology for the senses, a means of enhancing his own drama. The stations of the cross provide fantasies for self-eroticizing performances: for example, an offstage parody of the pillar scourging between the Marquis and a prostitute (29). No redemptive model leads the soul to salvation or justification. Rather than a Christic incarnation (word becoming flesh), the suffering eros is elevated, acquiring the sublimity of Logos through increasingly taboo sexual practices. Flesh becomes the Word through an excessive identification with images. Thus, the pinnacle of Sade's profanation of his own Christhood is to conduct a Black Mass (in a style later described by Huysmans in *Là-Bas*) with a bodily Eucharist. Sade's positioning of himself as the inverted or anti-Christ points to the diverse connotations of the original Greek term: to be not only *against* Christ, or in *opposition* to Christ, but also to be a substitute for his form and identity. In this substitutive fashion, Mishima's novel is *anti-christos* rather than *a-christos*.

Madame de Sade, who had no priestly role in this scandal, only learns of her husband's paschal infidelity second-hand. She must listen to a hearsay description from the woman who acted as the altar: "the blood of the lamb steamed over my nakedness" (52). Why would Madame de Sade carry out her duties as bride, a kind of apostolic church, to her anti-Christ? As she describes it herself, an emotive conflation between affect and piety leads to her confusion about the object of veneration and its theological truths. She asks, "Can you distinguish between loving roses and loving the scent of roses?" (31). The sensory thrills of affects, which also offer psychological succour, provide an experiential template for religious identification. The context never transcends itself, however. This is contrary to Balthasar, who advocates St. Aquinas's views. *Affectus* must subordinate itself to *pietas*, in that the sensual nature of the former must be configured as "the very desire to strive" for the latter (161). Renée uses theology to satisfy her own ends. She subordinates herself to an absent Marquis, thereby offering her body as a sacrifice (Romans 12:1), in part to satisfy her own confusion about Christ's essential nature.

Saint-Fond, the voice of carnality in this play, explains this desire to merge the carnal and the Christian in a new aesthetic: "I've become utterly bored with the artifices of love.... It occurred to me that if I could somehow add an element of the sacred..." (49). Such a view of satisfaction through sacred image in and for itself, certainly, contradicts the Catholic understanding of affective piety. But what recourse is there to transhistorical theology?

Curiously for a Passion play, the Marquis, as the messiah figure, actually remains outside of the visual register for the entire play. He never physically appears on stage, never speaks a word of dialogue, even after his release from prison, which should have entitled him to a Resurrection-like appearance to his women apostles outside a metaphorical tomb. Mishima thus suggests, ultimately, that religious suffering finds its meaning as a limited propitiation. Self-pleasuring relies on an absence of the sublime for its mystique. Once the pseudo-sublime returns to reality, the promulgation of some aesthetic mystery loses its raison d'être. There is, then, no *fumie* in *Madame de Sade*: there is no conversational encounter that unites affect with piety, immanence with transcendence, and aesthetics with theology. There is only Madame de Sade putting her foot down as an indication of denial, of both art and Eucharist: "That was the final stamp of the foot of the wine presser trampling the grapes" (90). Renée had read one of her husband's novels, *Justine*, his gospel of vice and lust, in which she features prominently as a ridiculous figure of naive devotion. Thus humiliated and without redemption, Renée comes to terms with her own motivations. Although dressed up in religious imagery, she is after all a crypto-atheist. Her narrative or martyrdom simply satisfied gender stereotypes and allowed her to indulge her own masochistic tendencies. What most disgusts Renée is that her faith only supplemented the Christological thrill of the Marquis's sense of himself as Passion proxy; this is the reason given for refusing to face her husband. She has, after all, played both Mary and Martha to a forged Christ with a delirious martyr complex. As she explains, the Marquis "has spun a thread of light from evil, created holiness from filth he has gathered" (104). Therefore, her final speech is an extended portrait of Sade as a righteous paladin, but one cloaked in romantic images that are subtly cast off. Renée de Sade's only option is to don the plain habit of a nun, leaving her husband, and his aesthetic anti-theology, for a form of sensory hermitage.[27]

Mishima submerges, rather than foregrounds, issues of ethnicity in relation to the dilemma of a multicultural Christology. The events of *Madame de Sade* occur shortly before and after the French Revolution. The original production of the play, performed at Kinokuniya Hall in Tokyo on November 14, 1965, included a highly stylized rococo set and an all-Japanese cast attired in French costumes, speaking of religion and society in Japanese. Despite the historical, geographical, and cultural complexity of *Madame de Sade*, the European Catholic content in the play arises out of a Japanese playwright's desire to examine what occurs to imported religious icons and doctrines. Mishima presents a miscalculating mimesis of Catholic imagery, in which the face of Christ is overtaken by a sensual aesthetic fantasy. In the process, Mishima reveals that the identity of Christ — and Christian theology in general — is contorted when it is recontextualized in a new culture. We are left not with a "clear vision of the things of Christ," but instead with an *incohatio visionis*. In this sense, *Madame de Sade* might be read as a skeptical retort to Balthasar's claims about an art of transcendental truth which is universally accessible.

Thus, both Mishima and Endō, while depicting the intense psychomachia of their characters, reveal that an individual's religious belief and experience cannot operate outside of — and is always uneasily shaped by — historical and cultural circumstance. Rodrigues's spiritual identity at the conclusion of *Silence* is hybridized and characterized by irrecoverable contradictions: he wears the attire of Buddhism but maintains an internal commitment to Christianity. Meanwhile, the appendix to *Silence* is written by a Dutch bookkeeper, who records the imports and exports of his company at Nagasaki, dutifully documenting the units of barter and exchange in operation between Asia and Europe while criticizing Rodrigues in derisive asides. This banal tabulation of profit reminds the reader that Christianity in Japan was, at least to some degree, an extension of a market society and not simply the glorious product of missionary zeal. The French Revolution, in *Madame de Sade*, likewise acts as a social force of class consciousness that impinges on the selfish paschal dramas of the aristocratic Sades.[28]

As Haight suggests, the irresolvable dialogues typical of intercultural communication compel us to take account of Christology in the postmodern age. Haight argues that Jesus as symbol *and* sacrament, a God in semiotics as well as human revelation, must be approached with dynamic diversity. "[O]ne cannot, or at least should not, relate to Christ undialectically," he insists.[29] While Haight recognizes the importance of a theological aesthetics in intercultural communication on religious belief, he rejects any simple interpretation of Christic imagery. He writes, "The problem with a poetic and imaginative Christology lies not in the Christology itself, but a literalist misreading and misunderstanding of it."[30] Balthasar makes few concessions for cultural processes that alter authoritative versions of Christ, thereby rendering him a pluralistic man. While both Balthasar and Haight affirm Christ's centrality as the salvific link, the former privileges a universal form that is unchanging: "the general conceptual content must be held *in suspenso* in view of the uniqueness of this particular application."[31]

The Haight/Balthasar dilemma, one that Asian writers such as Mishima and Endō explore in terms of personal and cultural faith dynamics, raises difficult questions on the role that mediation and adaptation should play during the cultural transmission of Christianity. As noted above, Haight emphasizes the vital role of historical and cultural context in the reception of Christianity by non-Christian societies attempting to comprehend Christology.[32] That Endō supports Haight's approach is evident in his narration of the culturally embedded imaginations of diverse characters who encounter the humanness, not authoritative aloofness, of Christ. Endō would be less tolerant of Balthasar's tendency to discount the significant ways in which different cultures can speak into Christianity; for Balthasar, Christ is expressive law, and it is societies that must adapt themselves to him: the "human must adapt itself to his essential living holiness."[33] While Haight and Endō understand the human condition as universal in sin, they do not accept that Christology should be (or can be) privatized to suit the perspectives of one socio-cultural group.[34]

These two Japanese authors, negotiating this debate at the receiving end of Christian evangelization, do present irreconcilable visions of *imitatio Christi*. The inevitable multiplicity of the paschal face is apparent. A Christian might dismiss Mishima's version of Christ as an outgrowth of his atheism. Endō, however, presents the challenge of a Japanese convert. Indeed, as Endō notes in his discussion with Johnston, his own efforts to bridge cultural gaps between Japan and Europe invariably displeased either the Japanese or Europeans. He does not believe, however, that any particular group of Christians is excused from Psalm 105's exhortation to *seek his face*. As the various manifestations of Catholicism in Japanese literature demonstrate, *seeing the form* of Christ does not involve pure vision (*theoria*), because his form is always viewed through a series of cultural lenses. The paschal face cannot be sketched according to a single cultural world view, nor can its dynamic character be unchangingly affixed, as unicursal image, to a wooden cross.

Notes

1 Raymond Cohen, "Intercultural Dissonance: A Theoretical Framework," *Negotiating across Cultures: International Communication in an Interdependent World*, rev. ed. (Washington, DC: United States Institute of Peace Press, 2002) 3, 25.

2 Hans Urs von Balthasar, *Seeing the Form* (vol. 1 of *The Glory of the Lord: A Theological Aesthetics*), ed. Joseph Fessio and John Riches, trans. Erasmo Leiva-Merikakis (San Francisco: Ignatius Press, 1982) 253.

3 Simon Blackburn, "hypostatic union," *The Oxford Dictionary of Philosophy*, 2008, *Oxford Reference Online*, Oxford University Press.
4 Balthasar, *Seeing the Form*, 137.
5 Hans Urs von Balthasar, *Dare We Hope "That All Men Be Saved"?* (San Francisco: Ignatius Press, 1988). I would like to thank Jens Zimmermann for his insightful comments and references for my phrasing of Balthasar's relationship to Barth.
6 Balthasar, *Seeing the Form*, 576.
7 Roger Haight, *Jesus: Symbol of God* (Maryknoll, NY: Orbis, 2005).
8 Masuzawa Tomoko, *The Invention of World Religions* (Chicago: University of Chicago Press, 2005).
9 Yasuoka Shōtarō and Inoue Yōji, *Warera naze Kirisuto-kyōto to narishika* [*Why Did We Become Christians?*] (Tokyo: Kōbun-sha, 1999).
10 Endō seems to have shared Mishima's curiosity for the Marquis de Sade, having written a biography of the famous French anti-religionist (Francis Mathy, "Endō Shūsaku: White Man, Yellow Man," *Comparative Literature* 19.1 [1967]: 60).
11 Ellis Hanson, *Decadence and Catholicism* (Cambridge, MA: Harvard University Press, 1998) 27.
12 Endō Shūsaku, "Endō and Johnston Talk of Buddhism and Christianity," *America*, 171.16 (19 Nov. 1994): 18–20.
13 Endō Shūsaku, *A Life of Jesus*, trans. Richard A. Schuchert (New York: Paulist Press, 1978) 1.
14 Endō, "Endō and Johnston," 20.
15 Endō Shūsaku, *Silence*, trans. William Johnston (Marlboro, NJ: Taplinger, 1980) 12; future quotations from *Chinmoku*, or *Silence*, are from this edition and are referenced in the text by page number. I have also consulted the following Japanese edition: Endō Shūsaku, *Chinmoku*, 3 vols (Tokyo: Daikatsuji bunko, 2004).
16 Though the novel suggests that sacraments serve an important role in bringing the Word to Japan, Endō shows that despite the 300-year absence of the sacraments in Japan, the face of Christ remained in the minds of hidden believers.
17 Joseph Cardinal Ratzinger, *Pilgrim Fellowship of Faith: The Church as Communion*, ed. Stephan Otto Horn and Vinzenz Pfnür, trans. Henry Taylor (San Francisco, CA: Ignatius Press, 2002) 83.
18 Balthasar, *Seeing the Form*, 579.
19 Haight, *Jesus: Symbol of God*, 410.
20 Anscar Vonier, *A Key to the Doctrine of the Eucharist* (Bethesda, MD: Zaccheus, 2004) 32.
21 Haight, *Jesus: Symbol of God*, 429.
22 Inoue Yōji, *The Face of Jesus in Japan*, trans. Akamatsu Hisako (Tokyo: Kindai Bungei-sha, 1994) 3.
23 Haight, *Jesus: Symbol of God*, 420.
24 The *nō* drama *Sotoba komachi* also depicts this snowy martyrdom. Mishima had satirized academic interest in sado-masochism through the character of Imanishi Yasushi, a specialist in German literature, who appears as a pretentious dinner guest in *Temple of Dawn* [*Akatsuki no tera*] (1970).
25 See in particular *The Future of an Illusion* [*Die Zukunft einer Illusion*] (1927).
26 Mishima Yukio, *Madame de Sade*, trans. Donald Keene (New York: Grove Press, 1967) 107; future quotations are from this edition and will be referenced in the text

by page number. I have also consulted the following Japanese edition: Mishima Yukio, *Sado kōshaku fujin* [*Madame de Sade*] (Tokyo: Shinchō-sha, 2003).

27 Any discussion of martyrdom in Mishima's writing cannot avoid the biographical details of this writer's own act of seppuku, a ritual suicide. Mutaguchi Yoshirō, a correspondent for the *Asahi shinbun* in France, relayed the observations of a local priest concerning Mishima's very public demise: "He has been directing his life as if it were a play. He probably decided on a directed, aesthetic way of death to end his life" (qtd. in Darrell Houston, "The Mishima Incident: 'A Wasteful Way to Die,'" *APF Newsletters of Darrell Houston*, 4 Dec. 1970, http://www.aliciapatterson .org/APF001970/Houston/Houston07/Houston07.html).

28 Economically and historically, Francis Xavier, and his missionary influence, retains a strong presence in Kyūshū. Ōita City Hall features an enormous tableau depicting the arrival of the Portuguese. Nearby, at the train station, a statue commemorates the convert Ōtomo Sōrin. A popular rice cracker [*senbei*] is named Rosario, produced by a company named *Xavieru-d*.

29 Haight, *Jesus: Symbol of God*, 395, 457.

30 Ibid., 177.

31 Balthasar, *Seeing the Form*, 432.

32 Haight, *Jesus: Symbol of God*, 401.

33 Balthasar, *Seeing the Form*, 454.

34 Haight, *Jesus: Symbol of God*, 384. Haight's work was recently censured by Pope Benedict XVI (Joseph Ratzinger).

POSTMODERN AESTHETICS AND BEYOND

TESTIFYING TO THE INFINITY OF THE OTHER: THE SACRED AND ETHICAL DIMENSIONS OF SECONDARY WITNESSING IN ANNE KARPF'S *THE WAR AFTER*

Bettina Stumm

Witnessing is the fact of being present, observing something, and testifying to it.[1] In *Witnessing: Beyond Recognition*, Kelly Oliver observes that the practice of witnessing has both juridical and religious connotations: eyewitness testimony in a court of law testifies to that which can be seen, known, and told, while religious witnessing testifies to that "which cannot be seen," the ineffable otherness of an infinite and transcendent God.[2] In trauma and Holocaust studies, survivor testimonies tend to be approached in one of these two ways. Historians typically examine the testimonies of survivors within a juridical paradigm, as eyewitness accounts testifying to the veracity of the Holocaust event. Psychoanalytic and literary critics, alternatively, secularize a sacred conception of witnessing, as bearing witness to the incomprehensible suffering of trauma beyond that which can be expressed.

Dori Laub addresses this tension in his reflection on a lively debate between historians and psychoanalysts responding to a survivor's account of the Auschwitz uprising. At issue was the veracity of the survivor's testimony regarding the number of chimneys that had exploded during the revolt: she reported four chimneys going up in flames, but in fact only one had been consumed in the fiery explosion. The historians in the room argued that her testimony should be discredited because she was an unreliable witness. They were listening for the empirical facts of her testimony and felt they could not give her account credence if those facts were inaccurate. Laub, a psychoanalyst who interviewed the survivor, contests their position suggesting that she was bearing witness to something in her experience *beyond* the facts. "The woman was testifying, not to the number of chimneys blown up," he insists, "but to something else, more radical, more crucial: the reality of an unimaginable occurrence."[3] The fact that any chimneys were blown up in Auschwitz at all, he argues, was so incredible that it broke the imprisoning framework of that place for her, even if only momentarily: "She was testifying . . . to the very secret of survival and of resistance to extermination" in Auschwitz signified by that event.[4]

The distinction between these two approaches to testimony illuminates the multi-faceted nature of truth involved in witnessing: it is a matter of fact and experience, objectivity and subjectivity, the knowable and the incomprehensible, the seen and the unimaginable. The truth of testimony depends precisely on what the survivor is bearing witness to in a given context and how that event has been integrated and reformulated in her memory. Consequently, both dimensions of witnessing — the finite occurrence of trauma and the infinite qualities of the survivor and her experiences — are critical to the study of survivor testimonies and memories of trauma. And yet, for those like Laub and the historians who witness such testimonies, negotiating the facts of a specific event with the survivor's personal experience, memory, and telling of it proves difficult, to say the least. How does one witness the testimony of others without dismissing their stories as historically misleading or venerating their traumatic experiences as purely ineffable? How does one witness the proximate person giving testimony without over-identifying with her trauma or losing her personhood in the facts of her experience?

In this study, I focus on the position of the one who bears witness to the survivor, on the "second person" or secondary witness who hears and responds to the survivor's testimony and personhood.[5] These witnesses are separated from the Holocaust event but proximate to the survivor and implicated in her testimony through the dialogical process of its telling. In this witnessing relationship, the survivor's experience is completely "other" to the secondary witness, an "unimaginable occurrence" beyond what he can see and comprehend either factually or experientially. Likewise, the aspects of a survivor's personhood determined by the trauma remain inaccessible to the secondary witness. To negotiate this space between proximity and otherness is difficult for any secondary witness, as Laub illustrates. It requires navigating between what one already knows about the Nazi genocide or already feels in empathy with its survivors and what evades one's knowledge, emotional affinity, and assumptions of personal connection. But arguably, negotiating this space is most complicated in filial relationships, where children of survivors are intimately connected to and profoundly implicated in their parents' lives and stories of suffering. Their parents' traumatic memories are invariably passed down to them, becoming an inherited form of suffering that defines their own life narratives. In this process of *postmemory*, as Marianne Hirsch calls it, their own "needs, desires, and cares fade out in relation to the stories that surround [them]."[6] This relational proximity, identification, and kinship with their parents threatens to overwhelm the infinite qualities of their parents' past experiences and collapse the necessary distance between their identities. In light of these particular problems, what is the role of ineffability and the quality of infinity in one's relationship with others and their stories of trauma? How can secondary witnesses—particularly the children of survivors—bear witness to such "otherness" ethically and bring it to bear on what can be seen and known of the other person's experience and personhood?

The religious and ethical philosophy of Emmanuel Levinas seems a fruitful starting point from which to examine these questions. Described as a "thinker of testimony," Levinas develops a framework for witnessing the sacred—the unseen, incomprehensible mystery of divine otherness—in order to describe the significance of infinity for the ethics of bearing witness to others.[7] In *Ethics and Infinity* and *Otherwise Than Being*, Levinas reveals how witnessing the absolute alterity of a divine Other functions as a paradigm for ethical encounters between humans, particularly in response to those who are suffering or victimized. Himself a survivor of Nazism, he contends that engaging ethically with others requires awakening to them and acknowledging their complete alterity so as not to reduce them to a particular identity or category within a totalizing system of thought. Such an awakening to otherness disrupts sociopolitical schemas because it radically challenges one's own subjectivity in relation to others. To bear witness ethically, my "I" is destabilized so that I can truly testify to that which is infinite about the other, outside and beyond me.

In light of Levinas's insights, I argue that secondary witnesses necessarily participate in the ethical task of testifying to that which cannot be seen or known about survivors and their suffering. At the same time, however, secondary witnessing proves a relationally fraught and ethically complicated practice precisely in its appropriation of a sacred paradigm to witness another's trauma. For children of survivors particularly, that which is "infinite" about their parents' suffering *is* transmitted and tangled together with their own filial identity and relational connection to their parents. In her memoir, *The War After: Living with the Holocaust*, Anne Karpf speaks precisely to this dilemma. She relates how as a child of survivors growing up in England, she struggles to negotiate the generational proximity and distance between her parents and herself and to distinguish her identity from that of her parents' suffering. Her narrative illustrates how children of survivors are challenged by Levinas's witnessing posture of speaking to the infinity of "the other" in their proximate relationships with their parents and within the finite context of Holocaust narrative.[8] To what extent, then, might Levinas's metaphysical ethics of testimony translate the practical and personal experiences of witnessing another's trauma in this filial context?

Levinas on Infinity: The Sacred Dimension of Testimony

Levinas's ethics is motivated by socio-political failure: the domination of National Socialism, the Jewish Holocaust, and the Second World War. He introduces *Totality and Infinity* by observing the problem of war and the human tendency towards it. For him, war is the inevitable result of a system of politics or philosophy that tries to make itself complete in itself, what he calls *totality*. If totality can be defined as "a whole that integrates its parts," then any relationship among beings that destroys alterity by integrating others into "the same" is totalizing.[9] Simon Critchley draws attention to the intimate connection Levinas makes between political and philosophical totalities, pointing out that "the category of totality in Western philosophy, from the ancient Greeks to Heidegger, is linked to the domination of totalizing forms of politics."[10] For instance, Levinas perceives in Heidegger's ontological study of *Dasein* a totalizing position of *being for-itself*, a comprehensive mastery over being that reduces others to objects of one's own consciousness.[11] This "being for-itself," Levinas argues, is marked by self-interest and "takes dramatic form in egoisms struggling with one another, each against all, in the multiplicity of allergic egoisms which are at war with one another."[12] Indeed, such egoistic struggle leads to a state of war when applied on a political or national scale. In response, Levinas proposes an ethical state of peace that evades being for-one-self or systems of thought that rest on being for its own sake. "Being," he challenges, "is never its own reason for being,"[13] and as Richard Cohen adds, neither is "the human ... the measure" or the "source of all right and all meaning."[14] Consequently, engaging peaceably and ethically with others requires that being be interrupted or opened up by something wholly other, beyond being, and overflowing being as a surplus. Levinas calls this surplus "infinity."[15]

For Levinas, infinity is a defining attribute of God. God overflows the totalities of self and the limits of human systems of knowledge and representation. As Alphonso Lingis explains, "God, the Infinite, is properly neither designated by words nor even indicated or named."[16] The infinity or glory of God cannot be thematized or grasped but appears solely as a trace in language, in my own voice and words. The only suitable human response to infinity, then, is to bear witness or testify to it. Using the biblical prophets as an exemplar, Levinas argues that the testimony par excellence is "here I am" to the call of the Infinite Other. To say "here I am" is not an act of self-positing or reinforcement of being. Rather, in keeping with the double meaning of the German *es gibt* (being and giving), it is giving oneself over to the Other.[17] "Here I am" is an affirmation of being in the availability of giving oneself, a self signified by generosity and sacrifice.[18] As revealed in the responses of Abraham, Moses, Samuel, and Isaiah, "here I am" signifies obedience and passivity to God *before* knowing what the request is.[19] These biblical figures exemplify how testifying to infinity is an act of stepping out "here" into the open in front of the other, exposing oneself to listen, respond, and be fully available to another: to God and by extension to other people. To say "here I am" to the summons of an infinite God requires the response "here I am" to that which is infinite in my neighbour.

Like God, but on a finite scale, my neighbour interrupts my being. Levinas describes this interruption as a "trauma" that wounds my self-interest, opens me to alterity, and challenges my impulse to totalize him for my own sake.[20] Such trauma is, from his perspective, the necessary precursor to ethical responsibility. My neighbour resists my representations and themes. He cannot be apprehended in my gaze, mastered in mind, or intuited by my emotions. To do so would be to subsume his otherness in myself and to war against him, exactly the unethical position that Levinas contests. When I respond "here I am" to my neighbour I testify to the infinite in him by giving myself for him before thinking about it, before knowing the request, and before calculating the cost.[21] I am opened to him, making myself vulnerable to his suffering and subject to his summons. By this very opening, however, I equally risk the possibility of being wounded or oppressed by him. The other can use my passivity against me. The trauma of vulnerability is the perpetual gamble of responsibility, the risk inherent in giving myself to promote peaceful interactions between us. As Levinas puts it, in being given-over to my neighbour, "I announce peace, that is, my responsibility for the other."[22] "Here I am" is therefore *both* an ethical bearing towards the other, in which I open up my being for-myself to respond to the divine call or human need, *and* a testimony to the other's infinity and my incapability of apprehending or thematizing him or her. In short, to attest to the other's infinity *is* to bear oneself ethically towards him or her in a finite way.

Trauma Testimony: Conceptions of the Sacred Sublime

Where Levinas's description of testimony focuses on the infinity of the person in need, trauma theory centres on the infinity of suffering itself as the basis for determining how to witness the survivor ethically. Trauma theorists address the infinite nature of this suffering in at least two ways. First, traumatic suffering is described in terms of a secular and negative infinite: a stimulus that interrupts or breaches one's personhood and exceeds one's ability to fully grasp, integrate, or represent it.[23] Second, one's experience of another person's trauma is described as infinite: secondary witnesses outside the experience cannot apprehend or understand a suffering not their own. Testifying to trauma means testifying to these dimensions of infinite otherness in one's own or another's experience of suffering. Studies in Holocaust trauma have expressed this infinite excess in religious terminology, translating *infinity* into the *sacred*, that which is unspeakable or unnameable, and the *sublime*, that which transcends apprehension, representation, or comprehension. Dominick LaCapra discerns that trauma, and its preoccupations with aporias, hiddenness, death, or absence, involves "a more or less secularized displacement of the sacred and its paradoxes" and may translate certain events as "occasions of negative sublimity."[24] He explains that, not unlike the religious sublime, an ambivalent relation to "a hidden, radically transcendent divinity," the secular sublime "is evoked by [a] near-death experience, by coming to the brink of the abyss or of annihilation while escaping death and destruction oneself," as for survivors of the Holocaust.[25] As a result, Anne Karpf observes, "[i]t's hard to speak about Holocaust survivors in anything but a reverent tone or without turning their suffering into a sacrament" (249).

Secondary witnesses often find themselves at a loss to respond to the survivor outside a sacred paradigm. Trauma appears to form its own kind of religion, and one's intimate bond with its victims demands fidelity: one may feel obligated to keep faith with the trauma in order not to betray its sufferers. Survivors seem not unlike a congregation whose suffering and survival become valorized as the basis for their personal or group identity.[26] Secondary witnesses may want to join in or to question its dictates, but feel hardly traumatized enough for membership. Furthermore, being outside the trauma, on what authority can secondary witnesses speak it? When the infinite dimension of trauma is elevated to the status of the negative sublime, it becomes a totalizing infinity, a complete separation or aporia that cannot be bridged and therefore runs the risk of creating indifference or even aversion to its sufferers. Clearly this negative sublimity is a mistaken extreme of the infinite aspect of trauma, in which the interrupting otherness of trauma is taken for the whole understanding of suffering at the expense of that which *can* be known, imagined, and represented. Keeping such an excessive faith, LaCapra cautions, may in fact function to separate the survivor and his or her experience from others entirely and perpetuate his or her trauma.

When trauma *is* regarded as radically other, transmitting it to others proves an impossible task. Indeed, some trauma theorists suggest that Holocaust trauma, as an experience of the sublime, *cannot* be testified; that central to the experience is precisely the collapse of witnessing.[27] Victims of trauma are left "expressionless." Through crisis experiences or the violence of others, they have been reduced to silence, eclipsed, or treated as if already dead.[28] Trauma, however, cannot be defined exclusively in the negative as inexpressible or unrepresentable excess: many survivors are capable of expressing and feel morally compelled to express their trauma, though, granted, with indescribable elements.[29] Infinity describes the specific inabilities and gaps that interrupt language or comprehension that are inevitably part of any testimony of trauma, but it becomes problematic as the sole means by which to describe a finite traumatic event. Theorists such as Cathy Caruth and Laub more convincingly convey the traumatic experience as a story that *can* be transmitted but not fully understood. Caruth explains that, as part of their testimonies, survivors transmit a gap or a silence that is inaccessible to platitudes or projects of knowledge about the Holocaust but is not inexpressible per se.[30] As a result, secondary witnesses encounter something in a survivor's testimony of trauma that *could* be described as "infinitely other." Since secondary witnesses were not there—separated by time, space, and experience from the Holocaust event— the survivor's trauma *is* wholly other to them. But at the same time, in the act of testifying, the survivor is proximate and brings the traumatic experience near to the secondary witness. In light of this witnessing space between distance and proximity, secondary witnesses are called by survivors to respond ethically. These witnesses are summoned by the testimony of the survivor, as an expression of infinite otherness that interrupts their self-enclosed world and turns them outward to listen and respond.[31] They face the "trauma," in Levinas's ethical sense of the term, of being made to bear the infinite otherness of those suffering from a catastrophic event and its painful memories.[32] To respond ethically to the other person's suffering, the secondary witness who was not there testifies "here I am." Ideally, this testimony refuses the human inclination to project onto the other's infinity expressions of one's own selfhood: what *I* know or feel about your trauma. Rather it represents the possibility of opening one's self to be available for-the-other before mastering the trauma with concepts, over-empathizing with the survivor's experiences, or foreclosing the survivor's testimony by what one "already knows" about the Holocaust.

Secondary Witnessing: Necessary Infinity in Proximity

Considered in the abstract, the interruption of infinity is necessary for an ethical response to the survivor. In practice, however, an ethics of testifying "here I am" to the infinity of the other and his or her experience is a highly vexed, problematic, and perhaps even an impossible responsibility. Secondary witnesses strive for ethical bearing and response but continually fall short of this kind of posture towards survivors. Perhaps the reason is obvious. Witnessing others is inescapably self-referential: I experience others for myself through my sensory perceptions and identification with them, seeing them in relation *to me*. In Levinas's terms, secondary witnesses must contend with being for-oneself in witnessing others. This inherent self-centredness, Primo Levi observes, "is more pronounced the more distant [the other's] experiences are" from one's own.[33] Secondary witnesses are apt to assimilate the unfamiliar to that which they have experienced or can understand, "as if the hunger in Auschwitz were the same as that of someone who has skipped a meal, or as if escape from Treblinka were similar to an escape from any ordinary jail."[34] While an ethics for-the-other interrupts the human tendency towards being for-oneself, it cannot eradicate or abolish it. Hence, the witness condition fluctuates between a self-centred experience of the other person and moments of self-sacrifice in being given over for his or her sake.

Such oscillations can be seen in the narrative testimonies of the second generation (the children of Holocaust survivors), and their complications are explicitly revealed in Karpf's The War After. Above all, her narrative reveals the difficulty of ethically navigating the relational space between oneself and another. As she attempts to negotiate between herself and her parents, her personal suffering and her parents' verbal and non-verbal expressions of trauma, Karpf reveals her struggle with over-identifying with her parents' past and collapsing the infinity of their identities and experiences into her own. As a result, she finds it difficult to testify ethically to her parents, construing the ethical "here I am" as overextending herself to compensate for her parents' trauma. I will briefly touch on each of these struggles in order to illustrate the ethical necessity of infinity for negotiating the space between self and survivor.

Karpf's identity is inextricably linked to her parents' trauma, as their daughter and as a Jew. The title of the narrative itself, The War After, blurs the boundaries between identities: whose war after? Her parents' war with the memories of their Holocaust experiences? Or Karpf's own battle with her parents' past, her relationship to them, and her Jewish heritage? The narrative suggests both, though the focus is on Karpf's war, her struggle for an identity beyond her parents' trauma. In this struggle, she feels the infinity of their trauma as an unmovable burden and wants to collapse it, carry it, be included in it, or eliminate it somehow. Situated between her parents and herself, their Holocaust trauma acts both as a gap that she cannot bridge and a tether from which she cannot break free. It is the principal measure by which she gauges and evaluates her identity and her experiences.

Karpf determines her identity both against her parents' trauma and in relation to it and alternates between the two in her memoir. Most obviously, she defines herself against a trauma she has never experienced personally, feeling both envious of it and guilty for being exempt from it. As she confesses, "I'd always envied my parents their suffering," clarifying that this envy does not stem from an underestimation of the war's horrors or a masochistic seeking of pain, but from her inability to share in the history and experiences of her parents (126). "It was so excluding and unsharable," she laments. "It had originated before we were born, wasn't caused by us and, however much we tried, we would never be able to take it away" (126). Alongside her envy to be included, she resents that the horror and significance of her parents' trauma renders her suffering — a debilitating case of eczema, the loss of a lover, and an identity crisis — trivial or illegitimate in comparison. "Their terrible experiences," she writes, "seemed to diminish — even to taunt — anything bad which happened to us. In its drama, enormity, and significance, their war could never be matched" (126). At the same time, she feels guilty that she has been spared the suffering of her parents and alternates between creating her own discomfort and excluding happiness from her life to make up for it. In her guilt, the question, "[H]ow could you feel bad if you weren't in a concentration camp?" plagues her and functions as the rod she uses to punish herself: her "bad" is never as bad as her parents' and her "good" must make up for their bad (100).

In light of her feelings of exclusion, Karpf turns to identify herself by aligning her parents' suffering with her own. In her bouts of eczema, she literally embodies trauma in the self-inflicted wounds she scratches into her skin, wounds she at once despises and desires. Through them, she feels victim enough to access and procure something of her mother's trauma for herself: "It was as if I'd finally managed to prise off some particle of my mother's suffering and make it my own," she writes reflectively. "I'd grafted onto myself a bit of her pain" (126). Making pain the grounds on which to relate to her mother and assert herself within that relationship, she writes that eczema gives her a legitimate misery of her own: "Now, as well as feeling like a victim, I'd also acquired something to feel a victim about — I'd found an objective correlative (the best I could manage)" (126–27). By genuinely suffering herself, she feels kinship with her mother and included in the experience of feeling pain, despite the different form her pain takes.

Karpf further appropriates her mother's Holocaust trauma by narrating it to others. Deriving for herself "a bit" of her mother's pain, Karpf secures a "second-hand compassion" from others in telling and retelling her mother's story (95). In its successive tellings, she perceives it taking on an overdramatic and mythical quality that drifts from the events themselves. It becomes her version of the story, witnessed for her own benefit. She confesses that she uses her mother's life to "enthral and appal," a talent which "endowed [her] (in other people's eyes) with a kind of reflected martyrdom," although she admits that it leaves her with a "sour aftertaste" (94–95). The need to connect herself with her parents' suffering, however, appears stronger than her guilt for appropriating it. Her own suffering and her renditions of her mother's story are ways of sharing in a trauma not her own and removing the burden of its infinity that separates her from her parents.

Perhaps Karpf reveals her struggle with over-identification most explicitly in her fear of suffering any kind of loss, especially losing another person in death. Her fear of loss results in a literal inability to separate herself from her parents or to deal with endings of any kind. As she describes:

> Until an indecently advanced age, I was unable to imagine myself surviving away from my parents, or them without me. So chronic was this fear of separation and rupture (to me they were equivalent) that I balked at endings of any kind.... I treated all partings *as if* they were final: wherever you were going, you might never come back. When people packed during the war, they rarely did come back: my parents' life was full of such sudden fractures.... It was as if my parents' experience had become my own; I'd soaked up their fear of loss. (44)

Her parent's reality of loss becomes the fearful "what if" of loss in Karpf's life, *as if* what happened to them could happen to her. She later extends this fear of loss to postwar Jews in general, observing how they all seemed stalked by a sense of "what if" (315). As she applies this general fear of loss to the specific inability of separating from her parents, Karpf blurs the boundaries that distinguish her identity from her parents' suffering, collapsing the infinite aspects of her parents' trauma with her finite experiences and fears. Her response proves to be ethically fraught not through any malicious intention on her part, but because she is uncertain about who she is outside the context of her relationship with her parents and their suffering. Only later does she come to realize that she has mis-negotiated the space between her parents and herself. As she explains, she had confused intimacy with another person and merging with him or her, regarding "any kind of separateness or difference as threatening" (127).

Due to her overly intimate relationship with her parents, Karpf struggles to witness them and their suffering ethically. Responding "here I am" from her position of extreme identification means either taking on their experiences *as if* she could be them or successfully making up for and healing their losses. She describes herself wishing she could "take over some of [her] parents' bodily functions—[eating] for them, [breathing] for them. Or failing this, [suffering] for them" (53). But even success would not be enough: "I would never be able to match them in suffering" (53). This seemingly ethical stance of giving oneself over for the sake of another or suffering for-the-other is in actuality shot through with being for-itself, in this case, Karpf's own consuming need to suffer and her sense of guilt for not being capable of taking on someone else's pain. For Karpf, the responsibility to give herself and bear the pain of her parents becomes more about her and her inabilities—her failure to identify or suffer enough—than about her parents and their experiences. In a telling statement, she reveals this shift from other to self: "I came to abominate what [my mother] had been through no longer on her account, but on ours. Was everything she said and did beyond reproach because of her past" (38)? Karpf begins to resent the feeling that she needs to keep the peace—her adolescent interpretation of what giving herself up for them should look like—by avoiding conflicts with and criticism of her parents because of their past. This "keeping the peace" with resentment or fear brewing under the surface is a poor reflection of the ethical peace with others that Levinas espouses. Karpf's difficulty in ethically giving herself raises some important questions for determining what existential generosity in such contexts might entail: Where is the line between taking on another's pain and taking it over? How does one negotiate between ethical and self-centred peacekeeping? Does criticism or critique of the survivor's shortcomings factor into the ethical self-giving of "here I am"? Or does a survivor's past sufferings somehow cancel out his or her current failings or offences? Giving oneself for another becomes a blurry ethics in practice, primarily because it cannot be divided from the giver's perception of others' suffering and her position in relation to that suffering: what is the actual need, what must giving look like, what should it accomplish, and how is the sufferer expected to respond to it?

In struggling with her self-assigned role for peacekeeping and her need to take her parents' suffering upon herself, Karpf describes what she sees as her responsibility to bandage, fix, and make up for her parents' losses. Despite the fact that her parents seemed invincible—survivors characterized by optimism, energy, and animation—she senses their fragility: "They were like mended figurines liable to rebreak," she recalls. "We knew we played a critical role as their glue" (15). She describes her love as "a kind of bandage" meant to restore and compensate for her parents' losses (39), a tendency, she notes, common to children of survivors (231): "I think we understood from a very young age that we must look after them, or something bad could happen. We tried to keep them alive" (17). While empathically identifying with the suffering of others is arguably part of an ethical stance, Karpf's interpretation of ethical responsibility without the necessary infinity of her parents' personhood and their experiences becomes *solely* one of identification. Being given over results in over-giving herself for them.

And yet, throughout the course of her memoir, Karpf reveals that this self-imposed responsibility for her parents is repeatedly ruptured by actual calls of infinity. The actual other and concrete suffering keep interrupting her assumptions of ethical responsibility and suffering for the other. Two particular disruptions stand out. First, Karpf's vision of her parents' past and their geographical history are dismantled when she visits her parents' homeland of Poland. The place names and maps reflect her imaginings, and some of the sites—like her mother's house—still remain intact. However, Karpf discovers that the actual places—their changes over time and their present state—interrupt her expectations and her mythological rendering of them based on her parents' stories. Even where certain sites, like Auschwitz, remain, she finds that time has buried its events and its sorrows. She apprehends that she had "confused time and place, history and geography, as if coming in person to the site of terrible events which occurred fifty years ago could somehow yield them up to transform them" (300). This journey is one in which she realizes that she has reduced her parents' experience to a sentimentalized, mythologized, and even totalizing pre-war Jewish existence (303).

Second, Karpf's experience of the death of her father, her first concrete loss of a loved one, challenges her fears of separation and death. In her journal entries covering his deterioration and death, she recalls how she spent her childhood terrified that her parents would die and compares her fear to its painful and ordinary reality thirty years later: "[T]his drama is being played out and it's just a normal part of life" (268). In fact, she is able to write a year later how the experience of his passing had shifted her from fearing to accepting death as a natural part of living: "The fear that my father might die has been replaced by the knowledge that my mother—and P, and me, and even B —undeniably will.... For the first time, I recognise the meaning of the term 'a natural death'; death to me no longer seems necessarily unnatural" (282). She is surprised and even relieved to discover that her fears of death and loss do not resemble its reality and that she could move "death" from the centre of her life to the end, where it belonged (317). In these two experiences, Karpf is awakened to find infinity as an essential separation between herself and her parents, necessary for creating her own identity and responding to the actual, and not merely the feared or imagined, needs of others. As she concludes, "surveying things now, I can't believe how much connectedness and separateness I've attained" (317).

Karpf's memoir reveals that when we, naturally being for-ourselves, attempt to practice ethical responsibility for-the-other, this practice is even at its best shot through with self-centred interpretations of the other's call and one's own response. Since testimony is rooted in one's subject position and experiences, it inevitably slides between over-identification with the other, as Karpf illustrates, or exclusion from the other. Her account shows that actual ethical response comes in the interruption, in those moments of awakening that not only destabilize one's projections, imaginings, and fears about others, but also one's ethical ideals and self-directed acts of responsibility towards them. In these moments, she is surprised to find herself responding from what seems to me a Levinasian posture of "here I am," beyond what she thinks she sees, expects, or knows. She bears witness to the infinite by testifying to the actual people, places, and incidents that unsettle her assumptions and conceptions of her parents' Holocaust and cause her to revise her own implication in and inheritance of their trauma. To testify to the infinity of others practically, as her narrative shows, is not an ethical prescription for responsible interaction but a matter of being open to the way other people and actual experiences not only disrupt how one sees and knows them, but also how one sees and knows oneself.

Notes

1 "Witnessing," *The Canadian Oxford English Dictionary*, 1998.
2 Kelly Oliver, *Witnessing: Beyond Recognition* (Minneapolis: University of Minnesota Press, 2001) 16.
3 Dori Laub, "Bearing Witness, or the Vicissitudes of Listening," *Testimony: Crises of Witnessing in Literature, Psychoanalysis, and History*, ed. Shoshana Felman and Dori Laub (London and New York: Routledge, 1992) 60.
4 Ibid., 62.
5 Gillian Whitlock, "In the Second Person: Narrative Transactions in Stolen Generations Testimony," *Biography* 24.1 (2001): 199.
6 Marianne Hirsch, "Projected Memory: Holocaust Photographs in Personal and Public Fantasy," *Acts of Memory: Cultural Recall in the Present*, ed. Mieke Bal, Jonathan Crewe, and Leo Spitzer (Hanover, NH: University Press of New England, 1999) 8.
7 Paul Ricoeur, "Emmanuel Levinas: Thinker of Testimony," *Figuring the Sacred: Religion, Narrative, and Imagination* (Minneapolis, MN: Fortress, 1995) 108.
8 Anne Karpf, *The War After: Living with the Holocaust* (London: Heinemann, 1996); future citations from *The War After* are from this edition and are referenced in the text by page number.
9 William Schroeder, "Continental Ethics," *The Blackwell Guide to Ethical Theory*, ed. Hugh LaFollette (Oxford: Blackwell, 2000) 392. In *Totality and Infinity*, Levinas points to the totalizing force of my comprehension (subsuming the other in the self), representation (presenting the other as the same), being at home (belonging to me or possessed by me), freedom (capricious spontaneity of my own free will), and history (totalizing being in time), to name just a few.
10 Simon Critchley, introduction, *The Cambridge Companion to Levinas*, ed. Robert Bernasconi and Simon Critchley (Cambridge: Cambridge University Press, 2002) 24. For further discussion on the political dimensions of Levinas's thought, see Bettina Bergo, *Levinas between Ethics and Politics: For the Beauty That Adorns the Earth* (Dordrecht, Neth.: Kluwer, 1999); Robert Gibbs, "Philosophy and Law: Questioning Justice," *The Ethical*, ed. Edith Wyschogrod and Gerald P. McKenny (London: Blackwell, 2003) 101–16; and Asher Horowitz and Gad Horowitz, eds., *Difficult Justice: Commentaries on Levinas and Politics* (Toronto: University of Toronto Press, 2006).
11 For further discussion see Emmanuel Levinas, "Intention, Event, and the Other," *Is It Righteous to Be? Interviews with Emmanuel Levinas*, ed. Jill Robbins, trans. Andrew Schmitz (Stanford, CA: Stanford University Press, 2001) 140–57.
12 Emmanuel Levinas, *Otherwise Than Being or Beyond Essence*, trans. Alphonso Lingis (Pittsburgh: Duquesne University Press, 1998) 4.
13 Emmanuel Levinas, *Ethics and Infinity: Conversations with Philippe Nemo*, trans. Richard A. Cohen (Pittsburgh: Duquesne University Press, 1985) 123.
14 Richard A. Cohen, "Ricoeur and the Lure of Self-Esteem," ch. 9 of *Ethics, Exegesis and Philosophy: Interpretation after Levinas* (Cambridge: Cambridge University Press, 2001) 316.
15 Emmanuel Levinas, *Totality and Infinity: An Essay on Exteriority*, trans. Alphonso Lingis (The Hague: Martinus Nijhoff, 1979) 23.
16 Alphonso Lingis, translator's introduction, *Otherwise Than Being or Beyond Essence*, by Emmanuel Levinas (The Hague: Martinus Nijhoff, 1981) xxxiv.

17 Ricoeur, "Emmanuel Levinas, Thinker of Testimony," 125.

18 Indeed, in both its Hebrew rendering, *hineni*, and in the French, *me voici*, "here I am" is not a reference to oneself in the nominative, but the subject grammatically in the accusative. Levinas extends this grammar to signify an ethical position of the subject in this passive tense: assigned, accused, brought into question, subjected to the call of the other, and suffering for the sake of another. In shifting "here I am" from a statement of self-assertion to self-sacrifice, Levinas relegates the self to a passive, submissive, and responsive position in relation to the infinite Other. For further discussion, see Oona Ajzenstat, *Driven Back to the Text: The Premodern Sources of Levinas' Postmodernism* (Pittsburgh: Duquesne University Press, 2001).

19 Emmanuel Levinas, "God and Philosophy," *The Levinas Reader*, ed. Seán Hand, trans. Richard A. Cohen (Oxford: Blackwell, 1989) 184.

20 Levinas, *Otherwise Than Being*, 19.

21 Ibid., 150.

22 Levinas, "God and Philosophy," 185.

23 Mary S. Cerney, "Treating the 'Heroic Treaters,'" *Compassion Fatigue: Coping with Secondary Traumatic Stress Disorder in Those Who Treat the Traumatized*, ed. Charles R. Figley (London: Brunner-Routledge, 1995) 131.

24 Dominick LaCapra, *Writing History, Writing Trauma* (Baltimore: Johns Hopkins University Press, 2001) 23. For further discussion on the language of the sacred or sublime in relation to Holocaust suffering, see Thomas Trezise's article "Unspeakable," *Yale Journal of Criticism* 14.1 (2001): 39–66; and Michael Bernard-Donals and Richard Glejzer's chapters, "Sublimity, Redemption, Witness" and "Museums and the Imperative of Memory: History, Sublimity, and the Divine" in their co-authored book, *Between Witness and Testimony: The Holocaust and the Limits of Representation* (Albany: State University of New York Press, 2001).

25 Dominick LaCapra, *History and Memory after Auschwitz* (Ithaca, NY: Cornell University Press, 1998) 35.

26 LaCapra, *Writing History, Writing Trauma*, 23.

27 Dori Laub, "Truth and Testimony: The Process and the Struggle," *Trauma: Explorations in Memory*, ed. Cathy Caruth (Baltimore: Johns Hopkins University Press, 1995) 65–66.

28 Shoshana Felman, *The Juridical Unconscious: Trials and Traumas in the Twentieth Century* (Cambridge, MA: Harvard University Press, 2002) 13–14.

29 Ibid., 93.

30 Cathy Caruth, introduction, *Trauma: Explorations in Memory*, ed. Cathy Caruth (Baltimore: Johns Hopkins University Press, 1995) 3–12.

31 Levinas, *Otherwise Than Being*, 141.

32 Notably, this ethical sense of trauma is not the same as "vicarious trauma," the firsthand trauma of others empathically (and often problematically) assumed or appropriated by many secondary witnesses. For further discussion on vicarious trauma, see E. Ann Kaplan, "Vicarious Trauma and 'Empty' Empathy," *Trauma Culture: The Politics of Terror and Loss in Media and Literature* (New Brunswick, NJ: Rutgers University Press, 2005) 87–100.

33 Primo Levi, *The Drowned and the Saved*, trans. Raymond Rosenthal (New York: Vintage, 1989) 158.

34 Ibid.

SACRED SPACE AND THE FELLOWSHIP OF SUFFERING IN THE POSTMODERN SUBLIME

Richard J. Lane

One of the intriguing aspects of the turn to religion in contemporary theory is the way in which much of the new work conforms to now normative deconstructive strictures, rather than adopting any particular faith perspective; I argue that this conforming, as it is staged in the postmodern sublime, is a foreclosure of the sacred, but in turn, such a foreclosure inadvertently reveals the constitutive nature of the sacred for the postmodern sublime, as well as the eschatological tension which is its time. My argument is that entering the sacred space of the postmodern sublime is to expose oneself to the possibility not of conforming to mundane deconstructive strictures, but of being conformed per se (συμμορφίζομαι). What are we conformed to? The answer may be to the fellowship of suffering, as the Apostle Paul puts it (Phil. 3:10).[1]

What is the postmodern sublime? Following Jean-François Lyotard, the postmodern sublime is "the presentation of the unpresentable in presentation itself."[2] A slightly longer quotation from Lyotard reveals a difference between the modern and postmodern:

> Here, then, lies the difference: modern aesthetics is an aesthetics of the sublime, though a nostalgic one. It allows the unpresentable to be put forward only as the missing contents; but the form, because of its recognizable consistency, continues to offer the reader or viewer matter for solace and pleasure. The postmodern would

be that which, in the modern, puts forward the unpresentable in presentation itself; that which denies itself the solace of good forms, the consensus of taste which would make it possible to share collectively the nostalgia for the unattainable; that which searches for new presentations, not in order to enjoy them but in order to impart a stronger sense of the unpresentable.[3]

In two key essays on Barnett Newman — "The Sublime and the Avant Garde" and "Newman: The Instant" — Lyotard argues that the site of the sublime has a complex spatiality and temporality; the "now" of Newman's work can be related to creation per se, or, the now is site-specific, where there is an intersection of time, place, and *name*: "Newman's time was the *Makom* or the *Hamakom* of Hebraic tradition — the *there*, the site, the place, which is one of the names given by the Torah to the Lord, the Unnameable."[4] Naming as a process of unnameability, like "the presentation of the unpresentable in presentation itself," collapses or condenses the spacing or sequencing of narrative into a moment. Lyotard's striking example of this moment is the *Akedah*, Abraham's binding of Isaac in Genesis 22:1–18. As Lyotard says in reference to Newman's painting and the *Akedah*:

> The time of what is recounted (the flash of the knife raised against Isaac) and the time taken to recount that time (the corresponding verses of Genesis) cease to be dissociated. They are condensed into the plastic (linear, chromatic, rhythmic) instant that *is* the painting. [Thomas B.] Hess would say that the painting rises up (*se dresse*), like the appeal from the Lord that stays the hand of Abraham. One might say … in more sober terms that it arises, just as an occurrence arises. The picture presents the presentation, being offers itself up in the here and now.[5]

From a contemporary theoretical perspective it is remarkable that the "instant" whereby the spacing and the moment are "condensed" is the event of the *Akedah*, one of the core narratives within the book of Genesis. At a practical level, Lyotard merely draws upon the logic of the *Akedah* to explain a particular painting; yet at a more profound level, Lyotard is asserting that the *Akedah* binds time (narrative sequence) and place, where "place" is the unnameable name of the Lord. The *Akedah*, however, does more than bind together narrative, place, and name: in a typological reading it also binds the two covenants, with Isaac standing in for, or prefiguring, the sacrifice of Christ.[6] Why does Lyotard not recognize Christ here? This is an example of the foreclosure of the sacred in the post-structuralist dwelling upon suffering, a gesture that Jacques Derrida repeats in *The Gift of Death* in his discussion of the *Akedah* and Søren Kierkegaard in chapter 3, "Whom to Give To (Knowing Not to Know)."[7] Derrida does refer to "the lamb" from Genesis 22:8 which "God will provide," as well as the fact that the *Akedah* is what Derrida refers to as "Judeo-Christian-Islamic."[8] But it is only in the last paragraph of the chapter, a citation from Kierkegaard's concluding comments in *Fear and Trembling*, that Derrida observes the references to Matthew 6 (verses 4, 6, and 18), with the phrase spoken by Christ "for he sees in secret."[9] Yet even here Christ remains unnamed by Derrida, perhaps his name being an aporia, or that which Derrida calls "sacrifice, the revelation of conceptual thinking at its limit, its death and finitude."[10] Derrida in effect mimics or repeats the unnaming of the *Akedah*, where Christ is the sacrificial lamb, the doubled event of the binding or holocaust of Genesis 22; this name not spoken is profoundly present-via-absence in *The Gift of Death*, as a limit (in Jaspers's sense), "something we can grasp only as empirical reality but cannot explore because it exceeds that reality."[11] As Bill Readings notes, "when an 'event' occurs … something happens which disrupts the pre-existent frame of reference, so that we don't know how to understand it, at the time. Indeterminate or reflective judgement is required, in which the imagination experiments, inventing ways of understanding the event."[12] Indeterminate judgement occurs in the *Jetztzeit* or "now-time," to use Walter Benjamin's phrase, or, as Readings puts it, "[i]ndeterminate judgement deals with the 'it is happening,' not with the '*what is happening*.'"[13] The postmodern sublime is thus the "sensation of time."[14] Lyotard ultimately utilizes the now-time of the sublime for political purposes, but this would appear to be a foreclosure of the sublime's sacred quality, precisely the quality recognized by Lyotard's example of the *Akedah*.

In "The Sublime and the Avant-Garde," Lyotard argues that the "now" of Newman's work is beyond consciousness per se, even that of ecstasy, and furthermore, the now-time of Newman's paintings "dismantles consciousness."[15] The event is a now-time or an "occurrence" that Lyotard re-articulates using Heidegger's term *Ereignis*. Silverman usefully expands upon and explicates this term, suggesting that "*Ereignis* is the event, the happening, the occurrence, the appropriation of *what is* in its relation to Being."[16] Silverman, unlike Lyotard, also links the constitutive, yet also frame-breaking, or *ec-stasis* of the event, with Joyce's "epiphany."[17] Thinking about *Ereignis* as the postmodern sublime, the "event that is happening now," *Ereignis* is unpresentable; as epiphany, the event happens, yet if this happening or experience is denied epiphanic status, then it is not as such a "withdrawal" of the Absolute, as Hegel would have it, but again, a foreclosure.[18] Such a foreclosure can happen at the level of translation, in this case rejecting the use of the word "event" itself, as do the translators of Heidegger's *Contributions*: "[E]vent, does not even remotely approximate *Ereignis*, because 'event' immediately evokes the metaphysical notions of the unprecedented and the precedent that are totally alien to *Ereignis*. Moreover, as born out by sections 238 to 242 of the *Contributions*, 'event' cannot live up to the demands put on it by *Ereignis* because 'event' emerges from within 'time-space' and as such is *itself* enowned by *Ereignis*."[19]

The translators conclude that "[t]his means that 'event' must be understood from within *Ereignis* and cannot function as its approximation."[20] There is a vicious circle here, because this denial or rejection of "event" is in line with the deconstructive understanding of the postmodern sublime that is in part drawn from Heidegger's work—that is Heidegger's rejection of transcendence in his description of the clearing in which the possibility of the person arises.[21] Of course beyond the debates concerning the translation of *Ereignis*, other approaches can be taken: for example, simply noting the way in which *Ereignis* is used differently in different "periods" of Heidegger's work. In the *Contributions* period, *Ereignis* signifies (among other things) an experiential living-through of be-ing (*Seyn*): "*Be-ing essentially happens as Ereignis.*"[22] As Richard Polt summarizes, "*Ereignis* is the way in which the givenness of given beings—including ourselves—comes into question for us. This happening is an urgent inception that grounds a site and initiates an age that has its own unique relation to the divine."[23] In the *Contributions*, *Ereignis* has both happened—uniquely—and not happened; it is yet to come:

> Not only is *Ereignis* in the *Contributions* rare and elusive, but it is arguably one, solitary event. Some passages suggest that be-ing can take place many times, but each time in a distinctive way; Heidegger speaks of be-ing's "uniqueness in each case." But at other times, he seeks "what happens one time, this time." *Ereignis*, like *physis* in the first inception, is "unique and singular."... We can go farther: maybe *Ereignis* has never yet happened at all. *Ereignis* is history, but "so far, man has never yet *been* historical." Heidegger thus invokes "the future ones," those who can engage with the sweep of the first inception and open the possibility of another unique inception. The *Contributions* are thought in the future tense and subjunctive mood.[24]

Be-ing is thus a "between" state (or *das Zwischen*), not just as Heidegger argues "between man (as history-grounding) and gods (in their history)," but also between the inception and that which is yet to come.[25] Be-ing may be time, but at the point of the postmodern sublime, Be-ing foregrounds the experience of eschatological time, and this experiential event does suggest something that precedes and will come after, as Heidegger says in a footnote in *Being and Time*: "If God's eternity can be 'construed' philosophically, then it may be understood only as a more primordial temporality which is 'infinite.'"[26] To put this reading of the event another way, the event is the primordial logos, where, as Peter C. Hodgson argues, there is a correspondence between Be-ing and the Word of God.[27] Hodgson also points out that "Heidegger learned from Paul (1 Thess. 5:1–3) that thinking which closes itself to the incalculable future by reckoning the times and applying itself to an objective content faces destruction."[28] But there is also a danger here of simply overturning the deconstruction of "logocentrism" in favour of the "event-logos" equation in the postmodern sublime, without an understanding of John 1:1–5; in other words, the turn to religion within contemporary theory becomes a Marcionism in reverse: the "progenitor" God is now held in favour of the "symbolic" New Testament Father.[29]

The event of the postmodern sublime, I have argued, might be read as a *Jetztzeit* or "now-time." The phrase is key in understanding Benjamin's notion of the dialectical image, or dialectics at a standstill, but it also leads to the possibility of acknowledging the Christological component of Benjamin's thought (given that Benjamin is an iconic figure for contemporary theory, and this aspect has long been, on the whole, ignored or effaced) as well as his sense of sacred community from his "youth movement" writings. In *The Arcades Project* Benjamin writes that "[e]very present day is determined by the images that are synchronic with it: each 'now' is the now of a particular recognizability. In it, truth is charged to the bursting point with time.… It is not that what is past casts its light on what is present, or what is present its light on what is past; rather, image is that wherein what has been comes together in a flash with the now to form a constellation. In other words: image is dialectics at a standstill."[30] *Jetztzeit* can be read negatively, as a cancelling-out or deconstruction of a messianic impulse, or positively. Giorgio Agamben charts some of the negative usages in Arthur Schopenhauer — "only the now is thought and the time that comes and judges is not even glanced at" — and Heidegger — "everyday time as it appears in the clock that counts the 'nows.'"[31] However, Agamben also shows how Benjamin "dispels" these negative usages "and endows the term with the same qualities as those pertaining to the *ho nyn kairos* in Paul's paradigm of messianic time."[32] I suggest that Benjamin's messianism is not just part of his Jewish heritage, but also involves his exploration of Christianity during his youth-movement period and his continual use of scriptural citations up to and including his last major work; I argue further that his messianism should be read in the sense of Rosenzweig's "two covenant theory." For example, Agamben, after examining the *Handexemplar* of Benjamin's "Theses on the Philosophy of History," discovers an embedded and virtually hidden (in re-typed translation) citation from Saint Paul. In the "Theses" Agamben points out a textual marker which is the proof of the citation: "Like every generation that preceded us, we have been endowed with a w e a k messianic power" ("*Dann ist uns wie jedem Geschlecht, das vor uns war, eine s c h w a c h e messianische Kraft mitgegeben*");[33] the word "weak" has been spaced out by Benjamin in the *Handexemplar* to give it emphasis, and thus the embedded, virtually hidden, citation: "power fulfils itself in weakness" ("*hē gar dynamis en astheneia teleitai*"), that is, Saint Paul's 2 Corinthians 12:9.[34] A more explicit example is Benjamin's condensation of Luke 17:20–21 and John 18:36, cited in a letter to Carla Seligson in 1913: "Today I felt the awesome truth of Christ's

words: Behold, the kingdom of God is not of this world, but within us."[35]
Bernd Witte calls Benjamin's statement the "most explicit formulation" of
"the life context and the religious grounding of Benjamin's 'metaphysics of
youth.'"[36] But of course this "explicit formulation" must be foreclosed as an
"offence" to an anti-metaphysical postmodernism, since power through weakness is also another way of saying "power through suffering," or, the event of
the cross. Salvation, as Bultmann formulates it, is the name of that offence.[37]

In recounting to Carla Seligson an awkward personal encounter with C.F.
Heinle, Benjamin sketches further such a religious context and grounding,
noting that he recognizes the "*inevitability of the idea*" and fulfillment that
can only be anticipated: "fulfillment is something too serene and divine for it
to issue from anything other than a burning wind."[38] Benjamin utilizes the
eschatological tension with his notion of youth as both fulfilled/actualized
Spirit and anticipatory, waiting-for-fulfilment (or, messianic hope):

> [T]o be young does not mean so much serving the spirit as *awaiting* it. To see it in
> every person and in the most remote thought. This is the most important thing: we
> must not commit ourselves to one specific idea. For us, the concept of youth cul-
> ture should simply be illumination that draws even the most remote spirit to its
> light. For many people, however, even Wyneken, even the Discussion Hall, will be
> merely a "movement." They will have committed themselves and will no longer see
> the spirit where it manifests itself as freer and more abstract. This constantly rever-
> berating feeling for the abstractness of pure spirit I would like to call youth. For
> then (if we do not turn ourselves into nothing more than workers in a movement),
> if we keep our gaze free to see the spirit wherever it may be, we will be the ones who
> actualize it. Almost everybody forgets that *they themselves* are the place where spirit
> actualizes itself. However, because they have made themselves inflexible, turned
> themselves into the pillars of a building instead of into vessels or bowls that can
> receive and shelter an ever-purer content, they despair of the actualization we feel
> within ourselves. This soul is the *eternally actualizing soul*.[39]

Benjamin's abstract theological language here bifurcates this statement via the
two covenants of Christianity and Judaism. As Franz Rosenzweig writes,
"Chosen by its Father, the people of Israel gazes fixedly across the world and
history, over to that last, most distant time when the Father, the One and Only,
will be 'all in all.' Then, when Christ ceases to be the Lord, Israel will cease to
be the chosen people."[40] As a formulation of "religious grounding," it is apparent that any notion of a *choice*, between Christianity or Judaism, is in itself to
misread Benjamin's metaphysics of youth; the two covenants coexist in his
"religious grounding" as being already/not-yet, just as the Jewish culture is
"already" and the messianic arrival (from a Christian perspective) is "already,"
while both notions of the messiah are potentially to be read as "not-yet": "On
this day [the end of human time], God will lose the name by which only Israel

calls him; God will then no longer be 'its' God. But until that day dawns, the lifework of Israel is to anticipate the eternal day, in profession and in action, to be its living presage, to hallow the name of God through its, Israel's, own holiness and with its Law as a people of priests."[41]

The *Jetztzeit* of the postmodern sublime, traced via Benjamin's Christian, not just Jewish, understanding of "now-time" in his working towards such a concept, is thus one which partakes of the Pauline eschatological tension. As noted, Lyotard forecloses the sacred in the postmodern sublime in favour of political purposes: "Lyotard finally finds what he is seeking for the political: the theory of a judgement regulated by Ideas without content, without any possible representation or even presentation, the theory of a feeling of the ethical without any overly moral prescription telling us '*what* there is to be done.'"[42] More technically, one can ask, what does it *mean* to foreclose the sacred as, or into, the (Lacanian) Real, since within postmodernity, the Lacanian coordinates are more relevant than the Freudian understanding of *Verwerfung*?[43] In *The Puppet and the Dwarf: The Perverse Core of Christianity*, Slavoj Žižek argues that "the Real is not external to the Symbolic: the Real is the Symbolic itself in the modality of non-All, lacking an external Limit/Exception. In this precise sense, the line of separation between the Symbolic and the Real is not only a symbolic gesture *par excellence*, but the very founding gesture of the Symbolic and to step into the Real does not entail abandoning language, throwing oneself into the abyss of the chaotic Real, but, on the contrary, dropping the very allusion to some external point of reference which eludes the Symbolic."[44] The postmodern sublime functions via its foreclosure of the sacred, yet, the sacred *is its Real*; that is to say, in separating the sacred from the symbolic universe of post-structuralism and postmodernism, theory repeats the symbolic gesture of foreclosure. As I have written elsewhere, "foreclosed signifiers are not integrated in the subject's unconscious and... they return not from some inner realm of subjectivity but emerge in (the Lacanian concept of) the Real."[45] I make the parallel with Gayatri Spivak's use of foreclosure in her post-colonial theory; thus for Spivak, "[t]he native informant is not simply cast 'outside' of colonial networks of power-knowledge, but [he or she] is foreclosed: expulsed, unintegrated, beyond reach but constitutive of the colonial Real; the native informant is thus simultaneously perceived by Spivak here as an oppressed *and* a powerful subject, repeatedly denied, but always haunting and... constitutive of the discursive reasoning of the West."[46] I am suggesting that the sacred is therefore not only that which is "expulsed" and "unintegrated" within the postmodern sublime, but that which is also constitutive. As Žižek says, "the Real is thus the disavowed X on account of which our vision of reality is anamorphically distorted."[47] I argue that the disavowal in postmodernism is one which pertains not just to the sacred, but also to suffering understood in a theological, and ultimately redemptive, sense. In refusing the sacred, the representation of suffering is also distorted to such an extent that it eventually breaks down entirely, the unrepresentable becoming an absent, yet still adjacent, core of representation. As Žižek suggests in *Tarrying with the Negative*, "every exclusion of the Real…is a symbolic act par excellence."[48]

I want to turn, by way of an extended conclusion, to an example of the postmodern sublime as an experience of suffering and the sacred; my example is a work by the British artist Rachel Whiteread called *The Nameless Library*, situated in Judenplatz, Vienna.[49] I am calling it a "work" because it is a work of art that exceeds the aesthetic, or, to use Leora Batnitzky's phrase, it is an "art form beyond aestheticism."[50] Batnitzky is commenting on Franz Rosenzweig's thoughts on art and Christianity in *The Star of Redemption*; thus, "Rosenzweig argues that the Christian life is a life of structured passion. To structure passion is not to control passion; it is rather to live with the tensions of passion. In Rosenzweig's words, 'Structure must be shaped, brought forth, constructed.' Structure is not something that can be mastered once and for all; it must be continually constructed and managed."[51] Rosenzweig sets up a complex comparison and contrast in this section of *The Star of Redemption* between secular and Christian art, and secular art and Judaism.[52] Batnitzky quotes the first part of Rosenzweig's "The Structuring of the Passion":

> In the Christian, those forces intersect which elsewhere appear to cancel each other out. Christianity affords them no refuge beyond these contradictions. It absorbs them all within itself and inserts the Christian into their midst, into a middle which— for him who stands there—is at the same time a beginning. The cross neither negates the contradiction, nor annihilates it; rather it articulates it as structure. Structure is not created by fiat, nor is it brute force. Structure must be shaped, brought forth, constructed. The way of the Christian is at every station a crossroad.[53]

The key phrase here, in the original, is "Der Weg des Christen ist in jedem Augenblick Kreuzweg."[54] Hallo's translation neatly captures the meaning of "stations of the cross,"[55] but a more literal translation also brings out Rosenzweig's notion that at "any moment" the "way of the cross" presents itself: this moment should not be read neutrally, or as some kind of simple positivity; rather, it is the awareness of the suffering, which is "lacking" as Paul puts it (Col. 1:24). If the subject is at a crossroads, that intersection is also one where the already meets the not-yet; Batnitzky argues that this crossroads or "midpoint" in Rosenzweig is perceived as performative: "The midpoint is…constructed and managed as a depiction of universal suffering. The Christian midpoint that defines both Christian eternity in time and an acknowledgment of the tragic fate of finite man is never achieved but must always be performed."[56] Rosenzweig argues that at the crossroads there is a competing, structuring force: that of art, where art is that which fundamentally depicts suffering. Art thus *memorializes* suffering in this depiction, yet it also structures the passion of suffering in such a way that it is both heightened in intensity, and, paradoxically, is "overcome without forgetting": "Sie lehrt ihn, überwinden ohne zu vergessen."[57] This "overcoming" is thus no less an intensity than the memorializing force, the explosive energies that are both contained and unleashed therein. Rosenzweig's "structuring passion" ("das Leiden gestaltet") creates a dialectical image whereby "[p]ast pains, not past joys, are the delight of the soul in every present moment" ("Nicht vergangenes Glück, nur vergangene Schmerzen sind die Seligkeit der Seele in jeder Gegenwart").[58]

Norbert Samuelson notes that Rosenzweig's underlying ethical argument here is that "secular art is morally irresponsible" because it engenders an entirely private mode of suffering, not one which is corporate and redemptive, as with the symbol of the cross, where the dialectical image is messianic and wholly redemptive.[59] In other words, the "private mode" denies a reciprocal relationship or community forged by redemptive suffering; community thus becomes the "whatever" (*qualunque*)[60] community, not one called to sustained[61] partnership[62] or fellowship. There is the additional comparison underlying this part of the *Star of Redemption* which comments on aesthetics, Judaism, and community, that is to say between the overtly stated Christian and secular art, and the covertly addressed secular art and Judaism: unlike the private and "morally irresponsible" secular art patron, in Judaism the "removal [from temporality] is morally responsible for three reasons."[63] As Samuelson sketches them, "First, it expresses reality, not illusion. Second, it occurs in community and it is not entirely individual. Third, it provides a model for the Christian to transform (i.e., redeem) the world."[64]

I am deliberately using Rosenzweig to think about *The Nameless Library*, a concrete cast of a library, with the bindings all hidden from view, representing the Jewish people murdered in the Shoah; I use Rosenzweig here because *The Nameless Library* not only "presents the unpresentable" but is a sign of the multiple events of the unpresentable. As Silverman notes, "While Lyotard has called this 'presentation of the unpresentable in presentation itself' the postmodern, it also has another name: *the sublime*. And because the sublime does not characterize an object but rather an event, and there are such events in many places, the sites of the sublime are also multiple."[65] *The Nameless Library* is a binding of the multiple events not just into one site of remembrance, but also into a now-time of suffering and the sacred; moreover, it is a structuring of suffering and the sacred. Rosenzweig's two covenant theory helps us account for the fact that in the face of this suffering and sacred site of the experience of the postmodern sublime, two parallel faiths coexist and interact. This is not to be naive in relation to the history of Christianity and the Shoah;

rather, I am inspired by the two covenant theory which offers the hope of a "*mahloket leshem shamayim*," or "a struggle in the name, and for the sake, of Heaven."[66] The two covenant "fellowship of… suffering" (Phil. 3:10) is an experience of the postmodern sublime that is very different from the "permanent revisionism" of standard conceptions of the postmodern "subject," where the word "subject" is of course placed and held under erasure;[67] this experience is also radically different from the Hegelian teleological subject, where again there is a "permanent revisionism" of the subject on the road to absolute knowledge or spirit, "in which," Jacques Lacan says, "what is disturbing about truth is constantly being reabsorbed, truth being in itself but what is lacking in the realization of knowledge.… Truth is nothing but what knowledge can learn that it knows merely by putting its ignorance to work."[68] Lacan concludes that the Hegelian dialectic is thus "the conjunction of the symbolic with a real from which nothing more can be expected."[69] Contra the standard postmodern *or* dialectical experience of the subject, I suggest that at the point of the postmodern sublime, the experience is not so much one of lack, but of a *plenitude of suffering*; this strange phrase — *plenitude of suffering* — is my description of the intersection of the sacred and the suffering in the sublime, whereby we can understand Lacan's phrase "permanent revisionism" in an eschatological way, via Colossians 1:24: "I now rejoice in my sufferings for you, and fill up in my flesh what is lacking in the afflictions of Christ, for the sake of His body, which is the church."

Notes

1 James D.G. Dunn, *The Theology of Paul the Apostle* (Grand Rapids, MI: Eerdmans, 1998) 486–87.

2 Qtd. in Hugh J. Silverman, "Lyotard and the Events of the Postmodern Sublime," *Lyotard: Philosophy, Politics, and the Sublime*, ed. Hugh J. Silverman (London and New York: Routledge, 2002) 227.

3 Qtd. in Serge Trottein, "Lyotard: Before and After the Sublime," *Lyotard*, ed. Silverman, 197.

4 Jean-François Lyotard, "The Sublime and the Avant Garde," *The Lyotard Reader*, ed. Andrew Benjamin (Oxford: Blackwell, 1989) 196.

5 Jean-François Lyotard, "Newman: The Instant," *The Lyotard Reader*, 244.

6 See, for example, the following essays in *The Sacrifice of Isaac in the Three Monotheistic Religions*, ed. Frédéric Manns (Jerusalem: Franciscan, 1995): Frédéric Manns, "Note on the Sacrifice of Isaac in the Fourth Gospel" (99–100); Mieczyslaw C. Paczkowski, "The Sacrifice of Isaac in Early Patristic Exegesis" (101–21); and Lino Cignelli, "The Sacrifice of Isaac in Patristic Exegesis" (123–26).

7 Jacques Derrida, *The Gift of Death*, trans. David Wills (Chicago: University of Chicago Press, 1995).

8 Ibid., 64.

9 Ibid., 81, quoting Kierkegaard's *Fear and Trembling*.

10 Ibid., 68. Derrida's extended discussion of the name(s) of God is found in "Des Tours de Babel" in Jacques Derrida, *Acts of Religion*, ed. Gil Anidjar (London and New York: Routledge, 2002) 104–36.

11 Karl Jaspers, *Philosophy*, trans. E.B. Ashton, vol. 3 (Chicago: University of Chicago Press, 1971) 8.

12 Bill Readings, *Introducing Lyotard: Art and Politics*, qtd. in Brad Prager, "Kant in Caspar David Friedrich's Frames," *Art History* 25.1 (2002): 78–79.

13 Qtd. in Prager, "Kant in Caspar David Friedrich's Frames," 79.

14 Qtd. in Thomas B. Hess, *Barnett Newman* (New York: Museum of Modern Art, 1971) 73.

15 Lyotard, "The Sublime and the Avant Garde," 197.

16 Silverman, "Lyotard and the Events of the Postmodern Sublime," 225.

17 Ibid.

18 Ibid., 227; G.W.F. Hegel, *Aesthetics: Lectures on Fine Art*, trans. T.M. Knox, vol. 1 (Oxford: Clarendon, 1988) 339.

19 Parvis Emad and Kenneth Maly, translators' foreword, Martin Heidegger, *Contributions to Philosophy (From Enowning)*, trans. Parvis Emad and Kenneth Maly (Bloomington: Indiana University Press, 1999) xx–xxi.

20 Ibid.

21 Ronald P. Morrison, "Kant, Husserl, and Heidegger on Time and the Unity of 'Consciousness,'" *Philosophy and Phenomenological Research* 39.2 (1978): 196.

22 Heidegger, qtd. in Richard Polt, "*Ereignis*," *A Companion to Heidegger*, ed. Hubert L. Dreyfus and Mark A. Wrathall (Oxford: Blackwell, 2005) 381.

23 Polt, "*Ereignis*," 383.

24 Ibid., 384.

25 Heidegger, *Contributions to Philosophy*, 219.

26 Martin Heidegger, *Being and Time*, trans. John Macquarrie and Edward Robinson (Oxford: Blackwell, 1990), 499n13 (H.427).

27 Peter C. Hodgson, "Heidegger, Revelation, and the Word of God," *Journal of Religion* 49.3 (1969): 243.

28 Ibid., 245.

29 Alain Badiou, *Saint Paul: The Foundation of Universalism*, trans. Ray Brassier (Stanford, CA: Stanford University Press, 2003) 34–35.

30 Walter Benjamin, *The Arcades Project*, trans. Howard Eiland and Kevin McLaughlin (Cambridge, MA: Belknap-Harvard University Press, 1999) 462–63 (N3, 1).

31 Qtd. in Giorgio Agamben, *The Time That Remains: A Commentary on the Letter to the Romans*, trans. Patricia Dailey (Stanford, CA: Stanford University Press, 2005) 143.

32 Agamben, *The Time That Remains,* 143.

33 Qtd. in Agamben, *The Time That Remains,* 139; Agamben's translation.

34 Ibid., 140; Agamben's translation.

35 Walter Benjamin, *The Correspondence of Walter Benjamin: 1910–1940*, ed. Gershom Scholem and Theodor W. Adorno, trans. Manfred R. Jacobson and Evelyn M. Jacobson (Chicago: University of Chicago Press, 1994) 54.

36 Bernd Witte, *Walter Benjamin: An Intellectual Biography*, trans. James Rolleston (Detroit: Wayne State University Press, 1997) 29.

37 Rudolf Bultmann, *The Gospel of John*, trans. G.R. Beasley-Murray, R.W.N. Hoare, and J.K. Riches (Philadelphia: Westminster Press, 1971) 433.
38 Benjamin, *The Correspondence of Walter Benjamin*, 56–57.
39 Ibid., 54–55.
40 Qtd. in Nahum N. Glatzer, *Franz Rosenzweig: His Life and Thought* (New York: Schocken, 1953) 341–42.
41 Glatzer, *Franz Rosenzweig*, 342.
42 Trottein, "Lyotard: Before and After the Sublime," 196.
43 Jean-François Lyotard, "Figure Foreclosed," *The Lyotard Reader*, 88.
44 Slavoj Žižek, *The Puppet and the Dwarf: The Perverse Core of Christianity* (Cambridge, MA: MIT Press, 2003) 69–70.
45 Richard J. Lane, *Fifty Key Literary Theorists* (London and New York: Routledge, 2006) 249.
46 Ibid.
47 Slavoj Žižek, *Interrogating the Real*, ed. Rex Butler and Scott Stephens (London: Continuum, 2005) 339.
48 Slavoj Žižek, *Tarrying with the Negative: Kant, Hegel, and the Critique of Ideology* (Durham, NC: Duke University Press, 1993) 129.
49 See Richard J. Lane, *Reading Walter Benjamin: Writing through the Catastrophe* (Manchester, UK: Manchester University Press, 2005); Richard Lane, "Kant's 'Safe Place': Security and the Sacred in the Concept of Sublime Experience," *Sublimer Aspects: Interfaces between Literature, Aesthetics, and Theology, 1715–1885*, ed. Natasha Duquette (Newcastle, UK: Cambridge Scholars Publishing, 2007); Richard Lane, "The Hidden and the Exposed: 'One-Time Appearance' in Walter Benjamin and Rachel Whiteread's *Holocaust Memorial* (a reading of Section iv of 'The Work of Art in the Age of Its Technical Reproducibility,' 2nd version)," *Reproducing Art: Walter Benjamin's "Work of Art" Essay Reconsidered*, ed. Patricia Allmer and John Sears, spec. issue of *InterCulture* 4.2 (2008), http://iph.fsu.edu/interculture/benjamin.html.
50 Leora Batnitzky, *Idolatry and Representation: The Philosophy of Franz Rosenzweig Reconsidered* (Princeton, NJ: Princeton University Press, 2000) 150.
51 Ibid.
52 See Norbert M. Samuelson, *A User's Guide to Franz Rosenzweig's "Star of Redemption"* (Richmond, UK: Curzon Press, 1999) 298–99.
53 Franz Rosenzweig, *The Star of Redemption*, trans. William W. Hallo (Notre Dame, IN: University of Notre Dame Press, 1985) 376, qtd. in Batnitzky, *Idolatry and Representation*, 150.
54 Franz Rosenzweig, *Der Stern der Erlösung, Gesammelte Schriften II*, ed. Reinhold Mayer (The Hague: Martinus Nijhoff, 1976) 418.
55 Also the title of fourteen paintings by Barnett Newman. Lyotard observes that the subtitle for this series is "Lama Sabachthani," "the cry of despair uttered by Jesus on the cross: *My God, why hast thou forsaken me?*" (Lyotard, "Newman: The Instant," 248).
56 Batnitzky, *Idolatry and Representation*, 150.
57 Rosenzweig, *The Star of Redemption*, 377; Rosenzweig, *Der Stern der Erlösung*, 419.
58 Ibid.
59 Samuelson, *A User's Guide*, 298.

60 See translator's note number 1, Giorgio Agamben, *The Coming Community*, trans. Michael Hardt (Minneapolis: University of Minnesota Press, 2007) 107.

61 Dietrich Bonhoeffer, *Sanctorum Communio*, trans. Reinhard Krauss and Nancy Lukens (Minneapolis: Fortress, 1998) 160.

62 *The Message* translation of the Bible, translating κοινωνία, Philippians 3:10 (Eugene H. Peterson, *The Message: The Bible in Contemporary Language* [Colorado Springs, CO: NavPress, 2002]).

63 Samuelson, *A User's Guide*, 299.

64 Ibid.

65 Silverman, "Lyotard and the Events of the Postmodern Sublime," 228.

66 Maurice G. Bowler, "Rosenzweig on Judaism and Christianity—The Two Covenant Theory," *Judaism* 22.4 (1973): 481.

67 Subsequent biblical quotations are taken from the New King James Version; Jacques Lacan, *Ecrits*, trans. Bruce Fink (New York: Norton, 2004) 285.

68 Ibid.

69 Ibid.

SUFFERING DIVINE THINGS: CRUCIFORM REASONING OR INCARNATIONAL HERMENEUTICS

Jens Zimmermann

In the essay which opens this volume, David Lyle Jeffrey suggests that contemporary consciousness has difficulty holding together the three principal concepts of "suffering, the sacred, and the sublime" that motivate and integrate the contributions to this essay collection. This difficulty arises from the forgetfulness of the Judeo-Christian roots which enable the conjunction of these terms and elevate them beyond their preceding ancient Greek or Roman definitions. As Jeffrey points out, this loss renders much of Christian poetry and other works of art inspired by Christianity largely unintelligible to the modern secularist reader. But the effects of becoming unmoored from the founding traditions of Western culture go far beyond our inability to understand art and literature or to connect meaningfully the human experiences of "suffering, the sacred, and the sublime." As I argue in this closing contribution, the very nature of human reason and solidarity are at stake. This argument requires the reader's willingness to enter into a discussion of intellectual history which may appear rather abstract. And yet this effort takes us to the heart of the matter — that the Christian doctrine of the Incarnation made possible a humanism that enabled a rich concept of reason and correlated it with religious belief in such a way that human solidarity, even empathy, became constitutive of one's deepest religious convictions. In this concluding contribution, I want to show the importance of this "incarnational humanism." The Christian sacred is sublime within the unique context of God's becoming human, the judgment of evil at the Cross, and the redemption of humanity in the Resurrection. The divine sublime is brought into the human realm of understanding and is defined equally by the incomprehensible kenosis of divine suffering and the restoration of humanity in the Resurrection. In the Christian religion, true humanity is defined as participation in this divine event, keeping the believer's horizon in line with the Incarnation as "being-for-another." In order to appreciate fully the implications of this humanism for the nature of human reason, we need to grasp the current cultural context resulting from the loss of our Judeo-Christian roots.

Western Identity, the Exhaustion of Secular Reason, and the Return to Religion

Western culture needs to come to terms with two crucial losses: first, with a loss of identity accompanied by the consequent failure to mount a convincing defence of its values in light of current global developments; second, with the loss of a clear goal for the education of its citizens. Terry Eagleton's voice is representative of other cultural critics, intellectuals, and politicians in his assessment that global political pressures, including religious confrontations, force the West "more and more to reflect on the foundations of its own civilization" at a time when we have lost the ability to think deeply.[1] According to Eagleton, postmodernity has rightly criticized naive and oppressive notions of universal reason, but it has also left us without any common ground for a universal sense of human dignity. Postmodern cultural theory has taught us to dislike universal truth claims and feel "embarrassed by fundamentals."[2] Yet world events require that we discuss human nature in terms of universal purpose and ask once again, in all seriousness, "What is the function of human beings? What are human beings for?"[3]

This loss of common ground has also affected Western educational ideals and their institutions. In his book *Simulacra and Simulation*, Jean Baudrillard, an important postmodern cultural critic, writes about the loss of purpose in university education and the consequent fragmentation of the disciplines. Designating the contemporary culture of knowledge as a "spiraling cadaver," he concludes that "the university is in ruins; nonfunctional in the social arenas of the market and employment, lacking cultural substance or an end purpose of knowledge."[4] He argues that since we have lost an ultimate unifying reason for knowledge, especially for knowledge of seemingly impractical values such as truth, justice, goodness, and beauty, we no longer know why we should invest real work in knowledge. The value of a university education and graduate certificates is no longer connected to any real ultimate content, and so we have a kind of inflation: university degrees are still valuable to get us someplace in society, a kind of job requirement, but they are actually increasingly worthless in themselves.[5]

In case you suspect that only a crazy French intellectual could come up with such a depressing view of higher education, a recent article in the *National Post* entitled "Hollow Halls of Academe" confirms Baudrillard's judgment almost verbatim. The modern Canadian university is a place "where students are more interested in the piece of paper they get at the end of their programs than in the intellectual journey along the way, where professors are cowed into watering down courses and bumping up grades, and where universities are run like corporations hawking mass-produced *degrees which are increasingly in demand but increasingly meaningless*."[6]

Uncertainties about the essence of human nature, the loss of cultural identity, and the purpose of knowledge are all rooted in one basic problem: the exhaustion of secular reason. Precipitated by postmodernity, what Charles Taylor asserted decades ago has now trickled down fully into the public cultural arena: the malaise of modernity is that we have lost horizons of significance. The malaise of postmodernity, on the other hand, is its inability to provide us with a much-needed unified notion of rationality.

By the exhaustion of secular reason, I mean the breakdown of scientific objectivism. Following a fascination with the pristine clarity of mathematical certainty and geometrical purity which promised to transcend the murkiness of shifting historical circumstances and the emotionally unstable quality of religious truth, academics and, later, popular culture identified the rational with the scientific method. This test-tube epistemology makes short shrift of any human knowledge which does not show up under the microscope. Since religion, tradition, love, and ultimate questions concerning our humanity usually do not appear in a test tube, they do not count as real knowledge. It is no wonder that the human sciences have taken a back seat to the supposedly more practical rational or scientific disciplines such as the natural sciences, economics, or whatever else we count as conforming to the ideal of verifiable and calculable knowledge.

Thankfully, however, for a number of reasons we cannot enumerate here, scientific objectivism as the secular common sense idea of truth has run its course. We live not only in a post-*Christian* world but also in a post-*secular* one. Atheism and secular humanism, both in substance and rhetoric, depend on scientific objectivism, the very idea of truth as a neutral fact-finding mission that has failed. It has failed because scientific objectivism cannot generate by itself the values and interpretive frameworks that sustain its own scientific enterprise and which we require for a human way of being. It no longer is, because it never was, an adequate source for human self-understanding.

The identity crisis of the West, and the exhaustion of secular reason, has a number of philosophers and politicians calling for a return of religion into the heart of the academy and public policy. Especially in Europe, politicians and public intellectuals are recognizing the dependence of Western culture on Christian roots. The Italian statesman Marcello Pera, for example, proclaims specifically the Incarnation as the root of human rights, solidarity, equality, compassion, and the institutions shaped through them.[7]

Closer to home, North American academics are beginning to realize the importance of religion for keeping alive the distinction between nature and humanity, a crucial and foundational difference for any research. The historian John Sommerville explains in *The Decline of the Secular University* that "if the point of the secular university was to eliminate the religious dimension, it will eventually find that it has eliminated the human distinction as well, and be unable to make sense of any of its intellectual and professional disciplines."[8] Sommerville warns that, in light of the returning interest in religion, universities will completely lose touch with society unless they can adopt "an intellectual framework that is religiously suggestive."[9]

Many of us may also recall Stanley Fish's announcement several years ago in the *Chronicle of Higher Education* that religion will form the next research focus in North American literature departments, even in the university as a whole. The reason, Fish argues, is that one of the things 9/11 has taught us is that most people in the world are in fact religious. The time has now come for the small secular elite governing the overall outlook of university curricula to reinstitute religion as a real "candidate for the truth."[10] We find ourselves in a cultural situation where the weakening of secularism, in part effected by the postmodern critique of scientific objectivism, opens up space for less narrow conceptions of rationality that include religion.

A paradigmatic example of this new openness toward religion is the exchange between the current champion of recovering the Christian roots of reason, Joseph Ratzinger, Pope Benedict XVI, and the grey eminence of the Frankfurt school of social philosophy, Jürgen Habermas.[11] Benedict, both in his public debate with Habermas and later in his Regensburg address, calls for recovering a wider notion of human rationality that includes religion and offers the Christian model of reason that takes up, elevates, and transforms the Greek logos into the Christian incarnate Logos. Standing in the tradition of Augustine, Benedict argues that the concrete historical tie of the divine to the suffering and self-giving god-man of love ensures that religious reason is non-violent, and he calls for the "co-rationality of reason and faith, reason and religion, which are destined to reciprocal cleansing and healing, and which need one another and have to recognize this need."[12]

While he fully admits that secular reason cannot provide of itself the ultimate transcendent values to make human life worth living, Habermas still refuses to buy into Benedict's all too easy return to a Thomistic merger of faith and reason. Habermas is not quite so ready to rush into the embrace of Queen Theology and asks whether her rational subjects did not have good reason to revolt. The very intellectual developments Benedict cites as detrimental to a healthy relationship between faith and reason Habermas regards as positive achievements of secular rationality: "The step taken by Duns Scotus toward Nominalism did not lead only to the Protestant God of voluntarism but also paved the way for modern natural science. Kant's critical turn not only dismantled proofs of God's existence but also led to the modern concept of autonomy which shaped our modern understanding of rights and democracy. Nor does historicism lead necessarily to a relativistic self-denial of reason, but ... sensitizes us to cultural differences and protects us from generalizing judgments which depend on concrete historical contexts."[13]

It is safe to say that Habermas's warning not to ignore this secular legacy of reason is uttered with an eye to U.S. politics and political Islamic jihad. Yet as Benedict has pointed out, pathological developments have occurred in secular reason as well as in religion. And, surely, he is correct in identifying Western intellectual history as the fruitful correlation of faith and reason. Tracing this synthesis from the emergence of the Christian church to the present shows just how much this is a history of reason and self-understanding.

At the deepest conceptual level, the intellectual history of the West and its cultural identity is the story of reason. Western intellectual history is to a great part the history of logos, of rationality and its social implications. Human culture and its institutions are the expression both consciously and unconsciously of what is considered most rational and therefore most human. In the West, the question of human identity *is* the question of rationality. This Western ethos of rational human identity is most easily traced in the concept of humanism. Humanism in its broadest sense is the rational creature's question "Who am I?" or "What makes me most fully human?"[14]

Western rationality and identity have been shaped profoundly by the synthesis of Greek and Judeo-Christian ideals. The Delphic oracle's demand "know thyself," this ancient desire for self-knowledge, was taken up by Christianity and answered by elevating and transforming the Greek logos into the eternal Word of God and its incarnation in Jesus. This synthesis so closely knit together the question of reason, words, language, meaning, and human identity that in the West, try as we might, we cannot talk about any of these things without talking about Christianity, nor can we do so without talking about humanism.

It is equally true that this humanism was preoccupied with self-under-standing. We do not need a modern humanist such as Hans-Georg Gadamer to tell us that "in the final analysis, *all* human understanding is self-under-standing."[15] The Italian humanist Giambattista Vico summarized the human-ist tradition in his orations on humanism when he announced to prospective students that "knowledge of oneself is for everyone the greatest incentive to acquire the universe of learning in the shortest possible time."[16] Yet this knowledge is by no means interior or private only. Even in the opening of the very first lecture, Vico makes an immediate connection between humanistic learning and the political life. Professors like him must convince the students "to take up the studies of liberal arts and sciences, which can be acquired only with strong dedication of the mind, with long and late hours of application, with sweat, with persistent discipline, and with punctilious discipline" because "our peaceful society" and its fruits are "for the most part based on the culti-vation of these studies."[17]

For the classical humanists, studying the texts of the great orators, poets, and historians trained students in "breadth of learning and grace of style," and acquainted them with religion and "our duties in the world."[18] Reading of texts, learning of languages, and knowing how to argue and express oneself were eminently practical in producing good citizens — "the complete human being" — whose interest was the common weal of their society and of humanity.

At bottom, however, the humanistic ideal derives from a neo-Platonic view of reason transformed by Christianity into learning as reflection of and par-ticipation in the image of God. Vico writes, "As God is known by those things that have been created and are contained within this universe, so the spirit is recognized as divine by reason, in which it is pre-eminent, and by its sagacity, ability, memory, and ingenuity. The spirit is the most manifest image of God."[19] Such a universal notion of reason, let alone a participatory one, has been renounced by postmodern philosophers, who emphasize the particular over the universal and subscribe to the general argument that universal reason is an oppressive metaphysical construct favouring — mostly male — power brokers.

Given the historical development of rationality from Greek and Christian thought, Benedict is right in defining the Western intellectual ethos as a humanistic synthesis of faith and reason, but Habermas is equally correct in pointing out its problems. We must not bypass but integrate the correctives of postmodernity's critique of reason into recovering a broader concept of human reason. While many offer up silent prayers of thanksgiving that post-modernity and deconstruction seem to fade from prominence, we should not forget that postmodernism is itself an important part of the history of the Logos. Postmodernism is in essence a criticism of Western rationality, includ-ing scientific objectivism, a critique with an ethical focus that tries to examine the very nature of reason and the self. Let us take, for example, Nietzsche, Heidegger, Levinas, and Derrida. All four want to recall us to the historical dimensions of truth, reason, and the self, and all four understand that we cannot talk about reason and self-understanding without also always talking about the divine Logos and the humanistic tradition.

For example, Nietzsche's philosophy may be read as the overcoming of Platonic idealism. Instead of a direct interface or a "Vulcan mind-meld" with eternal forms that bypass life and body, Nietzsche suggests an anti-metaphysical approach to truth motivated by the highest value of the will to power. Heidegger certainly reads Nietzsche this way and derives from this impulse his own version of Western intellectual history as the departure from a dynamic and holistic way of thinking in which man thought of himself as embedded into a greater horizon of being toward the reductive, modern attitude of human-centered thinking. Heidegger regards the humanistic synthesis of faith and reason as a disaster, and Christianity is much to blame because it combined the Greek idea of logos with God: "logos in the New Testament does not, as in Heraclitus, mean the being of the beings, the gathering together of the conflicting; it means *one* particular being, namely the son of God [....] a whole world separates all this from Heraclitus."[20] With this move, God turned into a metaphysical concept, the God of ontotheology; logos became logic; a more original unity between existence and thought was severed; and an opposition between logos and being was inscribed into Western thought.

From this misinterpretation of logos as reason, as meaning, even as word, stem all humanisms as a kind of Platonic disease that turns knowledge into objectification and splits thinking from being. Being and experience become objective, while thinking becomes subjective. For Heidegger, this split is responsible for the alienation of modern man from himself and the world. Only a philosophy that recognizes how reasoning works within and through history can heal this alienation by recovering the original meaning of logos as "the primal gathering principle." Only with this recovery can we overcome the separation of existence and thinking. Why? Because the human being, as the only truly reflective being, is in fact the place where the gathering logos appears. The really real, the *essent* of being, makes itself known through human being. This is why Heidegger can say, "Apprehension is not a function that man has as an attribute, but rather the other way around: apprehension is the happening that has man."[21]

Heidegger knows all about Faust's desire to combine being and knowing and he gets thinking on the right track by presenting a possible *participatory* model of reason. Rationality, historical being-in-the-world, and the question of human identity or self-understanding all come together. He writes, "[O]nly as a questioning, historical being does man come to himself; only as such is he a self. Man's selfhood means this: he must transform the being that discloses itself to him into history and bring himself to stand in it. Selfhood does not mean he is primarily an 'ego' and an individual. This he is no more than he is a we, a community.... Because man as a historical being is himself, the question about his own being must be reformulated. Rather than 'what is man,' we should say 'who is man?'"[22]

Heidegger answers this question in his *Letter on Humanism*, which aspires to a new humanism by designating human beings, poets in particular (especially German philosopher poets who read Trakl, Hölderlin, and Rilke), as shepherds of being. However fuzzy in substance, Heidegger's *Letter on Humanism* directly answers the questions of identity, reason, and self-understanding. All three are, or at least *seem*, radically and hermeneutically open: "We do not learn who man is by learned definitions; we learn it only when man contends with the essent, striving to bring it into its being, i.e. into limit and form, that is to say when he projects something new (not yet present), when he creates original poetry, when he builds poetically."[23] While a student may not understand the comment on his paper, "C+; not enough striving with the *Being* of being," Heidegger nonetheless offers an important justification for reading poetry and literature.[24] Literature and poetry are portals to self-understanding which move thinking closer to the perennial human questions of purpose and identity.

Heidegger is a central thinker for our discussion because he anticipates the postmodern demands on rationality and religion. By bringing together existence and reflection, Heidegger saves poetry and the humanities from disappearing in the dualistic abyss of opposing experiential and intellectual knowledge. In contrast to all forms of philosophical idealism, Heidegger's hermeneutic ontology valiantly struggles against subjectivism and calls for some kind of participation in being itself. The negative effect of this participation—at least according to the Jewish philosopher Emmanuel Levinas, one of Heidegger's severest critics—is that Heidegger's supposed openness to Being poses a threat to human dignity.

We cannot overlook in Heidegger a certain disdain, in the name of Being, not only for subjectivism, rationalism, and individualism, but also for community. We are neither fundamentally an *I* nor a *we* but the ears and mouthpiece of being. Levinas noticed this problem too. Since Heidegger's ontology is participation in an impersonal pagan notion of Being, which is rather flexible in its ethics, human dignity gets sold to the highest paid interpreter of what Being discloses to us. To forestall this disaster, Levinas argues that ethics has to be more primordial than ontology. He reintroduces the social and ethical categories of encounter and responsibility into human reason. The primary category of the human is the mode of revelation of address by another.

Moreover, Levinas does not accept Heidegger's openness toward Being as transcendence, but accuses him of creating yet other totalities. Levinas thus issues a fundamental challenge to interpretation because he realizes that the hermeneutical circle of understanding implies a totality: self-understanding always requires a whole, at least an anticipation of a prior whole in light of which we continue to develop our understanding of who we are. In other words, hermeneutics, contrary to Heidegger's claim, is not radically open but lacks transcendence because in its encounter with texts and with other people, it will never be able to have them fully appear on their own terms. Heidegger can talk about ethics as little as he can talk about God.[25]

Levinas, this philosophical Moses, holds up the command "thou shalt not kill" as the ethical imposition by the other who founds my human identity with this call. He calls for nothing less than recovering a concept of rationality that is intrinsically ethical, beyond any totalizing structures, a "humanism of the other" configured primarily as responsibility for the other.[26] It is true what Levinas claims—namely, that he has no need of the Incarnation. God shows up in history through my ethical response to the other. Yet I would argue that Levinas does need the Incarnation, not least to relieve the traumatic experience of the ethical call. Some may be drawn to this concept of the open wound of subjectivity, constantly exposed to the trauma of substitution, of being taken hostage to the other, as wholesome, but I find it too hard.[27]

Moreover, Levinas also leaves us with a fear of the ontological as that which tends to objectify and distort human dignity. It is no surprise that Levinas, despite his own frequent use of literary texts, can never quite shake off an intrinsic fear that writing and artwork is less a source of otherness than an ethical death trap, a form of idolatry which obscures the face of the other by freezing it into literary or artistic timelessness.

Another postmodern thinker who takes up Heidegger's questions concerning ontology and human rationality is Jacques Derrida, whose life's work constitutes a sweeping critique of Western rationality. Derrida's central argument is that Western philosophy has always defined human understanding with the Greeks as "sameness." We define understanding as participating in a common logos, in terms of familiarity and likeness, therefore suppressing difference. Derrida's observations on the abusive potential of defining "logos" in the West as immediate presence chide Heidegger for his belief in unified meaning and Levinas for his fear of mediated truth within ontology.[28] Yet somehow his criticism of rationality as logocentric lands him in a similar place as Heidegger and Levinas. All three long to escape rationalism and seek to recover a more human way of being and reasoning, but their fear of unifying and objectifying statements does not allow them to say anything universally substantive about human nature, ethics, or justice.

When we understand the rejection of metaphysics by postmodern critics in the light of their critique of Western rationality, two main and contrary emphases come to light: (a) the historical dimension of reason's unfolding in its linguistic and social determination, and (b) the ethical issue of sameness and difference. The first issue is the question of philosophical hermeneutics and the nature of reason: How does universal reason unfold in the cultural particularities of language and interpretation without becoming relativistic? How can we ever reach a universally acknowledged sense of who we are and what we live for? The second emphasis is the ethical question of identity and difference: how can we have a unified, universal ideal of reason and humanity which recognizes cultural and individual differences as intrinsic to self-understanding? This basic question of identity and difference is also the source for the common prejudice we mentioned earlier: that religious conviction necessarily results in intolerance and violence. According to this prejudice, religion stands for certain self-knowledge and identity, which inevitably creates the desire to make both God and others in the image of our particular interpretation of religion.

At the deepest and most abstract philosophical level, all of these questions boil down to the balance between immanence and transcendence. When all is said and done in postmodern theory, we are left with an emphasis on historicity on the one hand and ineffable transcendent otherness that cannot say anything substantive about ethics and justice on the other. The problem of exaggerated particularity is confirmed by Terry Eagleton's claim in *After Theory* that postmodern cultural theory has little to say about ultimate values and the big topics such as morality, metaphysics, love, biology, religion, revolution, evil, death, suffering, essences, and universal foundations. This, as he concludes, is indeed "on any estimate a rather large slice of human existence to fall down on."[29]

As Richard Kearney has shown so convincingly in *Strangers, Gods, and Monsters*, on the other hand, when postmodern thinkers try to come up with ethics, radical otherness or alterity tends to lose all human contours. In the white, unspeakable space of transcendence, there is little difference between the monstrous and the divine. Even Levinas, who reintroduces Hebraic categories of personal transcendence into the project of self-understanding, overemphasizes this ethical transcendence so much that he renders it more traumatic, resorting to the hyperbolic expression of being taken hostage by the other. Too much transcendence can be a bad thing, because while it correctly limits human reason from colonizing the other, it leaves us still in opposition to the other; it traumatizes us with a sublime from on high which seems to prohibit real communion. Benedict affirmed the same problem for religious views of transcendence in his Regensburg lecture. If God transcends our human sense of reason, justice, and goodness absolutely, then violence may indeed be commanded in the name of God.[30] As a foundation for truly human dialogue, I must be able to know whether the other, whether human or divine, is intrinsically good and well disposed toward me.

What we need, in other words, is an ethical measure of our humanity and reason in which we participate ontologically and which unfolds hermeneutically but also transcends time, history, and culture. And this measure must have a face, preferably a human face. Reason should be intrinsically human and yet it cannot be fabricated by us. Where do we find such a concept? We could go to the work of Richard Kearney, who has written three books that chart a hermeneutical middle way between idolatrous views of religion and humanity and radical otherness. Kearney is an incarnational thinker who recognizes the human need for divine epiphanies, but he also knows the danger of truth-possession, hence his effort in establishing an eschatological hermeneutic of possibility, of the God who may be, and who becomes God when we "recreate the world for God."[31] Without question, Kearney is currently one of the most lucid, mediating philosophers of religion in the continental tradition, who combines the best of Levinas, Marion, and especially Ricoeur by emphasizing a narrative conception of the self and the realization of the divine in concrete human action.

The reason, however, I will not end with Kearney's eschatological hermeneutic of possibility is that his work is still too uneasy about God's presence. God is only real in this world, if we help God be God by helping "the least of these." Kearney touches here on the deep truth which applies to all human knowing, namely, that faith unfolds only in action. Yet his hermeneutic does not take full account of participation in the divine. To put it bluntly, it is not clear what role the institutional, visible church and its traditions have in Kearney's hermeneutic, and yet the incarnation demands a communal body, the church as the body of Christ, and the embryonic new humanity.[32]

This criticism of Kearney is not born from the usual academic need to save one's professional honour by finding fault in another's work. On the contrary, I am so impressed by Kearney's ability and desire to bring the transcendent into the human imagination, into human works and hence into literature, that I couldn't explain a feeling of unease in reading his work. It was not until Kearney clearly expressed his fundamental conviction in a CBC interview that the problem became clearer. Kearney opens the interview with this sentence: "In the beginning is hermeneuein — interpretation. In the beginning is the word. Not a stone, not a certitude.... In the beginning is the *word*; and as we know words are dialogical and you've got to listen and to respond."[33]

This primordial importance of interpretation frightens the fundamentalist evangelical. Yet after teaching for years in the climate of North American evangelicalism, I have come to understand that the evangelical may actually merely distort a fundamentally correct hermeneutical insight: his desire to reduce religion to absolute propositions is the survival instinct of the self, the *correct* desire for *having*, for *possessing*, an identity. Self-understanding as a hermeneutical process requires indeed, as Heidegger and later Gadamer have pointed out, a participation in universal reason, the ultimate whole of the hermeneutic circle by which we understand the penultimate part. Withholding this whole in the name of hermeneutics is not only cruel but self-defeating. Yet neither do we want this whole to turn into a totality by which we assimilate the other.

To emphasize a hermeneutical self, a narrative self that always develops and whose identity can only be deduced from what remains constant throughout this journey of the self, does not satisfy the human desire for identity but sacrifices it on the altar of hermeneutics to appease the idol of fundamentalism. We need a hermeneutic whole which grants us self-identity and in so doing — that is, in its very being — structures identity ontologically in its humanity as hermeneutical, ethical, and transcendent. This becomes possible when we change Kearney's sentence slightly from "in the beginning was interpretation" to "in the beginning was communion," or community. It is of course true that "in the beginning was the Word," but we cannot forget that the same text also tells us that "the Word was *with* God."

An incarnational hermeneutic must begin with this Trinitarian communal dimension at the heart of ontology; incarnational thinking proceeds from the realized communion of God with his people, the Incarnation of God in the church as the first Eucharist. It is from this first communion that all other Eucharistic acts, all other incarnations of the Divine into the lives of others, flow. No one makes this clearer than the Apostle Paul, whose advice to Christians is always "become what you already are." Possibility becomes actual only because of the actual already realized in Christ. But does not this view regress into sectarianism and triumphalism, into the hived-off "us" from the rest of humanity? This depends on our theology. By defining human identity Christologically, the Christian self is linked to the rest of humanity not "merely" as fellow creature, but also as a participant in the Christ event, which ensures that one's very being is shaped as "being-for-the-other."

Incarnational Hermeneutics
In the final portion of this essay, I want to briefly outline how incarnational thought addresses the current cultural demands on reason and self-understanding — that reason should be grounded in ontology, intrinsically ethical in its orientation to the other, and hermeneutical. The following provides merely a sketch of how incarnational thinkers in the Christian tradition have com-

bined the identity of "being in Christ" with a hermeneutical unfolding of this existence that structures being human ontologically as being for the other.

The trendsetter of Christianity as an "all-embracing humanism" is the second-century theologian Irenaeus:[34] "In all things, however, [Christ] is human, the formation of God. Recapitulating human being in Himself, the invisible is made visible, the incomprehensible is made comprehensible, and that which is not subject to suffering is made subject to suffering. The Word becoming human being recapitulates all things in Himself, so that just as the Word of God is foremost in things super-celestial, spiritual, and invisible, so also in things visible and corporeal He might have the primacy; and so that, in taking the primacy to Himself, and in constituting Himself the Head of the Church, He might at the proper time draw all things to Himself."[35]

From its beginnings in the church father Irenaeus, incarnational humanism expresses a fundamental ontological unity of all human beings in the divine Logos become flesh. For Irenaeus, the Incarnation draws into itself *all* of humanity, offering to the Father true humanity, the true *imago dei*.[36] Christ is "the perfect human being," the embodied communion of immanence and transcendence, identity and difference, consisting "in the co-mingling and the union of the soul receiving the spirit of the Father, and the admixture of that fleshly nature which was moulded after the image of God."[37] The Incarnation is a "recapitulation" of humanity, and thus an affirmation of the human as it was created.[38] In the Incarnation, history and the wholly other transcendence of God are fused into one particular and yet universal ideal of what it means to be human. As Henri de Lubac puts it, "Christ is not only the bearer of an eternal message which he repeats to the astonished ears of successive individuals, but also he in whom humanity finds an unexpected answer to the problems of its organic unity."[39]

This answer to the problem of unity is also God's response to the humanistic concern of self-knowledge. We find here the certainty of identity which nonetheless allows for difference and hermeneutical unfolding of this self. Henri de Lubac in his book *Catholicism: Christ and the Common Destiny of Man* argues that the Incarnation is the ultimate word concerning human self-understanding:[40]

> By revealing the Father and by being revealed by him, Christ completes the revelation of man to himself. By taking possession of man, by seizing hold of him and by penetrating to the very depths of his being Christ makes man go deep down within himself, there to discover in a flash regions hitherto unsuspected. It is through Christ that the person reaches maturity, that man emerges definitively from the universe and becomes conscious of his own being.... The wise man's precept "know thyself" takes on a new meaning. Every man who says "I" gives utterance to something that is absolute and definitive.[41]

It is definitive because in the Incarnation, with its unique union of human and divine, of the particular and the transcendent, of the historical and the eternal, of the cultural and the collective human race, here the very "idea of human unity is born. That image of God, the image of the Word, which the incarnate Word restores and gives back to its glory, is 'I myself'; it is also the other, *every* other. It is that aspect of *me* in which I coincide with every other man, it is the hallmark of our common origin and the summons to our common destiny. It is our very unity in God."[42]

This unity of all human beings in God is most fully realized in the Christian and the Church as the embryonic new humanity. And so the deepest mystery of our unity with the Trinity defines our humanity: "[W]e are fully persons only within the Person of the Son, by whom and with whom we share in the circumcession [mutual co-inhabiting] of the Trinity."[43] Only here do we find the fullest understanding of what it means to be human according to the Trinitarian pattern. The subject is founded primordially neither in the other human being nor in narrative, but called into being by the wholly other who demonstrated his goodness by dying for the other.

Yet at the same time, this ontological participation in Christ does not separate the Church from the rest of humanity but rather establishes an intrinsic connection between the two. At the very heart of the Church, in the encounter with the incarnate Word of God, through preaching and the Eucharist, we participate in Christ's humanity, which is ontologically structured as *being-for-others*. Without lapsing into a neo-Platonic or Romantic panentheism, we can nonetheless affirm that Eucharistic participation in the Incarnation links us, in Christ, to all of humanity and thus with the suffering of all of humanity. As one theologian put it, in the Church, the reconciling power of the Cross is "grafted onto the great pain-ridden body of human kind."[44]

Benedict, standing in the same tradition, can therefore recover in the Eucharistic theology of the Church Fathers a vision not only for the unity of the Church but also for the nations: "The being of Jesus Christ and his message brought a new dynamic into humanity, the transitional dynamic from the ruptured being of many individuals into the unity of Jesus Christ, into the unity of God. And the church is basically nothing else but this dynamic, this setting into motion of humanity toward the unity of God." And because in Christ this unity concerns not just Christians but the entire human race, the Communion table emphasizes the common brotherhood of all human beings: while we feed on the body of Christ at the Communion table, writes Benedict, we are at the same time participating in *human* intercommunication. The Church models the "melting of individuals into one new human being."[45] This Eucharistic definition of human existence as participating in the Logos "in whom all things hang together" provides the Christological foundation for a Eucharistic hermeneutic as admirably described by Valentine Cunningham in his *Reading after Theory*: "Here's a body of text, and the text as body, the body of the other, the text as other, to be consumed, ingested, in a memorial act, an act of personal reception and reflection, an inward event which is also an outward-working act, an act of testimony, of worldly witness.... In ... holy communion, the believer is blessed and graced, signed as Christ's own, marked as sanctified. In reading on this [Eucharistic] model, the reader is, in some way or another, also graced, blessed, marked as the text's own."[46] As Cunningham explains, texts are to be treated with tact and respect, and texts have a transformative effect because the fragments of interpretation find an ultimate common ground in the Logos in whom our common humanity exists.

I hope to have made a plausible case for the intrinsic connection between Christology, ecclesiology, and our professional activities for the good of humanity, including the activities of studying, learning, and teaching, all the things we commonly subsume under the notion of "the life of the mind." By virtue of this link, the Christian is called to labour for the good of humanity, to suffer with humanity in its common problems. Have we forgotten completely, now, Habermas's post-metaphysical worries? In embracing the Church as a sacrament for humanity, and in speaking so clearly about the unified goal of humanity in Christ, are we not in fact confirming the suspicions that the Christian religion knows nothing about the interpretive dimension of reason?

On the contrary. As Luther already put it so well, Christians as the embryonic new humanity inaugurated by Christ live not as in a completely different realm but live differently in the same world, now in faith and in an "unclear Word" through the incarnate Christ. For Luther, Christ is the "glass darkly" through whom we perceive our humanity.[47] Faith is first of all a being in Christ, and out of this community we unfold interpretively what it means to be Christ for the other, because every other is presented as an image of God in Christ.

The Lutheran theologian Dietrich Bonhoeffer confirms this interpretive emphasis of the Christian faith. With the Church Fathers, Bonhoeffer can affirm that "[t]he new humanity is altogether concentrated in one single historical locus, in Jesus Christ, and only in him is it [humanity] understood as a whole.... Now, because in Jesus Christ the entire new humanity is truly established, he represents in his historical life the entire history of humanity."[48] Consequently, "[t]he church may be called the body of Christ, because in the body of Jesus Christ *human being per se* (and therefore all human beings) has really been taken on. The church now bears the form that in truth is meant for all people. The image according to which it is being formed is the image of humanity. What takes place in the church happens vicariously and representatively as a model of all human beings."[49]

Bonhoeffer insists on Christian identity as participation in the Trinity, which is unfolded reflectively with an ontological structure as "being-for-the-other," as "suffering for the world."[50] This reflective unfolding within the interpretive tradition of the Church transpires by availing ourselves of all human reflection by the best thinkers, because they too are illumined by the same Logos, even if they do not enjoy relational participation in him ("The word shines in all, but all do not have it in them").[51]

Not only is the very process of knowing God unfolding interpretively, but the Christian's relation to culture, to the world, is also deeply hermeneutical. Bonhoeffer captures this eschatological tension of Christian existence between the ultimate redeemed humanity and the continuation of the current fallen world in his distinction of the ultimate-penultimate relation. Bonhoeffer boldly affirms the incarnate, resurrected Logos as the center of reality. If Christianity is true, to be reasonable and to be realistic is to view the world as united in the living Word of God: "Secular and sacred are not opposed but find their unity in Christ. At the deepest level of reality, we cannot speak about the reality of religion and the reality of secular life; rather we must speak about the divine and cosmic reality of Christ. The world, the natural, the profane, and reason are now all taken up into God from the outset. They do not exist in themselves and on their own account. *They have their reality nowhere save in the reality of God in Christ.*"[52]

But because the eternal Logos has entered reality in the flesh, has taken up creation and transformed it, so our understanding of the Christian faith must follow this pattern: "Just as in Christ the reality of God entered into the reality of the world, so, too, is that which is Christian to be found only in the natural, the holy only in the profane, and the revelational only in the rational." While human reason is unified in Christ, unfolding this unity is an all-demanding struggle bearing the full risk and responsibility of interpretation.[53]

Conclusion

An incarnational hermeneutic seeks to combine the Passion of Christ with the passion of the intellect in two meanings of the word passion. First of all, incarnational humanism champions a passionate intellect by denouncing dualistic views of Church and culture. In the idea of Christ as the universal Logos whose Incarnation and Resurrection inaugurates the new humanity, we find an immediate transcendent unity and goal for human reason. Moreover, because of this unity of a common reason and humanity in Christ, incarnational humanism stresses an interpretive Christian life in the common public sphere.

Secondly, because the Christian mode of existence is ontologically cruciform, an incarnational hermeneutic implies an intellect which is passionate in the second sense of the word, as "suffering." The Eucharist serves as a reminder that our lives and intellectual activities are a suffering with humanity in Christ.[54] The Incarnation defines reason as pathic, as suffering-with. Not at all do we have to hide our religious passion and conviction. As Benedict put it in his apostolic letter on the Eucharist, "Our communities, when they celebrate the Eucharist, must become ever more conscious that the sacrifice of Christ is for all, and that the Eucharist thus compels all who believe in him to become 'bread that is broken' for others."[55] This means that for the Christian, the deepest mystery of the Incarnation and the passions it evokes link directly to all of our professional and everyday lives, because they are to be lived in service to the humanity for whom Christ gave himself.

The common fear that religious dogma must be avoided at all cost in order to assure peaceful coexistence with those of other convictions has it backwards. If we understand our Christian Logos-centric heritage correctly, the deeper our understanding of the mysteries of the faith, the richer our Christological doctrine, the more Christianity will become the solution rather than the problem in society. In our current intellectual culture it is important to understand that solidarity and common humanity are *intrinsic* to the Christian faith, and we should recover the passion antecedent Christian minds derived from the mystery of the Incarnation in this regard. One of the best literary illustrations of how contemplating this mystery is a participation in the Trinity that moves us to share in God's love for the world is Dante's beatific vision. In this vision we find all the aspects of the passionate intellect we have discussed: the nature of reason and its limits, the desire for self-understanding, the need for interpretation of knowing, the inexplicable correlation of ontology and transcendence, and the intrinsic structuring of being as suffering, as being-for-the-other, an encounter of otherness which bears the indelible stamp of love for me and is therefore not traumatic but attractive, drawing us toward action.

After a long ascent to the seat of God, Dante's pilgrim looks at the Trinity. This is what he sees:

> That circle—which begotten so, appeared
> In You as light reflected—when my eyes
> had watched it with attention for some time,
> within itself and colored like itself,
> to me seemed painted with our effigy,
> so that my sight was set on it completely.
> As the geometer intently seeks
> to square the circle, but he cannot reach,
> through thought on thought, the principle he needs,[56]
> so I searched that strange sight: I wished to see
> the way in which our human effigy

suited the circle and found place in it—
and my own wings [reason] were far too weak for that.
But then my mind was struck by light that flashed
and, with this light, received what it had asked.
Here force failed my high fantasy: but *my
desire and will were moved* already—like
a wheel revolving uniformly—by
the Love that moves the sun and the other stars.
      —*Paradiso*, canto 33, lines 127–45[57]

May our desire and will be moved likewise.

Notes

1 Terry Eagleton, *After Theory* (London: Allen Lane; New York: Basic Books, 2003) 15, 73.

2 Ibid., 72.

3 Ibid., 123, 120.

4 Jean Baudrillard, *Simulacra and Simulation*, trans. Sheila Faria Glaser (Ann Arbor: University of Michigan Press, 2004) 149. His words are "le cadavre en spirale."

5 "The values of the university (diplomas, etc.) will proliferate and continue to circulate, a bit like floating capital or Eurodollars, they will spiral without referential criteria, completely devalorized in the end, but that is unimportant: their circulation alone is enough to create a social horizon of value, and the ghostly presence of the phantom value will even be greater, even when its reference point (its use value, its exchange value, the academic 'work force' that the university recoups) is lost. Terror of value without equivalence" (Baudrillard, *Simulacra and Simulation*, 155).

6 *National Post*, 28 Apr. 2007: A1; italics mine.

7 Pera recognizes the centrality of the Incarnation for Western liberal humanism when he writes, "[I]t is true that almost all of the achievements that we consider most laudable are derived from Christianity or were influenced by Christianity, by the message of God become Man. In truth without this message, which has transformed all human beings into persons in the image of God, individuals would have no dignity. In truth our values, rights, and duties of equality, tolerance, respect, solidarity, and compassion are born from God's sacrifice. In truth, our attitude toward others, toward all others, whatever their condition, class, appearance or culture is shaped by the Christian revolution. In truth, even our institutions are inspired by Christianity, including the secular institutions of government that render unto Caesar that which is Caesar's" (Joseph Ratzinger [Pope Benedict XVI] and Marcello Pera, *Without Roots: The West, Relativism, Christianity, Islam*, trans. Michael F. Moore [New York: Basic Books, 2006] 36–37).

8 John Sommerville, *The Decline of the Secular University* (Oxford: Oxford University Press, 2006) 38.

9 Ibid., 26.

10 Stanley Fish, "One University under God?" *Chronicle of Higher Education*, 7 Jan. 2005, http://chronicle.com/article/One-University-Under-God-/45077.

11 Hereafter, Joséph Ratzinger, Pope Benedict XVI, will be identified in the body of the essay as Benedict.

12 Jürgen Habermas and Joseph Ratzinger (Pope Benedict XVI), *Dialektik der Säkularisierung: Über Vernunft und Religion*, ed. Florian Schuller (Freiburg: Herder, 2005) 57; unless otherwise noted, all translations from the German are mine.

13 Ibid., 4.

14 For example, the humanist Erasmus of Rotterdam writes, "And what is it that properly belongeth unto man? Verily, to live according to reason, and for that is called a reasonable creature and divided from those that cannot speak" (qtd. in Joanna Martindale, ed. *English Humanism: Wyatt to Cowley* [London: Croom Helm, 1985] 59). Also, the Reformers were united on this point, continuing the tradition of Augustine and Aquinas, who saw reason as part of the image of God in man, and made reason, any good reasoning or discovery of truth, dependent on divine illumination. Like Augustine before and John Calvin after him, Luther believed that even the achievements of the ungodly are witnesses to the divine likeness in human beings. Reason and culture generally point to God because, in contrast with the animals, humanity enjoys not merely a natural awareness but, by virtue of his divine likeness, also the light of reason: "but man (*der Mensch*) is especially gifted with the glorious light of reason and understanding. That human beings thought up and invented so many noble arts, be it wisdom, dexterity, or skilfulness, all this derives from this light, or from this Word, which was the life of humanity. In such a way this life, Christ, is not only a light to himself, but illumines all human beings with this light, so that all understanding, cleverness and skilfulness, as far as they are not deceptive and demonic, flow from this light as Wisdom of the eternal father" ("Auslegung über den Evangelisten Johannes" in Martin Luther's *Sämtliche Schriften*, Band 7, ed. Johann G. Walch [Groß Oesingen, Ger.: Verlag der Lutherischen Buchhandlung Heinrich Harms, 1986], S. 1567). Also found in *Sermons on the Gospel of St. John: Chapters 1-4, Luther's Works*, gen. ed. J. J. Pelikan, vol. 22 [St. Louis, MO: Concordia Publishing House, 1956], 30). Clearly Jesus is here equated with logos, the word of God with reason.

15 Hans-Georg Gadamer, *Philosophical Hermeneutics*, ed. and trans. David E. Linge (Berkeley: University of California Press, 1976) 55; see also *Gesammelte Werke*, vol. 2 (Tübingen, Ger.: J.C.B. Mohr, 1985), 40–41; hereafter *Gesammelte Werke* will be abbreviated *GW*.

16 Giambattista Vico, *On Humanistic Education (Six Inaugural Orations, 1699–1707)*, trans. Giorgio A. Pinto and Arthur W. Shippee (Ithaca, NY: Cornell University Press, 1993) 37–38.

17 Ibid., 35.

18 William Harrison Woodward, *Vittorino Dà Feltre and Other Humanist Educators*, Renaissance Society of America Reprint Texts Series 5 (Toronto: University of Toronto Press; New York: Renaissance Society of America, 1996) 133.

19 Vico, *On Humanistic Education*, 41.

20 Martin Heidegger, *An Introduction to Metaphysics*, trans. Ralph Manheim (New Haven, CT: Yale University Press, 1987) 134–35.

21 Ibid., 141.

22 Ibid., 143–44.

23 Ibid., 144.

24 Gadamer in principle adopts Heidegger's model of reason but tones down the the-
    ological mysticism of Being to·a more sober Greek idea of logos participation in
    suggesting the "mid-world" of language and the universality of interpretation on
    account of our existence in language as an expression of rationality; "understand-
    ing is inseparably tied to language (*sprachgebunden*); that is how one should
    understand the universal claim of the hermeneutical dimension" (*GW* 2.231). This
    is summarized in his well-known motto: "Being that can be expressed is language."

25 His former student Gadamer revealed in his last substantial interview that Mitsein
    and the other were concessions by Heidegger rather than intrinsic elements of his
    philosophy: "Mitsein is a concession for Heidegger that he had to make but which
    he didn't really believe in. Already back then when he developed this notion [of
    Mitsein], he really was not talking about the other. It can be said that Mit-sein is
    a statement about Dasein which, of course, has to allow for the existence of
    Mitsein.... His notion of 'Care' (*Sorge*) is always care about one's own being, and
    Mit-sein is in truth a very weak thought of the other, indicating more a 'letting the
    other be' than a being-turned-toward-the-other" (Hans-Georg Gadamer, *Die Lek-
    tion des Jahrhunderts* [Münster: Lit Verlag, 2002] 26). Gadamer adds that Heideg-
    ger recognized this difference: "He acknowledged that I associated more with the
    thought about the other than he did with his Mit-sein. Mit-sein is a weak expres-
    sion because it leaves open the 'with,' that the other is also a Dasein; 'this also' then
    becomes, so to speak, his justification for his conscience" (ibid., 27).

26 Emmanuel Levinas, *Humanismus des anderen Menschen*, ed. Ludwig Wenzler and
    Christoph von Wolzogen, Philosophische Bibliothek (Hamburg: F. Meiner, 2005) 90.

27 See Simon Critchley's description of this trauma and its need for sublimation:
    "Levinas seems to be describing ethical responsibility as the maintenance of a per-
    manent state of Trauma." Critchley finds the necessary sublimation of this trauma
    in the discourse of philosophy, a return to ontology and reflection, but now to a
    same that had been altered through the ethical encounter. However, this depends
    on the nature of philosophy, and reflection here remains the constant ontological
    menace that threatens to ossify the saying in the said (Simon Critchley, *Ethics, Pol-
    itics, Subjectivity: Essays on Derrida, Levinas and Contemporary French Thought*
    [London: Verso, 1999] 205–6).

28 While Levinas can still tie this notion of difference to a radically transcendent bib-
    lical God, Derrida can only talk about difference as such. His work constitutes,
    again, an examination of the nature of reason. All of humanity, says Derrida, is
    plagued by the desire for immediacy, for unmediated knowledge through the inner
    voice. In Western philosophy from Plato onward, this desire has expressed itself
    through the definition of reason, or the logos, as pure unmediated communica-
    tion between minds or the full presence of truth. Hence his term "Logocentrism,"
    which, to add to our problems, was largely defined in favour of male rationality, so
    that we end up with phallo-logo-centrism. Derrida thus becomes an inverted Pla-
    tonist, driven by the fear of immediate presence which objectifies. Derrida leaves
    us with the fear of presence, and many have taken up his misunderstanding of
    presence as objectification into the discussion of religion. Presence becomes
    equated with assimilation, with foreshortening interpretive possibilities, even with
    violence. Theologically, this fear of ontological participation is the soil from which
    sprout the gods without being (Jean-Luc Marion) and the gods who may be
    (Richard Kearney).

29 Eagleton, *After Theory*, 102.

30 Ratzinger, Joseph (Pope Benedict XVI), *Der Glaube ist Einfach! Ansprachen, Meditationen, Predigten während des Besuches in Bayern* (Leipzig: St. Benno Verlag, 2006) 112.

31 Richard Kearney, *The God Who May Be: A Hermeneutics of Religion*, Indiana Series in the Philosophy of Religion (Bloomington: Indiana University Press, 2001) 110.

32 There are statements in which Kearney specifies that his emphasis is a correction to excessive focus on God as substance: "It is my wager in this chapter that one of the main ways in which the infinite comes to be experienced and imagined by finite minds is as *possibility*—that is, as *the ability to be*. Even, and especially, when such possibility seems impossible to us. I am not saying this is the only way… just that it is a very telling way, and one that has been largely neglected in the history of Western metaphysics and theology in favor of categories such as substance, cause, actuality, absolute spirit, and sufficient reason" (Richard Kearney, "Hermeneutics of the Possible God," *Givenness and God: Questions of Jean-Luc Marion*, ed. Ian Leask and Eoin Cassidy [New York: Fordham University Press, 2005] 220).

33 Richard Kearney, "The God Who May Be," conversation with David Cayley, *Ideas*, CBC Radio, 20 Feb., 27 Feb., and 6 Mar. 2006 (*Ideas* Transcripts ID 2964).

34 Henri de Lubac, *Catholicism: Christ and the Common Destiny of Man*, trans. Lancelot C. Sheppard and Elizabeth Englund (San Francisco: Ignatius Press, 1988) 321.

35 Irenaeus, *Adversus haereses*, 3.17.1 (*Against Heresies*, in *The Apostolic Fathers with Justin Martyr and Irenaeus*, ed. Alexander Roberts, James Donaldson, and Arthur Cleveland Coxe [Grand Rapids, MI: Hendrickson, 2004] 443, left column).

36 Irenaeus argues that the Christ ascended to heaven, "commending to his Father that human nature (*hominem*) [i.e., "*den Menschen*"] which had been found, making in His own person the first-fruits of the resurrection of man." In Christ all those who are members of this new body, this new humanity, will find a place in heaven when rising again (ibid., 3.19.1., 449, right column).

37 Ibid., 5.6.1, 531, right column (see also 532, left column).

38 Ibid., 5.25.4, 554, left column. See also Irenaeus's comment that "[the framer of the whole creation's] son was his Word, by whom He founded all things; and that He, in the last times, was made a man among men; that He re-formed the human race, but destroyed and conquered the enemy of man, and gave to his handiwork victory against the adversary" (ibid., 4.24.1., 495, left column). See also 5.23.2, 551, right column: "His sufferings upon the day preceding the Sabbath, that is, the sixth day of the creation, on which day man was created; thus granting him a second creation by means of His passion, which is that [creation] out of death."

39 Henri de Lubac, *Catholicism*, 356; de Lubac cites Canon Masure.

40 See also Eberhard Jüngel's statement to the same effect in *God as the Mystery of the World*, which captures the idea of Christ as the incarnation of human self-understanding (Eberhard Jüngel, *Gott als Geheimnis der Welt: Zur Begründung d. Theologie d. Gekreuzigten im Streit zwischen Theismus u. Atheismus*, 3rd ed. [Tübingen, Ger.: Mohr, 1978] 207).

41 See de Lubac, *Catholicism*, 339–40.

42 Ibid.

43 Ibid., 342.

44 God's "salvation through agape and communion is realized in this: in his historical work, the Son assumed everything in the human condition (by taking it on

himself); at the same time, since the resurrection, he continues to live in his members the human tragedy in all its truth and all its reality. What this means is not a 'continued incarnation' but the fulfillment (teleiosis) of the work of the incarnation in the power of the Spirit" (ibid., 138).

45 Joseph Ratzinger (Pope Benedict XVI), *Die Einheit der Nationen. Eine Vision d. Kirchenväter* (Salzburg and Munich: Pustet, 2005) 35.

46 Valentine Cunningham, *Reading after Theory* (Oxford: Blackwell, 2002) 148.

47 "Nicht als ob es ein völlig anderes Reich wäre, sondern ganz anders ist nur die Art und Weise, wie darin regiert wird, jetzt im Glauben, und in einem 'dunklen Wort' durch den menschgewordenen Christus, einst im Schauen und der Offenbarung der göttlichen Natur (2 Kor. 5, 7; 1 Kor. 13, 12)" (Martin Luther, *Kommentar zum Galaterbrief 1519*, ed. Wolfgang Metzler, Calwer Luther-Ausgabe, Band 10 [Stuttgart: Calwer Verlag, 1996] 26.

48 *Dietrich Bonhoeffer Werke*, ed. Eberhard Bethge et al., 17 vols. (Munich: Chr. Kaiser Verlag, 1986–1999), 1.91–92; *Dietrich Bonhoeffer Werke* is hereafter abbreviated *DBW*.

49 *Ethics*, vol. 6 of *Dietrich Bonhoeffer's Works*, ed. Clifford J. Green, trans. Reinhard Krauss, Charles C. West, and Douglas W. Stott (Minneapolis: Fortress, 2004) 96–97; (*DBW*, 6.85); *Ethics* is hereafter abbreviated *DBWE*, 6.

50 *DBW* 8.558: "Encounter with Jesus Christ. Experience that here a complete reversal of human existence occurs, namely in the fact that Jesus is only 'there for others.' This 'being-there-for-others' of Jesus is experience of transcendence as such. In freedom on his own accord, in the 'being-for-others' to the death does omnipotence, omniscience, omnipresence derive in the first place. Faith is participation in this being of Christ (Incarnation, Cross, Resurrection)." That is why faith is not a religious relation to God, to a "highest, most powerful, most good being—that is not real transcendence—but our relation to God is a new life in 'being-there-for-others,' in participation in Jesus' being. Not the infinite, unreachable tasks, but the respective given reachable neighbour is the transcendent. God in human form!" This is what sets Christianity apart from other religions (ibid.).

51 *DBW* 2.110: "Theology is a function of the church, because church is not without preaching, preaching not without memory; theology, however, is the memory of the church." Theological knowledge, says Bonhoeffer, "is not existential knowledge; its object is that memory of what happened in the Christian community, in the Bible, in the sermon and sacrament, prayer, confession, in the words of Christ, which is kept [*aufbewahrt*] as existent [*als Seiendes*] in the church"; Maurice Blondel, *Action (1893): Essay on a Critique of Life and a Science of Practice*, trans. Oliva Blanchette (Notre Dame, IN: University of Notre Dame, 1984) 393.

52 Bonhoeffer, *DBW*, 6.44 (*DBWE*, 6.59).

53 According to Bonhoeffer, living out the Christ reality of the new humanity is an interpretive effort, a concrete ethic which applies Christ's humanity to every cultural situation anew: "The unity of the reality of God and of the world, which has been accomplished in Christ, is repeated, or, more exactly, is realized, ever afresh in the life of men. And yet what is Christian is not identical with what is of the world. The natural is not identical with the supernatural or the revelational with the rational. But between the two there is in each case a unity which derives solely from the reality of Christ" (ibid.).

54 "[B]y sharing the sacrifice of the Cross, the Christian partakes of Christ's self-giving love and is equipped and committed to live this same charity in all his thoughts and deeds" (Joseph Ratzinger [Pope Benedict XVI], *The Sacrament of Charity* [Washington, DC: USCCB Publishing, 2007] 69).

55 *Post-synodal Apostolic Exhortation Sacramentum Caritatis*, 42. http://www.vatican.va/holy_father/benedict_xvi/apost_exhortations/documents/hf_ben-xvi_ exh_ 20070222_sacramentum-caritatis_en.html.

56 A geometer is a mathematician specializing in geometry. Just as the mathematical mind, seeking to understand the highest impossibility of geometric math, the squaring of the circle, so the pilgrim seeks to understand how something human can fit the perfection of the Trinity. The answer is not mathematical understanding but goes beyond reason to movement with the love of God.

57 Dante Alighieri, *The Divine Comedy of Dante Alighieri: Paradiso*, trans. Allen Mandelbaum (New York: Bantam, 1982) 109; italics mine.

BIBLIOGRAPHY

Aalders, Cynthia. "'Hymns and music were poured out': Moravian Hymnody and the Evangelical Revival." Unpublished paper. Regent College, Vancouver, 2007.

Abrams, M.H. *Natural Supernaturalism: Tradition and Revolution in Romantic Literature.* New York: Norton, 1973.

Addison, Joseph. "XXII. Pleasures of Imagination." *The Spectator* 411 (21 June 1712).

Aelred of Rievaulx. *Aelred of Rievaulx's De Institutione Inclusarum: Two English Versions.* Ed. John Ayto and Alexandra Barratt. Early English Text Society, o.s., 287. London: Oxford University Press, 1984.

———. *De Institutione Inclusarum.* Eng. poet. a.l. Vernon MS. Bodleian Library, Oxford.

———. *De Institutione Inclusarum.* MS Bodley 423. Bodleian Library, Oxford.

Aers, David. "*The Parliament of Fowls*: Authority, the Knower and the Known." *Chaucer Review* 16.1 (1981): 1–17.

Aers, David, and Lynne Staley. *The Powers of the Holy: Religion, Politics, and Gender in Late Medieval English Culture.* University Park: Pennsylvania State University Press, 1996.

Agamben, Giorgio. *The Coming Community.* Trans. Michael Hardt. Minneapolis: University of Minnesota Press, 2007.

———. *The Time That Remains: A Commentary on the Letter to the Romans.* Trans. Patricia Dailey. Stanford, CA: Stanford University Press, 2005.

Aikenside, Mark. *The Pleasures of Imagination: A Poem in Three Books.* London, 1744.

Ajzenstat, Oona. *Driven Back to the Text: The Premodern Sources of Levinas' Postmodernism.* Pittsburgh: Duquesne University Press, 2001.

Anchoritic Spirituality: Ancrene Wisse and Associated Works. Trans. Anne Savage and Nicholas Watson. New York: Paulist Press, 1991.

Ancrene Wisse: A Corrected Edition of the Text in Cambridge, Corpus Christi College, MS 402, with Variants from Other Manuscripts: Drawing on the Uncompleted Edition by E.J. Dobson, with a Glossary and Additional Notes by Richard Dance. Ed. Bella Millett. Vol. 1. Early English Text Society, o.s., 325. Oxford: Oxford University Press, 2005.

Anderson, J.J. "The Narrators in the *Book of the Duchess* and the *Parlement of Foules*." *Chaucer Review* 26.3 (1992): 219–35.

Anderson, Judith H. "The 'couert vele': Chaucer, Spenser, and Venus." *English Literary Renaissance* 24.3 (1994): 638–59.

Ankersmit, F.R. *Sublime Historical Experience.* Stanford, CA: Stanford University Press, 2005.

Anselm, Saint. *The Prayers and Meditations of St. Anselm.* Trans. Sister Benedicta Ward, S.L.G. London: Penguin, 1973.

Arseneau, Mary. *Recovering Christina Rossetti: Female Community and Incarnational Poetics.* New York: Palgrave, 2004.

Asals, Heather. "The Voice of George Herbert's 'The Church.'" *ELH* 36.3 (Sept. 1969): 511–28.

Atwood, Margaret. Introduction. *Alice Munro's Best: Selected Stories.* By Alice Munro. Toronto: McClelland and Stewart, 2006.

———. Contribution. "Appreciations of Alice Munro." Comp. Lisa Dickler Awano. *Virginia Quarterly Review* 82.3 (2006): 91–107.

Auerbach, Erich. *Mimesis: The Representation of Reality in Western Literature.* Princeton, NJ: Princeton University Press, 1968.

Augustine. *Concerning the City of God against the Pagans.* London: Penguin, 1984.

Badiou, Alain. *Saint Paul: The Foundation of Universalism.* Trans. Ray Brassier. Stanford, CA: Stanford University Press, 2003.

Baillie, Joanna. *The Dramatic and Poetical Works.* 1851. New York: Georg Olms Verlag, 1976.

———. *The Dream. Six Gothic Dramas.* Chicago: Valancourt, 2007.

———. *Joanna Baillie: A Selection of Plays and Poems.* Ed. Amanda Gilroy and Keith Hanley. London: Pickering and Chatto, 2002.

———. *A View of the General Tenour of the New Testament Regarding the Nature and Dignity of Jesus Christ.* London, 1831.

Baker, Brian. "The Map of Apocalypse: Nuclear War and the Space of Dystopia in American Science Fiction." *Histories of the Future: Studies in Fact, Fantasy, and Science Fiction.* Ed. Alan Sandison and Robert Dingley. London: Palgrave, 2000. 124–36.

Bald, R.C. *John Donne: A Life.* New York: Oxford University Press, 1970.

Balthasar, Hans Urs von. *Dare We Hope "That All Men Be Saved"?* San Francisco: Ignatius Press, 1988.

———. *Seeing the Form.* Ed. Joseph Fessio and John Riches. Trans. Erasmo Leiva-Merikakis. San Francisco: Ignatius Press, 1982. Vol. 1 of *The Glory of the Lord: A Theological Aesthetics.*

Banks, Russell. Contribution. "Appreciations of Alice Munro." Comp. Lisa Dickler Awano. *Virginia Quarterly Review* 82.3 (2006): 91–107.

Barratt, Alexandra. Introduction. *Women's Writing in Middle English.* Ed. Alexandra Barratt. London: Longman, 1992. 1–23.

Batnitzky, Leora. *Idolatry and Representation: The Philosophy of Franz Rosenzweig Reconsidered.* Princeton, NJ: Princeton University Press, 2000.

Baudrillard, Jean. *Simulacra and Simulation.* Trans. Sheila Faria Glaser. Ann Arbor: University of Michigan Press, 2004.

Bauerschmidt, Frederick Christian. "Loosening Our Grip: Julian of Norwich." *Mysticism.* Ed. Robert B. Kruschwitz. Waco, TX: Baylor University Center for Christian Ethics, 2005. 29–36. Vol. 17 of *Christian Reflection: A Series in Faith and Ethics.*

Bawer, Bruce. "Quiet—Author Suffering." Rev. of *The Writing Life*, by Annie Dillard. *American Scholar* 59.3 (1990): 445–49.

Beer, Gillian. "Negation in *A Passage to India.*" *A Passage to India: Essays in Interpretation*. Ed. John Beer. Towtowa, NJ: Barnes and Noble, 1986. 44–58.

Beilin, Elaine V., ed. *The Examinations of Anne Askew*. Oxford: Oxford University Press, 1996.

Belsey, Catherine. "Tarquin Dispossessed: Expropriation and Consent in 'The Rape of Lucrece.'" *Shakespeare Quarterly* 52.3 (2001): 315–35.

Benjamin, Walter. *The Arcades Project*. Trans. Howard Eiland and Kevin McLaughlin. Cambridge, MA: Belknap-Harvard University Press, 1999.

———. *The Correspondence of Walter Benjamin: 1910–1940*. Ed. Gershom Scholem and Theodor W. Adorno. Trans. Manfred R. Jacobson and Evelyn M. Jacobson. Chicago: University of Chicago Press, 1994.

———. "The Image of Proust." *Illuminations: Essays and Reflections*. Ed. Hannah Arendt. Trans. Harry Zohn. New York: Schocken, 1985. 201–16.

———. "On the Concept of History." *Walter Benjamin: Selected Writings, Volume 4, 1938–1940*. Ed. Howard Eiland and Michael W. Jennings. Cambridge, MA: Belknap-Harvard University Press, 2006. 389–400.

———. "Theses on the Philosophy of History." *Illuminations: Essays and Reflections*. Ed. Hannah Arendt. Trans. Harry Zohn. New York: Schocken, 1985. 253–64.

Bennett, J.A.W. *The Parlement of Foules: An Interpretation*. Oxford: Clarendon, 1957.

Bergo, Bettina. *Levinas between Ethics and Politics: For the Beauty That Adorns the Earth*. Dordrecht, Neth.: Kluwer, 1999.

Bernand, Carmen. *The Incas: People of the Sun*. London: Harry N. Abrams, 1994.

Bernard of Clairvaux. "Sermon 61." *On the Song of Songs III: Bernard of Clairvaux*. Ed. and trans. Kilian Walsh and Irene M. Edmonds. Kalamazoo, MI: Cistercian Publications, 1976. 144–45.

Bernard-Donals, Michael, and Richard Glejzer. *Between Witness and Testimony: The Holocaust and the Limits of Representation*. Albany: State University of New York Press, 2001.

Besse, Joseph. *A Collection of the Sufferings of the People Called Quakers*. London, 1753. 2 vols.

Bhabha, Homi K. *The Location of Culture*. London and New York: Routledge, 1994.

Bittle, William M. *James Nayler (1618–1660): The Quaker Indicted by Parliament*. York, UK: Friends United Press, 1986.

Blackburn, Simon. "Hypostatic union." *The Oxford Dictionary of Philosophy*. 2008.

Blakemore, Steven. *Crisis in Representation: Thomas Paine, Mary Wollstonecraft, Helen Maria Williams*. Madison, NJ: Fairleigh Dickinson University Press, 1997.

Bloch, Chana. *Spelling the Word: George Herbert and the Bible*. Berkeley: University of California Press, 1985.

Blondel, Maurice. *Action (1893): Essay on a Critique of Life and a Science of Practice*. Trans. Oliva Blanchette. Notre Dame, IN: University of Notre Dame, 1984.

Blumenthal, David. *Facing the Abusing God: A Theology of Protest*. Louisville, KY: Westminster/John Knox Press, 1993.

Boccaccio, Giovanni. *The Book of Theseus*. Trans. Bernadette Marie McCoy. New York: Medieval Text Association, 1974.

Boitani, Piero. "Old books brought to life in dreams: The *Book of the Duchess*, the *House of Fame*, the *Parliament of Fowls.*" *The Cambridge Companion to Chaucer*.

Ed. Piero Boitani and Jill Mann. 2nd ed. Cambridge: Cambridge University Press, 2003. 58–77.

Bonaventure. *Commentary on the Gospel of Luke*. Ed. and Trans. Robert J. Karris. 3 vols. St. Bonaventure, NY: Franciscan Institute Publications, 2001–3.

Bonhoeffer, Dietrich. *Dietrich Bonhoeffer Werke*. Ed. Eberhard Bethge et al. 17 vols. Munich: Chr. Kaiser Verlag, 1986–99.

———. *Ethics*. Ed. Clifford J. Green. Trans. Reinhard Krauss, Charles C. West, and Douglas W. Stott. Minneapolis: Fortress, 2004. Vol. 6 of *Dietrich Bonhoeffer's Works*.

———. *Sanctorum Communio*. Trans. Reinhard Krauss and Nancy Lukens. Minneapolis: Fortress, 1998.

Booy, David. *Autobiographical Writings by Early Quaker Women*. Aldershot, UK: Ashgate, 2004.

Boulton, J.T. Introduction. *A Philosophical Enquiry into the Origin of Our Ideas of the Sublime and Beautiful*. By Edmund Burke. New York: Columbia University Press, 1958.

Bowers, Fredson. "Herbert's Sequential Imagery: 'The Temper.'" *Modern Philology* 59 (1962): 202–13.

Bowler, Maurice G. "Rosenzweig on Judaism and Christianity—The Two Covenant Theory." *Judaism* 22.4 (1973): 475–81.

Boykan, Martin. *Silence and Slow Time: Studies in Musical Narrative*. Oxford: Scarecrow, 2004.

Boyle, Robert. *James Joyce's Pauline Vision: A Catholic Exposition*. Carbondale: Southern Illinois University Press, 1978.

Brailsford, Mabel Richmond. *Quaker Women 1650–1690*. London: Duckworth, 1915.

Bray, Matthew. "Helen Maria Williams and Edmund Burke: Radical Critique and Complicity." *Eighteenth-Century Life* 16 (1992): 1–24.

Breton, Stanislas. *The Word and the Cross*. Trans. Jacquelyn Porter. New York: Fordham University Press, 2002.

Brewer, D.S., ed. *The Parlement of Foulys*. By Geoffrey Chaucer. 2nd. ed. Manchester, UK: Manchester University Press, 1972.

Brinton, Anna Cox. *The Function of Quaker Literature: An Address Delivered at the Friends' Meeting House in Dublin, April 27th, the First Day of the Yearly Meeting of 1932*. Leominster, UK: The Orphans' Printing Press, n.d. In CYMA.

Bromley, Laura. "Lucrece's Re-Creation." *Shakespeare Quarterly* 34.2 (1983): 200–211.

Bultmann, Rudolf. *The Gospel of John*. Trans. G.R. Beasley-Murray, R.W.N. Hoare, and J.K. Riches. Philadelphia: Westminster Press, 1971.

Burke, Edmund. *A Philosophical Enquiry into the Origin of Our Ideas of the Sublime and Beautiful*. London, 1757.

———. *A Philosophical Enquiry into the Origin of Our Ideas of the Sublime and Beautiful*. Ed. James T. Boulton. London and New York: Routledge; New York: Columbia University Press, 1958.

———. *A Philosophical Enquiry into the Origin of Our Ideas of the Sublime and Beautiful*. Ed. David Womersley. London: Penguin, 2004.

———. *Reflections on the Revolution in France*. Ed. Frank M. Turner. New Haven, CT: Yale University Press, 2003.

Butler, Judith. "Desire." *Critical Terms for Literary Study*. Ed. Frank Lentricchia and Thomas McLaughlin. 2nd ed. Chicago: University of Chicago Press, 1995. 369–86.

Bynum, Caroline Walker. *Holy Feast and Holy Fast: The Religious Significance of Food to Medieval Women*. Berkeley: University of California Press, 1987.

———. *Jesus as Mother: Studies in the Spirituality of the High Middle Ages*. Berkeley: University of California Press, 1982.

Byrd, Ann. *Narratives, Pious Meditations, and Religious Exercises of Ann Byrd, Late of the City of New York, Deceased*. Philadelphia: J. Richards, Printer, 1843. In CYMA.

Cage, John. *Silence*. Middletown, CT: Wesleyan University Press, 1961.

Calvin, John. *Commentary on the Book of Psalms*. Trans. James Anderson. 5 vols. Edinburgh: Calvin Translation Society, 1843–55. Grand Rapids, MI: Eerdmans, 1963.

———. *Institutes of the Christian Religion*. Ed. John T. McNeill. Trans. F. L. Battles. 2 vols. Philadelphia: Westminster, 1960.

———. "Section III: A Selection from the Preface to the Commentary on Psalms, 1557." *John Calvin: Writings on Pastoral Piety*. Ed. and trans. Elsie Anne McKee. New York: Paulist Press, 2001. 55–63.

———. *Sermons of Maister Iohn Caluin, vpon the booke of Iob*. Trans. Arthur Golding. London, 1584.

Caputo, John D. *The Weakness of God: A Theology of the Event*. Bloomington: Indiana University Press, 2006.

Carlson, Julie. "Command Performances: Burke, Coleridge, and Schiller's Dramatic Reflections on the Revolution in France." *Wordsworth Circle* 23.2 (1992): 117–34.

Carney, Sean. "The Passion of Joanna Baillie: Playwright as Martyr." *Theatre Journal* 52 (2000): 227–52.

Carrier, Peter. *Holocaust Monuments and National Memory Cultures in France and Germany Since 1989*. New York: Berghahn, 2005.

Carter, Stephen J. "Lucrece's Gaze." *Shakespeare Studies* 23 (1995): 210–24.

Caruth, Cathy. Introduction. *Trauma: Explorations in Memory*. Ed. Cathy Caruth. Baltimore: John Hopkins University Press, 1995. 3–12.

———. *Unclaimed Experience: Trauma, Narrative, and History*. Baltimore: Johns Hopkins University Press, 1996.

Cefalu, Paul. "Godly Fear, Sanctification, and Calvinist Theology in the Sermons and 'Holy Sonnets' of John Donne." *Studies in Philology* 100.1 (2003): 71–86.

Cerney, Mary S. "Treating the 'Heroic Treaters.'" *Compassion Fatigue: Coping with Secondary Traumatic Stress Disorder in Those Who Treat the Traumatized*. Ed. Charles R. Figley. London: Brunner-Routledge, 1995. 131–49.

Charman, Caitlin J. "There's Got to Be Some Wrenching and Slashing: Horror and Retrospection in Alice Munro's 'Fits.'" *Canadian Literature* 191 (Winter 2006): 13–30.

Chaucer, Geoffrey. *Chaucer's Dream Poetry*. Ed. Helen Phillips and Nick Havely. London: Longman, 1997.

———. *The Complete Poetry and Prose of Geoffrey Chaucer*. Ed. John H. Fisher. New York: Holt, Rinehart and Winston, 1977.

———. *The Parliament of Fowls. The Riverside Chaucer*. Ed. Larry D. Benson et al. 3rd ed. Boston: Houghton Mifflin, 1987. 383–94.

———. *The Riverside Chaucer*. Ed. Larry D. Benson et al. 3rd ed. Boston: Houghton Mifflin, 1987.

Chauvet, Louis-Marie. *Symbol and Sacrament: A Sacramental Reinterpretation of Christian Experience*. Trans. Patrick Madigan and Madeleine Beaumont. Collegeville, MN: Liturgical Press, 1995.

Childs, Peter. "*A Passage to India.*" *The Cambridge Companion to E.M. Forster.* Ed. David Bradshaw. Cambridge: Cambridge University Press, 2007. 188–208.

Clark, Freeman. *A Memorial Concerning Deborah Clark, Deceased, by Her Husband, Freeman Clark; Reprinted by Direction of Genesee Yearly Meeting.* Rochester, NY: William S. Falls, 1874. In CYMA.

Clarke, Elizabeth. *Theory and Theology in George Herbert's Poetry: 'Divinitie, and Poesie, Met.'* Oxford: Clarendon, 1997.

Clayden, Peter. *The Early Life of Samuel Rogers.* London: Smith, Elder, 1887.

Clement of Alexandria. *Christ the Educator.* Trans. Simon P. Wood. The Fathers of the Church 23. Washington, DC: The Catholic University of America Press, 1954.

Clemons, Walter. "A Gravestone of Memories." *Newsweek* 28 Sept. 1987: 75.

Cohen, Raymond. "Intercultural Dissonance: A Theoretical Framework." Chapter 3. *Negotiating across Cultures. International Communication in an Interdependent World.* Rev. ed. Washington, DC: United States Institute of Peace Press, 2002.

Cohen, Richard A. "Ricoeur and the Lure of Self-Esteem." Chapter 9. *Ethics, Exegesis and Philosophy: Interpretation after Levinas.* Cambridge: Cambridge University Press, 2001.

Coleridge, Samuel Taylor. *Coleridge on the Seventeenth Century.* Ed. Roberta F. Brinkley. Durham, NC: Duke University Press, 1955.

———. *Notes and Lectures upon Shakespeare and Some of the Old Poets and Dramatists with Other Literary Remains of S.T. Coleridge.* Ed. H.N. Coleridge. Vol. 1. London: William Pickering, 1849.

Conner, Marc C., "From the Sublime to the Beautiful: The Aesthetic Progression of Toni Morrison." *The Aesthetics of Toni Morrison: Speaking the Unspeakable.* Ed. Marc C. Conner. Jackson: University of Mississippi Press, 2000. 49–76.

Cooke, George Willis. *George Eliot: A Critical Study of Her Life, Writings and Philosophy.* Boston: J.R. Osgood, 1883.

Cooney, Helen. "The *Parlement of Foules:* A Theodicy of Love." *Chaucer Review* 32.4 (1998): 339–76.

Cooper, Helen. "Chaucerian Representation." *New Readings of Chaucer's Poetry.* Ed. Robert G. Benson and Susan J. Ridyard. Cambridge: D.S. Brewer, 2003. 7–30.

Copley, Antony. *A Spiritual Bloomsbury.* Lanham, MD: Lexington Books, 2006.

Coquerel, Athanase. *Cours de Religion Chretienne.* Paris: Ab. Cherbuliez, 1833.

Corner, Martin. "Mysticism and Atheism in *To the Lighthouse.*" *Virginia Woolf's To the Lighthouse.* Ed. Harold Bloom. New York: Chelsea House, 1988.

Cousins, A.D. "Subjectivity, Exemplarity and the Establishing of Characterization in *Lucrece.*" *Studies in English Literature 1500–1900* 38 (1998): 45–60.

Crashaw, Richard. *The Complete Poetry of Richard Crashaw.* Ed. George Walton Williams. New York: Anchor Books, 1970.

Critchley, Simon. *Ethics, Politics, Subjectivity: Essays on Derrida, Levinas and Contemporary French Thought.* London: Verso, 1999.

———. Introduction. *The Cambridge Companion to Levinas.* Ed. Robert Bernasconi and Simon Critchley. Cambridge: Cambridge University Press, 2002. 1–32.

Crockett, Clayton. *Interstices of the Sublime: Theology and Psychoanalytic Theory.* New York: Fordham University Press, 2007.

———. *A Theology of the Sublime.* London and New York: Routledge, 2001.

Crowther, Paul. "*Les Immatériaux* and the Postmodern Sublime." *Judging Lyotard.* Ed. Andrew Benjamin. London and New York: Routledge, 1992. 192–205.

Cunningham, Michael. Contribution. "Appreciations of Alice Munro." Comp. Lisa Dickler Awano. *Virginia Quarterly Review* 82.3 (2006): 91–107.

Cunningham, Valentine. *Reading after Theory*. Oxford: Blackwell, 2002.

CYMA (Canadian Yearly Meeting Archives). The Quaker Archives and Library of Canada. Pickering College, Newmarket, Ontario.

D'Amico, Diane. *Christina Rossetti: Faith, Gender and Time*. Baton Rouge: Louisiana State University Press, 1999.

———. "Christina Rossetti's Breast Cancer: 'Another Matter, Painful to Dwell Upon,'" *Journal of Pre-Raphaelite Studies* 15 (Fall 2006): 28–50.

D'Amico, Diane, and David A. Kent. "Rossetti and the Tractarians." *Victorian Poetry* 44.1 (2006): 93–103.

Dante Alighieri. *The Divine Comedy of Dante Alighieri: Paradiso*. Trans. Allen Mandelbaum. New York: Bantam, 1982.

Dawson, Carrie. "Skinned: Taxidermy and Pedophilia in Alice Munro's 'Vandals.'" *Canadian Literature* 184 (Spring 2005): 69–83.

Deleuze, Gilles. *Proust and Signs*. Trans. Richard Howard. London: Athlone, 2000.

Deleuze, Gilles, and Felix Guattari. *A Thousand Plateaus: Capitalism and Schizophrenia*. Trans. Brian Massumi. Minneapolis: University of Minnesota, 1987.

de Lubac, Henri. *Catholicism: Christ and the Common Destiny of Man*. Trans. Lancelot C. Sheppard and Elizabeth Englund. San Francisco: Ignatius Press, 1988.

Dennis, John. *The Critical Works of John Dennis*. Ed. E.N. Hooker. 2 vols. Baltimore: Johns Hopkins University Press, 1939.

Derrida, Jacques. *Adieu to Emmanuel Levinas*. Trans. Pascale-Anne Brault and Michael Naas. Stanford, CA: Stanford University Press, 1999.

———. "Des Tours de Babel." *Acts of Religion*. Ed. Gil Anidjar. London and New York: Routledge, 2002. 104–36.

———. *The Gift of Death*. Trans. David Wills. Chicago: University of Chicago Press, 1995.

———. *On the Name*. Ed. Thomas Dutoit. Trans. David Wood, John P. Leavey, and Ian McLeod. Stanford, CA: Stanford University Press, 1995.

———. *Specters of Marx: The State of the Debt, the Work of Mourning, and the New International*. Trans. Peggy Kamuf. London and New York: Routledge, 1994.

———. *Ulysse Gramophone: Deux mots pour Joyce*. Paris: Galilee, 1987.

———. "Ulysses Gramophone: Hear Say Yes in Joyce." *Acts of Literature*. Ed. Derek Attridge. London and New York: Routledge, 1992. 253–309.

———. *Writing and Difference*. Trans. Alan Bass. Chicago: University of Chicago Press, 1978.

Desjardins, Michel, and Harold Remus, eds. *Tradition and Formation: Claiming an Inheritance: Essays in Honour of Peter C. Erb*. Kitchener, ON: Pandora Press, 2009.

Detmer-Goebel, Emily. "The Need for Lavinia's Voice: *Titus Andronicus* and the Telling of Rape." *Shakespeare Studies* 29 (2001): 75–92.

Deutsch, Eliot, and Rohit Dalvi, eds. *The Essential Vedanta: A New Source Book of Advaita Vedanta*. Bloomington, IN: World Wisdom, 2004.

Dillard, Annie. *Holy the Firm*. New York: Harper and Row, 1977.

———. *Teaching a Stone to Talk: Expeditions and Encounters*. New York: Harper, 1982.

Discipline of the Yearly Meeting of Friends, held in New-York… revised, in the sixth month, 1810. New York Yearly Meeting of the Religious Society of Friends. In CYMA.

Doerksen, Daniel W. *Conforming to the Word: Herbert, Donne, and the English Church before Laud.* Lewisburg, PA: Bucknell University Press, 1997.

———. "'Growing and Groning': Herbert's 'Affliction' (I)." *English Studies in Canada* 8 (1982): 1–8.

———. "Polemist or Pastor? Donne and Moderate Calvinist Conformity." *John Donne and the Protestant Reformation: New Perspectives.* Ed. Mary Arshagouni Papazian. Detroit: Wayne State University Press, 2003. 12–34.

Doherty, Robert W. *The Hicksite Separation: A Sociological Analysis of Religious Schism in Early Nineteenth Century America.* New Brunswick, NJ: Rutgers University Press, 1967.

Donne, John. *The Divine Poems.* Ed. Helen Gardner. 2nd ed. Oxford: Clarendon, 1978.

———. *Poetical Works.* Ed. Herbert J.C. Grierson. Oxford: Oxford University Press, 1991.

———. *Sermons.* Ed. G.R. Potter and E.M. Simpson. Berkeley: University of California Press, 1953–62.

———. "Upon the Annunciation and Passion, falling upon one day. 1608 [March 25]." *John Donne: Selections from Divine Poems, Sermons, Devotions, and Prayers.* Ed. John Booty. New York: Paulist Press, 1990. 98–99.

Donnelly, Phillip. "Enthusiastic Poetry and Rationalized Christianity: The Poetic Theory of John Dennis." *Christianity and Literature* 54.2 (2005): 236–64.

Dubrow, Heather. "The Rape of Clio: Attitudes to History in Shakespeare's *Lucrece*." *English Literary Renaissance* 16.3 (1986): 425–41.

Dunn, James D.G. *The Theology of Paul the Apostle.* Grand Rapids, MI: Eerdmans, 1998.

Eagleton, Terry. *After Theory.* London: Allen Lane; New York: Basic Books, 2003.

Eaton, Sara. "A Woman of Letters: Lavinia in *Titus Andronicus*." *Shakespearean Tragedy and Gender.* Ed. Shirley Nelson Garner and Madelon Sprengnether. Bloomington: Indiana University Press, 1996. 54–74.

Edwards, David L. *John Donne: Man of Flesh and Spirit.* Grand Rapids, MI: Eerdmans, 2001.

Eliot, George. *Adam Bede.* Ed. Stephen Gill. London: Penguin, 1980.

———. *Daniel Deronda.* Ed. Terence Cave. London: Penguin, 1995.

———. *Essays of George Eliot.* Ed. Thomas Pinney. New York: Columbia University Press, 1963.

———. *George Eliot: Collected Poems.* Ed. Lucien Jenkins. London: Skoob, 1989.

———. *The George Eliot Letters.* Ed. Gordon S. Haight. New Haven, CT: Yale University Press, 1955.

———. *The Impressions of Theophrastus Such.* Ed. Nancy Henry. Iowa City: University of Iowa Press, 1994.

———. *The Mill on the Floss.* Ed. A.S. Byatt. London: Penguin, 1979.

———. "The Morality of Wilhelm Meister." *Leader* 6 (21 July 1855): 247–51. Reprinted in *Essays of George Eliot.* Ed. Thomas Pinney. New York: Columbia University Press, 1963.

———. *Romola.* Ed. Andrew Sanders. London: Penguin, 1980.

———. *Scenes of Clerical Life.* Ed. Jennifer Gribble. London: Penguin, 1998.

———. *Silas Marner.* Ed. David Carroll. London: Penguin, 1996.

———. *The Works of George Eliot.* Ed. J.W. Cross. 21 vols. Boston: Little, Brown, 1908.

Eliot, George, trans. *The Essence of Christianity*. By Ludwig Feuerbach. London: Trübner, 1854.

Eliot, T.S. *Four Quartets*. London: Faber and Faber, 1944.

Empson, William. *Seven Types of Ambiguity*. London: Chatto and Windus, 1930.

Endō Shūsaku. *Chinmoku [Silence]*. 3 vols. Tokyo: Daikatsuji bunko, 2004.

———. "Endō and Johnston Talk of Buddhism and Christianity." *America* 171.16 (19 Nov. 1994): 18–20.

———. *A Life of Jesus*. Trans. Richard A. Schuchert. New York: Paulist Press, 1978.

———. *Silence*. Trans. William Johnston. Marlboro, NJ: Taplinger, 1980.

Engström, Timothy H. "The Postmodern Sublime? Philosophical Rehabilitations and Pragmatic Evasions." *Boundary 2* 20.2 (1993): 190–204.

Entzminger, Robert L. "The Pattern of Time in *The Parlement of Foules*." *Journal of Medieval and Renaissance Studies* 5 (1975): 1–11.

Erler, Mary, and Maryanne Kowaleski, eds. Introduction. *Gendering the Master Narrative: Women and Power in the Middle Ages*. Ithaca, NY: Cornell University Press, 2003. 1–16.

Fawcett, Mary Laughlin. "Arms/Words/Tears: Language and the Body in *Titus Andronicus*." *ELH* 50.2 (1983): 261–77.

Feder, Lillian, ed. *The Handbook of Classical Literature*. New York: De Capo, 1998.

Fein, Susanna Greer, ed. *Moral Love Songs and Laments*. Kalamazoo, MI: Medieval Institute Publications, 1998.

Felman, Shoshana. "Education and Crisis, or the Vicissitudes of Teaching." *Trauma: Explorations in Memory*. Ed. Cathy Caruth. Baltimore: Johns Hopkins University Press, 1995. 13–60.

———. *The Juridical Unconscious: Trials and Traumas in the Twentieth Century*. Cambridge, MA: Harvard University Press, 2002.

Felski, Rita. *Doing Time: Feminist Theory and Postmodern Culture*. New York: New York University Press, 2000.

Ferguson, Moira. *Subject to Others: British Women Writers and Colonial Slavery, 1670–1834*. London and New York: Routledge, 1992.

Feuerbach, Ludwig. *The Essence of Christianity*. Trans. Marian Evans. London: Trübner, 1854.

Firpo, Massimo. "Storia religiosa e storia dell'arte. I casi di Iacopo Pantormo e Lorenzo Lotto." *Belfagor: Rassegna di Varia Umanità* 59 (2004): 571–90.

Fish, Stanley. "One University under God?" *Chronicle of Higher Education*, 7 Jan. 2005. http://chronicle.com/article/One-University-Under-God-/45507.

Forbes, Aileen. "'Sympathetic Curiosity' in Joanna Baillie's Theater of the Passions." *European Romantic Review* 14.1 (2003): 31–48.

Forest, James. "What Merton Came to Know through Icons." *U.S. Catholic* 20 (1993): 21–29.

Forster, E.M. *The Hill of Devi and Other Indian Writings*. Ed. Elizabeth Heine. Abinger Edition. Vol. 14. London: Edward Arnold, 1983.

———. *The Manuscripts of* A Passage to India. Ed. Oliver Stallybrass. Abinger Edition. Vol. 6a. London: Edward Arnold, 1978.

———. *A Passage to India*. Ed. Oliver Stallybrass. Abinger Edition. Vol. 6. London: Edward Arnold, 1979.

———. *Selected Letters of E.M. Forster: Vol. 1, 1879–1920*. Ed. Mary Lago and P.N. Furbank. London: Arena, 1983.

———. *Two Cheers for Democracy*. Ed. Oliver Stallybrass. Abinger Edition. Vol. 11. London: Edward Arnold, 1972.

Fowler, Anne C. "'With Care and Courage': Herbert's '*Affliction*' Poems." In *"Too Rich to Clothe the Sunne": Essays on George Herbert*. Ed. Claude J. Summers and Ted-Larry Pebworth. Pittsburgh: University of Pittsburgh Press, 1980. 129–45.

Foxton, Rosemary. *"Hear the Word of the Lord": A Critical and Biographical Study of Quaker Women's Writing, 1650–1700*. Melbourne: Bibliographical Society of Australia and New Zealand, 1994.

Freeman, Barbara Claire. *The Feminine Sublime: Gender and Excess in Women's Fiction*. Berkeley: University of California Press, 1995.

Fried, Lewis. "*A Canticle for Leibowitz*: A Song for Benjamin." *Extrapolation* 42.4 (2001): 362–73.

Frye, Northrop. "Conclusion." *Literary History of Canada: Canadian Literature in English*. Ed. C.F. Klinck. Toronto: University of Toronto Press, 1965. 821–49.

Fulford, Robert. "An Interview with Hugh Hood." *Tamarack Review* 66 (1975): 65–77.

Gadamer, Hans-Georg. *Die Lektion des Jahrhunderts*. Münster, Ger.: Lit Verlag, 2002.

———. *Gesammelte Werke*. Vol. 2. Tübingen, Ger.: J.C.B. Mohr, 1985.

———. *Philosophical Hermeneutics*. Ed. and trans. David E. Linge. Berkeley: University of California Press, 1976.

Gasché, Rodolphe. *Inventions of Difference: On Jacques Derrida*. Cambridge, MA: Harvard University Press, 1994.

Gibbs, Robert. "Philosophy and Law: Questioning Justice." *The Ethical*. Ed. Edith Wyschogrod and Gerald P. McKenny. London: Blackwell, 2003. 101–16.

Gilbert, Sandra, and Susan Gubar. *The Madwoman in the Attic: The Woman Writer and the Nineteenth-Century Literary Imagination*. New Haven, CT: Yale University Press, 1979.

Gildersleeve, D. Britton. "'I Had a Religious Mother': Maternal Ancestry, Female Spaces, and Spiritual Synthesis in Elizabeth Ashbridge's *Account*." *Early American Literature* 36.3 (2001): 371–94.

Gill, Catie. *Women in the Seventeenth-Century Quaker Community*. Aldershot, UK: Ashgate, 2005.

Gilroy, Paul. *The Black Atlantic: Modernity and Double Consciousness*. London: Verso, 1993.

Gilson, Étienne. *The Unity of Philosophical Experience*. 1937. San Francisco: Ignatius Press, 1999.

Glatzer, Nahum N. *Franz Rosenzweig: His Life and Thought*. New York: Schocken, 1953.

Glowacka, Dorota, and Stephen Boos. Introduction. *Between Ethics and Aesthetics: Crossing the Boundaries*. Ed. Glowacka and Boos. Albany: State University of New York Press, 2002. 1–11.

Graffigny, Françoise de. *Letters Written by a Peruvian Princess*. Translated from the French. London, 1748.

———. *Lettres d'une Peruvienne*. Paris, 1747.

Gransden, K.W. *John Donne*. London: Longmans, Green, 1954.

Gregory, G. Translator's Preface. *Lectures on the Sacred Poetry of the Hebrews*. By Robert Lowth. New York: Garland, 1971.

Grubb, Sarah Lynes. *A Selection from the Letters of the Late Sarah Grubb (Formerly Sarah Lynes)*. Sudbury, UK: J. Wright, 1848. In CYMA.

Gutiérrez, Gustavo. *Las Casas: In Search of the Poor of Jesus Christ.* Trans. Robert Barr. New York: Orbis, 1993.

Habermas, Jürgen, and Joseph Ratzinger (Pope Benedict XVI). *Dialektik der Säkularisierung: Über Vernunft und Religion.* Ed. Florian Schuller. Freiburg, Ger.: Herder, 2005.

Haight, Roger. *Jesus: Symbol of God.* Maryknoll, NY: Orbis, 2005.

Hale, Victoria. "An Interview with Hugh Hood." *World Literature Written in English* 11.1 (1972): 35–41.

Halewood, William H. *The Poetry of Grace: Reformation Themes and Structures in English Seventeenth-Century Poetry.* New Haven, CT: Yale University Press, 1970.

Hamm, Thomas. *The Quakers in America.* New York: Columbia University Press, 2003.

———. *The Transformation of American Quakerism: Orthodox Friends, 1800–1907.* Bloomington: Indiana University Press, 1988.

Hammond, Karla M. "Drawing the Curtains: An Interview with Annie Dillard." *Bennington Review* 10 (1981): 30–38.

Handelman, Susan H. *The Slayers of Moses: The Emergence of Rabbinic Interpretation in Modern Literary Theory.* Albany: State University of New York Press, 1982.

Hanson, Ellis. *Decadence and Catholicism.* Cambridge, MA: Harvard University Press, 1998.

Hanzo, Thomas. "The Past of Science Fiction." *Bridges to Science Fiction.* Ed. George E. Slusser, George R. Guffey, and Mark Rose. Carbondale: Southern Illinois University Press, 1980. 131–46.

Harman, Barbara Leah. "George Herbert's *Affliction (I)*: The Limits of Representation." *ELH* 44. 2 (1977): 267–85.

Harris, Bernice. "Sexuality as a Signifier for Power Relations: Using Lavinia, of Shakespeare's *Titus Andronicus*." *Criticism* 38.3 (1996): 383–406.

Hart, Kevin. "God and the Sublime." *God Out of Place? A Symposium on L.P. Hemming's Postmodernity's Transcending, Devaluing God.* Ed. Yves de Maeseneer. Utrecht, Neth.: Ars Disputandi, 2005. 33–38.

———. "Postmodernism." *The Oxford Handbook of English Literature and Theology.* Ed. Andrew Hass, David Jasper, and Elisabeth Jay. Oxford: Oxford University Press, 2007. 180–94.

Healey, Robynne Rogers. "Building, Sustaining, and Reforming Quaker Community in Upper Canada: Informal Education and the Yonge Street Women Friends." *Quaker History* 94.1 (2005): 1–23.

———. *From Quaker to Upper Canadian: Faith and Community among Yonge Street Friends, 1801–1850.* Montreal and Kingston: McGill-Queen's University Press, 2006.

Hegel, G.W.F. *Aesthetics: Lectures on Fine Art.* Trans. T.M. Knox. Vol. 1. Oxford: Clarendon, 1988.

Heidegger, Martin. *Being and Time.* Trans. John Macquarrie and Edward Robinson. Oxford: Blackwell, 1990.

———. *Contributions to Philosophy (From Enowning).* Trans. Parvis Emad and Kenneth Maly. Bloomington: Indiana University Press, 1999.

———. *An Introduction to Metaphysics.* Trans. Ralph Manheim. New Haven, CT: Yale University Press, 1987.

Herbert, George. "The H. Scriptures I." *George Herbert: The Complete English Works.* Ed. Ann Pasternak Slater. New York: Alfred A. Knopf, 1995. 56.

———. *The Works of George Herbert.* Ed. F.E. Hutchinson. Corrected ed. Oxford: Oxford University Press, 1945.

Hess, Thomas B. *Barnett Newman.* New York: Museum of Modern Art, 1971.

Hewitt, Nancy. "The Fragmentation of Friends: The Consequences for Women in Antebellum America." *Witnesses for Change.* Ed. Elizabeth Brown and Susan Stuard. New Brunswick, NJ: Rutgers University Press, 1989. 93–108.

Hillesum, Etty. *An Interrupted Life.* Trans. Arnold J. Pomerans. London: Jonathan Cape, 1983.

Hinds, Hilary. *God's Englishwomen: Seventeenth-Century Radical Sectarian Writing and Feminist Criticism.* Manchester, UK: Manchester University Press, 1996.

Hirsch, Marianne. "Projected Memory: Holocaust Photographs in Personal and Public Fantasy." *Acts of Memory: Cultural Recall in the Present.* Ed. Mieke Bal, Jonathan Crewe, and Leo Spitzer. Hanover, NH: University Press of New England, 1999. 3–23.

Hoag, Huldah. *Memoir of Huldah Hoag.* In CYMA.

Hodgson, Peter C. "Heidegger, Revelation, and the Word of God." *Journal of Religion* 49.3 (1969): 228–52.

Holden, David E.W. *Friends Divided: Conflict and Division in the Society of Friends.* Richmond, IN: Friends United Press, 1988.

Holden-Kirwan, Jennifer L. "Looking into the Self That Is No Self: An Examination of Subjectivity in *Beloved." African American Review* 32.3 (1998): 415–26.

"Hollow Halls of Academe." *National Post,* 28 Apr. 2007: A1.

Hood, Hugh. *Be Sure to Close Your Eyes.* Toronto: Anansi, 1993.

———. *Black and White Keys.* Toronto: ECW Press, 1982.

———. *Dead Men's Watches.* Toronto: Anansi, 1995.

———. *The Governor's Bridge Is Closed.* Ottawa: Oberon, 1973.

———. *Great Realizations.* Toronto: Anansi, 1997.

———. "Letter." *Essays on Canadian Writing* 9 (Winter 1977–1978): 139–41.

———. *The Motor Boys in Ottawa.* Toronto: Stoddart, 1986.

———. *Near Water.* Toronto: Anansi, 2000.

———. *A New Athens.* Ottawa: Oberon, 1977.

———. *Property and Value.* Toronto: Anansi, 1990.

———. *Reservoir Ravine.* Ottawa: Oberon, 1979.

———. *The Scenic Art.* Toronto: Stoddart, 1984.

———. *The Swing in the Garden.* Ottawa: Oberon, 1975.

———. *Tony's Book.* Toronto: Stoddart, 1988.

Hood, Hugh, and John Mills. "Hugh Hood and John Mills in Epistolary Conversation." *Fiddlehead* 116 (Winter 1978): 133–46.

Hopkins, Gerard Manley. *Poems and Prose of Gerard Manley Hopkins.* Ed. W.H. Gardner. 1953. New York: Penguin, 1985.

Horowitz, Asher, and Gad Horowitz, eds. *Difficult Justice: Commentaries on Levinas and Politics.* Toronto: University of Toronto Press, 2006.

Houbedine, Jean-Louis. *Excès de langage: Holderlin, Joyce, Duns Scot, Hopkins, Cantor, Sollers.* New York: Denoël, 1984.

Houston, Darrell. "The Mishima Incident: 'A Wasteful Way to Die.'" *APF Newsletters of Darrell Houston.* 4 Dec. 1970. http://www.aliciapatterson.org/APF001970/ Houston/Houston07/Houston07.html).

Howells, Coral Ann. *Alice Munro*. Manchester, UK: Manchester University Press, 1998.

Hu, Esther T. "Christina Rossetti, John Keble, and the Divine Gaze." *Victorian Poetry* 46.2 (2008): 175–89.

Hulse, S. Clark. "Wresting the Alphabet: Oratory and Action in *Titus Andronicus*." *Criticism* 21 (1979): 106–18.

Hunt, Sarah. *Journal of the Life and Religious Labors of Sarah Hunt: (Late of West Grove, Chester County, Pennsylvania)*. Philadelphia: Friends' Book Association, 1892. In CYMA.

Hunter, Jeanne. "Herbert's 'Water-Course': Notorious and Neglected." *Notes and Queries* 34 (1987): 310–12.

Ingle, Larry H. *Quakers in Conflict: The Hicksite Reformation*. Knoxville: University of Tennessee Press, 1986.

Inoue Yōji. *The Face of Jesus in Japan [Nihon to Iesu no kao]*. Trans. Akamatsu Hisako. Tokyo: Kindai Bungei-sha, 1994.

Irenaeus. "*Adversus haereses* [Against Heresies]." *The Apostolic Fathers with Justin Martyr and Irenaeus*. Ed. Alexander Roberts, James Donaldson, and Arthur Cleveland Coxe. Grand Rapids, MI: Hendrickson, 2004. Vol. 1 of *The Ante-Nicene Fathers: The Writings of the Fathers down to A.D. 325*.

Irlam, Shaun. *Elations: The Poetics of Enthusiasm in Eighteenth-Century Britain*. Stanford, CA: Stanford University Press, 1999.

James, Trevor. *The Metaphysical Poets*. Essex, UK: Longman, 1988.

James, William Closson. *Locations of the Sacred: Essays on Religion, Literature, and Canadian Culture*. Waterloo, ON: Wilfrid Laurier University Press, 1998.

Jameson, Fredric. *Archaeologies of the Future: The Desire Called Utopia and Other Science Fictions*. New York: Verso, 2005.

Jaspers, Karl. *Philosophy*. Trans. E.B. Ashton. Vol. 3. Chicago: University of Chicago Press, 1971.

Jed, Stephanie. *Chaste Thinking: The Rape of Lucretia and the Birth of Humanism*. Bloomington: Indiana University Press, 1989.

Jeffrey, David Lyle. *People of the Book: Christian Identity and Literary Culture*. Grand Rapids, MI and Cambridge: Eerdmans, 1996.

Jeffrey, Francis. Rev. of *A Series of Plays (Vol. II)*, by Joanna Baillie. *Edinburgh Review* 2 (1803): 269–86.

Johnson, Sandra Humble. *The Space Between: Literary Epiphany in the Work of Annie Dillard*. Kent, OH: Kent State University Press, 1992.

Jones, Chris. *Radical Sensibility: Literature and Ideas in the 1790s*. London and New York: Routledge, 1993.

Jones, Vivien. "Women Writing Revolution: Narratives of History and Sexuality in Wollstonecraft and Williams." *Beyond Romanticism: New Approaches to Texts and Contexts, 1780–1832*. Ed. Stephen Copley and John Whale. London and New York: Routledge, 1992. 190–97.

Joyce, James. *A Portrait of the Artist as a Young Man*. London: Penguin, 1992.

———. *Ulysses*. Introd. Declan Kiberd. 1960. London: Penguin, 2000.

Joyce, Stanislaus. *My Brother's Keeper: James Joyce's Early Years*. Ed. Richard Ellmann. Cambridge, MA: Da Capo, 2003.

Judson, Barbara. "'Sympathetic Curiosity': The Theater of Joanna Baillie." *Tulsa Studies in Women's Literature* 25.1 (2006): 49–70.

Julian of Norwich. *Julian of Norwich: Showings*. Trans. Edmund Colledge and James Walsh. New York: Paulist Press, 1978.

———. *The Showings of Julian of Norwich*. Ed. Denise N. Baker. New York: Norton, 2005.

Jüngel, Eberhard. *Gott als Geheimnis der Welt: Zur Begründung d. Theologie d. Gekreuzigten im Streit zwischen Theismus u. Atheismus*. 3rd ed. Tübingen, Ger.: Mohr, 1978.

Kant, Immanuel. *Critique of the Power of Judgment*. Ed. Paul Guyer. Trans. Paul Guyer and Eric Matthews. Cambridge: Cambridge University Press, 2000.

———. *Observations on the Feeling of the Beautiful and Sublime*. 1764. Trans. John Goldthwait. Berkeley: University of California Press, 1965.

Kaplan, E. Ann. "Vicarious Trauma and 'Empty' Empathy." *Trauma Culture: The Politics of Terror and Loss in Media and Literature*. New Brunswick, NJ: Rutgers University Press, 2005. 87–100.

Karpf, Anne. *The War After. Living with the Holocaust*. London: Heinemann, 1996.

Kearney, Richard. *Anatheism: Returning to God after God*. New York: Columbia University Press, 2009.

———. "Enabling God." Manoussakis, *After God* 39–54.

———. "Epiphanies of the Everyday: Toward a Micro-Eschatology." Manoussakis, *After God* 3–20.

———. *The God Who May Be: A Hermeneutics of Religion*. Indiana Series in the Philosophy of Religion. Bloomington: Indiana University Press, 2001.

———. "The God Who May Be." Conversation with David Cayley, in three parts. *Ideas*. CBC Radio. 20 Feb., 27 Feb., and 6 Mar. 2006. *Ideas* Transcripts ID 2964.

———. "Hermeneutics of the Possible God." *Givenness and God: Questions of Jean-Luc Marion*. Ed. Ian Leask and Eoin Cassidy. Perspectives in Continental Philosophy 43. New York: Fordham University Press, 2005. 220–42.

———. *Navigations: Collected Irish Essays 1976–2006*. Dublin: Lilliput, 2006.

———. *On Stories: Thinking in Action*. London and New York: Routledge, 2002.

———. *Poetics of Imagining: Modern to Post-modern*. Edinburgh: Edinburgh University Press, 1998.

———. "The Shulammite's Song: Divine Eros, Ascending and Descending." *Toward a Theology of Eros: Transfiguring Passion at the Limits of Discipline*. Ed. Virginia Burrus and Catherine Keller. New York: Fordham University Press, 2006. 306–40.

———. *Strangers, Gods and Monsters: Interpreting Otherness*. London and New York: Routledge, 2003.

———. "Traversals and Epiphanies in Joyce and Proust." *Traversing the Imaginary: Richard Kearney and the Postmodern Challenge*. Ed. Peter Gratton and John Panteleimon Manoussakis. Evanston, IL: Northwestern University Press, 2007. 183–208.

———. *The Wake of Imagination*. London: Hutchinson; Minneapolis: University of Minnesota Press, 1988.

Keats, John. John Keats to Richard Woodhouse, 27 October 1818. *The Poems of John Keats: A Sourcebook*. Ed. John Strachan. New York: Routledge, 2003.

Keble, John. *Sermons for Christmas and Epiphany*. Oxford: James Parker, 1875.

Keith, W.J. *Canadian Odyssey: A Reading of Hugh Hood's* The New Age / Le nouveau siècle. Montreal and Kingston: McGill-Queen's University Press, 2002.

Keller, Catherine. *Face of the Deep: A Theology of Becoming*. London and New York: Routledge, 2003.

Kelly, Gary. *Women, Writing, and Revolution 1790–1827*. Oxford: Clarendon, 1993.

Kennedy, Deborah. *Helen Maria Williams and the Age of Revolution*. Lewisburg, PA: Bucknell University Press; London: Associated University Presses, 2002.

Kiberd, Declan, ed. Introduction. *Ulysses*. By James Joyce. London: Penguin, 1992.

Kierkegaard, Søren. *Repetition*. Trans. Walter Lowrie. Princeton, NJ: Princeton University Press, 1941.

Kilcourse, George. *Ace of Freedoms: Thomas Merton's Christ*. Notre Dame, IN: University of Notre Dame Press, 1993.

Kippis, Andrew. *Sermons on Practical Subjects*. London: T. Cadell, 1791.

Kivy, Peter. *Introduction to a Philosophy of Music*. Oxford: Clarendon, 2002.

Klassen, Norman. "A Note on 'Hyre' in *Parliament of Fowls*, 284." *Notes and Queries* 251.2 (June 2006): 154–57.

Knights, L.C. "George Herbert." *Scrutiny* 12 (1944): 171–86.

Kristeva, Julia. "Joyce 'The Gracehoper' or Orpheus' Return." *New Maladies of the Soul*. Trans. Ross Guberman. New York: Columbia University Press, 1997. 172–88.

———. *Strangers to Ourselves*. Trans. Leon S. Roudiez. New York: Columbia University Press, 1991.

———. "Strangers to Ourselves: The Hope of the Singular." *States of Mind: Dialogues with Contemporary Thinkers on the European Mind*. Ed. Richard Kearney. New York: New York University Press, 1995. 6–13.

———. *Tales of Love*. Trans. Leon Roudiez. New York: Columbia University Press, 1987.

———. *Time and Sense: Proust and the Experience of Literature*. Trans. Ross Guberman. New York: Columbia University Press, 1996.

Kunze, Bonnelyn Young. *Margaret Fell and the Rise of Quakerism*. London: Macmillan, 1994.

Kushner, Harold S. *Overcoming Life's Disappointments*. New York: Alfred A. Knopf, 2006.

———. *When Bad Things Happen to Good People*. New York: Schocken, 1981.

Lacan, Jacques. *Ecrits*. Trans. Bruce Fink. New York: Norton, 2004.

LaCapra, Dominick. *History and Memory after Auschwitz*. Ithaca, NY: Cornell University Press, 1998.

———. *Writing History, Writing Trauma*. Baltimore: Johns Hopkins University Press, 2001.

Lane, Richard J. *Fifty Key Literary Theorists*. London and New York: Routledge, 2006.

———. "The Hidden and the Exposed: 'One-Time Appearance' in Walter Benjamin and Rachel Whiteread's *Holocaust Memorial* (a reading of Section iv of 'The Work of Art in the Age of Its Technical Reproducibility,' Second Version)." *Reproducing Art — Walter Benjamin's "Work of Art" Essay Reconsidered*. Ed. Patricia Allmer and John Sears. Spec. issue *InterCulture* 4.2 (2008). http://iph.fsu.edu/interculture/benjamin.html.

———. "Kant's 'Safe Place': Security and the Sacred in the Concept of Sublime Experience." *Sublimer Aspects: Interfaces between Literature, Aesthetics, and Theology, 1715–1885*. Ed. Natasha Duquette. Newcastle, UK: Cambridge Scholars Publishing, 2007. 51–61.

———. *Reading Walter Benjamin: Writing through the Catastrophe*. Manchester, UK: Manchester University Press, 2005.

Lang, Monique. "Trauma and Spirituality." *Healing from Post-Traumatic Stress: A Workbook for Recovery*. New York: McGraw-Hill, 2007. 163–76.

Las Casas, Bartolomé de. *Brevísima Relación de la Destruyción de las Indias [A Short Account of the Destruction of the Indies]*. 1542. Ed. Jean-Paul Duviols. Buenos Aires: Stockero, 2006.

Laub, Dori. "Bearing Witness, or the Vicissitudes of Listening." *Testimony: Crisis of Witnessing in Literature, Psychoanalysis, and History*. Ed. Shoshana Felman and Dori Laub. London and New York: Routledge, 1992. 57–74.

———. "Truth and Testimony: The Process and the Struggle." *Trauma: Explorations in Memory*. Ed. Cathy Caruth. Baltimore: Johns Hopkins University Press, 1995. 61–75.

Lawrence, D.H. *Apocalypse*. New York: Viking, 1932.

Lawrence, T.E., ed. *The Odyssey of Homer*. New York: Oxford University Press, 1991.

Lawton, David. *Chaucer's Narrators*. Cambridge: D.S. Brewer, 1985.

Leclercq, Jean. Preface. *Julian of Norwich: Showings*. By Julian of Norwich. Trans. Edmund Colledge and James Walsh. New York: Paulist Press, 1978.

L'Engle, Madeleine. *A Circle of Quiet*. New York: HarperSanFrancisco, 1972.

———. *A Swiftly Tilting Planet*. New York: Dell, 1978.

———. *Walking on Water: Reflections on Faith and Art*. Wheaton, IL: Harold Shaw, 1980.

———. *A Wind in the Door*. New York: Dell, 1973.

———. *A Wrinkle in Time*. New York: Dell, 1962.

Levenduski, Cristine. *Peculiar Power: A Quaker Woman Preacher in Eighteenth-Century America*. Washington: Smithsonian Institution Press, 1996.

———. "'Remarkable Experiences in the Life of Elizabeth Ashbridge': Portraying the Public Woman in Spiritual Autobiography." *Women's Studies* 19 (1991): 271–81.

Levertov, Denise. *Denise Levertov: Selected Poems*. New York: New Directions, 2002.

Levi, Primo. *The Drowned and the Saved*. Trans. Raymond Rosenthal. New York: Vintage, 1989.

Levinas, Emmanuel. *Ethics and Infinity: Conversations with Philippe Nemo*. Trans. Richard A. Cohen. Pittsburgh: Duquesne University Press, 1985.

———. "Ethics of the Infinite." *States of Mind: Dialogues with Contemporary Thinkers on the European Mind*. Ed. Richard Kearney. New York: New York University Press, 1995. 177–99.

———. "God and Philosophy." Trans. Richard A. Cohen. *The Levinas Reader*. Ed. Seán Hand. Oxford: Blackwell, 1989. 166–89.

———. *Humanismus des anderen Menschen*. Ed. Ludwig Wenzler and Christoph von Wolzogen. Philosophische Bibliothek. Hamburg: F. Meiner, 2005.

———. "Intention, Event, and the Other." *Is It Righteous to Be? Interviews with Emmanuel Levinas*. Ed. Jill Robbins. Trans. Andrew Schmitz. Stanford, CA: Stanford University Press, 2001. 140–57.

———. *Otherwise Than Being or Beyond Essence*. Trans. Alphonso Lingis. The Hague: Martinus Nijhoff, 1981.

———. *Totality and Infinity: An Essay on Exteriority*. Trans. Alphonso Lingis. The Hague: Martinus Nijhoff, 1979.

Levinson, Jerrold. Introduction. *Aesthetics and Ethics: Essays at the Intersection*. Ed. Jerrold Levinson. Cambridge: Cambridge University Press, 1998. 1–25.

Lewalski, Barbara K. *Protestant Poetics and the Seventeenth-Century Religious Lyric.* Princeton, NJ: Princeton University Press, 1979.

Lewis, C. S. *The Horse and His Boy.* 1954. Harmondsworth, UK: Puffin, 1975.

———. *The Last Battle.* 1956. Harmondsworth, UK: Puffin, 1975.

———. *The Magician's Nephew.* 1955. Harmondsworth, UK: Puffin, 1975.

———. "On Three Ways of Writing for Children." 1952. *The Riverside Anthology of Children's Literature.* Ed. Judith Saltman. 6th ed. Boston: Houghton Mifflin, 1985. 1075–81.

———. *The Silver Chair.* 1953. Harmondsworth, UK: Puffin, 1975.

———. *Studies in Words.* 1960. Cambridge: Cambridge University Press, 1990.

———. "What Chaucer Really Did to *Il Filostrato.*" *Essays and Studies* 17 (1932): 56–75.

Lingis, Alphonso. Translator's Introduction. *Otherwise than Being or Beyond Essence.* By Emmanuel Levinas. The Hague: Martinus Nijhoff, 1981. xi–xxxix.

Livy. "The Rape of Lucretia." *The History of Rome.* Trans. B.O. Foster. *World Civilizations: An Internet Classroom and Anthology.* Ed. Richard Hooker, et al. Washington State University, 1996. http://www.wsu.edu/~dee/.

Longinus. "On the Sublime." *Classical Literary Criticism.* Orig. trans. T.S. Dorsch. Rev. trans. Penelope Murray. London: Penguin, 2000. 113–34.

Lonsdale, Roger, ed. *Eighteenth-Century Women Poets: An Oxford Anthology.* Oxford: Oxford University Press, 1990.

Low, Anthony. "Absence in Donne's Holy Sonnets: Between Catholic and Calvinist." *John Donne Journal* 23 (2004): 95–115.

Lowth, Robert. *Lectures on the Sacred Poetry of the Hebrews.* Trans. G. Gregory. 1829. New York: Garland, 1971.

Luther, Martin. *Kommentar zum Galaterbrief 1519.* Ed. Wolfgang Metzler. Calwer Luther-Ausgabe. Band 10. Stuttgart: Calwer Verlag, 1996.

———. *Sämtliche Schriften.* Band 7. Ed. Johann G. Walch. Groß Oesingen, Ger.: Verlag der Lutherischen Buchhandlung Heinrich Harms, 1986.

———. *Sermons on the Gospel of St. John: Chapters 1-4, Luther's Works.* Gen. ed. J. J. Pelikan. Vol. 22. St. Louis, MO: Concordia Publishing House, 1956.

Lynch, Kathryn L. "Diana's 'Bowe Ybroke': Impotence, Desire, and Virginity in Chaucer's *Parliament of Fowls.*" *Menacing Virgins: Representing Virginity in the Middle Ages and Renaissance.* Ed. Kathleen Coyne Kelly and Marina Leslie. Newark: University of Delaware Press, 1999. 83–96.

Lyotard, Jean-François. "Answering the Question: What Is Postmodernism?" *The Postmodern Condition.* Trans. R. Durand. 1979. Manchester, UK: Manchester University Press, 1986. 71–82.

———. *The Differend: Phrases in Dispute.* Trans. Georges Van Den Abbeele. Minneapolis: University of Minnesota Press; Manchester, UK: Manchester University Press, 1988.

———. *The Inhuman: Reflections on Time.* Trans. Geoff Bennington and Rachel Bowlby. Cambridge: Polity, 1991.

———. *Lessons on the Analytic of the Sublime.* Trans. Elizabeth Rottenburg. Stanford, CA: Stanford University Press, 1994.

———. *The Lyotard Reader.* Ed. Andrew Benjamin. Oxford: Blackwell, 1989.

———. *The Postmodern Condition.* Trans. Geoffrey Bennington and Brian Massumi. Manchester, UK: Manchester University Press, 1984.

————. *The Postmodern Explained: Correspondence 1982–1985*. Ed. Julian Pefanis and Morgan Thomas. Trans. Don Barry et al. Minneapolis: University of Minnesota Press, 1992.

MacDonald, George. *At the Back of the North Wind*. 1871. London: Octopus, 1979.

MacDonald, Joyce Green. "Speech, Silence and History in *The Rape of Lucrece*." *Shakespeare Studies* 22 (1994): 77–103.

Macfarland, Ellen. *The Sacred Path Beyond Trauma: Reaching the Divine through Nature's Healing Symbols*. Berkeley, CA: North Atlantic Books, 2008.

Mack, Phyllis. *Visionary Women: Ecstatic Prophecy in Seventeenth-Century England*. Berkeley: University of California Press, 1992.

Madden, Etta M. "Quaker Elizabeth Ashbridge as 'The Spectacle & Discourse of the Company': Metaphor, Synecdoche, and Synthesis." *Early American Literature* 34 (1999). 171–89.

Mahony, Patrick J. "Hugh Hood's Edenic Garden: Psychoanalysis among the Flowerbeds; with a reply by Hugh Hood." *Canadian Literature* 96 (Spring 1983): 37–48.

Makransky, John. *Awakening through Love: Unveiling Your Deepest Goodness*. Boston: Wisdom Publications, 2007.

Manganiello, Dominic. "History as Judgment and Promise in *A Canticle for Leibowitz*." *Science-Fiction Studies* 13, part 2 (1986): 159–69.

Manns, Frédéric, ed. *The Sacrifice of Isaac in the Three Monotheistic Religions*. Jerusalem: Franciscan, 1995.

Manoussakis, John Panteleimon, ed. *After God: Richard Kearney and the Religious Turn in Continental Philosophy*. Perspectives in Continental Philosophy 49. New York: Fordham University Press, 2006.

————. *God after Metaphysics: A Theological Aesthetics*. Bloomington: Indiana University Press, 2007.

Marcel, Gabriel. "Desire and Hope." *Readings in Existential Phenomenology*. Ed. Nathaniel Lawrence and Daniel O'Connor. Englewood Cliffs, NJ: Prentice-Hall, 1967. 277–85.

Marietta, Jack D. *The Reformation of American Quakerism, 1748–1783*. Philadelphia: University of Philadelphia Press, 1984.

Marmontel, Jean-François. *Les Incas ou la destruction de l'empire du Pérou*. Paris, 1777.

Martin, Catherine Gimelli. "'Unmeete Contraryes': The Reformed Subject and the Triangulation of Religious Desire in Donne's *Anniversaries* and *Holy Sonnets*." *John Donne and the Protestant Reformation: New Perspectives*. Ed. Mary Arshagouni Papazian. Detroit: Wayne State University Press, 2003. 193–220.

Martindale, Joanna, ed. *English Humanism: Wyatt to Cowley*. London: Croom Helm, 1985.

Martz, Louis L. *The Poetry of Meditation*. New Haven, CT: Yale University Press, 1954. Rev. ed. New Haven, CT: Yale University Press, 1962.

Masuzawa Tomoko. *The Invention of World Religions*. Chicago: University of Chicago Press, 2005.

Mathews, Lawrence. Rev. of *Near Water*, by Hugh Hood. *Essays on Canadian Writing* 72 (Winter 2000): 109–17.

Mathy, Francis. "Endō Shūsaku: White Man, Yellow Man." *Comparative Literature* 19.1 (1967): 58–74.

Maus, Katharine Eisaman. Introduction. *The Rape of Lucrece*. By William Shakespeare. *The Norton Shakespeare*. Ed. Stephen Greenblatt et al. 2nd ed. New York: Norton, 2008. 663–67.

McDowell, Sean. "*W;t*, Donne's Holy Sonnets, and the Problem of Pain." *John Donne Journal* 23 (2004): 161–83.

McDuffie, Felecia Wright. *To Our Bodies Turn We Then: Body as Word and Sacrament in the Works of John Donne*. New York: Continuum, 2005.

McGillis, Roderick. Introduction. *For the Childlike: George MacDonald's Fantasies for Children*. Ed. Roderick McGillis. Metuchen, NJ: Scarecrow, 1992. 1–15.

McGrath, Alister E. *Christian Theology: An Introduction*. 2nd ed. Oxford: Blackwell, 1997.

McLaughlin, Eleanor. "Christ My Mother: Feminine Naming and Metaphor in Medieval Spirituality." *Nashota Review* 15 (1975): 228–48.

McMullan, Lorraine. "'Shameless, Marvellous, Shattering Absurdity': The Humour of Paradox in Alice Munro." *Probable Fictions: Alice Munro's Narrative Acts*. Ed. Louis MacKendrick. Downsview, ON: ECW Press, 1983. 144–62.

Mead, Stephen X. "The Crisis of Ritual in *Titus Andronicus*." *Exemplaria* 6.2 (1994): 459–79.

Mee, Jon. *Romanticism, Enthusiasm, and Regulation*. Oxford: Oxford University Press, 2003.

Mellor, Anne. "The Female Poet and the Poetess." *Women's Poetry in the Enlightenment*. Ed. Isobel Armstrong and Virginia Blain. London: Macmillan, 1999. 81–98.

Merkle, John C. *Approaching God: The Way of Abraham Joshua Heschel*. Collegeville, MN: Liturgical Press, 2009.

———. "The Sublime, the Human, and the Divine in the Depth-Theology of Abraham Joshua Heschel." *Journal of Religion* 58.4 (1978): 365–79.

Merleau-Ponty, Maurice. *Eye and Mind. Continental Aesthetics: Romanticism to Postmodernism: An Anthology*. Ed. Richard Kearney and David Rasmussen. Oxford: Blackwell, 2001. 288–306.

———. *Phenomenology of Perception*. Trans. Colin Smith. London and New York: Routledge, 2002.

———. *Signs*. Trans. Richard C. McCleary. Evanston, IL: Northwestern University Press, 1964.

———. *The Visible and the Invisible*. Ed. Claude Lefort. Trans. Alphonso Lingis. Evanston, IL: Northwestern University Press, 1968.

Merton, Thomas. *The Climate of Monastic Prayer*. Spencer, MA: Cistercian Publications, 1969.

———. *The Collected Poems of Thomas Merton*. New York: New Directions, 1977.

———. *Contemplative Prayer*. New York: Doubleday, 1996.

———. *Dialogues with Silence: Prayers & Drawings*. Ed. Jonathan Montaldo. San Francisco: HarperSanFrancisco, 2001.

———. *The Hidden Ground of Love: The Letters of Thomas Merton on Religious Experience and Social Concerns*. Ed. William H. Shannon. New York: Farrar, Straus and Giroux, 1985.

———. *"Honorable Reader": Reflections on My Work*. Ed. Robert E. Daggy. New York: Crossroad, 1991.

———. *In The Dark Before Dawn: New Selected Poems of Thomas Merton*. Ed. Lynn R. Szabo. New York: New Directions, 2005.

———. *The Intimate Merton: His Life from His Journals*. Ed. Patrick Hart and Jonathan Montaldo. San Francisco: HarperSanFrancisco, 1999.

————. "John Crowe Ransom—Standards for Critics." Rev. of *The World's Body*, by John Crowe Ransom. *New York Herald Tribune*. 8 May 1938. *The Literary Essays of Thomas Merton*. Ed. Patrick Hart. New York: New Directions, 1981.

————. *The New Man*. New York: Farrar, Straus and Cudahy, 1961.

————. *New Seeds of Contemplation*. New York: New Directions, 1961.

————. "Night-Flowering Cactus." *In The Dark Before Dawn*. Ed. Lynn R. Szabo. New York: New Directions, 2005. 98–99.

————. "Notes for a Philosophy of Solitude." *Disputed Questions*. New York: Farrar, Straus and Giroux, 1960. 177–207.

————. *Seasons of Celebration: Meditations on the Cycle of Liturgical Feasts*. New York: Farrar, Straus and Giroux, 1977.

————. *The Seven Storey Mountain*. 1948. New York: Farrar, Straus and Giroux, 1998.

————. *Thoughts in Solitude*. New York: Farrar, Straus and Giroux, 1958.

————. *What Is Contemplation?* Springfield, IL: Templegate, 1950.

————. *The Wisdom of the Desert*. New York: New Directions, 1960.

Miller, J. Hillis. *Fiction and Repetition*. Cambridge, MA: Harvard University Press, 1982.

————. "The Rhythm of Creativity: *To the Lighthouse*." *Tropes, Parables, Performatives: Essays on Twentieth-Century Literature*. Durham, NC: Duke University Press, 1991.

Miller, Walter. *A Canticle for Leibowitz*. 1959. New York: Bantam, 1997.

Minnis, A.J. et al. *Oxford Guides to Chaucer: The Shorter Poems*. Oxford: Clarendon, 1995.

Mishima Yukio. *Madame de Sade*. Trans. Donald Keene. New York: Grove Press, 1967.

————. *Sado kōshaku fujin [Madame de Sade]*. Tokyo: Shinchō-sha, 2003.

Mitchell, Robert Edward. "'The soul that dreams it shares the power it feels so well': The Politics of Sympathy in the Abolitionist Verse of Williams and Yearsley." *Romanticism on the Net* 29/30 (2003). http://id.erudit.org/iderudit/007719ar.

Moore, Rosemary. *The Light in Their Consciences: Early Quakers in Britain, 1646–1666*. University Park: Pennsylvania State University Press, 2000.

Morgan, Gerald. "Chaucer's Adaptation of Boccaccio's Temple of Venus in *The Parliament of Fowls*." *Review of English Studies*, n.s. 56 (2005): 1–36.

Morrison, Ronald P. "Kant, Husserl, and Heidegger on Time and the Unity of 'Consciousness.'" *Philosophy and Phenomenological Research* 39.2 (1978): 182–98.

Morrison, Toni. *Beloved*. London: Picador, 1987.

————. *Conversations with Toni Morrison*. Ed. Danille Taylor-Guthrie. Jackson: University Press of Mississippi, 1994.

————. *The Nobel Lecture*. New York: Norton, 1993.

————. *Playing in the Dark: Whiteness and the Literary Imagination*. Cambridge, MA: Harvard University Press, 1992.

————. "Rediscovering Black History." *New York Times Magazine*. 11 Aug. 1974: 14–24.

————. "The Site of Memory." *Inventing the Truth: The Art and Craft of Memoir*. Ed. William Zinsser. New York: Mariner Books, 1998. 183–200.

————. "Unspeakable Things Unspoken: The Afro-American Presence in American Literature." *Michigan Quarterly Review* 28.1 (1989): 1–34.

Moss, John. *Sex and Violence in the Canadian Novel: The Ancestral Present*. Toronto: McClelland and Stewart, 1977.

Mott, Richard, and Abigail Mott. *A Short Account of the Last Sickness and Death of Maria Mott, Daughter of Richard and Abigail Mott, of Mamaroneck, in the State of New York*. New York: Samuel Wood and Sons, 1817. In CYMA.

Munro, Alice. "Alice Munro: A Life in Writing." Interview with Eleanor Wachtel. *Queen's Quarterly* 112.2 (2005): 267–81.

———. "Art of Fiction." Interview with Jeanne McCulloch and Mona Simpson. *Paris Review*, 137 (1994): 226–64.

———. "Carried Away." *Open Secrets*. New York: Alfred A. Knopf, 1994.

———. Interview with Geoff Hancock. *Canadian Fiction Magazine* 43 (1982): 74–114.

———. Introduction. *Selected Stories*. By Alice Munro. New York: Vintage Books, 1996.

———. *Lives of Girls and Women*. 1971. Toronto: Penguin Canada, 2005.

Murphy, Georgeann. "The Art of Alice Munro: Memory, Identity, and the Aesthetics of Connection." *Canadian Women Writing Fiction*. Ed. Mickey Pearlman. Jackson: University Press of Mississippi, 1993. 12–27.

Murray, Julie. "Governing Economic Man: Joanna Baillie's Theatre of Utility." *ELH* 70 (2003): 1043–65.

Myers, Carol. "Deborah." *The Oxford Companion to the Bible*. Ed. Bruce Metzger and Michael Cogan. Oxford: Oxford University Press, 1993. 161.

Myers, Victoria. "Joanna Baillie's Theatre of Cruelty." *Joanna Baillie, Romantic Dramatist: Critical Essays*. Ed. Thomas C. Crochunis. New York: Routledge, 2004. 87–107.

Myles, Anna G. "From Monster to Martyr: Re-Presenting Mary Dyer." *Early American Literature* 36.1 (2001): 1–30.

Nancy, Jean-Luc. *La Déclosion: Déconstruction du christianisme, 1*. Paris: Galilée, 2005.

Newman, John Henry. *Parochial and Plain Sermons*. Vol. 5. London: Longmans, Green, 1907.

Nicholls, Peter. "The Belated Postmodern: History, Phantoms and Toni Morrison." *Psychoanalytic Criticism: A Reader*. Ed. Sue Vice. Cambridge: Polity, 1996. 50–74.

Noon, William T. *Joyce and Aquinas*. New Haven, CT: Yale University Press, 1957.

"Nou goth sonne under wode." *English Lyrics of the XIIIth Century*. Ed. Carleton Fairchild Brown. Oxford: Clarendon, 1932. 165–66.

Nuttall, A.D. *Overheard by God: Fiction and Prayer in Herbert, Milton, Dante and St. John*. London: Methuen, 1980.

O'Connor, Flannery. *Mystery and Manners: Occasional Prose*. Ed. Sally Fitzgerald and Robert Fitzgerald. New York: Farrar, Straus and Giroux, 1969.

O'Leary, Joseph. "Enclosed Spaces in 'The Dead.'" *English Literature and Language*. Vol. 34. Tokyo: University of Sophia, 1997. 33–52.

Oliver, Kelly. *Witnessing: Beyond Recognition*. Minneapolis: University of Minnesota Press, 2001.

Olivier, Bert. "The Sublime, Unpresentability and Postmodern Cultural Complexity." *South African Journal of Philosophy* 16.1 (1997): 7–13.

O'Neill, Samuel. "The Mystic Way in Two Works by Annie Dillard." Master's thesis. Georgetown University, 1993.

Ottway, Sheila. *Desiring Disencumbrance: The Representation of the Self in Autobiographical Writings by Seventeenth-Century Englishwomen*. Groningen, Neth.: University of Groningen Press, 1998.

Pell, Barbara. "Divine Tragicomedy: A Theological/Tropological Reading of Hugh Hood's 'Marriage Group.'" *English Studies in Canada* 28 (2002): 685–713.

———. *Faith and Fiction: A Theological Critique of the Narrative Strategies of Hugh MacLennan and Morley Callaghan*. Waterloo, ON: Wilfrid Laurier University Press, 1998.

Peterson, Eugene H. *The Message: The Bible in Contemporary Language*. Colorado Springs, CO: NavPress, 2002.

Picard, Max. *The World of Silence*. Chicago: Henry Regnery, 1952.

Pinney, Thomas. "More Leaves from George Eliot's Notebook." *Huntington Library Quarterly* 29.4 (1966): 353–76.

Polt, Richard. "*Ereignis.*" *A Companion to Heidegger*. Ed. Hubert L. Dreyfus and Mark A. Wrathall. Oxford: Blackwell, 2005. 375–91.

Prager, Brad. "Kant in Caspar David Friedrich's Frames." *Art History* 25.1 (2002): 68–86.

Proust, Marcel. *The Captive, The Fugitive. In Search of Lost Time*. Trans. C.K. Scott Moncrieff and Terence Kilmartin. Rev. D.J. Enright. Vintage Classics Series. Vol. 5. London: Vintage, 1996.

———. *Swann's Way. In Search of Lost Time*. Trans. C.K. Scott Moncrieff and Terence Kilmartin. Rev. D.J. Enright. Vol. 1. New York: Modern Library, 1998.

———. *Time Regained. In Search of Lost Time*. Trans. Andreas Mayor and Terence Kilmartin. Rev. D.J. Enright. Vol. 6. New York: Modern Library, 1999.

———. *Within a Budding Grove. In Search of Lost Time*. Trans. C.K. Scott Moncrieff and Terence Kilmartin. Rev. D.J. Enright. Vol. 2. New York: Modern Library, 1998.

Pseudo-Dionysius: The Complete Works. Ed. and trans. Colm Luibheid. New York: Paulist Press, 1987.

Pusey, E.B. *Parochial Sermons*. 3 vols. Oxford: James Parker, 1873.

———. *Parochial Sermons III. The Mind of the Oxford Movement*. Ed. Owen Chadwick. Stanford, CA: Stanford University Press, 1960. 129–32, 137–38.

"Quaker Women's Diaries: The Diaries of Elizabeth Robson, 1813–43." *Quaker Women's Diaries of the 18th and 19th Centuries, from Friends House Library*. Reels 6 and 7.

Quay, Sara E. "'Lucrece the chaste': The Construction of Rape in Shakespeare's *The Rape of Lucrece.*" *Modern Language Studies* 25.2 (1995): 3–17.

Radcliffe, Anne. *The Romance of the Forest*. Ed. Chloe Chard. Oxford: Oxford University Press, 1986.

Raspa, Anthony. Introduction. *Devotions upon Emergent Occasions*. Ed. Anthony Raspa. Montreal and Kingston: McGill-Queen's University Press, 1975.

Ratzinger, Joseph (Pope Benedict XVI). *Die Einheit der Nationen. Eine Vision d. Kirchenväter*. Salzburg and Munich: Pustet, 2005.

———. *Encyclical Letter Deus Caritas Est of the Supreme Pontiff Benedict XVI to the Bishops, Priests and Deacons, Men and Women Religious, and all the Lay Faithful on Christian Love*. Libreria Editrice Vaticana, 2005. http://www.vatican.va/holy_father/benedict_xvi/encyclicals/documents/hf_ben-xvi_enc_20051225_deus-caritas-est_en.html.

———. *Der Glaube ist Einfach! Ansprachen, Meditationen, Predigten während des Besuches in Bayern*. Leipzig: Ger.: St. Benno Verlag, 2006.

———. *Pilgrim Fellowship of Faith: The Church as Communion*. Ed. Stephan Otto Horn and Vinzenz Pfnür. Trans. Henry Taylor. San Francisco: Ignatius Press, 2002.

———. *Post-synodal Apostolic Exhortation Sacramentum Caritatis of the Holy Father Benedict XVI to the Bishops, Clergy, Consecrated Persons and the Lay Faithful on the Eucharist as the Source and Summit of the Church's Life and Mission*, 22 February 2007. http://www.vatican.va/holy_father/benedict_xvi/apost_exhortations/documents/hf_ben-xvi_exh_20070222_sacramentum-caritatis_en.html.

————. *The Sacrament of Charity*. Washington, DC: USCCB Publishing, 2007.

Ratzinger, Joseph (Pope Benedict XVI), and Marcello Pera. *Without Roots: The West, Relativism, Christianity, Islam*. Trans. Michael F. Moore. New York: Basic Books, 2006.

Rhiele, Wolfgang. *The Middle English Mystics*. London: Routledge and Kegan Paul, 1981.

Richardson, Alan. "Epic Ambivalence: Imperial Politics and Romantic Deflection in Williams's *Peru* and Landor's *Gebir*." *Romanticism, Race, and Imperial Culture, 1780–1834*. Ed. Alan Richardson and Sonia Hofkosh. Bloomington: Indiana University Press, 1996. 265–82.

Ricoeur, Paul. "Emmanuel Levinas: Thinker of Testimony." *Figuring the Sacred: Religion, Narrative, and Imagination*. Minneapolis, MN: Fortress, 1995. 108–126.

————. "Life in Quest of Narrative." *On Paul Ricoeur: Narrative and Interpretation*. Ed. Derek Wood. London and New York: Routledge, 1991. 20–33.

————. *On Translation*. Trans. Eileen Brennan. London and New York: Routledge, 2006.

————. *The Philosophy of Paul Ricoeur: An Anthology of His Work*. Ed. Charles E. Regan and David Stuart. Boston: Beacon, 1978.

————. *Time and Narrative*. Trans. Kathleen McLaughlin and David Pellauer. 3 vols. Chicago: University of Chicago Press, 1984–88.

————. *Vivant jusqu'à la mort*. Paris: Editions du Seuil, 2007.

Roberts, Lorraine M., and John R. Roberts. "Crashavian Criticism: A Brief Interpretive History." *New Perspectives on the Life and Art of Richard Crashaw*. Ed. John R. Roberts. Columbia: University of Missouri Press, 1990. 1–29.

Roberts, Sasha. "Editing Sexuality, Narrative and Authorship: The Altered Texts of Shakespeare's *Lucrece*." *Texts and Cultural Change in Early Modern England*. Ed. Cedric C. Brown and Arthur F. Marotti. New York: St. Martin's Press, 1997. 124–52.

Robertson, William. *The History of America*. 2 vols. London, 1777.

Roe, Dinah. *Christina Rossetti's Faithful Imagination: The Devotional Poetry and Prose*. New York: Palgrave, 2007.

Roeschlein, Michael. "E.M. Forster and 'The Part of the Mind that Seldom Speaks': Mysticism, Mythopoeia and Irony in *A Passage to India*." *Religion and Literature* 36.1 (2004): 67–99.

Rosenzweig, Franz. *Der Mensch und sein Werk. Gesammelte Schriften*, II. Bd: *Der Stern der Erlösung*. Ed. Reinhold Mayer. The Hague: Martinus Nijhoff, 1976.

————. *The Star of Redemption*. Trans. William W. Hallo. Notre Dame, IN: University of Notre Dame Press, 1985.

Rossetti, Christina. *Annus Domini: A Prayer for Each Day of the Year, Founded on a Text of Holy Scripture*. Oxford: James Parker, 1874.

————. *Christina Rossetti: The Complete Poems*. Text R.W. Crump. Notes and introduction Betty S. Flowers. London: Penguin, 2001.

————. *The Face of the Deep: A Devotional Commentary on the Apocalypse*. London: Society for Promoting Christian Knowledge, 1892.

————. *The Letters of Christina Rossetti: Vol. 4*. Ed. Antony H. Harrison. Charlottesville: University of Virginia Press, 2004.

Salter, Elizabeth. "Chaucer and Medieval English Tradition." *Fourteenth-Century English Poetry: Contexts and Readings*. Oxford: Clarendon, 1983. 117–40.

Samuelson, Norbert M. *A User's Guide to Franz Rosenzweig's* Star of Redemption. Richmond, UK: Curzon Press, 1999.

Sandler, Linda. "Between Proust and Yonge." *Books in Canada* 4 (December 1975): 5–7.

Saunders, Ben. *Desiring Donne: Poetry, Sexuality, Interpretation*. Cambridge, MA: Harvard University Press, 2006.

Saunders, Max. "Forster's Life and Life-Writing." *The Cambridge Companion to E.M. Forster*. Ed. David Bradshaw. Cambridge: Cambridge University Press, 2007. 8–31.

Schloesser, Steven. *Jazz Age Catholicism: Mystic Modernism in Postwar Paris: 1919–1923*. Toronto: University of Toronto Press, 2005.

Schneider, Helmut J. "Nature." *Romanticism*. Ed. Marshall Brown. Cambridge: Cambridge University Press, 2000. 92–114. Vol. 5 of *The Cambridge History of Literary Criticism*.

Scholes, Robert, and Eric Rabkin. *Science Fiction: History, Science, Vision*. New York: Oxford University Press, 1977.

Scholz, Suzanne. "Textualizing the Body Politic: National Identity and the Female Body in *The Rape of Lucrece*." *Shakespeare Jahrbuch* 132 (1996): 103–13.

Schroeder, William. "Continental Ethics." *The Blackwell Guide to Ethical Theory*. Ed. Hugh LaFollette. Oxford: Blackwell, 2000. 375–99.

Seasoltz, R. Kevin. *A Sense of the Sacred: Theological Foundations of Christian Architecture and Art*. New York: Continuum, 2005.

Seed, David. "Recycling the Texts of the Culture: Walter M. Miller's *A Canticle for Leibowitz*." *Extrapolation* 37.3 (1996): 257–71.

Shakespeare, William. *The Rape of Lucrece. The Riverside Shakespeare*. Ed. G. Blakemore Evans, with the assistance of J.J.M. Tobin. 2nd ed. Boston: Houghton Mifflin, 1997. 1816–38.

———. *Titus Andronicus*. Ed. and introd. Eugene M. Waith. Oxford: Oxford University Press, 1984.

Shea, Daniel, Jr. "Elizabeth Ashbridge and the Voice Within." *Journeys in New Worlds: Early American Women's Narratives*. Ed. William L. Andrews. Madison: University of Wisconsin Press, 1990. 119–46.

Sherwood, Terry G. *Herbert's Prayerful Art*. Toronto: University of Toronto Press, 1989.

Sievers, Julie. "Awakening the Inner Light: Elizabeth Ashbridge and the Transformation of Quaker Community." *Early American Literature* 36.2 (2001): 235–62.

Silver, Brenda R. "Periphrasis, Power, and Rape in *A Passage to India*." *Novel* 22.1 (1988): 86–105.

Silverman, Hugh J. "Lyotard and the Events of the Postmodern Sublime." *Lyotard: Philosophy, Politics, and the Sublime*. Ed. Hugh J. Silverman. London and New York: Routledge, 2002. 222–30.

Sirbu, Rebecca W. *Theologies of Suffering: How Judaism Can Help You Cope*. 2007. http://www.huc.edu/kalsman/articles/Rebecca.pdf.

Slights, William W.E. "The Sacrificial Crisis in *Titus Andronicus*." *University of Toronto Quarterly* 49.1 (1979): 18–32.

Smith, Adam. *The Theory of Moral Sentiments*. 2 vols. 1759. New York: Duyckinck, 1822.

Smith, Linda L. *Annie Dillard*. New York: Twayne, 1991.

Smith, Nigel. "Hidden Things Brought to Light: Enthusiasm and Quaker Discourse." *The Emergence of Quaker Writing: Dissenting Literature in Seventeenth-Century*

England. Ed. Thomas N. Corns and David Loewenstein. London: Frank Cass and Co., 1995. 57–69.

———. *Perfection Proclaimed: Language and Literature in English Radical Religion, 1640–1660*. Oxford: Clarendon, 1989.

Smith, Pamela A. "The Ecotheology of Annie Dillard: A Study in Ambivalence." *Cross Currents* 45.3 (1995): 341–58.

Sommerville, John. *The Decline of the Secular University*. Oxford: Oxford University Press, 2006.

Spearing, A.C. *Medieval Dream-Poetry*. Cambridge: Cambridge University Press, 1976.

Spencer, Susan. "The Post-Apocalyptic Library: Oral and Literate Culture in *Fahrenheit 451* and *A Canticle for Leibowitz*." *Extrapolation* 32.4 (1991): 331–42.

Spenser, Edmund. *The Faerie Queene*. Harmondsworth, UK: Penguin, 1987.

Stachniewski, John. "John Donne: The Despair of the 'Holy Sonnets.'" *ELH* 48.4 (1981): 677–705.

Stead, Christopher. *Philosophy in Christian Antiquity*. Cambridge: Cambridge University Press, 1994.

Steiner, George. *Language and Silence: Essays on Language, Literature, and the Inhuman*. New York: Atheneum, 1967.

———. *Real Presences*. London: Faber and Faber, 1989.

Stewart, Stanley. *George Herbert*. Boston: Twayne, 1986.

Stovel, Nora Foster. "Temples and Tabernacles: Alternative Religions in the Fictional Microcosms of Robertson Davies, Margaret Laurence, and Alice Munro." *International Fiction Review* 31.1–2 (2004): 65–77.

Stratford, Philip. *Faith and Fiction: Creative Process in Greene and Mauriac*. Notre Dame, IN: University of Notre Dame Press, 1964.

Strier, Richard. *Love Known: Theology and Experience in George Herbert's Poetry*. Chicago: University of Chicago Press, 1983.

Struthers, J.R. (Tim). "An Interview with Hugh Hood." *Hugh Hood's Work in Progress. Essays on Canadian Writing* 13/14 (1978–79): 21–93.

Summers, Claude J., and Ted-Larry Pebworth. "The Politics of *The Temple*: 'The British Church' and 'The Familie.'" *George Herbert Journal* 8.1 (1984): 1–15.

Szabo, Lynn. "The Sound of Sheer Silence: A Study in the Poetics of Thomas Merton." *Merton Annual* 13 (2000): 208–21.

Tarter, Michele Lise. "Reading *A Quaker's Book*: Elizabeth Ashbridge's Testimony of Quaker Literary Theory." *Quaker Studies* 9.2 (2005): 176–90.

A Testimony of Falls Monthly Meeting of Friends, Concerning Lucy B. Cadwallader, a Minister, Deceased. Philadelphia: William H. Pile's Sons, 1900. In CYMA.

Thomas, Keith. *Religion and the Decline of Magic*. New York: Charles Scribner's Sons, 1971.

Todd, Janet. *Sensibility: An Introduction*. London: Methuen, 1986.

Tolkien, J.R.R. "Beowulf: The Monsters and the Critics." *The Monsters and the Critics, and Other Essays*. Ed. Christopher Tolkien. Boston: Houghton Mifflin, 1984. 5–45.

———. "On Fairy-Stories." *The Tolkien Reader*. New York: Ballantine, 1977. 3–84.

Toplady, Augustus. *Psalms and Hymns for Public and Private Worship: Collected... and published by Augustus Toplady, A.B. Vicar of Broad Hembury*. London, 1776.

Traherne, Thomas. *Centuries of Meditations*. London: A.R. Mowbray, 1960. Wilton, CT: Morehouse, 1985.

"Transubstantiation." *The Shorter Oxford English Dictionary*. 5th ed. 2002.

Trevett, Christine. *Quaker Women Prophets in England and Wales, 1650–1700*. Lewiston, NY: Edwin Mellen, 2000.

———. *Women and Quakerism in the 17th Century*. York, UK: Sessions Book Trust, Ebor Press, 1991.

Trezise, Thomas. "Unspeakable." *Yale Journal of Criticism* 14.1 (2001): 39–66.

Trottein, Serge. "Lyotard: Before and After the Sublime." *Lyotard: Philosophy, Politics, and the Sublime*. Ed. Hugh J. Silverman. London and New York: Routledge, 2002. 192–200.

Tucker, Sarah Fish. *Memoirs of the Life and Religious Experience of Sarah Tucker, a Minister of the Society of Friends, Written by Herself*. Providence, R.I., 1848. In CYMA.

Tuve, Rosemond. *A Reading of George Herbert*. Chicago: University of Chicago Press, 1952.

Updike, John. "Magnetic North." Rev. of *Selected Stories*, by Alice Munro. *New York Times* 27 Oct. 1996. http://www.nytimes.com/1996/10/27/books/review/1996 munro.html.

Vattimo, Gianni, and Richard Rorty. *The Future of Religion*. Ed. Santiago Zabala. New York: Columbia University Press, 2005.

Veith, Gene Edward, Jr. *Reformation Spirituality: The Religion of George Herbert*. Lewisburg, PA: Bucknell University Press, 1985.

Vendler, Helen. *The Poetry of George Herbert*. Cambridge, MA: Harvard University Press, 1975.

Vico, Giambattista. *On Humanistic Education (Six Inaugural Orations, 1699–1707)*. Trans. Giorgio A. Pinto and Arthur W. Shippee. Ithaca, NY: Cornell University Press, 1993.

"Villain." Def. 4b. *The Oxford English Dictionary*. 2nd ed. 1989.

Virgil. *Eclogues, Georgics, Aeneid 1–6*. Trans. H. Rushton Fairclough. Rev. and ed. G.P. Goold. Loeb Classical Library 63. Rev. ed. Cambridge, MA: Harvard University Press, 1916.

Vonier, Anscar. *A Key to the Doctrine of the Eucharist*. Bethesda, MD: Zaccheus, 2004.

Waith, Eugene M. Introduction. *Titus Andronicus*. By William Shakespeare. Oxford: Oxford University Press, 1984. 1–69.

Walker, Evan Harris. *The Physics of Consciousness: The Quantum Mind and the Meaning of Life*. Cambridge, MA: Perseus, 2000.

Wallace, R.S. *Calvin's Doctrine of the Christian Life*. Edinburgh: Oliver and Boyd, 1959.

Walpole, Horace. *Castle of Otranto*. London, 1765.

Walton, Izaak. *The Lives of John Donne, Sir Henry Wotton, Richard Hooker, George Herbert, and Robert Sanderson*. 1927. London: Oxford University Press, 1962.

Watson, J.R., ed. *An Annotated Anthology of Hymns*. Oxford: Oxford University Press, 2002.

Watts, Isaac. *The Psalms and Hymns of the Rev. Isaac Watts, D.D.: A New Edition… corrected and revised by the Rev. G. Burder*. London: Whittingham, 1806.

Wessells, Michael G., and Carlinda Monteiro. "Healing the Wounds following Protracted Conflict in Angola: A Community-Based Approach to Assisting War-affected Children." *Handbook of Culture, Therapy, and Healing*. Ed. Uwe Peter Gielen, Jefferson M. Fish, and Juris G. Draguns. New York and London: Routledge, 2004. 321–41.

West, Grace Starry. "Going by the Book: Classical Allusions in Shakespeare's *Titus Andronicus*." *Studies in Philology* 79.1 (1982): 62–77.

Westling, Louise. "Virginia Woolf and the Flesh of the World." *New Literary History* 30.4 (1999): 855–75.

Whalen, Robert. *The Poetry of Immanence: Sacrament in Donne and Herbert*. Toronto: University of Toronto Press, 2002.

Whitlock, Gillian. "In the Second Person: Narrative Transactions in Stolen Generations Testimony." *Biography* 24.1 (2001): 197–214.

Wilbur, Richard. *The Poems of Richard Wilbur*. New York: Harcourt Brace, 1963.

Wilcox, Catherine M. *Theology and Women's Ministry in Seventeenth-Century English Quakerism*. Lewiston, NY: Edwin Mellen, 1995.

William of St. Thierry. *The Meditations of William of St. Thierry: Meditativae Orationes*. Trans. from the Latin by a Religious of C.S.M.V. London: A.R. Mowbray, 1954.

Williams, Carolyn D. "'Silence, Like a Lucrece Knife': Shakespeare and the Meanings of Rape." *Yearbook of English Studies* 23 (1993): 93–110.

Williams, Helen Maria. *Poems 1786*. Introd. Jonathan Wordsworth. Oxford: Woodstock, 1994.

———. *Poems on Various Subjects with Introductory Remarks on the Present State of Science and Literature in France*. London: Whittaker, 1823.

———. *Recueil de Poésies Extraites des Ouvrages d'Helena Maria Williams, Traduites de l'Anglais par M. Stanislas de Boufflers et M. Esménard*. Paris: Fr. Cocheris Fils, 1808.

Williams, Roger W. "Man of Sorrows." *A Dictionary of Biblical Tradition in English Literature*. Ed. David Lyle Jeffrey. Grand Rapids, MI: Eerdmans, 1992. 476.

Williams, Rowan. *Grace and Necessity: Reflections on Art and Love*. London: Continuum, 2005.

Winny, James. *A Preface to Donne*. New York: Charles Scribner's Sons, 1970.

"Witnessing." *The Canadian Oxford English Dictionary*. 1998.

Witte, Bernd. *Walter Benjamin: An Intellectual Biography*. Trans. James Rolleston. Detroit: Wayne State University Press, 1997.

Wollstonecraft, Mary. *The Works of Mary Wollstonecraft*. Ed. Janet Todd and Marilyn Butler. 7 vols. London: William Pickering, 1989.

Wood, Ralph C. "Lest the World's Amnesia Be Complete: A Reading of Walter Miller's *A Canticle for Leibowitz*." *Religion and Literature* 33.1 (2001): 23–41.

Woodward, William Harrison. *Vittorino Da Feltre and Other Humanist Educators*. Renaissance Society of America Reprint Texts Series 5. Toronto: University of Toronto Press; New York: Renaissance Society of America, 1996.

Woolf, Virginia. *The Diary of Virginia Woolf*. Ed. Anne Olivier Bell, with Andrew McNeillie. 5 vols. New York: Harcourt Brace Jovanovich; London: Hogarth, 1977–1984.

———. *To the Lighthouse*. New York: Harcourt Brace Jovanovich, 1927. Orlando, FL: Harcourt, 1981.

Wordsworth, William. *Guide to the Lakes*. London: R. Ackermann, 1810.

———. "Lines written a few miles above Tintern Abbey." *William Wordsworth: The Major Works*. Ed. Stephen Gill. Oxford World's Classics. 1984. Oxford: Oxford University Press, 2000. 131–35.

Wright, Luella M. *The Literary Life of Early Friends, 1650–1725*. New York: Columbia University Press, 1932.

Wright, T.R. *Theology and Literature.* Oxford: Blackwell, 1988.

Yaeger, Patricia. "The 'Language of Blood': Toward a Maternal Sublime." *Genre* 25 (1992): 5–24.

Yasuoka Shōtarō, and Inoue Yōji. *Warera naze Kirisuto-kyōto to narishika* [*Why Did We Become Christians?*]. Tokyo: Kōbun-sha, 1999.

Young, Edward. *The Complaint, or Night Thoughts on Life, Death, and Immortality.* London, 1742.

Zinzendorf, Count Nicolaus Ludwig von. *Hymns Composed for the Use of the Brethren.* London, 1749.

Žižek, Slavoj. *The Fragile Absolute—or, Why Is the Christian Legacy Worth Fighting For?* London: Verso, 2000.

———. *Interrogating the Real.* Ed. Rex Butler and Scott Stephens. London: Continuum, 2005.

———. *The Puppet and the Dwarf: The Perverse Core of Christianity.* Cambridge, MA: MIT Press, 2003.

———. *The Sublime Object of Ideology.* London: Verso, 1989.

———. *Tarrying with the Negative: Kant, Hegel, and the Critique of Ideology.* Durham, NC: Duke University Press, 1993.

NOTES ON CONTRIBUTORS

David Anonby is a lecturer in English at Trinity Western University. His research areas are early modern devotional literature and religion and literature. He is currently working on the theology of John Donne, an interest that developed during graduate studies at the University of British Columbia under Paul Stanwood. Other areas of interest include the Bible as literature, Shakespeare, and the relationship between sexuality and spirituality.

Deborah C. Bowen is an associate professor and the current chair of English at Redeemer University College in Ancaster, Ontario. She is the author of *Stories of the Middle Space: Reading the Ethics of Postmodern Realisms* (2010) and the editor of *The Strategic Smorgasbord of Postmodernity: Literature and the Christian Critic* (2007). Recent and forthcoming publications include articles in *The Journal of Education and Christian Belief* and a chapter on Carol Shields's *The Stone Diaries* in *Re: Reading the Postmodern: A Canadian Literature Symposium*. Bowen regularly reviews new Canadian poetry and is presently working on the interface of poetry, ecology, and spirituality.

Christine A. Colón is an associate professor of English at Wheaton College in Illinois, where she teaches courses in writing, English literature, global literature, modern drama, and Jane Austen. She has published articles on Jane Austen, Joanna Baillie, Anne Brontë, Adelaide Procter, Caryl Churchill, Wilkie Collins, and John Keats. She is the author of the introduction to the Valancourt edition of Joanna Baillie's Gothic dramas, and she has recently published a monograph entitled *Joanna Baillie and the Art of Moral Influence*.

Daniel W. Doerksen is Honorary Research Professor, Department of English, University of New Brunswick, Fredericton. Originally from Winnipeg, he received his Ph.D. from the University of Wisconsin, Madison in 1973. He has published *Conforming to the Word: Herbert, Donne, and the English Church* *before Laud* (1997) and co-edited with Christopher Hodgkins *Centered on the Word: Literature, Scripture, and the Tudor-Stuart Middle Way* (2004). His book manuscript "Picturing Spiritual Conflicts: Herbert, Calvin, and Scriptural Portrayals of Experience" is currently under review. He has authored articles on Spenser, Donne, Herbert, and Milton. Recent work includes "'Generous Ambiguity' Revisited: A Herbert for All Seasons" (*George Herbert Journal* 30.1–2 [2006–2007]: 19–41) and "George Herbert, Calvinism, and Reading 'Mattens,'" forthcoming in *Christianity and Literature*.

Natasha Duquette teaches eighteenth-century literature and critical theory at Biola University in Southern California. She has published articles in *Mosaic, Notes and Queries, Christianity and Literature,* and *Persuasions-Online*. She has also edited the essay collection *Sublimer Aspects: Interfaces between Literature, Aesthetics, and Theology* (2007) and recently contributed to *Jane Austen Sings the Blues* (2009). She is currently producing a new, annotated edition of Helen Maria Williams's novel *Julia* for Pickering & Chatto's Chawton House Library series.

Constance M. Fulmer holds the Blanche E. Seaver Chair in English Literature and is the associate dean of Seaver College at Pepperdine University in Malibu, California. She is working on a biography of Edith J. Simcox and a book on George Eliot's moral aesthetic. She has published an annotated bibliography of George Eliot criticism (1977) and with Margaret Barfield edited *A Monument to the Memory of George Eliot: Edith J. Simcox's Autobiography of a Shirtmaker* (1998) as well as several articles on George Eliot and Edith Simcox. She is president of the Victorian Interdisciplinary Studies Association of the Western United States.

Robynne Rogers Healey is an associate professor of history at Trinity Western University in Langley, British Columbia. She is the author of *From Quaker to Upper Canadian: Faith and Community among Yonge Street Friends, 1801–1850* (2006). Her articles have appeared in journals such as *Quaker History*, the *Canadian Quaker History Journal*, the *York Pioneer*, and *Past Imperfect*, and her essay on the diary of Sarah Welch Hill is included in *The Small Details of Life: Twenty Diaries by Women in Canada, 1830–1996* (2002).

Monika B. Hilder is an associate professor of English at Trinity Western University. She specializes in children's literature and fantasy literature, and her research interests include literature as moral education, imaginative education, gender criticism, and literature and spirituality, with a focus on George MacDonald, C.S. Lewis, Madeleine L'Engle, and L.M. Montgomery. Recent publications include journal articles and book chapters on C.S. Lewis, George MacDonald, L.M. Montgomery, and moral education.

Esther T. Hu, who received her Ph.D. from Cornell University, teaches literature and writing at Boston University. Her publications include "Christina Rossetti, John Keble, and the Divine Gaze" in *Victorian Poetry* (2008) and a translation, "Mother Goose Got Married," in *Taiwan Literature: English Translation Series* (2007). She is writing a book on Christina Rossetti's religious poetry and has completed the translation of *Heaven and Earth: The Love Story of General Hu Tsung-Nan and Dr. Hsia-Ti Yeh* into English.

David Lyle Jeffrey, Ph.D. (Princeton) and Fellow of the Royal Society of Canada, is Distinguished Professor of Literature and Humanities at Baylor University. He is also Professor Emeritus of English literature at the University of Ottawa, and has been Guest Professor at Peking University (Beijing) since 1996 and Honorary Professor at the University of International Business and Economics (Beijing) since 2005. His books include *A Dictionary of Biblical Tradition in English Literature* (1992); *The Early English Lyric and Franciscan Spirituality* (1975); *Chaucer and Scriptural Tradition* (1984); *English Spirituality in the Age of Wesley* (1987, 1994, 2000); *The Law of Love: English Spirituality in the Age of Wyclif* (1988, 2001); *People of the Book: Christian Identity and Literary Culture* (1996); and a co-authored book on *The Bible and the University* (2007). Currently he has forthcoming a book on Christianity and literature, co-authored by Greg Maillet (2010), and chapters for the *Cambridge History of Literary Criticism* and *Cambridge Companion to the Hebrew Bible*, and he is completing a commentary on Luke for the Brazos theological commentary series.

Heather G.S. Johnson received her Ph.D. in Renaissance English literature from Indiana University Bloomington and is an assistant professor of English at Southern Illinois University Edwardsville. Her current research explores seventeenth-century attitudes toward texts and textuality.

Richard Kearney holds the Charles B. Seelig Chair of Philosophy at Boston College. His publications include *Poétique du Possible* (1984); *Dialogues With Contemporary Continental Thinkers* (1984); *Modern Movements in European Philosophy* (1987); *Transitions: Narratives in Modern Irish Culture* (1987); *The Wake of the Imagination* (1988); *Poetics of Imagining: Modern and Post Modern* (1991, 1998); *Angel of Patrick's Hill* (1991); *Visions of Europe* (1993); *Poetics of Modernity* (1995); *States of Mind: Dialogues with Contemporary Thinkers* (1995); *Sam's Fall* (1995); *Walking at Sea Level* (1997); *Desiderio et Dio* (1996); *The God Who May Be: A Hermeneutics of Religion* (2001); *On Stories: Thinking in Action* (2001); *Strangers, Gods, and Monsters: Interpreting Otherness* (2002); *Debates in Continental Philosophy: Richard Kearney in Conversation with Contemporary Thinkers* (2004); *The Owl of Minerva: Encountering Paul Ricoeur* (2004); and *Navigations: Collected Irish Essays, 1976–2006* (2006).

Norm Klassen is an associate professor and the current chair of English at St. Jerome's University, federated with the University of Waterloo. He is the author of *Chaucer on Love, Knowledge, and Sight* (1995) and co-author of *The Passionate Intellect: Incarnational Humanism and the Future of University Education* (2006). Recent publications include notes and articles in *Notes and Queries* and *Quaderni d'Italianistica* as well as book chapters in *A Concise Companion to Chaucer* (2005), *The Strategic Smorgasbord of Postmodernity: Literature and the Christian Critic* (2007), and *Tradition and Formation: Claiming an Inheritance* (2009).

Richard J. Lane teaches in the English Department at Vancouver Island University, where he also directs the Literary Theory Research Group and the Seminar for Advanced Studies in the Humanities. He is the author or editor of nine academic books, including *Image Technologies in Canadian Literature* (2009), the single-authored *Fifty Key Literary Theorists* (2006), *The Postcolonial Novel* (2005), and *Reading Walter Benjamin: Writing through the Catastrophe* (2005). His *Jean Baudrillard* (2000, second expanded edition 2009) has been translated into Japanese and Korean. Lane writes the "Canada" section of *The Year's Work in English Studies* for Oxford University Press and The English Association.

Sean Lawrence is an assistant professor in the Department of Critical Studies at the University of British Columbia (Okanagan). He has published on Elizabethan drama in journals such as the *European Journal of English Studies, English Studies in Canada,* and *Renascence: Essays on Values in Literature.* He is currently completing a book project entitled *Forgiving the Gift: Exchange and Forgiveness in Marlowe and Shakespeare.*

Eleanor McCullough, a graduate of the University of Oxford and Regent College, is a Ph.D. candidate at the Centre for Medieval Studies at the University of York, England. Her current research involves investigating the ways in which late-medieval laypeople accessed the liturgy through vernacular lyrics and prayers in English and Anglo-Norman. She was recently granted a fellowship by the church of All Saints North Street to reconstruct a medieval mass for the Use of York, which was performed and published in 2009. McCullough lectures on medieval literature and theology in the Oxford Scholars and Christians in Residence summer program.

Holly Faith Nelson, an associate professor of English and co-director of the Gender Studies Institute at Trinity Western University, has co-edited *The Broadview Anthology of Seventeenth-Century Verse and Prose* (2000); *Of Paradise and Light: Essays on Henry Vaughan and John Milton* (2005); *Eikon Basilike with Selections from Eikonoklastes* (2006); and *James Hogg and the Literary*

Marketplace: Scottish Romanticism and the Working-Class Author (2009). Her articles have appeared in journals such as *Studies in English Literature, Studies in Philology, Eighteenth-Century Fiction, Scintilla, Studies in Hogg and his World,* and *The Year's Work in English Studies.*

Barbara Pell was a much loved and admired professor of English at Trinity Western University. She taught at Trinity for nearly twenty years before her death on March 9, 2009. Her publications include two monographs—*Faith and Fiction: A Theological Critique of the Narrative Strategies of Hugh MacLennan and Morley Callaghan* (1998) and *A Portrait of the Artist: Ernest Buckler's "The Mountain and the Valley"* (1995)—as well as numerous articles and book chapters on Canadian literature. She was the recipient of the Davis Distinguished Teaching Award in 2006 and a Leading Women Award in 2008.

George Piggford is an associate professor of English and Martin Fellow in Catholic Studies at Stonehill College in Easton, Massachusetts. He compiled and edited Forster's *The Feminine Note in Literature* (2000) and is co-editor of *Queer Forster* (1997). He has published on modernism and postmodernism in journals including *English Studies in Canada, Modern Drama,* and *Mosaic,* and in the collections *American Gothic* (1998), *American Modernism across the Arts* (1999), and *The Strategic Smorgasbord of Postmodernity* (2008). He is currently at work on a project on Flannery O'Connor and the languages of mysticism.

Deanna T. Smid is a Ph.D. candidate in the Department of English and Cultural Studies at McMaster University, Hamilton, Ontario. Her dissertation, "'The world in man's heart': The Faculty of Imagination in Early Modern English Literature," supervised by Mary Silcox, explores early modern perceptions of imagination as a medical, philosophical, and psychological construct which is then used and stimulated in works of literature. Studying imagination is one of the consequences of her interest in science fiction and in protoscientific literary works. Her research interests also include devotional poetry and English emblem books.

Sean Somers teaches in the English Department at the University of British Columbia. He has published several articles and book chapters on translation theory and the intercultural connections between Japan and Europe in the twentieth century. His monograph *Ancestral Recall: The Celtic Revival and Japanese Modernism* is currently under review.

Bettina Stumm is a Ph.D. candidate and a lecturer at the University of British Columbia. Her work examines the intersections between ethics and collaborative autobiography and develops an ethical framework for secondary witnessing in trauma communities. She recently assisted in writing the Holocaust memoir, *A Long Labour*, with survivor Rhodea Shandler and is currently the reviews editor for *Life Writing*.

Lynn R. Szabo is an associate professor of English at Trinity Western University where she teaches American literature and creative writing. She is a scholar of the poet and mystic Thomas Merton and is the editor of the first comprehensive edition of Merton's poetry, *In The Dark Before Dawn: New Selected Poems of Thomas Merton* (2005). She has written primarily on poetics and language, particularly on their relationship to silence and solitude in the American literary tradition.

John C. Van Rys, a graduate of Dalhousie, is a professor of English at Redeemer University College. He has written on a range of modern Canadian writers, including Al Purdy, Margaret Avison, Ernest Buckler, Robertson Davies, and Alice Munro, as well as on the theories of Mikhail Bakhtin. His current research focuses on cross-border writing, such as the fiction of Guy Vanderhaeghe and Annie Proulx; on the Canadian historical novel, particularly on suffering and trauma; and on the complexities of Munro's short stories, including their historical dimensions, their moral complexity, and their formal openness. He has also co-authored *The Research Writer: Curiosity, Discovery, Dialogue* (forthcoming).

Steve Vine is a senior lecturer in English at Swansea University, Wales, where he specializes in teaching Romantic literature and literary theory. As well as articles and book chapters on Romanticism and theory, his publications include *Blake's Poetry: Spectral Visions* (1993), the Penguin edition of D.H. Lawrence's *Aaron's Rod* (1995), *Emily Brontë* (1998), *Literature in Psychoanalysis: A Reader* (2005), and *William Blake* (2007). He is currently writing a book entitled *Reinventing the Sublime: Post-Romantic Literature and Theory*.

Jens Zimmermann is a professor of English and Canada Research Chair in Interpretation, Religion, and Culture at Trinity Western University. He is the author of *Recovering Theological Hermeneutics: An Incarnational-Trinitarian Theory of Interpretation* (2004) and *Theologische Hermeneutik* (2008); co-author of *The Passionate Intellect: Incarnational Humanism and the Future of University Education* (2006); and co-editor of *Bonhoeffer and Continental Thought: Cruciform Philosophy* (2009). His articles have appeared in journals such as *Christianity and Literature*, the *Journal of the British Society for Phenomenology*, the *Journal of Beliefs and Values: Studies in Religion and Education*, the *Journal for Hermeneutics and Postmodern Thought*, and *Philosophy Today*.

INDEX

Abraham (biblical), 194, 353, 364
Abrahamic religion, 224, 332, 334
Ackerley, J.R., 226
Adam (biblical), 10, 258, 259, 262, 335
Addison, Joseph, 4–6
Aelred of Rievaulx, 27
Aers, David, 51n5, 52n8, 52n15
aesthetic, xviii–xix, xxiv, 4–7, 134, 155,
  189–90, 196, 199, 206, 215n16,
  218n33, 220n48, 222n66, 258, 293,
  299, 301, 330–31, 333, 336–40,
  342–43, 346n27, 370; eucharistic,
  189,196, 199, 212; experience,
  xxviin18, 19, 332; incarnational,
  xxiii, 215n16; participatory, 40,
  49–50; sacramental, 197, 202, 209,
  215n16; of the sublime, xviii–xix,
  xxiv, 6, 289–90, 293–94, 302, 313n8,
  317, 321, 363; theory, xx, 6, 114; of
  transubstantiation, 186, 188–89, 197;
  vision, xx, 206, 208, 221n53
aesthetics, xv, xviii–xix, 124n14, 145,
  197, 202, 292–93, 301, 330–33, 338,
  342, 363, 371; theological, 331–33,
  338, 342–43
affliction, xxi–xxii, xxiv, 74, 88, 93–94,
  97–100, 102–5, 107n13, 108n32,
  109n35, 109nn37–38, 119, 160, 174,
  372. See also Herbert, George
Agamben, Giorgio, 367
Aikenside, Mark, 5
Akedah, the, 364–65

allusion: and the artist, xxiv; examples
  of, 29, 35n6, 37n41, 196, 261, 270; in
  Joyce's works, 190–91, 193; and the
  sublime, xvii, 318–19, 321; in Woolf's
  works, 199, 207, 221n49
anamnesis, 213, 222n65, 310–11
anatheism, 184, 213, 228
Anderson, Judith H., 43
Angelo, Bonnie, 301
Ankersmit, F.R., xvi, xxvn3
Annunciation, xx, 12, 16–19. See Weyden,
  Roger van der
Anonby, David, xxi
Anselm, Saint, 12, 26, 35n10, 93
aporia, 4, 19, 292, 354, 365
Aquinas. See Thomas Aquinas, Saint
Aristotle, 193
Arminian, 87–88, 90–91, 94
Ariminianism, 87–88, 90
Arminius, Jakob, 91
art, xviii, xix–xx, 4, 6, 42, 44, 49–50, 66,
  155, 189–90, 212, 217n29, 219n42,
  290, 295, 301, 320, 342, 370–71, 377;
  as artifice, 42–44; Chaucer's relation
  of, to Venus, 40, 42–45, 48; and
  Christianity, 329–32, 343, 370–71,
  377; and language, 186, 188; and
  love, xx, 39–44, 49; and nature, 43–45,
  61; relation of, to moral value, xix,
  146, 154n4, 371; and the sacred, 15,
  39–40, 42; and suffering, 301, 371; as
  transubstantiation, 190, 196–98, 212,

tion to suffering; sublime, the, in relation to suffering; theology, of suffering
Sutton, Mrs. Henry, 157
Szabo, Lynn R., xxiv

Tarter, Michele Lise, 170
Taylor, Charles, 379
Teilhard de Chardin, Pierre, 187, 221n49
Teresa of Avila, Saint, 30
terror, xix, 4–5, 113, 117–18, 129–30, 134–37, 141, 224, 289, 291, 296, 300–2, 313n3, 318, 321
theodicy, xvii, 211, 213
theology: aesthetic, 330–33, 337–38, 342; apophatic, 210, 228; Catholic, 90, 92, 258; Christian, xvii, xxiii, 264–65, 338–39, 343, 388, 398n51; and cross-cultural dialogue, 332–33; in Donne's *Holy Sonnets*, 88, 90–92, 94; Eucharistic, 390; in Herbert's poetry, 105, 107n17, 107n20; incarnational, 258; of light, 295; negative, xvii, 229. *See also* via negativa; ontotheology, 230, 289, 383; positive, xvii. *See also* via positiva; of presence, 226, 228; Quaker, xxii, 169, 172, 176; sacramental, 331; sacrificial, 209; of suffering, xvii–xviii, 92, 172; systematic, 339; Tractarian, xxii, 156
thisness, 183–84, 187, 192, 216n21
Time Regained, xxiii, 183, 195, 198–202, 219n42; and epiphany, 183, 195–96, 198, 208, 217n29, 218n31, 219n43; Kristeva's reading of, 196–99. *See also* Proust, Marcel
Thomas Aquinas, Saint, 50, 215n16, 341, 395n14
Tillich, Paul, xvii
Titus Andronicus, xx–xxi, 57–68; and demand for an ethical response, xx–xxi, 58, 60–62, 64–65, 67; and Lavinia as sign, 58–60, 65; and Lavinia as signifier, 58–60, 62, 67; and Levinas's "saying and the said," 58–62, 64–68; rape in, xx, 57, 59–62; and reducing Lavinia to silence, xx,

57–60, 66, 68; and the relationship between language and ethics, xxi, 58, 62, 68. *See also* Shakespeare, William
To the Lighthouse, xxiii, 183, 199, 202–8, 212; art in, 204–5, 207; eucharistic imagery in, 203–4, 206, 212; mysticism in, 202–8, 213. *See also* Woolf, Virginia
Todd, Janet, 116
Toplady, Augustus, 33, 37n39
Tolkien, J.R.R., 240, 241n6, 241n8
Traherne, Thomas, 7–8
Trakl, Georg, 384
transcendence, xvi–xvii, xxii–xxiii, 114, 174, 176, 186–87, 292, 303–5, 333–34, 365–66, 385–86, 389, 393, 398n50; divine, xxviin8, 335 and immanence, 187, 206–7, 210, 221n51, 319, 342, 386, 389; and trauma, xix, xxi, xxiii
transubstantiation, xxiii, 183, 186–87, 189, 195, 197, 200–1, 206, 208–9, 211–13, 214n12, 215n14, 336. *See also* aesthetic, of transubstantiation; art, as transubstantiation; Joyce, James, and transubstantiation
transfiguration, xxiii, 8, 183, 190, 299
trauma, xv–xvi, xviii, xxiii, 301, 305, 353–58, 360; of the ethical call, 385–86, 393, 396n27; examples of, in literature, 58, 67, 76, 302–3, 305–6, 308, 320; Holocaust, xvi, 349, 354–57, 360, 362n24; studies, xv–xvi, xix, 349; testifying to, xxiv–xxv, 349–58, 360, 362n32; theory and theorists, xvi, xviii, 353–54; victims of, xvi, xviii–xxiv, 349–50, 353–58, 360. *See also*, sublime, the, in relation to trauma; terror, and trauma
Travers, Rebecca, 172
Trinity, the, 90, 141n9, 194, 390, 392–93, 399n56
Tucker, Sarah Fish, 174–75

Ulysses, xxiii, 183, 190–95, 208, 216n28; and epiphany, 190–92, 194; pseudo-Eucharists in, 190–91, 193. *See also* Joyce, James
Updike, John, 269–70

van der Weyden, Rogier, xx, 17
Van Eyck brothers, 10, 15, 17
Van Rys, John C., xxiii
Vattimo, Gianni, 210
Vaughan, Henry, 8
Vendler, Helen, 108n29
Venus (goddess), xx, 39–49, 51n5, 51n8,
   52–53nn15–16, 53n24. *See also*
   Parliament of Fowls
via negativa, xvii, 191, 212–13, 224, 322
via positiva, xvii, 322
Vico, Giambattista, 382
Vine, Steve, xxiv
Virgil, xx, 4, 12
von Zinzendorf, Count Nicolaus
   Ludwig, 32

Wachtel, Eleanor, 271
Waith, Eugene M., 57, 64
Walker, Evan Harris, 295
Walpole, Horace, 5
Ward, Mrs. Humphrey, 223
Watts, Isaac, 33
Waugh, Dorothy, 173
Wesley, Charles, 32
Wessells, Michael G., xvi
West, Grace Starry, 61
Westling, Louise, 221n55
Whalen, Robert, 93
Whiteread, Rachel, xxv, 370; and *The
   Nameless Library*, xxv, 370–71
Wiesel, Elie, xviii
Wilbur, Richard, 19
William of St. Thierry, 27
Williams, Carolyn D., 59
Williams, Helen Maria, xxi, 113–22,
   122n2, 123nn5–7, 123n13, 124n16,
   125n22, 125n24, 126n28, 126n31,

126n34; and Burke's idea of punitive
   justice, xxi, 113–14, 116, 118, 120–21,
   123n13, 126n31; *Peru: A Poem in Six
   Cantos. See* Peru; *Poems*, 114, 123n5;
   and poetry as a vehicle for the sublime, xxi, 113, 118. *See also* justice,
   preventative; justice, punitive;
   justice, social
Williams, Rowan, 49
Wilson, John Dover, 57
Winny, James, 89
witnessing: the absolute alterity of
   divine Other, 351; and secondary
   witness, xxiv–xxv, 350–51, 354–55.
   See also trauma, testifying to
Witte, Bernd, 368
Wollstonecraft, Mary, 114, 123n4, 126n32
Wood, Ralph, 246
Woolf, Virginia, xxiii, 183, 187, 189–90,
   199, 202, 205–8, 212–13, 221n49,
   221n50, 221n55; and sacramental
   imaginary, 183, 190, 208; and use of
   indirect discourse, 202; *To the
   Lighthouse. See* To the Lighthouse
Wordsworth, Jonathan, 122n1, 125n24
Wordsworth, William, xx, 5, 124n13,
   258–59, 261
Wright, Luella, 171
Wriothesley, Henry, 80

Yaeger, Patricia, 115
Yasuoka Shōtar , 332
Young, Edward, 5

Zimmermann, Jens, xxv
Žižek, Slavoj, xviii, 78, 83n18, 304–6,
   369–70